An Introduction to Programming

USING VISUAL BASIC® 6.0

UPDATE EDITION

Fourth Edition

David I. Schneider
University of Maryland

Pearson Education, Inc.
Upper Saddle River, New Jersey 07458

Library of Congress Cataloging-in-Publication Data

Schneider, David I.
    An introduction to programming using Visual Basic 6.0 /
    David I. Schneider—Update, 4th ed.
    p.   cm.
    Includes index.
    ISBN: 0-13-142707-5
    1. Microsoft Visual BASIC. 2. BASIC (Computer program language).
    I. Title.

    QA76.73.B3S32 2004
    005.6′8—dc21

                              20030476181

Vice President and Editorial Director, ECS: *Marcia Horton*
Executive Editor: *Petra Recter*
Vice President and Director of Production and Manufacturing, ESM: *David W. Riccardi*
Executive Managing Editor: *Vince O'Brien*
Managing Editor: *Camille Trentacoste*
Production Editor: *Irwin Zucker*
Manufacturing Manager: *Trudy Pisciotti*
Manufacturing Buyer: *Lisa McDowell*
Director of Creative Services: *Paul Belfanti*
Art Editor: *Greg Dulles*
Creative Director: *Carole Anson*
Art Director: *Jayne Conte*
Cover Designer: *Maureen Eide*
Cover Art: *Tamara Newnam*
Executive Marketing Manager: *Pamela Shaffer*
Marketing Assistant: *Barrie Reinhold*

©2004, 1999, 1998, 1997, 1995 by Pearson Education, Inc.
Pearson Prentice Hall
Upper Saddle River, New Jersey 07458

The author and publisher of this book have used their best efforts in preparing this book. These efforts include the development, research, and testing of the theories and programs to determine their effectiveness. The author and publisher make no warranty of any kind, expressed or implied, with regard to these programs or the documentation contained in this book. The author and publisher shall not be liable in any event for incidental or consequential damages in connection with, or arising out of, the furnishing, performance, or use of these programs.

TRADEMARK INFORMATION: Microsoft and Visual Basic are registered trademarks of Micorsoft Corporation. IBM is a registered trademark of International Business Machines Corporation. Company and product names used in this text may be trademarks or registered trademark of the individual companies and are respectfully acknowledged.

Printed in the United States of America.

10 9 8 7 6 5 4 3 2 1

ISBN 0-13-142707-5

Pearson Education Ltd., *London*
Pearson Education Australia Pty. Limited, *Sydney*
Pearson Education Singapore Pte. Ltd.
Pearson Education North Asia Ltd., *Hong Kong*
Pearson Education Canada Inc., *Toronto*
Pearson Educación de Mexico, S.A. de C.V.
Pearson Education—Japan, Inc., *Tokyo*
Pearson Education—Malasia Pte. Ltd.
Pearson Education Inc., *Upper Saddle River, New Jersey*

CONTENTS

PREFACE

This text provides an introduction to programming using Microsoft® Visual Basic® 6.0 on computers running Microsoft Windows. Due to its extraordinary combination of power and ease of use, Visual Basic has been the tool of choice for developing user-friendly Windows applications in the business world. In addition, Microsoft has made Visual Basic the language used to take full control of its best selling Windows applications such as Microsoft Word, Access, and Excel. Not only is Visual Basic the state of the art in Basic programming, but Visual Basic is fun! Learning Visual Basic was very exciting to me, and most students have similar reactions when they see how easy it is to build powerful visual interfaces using it.

My objectives when writing this text were as follows:

1. To develop focused chapters. Rather than covering many topics superficially, I concentrate on important subjects and cover them thoroughly.

2. To use examples and exercises with which students can relate, appreciate, and feel comfortable. I frequently use real data. Examples do not have so many embellishments that students are distracted from the programming techniques illustrated.

3. To produce compactly written text that students will find both readable and informative. The main points of each topic are discussed first and then the peripheral details are presented as comments.

4. To teach good programming practices that are in step with modern programming methodology. Problem-solving techniques and structured programming are discussed early and used throughout the book.

5. To provide insights into the major applications of computers.

Unique and Distinguishing Features

Exercises for Most Sections. Each section that teaches programming has an exercise set. The exercises both reinforce the understanding of the key ideas of the section and challenge the student to explore applications. Most of the exercise sets require the student to trace programs, find errors, and write programs. The answers to all the odd-numbered exercises in Chapters 3 through 8 and selected odd-numbered exercises from Chapters 9 through 15 are given at the end of the text.

Practice Problems. Practice problems are carefully selected exercises located at the end of a section, just before the exercise set. Complete solutions are given following the exercise set. The practice problems often focus on points that are potentially confusing or are best appreciated after the student has worked on them. The reader should seriously attempt the practice problems and study their solutions before moving on to the exercises.

Programming Projects. Beginning with Chapter 3, nearly every chapter contains programming projects. The programming projects not only reflect the variety of ways that computers are used in the business community, but also present some games and general-interest topics. The large number and range of difficulty of the programming projects allow adapting the course to the students' interests and abilities. Some programming projects in later chapters can be assigned as end-of-the-semester projects.

Comments. Extensions and fine points of new topics are deferred to the "Comments" portion at the end of each section so that they will not interfere with the flow of the presentation.

Case Studies. Each of the four case studies focuses on an important programming application. The problems are analyzed and the programs are developed with hierarchy charts and pseudocode. The programs are available to students on an accompanying CD.

Chapter Summaries. In Chapters 3 through 14 the key results are stated and the important terms are summarized at the end of the chapter.

Procedures. The early introduction of general procedures in Chapter 4 allows structured programming to be used in simple situations before being applied to complex problems. However, the text is written so that the presentation of procedures easily can be postponed until decision and repetition structures have been presented. In Chapters 5 and 6 (and Sections 7.1 and 7.2), all programs using procedures appear at the ends of sections and can be deferred or omitted.

Arrays. Arrays are introduced gently in two sections in Chapter 7. The first section presents the basic definitions and avoids procedures. The second section presents the techniques for manipulating arrays and shows how to pass arrays to procedures.

Appendix on Debugging. Placing the discussion of Visual Basic's sophisticated debugger in Appendix D allows the instructor flexibility in deciding when to cover this topic.

Reference Appendices. Appendices serve as a compact reference manual for Visual Basic's environments and statements.

Visual Basic 6.0 Included. A Working Model Edition of Visual Basic 6.0 is packaged with every copy of this book. The Working Model is identical to the Learning Edition with the exceptions that it cannot compile to an EXE file and it does not have on-line help.

Examples and Case Studies Files. The programs from all examples and case studies from the text are provided on the accompanying CD. The CD also contains all databases and text files used in the examples, and many of the text files used in exercises.

Instructors' Resource Website. This password-protected Website, which contains every program in the text, the solution to every exercise and programming project, PowerPoint slides, and a test item file for each chapter, is available only to instructors.

What's New in the Update Edition

The fourth edition of *An Introduction to Programming Using Visual Basic 6.0* was written in 1998, the year VB 6.0 first appeared. Since then, two upgrades of the operating system, two upgrades of Microsoft Office, and a new version of Visual Basic (VB.NET) have been released. Also, some of the technologies and tools that were in vogue in 1998 have been replaced since then. The Update Edition of the book addresses these issues, modernizes the book, and responds to some requests from instructors. Some changes in the book are as follows:

1. Two substantial programming projects have been added to each of Chapters 3 through 13.

2. In Chapter 12, the use of DAO database technology has been replaced with the newer ADO technology. Also, a discussion of calculated columns has been added.

3. An additional chapter (Chapter 15) titled "Visual Basic .NET," has been added. The chapter introduces VB.NET and explains how to transition from VB 6.0 to VB.NET.

4. Named constants are now covered.

5. The discussion of VB Script has been revised to be more consistent with the way people currently write Web pages.

6. The discussion of computers and Windows in Sections 1.2 and 1.3 has been modernized.

7. Several advances in computers and computer science have been added to the Biographical History of Computing.

8. Screen captures have been upgraded to Windows XP style forms.

9. Many exercises and examples use real data. This data has been made current.

ACKNOWLEDGMENTS

Many talented instructors, students, and programmers provided helpful comments and thoughtful suggestions at each stage in the preparation of this text. I extend my gratitude for their contributions to the quality of the book to A. Abonomah, University of Akron; Timothy Babbitt, Rochester Institute of Technology; William Barnett, Northwestern State University; Sherry Barriclow, Grand Valley State University; Robert Berman, Wayne State University; William Burrows, University of Washington; David Chao, San Francisco State University; Christopher Chisolm, University of Nebraska, Omaha; Robert Coil, Cincinnati State Technical and Community College; Gary Cornell, University of Connecticut; Ronit Dancis; John DaPonte, Southern Connecticut State Univ.; Ward Deutschman, Briarcliff; Ralph Duffy, North Seattle Community College; Charles Fairchild; Pat Fenton, West Valley College; David Fichbohm, Golden Gate University; Robert Fritz, American River College; Matthew Goddard, New Hampshire Technical College; Mickie Goodro, Casper College; Wade T. Graves, Grayson Community College; Christine Griffin; Gary Haw, MIPS Software Dev. Inc.; Shelly Hawkins, Microsoft; Tom Janicki, Kent State University; Dana Johnson, North Dakota State University; Dan Joseph, Rochester Institute of Technology; Del Kimber, Clemson University; Wanda Kunkle, Rowan College; Paul Lecoq, San Francisco Community College; David Leitch, Devry Institute; David Letcher, The College of New Jersey; Kieran Mathieson, Oakland University; Charlie Miri, Delaware Tech; George Nezlek, DePaul University; Ron Notes, Hebrew Academy of Greater Washington; Mike Paul, Berry University; T. S. Pennington, Maple Woods Community College; Arland Richmond, Computer Learning Center; David Rosser, Essex County College; Arturo Salazar, San Francisco State; Susanne Peterson, Microsoft; Janie Schwark, Microsoft; Mike Talber, Portland Community College; Steve Turek, Devry Institute of Technology, Kansas City; Jac Van Deventer, Washington State University; Randy Weinberg, St. Cloud State University; Laurie Werner, Miami University; Melinda White, Santa Fe Community College; Ronald Williams, Central Piedmont Community College.

Two talented programmers, John Tarcza and Peter Rosenbaum, helped with the development of this revision of the book. They developed new programming projects, provided many helpful suggestions for improving the book, and proofread the book.

Many people were involved in the successful publication of this book. I wish to thank the dedicated team at Prentice Hall whose support and diligence made this textbook possible. Irwin Zucker did a fantastic job producing the book and keeping it on schedule. Marcia Horton provided the needed editorial support and assistance. Pam Schaffer has done a thorough job of presenting the book to the academic community. Sarah Parker has been very conscientious in handling the supplements and Websites for the book.

I extend special thanks to my editor Petra Recter and my compositor Rebecca Evans. Petra's ideas and enthusiasm helped immensely with the preparation of the book. Rebecca's considerable skills and congenial manner made for an uncomplicated and pleasant production process.

Last, but not least, I am grateful to the Microsoft Corporation for its commitment to producing outstanding programming languages and for its permission to include a copy of the Working Model Edition of Visual Basic 6.0 with each book.

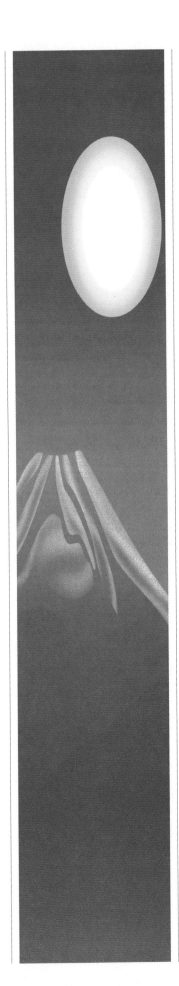

1 An Introduction to Computers and Visual Basic

1.1 AN INTRODUCTION TO COMPUTERS

An Introduction to Programming Using Visual Basic 6.0, Update Edition, is a book about problem solving using computers. The programming language used is Visual Basic, but the principles taught apply to many modern programming languages. The examples and exercises present a sampling of the ways that computers are used in society.

Computers are so common today that you certainly have heard some of the terminology applied to them. Here are some of the questions that you might have about computers and programming.

Question:	What is meant by a personal computer?
Answer:	The word "personal" does not mean that the computer is intended for personal, as opposed to business, purposes. Rather, it indicates that the machine is operated by one person at a time instead of by many people.
Question:	What are the main components of a personal computer?
Answer:	Hidden from view inside the system unit are several components including the microprocessor, memory, and hard drive of the computer. The *central processing unit* (CPU), sometimes referred to as the *microprocessor,* can be thought of as the computer's brain, which carries out all of the computations. The *memory,* often referred to as *random access memory* (RAM), stores instructions and data while they are being used by the computer. When the computer's power is turned off, the contents of memory are lost. A *hard disk drive* is used to store instructions and data when they are not being used in memory and when the computer is turned off. Inside the system unit there are also device cards such as a graphics card, sound card, and network card. A *graphics card* is used to send an image to the monitor, and a *sound card* is used to send audio to a set of speakers attached to the computer. *Network cards* can be used to connect to a local area network (LAN) of computers, while a *modem* uses a telephone line to connect to any computer that can be reached by a phone call.

The personal computer also has several *input* and *output devices,* which are used to communicate with the computer. Standard input devices include the keyboard and mouse. Standard output devices include the monitor and printer. Instructions are entered into the computer by typing them on the keyboard, clicking a mouse, or loading them from a file located on a disk drive or downloaded from a network. Information processed by the computer can be displayed on the monitor, printed on the printer, or recorded on a disk drive |
| **Question:** | What are some uses of computers in our society? |
| **Answer:** | The dramatic decrease in the cost of hardware and software technology has made computers widely available to consumers and corporations alike. Whenever we make a phone call, a computer determines how to route the call and calculates the cost of the call. Banks store all customer transactions on computers and process these transactions to revise the balance for each customer. Airlines record all reservations with computers. This information, which is stored in a database, can be accessed to determine the status of any flight. NASA uses computers to calculate the trajectories of satellites. Business analysts use computers |

to create pie and bar charts that give visual impact to data. With the Internet connecting millions of home computers, families and friends can exchange messages, information, and pictures. Consumers can shop from their PCs. Virtually no aspect of modern life is untouched by computer technology.

Question: What are some topics covered in this text that students can use immediately?

Answer: Computer files can be created to hold lists of names, addresses, and phone numbers, which can be alphabetized and printed in their entirety or selectively. Line graphs or attractive tables can be created to enhance the presentation of data in a term paper. Mathematical computations can be carried out for science, business, and engineering courses. Personal financial transactions, such as bank deposits and loans, can be recorded, organized, and analyzed.

Question: How do we communicate with the computer?

Answer: Many languages are used to communicate with the computer. At the lowest level, there is machine language, which is understood directly by the microprocessor but is awkward for humans. Visual Basic is an example of a higher-level language. It consists of instructions to which people can relate, such as Print, Input, and Do. The Visual Basic software translates Visual Basic programs into machine-language programs. This translation process is known as **compiling**.

Question: How do we get computers to perform complicated tasks?

Answer: Tasks are broken down into a sequence of instructions that can be expressed in a computer language. (This text uses the language Visual Basic.) The sequence of instructions is called a *program*. Programs range in size from two or three instructions to millions of instructions. Instructions are typed on the keyboard, or read in from a file on a disk, and stored in the computer's memory. The process of executing the instructions is called *running* the program.

Question: Are there certain features that all programs have in common?

Answer: Most programs do three things: take in data, manipulate them, and give desired information. These operations are referred to as input, processing, and output. The input data might be held in a portion of the program, reside on a disk drive, or be provided by the computer operator in response to requests made by the computer while the program is running. The processing of the input data occurs inside the computer and can take from a fraction of a second to many hours. The output data are either displayed on the screen, printed on the printer, or recorded on a disk. As a simple example, consider a program that computes sales tax. An item of input data is the cost of the thing purchased. The processing consists of multiplying the cost by a certain percentage. An item of output data is the resulting product, the amount of sales tax to be paid.

Question: What are the meanings of the terms *hardware* and *software*?

Answer: **Hardware** refers to the physical components of the computer, including all peripherals, the central processing unit, disk drives, and all mechanical and electrical devices. Programs are referred to as **software**.

Question: What are the meanings of the terms *programmer* and *user*?

Answer: A **programmer** is a person who solves problems by writing programs on a computer. After analyzing the problem and developing a plan for solving it, he or she writes and tests the program that instructs the computer how to carry out the plan. The program might be run many times, either by the programmer or by others. A **user** is any person who uses a program. While working through this text, you will function both as a programmer and as a user.

Question: What is meant by *problem solving*?

Answer: Problems are solved by carefully reading them to determine what data are given and what outputs are requested. Then a step-by-step procedure is devised to process the given data and produce the requested output. This procedure is called an **algorithm**. Finally, a computer program is written to carry out the algorithm. Algorithms are discussed in Section 2.2.

Question: What types of problems are solved in this text?

Answer: Carrying out business computations, creating and maintaining records, alphabetizing lists, and drawing line graphs are some of the types of problems we will solve.

Question: What is the difference between standard BASIC and Visual Basic?

Answer: In the early 1960s, two mathematics professors at Dartmouth College developed BASIC to provide their students with an easily learned language that could tackle complicated programming projects. As the popularity of BASIC grew, refinements were introduced that permitted structured programming, which increases the reliability of programs. Visual Basic is a version of BASIC released in 1991 by the Microsoft Corporation to allow easy, visually oriented development of Windows applications.

1.2 USING WINDOWS

Programs such as Visual Basic, which are designed for Microsoft Windows, are easy to use once you learn a little jargon and a few basic techniques. This section explains the jargon, giving you enough understanding of Windows to get you started in Visual Basic. Although Windows may seem intimidating if you've never used it before, you need to learn only a few basic techniques, which are covered in this section.

Mouse Pointers

When you use Windows, think of yourself as the conductor and Windows as the orchestra. The conductor in an orchestra points to various members and does something with his or her baton; then the orchestra members respond in certain ways. For a Windows user, the baton is called the **pointing device**; most often it is a **mouse**. As you move the mouse across your desk, a pointer moves along the screen in sync with your movements. Two basic types of mouse pointers you will see in Windows are an arrow and an hourglass.

The **arrow** is the ordinary mouse pointer you use to point at various Windows objects before activating them. You will usually be told to "Move the pointer to . . . ." This really means "Move the mouse around your desk until the mouse pointer is at . . . ."

The **hourglass** mouse pointer pops up whenever Windows is saying "Wait a minute; I'm thinking." This pointer still moves around when you move the mouse, but you can't tell Windows to do anything until it finishes what it's doing and the mouse pointer no longer resembles an hourglass. (Sometimes you can press the Esc key to tell Windows to stop what it is doing.)

Note: The mouse pointer can take on many other shapes, depending on which application you are using and what task you are performing. For instance, when entering text in a word processor or Visual Basic, the mouse pointer appears as a thin, large, uppercase I (referred to as an I-beam).

Mouse Actions

After you move the (arrow) pointer to a place where you want something to happen, you need to do something with the mouse. There are five basic things you can do—point, hover, click, double-click, and drag.

Pointing means moving your mouse across your desk until the mouse pointer is over the desired object on the screen.

Hovering means lingering the mouse at a particular place and waiting for a message or menu to appear.

Clicking (sometimes people say single-clicking) means pressing and releasing the left mouse button once. Whenever a sentence begins "Click on . . . ," you need to

1. Move the mouse pointer until it is at the object you are supposed to click on.

2. Press and release the left mouse button.

An example of a sentence using this jargon might be "Click on the button marked Yes." You also will see sentences that begin "Click inside the. . . ." This means to move the mouse pointer until it is inside the boundaries of the object, and then click.

Double-clicking means clicking the left mouse button twice in quick succession (that is, pressing it, releasing it, pressing it, and releasing it again *quickly* so that Windows doesn't think you single-clicked twice). Whenever a sentence begins "Double-click on . . . ", you need to

1. Move the mouse pointer until it is at the object you are supposed to double-click on.

2. Press and release the left mouse button twice in quick succession.

For example, you might be instructed to "Double-click on the little box at the far left side of your screen."

Note: An important Windows convention is that clicking selects an object so you can give Windows or the document further directions about it, but double-clicking tells Windows to perform a default operation. For example, double-clicking on a folder will open that folder.

Dragging usually moves a Windows object. If you see a sentence that begins "Drag the . . . ", you need to

1. Move the mouse pointer until it is at the object.

2. Press the left mouse button, and hold it down.

3. Now move the mouse pointer until the object moves to where you want it to be.

4. Finally, release the mouse button.

Sometimes this whole activity is called *drag and drop*.

Windows Start Button

Clicking on the **Start** button (at the bottom left corner of the screen) displays a menu that you can use to run programs, shut down Windows, and carry out several other tasks. The Start menu also can be accessed by pressing a special key labeled with the Windows logo (located next to the Alt key) or by pressing Ctrl+Esc. (In the notation "key1+key2", the plus sign (+) instructs you to hold down key1 and then press key2. There are many useful key combinations of this type.)

Windows and Its Little Windows

Windows gets its name from the way it organizes your screen into rectangular regions. When you run a program, the program runs inside a bordered rectangular box. Unfortunately Windows jargon calls all of these windows, so there's only a lowercase "w" to distinguish them from the operating system called Windows.

When Windows' attention is focused on a specific window, the Title bar at the top of the window is blue and the window is said to be **active**. (Inactive windows have a gray title bar.) The active window is the only one that can be affected by your actions. An example of a sentence you might see is "Make the window active." This means that if the Title bar of the window is gray, click inside the window. At this point, the active window will be responsive to your actions.

Using Notepad

We will explore the Windows application Notepad to illustrate the Windows environment. Notepad is used extensively in this text to create data files for programs. Most of the concepts learned here carry over to Visual Basic and other Windows applications.

To invoke Notepad from Windows, click the Start button, click on Run, type "Notepad" into the box labeled "Name:", and click the OK button. The window in Figure 1.1 will appear. As its name suggests, Notepad is an elementary word processor. You can type text into the Notepad window, edit the text, print the text on the printer, and save the text for later recall.

The blinking vertical line is called the **cursor**. Each letter you type will appear at the cursor. The Notepad window is divided into four parts. The part containing the cursor is called the **Work area**. It is the largest and most important part of the window because documents are typed into it.

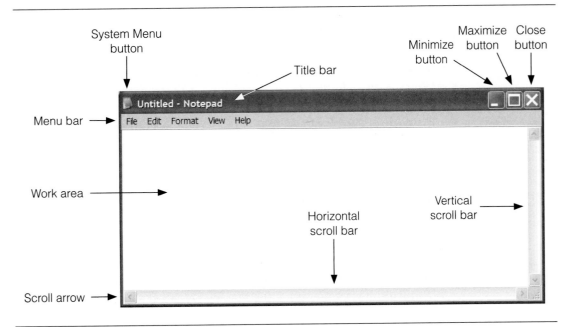

Figure 1.1 The Notepad window.

The **Title bar** at the top of the screen holds the name of the document currently being written. Until the document is given a name, the document is called "Untitled." The three buttons on the right side of the Title bar can be used to minimize, maximize, or close the window. You can click on the **Maximize button** to make the Notepad window fill the entire screen, click on the **Minimize button** to change the Notepad window into a button on the taskbar, or click on the **Close button** to exit Notepad. As long as a window isn't maximized or minimized, you can usually move it around the screen by dragging its Title bar. (Recall that this means to move the mouse pointer until it is in the Title bar, hold down the left mouse button, move the mouse until the window is where you want it to be, and then release the mouse button.) **Note 1:** If you have maximized a window, the Maximize button changes to a pair of rectangles called the **Restore button**. Click on this button to return the window to its previous size. **Note 2:** If the Notepad window has been minimized, it can be restored to its previous size by clicking on the button that was created on the task bar when the application was opened. (The three tasks discussed in this paragraph also can be carried out with the **System Menu button** in the upper-left corner of the window.)

You can change the Notepad window to exactly suit your needs. To adjust the size

1. Move the mouse pointer until it is at the place on the boundary you want to adjust. The mouse pointer changes to a double-headed arrow.

2. Drag the border to the left or right or up or down to make it smaller or larger.

3. When you are satisfied with the new size of the window, release the left mouse button.

If the Work area contains more information than can fit on the screen, you need a way to move through this information so you can see it all. For example, you will certainly be writing instructions in Visual Basic that are longer than one screen. You can use the mouse to scroll through your instructions with small steps or giant steps. A **Vertical scroll bar** lets you move from the top to the bottom of the window; a **Horizontal scroll bar** lets you move within the left and right margins of the window. Use this scroll bar when the contents of the window are too wide to fit on the screen. Figure 1.1 shows both Vertical and Horizontal scroll bars.

A scroll bar has two arrows at the end of a channel and sometimes contains a box called the **Scroll box**. The Scroll box is the key to moving rapidly; the arrows are the key to moving in smaller increments. Dragging the Scroll box enables you to quickly move long distances to an approximate location in your document. For example, if you drag the Scroll box to the middle of the channel, you'll scroll to approximately the middle of your document.

The **Menu bar** just below the Title bar is used to call up menus, or lists of tasks. Several of these tasks are described in this section.

Documents are created from the keyboard in much the same way they would be written with a typewriter. In computerese, writing a document is referred to as editing the document; therefore, the Notepad is called a **text editor**.

After Notepad has been invoked, the following routine will introduce you to using Notepad.

1. Click on the Work area of Notepad.

2. Type a few words into Notepad.

3. Press the **Home** key to move the cursor back to the beginning of the line. In general, the Home key moves the cursor to the beginning of the line on which it currently is located.

4. Now press the **End** key. The cursor will move to the end of the line.

5. Type some letters and then press the **Backspace** key a few times. It will erase letters one at a time. Another method of deleting a letter is to move the cursor to that letter and press the **Del** key. (Del stands for "Delete.") The backspace key erases the character to the left of the cursor, and the Del key erases the character to the right of the cursor.

6. Hold down the **Ctrl** key (Ctrl stands for "Control"), and press the **Del** key. This combination erases the portion of the line to the right of the cursor.

7. Type more characters than can fit on one line of the screen. Notice that the leftmost characters scroll off the screen to make room for the new characters.

8. Press Alt/O/W to turn on the Word Wrap feature. [The slash character (/), officially called a **solidus**, instructs you to release the character preceding it, before pressing the character following it.] Notice that Notepad broke the long line so that it fits in the Notepad.

9. Click Format on the menu bar and notice that there is a check mark in front of Word Wrap. To remove the check mark, turn the Word Wrap feature off by clicking once on Word Wrap.

10. The **Enter** key is used to begin a new line on the screen.

11. The **Alt** key activates the Menu bar and causes a letter from each menu to be underlined. Then, pressing one of the underlined letters, such as F, E, O, or

H, selects a menu. (From the Menu bar, a menu also can be selected by pressing the right-arrow key to highlight the name and then pressing the Enter key.) As shown in Figure 1.2, after a menu is opened, each option has one letter underlined. You can press an underlined letter to select an option. (Underlined letters are called **access keys**.) For instance, pressing A from the file menu selects the option "Save As". Selections also can be made with the cursor-movement keys and the Enter key. *Note 1:* You can select menus and options without the use of keys by clicking on them with the mouse. *Note 2:* You can close a menu, without making a selection, by clicking anywhere outside the menu or pressing the Esc key twice.

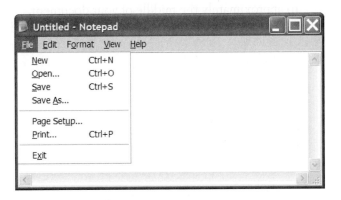

Figure 1.2 A menu and its options.

12. The **Esc** key (Esc stands for "Escape") is used to return to the Work area.

13. Press and release Alt, then press and release F, and then press and release N. (This key combination is abbreviated Alt/File/New or Alt/F/N.) The dialog box in Figure 1.3 will appear and ask you if you want to save the current document. Decline by pressing N or clicking on the No button.

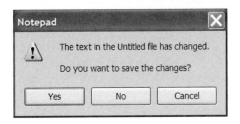

Figure 1.3 A "Do you want to save the changes?" dialog box.

14. Type the following information into Notepad. (It gives the names of employees, their hourly wages, and the number of hours worked in the past week.) This document is used in Section 3.5. **Note:** We follow the convention of surrounding words with quotation marks to distinguish words from numbers, which are written without quotation marks.

"Mike Jones", 7.35, 35
"John Smith", 6.75, 33

15. Store the document as a file on a disk. To save the document, press Alt/File/ Save As. A dialog box appears, requesting a file name for the document. The cursor is in a narrow rectangular box labeled "File name:". Type a drive letter, a colon, a backslash (\ ), and a name, and then press the Enter key or click on Save. For instance, you might type C:\STAFF. The document will then be stored on drive C. This process is called **saving** the document. Notepad automatically adds a period and the extension ".TXT" to the name. Therefore, the complete file name is STAFF.TXT on the disk. **Note:** If you want to save the document in a specific folder (directory) of the disk, also type the folder (directory). For instance, you might type C:\Myfiles\ STAFF. See Section 1.3 for a discussion of folders.

16. Press the key combination Alt/File/New to clear STAFF.TXT from Notepad.

17. To restore STAFF.TXT as the document in Notepad, press Alt/File/Open, type something like C:\STAFF in the "File name:" box, and then press the Enter key.

18. Move the cursor to the beginning of the document, and then press the keys Alt/Edit/Find (or Ctrl+F) to invoke the Find dialog box. This dialog box contains several objects that will be discussed in this book. The text to be found should be typed into the rectangle containing the cursor. Such a rectangle is called a *text box*. The phrase "Find what:", which identifies the type of information that should be placed into the text box, is referred to as the *caption* of a *label*.

19. Type "smith" into the text box, and then click on the "Find Next" button. This button is an example of a *command button*. Clicking on it carries out a task. Text boxes, labels, and command buttons are discussed in Section 3.2.

20. The small square to the left of the words "Match case" is called a *check box*. Click on it to see it checked, and then click again to remove the check mark.

21. The object captioned "Direction" is called a *frame*. It contains a pair of objects called *option buttons*. Click on the "Up" option button to select it, and then click on the "Down" option button. Only one option button at a time can be selected. Check boxes, frames, and option buttons are discussed in Section 11.2.

22. Press Alt/File/Exit to exit Notepad.

Comments

1. Two useful key combinations that we have not discussed yet are the following:

(a) Ctrl+Home moves the cursor to the beginning of the document.
(b) Ctrl+End moves the cursor to the end of the document.

2. When the work area is completely filled with lines of text, the document scrolls upward to accommodate additional lines. The lines that have scrolled off the top can be viewed again by pressing the **PgUp** key. The **PgDn** key moves farther down the document. The names of these keys are abbreviations for "Scroll one Page Up" and "Scroll one Page Down."

3. There are several ways to clear the work area. You can either erase the lines one at a time with Ctrl+Del, select the entire document with Alt/E/A and then erase all lines simultaneously with Del, or begin a new document with Alt/F/N. With the last method, a dialog box may query you about saving the current document. In this case, use Tab to select the desired option and press the Enter key. The document name in the Title bar will change to Untitled.

4. Notepad can perform many of the tasks of word processors, such as search and block operations. However, these features needn't concern us presently. A discussion of them can be found in Appendix B, under "HOW TO: Use the Editor."

✔ **PRACTICE PROBLEMS 1.2**

(Solutions to practice problems always follow the exercises.)
Assume that you are using Windows' Notepad.

1. Give two ways to open the Edit menu.

2. Assume the Edit menu has been opened. Give three ways to pick a menu item.

➤ **EXERCISES 1.2**

1. What does an hourglass pointer mean?

2. Describe "clicking" in your own words.

3. Describe "double-clicking" in your own words.

4. Describe "dragging" in your own words.

5. What is the blinking vertical line in Notepad called, and what is its purpose?

6. How can you tell when a window is active?

7. What is the difference between "Windows" and "windows"?

8. What is the purpose of the vertical scroll bar in Notepad?

9. By what name is a Notepad document known before it is named as part of being saved on disk?

In Exercises 10 through 28, select the key (or key combination) that performs the task in Windows' Notepad.

10. Scroll the document to view a higher part.

11. Scroll the document to view a lower part.

12. Erase the line containing the cursor.

13. Erase the character to the left of the cursor.

14. Access the Start menu.

15. Erase the character to the right of the cursor.

16. Move the cursor to the beginning of the line containing the cursor.

17. Move the cursor to the end of the line containing the cursor.

18. Exit Notepad.

19. Move the cursor to the beginning of the document.

20. Move the cursor to the end of the document.

21. Move from the Work area to the Menu bar.

22. Cancel a dialog box.

23. Move from the Menu bar to the Work area.

24. Move from one option rectangle of a dialog box to another rectangle.

25. Save the current document on a disk.

26. Clear the current document from the Work area and start a new document.

27. Create a blank line in the middle of a document.

28. Remove a pull-down menu from the screen.

✔✔ Solutions to Practice Problems 1.2

1. Press Alt/Edit or click on the word Edit in the Toolbar to display the Edit menu. The jargon says the menu is "dropped down" or "pulled down."

2. Press the down-arrow key to highlight the item. Then press the Enter key, press the underlined letter in the name of the item, or click on the item.

1.3   FILES AND FOLDERS

Modern computers have a hard disk, a diskette drive, and a CD (or DVD) drive. The hard disk is permanently housed inside the computer. You can read information from all three drives but can only write information easily to the hard disk and to diskettes. We use the word **disk** to refer to the hard disk, a diskette, a CD, or a DVD. Each drive is identified by a letter. Normally, the hard drive is identified by C, the diskette by A, and the CD (or DVD) drive by D or E. Disk management is handled by Windows.

Disks hold not only programs but also collections of data stored in **files.** The term **file** refers to either a program file, a text file, or some other kind of data file. We created a text file in Section 1.2. Each file has a name consisting of a base name followed by an optional extension consisting of a period and one or more characters (typically no more than three). The term **filename** refers to the combination of the base name, the period, and the extension. A filename can contain up to 215 characters, typically consisting of letters, digits, spaces, periods, and other assorted characters. (The only characters that cannot be used in filenames are \, /, :, *, ?, ", <, >, and | .) Extensions are normally used to identify the type of file. For example, spreadsheets created with Excel have the extension

".xls" (eXceL Spreadsheet), documents created with Word have the extension ".doc" (DOCument), and files created with Notepad have the extension txt (TeXT document). Some examples of file names are "Annual Sales.xls", "Letter to Mom.doc", and "Phone.txt".

Neither Windows nor Visual Basic distinguishes between uppercase and lowercase letters in folder and file names. For instance, the names COSTS03.TXT, Costs03.Txt, and costs03.txt are equivalent. We use uppercase letters in this book.

Because a disk is capable of holding thousands of files, locating a specific file can be quite time consuming. Therefore, related files are grouped into collections called **folders**. For instance, one folder might hold all your Visual Basic programs, and another the documents created with your word processor.

Think of a disk as a large folder, called the **root folder**, that contains several smaller folders, each with its own name. (The naming of folders follows the same rules as the naming of files.) Each of these smaller folders can contain yet other named folders. Any folder contained inside another folder is said to be a **subfolder** of that folder. Each folder is identified by listing its name preceded by the names of the successively larger folders that contain it, with each folder name preceded by a backslash. Such a sequence is called a **path**. For instance, the path \Sales\NY03\July identifies the folder July, contained in the folder NY03, which in turn is contained in the folder Sales. Think of a file, along with its name, as written on a slip of paper that can be placed into either the root folder or one of the smaller folders. The combination of a drive letter followed by a colon, a path, and a file name is called a **filespec**, an abbreviation of "file specification." Some examples of filespecs are C:\VB98\VB.EXE and A:\Personal\ INCOME03.TXT.

In early operating systems such as MS-DOS, folders were called **directories**. Many Visual Basic objects and commands still refer to folders as directories. The terms "root folder" and "path" are a reference to the "tree" metaphor commonly used to describe a computer's disk. In this metaphor, the large folder at the lowest level of the disk is called the "root" folder. The smaller folders contained in the root folder can be thought of as "branches" that emanate from the root. Each branch may have smaller branches, which in turn may have their own smaller branches, and so on. Finally, a file in one of these folders can be thought of as a leaf on a branch. The leaf is reached by starting at the root and following a "path" through the branches.

A program called Windows Explorer helps you view, organize, and manage the folders and files on your disks. We will learn how to use Windows Explorer to create, rename, copy, move, and delete folders and files.

Using Windows Explorer

To invoke Windows Explorer, click the Windows Start button, click on Run, type in the word "Explorer", and click on the OK button. The appearance of the Explorer window depends on the version of Windows being used and the values of certain settings. Figure 1.4 shows a possible Explorer window for Windows XP. The Folders pane on the left side of the window contains a folder tree with the My Documents folder highlighted. (Only one folder at a time can be highlighted. The icon for a highlighted folder appears to be physically open, and its name appears in the title bar at the top of the Explorer window.) The contents of the highlighted folder are displayed in the right pane of the Explorer window. In Figure 1.4, the highlighted folder contains six subfolders and two files. To highlight a different folder, just click on it with the left mouse button.

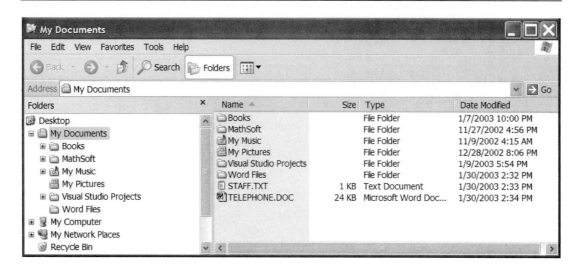

Figure 1.4 An Explorer window for Windows XP.

In the Folders pane, you can click on a plus box to expand the folder tree so that it reveals the subfolders of the folder next to the plus box. You click on a minus box to reverse the process. This process allows you to locate any file.

In Figure 1.4, the folders and files in the right pane are displayed in the so-called Details view. This view is invoked by pressing Alt/V/D. Also, in Figure 1.4, the extensions of the filenames are shown. By default, Windows shows only the base names of files. The following steps get it to also display the extensions:

1. From Windows Explorer, press Alt/T/O to display the Folders Options dialog box.

2. Click on the View tab in the dialog box.

3. If there is a check mark in the box next to "Hide file extensions for known file types", click on the box to remove the check mark.

4. Click on the OK button to close the Folders Options dialog box.

The following sets of instructions show how to create, rename, delete, copy, and move folders and files with Windows Explorer.

To create a new folder:

1. Highlight the folder that is to contain the new folder as a subfolder.

2. On the File menu, point to New, and then click Folder. (Or press Alt/File/New/Folder.) The new folder appears with the temporary name New Folder.

3. Type a name for the folder, and then press the Enter key. (The allowable names for folders are the same as for files. However, folders do not usually have an extension.)

To rename a folder or file:

1. Click on the folder or file in the right pane with the right mouse button.

2. In the Context menu that appears, click Rename. The current name will appear highlighted inside a rectangle.

3. Type the new name, and then press the Enter key.

To delete a folder or file:

1. Click on the folder or file with the right mouse button.

2. In the Context menu that appears, click Delete. A "Confirm Folder Delete" or a "Confirm File Delete" dialog box containing the name of the folder or file will appear.

3. Click the Yes button.

To copy a folder or file:

1. Click on the folder or file to be copied with the right mouse button.

2. In the Context menu that appears, click on Copy.

3. Open the folder where the copy is to be placed.

4. Click on the second folder with the right mouse button.

5. In the Context menu that appears, click on Paste.

To move a folder or file:

1. Click on the folder or file to be moved with the right mouse button.

2. In the Context menu that appears, click on Cut.

3. Open the folder where the copy is to be moved.

4. Click on the second folder with the right mouse button.

5. In the Context menu that appears, click on Paste.

You also can carry out some of the preceding operations by "drag and drop." For details, see the Help Topics accessed through the Windows Explorer Help menu. For instance, you can delete a folder or file by dragging it to the Recycle Bin and releasing the left mouse button.

Using the Open and Save As Dialog Boxes

In Section 1.2, we used the Open and Save As dialog boxes by just typing in the filespec for the desired file. These dialog boxes provide many features that assist with the locating of folders and files. Figure 1.5 shows an Open dialog box as it appears with Windows XP. In the Save As dialog box, "Look in:" is replaced with "Save in:", and "Files of type:" is replaced with "Save as type:".

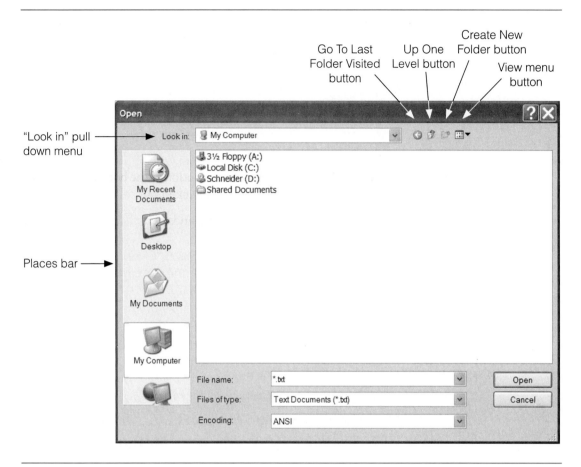

Figure 1.5 An Open dialog box from Windows XP.

You can begin the search by clicking on one of the icons in the Places bar. In Figure 1.5, the My Computer icon was pressed. The following steps would be used to locate the .txt file with filespec "C:\Programs\Ch06\USPRES.TXT".

1. Double-click on "Local Disk (C:)" to obtain a list of all the folders and files on the hard drive C:. (The text in the "Look in:" box will now read "Local Disk (C:)".

2. Double-click on the folder named "Programs" to obtain a list of its subfolders and files.

3. Double-click on "Ch06". The subfolders and files in the folder Ch06 will now be displayed. USPRES.TXT will be in the list.

4. Double-click on USPRES.TXT to open it.

The Save As dialog box operates in a similar way. However, after the desired folder is displayed in the "Save in:" box at the top of the dialog box, you would type the base name of the file into the "File name:" box.

Read-Only Attribute

Folders and files copied from a CD or DVD onto a hard disk are usually designated as read-only folders or files. You will be queried if you try to rename or delete read-only folders or files. Also, if you make changes to a read-only file with Notepad or Visual Basic, you will not be able to save the changes. (Read-only databases cannot even be accessed with Visual Basic.) The following steps change attributes of read-only folders and files.

1. From Windows Explorer, click on the folder or file with the right mouse button.

2. In the Context menu that appears, click on Properties. A Properties dialog box will appear.

3. Click on the General tab. In the Attributes section at the bottom of the window, the box next to "Read-only" will be checked.

4. Click on the box to remove the check mark, and then click on the OK button.

The above steps can be applied to a selected collection of files and folders. With Windows 2000 and XP, when you turn off the read-only attribute of a folder, the read-only attribute of each of its subfolders and files also can be turned off. We recommend that the Programs folder on the CD accompanying this book be copied onto your hard drive and that the read-only attribute of the folder (and its files) be turned off.

PRACTICE PROBLEMS 1.3

1. Where is the file having filespec "C:\TODAY.TXT" located?

2. Is "C:\Sales\New York" a filespec or a path?

EXERCISES 1.3

1. Explain why "Who is there?" is not a valid file name.

2. Explain why "FOUR STAR HOTEL ****" is not a valid name.

3. What is wrong with the filespec "C:/Sports/TENNIS.DOC"?

4. What is wrong with the filespec "A$:\Great\Films\CITIZEN KANE.TXT"?

5. What is the maximum number of characters in the name of a folder?

6. Why do files on CDs always have their read-only attribute turned on?

7. What is the path for a file whose filespec is "C:\Revenue\Chicago\MAIN .TXT"?

8. What is the filespec for the file PRES.TXT that is contained in the folder InfoUSA, where InfoUSA is a subfolder of the root directory of a diskette in the A drive?

9. Must the two files with filespecs "A:\DATA.TXT" and "A:\Info\ DATA.TXT" be identical—that is, copies of one another?

10. What is the difference between a filespec and a filename?

From Windows Explorer. highlight a folder on your computer that contains many files and then press Alt/V/D to select the Details option from the View menu. In Exercises 11–14, give the effect of clicking on the specified column head in the right pane.

11. Size

12. Type

13. Modified

14. Name

15. The CD accompanying this book has a folder named Pictures. With Windows 2000 or XP, use Windows Explorer to obtain a list of the files in this folder and then press Alt/V/H to select the Thumbnails option from the View menu. Describe what you see in the right pane.

16. Open the folder on your hard disk named My Documents. How many subfolders does the folder contain directly? How many files does the folder contain directly?

In Exercises 17 and 18, carry out the stated tasks.

17. (a) Take a blank diskette and create two folders named Laurel and Hardy.
(b) Create a subfolder of Laurel called Stan.
(c) Use Notepad to create a file containing the sentence "Here's another nice mess you've gotten me into." and save the file with the name QUOTE.TXT in the folder Laurel.
(d) Copy the file QUOTE.TXT into the folder Hardy.
(e) Rename the new copy of the file QUOTE.TXT as LINE.TXT.
(f) Delete the original copy of the file QUOTE.TXT.

18. (a) Take a blank diskette, create a folder named Slogans, and create two subfolders of Slogans named Coke and CocaCola.
(b) Use Notepad to create a file containing the sentence "It's the real thing." and save the file with the name COKE1970.TXT in the folder Coke.
(c) Use Notepad to create a file containing the phrase "The ideal brain tonic." and save the file with the name COKE1892.TXT in the folder Coke.
(d) Copy the two files in Coke into the folder CocaCola.
(e) Delete the folder Coke.
(f) Rename the folder CocaCola as Coke.

✔✔ **Solutions to Practice Problems 1.3**

1. The file is located in the root folder of the C drive.

2. It could be either. If "New York" is a folder, then it is a path. If "New York" is a file, it is a filespec. In this book, we always give extensions to files and never give extensions to folders. Therefore, by our conventions, "C:\Sales\New York" would be a path.

1.4 AN INTRODUCTION TO VISUAL BASIC

Visual Basic was designed to make user-friendly programs easier to develop. Prior to the creation of Visual Basic, developing a friendly user interface usually required a programmer to use a language such as C or C++, often requiring hundreds of lines of code just to get a window to appear on the screen. Now the same program can be created with much less time and fewer instructions using a language that is a direct descendant of BASIC—the language most accessible to beginning programmers. Visual Basic is used by millions of software developers.

Visual Basic 6.0 requires the Microsoft Windows operating system. Although you don't need to be an expert user of Microsoft Windows, you do need to know the basics before you can master Visual Basic—that is, you need to be comfortable with manipulating a mouse, you need to know how to manipulate a window, and you need to know how to use Notepad and Windows Explorer. However, there is no better way to master Microsoft Windows than to write applications for it—and that is what Visual Basic is all about.

Why Windows and Why Visual Basic?

What people call **graphical user interfaces**, or GUIs (pronounced "gooies"), have revolutionized the microcomputer industry. Instead of the confusing prompt that earlier users once saw, today's users are presented with a desktop filled with little pictures called icons. Icons provide a visual guide to what the program does or is used for.

Accompanying the revolution in how programs look was a revolution in how they feel. Consider a program that requests information for a database. Figure 1.6 shows how a program written before the advent of GUIs got its information. The program requests the six pieces of data one at a time, with no opportunity to go back and alter previously entered information. Then, the screen clears and the six inputs are again requested one at a time. Figure 1.7 shows how an equivalent Visual Basic program gets its information. The boxes may be filled in any order. When the user clicks on a box with the mouse, the cursor moves to that box. The user can either type in new information or edit the existing information. When the user is satisfied that all the information is correct, he or she just clicks on the Write to Database button. The boxes will clear and the data for another person can be entered. After all names have been entered, the user clicks on the Exit button. In Figure 1.6, the program is in control; in Figure 1.7, the user is in control!

```
Enter Name (Enter EOD to terminate): Mr. President
Enter Address: 1600 Pennsylvania Avenue
Enter City: Washington
Enter State: DC
Enter Zipcode: 20500
Enter Phone Number: 202-395-3000
```

Figure 1.6 Input screen of a DOS-based BASIC program to fill a database.

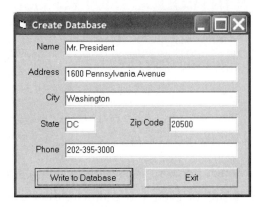

Figure 1.7 Input screen of a Visual Basic program to fill a database.

How You Develop a Visual Basic Application

One of the key elements of planning a Visual Basic application is deciding what the user sees—in other words, designing the screen. What data will he or she be entering? How large a window should the application use? Where will you place the command buttons—the "buttons" the user clicks on to activate the applications? Will the applications have places to enter text (text boxes) and places to display output? What kind of warning boxes (message boxes) should the application use? In Visual Basic, the responsive objects a program designer places on windows are called **controls**.

Two features make Visual Basic different from traditional programming tools.

1. You literally draw the user interface, much like using a paint program.

2. Perhaps more important, when you're done drawing the interface, the command buttons, text boxes, and other objects that you have placed in a blank window will automatically recognize user actions such as mouse movements and button clicks. That is, the sequence of procedures executed in your program is controlled by "events" that the user initiates rather than by a predetermined sequence of procedures in your program.

In any case, only after you design the interface does anything like traditional programming occur. Objects in Visual Basic recognize events like mouse clicks; how the objects respond to them depends on the instructions you write. You always need to write instructions in order to make controls respond to events. This makes Visual Basic programming fundamentally different from conventional programming.

Programs in traditional programming languages ran from the top down. For these programming languages, execution started from the first line and moved with the flow of the program to different parts as needed. A Visual Basic program works differently. Its core is a set of independent groups of instructions that are activated by the events they have been told to recognize. This event-driven methodology is a fundamental shift. The user decides the order in which things happen, not the programmer.

Most of the programming instructions in Visual Basic that tell your program how to respond to events like mouse clicks occur in what Visual Basic calls *event procedures*. Essentially, anything executable in a Visual Basic program is either in an event procedure or is used by an event procedure to help the procedure carry out its job. In fact, to stress that Visual Basic is fundamentally different from traditional programming languages, Microsoft uses the term *project*, rather than *program*, to refer to the combination of programming instructions and user interface that makes a Visual Basic application possible.

Here is a summary of the steps you take to design a Visual Basic application:

1. Design the appearance of the window that the user sees.

2. Determine the events that the controls on the window should recognize.

3. Write the event procedures for those events.

Now here is what happens when the program is running:

1. Visual Basic monitors the controls in the window to detect any event that a control can recognize (mouse movements, clicks, keystrokes, and so on).

2. When Visual Basic detects an event, it examines the program to see if you've written an event procedure for that event.

3. If you have written an event procedure, Visual Basic executes the instructions that make up that event procedure and goes back to Step 1.

4. If you have not written an event procedure, Visual Basic waits for the next event and goes back to Step 1.

These steps cycle continuously until the application ends. Usually, an event must happen before Visual Basic will do anything. Event-driven programs are reactive more than active—and that makes them more user friendly.

The Different Versions of Visual Basic

Visual Basic 1.0 first appeared in 1991. It was followed by version 2.0 in 1992, version 3.0 in 1993, version 4.0 in 1995, version 5.0 in 1997, and version 6.0 in 1998. Visual Basic 6.0 comes in four editions—Learning, Professional, Enterprise, and Working Model Edition. You can use any edition of Visual Basic 6.0 with this textbook.

Visual Basic .NET, released in February 2002, is not backward compatible with the earlier versions of Visual Basic. However, it has incorporated many features requested by software developers, such as true inheritance and powerful Web capabilities. Chapter 15 gives an introduction to Visual Basic .NET.

1.5 BIOGRAPHICAL HISTORY OF COMPUTING

The following people made important contributions to the evolution of the computer and the principles of programming. While we think of the computer as a modern technology, it is interesting to note that many of its technologies and concepts were developed decades before Silicon Valley became an address in American culture.

1800s

George Boole: a self-taught British mathematician; devised an algebra of logic that later became a key tool in computer design. The logical operators presented in Section 5.1 are also known as Boolean operators.

Charles Babbage: a British mathematician and engineer; regarded as the father of the computer. Although the mechanical "analytical engine" that he conceived was never built, it influenced the design of modern computers. It had units for input, output, memory, arithmetic, logic, and control. Algorithms were intended to be communicated to the computer via punched cards, and numbers were to be stored on toothed wheels.

Augusta Ada Byron: a mathematician and colleague of Charles Babbage; regarded as the first computer programmer. She encouraged Babbage to modify the design based on programming considerations. Together they developed the concepts of decision structures, loops, and a library of procedures. Decision structures, loops, and procedures are presented in Chapters 5, 6, and 4 of this text, respectively.

Herman Hollerith: the founder of a company that was later to become IBM; at the age of 20, he devised a computer that made it possible to process the data for the U.S. Census of 1890 in one-third the time required for the 1880 census. His electromagnetic "tabulating machine" passed metal pins through holes in punched cards and into mercury-filled cups to complete an electric circuit. Each location of a hole corresponded to a characteristic of the population.

1930s

Alan Turing: a gifted and far-sighted British mathematician; made fundamental contributions to the theory of computer science, assisted in the construction of some of the early large computers, and proposed a test for detecting intelligence within a machine. His theoretical "Turing machine" laid the foundation for the development of general-purpose programmable computers. He changed the course of the Second World War by breaking the German "Enigma" code, thereby making secret German messages comprehensible to the Allies.

John V. Atanasoff: a mathematician and physicist at Iowa State University; declared by a federal court in Minnesota to be the inventor of the first electronic digital special-purpose computer. Designed with the assistance of his graduate assistant, Clifford Berry, this computer used vacuum tubes (instead of the less efficient relays) for storage and arithmetic functions.

1940s

Howard Aiken: a professor at Harvard University; built the Mark I, a large-scale digital computer functionally similar to the "analytical engine" proposed by Babbage. This computer, which took five years to build and used relays for storage and computations, was technologically obsolete before it was completed.

Grace M. Hopper: retired in 1986 at the age of 79 as a rear admiral in the United States Navy; wrote the first major subroutine (a procedure that was used to calculate sin *x* on the Mark I computer) and one of the first assembly languages. In

1945, she found that a moth fused onto a wire of the Mark I was causing the computer to malfunction, thus the origin of the term "debugging" for finding errors. As an administrator at Remington Rand in the 1950s, Dr. Hopper pioneered the development and use of COBOL, a programming language for the business community written in English-like notation.

John Mauchley and J. Presper Eckert: electrical engineers working at the University of Pennsylvania; built the first large-scale electronic digital general-purpose computer to be put into full operation. The ENIAC used 18,000 vacuum tubes for storage and arithmetic computations, weighed 30 tons, and occupied 1500 square feet. It could perform 300 multiplications of two 10-digit numbers per second, whereas the Mark I required 3 seconds to perform a single multiplication. Later they designed and developed the UNIVAC I, the first commercial electronic computer.

John von Neumann: a mathematical genius and member of the Institute of Advanced Studies in Princeton, New Jersey; developed the stored program concept used in all modern computers. Prior to this development, instructions were programmed into computers by manually rewiring connections. Along with Hermann H. Goldstein, he wrote the first paper on the use of flowcharts.

Maurice V. Wilkes: an electrical engineer at Cambridge University in England and student of von Neumann; built the EDSAC, the first computer to use the stored program concept. Along with D. J. Wheeler and S. Gill, he wrote the first computer programming text, *The Preparation of Programs for an Electronic Digital Computer* (Addison-Wesley, 1951), which dealt in depth with the use and construction of a versatile subroutine library.

John Bardeen, Walter Brattain, and William Shockley: physicists at Bell Labs; developed the transistor, a miniature device that replaced the vacuum tube and revolutionized computer design. It was smaller, lighter, more reliable, and cooler than the vacuum tube.

1950s

John Backus: a programmer for IBM; in 1953, headed a small group of programmers who wrote the most extensively used early interpretive computer system, the IBM 701 Speedcoding System. An interpreter translates a high-level language program into machine language one statement at a time as the program is executed. In 1957, Backus and his team produced the compiled language Fortran, which soon became the primary academic and scientific language. A compiler translates an entire program into efficient machine language before the program is executed. (Visual Basic combines the best of both worlds. It has the power and speed of a compiled language and the ease of use of an interpreted language.)

Reynold B. Johnson: IBM researcher; invented the computer disk drive. His disk drive, known as the Ramac, weighed a ton and stored five megabytes of data. (In contrast, IBM recently released a drive that weighs less than a AA battery and stores 340 megabytes.) Mr. Johnson's other inventions include an electromechanical device that can read pencil-marked multiple-choice exams and grade them mechanically, the technology behind children's "Talk to Me Books," and major advances in the quality of tapes used in VCRs. He was a 1986 recipient of the National Medal of Technology.

Donald L. Shell: in 1959, the year that he received his Ph.D. in mathematics from the University of Cincinnati, published an efficient algorithm for ordering (or sorting) lists of data. Sorting has been estimated to consume nearly one-quarter of the running time of computers. The Shell sort is presented in Chapter 7 of this text.

1960s

John G. Kemeny and Thomas E. Kurtz: professors of mathematics at Dartmouth College and the inventors of BASIC; led Dartmouth to national leadership in the educational uses of computing. Kemeny's distinguished career included serving as an assistant to both John von Neumann and Albert Einstein, serving as president of Dartmouth College, and chairing the commission to investigate the Three Mile Island nuclear power plant accident. In recent years, Kemeny and Kurtz have devoted considerable energy to the promotion of structured BASIC.

Corrado Bohm and Guiseppe Jacopini: European mathematicians; proved that any program can be written with the three structures discussed in Section 2.2: sequence, decisions, and loops. This result led to the systematic methods of modern program design known as structured programming.

Edsger W. Dijkstra: professor of computer science at the Technological University at Eindhoven, The Netherlands; stimulated the move to structured programming with the publication of a widely read article, "Go To Statement Considered Harmful." In that article, he proposes that GOTO statements be abolished from all high-level languages such as BASIC. The modern programming structures available in Visual Basic do away with the need for GOTO statements.

Harlan B. Mills: IBM Fellow and professor of computer science at the University of Maryland; advocated the use of structured programming. In 1969, Mills was asked to write a program creating an information database for the *New York Times*, a project that was estimated to require 30 person-years with traditional programming techniques. Using structured programming techniques, Mills single-handedly completed the project in six months. The methods of structured programming are used throughout this text.

Donald E. Knuth: professor of computer science at Stanford University; generally regarded as the preeminent scholar of computer science in the world. He is best known for his monumental series of books, *The Art of Computer Programming*, the definitive work on algorithms.

Ted Hoff, Stan Mazer, Robert Noyce, and Federico Faggin: engineers at the Intel Corporation; developed the first microprocessor chip. Such chips, which serve as the central processing units for microcomputers, are responsible for the extraordinary reduction in the size of computers. A computer with greater power than the ENIAC now can be held in the palm of the hand.

Douglas Engelbart: human interface designer at the Stanford Research Institute; inventor of the computer mouse. While most of us would believe that the mouse is a new technology, the prototype was actually developed in the 1960s.

Funded by a government project, Engelbert and his team developed the idea of a mouse to navigate a computer screen with pop-up "windows" to present information to the user. In a contest to choose the best navigation tool, the mouse won over the light pen, a joystick, a "nose-pointing" device, and even a knee-pointing device!

1970s

Ted Codd: software architect; laid the groundwork for relational databases in his seminal paper, "A Relational Model of Data for Large Shared Data Banks," which appeared in the June 1970 issue of the *Communications of the ACM*. Relational databases are studied in Chapter 12 of this text.

Paul Allen and Bill Gates: cofounders of Microsoft Corporation; developed languages and the original operating system for the IBM PC. The operating system, known as PC-DOS, is a collection of programs that manage the operation of the computer. In 1974, Gates dropped out of Harvard after one year, and Allen left a programming job with Honeywell to write software together. Their initial project was a version of BASIC for the Altair, the first microcomputer. Microsoft is one of the most highly respected software companies in the United States and a leader in the development of programming languages.

Stephen Wozniak and Stephen Jobs: cofounders of Apple Computer Inc.; started the microcomputer revolution. The two had met as teenagers while working summers at Hewlett-Packard. Another summer, Jobs worked in an orchard, a job that inspired the names of their computers. Wozniak designed the Apple computer in Jobs's parents' garage, and Jobs promoted it so successfully that the company was worth hundreds of millions of dollars when it went public.

Dan Bricklin and Dan Fylstra: cofounders of Software Arts; wrote VisiCalc, the first electronic spreadsheet program. An electronic spreadsheet is a worksheet divided into rows and columns, which analysts use to construct budgets and estimate costs. A change made in one number results in the updating of all numbers derived from it. For instance, changing a person's housing expenses will immediately produce a change in total expenses. Bricklin got the idea for an electronic spreadsheet after watching one of his professors at Harvard Business School struggle while updating a spreadsheet at the blackboard. VisiCalc became so popular that many people bought personal computers just so they could run the program. A simplified spreadsheet is developed as a case study in Section 7.6 of this text. Chapter 14 shows how to use Visual Basic as a front end to access a spreadsheet.

Dennis Ritchie: member of the team at Bell Labs, creator of the C programming language. C is often referred to as a "portable assembly language." Programs developed in C benefit from speed of execution by being fairly low-level and close to assembly language, yet not being tied up in the specifics of a particular hardware architecture. This characteristic was particularly important to the development of the Unix operating system, which occurred around the same time as the development of C. Throughout the 1970s, 1980s, 1990s and even today, C has been a widely used language, particularly in situations where very fast program execution time is important.

Ken Thompson: member of the team at Bell Labs that created the Unix operating system as an alternative to the operating system for IBM's 360 mainframe computers. Unlike many other earlier operating systems, Unix was written in C instead of assembly language. This allowed it to be adapted to a wide variety of computer architectures. Programmers could then develop programs in C that were intended to run on a Unix operating system, avoiding much of the rewriting involved in porting (adapting) these programs from one type of machine to another. Over the past 30 years many variants of Unix have emerged, often referred to as different "flavors" of Unix. Unix and its variants have played a tremendous role in the growth of the Internet, as well as being an operating system used by many commercial, scientific, and academic institutions.

Alan Kay: a brilliant programmer at the University of Utah; crystallized the concept of reuseable building blocks of code to develop software programs. He developed a new language, Smalltalk, a pure object-oriented language, while at Xerox PARC in the 1970s. Most of today's programming languages such as C++, C#, Java, and Visual Basic make use of object-oriented features first developed in Smalltalk. Still, because of its conceptual purity, Kay believes that Smalltalk "is the only real object-oriented language."

Don Chamberlain: a Stanford Ph.D. and National Science Foundation scholar working at IBM; created a database programming language, later known as SQL (Structured Query Language). This innovative language was built on a "relational" model for data, where related data groups could be put into tables, then linked in various ways for easy programming and access. Very few people know that one of the world's largest software companies, Oracle Corporation, was founded on this technology, developed by IBM and published for all to use. SQL is covered in Chapter 12 of this book.

1980s

Phillip "Don" Estridge: head of a product group at IBM; directly responsible for the success of the personal computer. The ubiquity of the PC today can be attributed to a marketing decision by Estridge to make off-the-shelf, easily producible computers for a mass market, and to back that with IBM's huge marketing resources. Estridge's "skunk-works" group in Boca Raton broke many established IBM rules for product introduction. The IBM PC, introduced in 1981, chose an operating system from Microsoft and a processor chip from Intel over other vendors. This licensing deal opened the way for Microsoft's and Intel's successes today.

Mitchell D. Kapor: cofounder of Lotus Corporation; wrote the business software program 1-2-3, one of the most successful pieces of software for personal computers. Lotus 1-2-3 is an integrated program consisting of a spreadsheet, a database manager, and a graphics package. Databases are studied in Chapters 8 and 9 of this text and graphics in Chapter 10.

Tom Button: group product manager for applications programmability at Microsoft; headed the team that developed QuickBasic, QBasic, and Visual Basic. These modern, yet easy-to-use, languages have greatly increased the productivity of programmers.

Alan Cooper: director of applications software for Coactive Computing Corporation; considered the father of Visual Basic. In 1987, he wrote a program called Ruby that delivered visual programming to the average user. A few years later, Ruby was combined with QuickBasic to produce Visual Basic, the remarkably successful language that allows Windows programs to be written from within Windows easily and efficiently.

Tim Berners-Lee: British computer scientist, father of the World Wide Web. He proposed the Web project in 1989 while working in Switzerland. His brainchild has grown into a global phenomenon. Chapter 14 shows how to use Visual Basic to browse the Web.

Charles Simonyi: a Hungarian programmer; known to the industry as the "father of Word." He left his native Budapest as a 17-year-old prodigy to work at Xerox's prestigious Palo Alto Research Center (PARC), where he developed the capability of "What You See Is What You Get" (WYSIWYG) software. This technology, which allows users to define the fonts and presentations for computer output, opened the door to desktop publishing on the personal computer. In 1980, Simonyi joined a fledgling software company called Microsoft and developed Microsoft Word into one of the most widely used software programs ever.

Bjarne Stroustrup: a native of Denmark; creator of the C++ programming language. Stoustrup came to the United States to work for Bell Labs, during which time he created C++ to extend the C programming language with additional capabilities for object-oriented and generic programming. C++ has been one of the most widely used programming languages, combining the speed and efficiency of C with features that make the development of large-scale programs much simpler. Because of its ability to work at a low level in a manner similar to C, C++ remains the language of choice for many projects where other programming languages such as Java and Visual Basic are not suitable.

Richard M. Stallman: a star programmer at MIT's Artificial Intelligence Lab and a MacArthur Foundation Fellow; founded the Free Software Foundation (FSF). The FSF is an organization dedicated to promoting the free availablility of software for public access, modification, and improvement. This philosophy contrasts with that of a large part of the commercial software development world, where software is developed for sale, but the full rights to the source code are maintained by the company writing the software. Among his many technical accomplishments, Stallman created free versions of EMACS (a highly popular text editor on Linux/Unix systems) and GCC (a free C language compiler).

1990s

Marc Andreessen: a former graduate student at the University of Illinois; inventor of the Web browser. He led a small band of fellow students to develop Mosaic, a program that allowed the user to move around the World Wide Web by clicking on words and symbols. Andreessen went on to cofound NCSA and Netscape Communications Corporation. Netscape was the leading Web browser throughout the mid 1990s before being replaced by Microsoft's Internet Explorer. Chapter 14 shows how to use Visual Basic to build a simplified Web browser.

James Gosling: corporate vice president and Sun Fellow at Sun Microsystems; creator of the Java programming language. What started as an attempt to create a simple language for a networked world, Java, an object-oriented language, became a popular language for Internet programming. Java has become the primary teaching language at many universities.

Linus Torvalds: a graduate of the University of Helsinki in Finland; developed the popular Linux operating system. Linux began as a project by Linus to create a Unix operating system that could be used on personal computers. In the early 1990s, he began sharing the Linux source code with other OS programmers over the Internet, allowing them to contribute to and improve it. This philosophy resonated with the Internet culture, and the popularity of Linux grew quickly. Today, Linux is widely used, particularly as an operating system for Web servers. It is an open-source operating system, meaning that the source code (instructions) is made freely available for anyone to obtain, view, modify, and use.

2 Problem Solving

2.1   PROGRAM DEVELOPMENT CYCLE

We learned in the first chapter that hardware refers to the machinery in a computer system (such as the monitor, keyboard, and CPU) and software refers to a collection of instructions, called a **program** (or **project**), that directs the hardware. Programs are written to solve problems or perform tasks on a computer. Programmers translate the solutions or tasks into a language the computer can understand. As we write programs, we must keep in mind that the computer will only do what we instruct it to do. Because of this, we must be very careful and thorough with our instructions.

Performing a Task on the Computer

The first step in writing instructions to carry out a task is to determine what the **output** should be—that is, exactly what the task should produce. The second step is to identify the data, or **input**, necessary to obtain the output. The last step is to determine how to **process** the input to obtain the desired output—that is, to determine what formulas or ways of doing things can be used to obtain the output.

This problem-solving approach is the same as that used to solve word problems in an algebra class. For example, consider the following algebra problem:

How fast is a car traveling if it goes 50 miles in 2 hours?

The first step is to determine the type of answer requested. The answer should be a number giving the rate in miles per hour (the output). (The *rate* is also called *speed* or *velocity*.) The information needed to obtain the answer is the distance and time the car has traveled (the input). The formula

$$\text{rate} = \text{distance} / \text{time}$$

is used to process the distance traveled and the time elapsed in order to determine the rate. That is,

$$\text{rate} = 50 \text{ miles} / 2$$
$$= 25 \text{ miles} / \text{hour}$$

A pictorial representation of this problem-solving process is

We determine what we want as output, get the needed input, and process the input to produce the desired output.

In the following chapters we discuss how to write programs to carry out the preceding operations. But first we look at the general process of writing programs.

Program Planning

A baking recipe provides a good example of a plan. The ingredients and the amounts are determined by what is to be baked. That is, the *output* determines the *input* and the *processing*. The recipe, or plan, reduces the number of mistakes you might make if you tried to bake with no plan at all. Although it's difficult to imagine an architect building a bridge or a factory without a detailed plan, many programmers (particularly students in their first programming course) try to write programs without first making a careful plan. The more complicated the problem, the more complex the plan must be. You will spend much less time working on a program if you devise a carefully thought out step-by-step plan and test it before actually writing the program.

Many programmers plan their programs using a sequence of steps, referred to as the **program development cycle**. The following step-by-step process will enable you to use your time efficiently and help you design error-free programs that produce the desired output.

1. *Analyze:* Define the problem.

   Be sure you understand what the program should do—that is, what the output should be. Have a clear idea of what data (or input) are given and the relationship between the input and the desired output.

2. *Design:* Plan the solution to the problem.

   Find a logical sequence of precise steps that solve the problem. Such a sequence of steps is called an **algorithm**. Every detail, including obvious steps, should appear in the algorithm. In the next section, we discuss three popular methods used to develop the logic plan: flowcharts, pseudocode, and top-down charts. These tools help the programmer break a problem into a sequence of small tasks the computer can perform to solve the problem. Planning also involves using representative data to test the logic of the algorithm by hand to ensure that it is correct.

3. *Choose the interface:* Select the objects (text boxes, command buttons, etc.).

   Determine how the input will be obtained and how the output will be displayed. Then create objects to receive the input and display the output. Also, create appropriate command buttons and menus to allow the user to control the program.

4. *Code:* Translate the algorithm into a programming language.

   Coding is the technical word for writing the program. During this stage, the program is written in Visual Basic and entered into the computer. The programmer uses the algorithm devised in Step 2 along with a knowledge of Visual Basic.

5. *Test and debug:* Locate and remove any errors in the program.

   Testing is the process of finding errors in a program, and **debugging** is the process of correcting errors that are found. (An error in a program is called a **bug.**) As the program is typed, Visual Basic points out certain types of program errors. Other types of errors will be detected by Visual Basic when the program is executed; however, many errors due to typing mistakes, flaws in the algorithm, or incorrect usages of the Visual Basic language rules can be uncovered and corrected only by careful detective work. An example of such an error would be using addition when multiplication was the proper operation.

6. ***Complete the documentation:*** Organize all the material that describes the program.

Documentation is intended to allow another person, or the programmer at a later date, to understand the program. Internal documentation consists of statements in the program that are not executed, but point out the purposes of various parts of the program. Documentation might also consist of a detailed description of what the program does and how to use the program (for instance, what type of input is expected). For commercial programs, documentation includes an instruction manual and on-line help. Other types of documentation are the flowchart, pseudocode, and top-down chart that were used to construct the program. Although documentation is listed as the last step in the program development cycle, it should take place as the program is being coded.

2.2 PROGRAMMING TOOLS

This section discusses some specific algorithms and develops three tools used to convert algorithms into computer programs: flowcharts, pseudocode, and hierarchy charts.

You use algorithms every day to make decisions and perform tasks. For instance, whenever you mail a letter, you must decide how much postage to put on the envelope. One rule of thumb is to use one stamp for every five sheets of paper or fraction thereof. Suppose a friend asks you to determine the number of stamps to place on an envelope. The following algorithm will accomplish the task.

1. Request the number of sheets of paper; call it Sheets.   *(input)*

2. Divide Sheets by 5.   *(processing)*

3. Round the quotient up to the next highest whole number;
   call it Stamps.   *(processing)*

4. Reply with the number Stamps.   *(output)*

The preceding algorithm takes the number of sheets (Sheets) as input, processes the data, and produces the number of stamps needed (Stamps) as output. We can test the algorithm for a letter with 16 sheets of paper.

1. Request the number of sheets of paper; Sheets = 16.

2. Dividing 5 into 16 gives 3.2.

3. Rounding 3.2 up to 4 gives Stamps = 4.

4. Reply with the answer, 4 stamps.

This problem-solving example can be pictured by

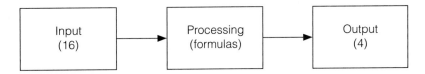

Of the program design tools available, three popular tools are the following:

Flowcharts: Graphically depict the logical steps to carry out a task and show how the steps relate to each other.

Pseudocode: Uses English-like phrases with some Visual Basic terms to outline the task.

Hierarchy charts: Show how the different parts of a program relate to each other.

Flowcharts

A flowchart consists of special geometric symbols connected by arrows. Within each symbol is a phrase presenting the activity at that step. The shape of the symbol indicates the type of operation that is to occur. For instance, the parallelogram denotes input or output. The arrows connecting the symbols, called **flowlines**, show the progression in which the steps take place. Flowcharts should "flow" from the top of the page to the bottom. Although the symbols used in flowcharts are standardized, no standards exist for the amount of detail required within each symbol.

A table of the flowchart symbols adopted by the American National Standards Institute (ANSI) follows. Figure 2.1 shows the flowchart for the postage stamp problem.

Symbol	Name	Meaning
⟶	*Flowline*	Used to connect symbols and indicate the flow of logic.
⬭	*Terminal*	Used to represent the beginning (Start) or the end (End) of a task.
▱	*Input/Output*	Used for input and output operations, such as reading and printing. The data to be read or printed are described inside.
▭	*Processing*	Used for arithmetic and data-manipulation operations. The instructions are listed inside the symbol.
◇	*Decision*	Used for any logic or comparison operations. Unlike the input/output and processing symbols, which have one entry and one exit flowline, the decision symbol has one entry and two exit paths. The path chosen depends on whether the answer to a question is "yes" or "no."
○	*Connector*	Used to join different flowlines.

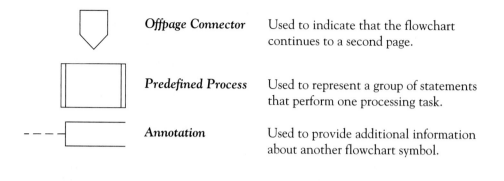

Offpage Connector	Used to indicate that the flowchart continues to a second page.
Predefined Process	Used to represent a group of statements that perform one processing task.
Annotation	Used to provide additional information about another flowchart symbol.

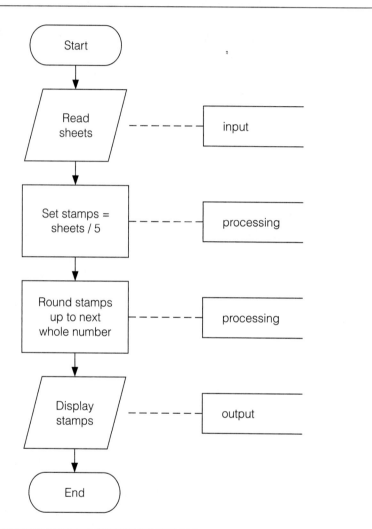

Figure 2.1 Flowchart for the postage stamp problem.

The main advantage of using a flowchart to plan a task is that it provides a pictorial representation of the task, which makes the logic easier to follow. We can clearly see every step and how each is connected to the next. The major disadvantage with flowcharts is that when a program is very large, the flowcharts may continue for many pages, making them difficult to follow and modify.

Pseudocode

Pseudocode is an abbreviated version of actual computer code (hence, *pseudocode*). The geometric symbols used in flowcharts are replaced by English-like statements that outline the process. As a result, pseudocode looks more like computer code than does a flowchart. Pseudocode allows the programmer to focus on the steps required to solve a problem rather than on how to use the computer language. The programmer can describe the algorithm in Visual Basic-like form without being restricted by the rules of Visual Basic. When the pseudocode is completed, it can be easily translated into the Visual Basic language.

The following is pseudocode for the postage stamp problem:

> **Program:** Determine the proper number of stamps for a letter
> Read Sheets   *(input)*
> Set the number of stamps to Sheets / 5   *(processing)*
> Round the number of stamps up to the next whole number   *(processing)*
> Display the number of stamps   *(output)*

Pseudocode has several advantages. It is compact and probably will not extend for many pages as flowcharts commonly do. Also, the plan looks like the code to be written and so is preferred by many programmers.

Hierarchy Chart

The last programming tool we'll discuss is the **hierarchy chart**, which shows the overall program structure. Hierarchy charts are also called structure charts, HIPO (Hierarchy plus Input-Process-Output) charts, top-down charts, or VTOC (Visual Table of Contents) charts. All these names refer to planning diagrams that are similar to a company's organization chart.

Hierarchy charts depict the organization of a program but omit the specific processing logic. They describe what each part, or **module**, of the program does and they show how the modules relate to each other. The details on how the modules work, however, are omitted. The chart is read from top to bottom and from left to right. Each module may be subdivided into a succession of submodules that branch out under it. Typically, after the activities in the succession of submodules are carried out, the module to the right of the original module is considered. A quick glance at the hierarchy chart reveals each task performed in the program and where it is performed. Figure 2.2 shows a hierarchy chart for the postage stamp problem.

The main benefit of hierarchy charts is in the initial planning of a program. We break down the major parts of a program so we can see what must be done in general. From this point, we can then refine each module into more detailed plans using flowcharts or pseudocode. This process is called the **divide-and-conquer** method.

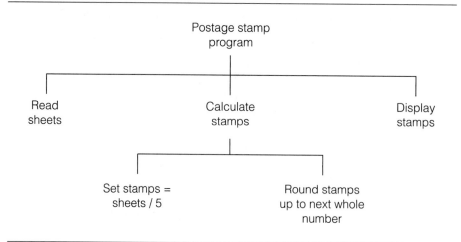

Figure 2.2 Hierarchy chart for the postage stamp problem.

The postage stamp problem was solved by a series of instructions to read data, perform calculations, and display results. Each step was in a sequence; that is, we moved from one line to the next without skipping over any lines. This kind of structure is called a **sequence structure**. Many problems, however, require a decision to determine whether a series of instructions should be executed. If the answer to a question is "Yes," then one group of instructions is executed. If the answer is "No," then another is executed. This structure is called a **decision structure**. Figure 2.3 contains the pseudocode and flowchart for a decision structure.

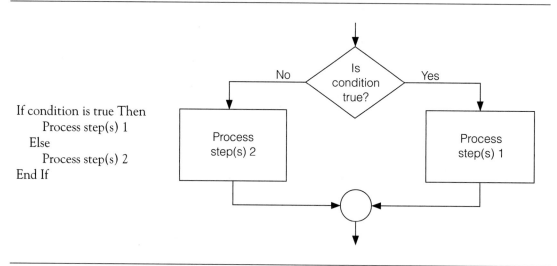

Figure 2.3 Pseudocode and flowchart for a decision structure.

The sequence and decision structures are both used to solve the following problem.

Direction of Numbered NYC Streets Algorithm

Problem: Given a street number of a one-way street in New York, decide the direction of the street, either eastbound or westbound.

Discussion: There is a simple rule to tell the direction of a one-way street in New York: Even-numbered streets run eastbound.

Input: Street number

Processing: Decide if the street number is divisible by 2.

Output: "Eastbound" or "Westbound"

Figures 2.4 through 2.6 show the flowchart, pseudocode, and hierarchy chart for the New York numbered streets problem.

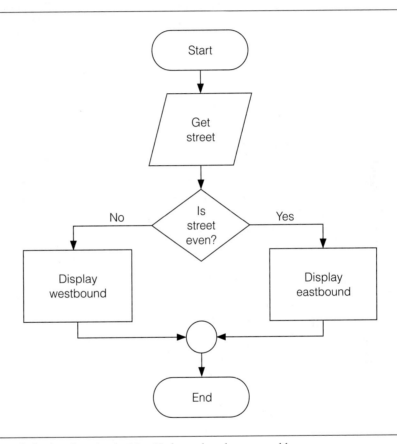

Figure 2.4 Flowchart for the New York numbered streets problem.

Program: Determine the direction of a numbered NYC street.

Get Street
If Street is even Then
    Display Eastbound
  Else
    Display Westbound
End If

Figure 2.5 Pseudocode for the New York numbered streets problem.

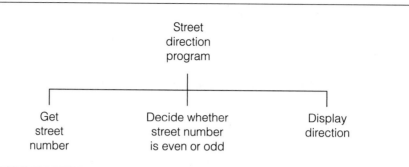

Figure 2.6 Hierarchy chart for the New York numbered streets problem.

The solution to the next problem requires the repetition of a series of instructions. A programming structure that executes instructions many times is called a **loop structure**.

We need a test (or decision) to tell when the loop should end. Without an exit condition, the loop would repeat endlessly (an infinite loop). One way to control the number of times a loop repeats (often referred to as the number of passes or iterations) is to check a condition before each pass through the loop and continue executing the loop as long as the condition is true. See Figure 2.7.

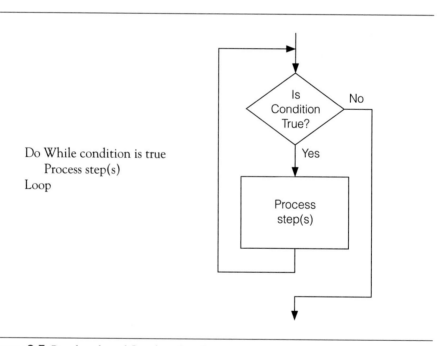

Do While condition is true
    Process step(s)
Loop

Figure 2.7 Pseudocode and flowchart for a loop.

Class Average Algorithm

Problem: Calculate and report the grade-point average for a class.

Discussion: The average grade equals the sum of all grades divided by the number of students. We need a loop to read and then add (accumulate) the grades for each student in the class. Inside the loop, we also need to total (count) the number of students in the class. See Figures 2.8 to 2.10.

Input: Student grades

Processing: Find the sum of the grades; count the number of students; calculate average grade = sum of grades / number of students.

Output: Average grade

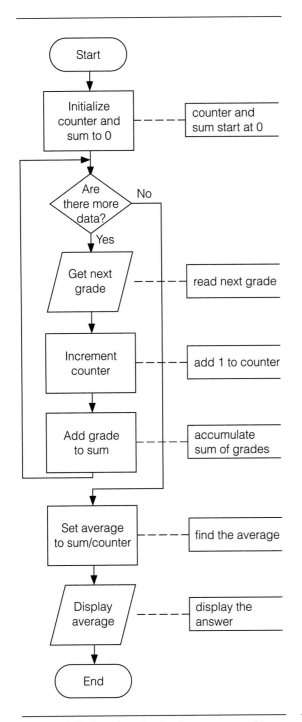

Figure 2.8 Flowchart for the class average problem.

Program: Determine the average grade of a class
Initialize Counter and Sum to 0
Do While there are more data
   Get the next Grade
   Add the Grade to the Sum
   Increment the Counter
Loop
Compute Average = Sum / Counter
Display Average

Figure 2.9 Pseudocode for the class average problem.

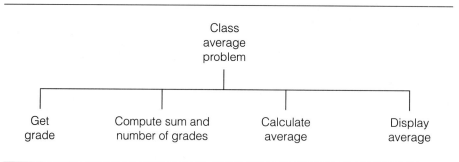

Figure 2.10 Hierarchy chart for the class average problem.

Comments

1. Tracing a flowchart is like playing a board game. We begin at the Start symbol and proceed from symbol to symbol until we reach the End symbol. At any time, we will be at just one symbol. In a board game, the path taken depends on the result of spinning a spinner or rolling a pair of dice. The path taken through a flowchart depends on the input.

2. The algorithm should be tested at the flowchart stage before being coded into a program. Different data should be used as input, and the output checked. This process is known as **desk checking**. The test data should include non-standard data as well as typical data.

3. Flowcharts, pseudocode, and hierarchy charts are universal problem-solving tools. They can be used to construct programs in any computer language, not just Visual Basic.

4. Flowcharts are used throughout this text to provide a visualization of the flow of certain programming tasks and Visual Basic control structures. Major examples of pseudocode and hierarchy charts appear in the case studies.

5. There are four primary logical programming constructs: sequence, decision, loop, and unconditional branch. Unconditional branch, which appears in some languages as Goto statements, involves jumping from one place in a program to another. Structured programming uses the first three constructs but forbids the fourth. One advantage of pseudocode over flowcharts is that pseudocode has no provision for unconditional branching and thus forces the programmer to write structured programs.

6. Flowcharts are time consuming to write and difficult to update. For this reason, professional programmers are more likely to favor pseudocode and hierarchy charts. Because flowcharts so clearly illustrate the logical flow of programming techniques, however, they are a valuable tool in the education of programmers.

7. There are many styles of pseudocode. Some programmers use an outline form, whereas others use a form that looks almost like a programming language. The pseudocode appearing in the case studies of this text focuses on the primary tasks to be performed by the program and leaves many of the routine details to be completed during the coding process. Several Visual Basic keywords, such as, Print, If, Do, and While, are used extensively in the pseudocode appearing in this text.

8. Many people draw rectangles around each item in a hierarchy chart. In this text, rectangles are omitted in order to make hierarchy charts easier to draw and thereby to encourage their use.

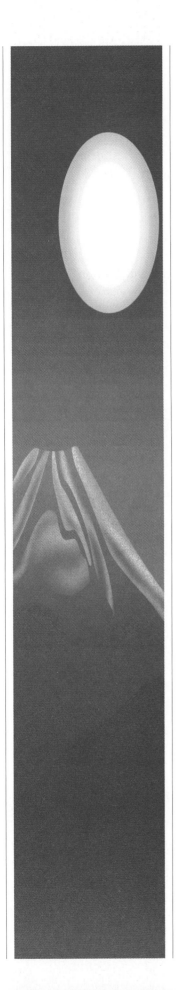

3 Fundamentals of Programming in Visual Basic

3.1 VISUAL BASIC OBJECTS

Visual Basic programs display a Windows style screen (called a **form**) with boxes into which users type (and in which users edit) information and buttons that they click to initiate actions. The boxes and buttons are referred to as **controls**. Forms and controls are called **objects**. In this section, we examine forms and four of the most useful Visual Basic controls.

Note: If Visual Basic has not been installed on your computer, you can install it by following the steps outlined on the first page of Appendix B.

Invoking Visual Basic 6.0: To invoke Visual Basic, click the Windows Start button, point to Programs (or All Programs), point to Microsoft Visual Basic 6.0, and click on Microsoft Visual Basic 6.0 in the final list.

With all versions of Visual Basic 6.0, the center of the screen will contain the New Project window of Figure 3.1. The main part of the window is a tabbed dialog box with three tabs—New, Existing, and Recent. (If the New tab is not in the foreground, click on it to bring it to the front.) The number of project icons showing are either three (with the Working Model and Learning Editions) or thirteen (with the Professional and Enterprise Editions).

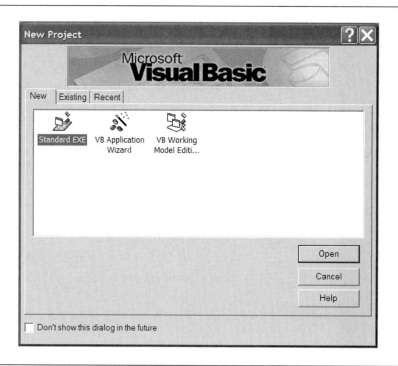

Figure 3.1 New Project window from the Working Model Edition of VB 6.0.

Double-click the Standard EXE icon to bring up the initial Visual Basic screen in Figure 3.2. The appearance of this screen varies slightly with the different versions of Visual Basic.

The **Menu bar** of the Visual Basic screen displays the commands you use to work with Visual Basic. Some of the menus, like File, Edit, View, and Window, are common to most Windows applications. Others, such as Project, Format, and Debug, provide commands specific to programming in Visual Basic.

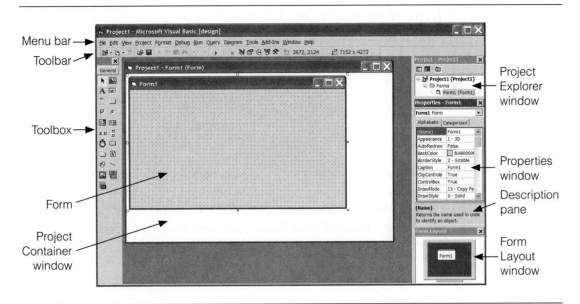

Figure 3.2 The initial Visual Basic screen.

The **Toolbar** is a collection of icons that carry out standard operations when clicked. For example, the fifth icon, which looks like a diskette, can be used to save the current program to a disk. To reveal the function of a Toolbar icon, hover the mouse pointer over the icon for a few seconds. The little information rectangle that pops up is called a **tooltip**.

The large stippled **Form window**, or **form** for short, becomes a Windows window when a program is executed. Most information displayed by the program appears on the form. The information usually is displayed in controls that the programmer has placed on the form. The **Form Layout window** allows you to position the location of the form at run time relative to the entire screen using a small graphical representation of the screen.

The **Project Explorer window** holds the names of the forms used in a program. The **Properties window** is used to change how objects look and react.

The icons in the **Toolbox** represent controls that can be placed on the form. The four controls discussed in this chapter are text boxes, labels, command buttons, and picture boxes.

Text boxes: You use a text box primarily to get information, referred to as **input**, from the user.

Labels: You place a label to the left of a text box to tell the user what type of information to enter into the text box. You also use labels to display output.

Command buttons: The user clicks a command button to initiate an action.

Picture boxes: You use a picture box to display text or graphics output.

A Text Box Walkthrough

1. Double-click on the text box icon. (The text box icon consists of the letters ab and a vertical bar cursor inside a rectangle and is the fourth icon in the

Toolbox.) A rectangle with eight small squares, called **sizing handles**, appears at the center of the form. See Figure 3.3.

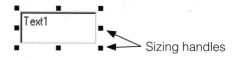

Figure 3.3 A text box with sizing handles.

2. Click anywhere on the form outside the rectangle to remove the handles.

3. Click on the rectangle to restore the handles. An object showing its handles is said to be **selected**. A selected object can have its size altered, location changed, and other properties modified.

4. Move the mouse arrow to the handle in the center of the right side of the text box. The cursor should change to a double arrow (↔). Hold down the left mouse button, and move the mouse to the right. The text box is stretched to the right. Similarly, grabbing the text box by one of the other handles and moving the mouse stretches the text box in another direction. For instance, you use the handle in the upper-left corner to stretch the text box up and to the left. Handles also can be used to make the text box smaller.

5. Move the mouse arrow to any point of the text box other than a handle, hold down the left mouse button, and move the mouse. You can now drag the text box to a new location. Using Steps 4 and 5, you can place a text box of any size anywhere on the form.

   Note: The text box should now be selected; that is, its sizing handles should be showing. If not, click anywhere inside the text box to select it.

6. Press the delete key, Del, to remove the text box from the form. Step 7 gives an alternative way to place a text box of any size at any location on the form.

7. Click on the text box icon in the Toolbox. Then move the mouse pointer to any place on the form. (When over the form, the mouse pointer becomes a pair of crossed thin lines.) Hold down the left mouse button, and move the mouse on a diagonal to generate a rectangle. Release the mouse button to obtain a selected text box. You can now alter the size and location as before.

   Note: The text box should now be selected; that is, its sizing handles should be showing. If not, click anywhere inside the text box to select it.

8. Press F4 to activate the Properties window. (You can also activate the Properties window by clicking on it or clicking on the Properties window icon in the Toolbar.) See Figure 3.4. The first line of the Properties window (called the **Object box**) reads "Text1 TextBox". Text1 is the current name of the text box. The two tabs permit you to view the list of properties either alphabetically or grouped into categories. Text boxes have 43 properties that can be grouped into 7 categories. Use the up- and down-arrow keys (or the up- and down-scroll arrows) to move through the list. The left column gives the property names and the right column gives the current settings of the prop-

erties. We discuss four properties in this walkthrough. **Note:** If the Description pane is not visible, right-click on the Properties window and then click on "Description." The Description pane describes the currently highlighted property.

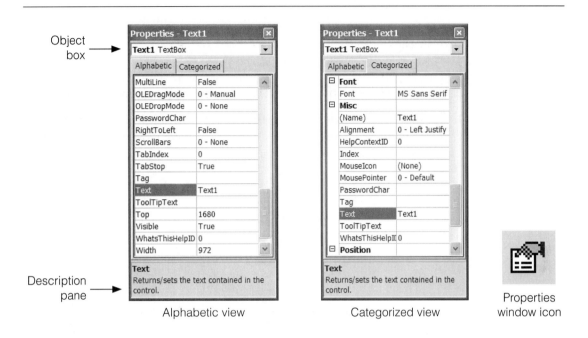

Object box

Description pane

Alphabetic view

Categorized view

Properties window icon

Figure 3.4 Text box Properties window.

9. Move to the Text property with the up- and down-arrow keys. (Alternatively, scroll until the property is visible and click on the property.) The Text property, which determines the words in the text box, is now highlighted. Currently, the words are set to "Text1" in the **Settings box** on the right.

10. Type your first name. As you type, your name replaces "Text1" in both the Settings box and the text box. See Figure 3.5. (Alternatively, you could have clicked on the Settings box and edited its contents.)

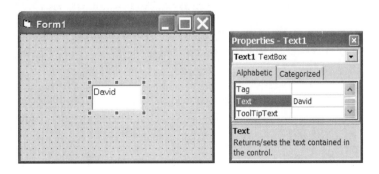

Figure 3.5 Setting the text property to David.

11. Click at the beginning of your name in the Settings box and add your title, such as Mr., Ms., or The Honorable. (If you mistyped your name, you can easily correct it now.)

12. Press Shift+Ctrl+F to move to the first property that begins with the letter F. Now use the down-arrow key or the mouse to highlight the property ForeColor. This property determines the color of the information displayed in the text box.

13. Click on the down arrow in the right part of the Settings box, and then click on the Palette tab to display a selection of colors. See Figure 3.6. Click on one of the colors, such as *blue* or *red*. Notice the change in the color of your name.

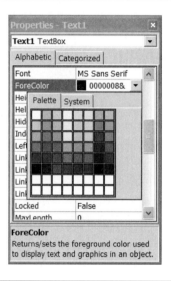

Figure 3.6 Setting the ForeColor property.

14. Highlight the Font property with a single click of the mouse. The current font is named MS Sans Serif.

15. Click on the ellipsis (...) box in the right part of the Settings box to display a dialog box. See Figure 3.7. The three lists give the current name (MS Sans Serif), current style (Regular), and current size (8) of the font. You can change any of these attributes by clicking on an item in its list or by typing into the box at the top of the list. Click on Bold in the style list, and click on 12 in the size list. Now click on the OK button to see your name displayed in a larger bold font.

16. Click on the text box and resize it to be about 3 inches wide and 1 inch high.

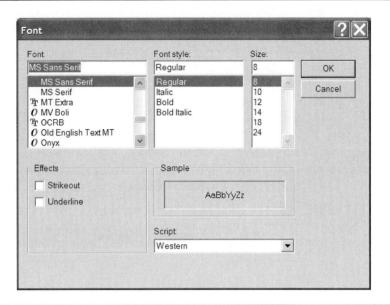

Figure 3.7 The Font dialog box.

Visual Basic programs consist of three parts—interface, values of properties, and code. Our interface consists of a form with a single object, a text box. We have set a few properties for the text box—the text (namely, your name), the foreground color, the font style, and the font size. In Section 3.2, we see how to place code into a program. Visual Basic endows certain capabilities to programs that are independent of any code we will write. We will now run the existing codeless program in order to experience these capabilities.

17. Press F5 to run the program. (Alternatively, a program can be run from the menu by pressing Alt/R/S or by clicking on the Start icon ▶, the twelfth icon on the Toolbar.) After a brief delay, a copy of the form appears that has no grid dots. (Grid dots are needed only when designing the form. Therefore, they disappear when the program is run.)

18. The cursor is at the beginning of your name. Press the End key to move the cursor to the end of your name. Now type in your last name, and then keep typing. Eventually, the words will scroll to the left.

19. Press Home to return to the beginning of the text. You have a miniature word processor at your disposal. You can place the cursor anywhere you like to add or delete text. You can drag the cursor across text to select a block, place a copy of the block in the clipboard with Ctrl+C, and then duplicate it anywhere with Ctrl+V.

20. To end the program, press Alt+F4. Alternatively, you can end a program by clicking on the End icon ■, the fourteenth icon on the Toolbar, or clicking on the form's close button ☒.

21. Select the text box, activate the Properties window, select the MultiLine property, click on the down-arrow button, and finally click on True. The MultiLine property has been changed from False to True.

22. Run the program, and type in the text box. Notice that now words wrap around when the end of a line is reached. Also, text will scroll up when it reaches the bottom of the text box.

23. End the program.

24. Press Alt/F/V, or click on the Save Project icon 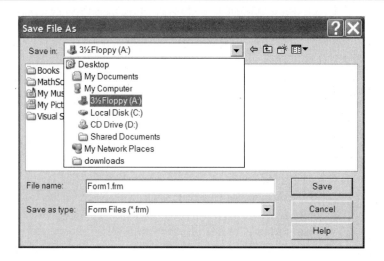 to save the work done so far. A Save File As dialog box appears. See Figure 3.8. Visual Basic creates two disk files to store a program. The first, with the extension ".frm," is entered into the Save File As dialog box and the second, with the extension ".vbp," into a Save Project As dialog box. Visual Basic refers to programs as **projects**.

Figure 3.8 The Save File As dialog box.

25. Type a file name, such as *testprog,* into the "File name" box. The extension ".frm" automatically will be appended to the name. Do not press the Enter key yet. (Pressing the Enter key has the same effect as clicking Save.) The selection in the "Save in" box tells where your program will be saved. Alter it as desired. (Suggestion: If you are using a computer in a campus computer lab, you probably should use a diskette to save your work. If so, place the diskette in a drive, say, the A drive, and select 3^1/$_2$ Floppy (A:) in the "Save in" box.)

26. Click the Save button when you are ready to go on. (Alternatively, press Tab several times until the Save button is highlighted and then press Enter.) The Save Project As dialog box appears.

27. Type a file name into the File name box. You can use the same name, such as *testprog*, as before. Then proceed as in Steps 25 and 26. (The extension .vbp will be added.)

28. Press Alt/F/N to begin a new program. (As before, select Standard EXE.)

29. Place three text boxes on the form. (If you use the double-click technique, move each text box out of the center of the form before creating the next.) Notice that they have the names Text1, Text2, and Text3.

30. Run the program. Notice that the cursor is in Text1. We say that Text1 has the **focus**. (This means that Text1 is the currently selected object and any keyboard actions will be sent directly to this object.) Any text typed will display in that text box.

31. Press Tab once. Now, Text2 has the focus. When you type, the characters appear in Text2.

32. Press Tab several times and then press Shift+Tab a few times. With Tab, the focus cycles through the objects on the form in the order the objects were created. With Shift+Tab, the focus cycles in the reverse order.

33. End the program.

34. Press Alt/F/O, or click on the Open Project icon 🖼 to reload your first program. When a dialog box asks if you want to save your changes, click the No button or press N. An Open Project dialog box appears on the screen. Click on the Recent tab to see a list of the programs most recently opened or saved. Your first program and its location should appear at the top of the list. (**Note:** You can also find any program by clicking on the Existing tab and using the dialog box to search for the program.)

35. Click on the name of your first program and then click on the Open button. Alternatively, double-click on the name. **Note:** If you do not see the program's form, open the Forms folder in the Project Explorer window and then double-click on Form1.

🖳 A Command Button Walkthrough

1. Press Alt/F/N and double-click on Standard EXE to start a new program. There is no need to save anything.

2. Double-click on the command button icon in the Toolbox to place a command button in the center of the form. (The rectangular-shaped command button icon is the sixth icon in the Toolbox.)

3. Activate the Properties window, highlight the Caption property, and type "Please Push Me". See Figure 3.9. Notice that the letters appear on the command button as they are typed. The button is too small.

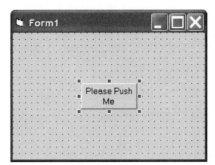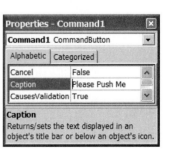

Figure 3.9 Setting the Caption property.

4. Click on the command button to select it, and then enlarge it to accommodate the phrase "Please Push Me" on one line.

5. Run the program, and click on the command button. The command button appears to move in and then out. In Section 3.2, we write code that is activated when a command button is pushed.

6. End the program, and select the command button.

7. From the Properties window, edit the Caption setting by inserting an ampersand (&) before the first letter, P. Notice that the ampersand does not show on the button. However, the letter following the ampersand is now underlined. See Figure 3.10. Pressing Alt+P while the program is running triggers the same event as clicking the command button. Here, P is referred to as the **access key** for the command button. (The access key is always specified by the character following the ampersand.)

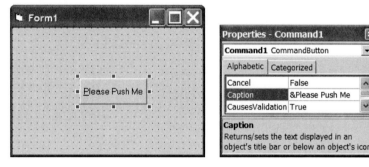

Figure 3.10 Designating P as an access key.

A A Label Walkthrough

1. Press Alt/F/N and double-click on Standard EXE to start a new program. There is no need to save anything.

2. Double-click on the label icon to place a label in the center of the form. (The label icon, a large letter A, is the third icon in the Toolbox.)

3. Activate the Properties window, highlight the Caption property, and type "Enter Your Phone Number". Such a label would be placed next to a text box into which the user will type a phone number.

4. Click on the label to select it, and then widen it until all words are on the same line.

5. Make the label narrower until the words occupy two lines.

6. Activate the Properties window, and double-click on the Alignment property. Double-click two more times and observe the label's appearance. The combination of sizing and alignment permits you to design a label easily.

7. Run the program. Nothing happens, even if you click on the label. Labels just sit there. The user cannot change what a label displays unless you write code to make the change.

8. End the program.

A Picture Box Walkthrough

1. Press Alt/F/N and double-click on Standard EXE to start a new program. There is no need to save anything.

2. Double-click on the picture box icon to place a picture box in the center of the form. (The picture box icon is the second icon in the Toolbox. It contains a picture of the sun shining over a desert.)

3. Enlarge the picture box.

4. Run the program. Nothing happens and nothing will, no matter what you do. Although picture boxes look like text boxes, you can't type in them. However, you can display text in them with statements discussed later in this chapter, you can draw lines and circles in them with statements discussed in Chapter 10, and you can insert pictures into them.

5. End the program and click the picture box to select it.

6. Activate the Properties window, and double-click on the Picture property. A Load Picture dialog box appears. See Figure 3.11.

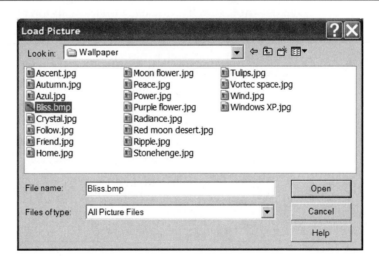

Figure 3.11 The Load Picture dialog box.

7. Locate a file with the extension *bmp* and then double-click on the file. With Windows XP, a good candidate is the file with filespec C:\Windows\Web\Wallpaper\Bliss.bmp displayed in Figure 3.12. (Also, the CD accompanying this textbook contains several picture files in the folder Pictures.)

Figure 3.12 A picture box filled with the Bliss.bmp picture.

8. Click on the picture box and press Del to remove the picture box.

Comments

1. When selecting from a list, double-clicking has the same effect as clicking once and pressing Enter.

2. On a form, the Tab key cycles through the objects that can get the focus, and in a dialog box, it cycles through the items.

3. The form itself is also an object and has properties. For instance, you can change the text in the title bar with the Caption property. You can move the form by dragging the title bar of its Project Container window.

4. The name of an object is used in code to refer to the object. By default, objects are given names like Text1 and Text2. You can use the Properties window to change the Name property of an object to a more meaningful name. (The Name property is always the first property in the list of properties. An object's name must start with a letter and can be a maximum of 40 characters. It can include numbers and underline (_) characters, but cannot include punctuation or spaces.) Also, Microsoft recommends that each name begin with a three-letter prefix that identifies the type of the object. See the table below. Beginning with Section 3.2, we will use suggestive names and these prefixes whenever possible.

Object	Prefix	Example
command button	cmd	cmdComputeTotal
form	frm	frmPayroll
label	lbl	lblInstructions
picture box	pic	picClouds
text box	txt	txtAddress

To display the name of the form, and the names of all the controls on the form, click on the down-arrow icon at the right of the Property window's Object box. You can make one of these items the selected item by clicking on its name.

5. The Name and Caption properties of a command button are both initially set to something like Command1. However, changing one of these properties does not affect the setting of the other property. Similarly for the Name and Caption properties of forms and labels, and for the Name and Text properties of text boxes.

6. The color settings appear as strings of digits and letters preceded by &H and trailed with &. Don't concern yourself with the notation.

7. Here are some fine points on the use of the Properties window.

(a) Press Shift+Ctrl+*letterkey* to highlight the first property that begins with that letter. Successive pressings highlight successive properties that begin with that letter.

(b) To change the selected object from the Properties window, click on the down-arrow icon at the right of the Object box of the Properties window. Then select the new object from the dropdown list.

8. Some useful properties that have not been discussed are the following:

(a) BorderStyle: Setting the BorderStyle to "0 – None" removes the border from an object.

(b) Visible: Setting the Visible property to False causes an object to disappear when the program is run. The object can be made to reappear with code.

(c) BackColor: This property specifies the background color for a text box, label, picture box, or form. It also specifies the background color for a command button having the Style property set to "1 – Graphical." (Such a command button can display a picture.)

(d) BackStyle: The BackStyle property of a label is opaque by default. The rectangular region associated with the label is filled with the label's background color and caption. Setting the background style of a label to transparent causes whatever is behind the label to remain visible; the background color of the label essentially becomes "see through."

(e) Font: Can be set to any of Windows' fonts, such as Courier New and Times New Roman. Two unusual fonts are Symbol and Wingdings. For instance, with the Wingdings font, pressing the keys for %, &, ', and J yields a bell, a book, a candle, and a smiling face, respectively. To view the character sets for the different Windows' fonts, click on Windows' Start button, and successively select Programs (or All Programs), Accessories, System Tools, and Character Map. (With older versions of Windows, skip System Tools.) Then click on Character Map or press the Enter key. After selecting a character in a font, you can place its corresponding keystroke into a property's Settings box by double-clicking on the character, clicking on the Copy button, highlighting the property, and pressing Ctrl+V.

9. When you click on a property in the Properties window, a description of the property appears just below the window. Additional information about many of the properties can be found in Appendix C. With the Learning, Professional, and Enterprise Editions of VB 6.0 you can obtain very detailed (and somewhat advanced) information about a property by clicking on the property and pressing F1 for Help.

10. Most properties can be set or altered with code as the program is running instead of being preset from the Properties window. For instance, a command button can be made to disappear with a line such as `Command1.Visible = False.` See Section 3.2 for details.

11. The BorderStyle and MultiLine properties of a text box can be set only from the Properties window. You cannot alter them during run time.

12. Of the objects discussed in this section, only command buttons have true access keys.

13. If you inadvertently double-click an object in a form, a window containing two lines of text will appear. (The first line begins Private Sub.) This is a Code window, which is discussed in the next section. Press Ctrl+Z to undo the addition of this new code. To return to the form, click its window or click on Object in the View menu.

14. To enlarge (or decrease) the Project Container window, position the mouse cursor anywhere on the right or bottom edge and drag the mouse. To enlarge (or decrease) the form, select the form and drag one of its sizing handles. Alternatively, you can enlarge either the Project Container window or the form by clicking on its Maximize button.

15. We will always be selecting the Standard EXE icon from the New Project window.

✔ **PRACTICE PROBLEMS 3.1**

1. What is the difference between the Caption and the Name properties of a command button?

2. Suppose in an earlier session you created an object that looks like an empty rectangle. It might be a picture box, a text box with Text property set to nothing (blanked out by deleting all characters), or a label with a blank caption and BorderStyle property set to Fixed Single. How might you determine which it is?

➤ **EXERCISES 3.1**

1. Why are command buttons sometimes called "push buttons"?

2. How can you tell if a program is running by looking at the screen?

3. Create a form with two command buttons, run the program, and click on each button. Do you notice anything different about a button after it has been clicked?

4. Place a text box on a form and select the text box. What is the effect of pressing the various arrow keys while holding down the Ctrl key? The Shift key?

5. Place three text boxes vertically on a form with Text3 above Text2 and Text2 above Text1. Then run the program and successively press Tab. Notice that the text boxes receive the focus from bottom to top. Experiment with vari-

ous configurations of command buttons and text boxes to convince yourself that objects get the focus in the order in which they were created.

6. While a program is running, an object is said to **lose focus** when the focus moves from that object to another object. In what three ways can the user cause an object to lose focus?

In Exercises 7 through 28, carry out the task. Use a new form for each exercise.

7. Place CHECKING ACCOUNT in the title bar of a form.

8. Create a text box containing the words PLAY IT, SAM in blue letters.

9. Create an empty text box with a yellow background.

10. Create a text box containing the word HELLO in large italic letters.

11. Create a text box containing the sentence "After all is said and done, more is said than done." The sentence should occupy three lines, and each line should be centered horizontally in the text box.

12. Create a borderless text box containing the words VISUAL BASIC in bold white letters on a red background.

13. Create a text box containing the words VISUAL BASIC in Courier font.

14. Create a command button containing the word PUSH.

15. Create a command button containing the word PUSH in large italic letters.

16. Create a command button containing the word PUSH in nonbold letters with the letter P underlined.

17. Create a command button containing the word PUSH with the letter H as access key.

18. Create a command button containing the caption HALF MOON, a white background, and the picture file MOON7.BMP from the Pictures folder of the CD accompanying this book.

19. Create a label containing the word ALIAS.

20. Create a label containing the word ALIAS in white on a blue background.

21. Create a label with a border containing the centered italicized word ALIAS.

22. Create a label containing VISUAL on the first line and BASIC on the second line. Each word should be right justified. (**Note:** An extra space will appear after "VISUAL".)

23. Create a label containing a picture of a diskette. (**Hint:** Use the Wingdings character <.) Make the diskette as large as possible.

24. Create a label with a border and containing the bold word ALIAS in the Terminal font.

25. Create a picture box with a yellow background.

26. Create a picture box with no border and a red background.

27. Create a picture box containing two command buttons.

28. Create a picture box with a blue background containing a picture box with a white background.

In Exercises 29 through 36, create the interface shown in the figure. (These exercises give you practice creating objects and assigning properties. The interfaces do not necessarily correspond to actual programs.)

29.

🔹 Dynamic Duo	▭ ☐ ✕

<u>B</u>atman

<u>R</u>obin

30.

🔹 Enter Names	▭ ☐ ✕

Name [   ]

Enter

31.

🔹 Fill in the Blank	▭ ☐ ✕

Toto, I don't think we're in [   ]

A Quote from the Wizard of Oz

32.

🔹 Wise Saying	▭ ☐ ✕

It is better to be a coward for a minute than dead for the rest of your life.

A Proverb

33.

🔹 An Uncle's Advice	▭ ☐ ✕

The three most important things in life are

1   Be kind.

2   Be kind.

3   Be kind.

Henry James' advice to his nephew.

34.

🔹 3 Rectangles	▭ ☐ ✕

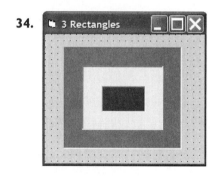

35.

🔹 Picture Box	▭ ☐ ✕

This picture is contained in the file picbox.bmp in the Pictures folder of the CD accompanying this book.

36.

🔹 Quiz	▭ ☐ ✕

Who wrote 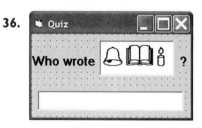 ?

[   ]

37. Create a replica of your bank check on a form. Words common to all checks, such as PAY TO THE ORDER OF, should be contained in labels. Items specific to your checks, such as your name at the top left, should be contained in text boxes. Make the check on the screen resemble your check as much as possible.

38. Create a replica of your campus ID on a form. Words that are on all student IDs, such as the name of the college, should be contained in labels. Information specific to your ID, such as your name and social security number, should be contained in text boxes. Simulate your picture with a text box containing a smiling face—a size 24 Wingdings J.

39. If you are familiar with Paint (one of the programs in the group Accessories), use Paint to make a drawing and then save it as a .bmp file. In Visual Basic, create a picture box containing the picture.

The following hands-on exercises develop additional techniques for manipulating and accessing controls placed on a form.

40. Place a text box on a form and select the text box. What is the effect of pressing the various arrow keys while holding down the Ctrl key?

41. Place a text box on a form and select the text box. What is the effect of pressing the various arrow keys while holding down the Shift key?

42. Place a command button on a form and select the button. Open the Format menu, hover the mouse arrow over "Center in Form," and click on "Horizontally." What happens?

43. Repeat Exercise 42, but click on "Vertically."

44. Place three text boxes vertically on a form with Text3 above Text2, and Text2 above Text1. Then run the program and successively press Tab. Notice that the text boxes receive the focus from bottom to top.

(a) Experiment with various configurations of buttons and text boxes to convince yourself that controls get the focus in the order in which they were created.
(b) Look at the settings of the TabIndex properties for one of the configurations from part (a) and interpret the settings. (**Note:** The order in which controls get the focus can be altered by changing the settings of their TabIndex properties.)

45. Place three text boxes vertically on a form. Make them of different sizes and so that their left sides do not line up. Click on the first text box. While holding down the Ctrl key, click on the second text box and then the third text box. Notice that the first two text boxes have white sizing handles and the third has black sizing handles. This process is referred to as **selecting multiple controls**.

(a) What is the effect of pressing the left-arrow key while holding down the Ctrl key?
(b) What is the effect of pressing the left-arrow key while holding down the Shift key?

(c) Press F4, set the ForeColor property to Blue, and press Enter. What happens?

(d) Open the Format menu and experiment with the Align and Make Same Size options.

✔✔ **Solutions to Practice Problems 3.1**

1. The Caption property specifies the words appearing on the command button, whereas the Name property specifies the designation used to refer to the command button. Initially, they have the same value, such as Command1. However, each can be changed independently of the other.

2. Click on the object to select it, and then press F4 to activate its Properties window. The Object box gives the Name of the object (in bold letters) and its type, such as Label, TextBox, or PictureBox.

   We have examined only four of the objects from the Toolbox. To determine the type of one of the other objects, hold the mouse pointer over it for a few seconds.

3.2 VISUAL BASIC EVENTS

When a Visual Basic program runs, the form and its controls appear on the screen. Normally, nothing happens until the user takes an action, such as clicking a control or pressing a key. We call such an action an **event**. The programmer writes code that reacts to an event by performing some functionality.

The three steps to creating a Visual Basic program are as follows:

1. Create the interface; that is, generate, position, and size the objects.

2. Set properties; that is, configure the appearance of the objects.

3. Write the code that executes when events occur.

Section 3.1 covered Steps 1 and 2; this section is devoted to Step 3.

Code consists of statements that carry out tasks. Visual Basic has a repertoire of over 200 statements, and we will use many of them in this text. In this section we limit ourselves to statements that change properties of objects while a program is running.

Properties of an object are changed in code with statements of the form

```
objectName.property = setting
```

where *objectName* is the name of the form or the control, *property* is one of the properties of the object, and *setting* is a valid setting for that object. Such statements are called **assignment statements**. They assign values to properties. Here are three other assignment statements.

The statement

```
txtBox.Font.Size = 12
```

sets the size of the characters in the text box named txtBox to 12 point.

The statement

```
txtBox.Font.Bold = True
```

converts the characters in the text box to boldface.

The statement

```
txtBox.Text = ""
```

clears the contents of the text box; that is, it invokes the blank setting.

Most events are associated with objects. The event "click on cmdButton" is different from the event "click on picBox." These two events are specified cmdButton_ Click and picBox_Click. The statements to be executed when an event occurs are written in a block of code called an **event procedure**. The structure of an event procedure is

```
Private Sub objectName_event()
   statements
End Sub
```

The word Sub in the first line signals the beginning of the event procedure, and the first line identifies the object and the event occurring to that object. The last line signals the termination of the event procedure. The statements to be executed appear between these two lines. (**Note:** The word Private indicates that the event procedure cannot be invoked by an event from another form. This will not concern us until much later in the text. The word Sub is an abbreviation of *Subprogram.*) For instance, the event procedure

```
Private Sub cmdButton_Click()
   txtBox.Text = ""
End Sub
```

clears the contents of the text box when the command button is clicked.

An Event Procedure Walkthrough

The form in Figure 3.13, which contains a text box and a command button, will be used to demonstrate what event procedures are and how they are created. Three event procedures will be used to alter the appearance of a phrase that is typed into the text box. The event procedures are txtPhrase_LostFocus, txtPhrase_GotFocus, and cmdBold_Click.

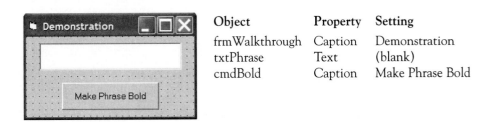

Object	Property	Setting
frmWalkthrough	Caption	Demonstration
txtPhrase	Text	(blank)
cmdBold	Caption	Make Phrase Bold

Figure 3.13 The interface for the event procedure walkthrough.

1. Create the interface in Figure 3.13. The Name properties of the form, text box, and command button should be set as shown in the Object column. The Caption property of the form should be set to Demonstration, the Text property of the text box should be made blank, and the Caption property of the command button should be set to Make Phrase Bold.

2. Double-click on the text box. A window, called a **Code window**, appears. See Figure 3.14. Just below the title bar are two dropdown list boxes. The left box is called the **Object box** and the right box is called the **Procedure box**. (When you position the mouse pointer over one of these list boxes, its type appears.)

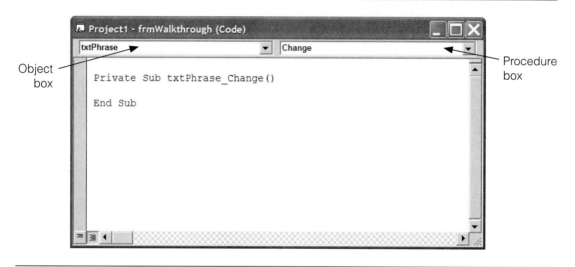

Figure 3.14 A Code window.

3. Click on the down-arrow button to the right of the Procedure box. The dropdown menu that appears contains a list of all possible event procedures associated with text boxes. See Figure 3.15.

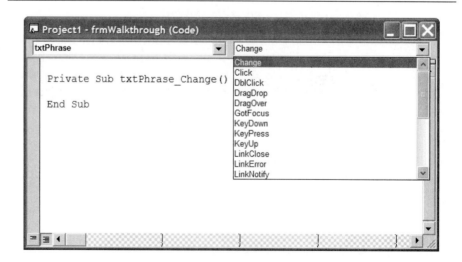

Figure 3.15 Dropdown menu of event procedures.

4. Scroll down the list of event procedures and click on LostFocus. (LostFocus is the 14th event procedure.) The lines

```
Private Sub txtPhrase_LostFocus()

End Sub
```

appear in the Code window with a blinking cursor poised at the beginning of the blank line. The first line is the declaration statement for the event procedure named txtPhrase_LostFocus. This procedure is triggered by the txtPhrase's LostFocus event. That is, whenever txtPhrase loses the focus, the code between the two lines shown above will be executed.

5. Type the line

```
txtPhrase.Font.Size = 12
```

between the existing two lines. (We usually indent lines inside procedures.) (After you type each period, the editor displays a list containing possible choices of items to follow the period. See Figure 3.16. This feature is called "List Properties/Methods" or "Statement Completion" and is one of the helpful features of Visual Basic 6.0 that use a Microsoft technology called IntelliSense. In Figure 3.16, instead of typing the word "Size," you can double-click on "Size" in the displayed list or highlight the word "Size" and press Tab.) The screen appears as in Figure 3.17. We have now created an event procedure that is activated whenever the text box loses the focus.

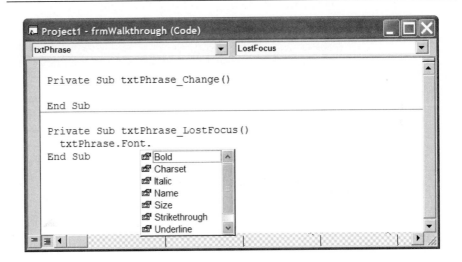

Figure 3.16 A LostFocus event procedure.

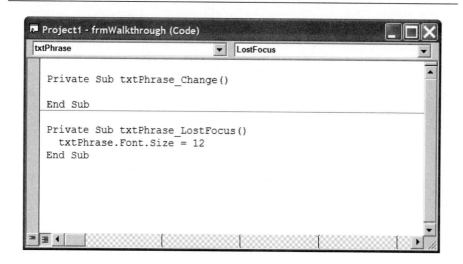

Figure 3.17 A LostFocus event procedure.

6. Let's create another event procedure for the text box. Click on the down-arrow button to the right of the Procedure box, scroll up the list of event procedures, and click on GotFocus. Then type the lines

```
txtPhrase.Font.Size = 8
txtPhrase.Font.Bold = False
```

between the existing two lines. See Figure 3.18.

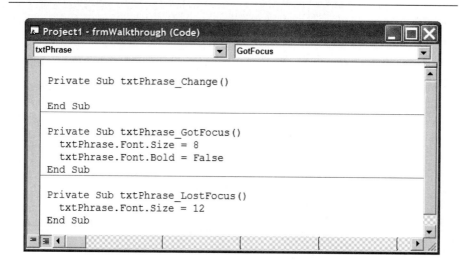

Figure 3.18 A GotFocus event procedure.

7. The txtPhrase_Change event procedure in Figure 3.18 was not used and can be deleted. To delete the procedure, highlight it by dragging the mouse across the two lines of code, and then press the Del key.

8. Let's now create an event procedure for the command button. Click on the down-arrow button to the right of the Object box. The dropdown menu contains a list of the objects, along with a mysterious object called (General). See Figure 3.19. [We'll discuss (General) in the next chapter.]

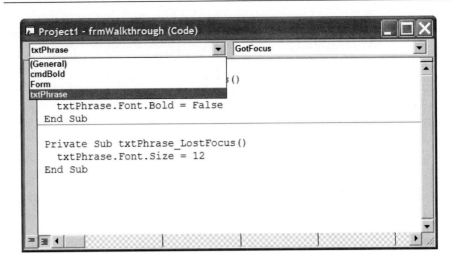

Figure 3.19 List of objects.

9. Click on cmdBold. The event procedure cmdBold_Click is displayed. Type in the line

```
txtPhrase.Font.Bold = True
```

The screen appears as in Figure 3.20, and the program is complete.

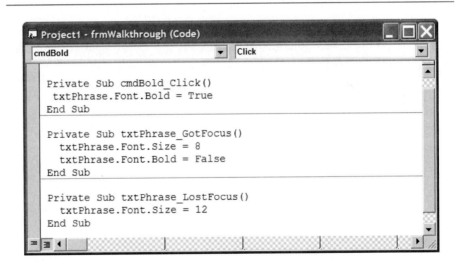

Figure 3.20 The three event procedures.

10. Now run the program by pressing F5.

11. Type something into the text box. In Figure 3.21, the words "Hello Friend" have been typed. (Recall that a text box has the focus whenever it is ready to accept typing—that is, whenever it contains a blinking cursor.)

Figure 3.21 Text box containing input.

12. Press the Tab key. The contents of the text box will be enlarged as in Figure 3.22. When Tab was pressed, the text box lost the focus; that is, the event LostFocus happened to txtPhrase. Thus, the event procedure txtPhrase_LostFocus was called, and the code inside the procedure was executed.

Figure 3.22 Text box after it has lost the focus.

13. Click on the command button. This calls the event procedure cmd-Bold_Click, which converts the text to boldface. See Figure 3.23.

Figure 3.23 Text box after the command button has been clicked.

14. Click on the text box or press the Tab key to move the cursor (and, therefore, the focus) to the text box. This calls the event procedure txtPhrase_GotFocus, which restores the text to its original state.

15. You can repeat Steps 11 through 14 as many times as you like. When you are finished, end the program by pressing Alt+F4, clicking the End icon on the Toolbar, or clicking the Close button (☒) on the form.

Comments

1. To hide the Code window, press the right mouse button and click on Hide. You can also hide it by clicking on the icon at the left side of the title bar and clicking on Close. To view a hidden Code window, press Alt/View/Code. To hide a form, close its container. To view a hidden form, press Alt/View/Object.

2. The form is the default object in Visual Basic code. That is, code such as

   ```
   Form1.property = setting
   ```

   can be written as

   ```
   property = setting
   ```

   Also, event procedures associated with Form1 appear as

   ```
   Form_event()
   ```

   rather than

   ```
   Form1_event()
   ```

3. Another useful command is SetFocus. The statement

   ```
   object.SetFocus
   ```

   moves the focus to the object.

4. We have ended our programs by clicking the End icon or pressing Alt+F4. A more elegant technique is to create a command button, call it cmdQuit, with caption Quit and the event procedure:

   ```
   Private Sub cmdQuit_Click()
     End
   End Sub
   ```

5. Certain words, such as Sub, End, and False, have special meanings in Visual Basic and are referred to as **keywords** or **reserved words**. The Visual Basic editor automatically capitalizes the first letter of a keyword and displays the word in blue.

6. The code editor can detect certain types of errors. For instance, consider the line

   ```
   txtPhrase.Font.Bold = False
   ```

   from the walkthrough. Suppose you neglected to type the word False to the right of the equal sign before leaving the line. The automatic syntax checker would tell you something was missing by displaying the left message box at the top of page 66. (Also, the line would turn red.) On the other hand, suppose in the cmdBold_Click procedure you misspell the keyword "Bold" as "bolt." You might notice something is wrong when the letter "b" is not capitalized. If not, you will certainly know about the problem when the program is run, because Visual Basic will display the right message box at the top of page 66 when you click on the command button. After you click on Debug, the line containing the offending word will be highlighted.

 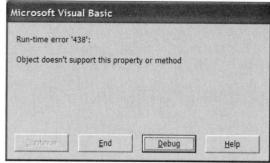

7. At design time, colors are selected from a palette. At run time, the eight most common colors can be assigned with the color constants vbBlack, vbRed, vbGreen, vbYellow, vbBlue, vbMagenta, vbCyan, and vbWhite. For instance, the statement

```
picBox.BackColor = vbYellow
```

gives picBox a yellow background.

8. For statements of the form *object.property* = *setting*, with properties Caption, Text, or Font.Name, the setting must be surrounded by quotes. (For instance, lblTwo.Caption = "Name", txtBox.Text = "Fore", and picBox.Font.Name = "Courier New".) When the words True or False appear to the right of the equal sign, they should *not* be surrounded by quotation marks.

9. Code windows have many features of word processors. For instance, the operations cut, copy, paste, find, undo, and redo can be carried out with the sixth through eleventh icons of the Toolbar. These operations, and several others, also can be initiated from the Edit menu.

10. Names of existing event procedures associated with an object are *not* automatically changed when you rename the object. You must change them yourself and also must change any references to the object. Therefore, you should finalize the names of your objects before you create their event procedures.

11. If you find the automatic List Properties/Methods feature distracting, you can turn it off by pressing Alt/Tools/Options, selecting the Editor page, and deselecting Auto List Members. If you do so, you can still display a list manually at the appropriate time by pressing Ctrl+J.

12. When you double-click on a control or a form, the first and last lines for the most common event procedure for the object are placed in the Code window. The event that appears most frequently in this book is the Click event for command buttons.

13. Assignment statements can be written preceded with the keyword Let. For instance, txtBox.Text = "Hello" also can be written Let txtBox.Text = "Hello". Therefore, assignment statements are also known as Let statements.

PRACTICE PROBLEM 3.2

1. You can always locate an existing event procedure by searching through the Code window with the Pg Up and Pg Dn keys. Give another way.

EXERCISES 3.2

In Exercises 1 through 6, describe the contents of the text box after the command button is clicked.

1.
```
Private Sub cmdButton_Click()
    txtBox.Text = "Hello"
End Sub
```

2.
```
Private Sub cmdButton_Click()
    txtBox.ForeColor = vbRed
    txtBox.Text = "Hello"
End Sub
```

3.
```
Private Sub cmdButton_Click()
    txtBox.Font.Italic = True
    txtBox.Text = "Hello"
End Sub
```

4.
```
Private Sub cmdButton_Click()
    txtBox.Font.Size = 24
    txtBox.Text = "Hello"
End Sub
```

5.
```
Private Sub cmdButton_Click()
    txtBox.Text = "Hello"
    txtBox.Visible = False
End Sub
```

6.
```
Private Sub cmdButton_Click()
    txtBox.Font.Bold = True
    txtBox.Text = "Hello"
End Sub
```

In Exercises 7 through 10, assume the three objects on the form were created in the order txtOne, txtTwo, and lblOne. Also assume that txtOne has the focus. Determine the output displayed in lblOne when Tab is pressed.

7.
```
Private Sub txtOne_LostFocus()
    lblOne.ForeColor = vbGreen
    lblOne.Caption = "Hello"
End Sub
```

8.
```
Private Sub txtOne_LostFocus()
    lblOne.Caption = "Hello"
End Sub
```

9.
```
Private Sub txtTwo_GotFocus()
    lblOne.Font.Name = "Courier"
    lblOne.Font.Size = 24
    lblOne.Caption = "Hello"
End Sub
```

10.
```
Private Sub txtTwo_GotFocus()
    lblOne.Font.Italic = True
    lblOne.Caption = "Hello"
End Sub
```

In Exercises 11 through 16, determine the errors.

11.
```
Private Sub cmdButton_Click()
    frmHi = "Hello"
End Sub
```

12.
```
Private Sub cmdButton_Click()
    txtOne.ForeColor = "red"
End Sub
```

13.
```
Private Sub cmdButton_Click()
    txtBox.Caption = "Hello"
End Sub
```

14.
```
Private Sub cmdButton_Click()
    lblTwo.Text = "Hello"
End Sub
```

15.
```
Private Sub cmdButton_Click()
    lblTwo.BorderStyle = 2
End Sub
```

16.
```
Private Sub cmdButton_Click()
    txtOne.MultiLine = True
End Sub
```

In Exercises 17 through 32, write a line (or lines) of code to carry out the task.

17. Display "E.T. phone home." in lblTwo.

18. Display "Play it, Sam." in lblTwo.

19. Display "The stuff that dreams are made of." in red letters in txtBox.

20. Display "Life is like a box of chocolates." in Courier New font in txtBox.

21. Delete the contents of txtBox.

22. Delete the contents of lblTwo.

23. Make lblTwo disappear.

24. Remove the border from lblTwo.

25. Give picBox a blue background.

26. Place a bold red "Hello" in lblTwo.

27. Place a bold italic "Hello" in txtBox.

28. Make picBox disappear.

29. Give the focus to cmdButton.

30. Remove the border from picBox.

31. Place a border around lblTwo and center its contents.

32. Give the focus to txtBoxTwo.

33. Describe the GotFocus event in your own words.

34. Describe the LostFocus event in your own words.

35. Labels and picture boxes have an event called DblClick that responds to a double-clicking of the left mouse button. Write a simple program to test this event. Determine whether or not you can trigger the DblClick event without also triggering the Click event.

36. Write a simple program to demonstrate that a command button's Click event is triggered when you press the Enter key while the command button has the focus. Does this also happen with text boxes and picture boxes?

In Exercises 37 through 42, the interface and initial properties are specified. Write the code to carry out the stated task.

37. When one of the three command buttons is pressed, the words on the command button are displayed in the label with the stated alignment.

Object	Property	Setting
frmEx37	Caption	Alignment
lblShow	BorderStyle	1-Fixed Single
cmdLeft	Caption	Left Justify
cmdCenter	Caption	Center
cmdRight	Caption	Right Justify

38. When one of the command buttons is pressed, the face changes to a smiling face (Wingdings character "J") or a frowning face (Wingdings character "L").

Object	Property	Setting
frmEx38	Caption	Face
lblFace	Font	Wingdings
	Caption	K
	Font Size	24
cmdSmile	Caption	Smile
cmdFrown	Caption	Frown

39. Pressing the command buttons alters the background and foreground colors in the text box.

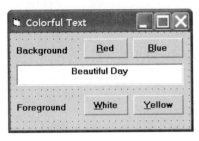

Object	Property	Setting
frmEx39	Caption	Colorful Text
lblBack	Caption	Background
cmdRed	Caption	&Red
cmdBlue	Caption	&Blue
txtShow	Text	Beautiful Day
	MultiLine	True
	Alignment	2 – Center
lblFore	Caption	Foreground
cmdWhite	Caption	&White
cmdYellow	Caption	&Yellow

40. While one of the three text boxes has the focus, its text is bold. When it loses the focus, it ceases to be bold. The command buttons enlarge text (Font.Size = 12) or return text to normal size (Font.Size = 8).

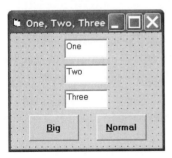

Object	Property	Setting
frmEx40	Caption	One, Two, Three
txtOne	Text	One
txtTwo	Text	Two
txtThree	Text	Three
cmdBig	Caption	&Big
cmdNormal	Caption	&Normal

41. When you click on one of the three small text boxes at the bottom of the form, an appropriate saying is displayed in the large text box. Use the sayings "I like life, it's something to do."; "The future isn't what it used to be."; and "Tell the truth and run."

Object	Property	Setting
frmEx41	Caption	Sayings
txtQuote	Text	(blank)
txtLife	Text	Life
txtFuture	Text	Future
txtTruth	Text	Truth

42. After the user types something into the text box, the user can change the font by clicking on one of the command buttons.

Object	Property	Setting
frmEx42	Caption	Fonts
txtShow	Text	(blank)
cmdCour	Caption	Courier
cmdSerif	Caption	MS Serif
cmdWing	Caption	Wingdings

In Exercises 43 through 48, write a program with a Windows-style interface to carry out the task.

43. Allow the user to click on command buttons to change the size of the text in a text box and alter its appearance between bold and italics.

44. A form contains two text boxes and one large label between them with no preset caption. When the focus is on the first text box, the label reads "Enter your full name." When the focus is on the second text box, the label reads "Enter your phone number, including area code."

45. Use the same form and properties as in Exercise 38, with the captions for the command buttons replaced with Vanish and Reappear. Clicking a button should produce the stated result.

46. Simulate a traffic light with three small square picture boxes placed vertically on a form. Initially, the bottom picture box is solid green and the other picture boxes are white. When the Tab key is pressed, the middle picture box turns yellow and the bottom picture box turns white. The next time Tab is pressed, the top picture box turns red and the middle picture box turns white. Subsequent pressing of the Tab key cycles through the three colors. *Hint:* First, place the bottom picture box on the form, then the middle picture box, and finally the top picture box.

47. The form contains four square buttons arranged in a rectangular array. Each button has the caption "Push Me." When you click on a button, the button disappears and the other three become or remain visible.

48. The form contains two text boxes into which the user types information. When the user clicks on one of the text boxes, it becomes blank and its contents are displayed in the other text box.

✔✔ Solution to Practice Problem 3.2

1. With the Code window showing, click on the arrow to the right of the Object box and then select the desired object. Then click on the arrow to the right of the Procedure box, and select the desired event procedure.

3.3 NUMBERS

Much of the data processed by computers consists of numbers. In "computerese," numbers are called **numeric constants**. This section discusses the operations that are performed with numbers and the ways numbers are displayed.

Arithmetic Operations

The five standard arithmetic operations in Visual Basic are addition, subtraction, multiplication, division, and exponentiation. (Because exponentiation is not as familiar as the others, it is reviewed in detail in Comment 9.) Addition, subtraction, and division are denoted in Visual Basic by the standard symbols +, −, and /, respectively. However, the notations for multiplication and exponentiation differ from the customary mathematical notations.

Mathematical Notation	Visual Basic Notation
$a \cdot b$ or $a \times b$	$a * b$
a^r	$a \wedge r$

(The asterisk [∗] is the upper character of the 8 key. The caret [∧] is the upper character of the 6 key.) **Note:** In this book, the proportional font used for text differs from the fixed-width font used for programs. In the program font, the asterisk appears as a five-pointed star (*).

One way to show a number on the screen is to display it in a picture box. If n is a number, then the instruction

```
picBox.Print n
```

displays the number n in the picture box. If the picBox.Print instruction is followed by a combination of numbers and arithmetic operations, it carries out the operations and displays the result. Print is a reserved word and the Print operation is called a **method**. (Generally, a method is a process that performs a task for a particular object.) Another important method is Cls. The statement

```
picBox.Cls
```

erases all text and graphics from the picture box picBox.

EXAMPLE 1　The following program applies each of the five standard arithmetic operations to the numbers 3 and 2. Preceding the program is the form design and a table showing the names of the objects on the form and the settings, if any, for properties of these objects. This form design is also used in the discussion and examples in the remainder of this section.

The word "Run" in the phrasing [Run . . .] indicates that F5 should be pressed to execute the program. Notice that in the output 3 / 2 is displayed in decimal form. Visual Basic never displays numbers as common fractions. **Note:** All programs appearing in examples and case studies are provided on the CD accompanying this book. See the discussion at the end of the book for details.

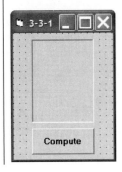

Object	Property	Setting
frm3_3_1	Caption	3-3-1
picResults		
cmdCompute	Caption	Compute

```
Private Sub cmdCompute_Click()
  picResults.Cls
  picResults.Print 3 + 2
  picResults.Print 3 - 2
  picResults.Print 3 * 2
  picResults.Print 3 / 2
  picResults.Print 3 ^ 2
  picResults.Print 2 * (3 + 4)
End Sub
```

[Run and then click the command button.]

Scientific Notation

Let us review powers of 10 and scientific notation. Decimal notation is based on a systematic use of exponents.

$$10^1 = 10 \qquad\qquad 10^{-1} = 1/10 = .1$$
$$10^2 = 100 \qquad\qquad 10^{-2} = .01$$
$$10^3 = 1000 \qquad\qquad 10^{-3} = .001$$
$$\vdots \qquad\qquad\qquad\qquad \vdots$$
$$10^n = \underbrace{1000...0}_{n \text{ zeros}} \qquad 10^{-n} = \underbrace{.000...01}_{n \text{ digits}}$$

Scientific notation provides a convenient way of writing numbers by using powers of 10 to stand for zeros. Numbers are written in the form $b \cdot 10^r$, where b is a number from 1 up to (but not including) 10, and r is an integer. For example, it is much more convenient to write the diameter of the sun (1,400,000,000 meters) in scientific notation: $1.4 \cdot 10^9$ meters. Similarly, rather than write .0000003 meters for the diameter of a bacterium, it is simpler to write $3 \cdot 10^{-7}$ meters.

Any acceptable number can be entered into the computer in either standard or scientific notation. The form in which Visual Basic displays a number depends on many factors, with size being an important consideration. In Visual Basic, $b \cdot 10^r$ is usually written as bEr. (The letter E is an abbreviation for *exponent*.) The following forms of the numbers just mentioned are equivalent.

1.4 * 10^9	1.4E+09	1.4E+9	1.4E9	1400000000
3 * 10^-7	3E-07	3E-7	.0000003	

Visual Basic displays r as a two-digit number, preceded by a plus sign if r is positive and a minus sign if r is negative.

EXAMPLE 2 The following program illustrates scientific notation. Visual Basic's choice of whether to display a number in scientific or standard form depends on the magnitude of the number.

```
Private Sub cmdCompute_Click()
  picResults.Cls
  picResults.Print 1.2 * 10 ^ 34
  picResults.Print 1.2 * 10 ^ 8
  picResults.Print 1.2 * 10 ^ 3
  picResults.Print 10 ^ -20
  picResults.Print 10 ^ -2
End Sub
```

[Run and then click the command button.]

Variables

In applied mathematics problems, quantities are referred to by names. For instance, consider the following high school algebra problem. "If a car travels at 50 miles per hour, how far will it travel in 14 hours? Also, how many hours are required to travel 410 miles?" The solution to this problem uses the well-known formula

$$\text{distance} = \text{speed} \times \text{time elapsed}$$

Here's how this problem would be solved with a computer program.

```
Private Sub cmdCompute_Click()
  picResults.Cls
  speed = 50
  timeElapsed = 14
  distance = speed * timeElapsed
  picResults.Print distance
  distance = 410
  timeElapsed = distance / speed
  picResults.Print timeElapsed
End Sub
```

[Run, and then click the command button. The following is displayed in the picture box.]

```
700
8.2
```

The third line of the event procedure sets the speed to 50, and the fourth line sets the time elapsed to 14. The fifth line multiplies the value for the speed by the value for the time elapsed and sets the distance to this product. The next line displays the answer to the distance-traveled question. The three lines before the End Sub statement answer the time-required question in a similar manner.

The names *speed*, *timeElapsed*, and *distance*, which hold numbers, are referred to as **variables**. Consider the variable *timeElapsed*. In the fourth line, its value was set to 14. In the eighth line, its value was changed as the result of a computation. On the other hand, the variable *speed* had the same value, 50, throughout the program.

In general, a variable is a name that is used to refer to an item of data. The value assigned to the variable may change during the execution of the program. In Visual Basic, variable names can be up to 255 characters long, must begin with a letter, and can consist only of letters, digits, and underscores. (The shortest variable names consist of a single letter.) Visual Basic does not distinguish between uppercase and lowercase letters used in variable names. Some examples of variable names are *total*, *numberOfCars*, *taxRate_2003*, and *n*. As a convention, we write variable names in lowercase letters except for the first letters of additional words (as in *gradeOnFirstExam*).

If *var* is a variable and *num* is a constant, then the statement

```
var = num
```

assigns the number *num* to the variable *var*. (Such a statement is another example of an **assignment statement**.) Actually, Visual Basic sets aside a location in memory with the name *var* and places the number *num* in it. The statement

```
picBox.Print var
```

looks into this memory location for the current value of the variable and displays the value in the picture box.

A combination of constants, variables, and arithmetic operations that can be evaluated to yield a number is called a **numeric expression**. Expressions are evaluated by replacing each variable by its value and carrying out the arithmetic. Some examples of expressions are 2 * distance + 7, n + 1, and (a + b) / 3.

EXAMPLE 3   The following program displays the value of an expression.

```
Private Sub cmdCompute_Click()
  picResults.Cls
  a = 5
  b = 4
  picResults.Print a * (2 + b)
End Sub
```

[Run, and then click the command button. The following is displayed in the picture box.]

30

If *var* is a variable, then the statement

```
var = expression
```

first evaluates the expression on the right and *then* assigns its value to the variable on the left. For instance, the event procedure in Example 3 can be written as

```
Private Sub cmdCompute_Click()
  picResults.Cls
  a = 5
  b = 4
  c = a * (2 + b)
  picResults.Print c
End Sub
```

The expression a * (2 + b) is evaluated to 30 and then this value is assigned to the variable *c*.

Because the expression on the right side of an assignment statement is evaluated *before* an assignment is made, a statement such as

```
n = n + 1
```

is meaningful. It first evaluates the expression on the right (that is, it adds 1 to the original value of the variable *n*), and then assigns this sum to the variable *n*. The effect is to increase the value of the variable *n* by 1. In terms of memory locations, the statement retrieves the value of *n* from *n*'s memory location, uses it to compute *n* + 1, and then places the sum back into *n*'s memory location.

Print Method

Consider the following event procedure.

```
Private Sub cmdDisplay_Click()
  picResults.Cls
  picResults.Print 3
  picResults.Print -3
End Sub
```

[Run, and then click the command button.]

Notice that the negative number –3 begins directly at the left margin, whereas the positive number 3 begins one space to the right. The Print method always displays nonnegative numbers with a leading space. The Print method also displays a trailing space after every number. Although the trailing spaces are not apparent here, we will soon see evidence of their presence.

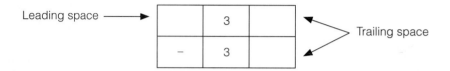

The Print methods used so far display only one number per line. After displaying a number, the cursor moves to the leftmost position and down a line for the next display. Borrowing from typewriter terminology, we say that the computer performs a carriage return and a line feed after each number is displayed. The carriage return and line feed, however, can be suppressed by placing a semicolon at the end of the number.

EXAMPLE 4 The following program illustrates the use of semicolons in Print methods. The output reveals the presence of the space trailing each number. For instance, the space trailing –3 combines with the leading space of 99 to produce two spaces between the numbers.

```
Private Sub cmdDisplay_Click()
  picResults.Cls
  picResults.Print 3;
  picResults.Print -3;
  picResults.Print 99;
  picResults.Print 100
End Sub
```

[Run, and then click the command button.]

Semicolons can be used to display several numbers with one Print method. If *m*, *n*, and *r* are numbers, a line of the form

```
picBox.Print m; n; r
```

displays the three numbers, one after another, separated only by their leading and trailing spaces. For instance, the Print methods in preceding Example 4 can be replaced by the single line

```
picResults.Print 3; -3; 99; 100
```

Comments

1. Numeric constants must not contain commas, dollar signs, or percent signs. Also, mixed numbers, such as 8 1/2, are not allowed.

2. Parentheses should be used when necessary to clarify the meaning of an expression. When there are no parentheses, the arithmetic operations are performed in the following order: (1) exponentiations; (2) multiplications and divisions; (3) additions and subtractions. In the event of ties, the leftmost operation is carried out first. Table 3.1 summarizes these rules. **Note:** If you use parentheses liberally, you will not have to remember the precedence table for arithmetic operations.

( )	Inner to outer, left to right
^	Left to right in expression
* /	Left to right in expression
+ −	Left to right in expression

Table 3.1 Level of precedence for arithmetic operations.

3. Keywords cannot be used as names of variables. For instance, the statements `print = 99` and `end = 99` are not valid. Some other common keywords are Call, If, Let, Select, and Sub. If a keyword is used as a variable name, you will soon be warned that something is wrong. As soon as the cursor is moved from the line, an error message will appear, and the line will turn red. The use of some other keywords (such as Error, Height, Name, Rate, Time, Val, Width, and Year) as variable names does not trigger an immediate warning, but generates an error message when the program is run. Although there is a way to get Visual Basic to accept this last group of keywords as variable names, we will never use keywords as variable names. Most of the items in Appendix C, other than properties, are keywords. You can tell immediately when you inadvertently use a keyword as a variable in an assignment statement because Visual Basic automatically capitalizes the first letter of keywords. For instance, if you type "rate = 50" and press the Enter key, the line will change to "Rate = 50".

4. Grammatical errors, such as misspellings, omissions, or incorrect punctuations, are called **syntax errors**. Certain types of syntax errors are spotted by the editor when they are entered; however, others are not detected until the program is executed. Some incorrect statements and their errors are given below.

Statement	Reason for Error
picBox.Primt 3	Misspelling of keyword
picBox.Print 2 +	No number follows the plus sign
9W = 5	9W is not a valid variable name

5. Errors that occur while a program is running are called **run-time errors**. They usually result from the inability of the computer to carry out the intended task. For instance, if the value of *numVar* is 0, then the statement

```
numVarInv = 1 / numVar
```

will cause the program to stop executing and produce a message box containing the statement "Division by zero." If the file DATA.TXT is not in the root folder of the C drive, then a statement that refers to the file by the filespec "C:\DATA.TXT" produces the run-time error "File not found."

The message box generated by a run-time error states the type of error and has a row of four command buttons captioned Continue, End, Debug, and Help. If you click on the Debug command button, Visual Basic will highlight in yellow the line of code that caused the error. (**Note:** After a run-time error occurs, the program is said to be in break mode. See the first page of Appendix D for a discussion of the three program modes.)

6. A third type of error is the so-called **logical error**. Such an error occurs when a program does not perform the way it was intended. For instance, the line

```
average = firstNum + secondNum / 2
```

is syntactically correct. However, the missing parentheses in the first line are responsible for an incorrect value being generated. Appendix D discusses debugging tools that can be used to detect and correct logical errors.

7. The omission of the asterisk to denote multiplication is a common error. For instance, the expression a(b + c) is not valid. It should read a * (b + c).

8. The largest number that most of the numeric variables considered in this text can represent is 3.402823E+38. Attempting to generate larger values produces the message "Overflow." The numbers generated by the programs in this text usually have a maximum of seven digits.

9. A *Review of Exponents*. The expression 2^3 means $2 \cdot 2 \cdot 2$, the product of three 2's. The number 3 is called the **exponent**, and the number 2 is called the **base**. In general, if r is a positive integer and a is a number, then a^r is defined as follows:

$$a^r = \underbrace{a \cdot a \ldots a}_{r \text{ factors}}$$

The process of calculating a^r is called *raising a to the rth power*. Some other types of exponents are the following:

$a^{1/2} = \sqrt{a}$		$9^{1/2} = 3$
$a^{1/n} = \sqrt[n]{a}$	n positive integer	$16^{1/4} = 2$
$a^{m/n} = (\sqrt[n]{a})^m$	m, n positive integers	$8^{2/3} = (\sqrt[3]{8})^2 = 4$
$a^{-r} = 1/a^r$	$a \neq 0$	$10^{-2} = .01$

10. More than one statement can be placed on a single line of a program provided the statements are separated by colons. For instance, the code inside the event procedure in Example 3 can be written as

```
picResults.Cls: a = 5: b = 4: picResults.Print a * (2 + b)
```

In general, though, programs are much easier to follow if just one statement appears on each line. In this text, we almost always use single-statement lines.

11. When you first open a program that has been saved on disk, neither the Code window nor the Form window may appear. If so, open the Forms folder in the Project Explorer window, right-click on the form name, and click on either View Code or View Form. Subsequently, you can use the View menu choices Code or Object to bring up the Code window or the Form window, respectively. (**Note:** If Project Explorer is not visible, press Ctrl+R.)

✔ **PRACTICE PROBLEMS 3.3**

1. Evaluate $2 + 3 * 4$.

2. Explain the difference between the assignment statement

```
var1 = var2
```

and the assignment statement

```
var2 = var1
```

3. Complete the table by filling in the value of each variable after each line is executed.

	a	b	c
`Private Sub cmdCompute_Click()`			
`a = 3`	3	–	–
`b = 4`	3	4	–
`c = a + b`			
`a = c * a`			
`picResults.Print  a - b`			
`b = b * b`			
`End Sub`			

➤ **EXERCISES 3.3**

In Exercises 1 through 6, evaluate the numeric expression without the computer, and then use Visual Basic to check your answer.

1. $3 * 4$

2. $7 \wedge 2$

3. $1 / (2 \wedge 5)$

4. $3 + (4 * 5)$

5. $(5 - 3) * 4$

6. $3 * ((-2) \wedge 5)$

In Exercises 7 through 10, write the number in scientific notation as it might be displayed by Visual Basic.

7. $3 \cdot 10^{15}$

8. .0000000000000007

9. $4 / (10 \wedge 20)$

10. $32 * (10 \wedge 20)$

In Exercises 11 through 16, determine whether or not the name is a valid variable name.

11. sales.2003

12. room&Board

13. fOrM_1040

14. 1040B

15. expenses?

16. INCOME 2002

In Exercises 17 through 22, evaluate the numeric expression where $a = 2$, $b = 3$, and $c = 4$.

17. $(a * b) + c$

18. $a * (b + c)$

19. $(1 + b) * c$

20. $a \wedge c$

21. $b \wedge (c - a)$

22. $(c - a) \wedge b$

In Exercises 23 through 28, write an event procedure to calculate, and display the value of the expression.

23. $7 \cdot 8 + 5$

24. $(1 + 2 \cdot 9)^3$

25. 5.5% of 20

26. $15 - 3(2 + 3^4)$

27. $17 (3 + 162)$

28. $4\ 1/2 - 3\ 5/8$

In Exercises 29 and 30, complete the table by filling in the value of each variable after each line is executed.

29.

	x	y
`Private Sub cmdCompute_Click()`		
`x = 2`		
`y = 3 * x`		
`x = y + 5`		
`picResults.Cls`		
`picResults.Print x + 4`		
`y = y + 1`		
`End Sub`		

30.

	bal	inter	withDr
Private Sub cmdCompute_Click()			
bal = 100			
inter = .05			
withDr = 25			
bal = bal + inter * bal			
bal = bal - withDr			
End Sub			

In Exercises 31 through 38, determine the output displayed in the picture box by the lines of code.

31.
```
amount = 10
picOutput.Print amount - 4
```

32.
```
a = 4
b = 5 * a
picOutput.Print a + b; b - a
```

33.
```
picOutput.Print 1; 2;
picOutput.Print 3; 4
picOutput.Print 5 + 6
```

34.
```
number = 5
number = 2 * number
picOutput.Print number
```

35.
```
picOutput.Print 0 + 1
a = 4
b = a ^ 2
picOutput.Print a * b
```

36.
```
tax = 200
tax = 25 + tax
picOutput.Print tax
```

37.
```
x = 3
picOutput.Print x ^ x; x + 3 * x
```

38.
```
n = 2
picOutput.Print 3 * n
n = n + n
picOutput.Print n + n
```

In Exercises 39 through 42, identify the errors.

39.
```
a = 2
b = 3
a + b = c
picOutput.Print c
```

40.
```
a = 2
b = 3
c = d = 4
picOutput.Print 5((a + b) / (c + d)
```

41.
```
balance = 1,234
deposit = $100
picOutput.Print balance + deposit
```

42.
```
.05 = interest
balance = 800
picOutput.Print interest * balance
```

In Exercises 43 and 44, rewrite the code with fewer lines.

43.
```
picOutput.Print 1;
picOutput.Print 2;
picOutput.Print 1 + 2
```

44.
```
a = 1
b = a + 2
picOutput.Print b
```

In Exercises 45 through 52, write an event procedure starting with Private Sub cmdCompute_Click() and picOutput.Cls statements, ending with an End Sub statement, and having one line for each step. Lines that display data should use the given variable names.

45. The following steps calculate a company's profit.

   (a) Assign the value 98456 to the variable *revenue*.
   (b) Assign the value 45000 to the variable *costs*.
   (c) Assign the difference between the variables *revenue* and *costs* to the variable *profit*.
   (d) Display the value of the variable *profit* in a picture box.

46. The following steps calculate the amount of a stock purchase.

   (a) Assign the value 25.625 to the variable *costPerShare*.
   (b) Assign the value 400 to the variable *numberOfShares*.
   (c) Assign the product of *costPerShare* and *numberOfShares* to the variable *amount*.
   (d) Display the value of the variable *amount* in a picture box.

47. The following steps calculate the price of an item after a 30% reduction.

   (a) Assign the value 19.95 to the variable *price*.
   (b) Assign the value 30 to the variable *discountPercent*.
   (c) Assign the value of (*discountPercent* divided by 100) times *price* to the variable *markDown*.
   (d) Decrease *price* by *markDown*.
   (e) Display the value of *price* in a picture box.

48. The following steps calculate a company's break-even point, the number of units of goods the company must manufacture and sell in order to break even.

   (a) Assign the value 5000 to the variable *fixedCosts*.
   (b) Assign the value 8 to the variable *pricePerUnit*.
   (c) Assign the value 6 to the variable *costPerUnit*.
   (d) Assign the value *fixedCosts* divided by (the difference of *pricePerUnit* and *costPerUnit*) to the variable *breakEvenPoint*.
   (e) Display the value of the variable *breakEvenPoint* in a picture box.

49. The following steps calculate the balance after three years when $100 is deposited in a savings account at 5% interest compounded annually.

   (a) Assign the value 100 to the variable *balance*.
   (b) Increase the variable *balance* by 5% of its value.
   (c) Increase the variable *balance* by 5% of its value.
   (d) Increase the variable *balance* by 5% of its value.
   (e) Display the value of the variable *balance* in a picture box.

50. The following steps calculate the balance at the end of three years when $100 is deposited at the beginning of each year in a savings account at 5% interest compounded annually.

   (a) Assign the value 100 to the variable *balance*.
   (b) Increase the variable *balance* by 5% of its value, and add 100.

(c) Increase the variable *balance* by 5% of its value, and add 100.
(d) Increase the variable *balance* by 5% of its value.
(e) Display the value of the variable *balance* in a picture box.

51. The following steps calculate the balance after 10 years when $100 is deposited in a savings account at 5% interest compounded annually.

(a) Assign the value 100 to the variable *balance*.
(b) Multiply the variable *balance* by 1.05 raised to the 10th power.
(c) Display the value of the variable *balance* in a picture box.

52. The following steps calculate the percentage profit from the sale of a stock:

(a) Assign the value 10 to the variable *purchasePrice*.
(b) Assign the value 15 to the variable *sellingPrice*.
(c) Assign, to the variable *percentProfit*, 100 times the value of the difference between *sellingPrice* and *purchasePrice* divided by *purchasePrice*.
(d) Display the value of the variable *percentProfit* in a picture box.

In Exercises 53 through 58, write an event procedure to solve the problem and display the answer in a picture box. The program should use variables for each of the quantities.

53. Suppose each acre of farmland produces 18 tons of corn. How many tons of corn can be produced on a 30-acre farm?

54. Suppose a ball is thrown straight up in the air with an initial velocity of 50 feet per second and an initial height of 5 feet. How high will the ball be after 3 seconds? **Note:** The height after t seconds is given by the expression $-16t^2 + v_0t + h_0$, where v_0 is the initial velocity and h_0 is the initial height.

55. If a car left Washington, D.C., at 2 o'clock and arrived in New York at 7 o'clock, what was its average speed? **Note:** New York is 233 miles from Washington.

56. A motorist wants to determine her gas mileage. At 23,340 miles (on the odometer), the tank is filled. At 23,695 miles the tank is filled again with 14.1 gallons. How many miles per gallon did the car average between the two fillings?

57. A U.S. geological survey showed that Americans use an average of 1600 gallons of water per person per day, including industrial use. How many gallons of water are used each year in the United States? **Note:** The current population of the United States is about 300 million people.

58. According to FHA specifications, each room in a house should have a window area equal to at least 10 percent of the floor area of the room. What is the minimum window area for a 14-ft by 16-ft room?

✔✔ Solutions to Practice Problems 3.3

1. 14. Multiplications are performed before additions. If the intent is for the addition to be performed first, the expression should be written (2 + 3) * 4.

2. The first assignment statement assigns the value of the variable *var2* to the variable *var1*, whereas the second assignment statement assigns *var1*'s value to *var2*.

3.

	a	b	c
Private Sub cmdCompute_Click()			
a = 3	3	–	–
b = 4	3	4	–
c = a + b	3	4	7
a = c * a	21	4	7
picResults.Print a - b	21	4	7
b = b * b	21	16	7
End Sub			

Each time an assignment statement is executed, only one variable (the variable to the left of the equal sign) has its value changed.

3.4 STRINGS

The most common types of data processed by Visual Basic are numbers and strings. Sentences, phrases, words, letters of the alphabet, names, telephone numbers, addresses, and social security numbers are all examples of strings. Formally, a **string constant** is a sequence of characters that is treated as a single item. String constants can be assigned to variables, displayed in picture boxes, and combined by an operation called concatenation (denoted by &).

Variables and Strings

A **string variable** is a name used to refer to a string. The allowable names of string variables are the same as those of numeric variables. The value of a string variable is assigned or altered with assignment statements and displayed with Print methods just like the value of a numeric variable.

EXAMPLE 1 The following code shows how assignment statements and the Print method are used with strings. The string variable *today* is assigned a value by the fourth line and this value is displayed by the fifth line. The quotation marks surrounding each string constant are not part of the constant and are not displayed by the Print method. (The form design for Examples 1 through 5 consists of a command button and a picture box.)

```
Private Sub cmdButton_Click()
  picBox.Cls
  picBox.Print "hello"
  today = "9/17/03"
  picBox.Print today
End Sub
```

[Run, and then click the command button. The following is displayed in the picture box.]

```
hello
9/17/03
```

If *x*, *y*, ..., *z* are characters and *strVar1* is a string variable, then the statement

```
strVar1 = "xy...z"
```

assigns the string constant *xy...z* to the variable, and the statement

```
picBox.Print "xy...z"
```

or

```
picBox.Print strVar1
```

displays the string *xy...z* in a picture box. If *strVar2* is another string variable, then the statement

```
strVar2 = strVar
```

assigns the value of the variable *strVar* to the variable *strVar2*. (The value of *strVar* will remain the same.) String constants used in assignment or picBox.Print statements must be surrounded by quotation marks, but string variables are never surrounded by quotation marks.

As with numbers, semicolons can be used with strings in picBox.Print statements to suppress carriage returns and line feeds. However, picBox.Print statements do not display leading or trailing spaces along with strings.

EXAMPLE 2   The following program illustrates the use of the assignment statement and Print method with text.

```
Private Sub cmdShow_Click()
  picOutput.Cls
  phrase = "win or lose that counts."
  picOutput.Print "It's not whether you "; phrase
  picOutput.Print "It's whether I "; phrase
End Sub
```

[Run, and then click the command button. The following is displayed in the picture box.]

```
It's not whether you win or lose that counts.
It's whether I win or lose that counts.
```

EXAMPLE 3

The following program has strings and numbers occurring together in a picBalance.Print statement.

```
Private Sub cmdCompute_Click()
  picBalance.Cls
  interestRate = 0.0655
  principal = 100
  phrase = "The balance after a year is"
  picBalance.Print phrase; (1 + interestRate) * principal
End Sub
```

[Run, and then click the command button. The following is displayed in the picture box.]

```
The balance after a year is 106.55
```

Concatenation

Two strings can be combined to form a new string consisting of the strings joined together. The joining operation is called **concatenation** and is represented by an ampersand (&). For instance, "good" & "bye" is "goodbye". A combination of strings and ampersands that can be evaluated to form a string is called a **string expression**. The assignment statement and the Print method evaluate expressions before assigning them to variables or displaying them.

EXAMPLE 4

The following program illustrates concatenation.

```
Private Sub cmdDisplay_Click()
  picQuote.Cls
  quote1 = "The ballgame isn't over, "
  quote2 = "until it's over."
  quote = quote1 & quote2
  picQuote.Print quote & "   Yogi Berra"
End Sub
```

[Run, and then click the command button. The following is displayed in the picture box.]

```
The ballgame isn't over, until it's over.   Yogi Berra
```

Declaring Variable Types

So far, we have not distinguished between variables that hold strings and variables that hold numbers. There are several advantages to specifying the type of values, string or numeric, that can be assigned to a variable. A statement of the form

```
Dim variableName As String
```

specifies that only strings can be assigned to the named variable. A statement of the form

```
Dim variableName As Single
```

specifies that only numbers can be assigned to the named variable. The term Single derives from *single-precision real number*. After you type the space after the word "As," the editor displays a list of all the possible next words. In this text we use only a few of the items from this list.

A Dim statement is said to **declare** a variable. From now on we will declare all variables. However, all the programs will run correctly even if the Dim statements are omitted. Declaring variables at the beginning of each event procedure is regarded as good programming practice because it makes programs easier to read and helps prevent certain types of errors.

EXAMPLE 5   The following rewrite of Example 3 declares all variables.

```
Private Sub cmdCompute_Click()
  Dim interestRate As Single
  Dim principal As Single
  Dim phrase As String
  picBalance.Cls
  interestRate = 0.0655
  principal = 100
  phrase = "The balance after a year is"
  picBalance.Print phrase; (1 + interestRate) * principal
End Sub
```

Several Dim statements can be combined into one. For instance, the first three Dim statements of Example 5 can be replaced by

```
Dim interestRate As Single, principal As Single, phrase As String
```

Visual Basic actually has several different types of numeric variables. So far, we have used only single-precision numeric variables. Single-precision numeric variables can hold numbers of magnitude from as small as 1.4×10^{-45} to as large as 3.4×10^{38}. Another type of numeric variable, called **Integer**, can hold only whole numbers from -32768 to 32767. Integer-type variables are declared with a statement of the form

```
Dim intVar As Integer
```

The Integer data type uses less memory than the Single data type, and statements using the Integer type execute faster. (This is useful only in programs with many calculations, such as the programs in later chapters that use For...Next loops.) Of course, Integer variables are limited because they cannot hold decimals or large numbers. We will use Integer variables extensively with For...Next loops in Chapter 6 and occasionally when the data clearly consist of small whole numbers.

Other types of numeric variables are Long, Double, and Currency. We do not use them in this text. If you want to learn about them, consult Appendix C. Whenever we refer to a numeric variable without mentioning a type, we mean Single or Integer.

Named Constants

Programs that use special constants are easier to read if the constants are given a name. For instance, a program involving social security taxes might give the constant 87000 (the largest amount of earnings subject to social security taxes in 2003) the name *wageBaseLimit03*. Ideally, we would like *wageBaseLimit03* to be a variable whose value cannot be changed during the execution of the program. Visual Basic provides such a construct—known as a **named constant**. A named constant is declared with a statement of the form

```
Const name As DataType = value
```

For instance, the named constant discussed above can be declared with the statement

```
Const wageBaseLimit03 As Single = 87000
```

The rules for naming named constants are the same as for variables, and named constants can be used in expressions along with variables and ordinary constants. The only difference between named constants and variables is that named constants cannot appear on the left side of an assignment statement.

EXAMPLE 6 The following program uses the named constant *pi*. Although the value of the variable *radius* changes during the execution of the program, the value of *pi* cannot be changed. For instance, the statement pi = 3.14159 would produce the error message "Assignment to constant not permitted."

```
Private Sub cmdCalculate_Click()
  Const pi As Single = 3.1416
  Dim radius As Single
  radius = 5
  picResults.Print "A circle of radius"; radius; "inches has area";
  picResults.Print pi * (radius * radius); "square inches."
  radius = 10
  picResults.Print "A circle of radius"; radius; "inches has area";
  picResults.Print pi * (radius * radius); "square inches."
End Sub
```

[Run, and then click the command button. The following is displayed in the picture box.]

```
A circle of radius 5 inches has area 78.54 square inches.
A circle of radius 10 inches has area 314.16 square inches.
```

Using Text Boxes for Input and Output

The contents of a text box is always a string. Therefore, statements such as

```
strVar = txtBox.Text
```

and

```
txtBox.Text = strVar
```

can be used to assign the contents of the text box to the string variable *strVar* and vice versa.

Numbers typed into text boxes are stored as strings. Therefore, they should be converted to numbers before being assigned to numeric variables. If *strng* is a string representation of a number, then

    Val(strng)

is that number. Conversely, if *num* is a number, then

    Str(num)

is a string representation of the number. Therefore, statements such as

    numVar = Val(txtBox.Text)

and

    txtBox.Text = Str(numVar)

can be used to assign the contents of the text box to the numeric variable *numVar* and vice versa. **Note:** When a non-negative number is converted to a string with Str, its first character (but not its last character) is a blank space.

EXAMPLE 7   The following program converts miles to furlongs and vice versa. **Note:** A furlong is 1/8th of a mile.

Object	Property	Setting
frm3_4_6	Caption	Convertor
lblMile	Caption	Miles
txtMile	Text	0
lblFurlong	Caption	Furlongs
txtFurlong	Text	0

The two text boxes have been named txtMile and txtFurlong. With the event procedures shown, typing a number into a text box and pressing Tab results in the converted number being displayed in the other text box.

```
Private Sub txtMile_LostFocus()
   txtFurlong.Text = Str(8 * Val(txtMile.Text))
End Sub

Private Sub txtFurlong_LostFocus()
   txtMile.Text = Str(Val(txtFurlong.Text) / 8)
End Sub
```

ANSI Character Set

Each of the 47 different keys in the center typewriter portion of the keyboard can produce two characters, for a total of 94 characters. Adding 1 for the space character produced by the space bar makes 95 characters. These characters have numbers ranging from 32 to 126 associated with them. These values, called the

ANSI (or ASCII) values of the characters, are given in Appendix A. Table 3.2 shows a few of the values.

32	(space)	48	0	66	B	122	z
33	!	49	1	90	Z	123	{
34	"	57	9	97	a	125	}
35	#	65	A	98	b	126	~

Table 3.2 A few ANSI values.

Most of the best-known fonts, such as Courier New, Microsoft Sans Serif, and Times New Roman, are essentially governed by the ANSI standard, which assigns characters to the numbers from 32 to 255. Table 3.3 shows a few of the higher ANSI values.

162	¢	177	±	181	μ	190	¾
169	©	178	^{2}	188	¼	247	÷
176	°	179	^{3}	189	½	248	Ø

Table 3.3 A few higher ANSI values.

If *n* is a number between 32 and 255, then

```
Chr(n)
```

is the string consisting of the character with ANSI value *n*. If *strng* is any string, then

```
Asc(strng)
```

is the ANSI value of the first character of *strng*. For instance, the statement

```
txtBox.Text = Chr(65)
```

displays the letter A in the text box and the statement

```
picBox.Print Asc("Apple")
```

displays the number 65 in the picture box.

Concatenation can be used with Chr to obtain strings using the higher ANSI characters. For instance, with one of the fonts that conforms to the ANSI standard, the statement

```
txtBox.Text = "32" & Chr(176) & " Fahrenheit"
```

displays 32° Fahrenheit in the text box.

The KeyPress Event Procedure

When a text box has the focus and the user presses a key, the KeyPress event procedure identifies the key pressed. When a key is pressed, the event procedure assigns the ANSI value of the key to an Integer variable called *KeyAscii*. The general form of the procedure is

```
Private Sub ControlName_KeyPress(KeyAscii As Integer)
    statements
End Sub
```

The statements usually involve the variable *KeyAscii*. Also, a character does not appear in the text box until End Sub is reached. At that time, the character with ANSI value *KeyAscii* is displayed.

EXAMPLE 8   The following program allows the user to determine the ANSI values of the standard (typewriter) keys of the keyboard. The statement `txtCharacter.Text =` `""` removes any previously typed character from the text box.

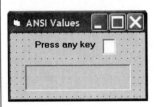

Object	Property	Setting
frm3_4_8	Caption	ANSI Values
lblPress	Caption	Press any key
txtCharacter	Text	(blank)
picOutput		

```
Private Sub txtCharacter_KeyPress(KeyAscii As Integer)
  txtCharacter.Text = ""
  picOutput.Cls
  picOutput.Print Chr(KeyAscii); " has ANSI value"; KeyAscii
End Sub
```

[Run, and then press a key. For instance, if A is pressed, the following is displayed in the picture box.]

```
A has ANSI value 65
```

The KeyPress event procedure can alter the character typed into the text box. For instance, if the statement

```
KeyAscii = 65
```

is placed in a KeyPress event procedure, the letter A is displayed when any standard key is pressed. In Chapter 5, we use a decision structure to prevent the user from typing unwanted keys. For instance, if we want the user to enter a number into a text box, we can intercept and discard any key presses that are not digits. The statement

```
KeyAscii = 0
```

placed in a KeyPress event procedure discards the key pressed. Finally, a program can be made more friendly by letting the Enter key (ANSI value 13) move the focus in the same way that the Tab key moves the focus. This requires having a KeyPress event procedure for each object that is to respond to the Enter key and then setting the focus to the next object when the value of *KeyAscii* is 13.

Comments

1. The string "", which contains no characters, is called the **empty string** or the **zero-length string**. It is different from " ", the string consisting of a single space. String variables that have not been assigned values initially have "" as their default values. (Numeric variables have default value 0.)

2. The statement picBox.Print, with no string or number, simply skips a line in the picture box.

3. Assigning a string value to a numeric variable can result in the error message "Type mismatch."

4. In Visual Basic 6.0, the maximum allowable number of characters in a string is approximately 2 billion.

5. The quotation-mark character (") can be placed into a string constant by using Chr(34). For example, after the statement

   ```
   txtBox.Text = "George " & Chr(34) & "Babe" & Chr(34) & " Ruth"
   ```

   is executed, the text box contains

   ```
   George "Babe" Ruth
   ```

6. Most major programming languages require that all variables be declared before they can be used. Although declaring variables with Dim statements is optional in Visual Basic, you can tell Visual Basic to make declaration mandatory. The steps are as follows:

   (a) From any code window, click on the down-arrow to the right of the Object box and click on (General).
   (b) Type

   ```
   Option Explicit
   ```

   and press Enter.

   Then, if you use a variable without first declaring it in a Dim statement, the message "Variable not defined" will appear as soon as you attempt to run the program. One big advantage of using Option Explicit is that mistypings of variable names will be detected. Otherwise, malfunctions due to typing errors are often difficult to detect.

7. You can have Visual Basic automatically place Option Explicit in every program you write. The steps are as follows:

   (a) Press Alt/T/O and click on the Editor tab to invoke the editor options.
   (b) If the square to the left of "Require Variable Declaration" does not contain a check mark, click on the square and press the OK button.

8. Variables that are not (explicitly) declared with Dim statements are said to be **implicitly declared**. Such variables, which have a data type called Variant, can hold strings, numbers, and several other kinds of information.

9. You can display the type of a variable with the following steps—position the cursor over the word, press the right mouse button, and click on Quick Info.

10. Val can be applied to strings containing nonnumeric characters. If the beginning of the string *str* represents a number, then Val(*str*) is that number; otherwise, it is 0. For instance, Val("123Blastoff") is 123, and Val("ab3") is 0.

11. The KeyPress event also applies to command buttons and picture boxes.

12. Concatenation of strings also can be represented by a plus sign (+). However, restricting the plus sign to operations on numbers eliminates ambiguity and provides self-documenting code.

13. If Val is omitted from the statement

    ```
    numVar = Val(txtBox.Text)
    ```

    or Str is omitted from the statement

    ```
    txtBox.Text = Str(numVar)
    ```

    Visual Basic does not complain, but simply makes the conversion for you. However, errors can arise from omitting Val and Str. For instance, if the contents of txtBox1.Text is 34 and the contents of txtBox2.Text is 56, then the statement

    ```
    numVar = txtBox1.Text + txtBox2.Text
    ```

    assigns the number 3456 rather than 90 to *numVar*. (This is because Visual Basic does not perform the conversion until just before the assignment.) If txtBox1 is empty, then the statement

    ```
    numVar = 3 * txtBox1.Text
    ```

    will stop the program and produce the error message "Type mismatch." We follow the standards of good programming practice by always using Val and Str to convert values between text boxes and numeric variables. Similar considerations apply to conversions involving label captions.

14. Variable names should describe the role of the variable. Also, some programmers use a prefix, such as *sng* or *str*, to identify the type of a variable. For example, they would use names like *sngInterestRate* and *strFirstName*.

✔ **PRACTICE PROBLEMS 3.4**

1. Compare the following two statements, where *phrase* is a string variable and *balance* is a numeric variable.

    ```
    picBox.Print "It's whether I "; phrase
    picBox.Print "The balance is"; balance
    ```

    Why is the space preceding the second quotation mark necessary for the first picBox.Print statement but not for the second picBox.Print statement?

2. A label's caption is a string and can be assigned a value with a statement of the form

    ```
    lblOne.Caption = strVar
    ```

What is one advantage to using a label for output as opposed to a text box?

3. Write code to add the numbers in txtBox1 and txtBox2, and place the sum in lblThree.

➤ ### EXERCISES 3.4

In Exercises 1 through 14, determine the output displayed in the picture box by the lines of code.

1.
```
picOutput.Print "Hello"
picOutput.Print "12" & "34"
```

2.
```
picOutput.Print "Welcome; my friend."
picOutput.Print "Welcome"; "my friend."
```

3.
```
picOutput.Print "12"; 12; "TWELVE"
```

4.
```
picOutput.Print Chr(104) & Chr(105)
```

5.
```
Dim r As String, b As String
r = "A ROSE"
b = " IS "
picOutput.Print r; b; r; b; r
```

6.
```
Dim n As Single, x As String
n = 5
x = "5"
picOutput.Print n
picOutput.Print x
```

7.
```
Dim houseNumber As Single
Dim street As String
houseNumber = 1234
street = "Main Street"
picOutput.Print houseNumber; street
```

8.
```
Dim p As String, word As String
p = "f"
word = "lute"
picOutput.Print p & word
```

9.
```
Dim quote As String, person As String, qMark As String
quote = "We're all in this alone."
person = "Lily Tomlin"
qMark = Chr(34)
picOutput.Print qMark & quote & qMark & "  " & person
```

10.
```
Dim letter As String
letter = "D"
picOutput.Print letter; " is the"; Asc(letter) - Asc("A") + 1;
picOutput.Print "th letter of the alphabet."
```

11.
```
picOutput.Print Str(17); Val("2B")
picOutput.Print Str(-20); Val("16.00")
```

12.
```
Dim a As Single, b As Single
a = 1
b = 2
picOutput.Print Val(Str(a)); Str(a + b)
picOutput.Print Str(4 - a)
```

13.
```
Dim num1 As Single, num2 As String
num1 = 3567
num2 = Str(num1)
picOutput.Print "The number of digits in"; num2; " is"; 4
```

14.
```
Const address As String = "1600 Pennsylvania Avenue"
picOutput.Print "George, your house number is"; Val(address)
```

In Exercises 15 through 20, identify any errors.

15.
```
Dim phone As Single
phone = "234-5678"
picOutput.Print "My phone number is "; phone
```

16.
```
Dim x As Integer, y As Integer
x = 10,000
y = 5 * x
picOutput.Print x + y
```

17.
```
Dim quote As String
quote = I came to Casablanca for the waters.
picOutput.Print quote; " "; "Bogart"
```

18.
```
Dim strVar As String
strVar = Str(23Skidoo)
picOutput.Print strVar
```

19.
```
Dim end As String
end = "happily ever after."
picOutput.Print "They lived "; end
```

20.
```
Const salesTaxRate As Single = .05
salesTaxRate = .055
picOutput.Print "Your sales tax is"; 8* salesTaxRate
```

21. Write an event procedure that causes an asterisk to appear in a text box when the text box has the focus and the user presses any key.

22. Describe the KeyPress event in your own words.

In Exercises 23 through 26, write an event procedure starting with Private Sub cmdDisplay_Click() and picOutput.Cls statements, ending with an End Sub statement, and having one line for each step. Lines that display data should use the given variable or named constant names.

23. The following steps give the name and birth year of a famous inventor.

   (a) Declare all variables used in steps (b)–(e).
   (b) Assign "Thomas" to the variable *firstName*.
   (c) Assign "Alva" to the variable *middleName*.
   (d) Assign "Edison" to the variable *lastName*.
   (e) Assign 1847 to the variable *yearOfBirth*.
   (f) Display the inventor's full name followed by a comma and his year of birth.

24. The following steps compute the price of ketchup.

   (a) Declare all variables used in steps (c) and (d).
   (b) Assign "ketchup" to the named constant *item*.
   (c) Assign 1.80 to the variable *regularPrice*.
   (d) Assign .27 to the variable *discount*.
   (e) Display the phrase "1.53 is the sale price of ketchup."

25. The following steps display a copyright statement.

    (a) Declare the variable used in step (b).
    (b) Assign "Prentice Hall, Inc." to the variable *publisher*.
    (c) Display the phrase "© Prentice Hall, Inc."

26. The following steps give advice.

    (a) Declare the variable used in step (b).
    (b) Assign "Fore" to the named constant *prefix*.
    (c) Display the phrase "Forewarned is Forearmed."

In Exercises 27 through 32, the interface and initial properties are specified. Write the code to carry out the stated task. (In Exercises 29–32, a sample run is shown.)

27. After values are placed in the x and y text boxes, pressing Compute Sum places x + y in the sum picture box. The other three command buttons clear controls.

Object	Property	Setting
frmEx27	Caption	Adder
lblX	Caption	x
txtNum1	Text	(blank)
cmdClearX	Caption	Clear x
lblY	Caption	y
txtNum2	Text	(blank)
cmdClearY	Caption	Clear y
cmdCompute	Caption	Compute Sum
lblSum	Caption	Sum
picSum		
cmdClearSum	Caption	Clear Sum

28. When cmdCelsius is pressed, the temperature in the text box is converted from Fahrenheit to Celsius, the title bar changes to Celsius, cmdCelsius is hidden, and cmdFahr becomes visible. If cmdFahr is now pressed, the temperature in the text box is converted from Celsius to Fahrenheit, the title bar reverts to Fahrenheit, cmdFahr is hidden, and cmdCelsius becomes visible. Of course, the user can change the temperature in the text box at any time. (**Note:** The conversion formulas are C = (5/9) ∗ (F − 32) and F = (9/5) ∗ C + 32.)

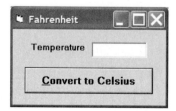

Object	Property	Setting
frmEx28	Caption	Fahrenheit
lblTemp	Caption	Temperature
txtTemp	Text	(blank)
cmdCelsius	Caption	Convert to Celsius
cmdFahr	Caption	Convert to Fahrenheit
	Visible	False

29. If *n* is the number of seconds between lightning and thunder, the storm is *n*/5 miles away. Write a program that requests the number of seconds between lightning and thunder and reports the distance of the storm.

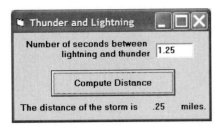

Object	Property	Setting
frmStorm	Caption	Thunder and Lightning
lblNumSec	Caption	Number of seconds between lightning and thunder
txtNumSec	Text	(blank)
cmdCompute	Caption	Compute Distance
lblDistance	Caption	The distance of the storm is
lblNumMiles	Caption	(blank)
lblMiles	Caption	miles.

30. Write a program to request the name of a baseball team, the number of games won, and the number of games lost as input, and then display the name of the team and the percentage of games won.

Object	Property	Setting
frmBaseball	Caption	Baseball
lblTeam	Caption	Team
txtTeam	Text	(blank)
lblWon	Caption	Games Won
txtWon	Text	(blank)
lblLost	Caption	Games Lost
txtLost	Text	(blank)
cmdCompute	Caption	Compute Percentage
picPercent		

31. The numbers of calories burned per hour by bicycling, jogging, and swimming are 200, 475, and 275, respectively. A person loses 1 pound of weight for each 3500 calories burned. Write a program that allows the user to input the number of hours spent at each activity and then calculates the number of pounds worked off.

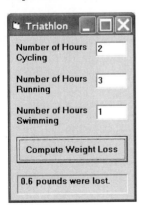

Object	Property	Setting
frmTriathlon	Caption	Triathlon
lblCycle	Caption	Number of Hours Cycling
txtCycle	Text	(blank)
lblRun	Caption	Number of Hours Running
txtRun	Text	(blank)
lblSwim	Caption	Number of Hours Swimming
txtSwim	Text	(blank)
cmdCompute	Caption	Compute Weight Loss
picWtLoss		

32. The American College of Sports Medicine recommends that you maintain your *training heart rate* during an aerobic workout. Your training heart rate is computed as $.7 * (220 - a) + .3 * r$, where a is your age and r is your resting heart rate (your pulse when you first awaken). Write a program to request a person's age and resting heart rate and then calculate the training heart rate. (Determine *your* training heart rate.)

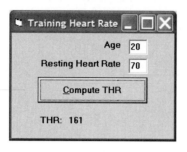

Object	Property	Setting
frmWorkout	Caption	Training Heart Rate
lblAge	Caption	Age
txtAge	Text	(blank)
lblRestHR	Caption	Resting Heart Rate
txtRestHR	Text	(blank)
cmdCompute	Caption	Compute THR
lblTHR	Caption	THR:
lblTrainHR	Caption	(blank)

In Exercises 33 through 41, write a program with a Windows-style interface to carry out the task. The program should use variables for each of the quantities and display the outcome with a complete explanation, as in Example 5.

33. Request a company's annual revenue and expenses as input, and display the company's net income (revenue minus expenses). (Test the program with the amounts $550,000 and $410,000.)

34. If the price of a 17-ounce can of corn is 68 cents, what is the price per ounce?

35. Request a company's earnings-per-share for the year and the price of one share of stock as input, and then display the company's price-to-earnings ratio (that is, price/earnings). (Test the program with the amounts $5.25 and $68.25.)

36. If the radius of the earth is 6170 kilometers, what is the volume of the earth? **Note:** The volume of a sphere of radius r is $(4/3) * (3.14159) * r^3$.

37. How many pounds of grass seed are needed to seed a lawn 40 feet by 75 feet if 40 ounces are recommended for 2000 square feet? **Note:** There are 16 ounces in a pound.

38. A store manager needs three shelf signs. Write a program to produce the output that follows. The words "SALE! Everything on this shelf" and "% off!" should appear only once in the program.

SALE! Everything on this shelf 10% off!
SALE! Everything on this shelf 30% off!
SALE! Everything on this shelf 50% off!

39. Write a program that uses a command button and a label on the form, with the label initially containing 0. Each time the command button is pressed, the number in the label should increase by 1.

40. Allow the user to enter any quantity of positive numbers. As each number is entered, display the sum of the numbers and the quantity of numbers entered. The user should be able to start anew at any time.

41. Calculate the amount of a waiter's tip, given the amount of the bill and the percentage tip as input. (Test the program with $20 and 15 percent.)

✔✔ **Solutions to Practice Problems 3.4**

1. In the second picBox.Print statement, the item following the second quotation mark is a positive number, which is displayed with a leading space. Because the corresponding item in the first picBox.Print statement is a string, which is *not* displayed with a leading space, a space had to be inserted before the quotation mark.

2. The user cannot enter data into a label from the keyboard. Therefore, if a control is to be used for output only, a label is preferred. **Note:** When using a label for output, you might want to set its BorderStyle property to "1-Fixed Single" so that it will be discernible.

3. `lblThree.Caption = Str(Val(txtBox1.Text) + Val(txtBox2.Text))`

3.5 INPUT AND OUTPUT

So far we have relied on assignment statements to assign values to variables. Data also can be stored in files and accessed through Input # statements, or supplied by the user in a text box or input dialog box. The Print method, with a little help from commas and the Tab function, can spread out and align the display of data in a picture box or on a printer. Message dialog boxes grab the user's attention and display temporary messages. Comment statements allow the programmer to document all aspects of a program, including a description of the input used and the output to be produced.

Reading Data from Files

In Chapter 1, we saw how to create text files with Windows' Notepad. (As a rule of thumb, and simply as a matter of style, we enclose each string in quotation marks.) A file can have either one item per line or many items (separated by commas) can be listed on the same line. Usually, related items are grouped together on a line. For instance, if a file consisted of payroll information, each line would contain the name of a person, their hourly wage, and the number of hours that person worked during the week, as shown in Figure 3.24.

```
"Mike Jones", 7.35, 35
"John Smith", 6.75, 33
```

Figure 3.24 Contents of STAFF.TXT.

The items of data will be assigned to variables one at a time in the order they appear in the file. That is, "Mike Jones" will be the first value assigned to a variable. After all the items from the first line have been assigned to variables, subsequent requests for values will be read from the next line.

Data stored in a file can be read in order (that is, sequentially) and assigned to variables with the following steps.

1. Choose a number from 1 to 255 to be the **reference number** for the file.

2. Execute the statement

`Open "filespec" For Input As #n`

where *n* is the reference number. This procedure is referred to as **Opening a file for input**. It establishes a communications link between the computer and the disk drive for reading data *from* the disk. Data then can be input from the specified file and assigned to variables in the program.

3. Read items of data in order, one at a time, from the file with Input # statements. The statement

```
Input #n, var
```

causes the program to look in the file for the next available item of data and assign it to the variable *var*. In the file, individual items are separated by commas or line breaks. The variable in the Input # statement should be the same type (that is, string versus numeric) as the data to be assigned to it from the file.

4. After the desired items have been read from the file, close the file with the statement

```
Close #n
```

EXAMPLE I Write a program that uses a file for input and produces the same output as the following code. (The form design for all examples in this section consists of a command button and a picture box.)

```
Private Sub cmdDisplay_Click()
  Dim houseNumber As Single, street As String
  picAddress.Cls
  houseNumber = 1600
  street = "Pennsylvania Ave."
  picAddress.Print "The White House is located at"; houseNumber; street
End Sub
```

[Run and then click the command button. The following is displayed in the picture box.]

```
The White House is located at 1600 Pennsylvania Ave.
```

SOLUTION Use Windows' Notepad to create the file DATA.TXT containing the following two lines:

1600
"Pennsylvania Ave."

In the following code, the fifth line looks for the first item of data, 1600, and assigns it to the numeric variable *houseNumber*. (Visual Basic records that this piece of data has been used.) The sixth line looks for the next available item of data, "Pennsylvania Ave.", and assigns it to the string variable *street*. **Note:** You will have to alter the Open statement in the fourth line to tell Visual Basic where the file DATA.TXT is located. For instance, if the file is in the root directory (that is, folder) of a diskette in drive A, then the line should read Open "A:\

DATA.TXT"For Input As #1. If the file is located in the folder VB6 of the C drive, then the statement should be changed to Open "C:\VB6\DATA.TXT"For Input As #1. See Comment 1 for another option.

```
Private Sub cmdDisplay_Click()
  Dim houseNumber As Single, street As String
  picAddress.Cls
  Open "DATA.TXT" For Input As #1
  Input #1, houseNumber
  Input #1, street
  picAddress.Print "The White House is located at"; houseNumber; street
  Close #1
End Sub
```

A single Input # statement can assign values to several different variables. For instance, the two Input # statements in the solution of Example 1 can be replaced by the single statement

```
Input #1, houseNumber, street
```

In general, a statement of the form

```
Input #n, var1, var2, ..., varj
```

has the same effect as the sequence of statements

```
Input #n, var1
Input #n, var2
      .
      .
      .
Input #n, varj
```

EXAMPLE 2 The following program uses the file STAFF.TXT in Figure 3.24 to compute weekly pay. Notice that the variables in the Input # statement are the same types (String, Single, Single) as the constants in each line of the file.

```
Private Sub cmdCompute_Click()
  Dim nom As String, wage As Single, hrs As Single
  picPay.Cls
  Open "STAFF.TXT" For Input As #1
  Input #1, nom, wage, hrs
  picPay.Print nom; hrs * wage
  Input #1, nom, wage, hrs
  picPay.Print nom; hrs * wage
  Close #1
End Sub
```

[Run, and then click the command button. The following will be displayed in the picture box.]

```
Mike Jones 257.25
John Smith 222.75
```

In certain situations, we must read the data in a file more than once. This is accomplished by closing the file and reopening it. After a file is closed and then reopened, subsequent Input # statements begin reading from the first entry of the file.

EXAMPLE 3   The following program takes the average annual amounts of money spent by single-person households for several categories and converts these amounts to percentages. The data are read once to compute the total amount of money spent and then read again to calculate the percentage for each category. **Note:** These figures were compiled for the year 2000 by the Bureau of Labor Statistics.

COSTS.TXT consists of the following four lines:

```
"Transportation", 4251
"Housing", 8929
"Food", 3414
"Other", 8829
```

```
Private Sub cmdCompute_Click()
  Dim total As Single, category As String, amount As Single
  Open "COSTS.TXT" For Input As #1
  picPercent.Cls
  total = 0
  Input #1, category, amount
  total = total + amount
  Input #1, category, amount
  total = total + amount
  Input #1, category, amount
  total = total + amount
  Input #1, category, amount
  total = total + amount
  Close #1
  Open "COSTS.TXT" For Input As #1
  Input #1, category, amount
  picPercent.Print category; amount / total
  Input #1, category, amount
  picPercent.Print category; amount / total
  Input #1, category, amount
  picPercent.Print category; amount / total
  Input #1, category, amount
  picPercent.Print category; amount / total
  Close #1
End Sub
```

[Run and then click the command button. The following is displayed in the picture box.]

```
Transportation 0.1672108
Housing 0.3512174
Food 0.1342878
Other 0.347284
```

Input from an Input Dialog Box

Normally, a text box is used to obtain input, where the type of information requested is specified in a label adjacent to the text box. Sometimes, we want just one piece of input and would rather not have a text box and label stay on the screen forever. The problem can be solved with an **input dialog box**. When a statement of the form

```
stringVar = InputBox(prompt, title)
```

is executed, an input dialog box similar to the one shown in Figure 3.25 pops up on the screen. After the user types a response into the text box at the bottom of the screen and presses Enter (or clicks OK), the response is assigned to the string variable. The *title* argument is optional and provides the caption to appear in the Title bar. The *prompt* argument is a string that tells the user what information to type into the text box.

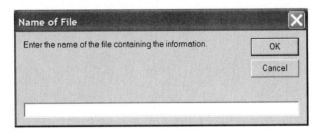

Figure 3.25 Sample input dialog box.

When you type the parenthesis following the word InputBox, the editor displays a line containing the general form of the InputBox statement. See Figure 3.26. This feature of IntelliSense is called **Quick Info**. Optional parameters are surrounded by brackets. All the parameters in the general form of the InputBox statement are optional except for *prompt*.

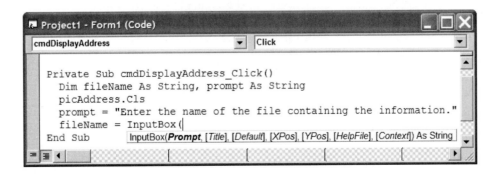

Figure 3.26 Quick Info feature of IntelliSense.

EXAMPLE 4   In the following enhancement to Example 1, the file name is provided by the user in an input dialog box.

```
Private Sub cmdDisplay_Click()
  Dim fileName As String, prompt As String, title As String
  Dim houseNumber As Single, street As String
  picAddress.Cls
  prompt = "Enter the name of the file containing the information."
  title = "Name of File"
  fileName = InputBox(prompt, title)
  Open fileName For Input As #1
  Input #1, houseNumber
  Input #1, street
  picAddress.Print "The White House is located at"; houseNumber; street
  Close #1
End Sub
```

[Run, and then click the command button. The input dialog box of Figure 3.25 appears on the screen. Type DATA.TXT (possibly preceded with a path) into the input dialog box and click on OK. The input dialog box disappears and the following appears in the picture box.]

```
The White House is located at 1600 Pennsylvania Ave.
```

The response typed into an input dialog box is treated as a single string value, no matter what is typed. (Quotation marks are not needed and, if included, are considered as part of the string.) Numeric data typed into an input dialog box should be converted to a number with Val before being assigned to a numeric variable or used in a calculation. Just as with a text box or file, the typed data must be a constant. It cannot be a variable or an expression. For instance, *num*, 1/2, and 2 + 3 are not acceptable.

Formatting Output with Print Zones

Each line in a picture box can be thought of as being subdivided into zones, as shown in Figure 3.27. Each zone contains 14 positions, where the width of a position is the average width of the characters in the font.

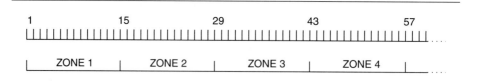

Figure 3.27 Print zones.

We have seen that when the Print method is followed by several items separated by semicolons, the items are displayed one after another. When commas are used instead of semicolons, the items are displayed in consecutive zones. For instance, if the Font property of picBox is set to Courier New, when the motto of the state of Alaska is displayed with the statements

```
picBox.Print "North", "to", "the", "future."
picBox.Print "123456789012345678901234567890123456789001234567890"
```

the resulting picture box is

```
North           to              the             future.
123456789012345678901234567890123456789001234567890
```

where each word is in a separate print zone. This same output can be achieved with the code

```
Dim a As String, b As String, c As String, d As String
a = "North"
b = "to"
c = "the"
d = "future."
picBox.Print a, b, c, d
picBox.Print "123456789012345678901234567890123456789001234567890"
```

EXAMPLE 5   The following program uses Print zones to organize expenses for public and private colleges into columns of a table. The data represent the average expenses for 2002–03. (The Font setting for picTable is Courier New.)

```
Private Sub cmdDisplay_Click()
  picTable.Cls
  picTable.Print " ", "Pb 2-yr", "Pr 2-yr", "Pb 4-yr", "Pr 4-yr"
  picTable.Print
  picTable.Print "Tuit & Fees", 1735, 9890, 4081, 18273
  picTable.Print "Bks & Suppl", 727, 766, 786, 807
  picTable.Print "Rm & Board", 5430, 5327, 5582, 6779
  picTable.Print "Trans", 1104, 1086, 1013, 957
  picTable.Print "Other Exp", 1462, 1476, 1643, 1419
  picTable.Print " ", "-------", "-------", "-------", "-------"
  picTable.Print "Total", 10458, 18545, 13105, 28235
End Sub
```

[Run and then click the command button. The following is displayed in the picture box.]

	Pb 2-yr	Pr 2-yr	Pb 4-yr	Pr 4-yr
Tuit & Fees	1735	9890	4081	18273
Bks & Suppl	727	766	786	807
Rm & Board	5430	5327	5582	6779
Trans	1104	1086	1013	957
Other Exp	1462	1476	1643	1419
	-------	-------	-------	-------
Total	10458	18545	13105	28235

Tab Function

If an item appearing in a Print statement is preceded by

```
Tab(n);
```

where n is a positive integer, that item will be displayed (if possible) beginning at the nth position of the line. (Exceptions are discussed in Comment 10.)

EXAMPLE 6
The following program uses the Tab function to organize data into columns of a table. The data represent the number of bachelor's degrees conferred (in units of 1000). (*Source:* National Center of Educational Statistics.)

```
Private Sub cmdDisplay_Click()
  picTable.Cls
  picTable.Print Tab(10); "1980-81"; Tab(20); "1990-91"; Tab(30); "2000-01"
  picTable.Print
  picTable.Print "Male"; Tab(10); 470; Tab(20); 490; Tab(30); 529
  picTable.Print "Female"; Tab(10); 465; Tab(20); 560; Tab(30); 706
  picTable.Print "Total"; Tab(10); 935; Tab(20); 1050; Tab(30); 1235
End Sub
```

[Run, and then click the command button. The resulting picture box is shown.]

	1980-81	1990-91	2000-01
Male	470	490	529
Female	465	560	706
Total	935	1050	1235

Using a Message Dialog Box for Output

Sometimes you want to grab the user's attention with a brief message such as "Correct" or "Nice try, but no cigar." You want this message to appear on the screen only until the user has read it. This task is easily accomplished with a **message dialog box** such as the one shown in Figure 3.28. When a statement of the form

```
MsgBox prompt, , title
```

is executed, where *prompt* and *title* are strings, a message dialog box appears with *prompt* displayed and the title bar caption *title*, and stays on the screen until the user presses Enter, clicks on the close box in the upper-right corner, or clicks OK. For instance, the statement `MsgBox "Nice try, but no cigar.", , "Consolation"` produces Figure 3.28. You can omit a value for *title* and just execute MsgBox *prompt*. If you do, the title bar will contain the name of the program.

Figure 3.28 Sample message dialog box.

Line Continuation Character

Up to 1023 characters can be typed in a line of code. If you use a statement with more characters than can fit in the window, Visual Basic scrolls the Code window toward the right as needed. However, most programmers prefer having lines that are no longer than the width of the Code window. A long statement can be split across two or more lines by ending each line (except the last) with the underscore character (_) preceded by a space. Make sure the underscore doesn't appear inside quotation marks, though. For instance, the line

```
msg = "640K ought to be enough for anybody. (Bill Gates, 1981)"
```

can be written as

```
msg = "640K ought to be enough for " & _
      "anybody. (Bill Gates, 1981)"
```

Output to the Printer

You print text on a sheet of paper in the printer in much the same way you display text in a picture box. Visual Basic treats the printer as an object named Printer. If *expr* is a string or numeric expression, then the statement

```
Printer.Print expr
```

sends *expr* to the printer buffer in exactly the same way picBox.Print sends output to a picture box. You can use semicolons, commas for print zones, and Tab.

Font properties can be set with statements like

```
Printer.Font.Name = "Script"
Printer.Font.Bold = True
Printer.Font.Size = 12
```

Another useful printer command is

```
Printer.NewPage
```

which starts a new page.

Windows' print manager usually waits until an entire page has been completed before starting to print. At any time, you can print the contents of the printer buffer by executing

```
Printer.EndDoc
```

The statement

```
PrintForm
```

prints the contents of the form.

Program Documentation

Program documentation is the inclusion of comments that specify the intent of the program, the purpose of the variables, and the tasks performed by individual portions of the program. To create a comment statement, just begin the line with an apostrophe. Such a statement is completely ignored when the program is executed. Comment lines appear whenever the program is displayed or printed. Also, a line of code can be documented by adding an apostrophe, followed by the desired information after the end of the line. Comments appear green on the screen.

EXAMPLE 7 The following rewrite of Example 2 uses program documentation. The first comment describes the entire program, the next three comments give the meanings of the variables, and the final comment describes the items in each line of the file.

```
Private Sub cmdCompute_Click()
  Dim nom As String     'Employee name
  Dim wage As Single    'Hourly pay
  Dim hrs As Single     'Number of hours worked during week
  'Compute weekly pay
  picPay.Cls
  Open "STAFF.TXT" For Input As #1
  'Get person's name, hourly pay, and hours worked
  Input #1, nom, wage, hrs
  picPay.Print nom; hrs * wage
  Input #1, nom, wage, hrs
  picPay.Print nom; hrs * wage
  Close #1
End Sub
```

Some of the benefits of documentation are as follows:

1. Other people can easily understand the program.

2. You can understand the program when you read it later.

3. Long programs are easier to read because the purposes of individual pieces can be determined at a glance.

Even though Visual Basic code is easy to read, it is difficult to understand the programmer's intentions without supporting documentation. Good programming practice dictates that developers document their code at the same time that they are writing it. In fact, many software companies require a certain level of documentation before they release a version, and some judge their programmers' performances on how well their code is documented. A rule of thumb is that 10% of the effort developing a software program is the initial coding, while the remaining 90% is maintenance. Much of the anxiety surrounding the fixing of the "Year 2000" problem was due to the enormous amount of effort required by programmers to read and fix old, undocumented code. The challenge was compounded by the fact that most of the original programmers of the code were retired or could not recall how their code was written.

Comments

1. Visual Basic provides a convenient device for accessing a file that resides in the same folder as the (saved) program. After a program has been saved in a folder, the value of App.Path is the string consisting of the path of the folder. Therefore, if a program contains a line such as

```
Open App.Path & "\DATA.TXT" For Input As #1
```

Visual Basic will look for the file DATA.TXT in the folder containing the program.

   The programs from this book, as well as the files they use, all are contained in the folder Programs on the CD accompanying this book. On the CD, App.Path is used in every Open statement. Therefore, even after you copy the contents of the Programs folder onto a hard drive or diskette, the programs will continue to execute properly without your having to alter any paths.

2. The text box and input dialog box provide a whole new dimension to the capabilities of a program. The user, rather than the programmer, can provide the data to be processed.

3. A string used in a file does not have to be enclosed by quotation marks. The only exceptions are strings containing commas or leading and trailing spaces.

4. If an Input # statement looks for a string and finds a number, it will treat the number as a string. Suppose the first two entries in the file DATA.TXT are the numbers 2 and 3.

```
Private Sub cmdButton_Click()
  Dim a As String, b As String
  picBox.Cls
  Open "DATA.TXT" For Input As #1
  Input #1, a, b
  picBox.Print a + b
  Close #1
End Sub
```

[Run, and then click the command button. The following is displayed in the picture box.]

23

5. If an Input # statement looks for a number and finds a string, the Input # statement will assign the value 0 to the numeric variable. For instance,

suppose the first two entries in the file DATA.TXT are "ten" and 10. Then after the statement

```
Input #1, num1, num2
```

is executed, where *num1* and *num2* are numeric variables, the values of these variables will be 0 and 10.

6. If all the data in a file have been read by Input # statements and another item is requested by an Input # statement, a box will appear displaying the message "Input past end of file."

7. Numeric data in a text box, input dialog box, or file must be a constant. It *cannot* be a variable or an expression. For instance, *var*, 2^3, and $2/3$ are not acceptable.

8. To skip a Print zone, just include two consecutive commas.

9. Print zones are usually employed to align information into columns. Since most fonts have proportionally-spaced characters, wide characters occupy more than one fixed-width column and narrow characters occupy less. The best and most predictable results are obtained when a fixed-pitch font (such as Courier New) is used with print zones.

10. The Tab function cannot be used to move the cursor to the left. If the position specified in a Tab function is to the left of the current cursor position, the cursor will move to that position on the next line. For instance, the line

```
picBox.Print "hello"; Tab(3); "good-bye"
```

results in the output

```
hello
  good-bye
```

11. The statement Close, without any reference number, closes all open files.

12. Windows allows you to alternate between Visual Basic and Notepad without exiting either application. After both Visual Basic and Notepad have been invoked, you can go from one application to the other by holding down the Alt key and repeatedly pressing the Tab key until the name of the other application appears. When the Alt key is released, the named application becomes active.

✔ **PRACTICE PROBLEMS 3.5**

1. What is the difference in the outcomes of the following sets of lines of code?

```
Input #1, num1, num2
picOutput.Print num1 + num2


Input #1, num1
Input #1, num2
picOutput.Print num1 + num2
```

2. What is the difference in the outcomes of the following sets of lines of code?

```
strVar = InputBox("How old are you?", "Age")
numVar = Val(strVar)
picOutput.Print numVar

numVar = Val(InputBox("How old are you?", "Age"))
picOutput.Print numVar
```

➤ **EXERCISES 3.5**

In Exercises 1 through 14, assume that the file DATA.TXT (shown to the right of the code) has been opened for input with reference number 1. Determine the output displayed in the picture box by the lines of code.

1.
```
Dim num As Single
Input #1, num
picOutput.Print num * num
```
DATA.TXT
4

2.
```
Dim word As String
Input #1, word
picOutput.Print "un" & word
```
DATA.TXT
"speakable"

3.
```
Dim str1 As String, str2 As String
Input #1, str1, str2
picOutput.Print str1; str2
```
DATA.TXT
"base"
"ball"

4.
```
Dim num1 As Single, num2 As Single
Dim num3 As Single
Input #1, num1, num2, num3
picOutput.Print (num1 + num2) * num3
```
DATA.TXT
3
4
5

5.
```
Dim yrOfBirth As Single, curYr As Single
Input #1, yrOfBirth
Input #1, curYr       'Current year
picOutput.Print "Age:"; curYr - yrOfBirth
```
DATA.TXT
1983
2003

6.
```
Dim str1 As String, str2 As String
Input #1, str1
Input #1, str2
picOutput.Print str1 & str2
```
DATA.TXT
"A, my name is "
"Alice"

7.
```
Dim word1 As String, word2 As String
Input #1, word1
Input #1, word2
picOutput.Print word1 & word2
```
DATA.TXT
"set", "up"

8.
```
Dim num As Single, sum As Single
sum = 0
Input #1, num
sum = sum + num
Input #1, num
sum = sum + num
picOutput.Print "Sum:"; sum
```
DATA.TXT
123, 321

9.
```
Dim building As String
Dim numRooms As Single
Input #1, building, numRooms
picOutput.Print "The "; building;
picOutput.Print " has"; numRooms; "rooms."
```
DATA.TXT
"White House", 132

10.
```
Dim nom As String        'Name of student
Dim grade1 As Single     'Grade on 1st exam
Dim grade2 As Single     'Grade on 2nd exam
Dim average As Single    'Ave of grades
Input #1, nom, grade1, grade2
average = (grade1 + grade2) / 2
picOutput.Print nom; " ======> "; average
Input #1, nom, grade1, grade2
average = (grade1 + grade2) / 2
picOutput.Print nom; " ======> "; average
```
DATA.TXT
"Al Adams", 72, 88
"Betty Brown", 76, 82

11.
```
Dim num1 As Single, num2 As Single
Dim str1 As String, str2 As String
Input #1, num1, str1
Input #1, str2, num2
picOutput.Print num1; str1; str2; num2
Close #1
Open "DATA.TXT" For Input As #1
picOutput.Print num2
Input #1, num2
picOutput.Print num2
```
DATA.TXT
1, "One", "Two", 2

12.
```
Dim num As Integer, strng As String
Input #1, num, strng
picOutput.Print num; strng
Close #1
Open "DATA.TXT" For Input As #1
Input #1, num, strng
picOutput.Print num, strng
```
DATA.TXT
4, "calling birds"
3, "French hens"

13.
```
Dim college As String
Dim yrFounded As Single
Dim yrStr As String, yr As Single
Input #1, college, yrFounded
yrStr = InputBox("What is the current year?")
yr = Val(yrStr)
picOutput.Print college; " is";
picOutput.Print yr - yrFounded; "years old."
```
DATA.TXT
"Harvard University", 1636

(Assume that the response is *2003*.)

14.
```
Dim hourlyWage As Single, nom As String
Dim hoursWorked As Single, message As String
Input #1, hourlyWage, nom
message = "Hours worked by " & nom & ":"
hoursWorked = Val(InputBox(message))
picOutput.Print "Pay for "; nom; " is";
picOutput.Print hoursWorked * hourlyWage
```
DATA.TXT
7.50, "Joe Smith"

(Assume that the response is *10*.)

In Exercises 15 through 28, determine the output displayed in the picture box by the lines of code.

15.
```
Dim bet As Single      'Amount bet at roulette
bet = Val(InputBox("How much do you want to bet?", "Wager"))
picOutput.Print "You might win"; 36 * bet; "dollars."
```

(Assume that the response is 5.)

16.
```
Dim word As String
word = InputBox("Word to negate:")
picOutput.Print "un"; word
```

(Assume that the response is *tied.*)

17.
```
Dim lastName As String, message As String, firstName As String
lastName = "Jones"
message = "What is your first name Mr. " & lastName & "?"
firstName = InputBox(message)
picOutput.Print "Hello "; firstName; " "; lastName
```

(Assume that the response is *John.*)

18.
```
Dim intRate As Single  'Current interest rate
intRate = Val(InputBox("Current interest rate?"))
picOutput.Print "At the current interest rate, ";
picOutput.Print "your money will double in";
picOutput.Print 72 / intRate; "years."
```

(Assume that the response is 6.)

19. `picOutput.Print 1; "one", "won"`

20. `picOutput.Print 1, 2; 3`

21.
```
picOutput.Print "one",
picOutput.Print "two"
```

22. `picOutput.Print "one", , "two"`

23.
```
picOutput.Font.Name = "Courier New"     'Fixed-width font
picOutput.Print "1234567890"
picOutput.Print Tab(4); 5
```

24.
```
picOutput.Font.Name = "Courier New"     'Fixed-width font
picOutput.Print "1234567890"
picOutput.Print "Hello"; Tab(3); "Good-bye"
```

25.
```
picOutput.Font.Name = "Courier New"
picOutput.Print "1234567890"
picOutput.Print Tab(3); "one"; Tab(8); "two"
```

26.
```
picOutput.Font.Name = "Courier New"
picOutput.Print "1234567890"
picOutput.Print Tab(3); "one"
picOutput.Print "    "; "two"
```

27.
```
picOutput.Font.Name = "Courier New"
picOutput.Print "12345678901234"
picOutput.Print "one", Tab(12); "two"
```

28.
```
picOutput.Font.Name = "Courier New"
picOutput.Print "1234567890"
picOutput.Print Tab(2); "1"; Tab(5); "2"
picOutput.Print 1; 2
```

In Exercises 29 through 40, assume that the file DATA.TXT (shown to the right of the code) has been opened for input with reference number 1. Identify any errors.

29.
```
Dim str1 As String, str2 As String
Input #1, str1, str2
picOutput.Print "Hello "; str1
```

DATA.TXT
"John Smith"

30.
```
Dim num As Single
Input #1, num
picOutput.Print 3 * num
```

DATA.TXT
1 + 2

31.
```
'Each line of DATA.TXT contains
'building, height, # of stories
Dim building As String
Dim ht As Single
Input #1, building, ht
picOutput.Print building, ht
Input #1, building, ht
picOutput.Print building, ht
```

DATA.TXT
"Empire State Building", 1250, 102
"Sears Tower", 1454, 110

32.
```
Dim num As Single
num = InputBox(Pick a number from 1 to 10.)
picOutput.Print "Your number is"; num
```

33.
```
Dim statePop As Single
statePop = Val(InputBox("State Population?"))
picOutput.Print "The population should grow to";
picOutput.Print 1.01 * statePop; "by next year."
```

(Assume that the response is 8,900,000.)

34. `info = InputBox()`

35. `Printer.Name = Courier New`

36. `txtBox.Text = "one", "two"`

37. `lblTwo.Caption = 1, 2`

38. `Printer.Print "Hello"; Tab(200); "Good-bye"`

39. `Form.Caption = "one"; Tab(10); "two"`

40.
```
Dim sub As Single  'Number to substitute
Input #1, sub
picOutput.Print "Don't forget to ";
picOutput.Print "substitute the number"; sub
```

DATA.TXT
4

41. Fill in the table with the substitute value of each variable after each line is executed. Assume the file DATA.TXT consists of the two lines

"phone", 35.25
"postage", 14.75

Event Procedure	category	amount	total
`Private Sub cmdDetermineTotal_Click()`			
`  Dim category As String`			
`  Dim amount As Single`			
`  Dim total As Single`			
`  Open "DATA.TXT" For Input As #1`			
`  Input #1, category, amount`			
`  total = total + amount`			
`  Input #1, category, amount`			
`  total = total + amount`			
`  picOutput.Print total`			
`  Close #1`			
`End Sub`			

42. Fill in the table with the value of each variable after each line is executed. Assume the file DATA.TXT consists of the single line

2, 3, 5

Event Procedure	num1	num2	num3
`Private Sub cmdButton_Click()`			
`  Dim num1 As Single, num2 As Single`			
`  Dim num3 As Single`			
`  Open "DATA.TXT" For Input As #1`			
`  Input #1, num1, num2, num3`			
`  num1 = num2 + num3`			
`  Close #1`			
`  Open "DATA.TXT" For Input As #2`			
`  Input #2, num1, num3`			
`  num3 = num3 + 1`			
`  Close #2`			
`End Sub`			

In Exercises 43 through 46, write an event procedure starting with Private Sub cmdDisplay_ Click() and picOutput.Cls statements, ending with an End Sub statement, and having one or two lines for each step. Lines that display data should use the given variable names.

43. The following steps display the changes in the percentage of declared majors for first-year college students from 2001 to 2002. Assume the file MAJORS .TXT consists of the two lines

"Business Administration", 3.7, 3.8
"Biology (general)", 4.1, 4.0

(a) Declare all variables used in step (c).
(b) Open the file MAJORS.TXT for input.
(c) Use an Input # statement to assign values to the variables *major*, *percent01*, and *percent02*.
(d) Display a sentence giving the change in the percentage of students majoring in a certain subject.
(e) Repeat steps (c) and (d).

44. The following steps display information about Americans' eating habits. Assume the file SODA.TXT consists of the single line

"soft drinks", "million gallons", 23

(a) Declare all variables used in step (c).
(b) Open the file SODA.TXT for input.
(c) Use an Input # statement to assign values to the variables *food*, *units*, and *quantityPerDay*.
(d) Display a sentence giving the quantity of a food item consumed by Americans in 1 day.

45. The following steps calculate the percent increase in a typical grocery basket of goods.

(a) Declare all variables used in steps (b)–(d).
(b) Assign 200 to the variable *begOfYearPrice*.
(c) Request the price at the end of the year with an input dialog box and assign it to the variable *endOfYearPrice*.
(d) Assign 100 ∗ (*endOfYearPrice* – *begOfYearPrice*) / *begOfYearPrice* to the variable *percentIncrease*.
(e) Display a sentence giving the percent increase for the year.

(Test the program with a $215 end-of-year price.)

46. The following steps calculate the amount of money earned in a walk-a-thon.

(a) Declare all variables used in steps (b) and (c).
(b) Request the amount pledged per mile from an input dialog box and assign it to the variable *pledge*.
(c) Request the number of miles walked from an input dialog box and assign it to the variable *miles*.
(d) Display a sentence giving the amount to be paid.

(Test the program with a pledge of $2.00 and a 15-mile walk.)

In Exercises 47 and 48, write a line of code to carry out the task.

47. Pop up a message dialog box stating "The future isn't what it used to be."

48. Pop up a message dialog box with "Taking Risks Proverb" in the title bar and the message "You can't steal second base and keep one foot on first."

49. Table 3.4 summarizes the month's activity of three checking accounts. Write a program that displays the account number and the end-of-month balance for each account and then displays the total amount of money in the three accounts. Assume the data are stored in a text file.

Account Number	Beginning-of-Month Balance	Deposits	Withdrawals
AB4057	1234.56	345.67	100.00
XY4321	789.00	120.00	350.00
GH2222	321.45	143.65	0.00

Table 3.4 Checking-account activity.

50. Table 3.5 contains a list of colleges with their student enrollments and faculty sizes. Write a program to display the names of the colleges and their student/faculty ratios, and the ratio for the total collection of students and faculty. Assume the data for the colleges are stored in a text file.

	Enrollment	Faculty
Ohio State	48477	3526
Univ. of MD, College Park	34160	2136
Princeton	6668	961

Table 3.5 Colleges.
Source: The World Almanac, 2003.

51. Write a program to compute semester averages. Each line in a text file should contain a student's social security number and the grades for three hourly exams and the final exam. (The final exam counts as two hourly exams.) The program should display each student's social security number and semester average, and then the class average. Use the data in Table 3.6.

Soc. Sec. No.	Exam 1	Exam 2	Exam 3	Final Exam
123-45-6789	67	85	90	88
111-11-1111	93	76	82	80
123-32-1234	85	82	89	84

Table 3.6 Student grades.

52. Table 3.7 gives the year 2000 populations of three New England states. Write a program that calculates the average population and then displays the name of each state and the difference between its population and the average population. The states and their populations should be stored in a text file.

Maine	1275
Massachusetts	6349
Connecticut	3406

Table 3.7 2000 Population (in thousands) of three New England states.

53. Write a program to produce Table 3.8. (The amounts are given in millions of dollars.) The name, sport, salary or winnings, and endorsements for the four people should be contained in a text file. The totals should be computed by the program.

Athlete	Sport	Salary or Winnings	Endorsements	Total
M. Jordan	basketball	29.3	193.2	222.5
E. Holyfield	boxing	110.3	7.5	117.8
A. Agassi	tennis	11.3	63.5	74.8
W. Gretsky	hockey	36.8	31.5	68.3

Table 3.8 1990–96 earnings (in millions) of athletes.

54. Write a program to calculate the amount of a server's tip given the amount of the bill and the percentage tip obtained via input dialog boxes. The output should be a complete sentence that reiterates the inputs and gives the resulting tip. For example, if $20 and 15% are the inputs, then the output might read "A 15 percent tip on 20 dollars is 3 dollars."

55. Design a form with two text boxes labeled "Name" and "Phone number". Then write an event procedure that shows a message dialog box stating "Be sure to include the area code!" when the second text box receives the focus.

In Exercises 56 and 57, write lines of code corresponding to the given flow-chart. Assume that the data needed are contained in a file.

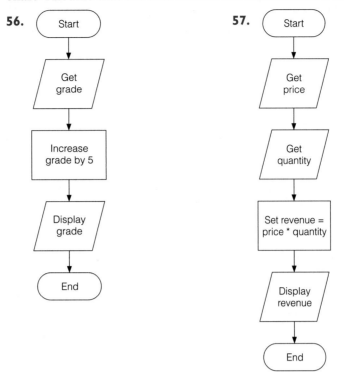

✔✔ Solutions to Practice Problems 3.5

1. The outputs are identical. In this text, we tend to use a single Input # statement for each line of the file.

2. The outcomes are identical. In this text, we use the second style.

3.6 BUILT-IN FUNCTIONS

Visual Basic has a number of built-in functions that greatly extend its capability. These functions perform such varied tasks as taking the square root of a number, counting the number of characters in a string, and capitalizing letters. Functions associate with one or more values, called the *input*, a single value, called the *output*. The function is said to **return** the output value. The three functions considered in what follows have numeric input and output.

Numeric Functions: Sqr, Int, Round

The function Sqr calculates the square root of a number. The function Int finds the greatest integer less than or equal to a number. Therefore, Int discards the decimal part of positive numbers. The value of Round (n, r) is the number n rounded to r decimal places. The parameter r can be omitted. If so, n is rounded to a whole number. Some examples follow:

```
Sqr(9) is 3.          Int(2.7) is 2.        Round(2.7) is 3.
Sqr(0) is 0.          Int(3) is 3.          Round(2.317, 2) is 2.32.
Sqr(2) is 1.414214.   Int(-2.7) is -3.      Round(2.317, 1) is 2.3.
```

The terms inside the parentheses can be either numbers (as shown), numeric variables, or numeric expressions. Expressions are first evaluated to produce the input.

EXAMPLE 1 The following program evaluates each of the functions for a specific input given by the value of the variable *n*.

```
Private Sub cmdEvaluate_Click()
  Dim n As Single, root As Single
  'Evaluate functions at a variable
  picResults.Cls
  n = 6.76
  root = Sqr(n)
  picResults.Print root; Int(n); Round(n,1)
End Sub
```

[Run, and then click the command button. The following is displayed in the picture box.]

```
2.6  6  6.8
```

EXAMPLE 2 The following program evaluates each of the preceding functions at an expression.

```
Private Sub cmdEvaluate_Click()
  Dim a As Single, b As Single
  'Evaluate functions at expressions
  picResults.Cls
  a = 2
  b = 3
  picResults.Print Sqr(5 * b + 1); Int(a ^ b); Round(a / b, 3)
End Sub
```

[Run, and then click the command button. The following is displayed in the picture box.]

```
4  8  0.667
```

EXAMPLE 3 The following program shows an application of the Sqr function.

```
Private Sub cmdComputeHyp_Click()
  Dim leg1 As Single, leg2 As Single, hyp As Single
  'Find the length of the hypotenuse of a right triangle
  picHyp.Cls
  leg1 = Val(txtFirst.Text)
  leg2 = Val(txtSecond.Text)
  hyp = Sqr(leg1 ^ 2 + leg2 ^ 2)
```

```
  picHyp.Print "The length of the hypotenuse is"; hyp
End Sub
```

[Run, type 3 and 4 into the text boxes, and then click the command button.]

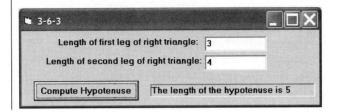

EXAMPLE 4 The following program shows how Int is used to carry out long division. When the integer *m* is divided into the integer *n* with long division, the result is a quotient and a remainder. See Figure 3.29.

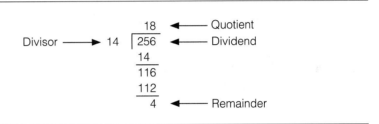

Figure 3.29 Long division.

```
Private Sub cmdDivide_Click()
  Dim divisor As Single, dividend As Single
  Dim quotient As Single, remainder As Single
  'Long division
  picResult.Cls
  divisor = Val(txtDivisor.Text)
  dividend = Val(txtDividend.Text)
  quotient = Int(dividend / divisor)
  remainder = dividend - quotient * divisor
  picResult.Print "The quotient is"; quotient
  picResult.Print "The remainder is"; remainder
End Sub
```

[Run, type 14 and 256 into the text boxes, and then click the command button.]

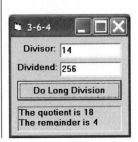

String Functions: Left, Mid, Right, UCase, Trim

The functions Left, Mid, and Right are used to extract a sequence of consecutive characters from the left end, middle, and right end of a string. Suppose *str* is a string and *m* and *n* are positive integers. Then Left(*str*, *n*) is the string consisting of the first *n* characters of *str* and Right(*str*, *n*) is the string consisting of the last *n* characters of *str*. Mid(*str*, *m*, *n*) is the string consisting of *n* characters of *str*, beginning with the *m*th character. UCase(*str*) is the string *str* with all of its lowercase letters capitalized. Trim(*str*) is the string *str* with all leading and trailing spaces removed. Some examples are as follows:

```
Left("fanatic", 3) is "fan".          Right("fanatic", 3) is "tic".
Left("12/15/99", 2) is "12".          Right("12/15/99", 2) is "99".
Mid("fanatic", 5, 1) is "t".          Mid("12/15/99", 4, 2) is "15".
UCase("Disk") is "DISK".              UCase("12three") is "12THREE".
Trim(" 1  2 ") is "1  2".             Trim("-12 ") is "-12".
```

The strings produced by Left, Mid, and Right are referred to as **substrings** of the strings from which they were formed. For instance, "fan" and "t" are substrings of "fanatic". The substring "fan" is said to begin at position 1 of "fanatic" and the substring "t" is said to begin at position 5.

Like the numeric functions discussed before, Left, Mid, Right, UCase, and Trim also can be evaluated for variables and expressions.

EXAMPLE 5 The following program evaluates the functions above for variables and expressions. Note that spaces are counted as characters.

```
Private Sub cmdEvaluate_Click()
  Dim str1 As String, str2 As String
  'Evaluate functions at variables and expressions.
  picResults.Cls
  str1 = "Quick as "
  str2 = "a wink"
  picResults.Print Left(str1, 7)
  picResults.Print Mid(str1 & str2, 7, 6)
  picResults.Print UCase(str1 & str2)
  picResults.Print "The average "; Right(str2, 4); " lasts .1 second."
  picResults.Print Trim(str1); str2
End Sub
```

[Run, and then click the command button. The following is displayed in the picture box.]

```
Quick a
as a w
QUICK AS A WINK
The average wink lasts .1 second.
Quick asa wink
```

String-Related Numeric Functions: Len, InStr

The functions Len and InStr operate on strings but produce numbers. The function Len gives the number of characters in a string. The function InStr searches for the first occurrence of one string in another and gives the position at which the string is found. Suppose *str1* and *str2* are strings. The value of Len(*str1*) is the number of characters in *str1*. The value of InStr(*str1, str2*) is 0 if *str2* is not a substring of *str1*. Otherwise, its value is the beginning position of the first occurrence of *str2* in *str1*. Some examples of Len and InStr follow:

```
Len("Shenandoah") is 10.         InStr("Shenandoah", "nand") is 4.
Len("Just a moment") is 13.      InStr("Just a moment", " ") is 5.
Len(" ") is 1.                   InStr("Croissant", "ist") is 0.
```

EXAMPLE 6   The following program parses a name. The ninth line locates the position, call it *n*, of the space separating the two names. The first name will end one position to the left of this position and the last name will consist of all but the first *n* characters of the full name.

```
Private Sub cmdAnalyze_Click()
  Dim nom As String      'Name
  Dim n As Integer       'Location of space
  Dim first As String    'First name
  Dim last As String     'Last name
  'Evaluate functions at variables and expressions.
  picResults.Cls
  nom = txtFullName.Text
  n = InStr(nom, " ")
  first = Left(nom, n - 1)
  last = Right(nom, Len(nom) - n)
  picResults.Print "Your first name is "; first
  picResults.Print "Your last name has"; Len(last); "letters."
End Sub
```

[Run, type John Doe into the text box, and then click the command button.]

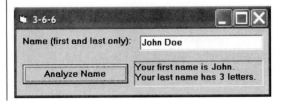

Format Functions

The Format functions are used to display numbers and dates in familiar forms and to right-justify numbers. Here are some examples of how numbers are converted to strings with Format functions.

```
Function                          String Value
FormatNumber(12345.628, 1)        12,345.6
FormatCurrency(12345.628, 2)      $12,345.63
FormatPercent(0.185, 2)           18.50%
```

The value of FormatNumber(n, r) is the string containing the number n rounded to r decimal places and displayed with commas as thousands separators. The value of FormatCurrency(n, r) is the string consisting of a dollar sign followed by the value of FormatNumber(n, r). FormatCurrency uses the accountant's convention of denoting negative amounts with surrounding parentheses. The value of FormatPercent(n, r) is the string consisting of the number n displayed as a percent and rounded to r decimal places.

With all three functions, r can be omitted. If so, the number is rounded to two decimal places. Strings corresponding to numbers less than one in magnitude have a zero to the left of the decimal point. Also, n can be a either a number, a numeric expression, or even a string corresponding to a number.

```
Function                   String Value
FormatNumber(1 + Sqr(2), 3)   2.414
FormatCurrency(-1000)         ($1,000.00)
FormatPercent(".005")         0.50%
```

If *dateString* represents a date in a form such as "7-4-2003", "7-4-03", or "7/4/03", then the value of FormatDateTime(*dateString*, vbLongDate) is a string giving the date as Friday, July 04, 2003.

```
Function                                 String Value
FormatDateTime("9-15-99", vbLongDate)    Wednesday, September 15, 1999
FormatDateTime("10-23-00", vbLongDate)   Monday, October 23, 2000
```

The value of Format(*expr*, "@@ ... @"), where "@@ ... @" is a string of n "at" symbols, is the string consisting of the value of *expr* right-justified in a field of n spaces. This function is used with fixed-width fonts, such as Courier New or Terminal, to display columns of numbers so that the decimal points and commas are lined up or to display right-justified lists of words. The following examples use a string of 10 "at" symbols.

```
Function                                      String Value
Format(1234567890, "@@@@@@@@@@")              1234567890
Format(FormatNumber(1234.5), "@@@@@@@@@@")       1,234.50
Format(FormatNumber(12345.67), "@@@@@@@@@@")    12,345.67
Format(FormatCurrency(13580.17), "@@@@@@@@@@")  $13,580.17
```

EXAMPLE 7   The following program produces essentially the first two columns of the table in Example 5 of Section 3.5. However, Format is used to right-justify the expense categories and to align the numbers.

Object	Property	Setting
frmExpenses	Caption	Public 2-year College Expenses
cmdDisplay	Caption	Display Expenses
picTable	Font.Name	Courier New

```
Private Sub cmdDisplay_Click()
  Dim fmt1 As String, fmt2 As String
  Dim col1 As String, col2 As String
  'Average expenses of commuter students (1995-96)
  picTable.Cls
  picTable.Print Tab(19); "Pb 2-yr"
  picTable.Print
  fmt1 = "@@@@@@@@@@@@@@@@@"    '17 @ symbols
  fmt2 = "@@@@@@"               '6 @ symbols
  col1 = Format("Tuition & Fees", fmt1)
  col2 = FormatNumber(1735, 0)
  col2 = Format(col2, fmt2)
  picTable.Print col1; Tab(19); col2
  col1 = Format("Books & Supplies", fmt1)
  col2 = FormatNumber(727, 0)
  col2 = Format(col2, fmt2)
  picTable.Print col1; Tab(19); col2
  col1 = Format("Rm & Board", fmt1)
  col2 = FormatNumber(5430, 0)
  col2 = Format(col2, fmt2)
  picTable.Print col1; Tab(19); col2
  col1 = Format("Transportation", fmt1)
  col2 = FormatNumber(1104, 0)
  col2 = Format(col2, fmt2)
  picTable.Print col1; Tab(19); col2
  col1 = Format("Other Expenses", fmt1)
  col2 = FormatNumber(1462, 0)
  col2 = Format(col2, fmt2)
  picTable.Print col1; Tab(19); col2
  picTable.Print Tab(19); "------"
  col1 = Format("Total", fmt1)
  col2 = FormatNumber(10458, 0)
  col2 = Format(col2, fmt2)
  picTable.Print col1; Tab(19); col2
End Sub
```

[Run, and then click the command button.]

```
                Pb 2-Yr

  Tuition & Fees   1,735
Books & Supplies     727
     Rm & Board   5,430
  Transportation   1,104
  Other Expenses   1,462
                  ------
          Total  10,458
```

Generating Random Numbers: Rnd

Consider a specific collection of numbers. We say that a process selects a number at **random** from this collection if any number in the collection is just as likely to be selected as any other and the number cannot be predicted in advance. Some examples follow:

Collection	Process
1, 2, 3, 4, 5, 6	toss a die
0 or 1	toss a coin: 0 = tails, 1 = heads
–1, 0, 1, . . . , 36	spin a roulette wheel (interpret –1 as 00)
1, 2, . . . , n	write numbers on slips of paper, pull one from hat
numbers from 0 to 1	flip the spinner in Figure 3.30

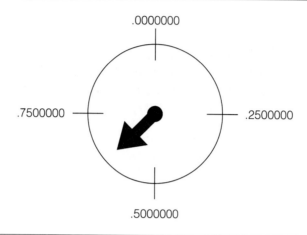

Figure 3.30 Spinner to randomly select a number between 0 and 1.

The function Rnd, which acts like the spinner in Figure 3.30, returns a random number. The statement

```
picBox.Print Rnd
```

randomly displays a number from 0 up to (but not including) 1. The statement

```
numVar = Rnd
```

randomly assigns a number between 0 and 1 to the variable *numVar*. A different number will be assigned each time Rnd is called in the program, and any number greater than or equal to 0 and less than 1 is just as likely to be generated as any other. Therefore, although Rnd looks like a numeric variable, it does not act at all like a variable.

With appropriate scaling, the Rnd function can generate random numbers from other collections. The statement

```
picBox.Print Int(6 * Rnd) + 1
```

displays a number from the set 1, 2, 3, 4, 5, 6. Because Rnd always has a value from 0 to 1, excluding 1, 6 * Rnd has a value from 0 to 6 (excluding 6), and Int(6 * Rnd) has one of the values 0, 1, 2, 3, 4, 5. Adding 1 shifts the resulting number into the desired range.

Suppose the preceding statement is repeated many times. The integers generated should exhibit no apparent pattern. They should look very much like a sequence of integers obtained from successively rolling a die. For instance, each of the six integers should appear about one-sixth of the time and be reasonably spread out in the sequence. The longer the sequence, the more likely this is to occur.

Rnd generates the same sequence of numbers each time a program is run. However, Visual Basic has another function, Randomize, that changes the sequence of numbers generated by Rnd. This statement will be used in all programs in this text.

EXAMPLE 8   The DC Lottery number is obtained by selecting a Ping-Pong ball from each of three separate bowls. Each ball is numbered with an integer from 0 through 9. The following program produces a lottery number. (Such a program is said to **simulate** the selection of Ping-Pong balls.) The value of Int(10 * Rnd) will be an integer from 0 through 9, and each of these integers has the same likelihood of occurring. Repeating the process three times produces the requested digits.

```
Private Sub cmdDisplayANumber_Click()
  'Display a lottery number
  picNumber.Cls
  Randomize
  picNumber.Print Int(10 * Rnd);
  picNumber.Print Int(10 * Rnd);
  picNumber.Print Int(10 * Rnd)
End Sub
```

[Run, and then click the command button. One possible output to be displayed in the picture box is as follows.]

```
8  3  9
```

Note: Run the program in Example 8 several times and notice that the output changes each time. Then delete the Randomize statement and run the program several times.

Comments

1. Requesting the square root of a negative number terminates the execution of the program and gives the error message "Invalid procedure call or argument."

2. If *n* is greater than the length of *str*, then the value of Left(*str*, *n*) will be the entire string *str*. A similar result holds for Mid and Right.

3. Visual Basic has a function called LCase that is analogous to UCase. LCase converts all uppercase letters in a string to lowercase letters.

4. Because the values of the functions Left, Mid, Right, UCase, and the Format functions are strings, they are referred to as **string-valued functions**.

5. Mid is an important function. It will be used several times in this book to examine each letter of a string.

6. Trim is useful when reading data from a text box. Sometimes users type spaces at the end of input. Unless the spaces are removed, they can cause

havoc elsewhere in the program. Also, Trim is useful in trimming the leading spaces from numbers that have been converted to strings with Str.

7. The InStr function has a useful extension. The value of InStr(n, *str1*, *str2*) is the position of the first occurrence of *str2* in *str1* in position n or greater. For instance, InStr(5, "Mississippi", "ss") is 6.

8. In Example 4, we found that 4 is the remainder when 256 is divided by 14. Mathematicians say "4 = 256 modulo 14." Visual Basic has an operation, Mod, that performs this calculation directly. If m and n are positive integers, then n Mod m is the remainder when n is divided by m. Visual Basic also has an operation called **integer division**, denoted by \, which gives the quotient portion of a long-division problem. For instance, 14/4 is 3.5 whereas 14\4 is the integer 3.

9. Recall that the function Mid has the form Mid(*str*, m, n) and returns the substring of *str* starting with position m and having length n. Visual Basic does its best to please for unexpected values of m and n. If m is greater than the length of the string or n is 0, then the empty string is returned. If $m + n$ is greater than the length of the string, then Mid(*str*, m, n) is the right part of the string beginning with the mth character. The same is true for Mid(*str*, m). For instance, the values of Mid("abcdef", 3, 9) and Mid("abcdef", 3) are both "cdef".

10. With FormatCurrency(n, r), fractional values are preceded by a leading zero, and negative values are surrounded by parentheses instead of beginning with a minus sign. The function has additional optional parameters. FormatCurrency(*exp*, , vbFalse) suppresses leading zeros for fractional values. FormatCurrency(*exp*, , , vbFalse) uses minus signs for negative numbers. For instance, the value of FormatCurrency(–3/4, 3, vbFalse, vbFalse) is –$.750.

11. With FormatNumber(n, r), fractional values are preceded by a leading zero. The function has additional optional parameters. FormatNumber(*exp*, , vbFalse) suppresses leading zeros for fractional values. For instance, the value of FormatNumber(3/4, 3) is 0.750 and the value of FormatNumber(3/4, 3, vbFalse) is .750. FormatNumber(*exp*, , , , vbFalse) suppresses commas.

12. When n is a number that is halfway between two successive whole numbers (such as 1.5, 2.5, 3.5, and 4.5), then n is rounded by the Round function to the nearest even number. For instance, Round(2.5) is 2 and Round(3.5) is 4. Similar results hold for any number whose decimal part ends in 5. For instance, Round(3.65, 1) is 3.6 and Round(3.75, 1) is 3.8. On the other hand, FormatNumber, FormatCurrency, and FormatPercent always round 5's up. For instance, FormatNumber(2.5) is "3.00".

13. The value of `FormatDateTime(Now,vbLongDate)` is today's date. For any positive number n, `FormatDateTime(Now +n, vbLongDate)` is the date n days from today and `FormatDateTime(Now - n, vbLongDate)` is the date n days ago.

14. Each time the function Rnd appears in a program, it will be reassigned a value. For instance, the task attempted (but not accomplished) by the first set of lines that follows is achieved by the second set of lines. Because each of

the Rnd's in the first set of lines will assume a different value, it is highly unlikely that the square of the first one will equal the product of the last two.

```
'Generate the square of a randomly chosen number
Randomize
picBox.Print "The square of"; Rnd; "is"; Rnd * Rnd

'Generate the square of a randomly chosen number
Randomize
numVar = Rnd
picBox.Print "The square of"; numVar; "is"; numVar * numVar
```

15. Additional information about the keywords, functions, methods, and properties discussed in this chapter appear in Appendix C. With the Learning, Professional, and Enterprise Editions of Visual Basic you can obtain a detailed (and somewhat advanced) discussion about an item appearing in code by clicking on the item and pressing F1. Other ways of obtaining help with these editions are presented in Appendix B.

✔ **PRACTICE PROBLEMS 3.6**

1. What is the value of InStr("Computer", "E")?

2. What is the value of Sqr(12 * Len("WIN"))?

3. Write an expression that will randomly select an uppercase letter from the alphabet.

4. When will Int(n / 2) be the same as n / 2?

➤ **EXERCISES 3.6**

In Exercises 1 through 20, find the value of the given function.

1. UCase("McD's")

2. Sqr(64)

3. Int(10.75)

4. Left("harp", 2)

5. Sqr(3 * 12)

6. Int(9 - 2)

7. Round(3.1279, 3)

8. Round(-2.6)

9. Left("ABCD", 2)

10. Mid("ABCDE", 2, 3)

11. Mid("shoe", 4, 1)

12. UCase("$2 bill")

13. Len("shoe")

14. InStr("shoe", "h")

15. InStr("shoe", "f")

16. Len("s" & Left("help", 2))

17. Right("snow", 3)

18. Right("123", 1)

19. Len(Trim(Str(32)))

20. Len(Trim(Str(-32)))

In Exercises 21 through 39, find the value of the given function where a and b are numeric variables, c and d are string variables; $a = 5$, $b = 3$, $c =$ "Lullaby", and $d =$ "lab".

21. `Len(d)`

22. `Sqr(4 + a)`

23. `Int(-a / 2)`

24. `UCase(d)`

25. `Round(a / b, 2)`

26. `Round(a + .5)`

27. `Sqr(a - 5)`

28. `Int(b * .5)`

29. `Left(c, Len(d))`

30. `Mid(c, a, 3)`

31. `Mid(c, a - b, 2 * a)`

32. `Left(d, b - 2)`

33. `UCase(c)`

34. `InStr(c, d)`

35. `InStr(c, "r")`

36. `Len(c & Left(d, 2))`

37. `Right(c, 2)`

38. `Right("Sky" & d, 5)`

39. `Trim(Str(a + b)) & d`

In Exercises 40 through 81, determine the output produced by the lines of code.

40.
```
numVar = 3.47
picOutput.Print Round(numVar)
numVar = Round(numVar, 1)
picOutput.Print Round(numVar)
```

41.
```
week = "SunMonTueWedThuFriSat"
strVar = InputBox("Day of week (1 to 7)")
picOutput.Print "Today is "; Mid(week, 3 * Val(strVar) - 2, 3)
```

(Assume that the response is 5.)

42.
```
today = InputBox("Date (mm/dd/yy)")
picOutput.Print "The year is 19" & Mid(today, 7, 2)
```

(Assume that the response is *10/23/99.*)

43.
```
word = "Hello"
picOutput.Print Mid(word, Len(word), 1)
```

44.
```
nom = txtName.Text
picOutput.Print Left(nom, 1) & Mid(nom, InStr(nom, " ") + 1, 1)
```

(Assume that txtName.Text is *Bob Clark.*)

45.
```
response = InputBox("Do you like jazz (yes or no)")
num = Int(InStr("YyNn", Left(response, 1)) / 2 + .5)
response = Mid("yesno ", 3 * num - 2, 3)
picOutput.Print "I guess your answer is "; response
```

(Assume that the response is *yup* or *Yeah.*)

46.
```
num = 123
strVar = Str(num)
picOutput.Print "xxx"; Right(strVar, Len(strVar) - 1)
```

47. `numStr = Trim(Str(37))`
    `strVar = " Yankees"`
    `picOutput.Print "19"; numStr; UCase(strVar)`

48. `txtBox.Text = FormatNumber(1234.56, 0)`

49. `txtBox.Text = FormatNumber(-12.3456, 3)`

50. `txtBox.Text = FormatNumber(1234, 1)`

51. `txtBox.Text = FormatNumber(12345)`

52. `txtBox.Text = FormatNumber(.012, 1)`

53. `txtBox.Text = FormatNumber(5 * (10 ^ -2), 1)`

54. `txtBox.Text = FormatNumber(-2/3)`

55. `txtBox.Text = FormatNumber(12345, 0, , , vbFalse)`

56. `txtBox.Text = FormatNumber(987654.128, 2, , , vbFalse)`

57. `numVar = Round(1.2345, 1)`
    `txtBox.Text = FormatNumber(numVar)`

58. `numVar = Round(12345.9)`
    `txtBox.Text = FormatNumber(numVar, 3)`

59. `numVar = Round(12.5)`
    `txtBox.Text = FormatNumber(numVar, 0)`

60. `numVar = Round(11.5)`
    `txtBox.Text = FormatNumber(numVar, 0)`

61. `txtBox.Text = FormatCurrency(1234.5)`

62. `txtBox.Text = FormatCurrency(12345.67, 0)`

63. `txtBox.Text = FormatCurrency(-1234567)`

64. `txtBox.Text = FormatCurrency(-.225)`

65. `txtBox.Text = FormatCurrency(-1234, , , vbFalse)`

66. `txtBox.Text = FormatCurrency(-.1234, 3, , vbFalse)`

67. `txtBox.Text = FormatCurrency(32 * (10 ^ 2))`

68. `txtBox.Text = FormatCurrency(4 / 5)`

69. `txtBox.Text = FormatPercent(.04, 0)`

70. `txtBox.Text = FormatPercent(.075)`

71. `txtBox.Text = FormatPercent(-.05, 3)`

72. `txtBox.Text = FormatPercent(1)`

73. `txtBox.Text = FormatPercent(100)`

74. `txtBox.Text = FormatPercent(2 / 3)`

75. `txtBox.Text = FormatPercent(3 / 4, 1)`

76. `txtBox.Text = FormatPercent(10 ^ -2)`

77. `txtBox.Text = FormatDateTime(Now + 1, vbLongDate)`

78. `txtBox.Text = FormatDateTime("7-4-1776", vbLongDate)`

    (*Note:* The Declaration of Independence was signed on a Thursday.)

79. `txtBox.Text = FormatDateTime("12-31-99", vbLongDate)`

    (*Note:* The year 2000 began on a Saturday.)

80. ```
strVar = FormatDateTime(Now, vbLongDate)
txtBox.Text = Left(strVar, Instr(strVar, ",") - 1)
```

81. ```
strVar = FormatDateTime(Now, vbLongDate)
txtBox.Text = Right(strVar, 4)
```

In Exercises 82 through 85, what will be displayed in the picture box by the following statements?

82. `picOutput.Print "Pay to France "; FormatCurrency(27267622)`

83. `picOutput.Print "Manhattan", FormatCurrency(24)`

84. ```
picOutput.Print "Name"; Tab(10); "Salary"
picOutput.Print "Bill"; Tab(10); FormatCurrency(123000)
```

85. ```
picOutput.Print "Name"; Tab(10); Format("Salary", "@@@@@@@@@@")
strVar = FormatCurrency(123000)
picOutput.Print "Bill"; Tab(10); Format(strVar, "@@@@@@@@@@")
```

    (Assume that the setting for Font.Name is "Courier New".)

In Exercises 86 through 91, determine the output displayed on the printer by the lines of code.

86. ```
Printer.Font.Name = "Courier New"   'Fixed-width font
Printer.Print "1234567890"
Printer.Print Format(123, "@@@@@@@@@@")
```

87. ```
Printer.Font.Name = "Courier New"     'Fixed-width font
Printer.Print "1234567890"
Printer.Print Format("abcd", "@@@@@@@@@@")
```

88. ```
Printer.Font.Name = "Courier New"   'Fixed-width font
Printer.Print "1234567890"
Printer.Print Format("$1,234.56", "@@@@@@@@@@")
```

89. ```
Printer.Font.Name = "Courier New"     'Fixed-width font
Printer.Print "1234567890"
strVar = Str(1234.559)
Printer.Print Format(strVar, "@@@@@@@@@@")
```

90. ```
Printer.Font.Name = "Courier New"   'Fixed-width font
Printer.Print "1234567890"
Printer.Print Format(1 / 4, "@@@@@@@@@@")
```
```

91.
```
Printer.Font.Name = "Courier New"     'Fixed-width font
Printer.Print "1234567890"
numVar = 25
strVar = FormatCurrency(numVar)
Printer.Print Format(strVar, "@@@@@@@@@@")
```

In Exercises 92 through 99, determine any errors.

92.
```
strVar = "Thank you"
picOutput.Print InStr(strVar, k)
```

93. `picOutput.Print Left(3, "goodbye")`

94.
```
firstName = InputBox("Enter your first name.")
picOutput.Print "Your first name is "; firstName
```

(Assume that the response is Left("John Doe", 4).)

95.
```
num1 = 7
num2 = 5
picOutput.Print Sqr(num1 - 2 * num2)
```

96.
```
Dim numString As String
numString = 123
picOutput.Print 2 * Val(numString)
```

97. `picOutput.Print Format(123.45, @@@@@@@)`

98. `txtBox.Text = FormatCurrency($7654.3)`

99. `txtBox.Text = (1234.568, 2)`

100. Is `Str(Val("32"))` the same string as `"32"`?

101. Is `Trim(Str(Val("32")))` the same string as `"32"`?

102. Is `Str(123.45)` the same string as `FormatNumber(123.45)`?

103. Is `Str(Round(14.5))` the same string as `FormatNumber(14.5)`?

104. Is `Int(6.5 + .5)` the same number as `Round(6.5)`?

105. Does `picBox.Print FormatNumber(123.45)` produce the same result as `picBox.Print 123.45`?

In Exercises 106 through 111, determine the range of values that can be generated by the given expression.

106. `Int(38 * Rnd) - 1`

107. `Int(10 * Rnd) + 10`

108. `2 * Rnd`

109. `Int(52 * Rnd) + 1`

110. `Chr(Int(3 * Rnd) + 65)`

111. `Chr(Int(26 * Rnd) + 97)`

In Exercises 112 through 117, write an expression that will randomly select a value from the given range.

112. An integer from 1 through 100

113. A number from 2 through 4 (excluding 4)

114. An even integer from 2 through 100

115. Either 0 or 1

116. The answer to a multiple-choice question, where the answers range from a to d

117. A white piano key from an octave; that is, one of the letters A through G

118. Suppose a text box contains a positive number. Write code to replace this number with its units digit.

119. Suppose a text box contains a (complete) phone number. Write code to display the area code.

120. The formula $s = \sqrt{24d}$ gives an estimate of the speed of a car in miles per hour that skidded d feet on dry concrete when the brakes were applied. Write a program that requests the distance skidded and then displays the estimated speed of the car. (Try the program for a car that skids 54 feet.)

121. A college graduation is to be held in an auditorium with 2000 seats available for the friends and relatives of the graduates. Write a program that requests the number of graduates as input and then displays the number of tickets to be distributed to each graduate. Assume each graduate receives the same number of tickets. (Try the program for 325 graduates.)

122. Suppose you decide to give three pieces of Halloween candy to each trick-or-treater. Write a program that requests the number of pieces of candy you have and displays the number of children you can treat. (Try the program for 101 pieces of candy.)

123. The optimal inventory size for a specific item is given by the formula $s = \sqrt{2qh/c}$, where q is the quantity to be sold each year, h is the cost of placing an order, and c is the annual cost of stocking one unit of the item. Write a program that requests the quantity, ordering cost, and storage cost as input and displays the optimum inventory size. (Use the program to compute the optimal inventory size for an item selling 3025 units during the year, where placing an order costs $50, and stocking a unit for 1 year costs $25.)

124. Write a program that requests a whole number of inches and converts it to feet and inches. (Try the program with 72, 53, and 8 inches.)

125. Write a program that requests a person's date of birth in the form mm-dd-yyyy in a text box and then tells the person what day of the week they were born.

126. Write a program that requests a letter, converts it to uppercase, and gives its first position in the sentence "THE QUICK BROWN FOX JUMPS OVER A LAZY DOG." For example, if the user responds by typing *b* into the text box, then the message *B first occurs in position 11* is displayed.

127. Write a program that requests an amount of money between 1 and 99 cents and gives the number of quarters to be used when making that amount of change. (Try each of the amounts 85, 43, and 15 as input.)

128. Write a program that requests a day of the week (Sunday, Monday, . . . , Saturday) and gives the numerical position of that day in the week. For example, if the user responds by typing *Wednesday* into the text box, then the message *Wednesday is day number 4* is displayed.

129. Write a program to calculate a baseball player's batting average from his times at bat and number of hits. **Note:** Batting averages are displayed to 3 decimal places with no preceding zero.

130. Write a program that requests a sentence, a word in the sentence, and another word, and then displays the sentence with the first word replaced by the second. For example, if the user responds by typing "What you don't know won't hurt you." into the first text box and *know* and *owe* into the second and third text boxes, then the message "What you don't owe won't hurt you." is displayed.

131. Write a program that requests a positive number containing a decimal point as input, and then displays the number of digits to the left of the decimal point and the number of digits to the right of the decimal point.

132. When *P* dollars are deposited in a savings account at interest rate *r* compounded annually, the balance after *n* years is $P(1 + r)^n$. Write a program to request the principal *P* and the interest rate *r* as input, and compute the balance after 10 years, as shown in the sample output on the left below.

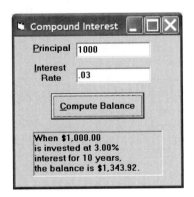 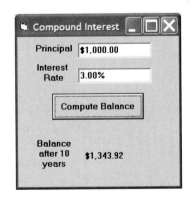

133. Redo Exercise 132 to achieve the output shown on the right above. The principal and interest should be entered as 1000 and .05, but should be converted to nice forms when the button is pressed. (The balance is displayed in a label.) Also, the two text boxes should become empty when they receive the focus to allow for additional computations.

134. Write a program to generate a rent receipt. The program should request the person's name, amount received, and the current date in text boxes and print a receipt of the type shown on the right below.

Receipt for Payment
Name Jane Smith
Amount 645.50
Date 4/7/03
Print Receipt

Received from Jane Smith the sum of $645.50

Signed _____
Monday, April 07, 2003

135. Write a program to produce Table 3.9 on the printer. (The population is the projection for the year 2005, the area is given in square miles, and the density is in people per square mile.) For each state, the name, capital, population, and area are contained in the file STATES.TXT. The densities should be computed by the program.

State	Capital	Population	Area	Density
Alaska	Juneau	700,000	570,374	1.23
New York	Albany	18,250,000	47,224	386.46
Texas	Austin	21,487,000	261,914	82.04

Table 3.9 State Data.
Source: U.S. Bureau of the Census.

136. Table 3.10 provides approximate information about certain occupations and projects the percent change in job openings from 1990 to 2005. Write a program to produce this table on the printer. Place the data in a file. Notice that the names of the occupations and the numbers are right-justified.

Occupation	Current Number of Jobs	% Change	Weekly Median Earning
Computer Programmer	565,000	63	$653
Teacher, Secondary School	1,280,000	45	$648
Physician	580,000	41	$2,996

Table 3.10 Job openings to 2005 and 1990 earnings.
Source: Bureau of Labor Statistics.

137. Write a program to randomly select a month and year during the 1990s. A typical outcome is 6 / 1997.

138. Write a program to randomly select one of the 64 squares on a chess board. *Note:* Each square is represented by a letter (from *a* to *h*, giving the column starting from white's left) and a number (from 1 to 8, giving the row starting from white's side). A typical outcome is d5.

139. Write an event procedure to drive the user crazy. Assume that the focus is on a text box. Each time the user presses a key, have a randomly selected letter from *A* to *Z* appear in the text box.

✔✔ **Solutions to Practice Problems 3.6**

1. 0. There is no uppercase letter E in the string "Computer". InStr distinguishes between upper and lower case.

2. 6. Len("WIN") is 3, 12 * 3 is 36, and Sqr(36) is 6. This expression is an example of function composition. The inner function will be evaluated first.

3. Chr(Int(26 * Rnd) + 65). Uppercase letters have the 26 ANSI values ranging from 65 to 90. The value of 26 * Rnd is a number from 0 through 26 (excluding 26). The value of Int(26 * Rnd) is a whole number from 0 to 25, and therefore the value of Int(26 * Rnd) + 65 is a whole number from 65 to 90.

4. When $n / 2$ is an integer—that is, when n is an even number. (This idea will be used later in the text to determine whether an integer is even.)

CHAPTER 3   SUMMARY

1. The Visual Basic window consists of a form holding a collection of *controls* for which various properties can be set. Some examples of controls are text boxes, labels, command buttons, and picture boxes. Some useful properties are Text (set the text displayed by a text box), Caption (set the title of a form, the contents of a label, or the words on a command button), Font.Size (set the size of the characters displayed), Alignment (set the placement of the contents of a label), MultiLine (text box to display text on several lines), Picture (display drawing in picture box), ForeColor (set the color of text), BackColor (set background color), Visible (show or hide object), BorderStyle (alter and possibly remove border), Font.Bold (display boldface text), and Font.Italic (display italic text).

2. An *event procedure* is executed when something happens to a specified object. Some event procedures are *object*_Click (*object* is clicked), *object*_LostFocus (*object* loses the focus), *object*_GotFocus (*object* receives the focus), and *object*_KeyPress (a key is pressed while *object* has the focus).

3. Visual Basic methods such as Print and Cls are applied to objects and are coded as *object*.Print and *object*.Cls.

4. Two types of *constants* that can be stored and processed by Visual Basic are *numbers* and *strings*.

5. The standard arithmetic *operations* are +, −, *, /, and ^. The only string operation is &, concatenation. An *expression* is a combination of constants, variables, functions, and operations that can be evaluated.

6. A *variable* is a name used to refer to data. Variable names can be up to 255 characters long, must begin with a letter, and may contain letters, digits, and underscores. Dim statements explicitly declare variables and specify the types of the variables. In this book, most variables have types Single, Integer, and String.

7. Named constants store values that do not change throughout the execution of a program. They are declared with Const statements and given meaningful names that take the place of a number or string and make code more readable.

8. Values are assigned to variables by *assignment statements* and *Input # statements*. The values appearing in assignment statements can be constants, variables, or expressions. Input # statements look to text files for constants. String constants used in assignment statements must be surrounded by quotation marks, whereas quotation marks are optional for string constants input with Input #. InputBox can be used to request that the user type in data.

9. The Print method displays information in a picture box or on the printer. *Semicolons*, *commas*, and *Tab* control the placement of the items on a particular line. A temporary message can be displayed on the screen using the MsgBox statement.

10. You control the printer with the *Printer object* and write to it with statements of the form Printer.Print *expression*. You set properties with statements of the form Printer.*property* = *setting*. Printer.NewPage starts a new page and PrintForm does a screen dump. A series of commands to the Printer object must end with EndDoc, which actually produces the final printed page.

11. *Comment statements* are used to explain formulas, state the purposes of variables, and articulate the purposes of various parts of a program.

12. The Format functions provide detailed control of how numbers, dates, and strings are displayed. Numbers can be made to line up uniformly and be displayed with dollar signs, commas, and a specified number of decimal places. Dates can be converted to a long form. Strings can be right-justified.

13. *Functions* can be thought of as accepting numbers or strings as input and returning numbers or strings as output.

Function	Input	Output
Asc	string	number
Chr	number	string
InStr	string, string	number
Int	number	number
LCase	string	string
Left	string, number	string
Len	string	number
Mid	string, number, number	string
Right	string, number	string
Rnd		number
Round	number, number	number
Sqr	number	number
Str	number	string
Trim	string	string
UCase	string	string
Val	string	number

CHAPTER 3 **PROGRAMMING PROJECTS**

1. Write a program that allows the user to specify two numbers and then adds, subtracts, or multiplies them when the user clicks on the appropriate command button. The output should give the type of arithmetic performed and the result.

2. Suppose automobile repair customers are billed at the rate of $35 per hour for labor. Also, costs for parts and supplies are subject to a 5% sales tax. Write a program to print out a simplified bill. The customer's name, the number of hours of labor, and the cost of parts and supplies should be entered into the program via text boxes. When a command button is clicked, the customer's name (indented) and the three costs should be displayed in a picture box, as shown in the sample run in Figure 3.31.

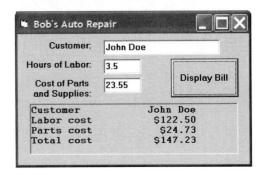

Figure 3.31 Sample run for Programming Project 2.

3. Write a program to generate the following personalized form letter. The person's name and address should be read from text boxes.

```
Mr. John Jones
123 Main Street
Juneau, Alaska  99803

Dear Mr. Jones,

    The Jones family has been selected as the
first family on Main Street to have the opportunity
to purchase an Apex solar-powered flashlight. Due to limited
supply, only 1000 of these amazing inventions will be available
in the entire state of Alaska. Don't delay. Order today.

                        Sincerely,
                        Cuthbert J. Twillie
```

4. At the end of each month, a credit card company constructs the table in Figure 3.32 to summarize the status of the accounts. Write a program to produce this table. The first four pieces of information for each account should be read from a text file. The program should compute the finance charges (1.5% of the unpaid past due amount) and the current amount due. Format the last column to be aligned right.

```
Account    Past Due   Payments   Purchases   Finance    Current
Number     Amount                            Charges    Amt Due

123-AB     123.45     10.00      934.00      1.70       $1,049.15
456-CD     134.56     134.56     300.00      0.00         $300.00
```

Figure 3.32 Status of credit card accounts.

5. Table 3.11 gives the projected 2005 distribution of the U.S. population (in thousands) by age group and sex. Write a program to produce the table shown in Figure 3.33. For each age group, the column labeled %Males gives the percentage of the people in that age group that are male, and similarly for the column labeled %Females. The last column gives the percentage of the total population in each age group. (**Note:** Store the information in Table 3.11 in a text file. For instance, the first line in the file should be "Under 25", 51210, 48905. Read and add up the data once to obtain the total population, and then read the data again to produce the table.)

Age Group	Males	Females
Under 25	51,210	48,905
25–64	74,169	77,059
Over 64	15,319	21,051

Table 3.11 Projected U.S. resident population in thousands (2005).

```
                  U.S. Population (in thousands)

Age group   Males    Females   %Males   %Females   %Total

Under 25    51,210   48,905    51.15%   48.85%     34.80%
25-64       74,169   77,059    49.04%   50.96%     52.56%
Over 64     15,319   21,051    42.12%   57.88%     12.64%
```

Figure 3.33 Output of Programming Project 5.

6. Write a program to convert a U.S. Customary System length in miles, yards, feet, and inches to a Metric System length in kilometers, meters, and centimeters. A sample run is shown in Figure 3.34. After the numbers of miles, yards, feet, and inches are read from the text boxes, the length should be converted entirely to inches and then divided by 39.37 to obtain the value in meters. The Int function should be used to break the total number of meters into a whole number of kilometers and meters. The number of centimeters should be displayed to one decimal place. Some of the needed formulas are as follows:

total inches = 63360 * miles + 36 * yards + 12 * feet + inches
total meters = total inches / 39.37
kilometers = Int(meters / 1000)

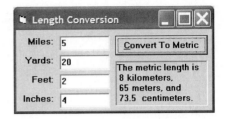

Figure 3.34 Sample run for Programming Project 6.

7. Write a program to produce the types of information shown in Figure 3.35. Your name should be entered with the last name first and separated from the last name with a comma and a space. As characters are typed into the second text box, the KeyPress event should be used to capture the character typed, store it in an invisible label, and replace it in the text box with an asterisk. The FormatDateTime function should be applied to the text in the third text box to determine the full date of birth. Then, the day of the week should be extracted from the full date.

Figure 3.35 A sample run of Practice Problem 7.

8. Write a program to simulate a farecard vending machine for a rapid transit rail system such as BART (San Francisco, CA) or Metro (Washington, DC). Farecard machines accept nickels, dimes, quarters, and $1, $5, $10, and $20 bills. In addition, you can insert a previously purchased farecard and receive credit for the unused value. Fares begin at $1.10 and are always a multiple of 5 cents. The program should accept the amount of money inserted, the unused value of a previously purchased farecard, and the amount of the new farecard to be purchased, and calculate the change as shown in Figure 3.36. The farecard (contained in the picture file METRO.BMP) should not appear until the command button is pressed. (**Note:** Set the AutoRedraw property of the right-hand picture box to True at design time. This will allow you to display the value of the farecard on top of the farecard picture with a Print method.)

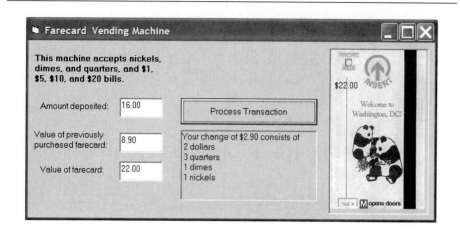

Figure 3.36 Sample run for Programming Project 8.

4 General Procedures

4.1 SUB PROCEDURES, PART I

Visual Basic has two devices, **Sub procedures** and **Function procedures**, that are used to break problems into small problems to be solved one at a time. To distinguish them from event procedures, Sub and Function procedures are referred to as **general procedures**. General procedures also eliminate repetitive code, can be reused in other programs, and allow a team of programmers to work on a single program.

In this section we show how Sub procedures are defined and used. The programs in this section are designed to demonstrate the use of Sub procedures rather than to accomplish sophisticated programming tasks. Later chapters of the book use them for more substantial programming efforts.

A **Sub procedure** is a part of a program that performs one or more related tasks, has its own name, and is written as a separate part of the program. The simplest type of Sub procedure has the form

```
Private Sub ProcedureName()
  statement(s)
End Sub
```

A Sub procedure is invoked with a statement of the form

```
Call ProcedureName
```

The rules for naming general procedures are identical to the rules for naming variables. The name chosen for a Sub procedure should describe the task it performs. Sub procedures can be typed either directly into the Code window or into a template created with the following steps:

1. Press Alt/T/P to select Add Procedure from the Tools menu.

2. Type in the name of the procedure. (Omit parentheses.)

3. Select Sub from the Type box.

4. Select Private from the Scope box. **Note:** Actually either Public or Private is OK. A Public procedure is available to all forms, whereas a Private procedure is only available to the form in which it is defined.

5. Press the Enter key or click on OK.

Note: When you type a procedure name directly into the Code window and then press the Enter key, the editor automatically inserts the parentheses, the line End Sub, and a blank line separating the two lines of code.

Consider the following program that calculates the sum of two numbers. This program will be revised to incorporate Sub procedures.

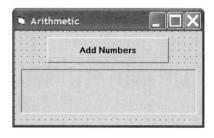

Object	Property	Setting
frmArithmetic	Caption	Arithmetic
cmdAdd	Caption	Add Numbers
picResult		

```
Private Sub cmdAdd_Click()
  Dim num1 As Single, num2 As Single
  'Display the sum of two numbers
  picResult.Cls
  picResult.Print "This program displays a sentence "
  picResult.Print "identifying two numbers and their sum."
  picResult.Print
  num1 = 2
  num2 = 3
  picResult.Print "The sum of"; num1; "and"; num2; "is"; num1 + num2
End Sub
```

[Run, and then click the command button. The following is displayed in the picture box.]

```
This program displays a sentence
identifying two numbers and their sum.

The sum of 2 and 3 is 5
```

The tasks performed by this program can be summarized as follows:

Explain purpose of program.
Display numbers and their sum.

Sub procedures allow us to write and read the program in such a way that we first focus on the tasks and later on how to accomplish each task.

EXAMPLE 1   The following program uses a Sub procedure to accomplish the first task of the preceding program. When the statement Call ExplainPurpose is reached, execution jumps to the Sub ExplainPurpose statement. The lines between Sub ExplainPurpose and End Sub are executed, and then execution continues with the line following the Call statement.

```
Private Sub cmdAdd_Click()
  Dim num1 As Single, num2 As Single
  'Display the sum of two numbers
  picResult.Cls
  Call ExplainPurpose
  picResult.Print
  num1 = 2
  num2 = 3
  picResult.Print "The sum of"; num1; "and"; num2; "is"; num1 + num2
End Sub

Private Sub ExplainPurpose()
  'Explain the task performed by the program
  picResult.Print "This program displays a sentence"
  picResult.Print "identifying two numbers and their sum."
End Sub
```

In Example 1, the cmdAdd_Click event procedure is referred to as the **calling procedure** and the Explain Purpose Sub procedure is referred to as the **called procedure**. The second task performed by the addition program also can be handled by a Sub procedure. The values of the two numbers, however, must be transmitted to the Sub procedure. This transmission is called **passing**.

EXAMPLE 2 The following revision of the program in Example 1 uses a Sub procedure to accomplish the second task. The statement `Call Add(2, 3)` causes execution to jump to the `Private Sub Add(num1 As Single, num2 As Single)` statement, which assigns the number 2 to *num1* and the number 3 to *num2*.

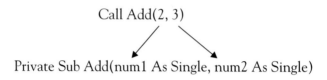

$$\text{Call Add(2, 3)}$$

$$\text{Private Sub Add(num1 As Single, num2 As Single)}$$

After the lines between `Private Sub Add (num1 As Single, num2 As Single)` and `End Sub` are executed, execution continues with the line following `Call Add(2, 3)`, namely, the `End Sub` statement in the event procedure. *Note:* When you create the Sub procedure Add with the Add Procedure dialog box, you must type in "num1 As Single, num2 As Single" after leaving the dialog box.

```
Private Sub cmdAdd_Click()
  'Display the sum of two numbers
  picResult.Cls
  Call ExplainPurpose
  picResult.Print
  Call Add(2, 3)
End Sub

Private Sub Add(num1 As Single, num2 As Single)
  'Display numbers and their sum
  picResult.Print "The sum of"; num1; "and"; num2; "is"; num1 + num2
End Sub

Private Sub ExplainPurpose()
  'Explain the task performed by the program
  picResult.Print "This program displays a sentence"
  picResult.Print "identifying two numbers and their sum."
End Sub
```

Sub procedures make a program easy to read, modify, and debug. The event procedure gives a description of what the program does and the Sub procedures fill in the details. Another benefit of Sub procedures is that they can be called several times during the execution of the program. This feature is especially useful when there are many statements in the Sub procedure.

EXAMPLE 3 The following extension of the program in Example 2 displays several sums.

```
Private Sub cmdAdd_Click()
  'Display the sums of several pairs of numbers
  picResult.Cls
  Call ExplainPurpose
  picResult.Print
  Call Add(2, 3)
  Call Add(4, 6)
  Call Add(7, 8)
End Sub

Private Sub Add(num1 As Single, num2 As Single)
  'Display numbers and their sum
  picResult.Print "The sum of"; num1; "and"; num2; "is"; num1 + num2
End Sub

Private Sub ExplainPurpose()
  'Explain the task performed by the program
  picResult.Print "This program displays sentences"
  picResult.Print "identifying pairs of numbers and their sums."
End Sub
```

[Run, and then click the command button. The following is displayed in the picture box.]

```
This program displays sentences
identifying pairs of numbers and their sums.

The sum of 2 and 3 is 5
The sum of 4 and 6 is 10
The sum of 7 and 8 is 15
```

The variables *num1* and *num2* appearing in the Sub procedure Add are called **parameters**. They are merely temporary place holders for the numbers passed to the Sub procedure; their names are not important. The only essentials are their type, quantity, and order. In this Add Sub procedure, the parameters must be numeric variables and there must be two of them. For instance, the Sub procedure could have been written

```
    Private Sub Add(this As Single, that As Single)
      'Display numbers and their sum
      picResult.Print "The sum of"; this; "and"; that; "is"; this + that
    End Sub
```

When a parameter is defined in a Sub procedure, it is automatically available to the code between the Private Sub and End Sub lines. That is, the code "this As Single" that defines a parameter behaves similarly to the "Dim this As Single" code that defines a variable. A string also can be passed to a Sub procedure. In this case, the receiving parameter in the Sub procedure must be followed by the declaration As String.

EXAMPLE 4   The following program passes a string and two numbers to a Sub procedure. When the Sub procedure is first called, the string parameter *state* is assigned the string constant "Hawaii", and the numeric parameters *pop* and *area* are assigned the numeric constants 1212000 and 6471, respectively. The Sub procedure then uses these parameters to carry out the task of calculating the population density of Hawaii. The second Call statement assigns different values to the parameters.

Object	Property	Setting
frmStates	Caption	State Demographics
cmdDisplay	Caption	Display Demographics
picDensity		

```
Private Sub cmdDisplay_Click()
  'Calculate the population densities of states
  picDensity.Cls
  Call CalculateDensity("Hawaii", 1212000, 6471)
  Call CalculateDensity("Alaska", 627000, 591000)
End Sub

Private Sub CalculateDensity(state As String, pop As Single, area As Single)
  Dim rawDensity As Single, density As Single
  'The density (number of people per square mile)
  'will be displayed rounded to a whole number
  rawDensity = pop / area
  density = Round(rawDensity)  'round to whole number
  picDensity.Print "The density of "; state; " is"; density;
  picDensity.Print "people per square mile."
End Sub
```

[Run, and then click the command button. The following is displayed in the picture box.]

```
The density of Hawaii is 187 people per square mile.
The density of Alaska is 1 people per square mile.
```

The parameters in the density program can have any valid variable names, as with the parameters in the addition program of Example 3. The only restriction is that the first parameter be a string variable and that the last two parameters have type Single. For instance, the Sub procedure could have been written

```
Private Sub CalculateDensity(x As String, y As Single, z As Single)
  Dim rawDensity As Single, density As Single
  'The density (number of people per square mile)
  'will be rounded to a whole number
  rawDensity = y / z
  density = Round(rawDensity)
  picDensity.Print "The density of "; x; " is"; density;
  picDensity.Print "people per square mile."
End Sub
```

When nondescriptive names are used for parameters, the Sub procedure should contain comments giving the meanings of the variables. Possible comments for the preceding program are

```
'x    name of the state
'y    population of the state
'z    area of the state
```

Variables and Expressions as Arguments

The items appearing in the parentheses of a Call statement are called **arguments**. These should not be confused with parameters, which appear in the heading of a Sub procedure. Each parameter defined for a Sub procedure corresponds to an argument passed in a Call statement for that procedure. In Example 3, the arguments of the Call Add statements were constants. These arguments also could have been variables or expressions. For instance, the event procedure could have been written as follows. See Figure 4.1.

```
Private Sub cmdAdd_Click()
    Dim x As Single, y As Single, z As Single
    'Display the sum of two numbers
    picResult.Cls
    Call ExplainPurpose
    picResult.Print
    x = 2
    y = 3
    Call Add(x, y)
    Call Add(x + 2, 2 * y)
    z = 7
    Call Add(z, z + 1)
End Sub
```

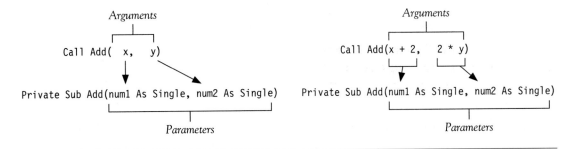

Figure 4.1 Passing arguments to parameters.

This feature allows values obtained as input from the user to be passed to a Sub procedure.

EXAMPLE 5

The following variation of the addition program requests the two numbers as input from the user. Notice that the names of the arguments, *x* and *y*, are different from the names of the parameters. The names of the arguments and parameters may be the same or different; what matters is that the order, number, and types of the arguments and parameters match.

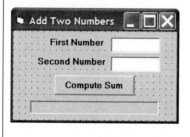

Object	Property	Setting
frmAdd	Caption	Add Two Numbers
lblFirstNum	Caption	First Number
txtFirstNum	Text	(blank)
lblSecondNum	Caption	Second Number
txtSecondNum	Text	(blank)
cmdCompute	Caption	Compute Sum
picResult		

```
Private Sub cmdCompute_Click()
  Dim x As Single, y As Single
  'This program requests two numbers and
  'displays the two numbers and their sum.
  x = Val(txtFirstNum.Text)
  y = Val(txtSecondNum.Text)
  Call Add(x, y)
End Sub

Private Sub Add(num1 As Single, num2 As Single)
  'Display numbers and their sum
  picResult.Cls
  picResult.Print "The sum of"; num1; "and"; num2; "is"; num1 + num2
End Sub
```

[Run, type 23 and 67 into the text boxes, and then click the command button.]

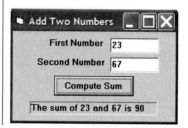

EXAMPLE 6

The following variation of Example 4 obtains its input from the file DEMOGRAPHICS.TXT. The second Call statement uses different variable names for the arguments to show that using the same argument names is not necessary. See Figure 4.2.

DEMOGRAPHICS.TXT contains the following two lines:

"Hawaii", 1212000, 6471
"Alaska", 627000, 591000

```
Private Sub cmdDisplay_Click()
  Dim state As String, pop As Single, area As Single
  Dim s As String, p As Single, a As Single
  'Calculate the population densities of states
  picDensity.Cls
  Open "DEMOGRAPHICS.TXT" For Input As #1
  Input #1, state, pop, area
  Call CalculateDensity(state, pop, area)
  Input #1, s, p, a
  Call CalculateDensity(s, p, a)
  Close #1
End Sub

Private Sub CalculateDensity(state As String, pop As Single, area As Single)
  Dim rawDensity As Single, density As Single
  'The density (number of people per square mile)
  'will be rounded to a whole number
  rawDensity = pop / area
  density = Round(rawDensity)
  picDensity.Print "The density of "; state; " is "; density;
  picDensity.Print "people per square mile."
End Sub
```

[Run, and then click the command button. The following is displayed in the picture box.]

```
The density of Hawaii is 187 people per square mile.
The density of Alaska is 1 people per square mile.
```

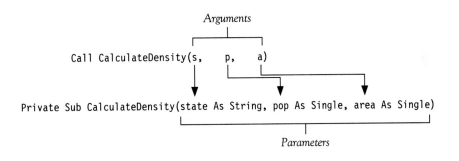

Figure 4.2 Passing arguments to parameters in Example 6.

Arguments and parameters also can be used to pass values from Sub procedures back to event procedures or other Sub procedures. This important property is explored in detail in the next section.

Comments

1. In this text, Sub procedure names begin with uppercase letters in order to distinguish them from variable names. Like variable names, however, they can be written with any combination of upper- and lowercase letters. To improve readability, the Visual Basic editor will automatically ensure that the capitalization of a Sub procedure name is consistent throughout a pro-

gram. For instance, if you type Private Sub PROCEDURENAME and also type Call ProcedureName, the second name will be changed to match the first. *Note:* Parameters appearing in a Sub statement are not part of the Sub procedure name.

2. To obtain a list of the general procedures in a program, select (General) from the Code window's Object box and then click on the down-arrow at the right side of the Procedure box.

3. Sub procedures allow programmers to focus on the main flow of a complex task and defer the details of implementation. Modern programs use them liberally. This method of program construction is known as **modular** or **top-down** design.

4. As a rule, a Sub procedure should perform only one task, or several closely related tasks, and should be kept relatively small.

5. After a Sub procedure has been defined, Visual Basic automatically reminds you of the Sub procedure's parameters when you type in a Call statement. As soon as you type in the left parenthesis of a Call statement, a Parameter Info banner appears giving the names and types of the parameters. See Figure 4.3.

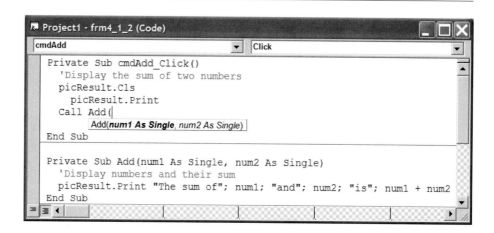

Figure 4.3 The Parameter Info help feature.

6. In this text, the first line after the Dim statements inside a Sub procedure is often a comment statement describing the task performed by the Sub procedure. If necessary, several comment statements are devoted to this purpose. Conventional programming practice also recommends that all variables used by the Sub procedure be listed in comment statements with their meanings. In this text, we give several examples of this practice but only adhere to it when the variables are especially numerous or lack descriptive names.

7. Although both constants and expressions can be used as arguments in Call statements, only variables can be used as parameters in Sub statements.

8. A Sub procedure can call another Sub procedure. If so, after the End Sub of the called Sub procedure is reached, execution continues with the line in the calling Sub procedure that follows the Call statement.

9. When you write a Sub procedure without parameters, Visual Basic automatically adds a pair of empty parentheses at the end of the Sub procedure name. However, Call statements should not use the empty parentheses.

10. The first lines of event procedures and Sub procedures end with a pair of parentheses. With the event procedures we have discussed, the parentheses are usually empty, whereas with Sub procedures, the parentheses often contain parameters.

 PRACTICE PROBLEMS 4.1

1. What is displayed in the picture box by the following code when the command button is clicked?

```
Private Sub cmdButton_Click()
  'Demonstrate Sub procedures calling other Sub procedures
  Call FirstPart
  picOutput.Print 4;
End Sub

Private Sub FirstPart()
  picOutput.Print 1;
  Call SecondPart
  picOutput.Print 3;
End Sub

Private Sub SecondPart()
  picOutput.Print 2;
End Sub
```

2. What is wrong with the following code?

```
Private Sub cmdDisplay_Click()
  Dim phone As String
  phone = txtPhoneNum.Text
  Call AreaCode(phone)
End Sub

Private Sub AreaCode()
  picOutput.Print "Your area code is "; Left(phone, 3)
End Sub
```

 EXERCISES 4.1

In Exercises 1 through 34, determine the output displayed in the picture box when the command button is clicked.

```
1. Private Sub cmdDisplay_Click()
     'Quote from Kermit
     Call Quotation
     picOutput.Print "          Kermit the frog"
   End Sub
```

```
     Private Sub Quotation()
       'Display a quotation
       picOutput.Print "It isn't easy being green."
     End Sub
```

2.
```
Private Sub cmdDisplay_Click()
    picOutput.Print "Today ";
    Call WhatDay
    picOutput.Print "of the rest of your life."
End Sub

Private Sub WhatDay()
  picOutput.Print "is the first day ";
End Sub
```

3.
```
Private Sub cmdDisplay_Click()
    Call Question
    Call Answer
End Sub

Private Sub Answer()
  picOutput.Print "Because they were invented in the northern"
  picOutput.Print "hemisphere, where sundials move clockwise."
End Sub

Private Sub Question()
  picOutput.Print "Why do clocks run clockwise?"
End Sub
```

4.
```
Private Sub cmdDisplay_Click()
    Call FirstName
    picOutput.Print "How are you today?"
End Sub

Private Sub FirstName()
  Dim nom As String
  nom = InputBox("What is your first name?", "Name")
  picOutput.Print "Hello " + UCase(nom)
End Sub
```

(Assume that the response is *Bill.*)

5.
```
Private Sub cmdDisplay_Click()
    'The fates of Henry the Eighth's six wives
    Call CommonFates
    picOutput.Print "died,"
    Call CommonFates
    picOutput.Print "survived."
End Sub

Private Sub CommonFates()
  'The most common fates
  picOutput.Print "Divorced, beheaded, ";
End Sub
```

6.
```
Private Sub cmdDisplay_Click()
    picOutput.Print "A rose";
    Call Rose
    Call Rose
    picOutput.Print "."
End Sub

Private Sub Rose()
    picOutput.Print ", is a rose";
End Sub
```

7.
```
Private Sub cmdDisplay_Click()
    'Good advice to follow
    Call Advice
End Sub

Private Sub Advice()
    picOutput.Print "Keep cool, but don't freeze."
    Call Source
End Sub

Private Sub Source()
    picOutput.Print "Source: A jar of mayonnaise."
End Sub
```

8.
```
Private Sub cmdDisplay_Click()
    Call Answer
    Call Question
End Sub

Private Sub Answer()
    picOutput.Print "The answer is 9W."
    picOutput.Print "What is the question?"
End Sub

Private Sub Question()
    'Note: "Wagner" is pronounced "Vagner"
    picOutput.Print
    picOutput.Print "Do you spell your name with a V, Mr. Wagner?"
End Sub
```

9.
```
Private Sub cmdDisplay_Click()
    Call Piano(88)
End Sub

Private Sub Piano(num As Integer)
    picOutput.Print num; "keys on a piano"
End Sub
```

10.
```
Private Sub cmdDisplay_Click()
    'Opening line of Moby Dick
    Call FirstLine("Ishmael")
End Sub

Private Sub FirstLine(nom As String)
    'Display first line
    picOutput.Print "Call me "; nom
End Sub
```

11. ```
Private Sub cmdDisplay_Click()
    'Beginning of Tale of Two Cities
    Call Times("best")
    Call Times("worst")
End Sub

Private Sub Times(word As String)
    'Display sentence
    picOutput.Print "It was the "; word; " of times."
End Sub
```

12. ```
Private Sub cmdDisplay_Click()
    Call Potato(1)
    Call Potato(2)
    Call Potato(3)
    picOutput.Print 4
End Sub

Private Sub Potato(quantity As Integer)
    picOutput.Print quantity; "potato,";
End Sub
```

13. ```
Private Sub cmdDisplay_Click()
    Dim nom As String
    'Analyze a name
    nom = "Gabriel"
    Call AnalyzeName(nom)
End Sub

Private Sub AnalyzeName(nom As String)
    'Display length and first letter
    picOutput.Print "Your name has"; Len(nom); "letters."
    picOutput.Print "The first letter is "; Left(nom, 1)
End Sub
```

14. ```
Private Sub cmdDisplay_Click()
    Dim color As String
    color = InputBox("What is your favorite color?")
    Call Flattery(color)
End Sub

Private Sub Flattery(color As String)
    picOutput.Print "You look dashing in "; color
End Sub
```

(Assume that the response is *blue*.)

15. ```
Private Sub cmdDisplay_Click()
    Dim num As Integer
    num = Val(InputBox("Give a number from 1 to 26."))
    Call Alphabet(num)
End Sub

Private Sub Alphabet(num As Integer)
    picOutput.Print Left("abcdefghijklmnopqrstuvwxyz", num)
End Sub
```

(Assume that the response is *5*.)
```

16. `Private Sub cmdDisplay_Click()`
     `Dim size As Single`
     `size = 435`
     `Call House(size)`
     `picOutput.Print "of Representatives"`
   `End Sub`

   `Private Sub House(size As Single)`
     `picOutput.Print size; "members in the House ";`
   `End Sub`

17. `Private Sub cmdDisplay_Click()`
     `Dim num As Single`
     `num = 144`
     `Call Gross(num)`
   `End Sub`

   `Private Sub Gross(amount As Single)`
     `picOutput.Print amount; "items in a gross"`
   `End Sub`

18. `Private Sub cmdDisplay_Click()`
     `Dim a As String`
     `a = "mile"`
     `Call Acres(a)`
   `End Sub`

   `Private Sub Acres(length As String)`
     `picOutput.Print "640 acres in a square "; length`
   `End Sub`

19. `Private Sub cmdDisplay_Click()`
     `Dim candy As String`
     `candy = "M&M's Plain Chocolate Candies"`
     `Call Brown(candy)`
   `End Sub`

   `Private Sub Brown(item As String)`
     `picOutput.Print "30% of "; item; " are brown."`
   `End Sub`

20. `Private Sub cmdDisplay_Click()`
     `Dim annualRate As Single`
     `annualRate = .04`
     `Call Balance(annualRate)`
   `End Sub`

   `Private Sub Balance(r As Single)`
     `Dim p As Single`
     `p = Val(InputBox("What is the principal?"))`
     `picOutput.Print "The balance after 1 year is"; (1 + r) * p`
   `End Sub`

   (Assume that the response is *100*.)

21.
```
Private Sub cmdDisplay_Click()
    Dim hours As Single
    hours = 24
    Call Minutes(60 * hours)
End Sub

Private Sub Minutes(num As Single)
    picOutput.Print num; "minutes in a day"
End Sub
```

22.
```
Private Sub cmdDisplay_Click()
    Dim a As String, b As String
    a = "United States"
    b = "acorn"
    Call Display(Left(a, 3) & Mid(b, 2, 4))
End Sub

Private Sub Display(word As String)
    picOutput.Print word
End Sub
```

23.
```
Private Sub cmdDisplay_Click()
    Dim word As String
    word = InputBox("Enter a word.")
    Call T(InStr(word, "t"))
End Sub

Private Sub T(num As Integer)
    picOutput.Print "t is the"; num; "th letter of the word."
End Sub
```

(Assume that the response is *computer.*)

24.
```
Private Sub cmdDisplay_Click()
    Dim states As Single, senators As Single
    states = 50
    senators = 2
    Call Senate(states * senators)
End Sub

Private Sub Senate(num As Single)
    picOutput.Print "The number of members of the U.S. Senate is"; num
End Sub
```

25.
```
Private Sub cmdDisplay_Click()
    Call DisplaySource
    Call Database("Sybase SQL Server", 75633)
    Call Database("Oracle", 73607)
    Call Database("Microsoft SQL Server", 68295)
End Sub

Private Sub DisplaySource()
    picOutput.Print "The May 2001 salary survey of readers of the Visual"
    picOutput.Print "Basic Programmer's Journal gave average salaries of"
    picOutput.Print "database developers according to the database used."
    picOutput.Print
End Sub
```

```vb
Private Sub Database(db As String, salary As Single)
    picOutput.Print db; " database developers earned "; _
                  FormatCurrency(salary, 0)
End Sub
```

26.
```vb
Private Sub cmdDisplay_Click()
    'Sentence using number, thing, and place
    Call Sentence(168, "hour", "a week")
    Call Sentence(76, "trombone", "the big parade")
End Sub


Private Sub Sentence(num As Single, thing As String, where As String)
    picOutput.Print num; thing; "s in "; where
End Sub
```

27.
```vb
Private Sub cmdDisplay_Click()
    Dim pres As String, college As String
    Open "CHIEF.TXT" For Input As #1
    Input #1, pres, college
    Call PresAlmaMater(pres, college)
    Input #1, pres, college
    Call PresAlmaMater(pres, college)
    Close #1
End Sub


Private Sub PresAlmaMater(pres As String, college As String)
    picOutput.Print "President "; pres; " is a graduate of "; college
End Sub
```

(Assume that the file CHIEF.TXT contains the following two lines.)

"Clinton", "Georgetown University"
"Bush", "Yale University"

28.
```vb
Private Sub cmdDisplay_Click()
    Dim nom As String, yob As Integer
    nom = InputBox("Name?")
    yob = Val(InputBox( "Year of birth?"))
    Call AgeIn2005(nom, yob)
End Sub

Private Sub AgeIn2005(nom As String, yob As Integer)
    picOutput.Print nom; ", in the year 2005 your age will be"; 2005 - yob
End Sub
```

(Assume that the responses are *Gabriel* and *1980*.)

29.
```vb
Private Sub cmdDisplay_Click()
    Dim word As String, num As Integer
    word = "Visual Basic"
    num = 6
    Call FirstPart(word, num)
End Sub

Private Sub FirstPart(term As String, digit As Integer)
    picOutput.Print "The first"; digit; "letters are ";
    picOutput.Print Left(term, digit)
End Sub
```

30.
```
Private Sub cmdDisplay_Click()
    Dim object As String, tons As Single
    object = "The Statue of Liberty"
    tons = 250
    Call HowHeavy(object, tons)
End Sub

Private Sub HowHeavy(what As String, weight As Single)
  picOutput.Print what; " weighs"; weight; "tons"
End Sub
```

31.
```
Private Sub cmdDisplay_Click()
    Dim word As String
    word = "worldly"
    Call Negative("un" & word, word)
End Sub

Private Sub Negative(neg As String, word As String)
  picOutput.Print "The negative of "; word; " is "; neg
End Sub
```

32.
```
Private Sub cmdDisplay_Click()
    Dim age As Integer, yrs As Integer, major As String
    age = Val(InputBox("How old are you?"))
    yrs = Val(InputBox("In how many years will you graduate?"))
    major = InputBox("What sort of major do you have (Arts or Sciences)?")
    Call Graduation(age + yrs, Left(major, 1))
End Sub

Private Sub Graduation(num As Integer, letter As String)
  picOutput.Print "You will receive a B"; UCase(letter);
  picOutput.Print " degree at age"; num
End Sub
```

(Assume that the responses are *19, 3,* and *arts.*)

33.
```
Private Sub cmdDisplay_Click()
    Call HowMany(24)
    picOutput.Print "a pie."
End Sub

Private Sub HowMany(num As Integer)
  Call What(num)
  picOutput.Print " baked in ";
End Sub

Private Sub What(num As Integer)
  picOutput.Print num; "blackbirds";
End Sub
```

34.
```
Private Sub cmdDisplay_Click()
    picOutput.Print "All's";
    Call PrintWell
    Call PrintWords(" that ends")
    picOutput.Print "."
End Sub
```

```
Private Sub PrintWell()
  picOutput.Print " well";
End Sub


Private Sub PrintWords(words As String)
  picOutput.Print words;
  Call PrintWell
End Sub
```

In Exercises 35 through 38, find the errors.

35.
```
Private Sub cmdDisplay_Click()
  Dim n As Integer
  n = 5
  Call Alphabet
End Sub


Private Sub Alphabet(n As Integer)
  picOutput.Print Left("abcdefghijklmnopqrstuvwxyz", n)
End Sub
```

36.
```
Private Sub cmdDisplay_Click()
  Dim word As String, number As Single
  word = "seven"
  number = 7
  Call Display(word, number)
End Sub


Private Sub Display(num As Single, term As String)
  picOutput.Print num; term
End Sub
```

37.
```
Private Sub cmdDisplay_Click()
  Dim nom As String
  nom = InputBox("Name")
  Call Print(nom)
End Sub


Private Sub Print(handle As String)
  picOutput.Print "Your name is "; handle
End Sub
```

38.
```
Private Sub cmdDisplay_Click()
  Dim num As Integer
  num = 2
  Call Tea(num)
End Sub


Private Sub Tea()
  picOutput.Print "Tea for"; num
End Sub
```

In Exercises 39 through 42, rewrite the program so the output is performed by calls to a Sub procedure.

39.
```
Private Sub cmdDisplay_Click()
    Dim num As Integer
    'Display a lucky number
    picOutput.Cls
    num = 7
    picOutput.Print num; "is a lucky number."
End Sub
```

40.
```
Private Sub cmdDisplay_Click()
    Dim nom As String
    'Greet a friend
    picOutput.Cls
    nom = "Jack"
    picOutput.Print "Hi, "; nom
End Sub
```

41.
```
Private Sub cmdDisplay_Click()
    Dim tree As String, ht As Single
    'Information about trees
    picOutput.Cls
    Open "TREES.TXT" For Input As #1
    Input #1, tree, ht
    picOutput.Print "The tallest "; tree; " in the U.S. is"; ht; "feet."
    Input #1, tree, ht
    picOutput.Print "The tallest "; tree; " in the U.S. is"; ht; "feet."
    Close #1
End Sub
```

(Assume the file TREES.TXT contains the following two lines.)

"redwood", 362
"pine", 223

42.
```
Private Sub cmdDisplay_Click()
    Dim city As String, salary As Single
    picOutput.Cls
    Open "CITIES.TXT" For Input As #1
    Input #1, city, salary
    picOutput.Print "In 2000, the average starting salary for ";
    picOutput.Print city; " residents was "; FormatCurrency(salary, 0)
    Input #1, city, salary
    picOutput.Print "In 2000, the average starting salary for ";
    picOutput.Print city; " residents was "; FormatCurrency(salary, 0)
    Close #1
End Sub
```

(Assume that the file CITIES.TXT contains the following two lines.)

"San Jose", 76076
"Harford", 42349

Note: San Jose is located in Silicon Valley, and Hartford is the center of the insurance industry.

43. Write a program that requests a number as input and displays three times the number. The output should be produced by a call to a Sub procedure named Triple.

44. Write a program that requests a word as input and displays the word followed by the number of letters in the word. The output should be produced by a call to a Sub procedure named HowLong.

45. Write a program that requests a word and a column number from 1 through 10 as input and displays the word tabbed over to the column number. The output should be produced by a call to a Sub procedure named PlaceNShow.

46. Write a program that requests three numbers as input and displays the average of the three numbers. The output should be produced by a call to a Sub procedure named Average.

In Exercises 47 through 50, write a program that, when cmdDisplay is clicked, will display in picOutput the output shown. The last two lines of the output should be displayed by one or more Sub procedures using data passed by variables from an event procedure.

47. (Assume that the following is displayed.)

```
According to a 2002 survey of college freshmen
taken by the Higher Educational Research Institute:

16.2 percent said they intend to major in business
2.2 percent said they intend to major in computer science
```

48. (Assume that the current date is 12/31/2003, the label for txtBox reads "What is your year of birth?", and the user types 1980 into txtBox before cmdDisplay is clicked.)

```
You are now 23 years old.
You have lived for more than 8395 days.
```

49. (Assume that the label for txtBox reads "What is your favorite number?" and the user types 7 into txtBox before cmdDisplay is clicked.)

```
The sum of your favorite number with itself is 14
The product of your favorite number with itself is 49
```

50. (Assume that the following is displayed.)

```
In the year 1998,
657 thousand college students took a course in Spanish
199 thousand college students took a course in French
```

51. Write a program to display four verses of *Old McDonald Had a Farm*. The primary verse, with variables substituted for the animals and sounds, should be contained in a Sub procedure. The program should use the file FARM.TXT.

FARM.TXT contains the following four lines:

"lamb", "baa"
"firefly", "blink"
"chainsaw", "brraap"
"computer", "beep"

The first verse of the output should be

```
Old McDonald had a farm. Eyi eyi oh.
And on his farm he had a lamb. Eyi eyi oh.
With a baa baa here, and a baa baa there.
Here a baa, there a baa, everywhere a baa baa.
Old McDonald had a farm. Eyi eyi oh.
```

52. Write a program that displays the word WOW vertically in large letters. Each letter should be drawn in a Sub procedure. For instance, the Sub procedure for the letter W follows. *Hint:* Use the font *Courier New* in the picture box.

```
Private Sub DrawW()
  'Draw the letter W
  picWow.Print "**          **"
  picWow.Print " **        **"
  picWow.Print "  **  **  **"
  picWow.Print "   **    **"
  picWow.Print
End Sub
```

53. Write a program to display the data from Table 4.1. The occupations and numbers of people for 1998 and 2008 should be contained in the file GROWTH.TXT. A Sub procedure, to be called four times, should read the first three pieces of data for an occupation, calculate the percent increase from 1998 to 2008, and display the four items. **Note:** The percent increase is calculated as (2008 value − 1998 value)/(1998 value).

Occupation	1998	2008	Increase
Computer engineers	299	622	108%
Computer support specialists	429	869	103%
Systems analysts	617	1194	94%
Database administrators	87	155	78%

Table 4.1 Occupations projected to experience fastest job growth, 1998–2008. (numbers in thousands)

Source: U.S. Bureau of the Census.

54. Write a program to compute tips for services rendered. The program should request the person's occupation, the amount of the bill, and the percentage tip as input and pass this information to a Sub procedure to display the person and the tip. A sample run is shown in the following figure.

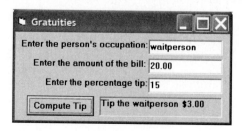

 **Solutions to Practice Problems 4.1**

1. 1 2 3 4

   After the Sub procedure SecondPart is called, execution continues with the remaining statements in the Sub procedure FirstPart before returning to the event procedure.

2. The statement Private Sub AreaCode( ) must be replaced by Private Sub AreaCode(phone As String). Whenever a value is passed to a Sub procedure, the Sub statement must provide a parameter to receive the value.

4.2 SUB PROCEDURES, PART II

The previous section introduced the concept of a Sub procedure but left some questions unanswered. Why can't the value of a variable be passed from an event procedure to a Sub procedure by just using the variable in the Sub procedure? How do Sub procedures pass values back to an event procedure? The answers to these questions provide a deeper understanding of the workings of Sub procedures and reveal their full capabilities.

Passing Values Back from Sub Procedures

Suppose a variable, call it *arg*, appears as an argument in a Call statement, and its corresponding parameter in the Sub statement is *par*. After the Sub procedure is executed, *arg* will have whatever value *par* had in the Sub procedure. Hence, not only is the value of *arg* passed to *par*, but the value of *par* is passed back to *arg*.

EXAMPLE 1 The following program illustrates the transfer of the value of a parameter to its calling argument.

```
Private Sub cmdDisplay_Click()
  Dim amt As Single
  'Illustrate effect of value of parameter on value of argument
  picResults.Cls
  amt = 2
  picResults.Print amt;
  Call Triple(amt)
  picResults.Print amt
End Sub

Private Sub Triple(num As Single)
  'Triple a number
  picResults.Print num;
  num = 3 * num
  picResults.Print num;
End Sub
```

[Run, and then click the command button. The following is displayed in the picture box.]

```
2  2  6  6
```

Although this feature may be surprising at first glance, it provides a vehicle for passing values from a Sub procedure back to the place from which the Sub procedure was called. Different names may be used for an argument and its corresponding parameter, but only one memory location is involved. Initially, the cmdDisplay_Click( ) event procedure allocates a memory location to hold the value of *amt* (Figure 4.4(a)). When the Sub procedure is called, the parameter *num* becomes the Sub procedure's name for this memory location (Figure 4.4(b)). When the value of *num* is tripled, the value in the memory location becomes 6 (Figure 4.4(c)). After the completion of the Sub procedure, the parameter name *num* is forgotten; however, its value lives on in *amt* (Figure 4.4(d)). The variable *amt* is said to be **passed by reference**.

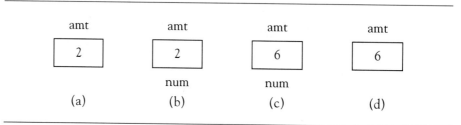

Figure 4.4 Passing a variable by reference to a Sub procedure.

Passing by reference has a wide variety of uses. In the next example, it is used as a vehicle to transport a value from a Sub procedure back to an event procedure.

EXAMPLE 2

The following variation of Example 5 from the previous section uses a Sub procedure to acquire the input. The variables *x* and *y* are not assigned values prior to the execution of the first Call statement. Therefore, before the Call statement is executed, they have the value 0. After the Call statement is executed, however, they have the values entered into the text boxes. These values then are passed by the second Call statement to the Sub procedure Add.

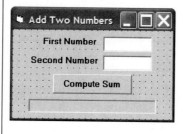

Object	Property	Setting
frmAdd	Caption	Add Two Numbers
lblFirstNum	Caption	First Number
txtFirstNum	Text	(blank)
lblSecondNum	Caption	Second Number
txtSecondNum	Text	(blank)
cmdCompute	Caption	Compute Sum
picResult		

```
Private Sub cmdCompute_Click()
  Dim x As Single, y As Single
  'Display the sum of the two numbers
  Call GetNumbers(x, y)
  Call Add(x, y)
End Sub
```

```
Private Sub GetNumbers(num1 As Single, num2 As Single)
  'Record the two numbers in the text boxes
  num1 = Val(txtFirstNum.Text)
  num2 = Val(txtSecondNum.Text)
End Sub

Private Sub Add(num1 As Single, num2 As Single)
  Dim sum As Single
  'Display numbers and their sum
  picResult.Cls
  sum = num1 + num2
  picResult.Print "The sum of"; num1; "and"; num2; "is"; sum
End Sub
```

[Run, type 2 and 3 into the text boxes, and then click the command button.]

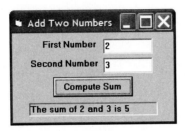

In most situations, a variable with no preassigned value is used as an argument of a Call statement for the sole purpose of carrying back a value from the Sub procedure.

EXAMPLE 3 The following variation of Example 2 allows the cmdCompute_Click event procedure to be written in the input-process-output style.

```
Private Sub cmdCompute_Click()
  Dim x As Single, y As Single, s As Single
  'Display the sum of two numbers
  Call GetNumbers(x, y)
  Call CalculateSum(x, y, s)
  Call DisplayResult(x, y, s)
End Sub

Private Sub GetNumbers(num1 As Single, num2 As Single)
  'Record the two numbers in the text boxes
  num1 = Val(txtFirstNum.Text)
  num2 = Val(txtSecondNum.Text)
End Sub

Private Sub CalculateSum(num1 As Single, num2 As Single, sum As Single)
  'Add the values of num1 and num2
  'and assign the value to sum
  sum = num1 + num2
End Sub
```

```
Private Sub DisplayResult(num1 As Single, num2 As Single, sum As Single)
  'Display a sentence giving the two numbers and their sum
  picResult.Cls
  picResult.Print "The sum of"; num1; "and"; num2; "is"; sum
End Sub
```

Passing by Value

Sometimes you want to pass a variable to a Sub procedure, but you want to ensure that the variable will retain its original value after the Sub procedure terminates—regardless of what was done to the corresponding parameter inside the Sub procedure. Such a variable is said to be **passed by value**. There are two ways to pass a variable by value.

1. In the Call statement, enclose the variable in an extra pair of parentheses.

2. In the Private Sub statement, precede the corresponding parameter with the word ByVal.

For instance, in Example 1, if you change the Call statement to

```
Call Triple((amt))
```

then the output will be

```
2   2   6   2
```

The same output results if you change the Private Sub statement to

```
Private Sub Triple(ByVal num As Single)
```

When a variable is passed by value, two memory locations are involved. At the time the Sub procedure is called, a temporary second memory location for the parameter is set aside for the Sub procedure's use and the value of the argument is copied into that location. After the completion of the Sub procedure, the temporary memory location is released and the value in it is lost. So, for instance, the outcome in the previous paragraph would be the same even if the name of the parameter was *amt*.

Local Variables

When a variable is declared in an event or Sub procedure with a Dim statement, a portion of memory is set aside to hold the value of the variable. As soon as the End Sub statement for the procedure executes, the memory location is freed up; that is, the variable ceases to exist. The variable is said to be **local** to the procedure.

When variables of the same name are declared with Dim statements in two different procedures (either event or Sub), Visual Basic gives the variables separate identities and treats them as two different variables. A value assigned to a variable in one part of the program will not affect the value of the like-named variable in the other part of the program. Also, each time a Sub procedure is called, all declared variables that are not parameters assume their default values. (Numeric variables have default value 0, and string variables default to the empty string.)

EXAMPLE 4 The following program illustrates the fact that each time a Sub procedure is called, its variables are set to their default values; that is, numerical variables are set to 0 and string variables are set to the empty string.

```
Private Sub cmdDisplay_Click()
  'Demonstrate that variables in a Sub procedure do
  'not retain their values in subsequent calls
  picResults.Cls
  Call Three
  Call Three
End Sub

Private Sub Three()
  Dim num As Single
  'Display the value of num and assign it the value 3
  picResults.Print num;
  num = 3
End Sub
```

[Run, and then click the command button. The following is displayed in the picture box.]

```
0  0
```

EXAMPLE 5 The following program illustrates the fact that variables are local to the part of the program in which they reside. The variable *x* in the event procedure and the variable *x* in the Sub procedure are treated as different variables. Visual Basic handles them as if their names were separate, such as *xcmdDisplay_Click* and *xTrivial*. Also, each time the Sub procedure is called, the value of variable *x* inside the Sub procedure is reset to 0.

```
Private Sub cmdDisplay_Click()
  Dim x As Single
  'Demonstrate the local nature of variables
  picResults.Cls
  x = 2
  picResults.Print x;
  Call Trivial
  picResults.Print x;
  Call Trivial
  picResults.Print x;
End Sub

Private Sub Trivial()
  Dim x As Single
  'Do something trivial
  picResults.Print x;
  x = 3
  picResults.Print x;
End Sub
```

[Run, and then click the command button. The following is displayed in the picture box.]

```
2   0   3   2   0   3   2
```

Form-Level Variables

Visual Basic provides a way to make a variable visible to *every* procedure in a form's code without being passed. Such a variable is called a **form-level variable**. The Dim statements for form-level variables appear at the top of the Code window and are separated from the rest of the code by a horizontal separator line. Inside the Code window, you can move to them either by pressing Ctrl+Home or by clicking on General in the Object list box. Form-level variables are said to reside in the (Declarations) section of (General) and are declared with the following steps.

1. Invoke a Code window if one is not already active.

2. Click on the down-arrow to the right of the Object list box.

3. Click on (General).

4. Click on (Declarations) in the Procedure list box.

5. Type in a declaration statement, such as Dim strVar As String, and press the Enter key.

When a form-level variable has its value changed by a procedure, the value persists even after the procedure has finished executing. We say that such a variable has **form-level scope**. Variables declared inside a procedure are said to have **local scope**. In this text, we rarely use form-level variables until Chapter 7.

EXAMPLE 6

The following program contains the form-level variables *num1* and *num2*. Their Dim statement does not appear inside a procedure.

```
Dim num1 As Single, num2 As Single    'In (Declarations) section of (General)

Private Sub cmdDisplay_Click()
  'Display the sum of two numbers
  num1 = 2
  num2 = 3
  picResults.Cls
  Call AddAndIncrement
  picResults.Print
  picResults.Print "num1 ="; num1
  picResults.Print "num2 ="; num2
End Sub
```

```
Private Sub AddAndIncrement()
  'Display numbers and their sum
  picResults.Print "The sum of"; num1; "and"; num2; "is"; num1 + num2
  num1 = num1 + 1
  num2 = num2 + 1
End Sub
```

[Run, and click the command button. The following is displayed in the picture box.]

```
The sum of 2 and 3 is 5

num1 = 3
num2 = 4
```

In the preceding example, we had to click a command button to assign values to the form-level variables. In some situations, we want to assign a value immediately to a form-level variable, without requiring the user to perform some specific action. Visual Basic has a special event procedure called Form_Load that is automatically activated as soon as the program is run, even before the form is created. The Form_Load template is invoked by double-clicking on the form itself.

EXAMPLE 7 The following program demonstrates the use of Form_Load.

```
Dim pi As Single     'In (Declarations) section of (General)

Private Sub Form_Load()
  'Assign a value to pi
  pi = 3.14159
End Sub

Private Sub cmdCompute_Click()
  'Display the area of a circle of radius 5
  picArea.Cls
  picArea.Print "The area of a circle of radius 5 is"; pi * 5 * 5
End Sub
```

[Run, and then click the command button. The following is displayed in the picture box.]

```
The area of a circle of radius 5 is 78.53975
```

Comments

1. In addition to the reasons presented earlier, some other reasons for using Sub procedures follow:

   (a) Programs with Sub procedures are easier to debug. Each Sub procedure can be checked individually before being placed into the program.

   (b) The task performed by a Sub procedure might be needed in another program. The Sub procedure can be reused with no changes. Programmers refer to the collection of their most universal Sub procedures as a **library** of Sub procedures. (The fact that variables appearing in Sub procedures are local to the Sub procedures is quite helpful when reusing Sub procedures in other programs. There is no need to worry if a variable name in the Sub procedure is used for a different purpose in another part of the program.)

(c) Often, programs are written by a team of programmers. After a problem has been broken into distinct and manageable tasks, each programmer is assigned a single Sub procedure to write.

(d) Sub procedures make large programs easier to understand. Some programming standards insist that each Sub procedure be at most two pages long.

(e) Sub procedures permit the following program design, which provides a built-in outline of an event procedure. A reader can focus on the main flow first, and then go into the specifics of accomplishing the secondary tasks.

```
Private Sub Object_Event()
  'An event procedure written entirely as Sub procedures
  Call FirstSubprocedure      'Perform first task
  Call SecondSubprocedure     'Perform second task
  Call ThirdSubprocedure      'Perform third task
End Sub
```

2. Sub procedures can call other Sub procedures. In such cases, the calling Sub procedure plays the role of the event procedure with respect to the called Sub procedure. Complex problems are thereby broken into simpler tasks, which are then broken into still more elementary tasks. This approach to problem solving is called **top-down design**.

3. In Appendix D, the section "Stepping Through a Program Containing a Procedure: Chapter 4" uses the Visual Basic debugger to trace the flow through a program and observe the interplay between arguments and parameters.

4. You can use the Print method in a Form_Load event procedure. If you do, you must set the AutoRedraw property of the picture box to True. Otherwise the contents of the picture box will be erased when the event procedure terminates.

✔ **PRACTICE PROBLEMS 4.2**

1. What does the following code display in the picture box when the command button is clicked?

```
Private Sub cmdDisplay_Click()
  Dim b As Integer, c As Integer
  b = 1
  c = 2
  Call Rhyme
  picOutput.Print b; c
End Sub
```

```
Private Sub Rhyme()
    Dim b As Integer, c As Integer
    picOutput.Print b; c; "buckle my shoe."
    b = 3
End Sub
```

2. Determine the output displayed in the picture box when the command button is clicked.

```
Private Sub cmdCompute_Click()
    Dim amt1 As Integer, amt2 As Integer
    amt1 = 1
    amt2 = 2
    picOutput.Print amt1; amt2
    Call Swap(amt1, amt2)
    picOutput.Print amt1; amt2
End Sub

Private Sub Swap(num1 As Integer, num2 As Integer)
    Dim temp As Integer
    temp = num1
    num1 = num2
    num2 = temp
    picOutput.Print num1; num2
End Sub
```

3. In Problem 2, change the Private Sub statement to

```
Private Sub swap(num1 As Integer, ByVal num2 As Integer)
```

and determine the output.

4. In Problem 2, change the Call statement to

```
Call swap((amt1), (amt2))
```

and determine the output.

EXERCISES 4.2

In Exercises 1 through 18, determine the output displayed in the picture box when the command button is clicked.

1.
```
Private Sub cmdDisplay_Click()
    Dim num As Single
    num = 7
    Call AddTwo(num)
    picOutput.Print num
End Sub

Private Sub AddTwo(num As Single)
    num = num + 2
End Sub
```

2.
```
Private Sub cmdDisplay_Click()
    Dim term As String
    term = "Fall"
    Call Plural(term)
    picOutput.Print term
End Sub

Private Sub Plural(term As String)
    term = term & "s"
End Sub
```

3.
```
Private Sub cmdDisplay_Click()
    Dim dance As String
    dance = "Can "
    Call Twice(dance)
    picOutput.Print dance
End Sub

Private Sub Twice(dance As String)
    dance = dance & dance
End Sub
```

4.
```
Private Sub cmdCompute_Click()
    Dim a As Integer, b As Integer
    a = 1
    b = 3
    picOutput.Print a; b
    Call Combine(a, b)
    picOutput.Print a; b
    Call Combine((a), b)
    picOutput.Print a; b
End Sub

Private Sub Combine(x As Integer, ByVal y As Integer)
    x = y - x
    y = x + y
    picOutput.Print x; y
End Sub
```

5.
```
Private Sub cmdDisplay_Click()
    Dim a As Single
    a = 5
    Call Square(a)
    picOutput.Print a
End Sub

Private Sub Square(num As Single)
    num = num * num
End Sub
```

6.
```
Private Sub cmdDisplay_Click()
    Dim state As String
    state = "NEBRASKA"
    Call Abbreviate(state)
    picOutput.Print state
End Sub

Private Sub Abbreviate(a As _
    String)
    a = Left(a, 2)
End Sub
```

7.
```
Private Sub cmdDisplay_Click()
    Dim word As String
    Call GetWord(word)
    picOutput.Print "Less is "; word
End Sub

Private Sub GetWord(w As String)
    w = "more"
End Sub
```

8.
```
Private Sub cmdDisplay_Click()
    Dim hourlyWage As Single, annualWage As Single
    hourlyWage = 10
    Call CalculateAnnualWage(hourlyWage, annualWage)
    picOutput.Print "Approximate Annual Wage:"; FormatCurrency(annualWage)
End Sub
```

```
    Private Sub CalculateAnnualWage(hWage As Single, aWage As Single)
      aWage = 2000 * hWage
    End Sub
```

9.
```
Private Sub cmdDisplay_Click()
    Dim nom As String, yob As Integer
    Call GetVita(nom, yob)
    picOutput.Print nom; " was born in the year"; yob
End Sub
```

```
    Private Sub GetVita(nom As String, yob As Integer)
      nom = "Gabriel"          'name
      yob = 1980               'year of birth
    End Sub
```

10.
```
Private Sub cmdDisplay_Click()
    Dim word1 As String, word2 As String
    word1 = "fail"
    word2 = "plan"
    picOutput.Print "If you ";
    Call Sentence(word1, word2)
    Call Exchange(word1, word2)
    picOutput.Print " then you ";
    Call Sentence(word1, word2)
End Sub
```

```
    Private Sub Exchange(word1 As String, word2 As String)
      Dim temp As String
      temp = word1
      word1 = word2
      word2 = temp
    End Sub
```

```
    Private Sub Sentence(word1 As String, word2 As String)
      picOutput.Print word1; " to "; word2;
    End Sub
```

11.
```
Private Sub cmdDisplay_Click()
    Dim state As String
    state = "Ohio "
    Call Team
End Sub

Private Sub Team()
    Dim state As String
    picOutput.Print state;
    picOutput.Print "Buckeyes"
End Sub
```

12.
```
Private Sub cmdDisplay_Click()
    Dim a As Single
    a = 5
    Call Multiply(7)
    picOutput.Print a * 7
End Sub

Private Sub Multiply(num As Single)
    Dim a As Single
    a = 11
    picOutput.Print a * num
End Sub
```

13.
```
Private Sub cmdDisplay_Click()
    Dim a As Single
    a = 5
    Call Multiply(7)
End Sub

Private Sub Multiply(num As Single)
    Dim a As Single
    picOutput.Print a * num
End Sub
```

14.
```
Private Sub cmdDisplay_Click()
    Dim nom As String, n As String
    nom = "Ray"
    Call Hello(nom)
    picOutput.Print n; " and "; nom
End Sub

Private Sub Hello(nom As String)
    Dim n As String
    n = nom
    nom = "Bob"
    picOutput.Print "Hello "; n; " and "; nom
End Sub
```

15.
```
Private Sub cmdDisplay_Click()
    Dim num As Single
    num = 1
    Call Amount(num)
    Call Amount(num)
End Sub

Private Sub Amount(num As Single)
    Dim total As Single
    total = total + num
    picOutput.Print total;
End Sub
```

16.
```
Private Sub cmdDisplay_Click()
    Dim river As String
    river = "Wabash"
    Call Another
    picOutput.Print river
    Call Another
End Sub

Private Sub Another()
    Dim river As String
    picOutput.Print river;
    river = "Yukon"
End Sub
```

17.
```
Private Sub cmdCompute_Click()
    Dim n As Integer, word As String
    n = 4
    word = "overwhelming"
    picOutput.Print n; word
    Call crop(n, word)
    picOutput.Print n; word
    Call crop(n, (word))
    picOutput.Print n; word
End Sub

Private Sub crop(ByVal n As Integer, word As String)
    n = Len(word) - n
    word = Right(word, n)
    picOutput.Print n; word
End Sub
```

18.
```
Private Sub cmdCompute_Click()
    Dim tax As Single, price As Single, total As Single
    tax = .05
    Call GetPrice("bicycle", price)
    Call ProcessItem(price, tax, total)
    Call DisplayResult(total)
End Sub

Private Sub DisplayResult(total As Single)
    picOutput.Print "With tax, the price is "; FormatCurrency(total)
End Sub

Private Sub GetPrice(item As String, price As Single)
    Dim strVar As String
    strVar = InputBox("What is the price of a " & item & "?")
    price = Val(strVar)
End Sub

Private Sub ProcessItem(price As Single, tax As Single, total As Single)
    total = (1 + tax) * price
End Sub
```

(Assume that the cost of the bicycle is $200.)

In Exercises 19 and 20, find the errors.

19.
```
Private Sub cmdCompute_Click()
    Dim a As Single, b As Single, c As Single
    a = 1
    b = 2
    Call Sum(a, b, c)
    picOutput.Print "The sum is"; c
End Sub

Private Sub Sum(x As Single, y As Single)
    Dim c As Single
    c = x + y
End Sub
```

20.
```
Private Sub cmdDisplay_Click()
    Dim ano As String
    Call GetYear(ano)
    picOutput.Print ano
End Sub

Private Sub GetYear(yr As Single)
    yr = 2004
End Sub
```

In Exercises 21 through 24, rewrite the program so input, processing, and output are each performed by Calls to Sub procedures.

21.
```
Private Sub cmdCompute_Click()
    Dim price As Single, tax As Single, cost As Single
    'Calculate sales tax
    picOutput.Cls
    price = Val(InputBox("Enter the price of the item:"))
    tax = .05 * price
    cost = price + tax
    picOutput.Print "Price: "; price
    picOutput.Print "Tax: "; tax
    picOutput.Print "--------------"
    picOutput.Print "Cost: "; cost
End Sub
```

22.
```
Private Sub cmdDisplay_Click()
    Dim nom As String, n As Integer, firstName As String
    'Letter of acceptance
    picOutput.Cls
    nom = InputBox("What is your full name?")
    n = InStr(nom, " ")
    firstName = Left(nom, n - 1)
    picOutput.Print "Dear "; firstName; ","
    picOutput.Print "We are proud to accept you to Gotham College."
End Sub
```

23.
```
Private Sub cmdDisplay_Click()
    Dim length As Single, width As Single, area As Single
    'Determine the area of a rectangle
    picOutput.Cls
    length = Val(txtLength.Text)
    width = Val(txtWidth.Text)
    area = length * width
    picOutput.Print "The area of the rectangle is"; area
End Sub
```

24.
```
Private Sub cmdCompute_Click()
    Dim a As String, feet As Single, inches As Single
    Dim totalInches As Single, centimeters As Single
    'Convert feet and inches to centimeters
    picOutput.Cls
    a =  "Give the length in feet and inches.  "
    feet = Val(InputBox(a & "Enter the number of feet."))
    inches = Val(InputBox(a & "Enter the number of inches. "))
    totalInches = 12 * feet + inches
    centimeters = 2.54 * totalInches
    picOutput.Print "The length in centimeters is"; centimeters
End Sub
```

In Exercises 25 and 26, write a line of code to carry out the task. Specify where in the program the line of code would occur.

25. Declare the variable *nom* as a string variable visible to all parts of the program.

26. Declare the variable *nom* as a string variable visible only to the Form_Click event procedure.

In Exercises 27 through 32, write a program to perform the stated task. The input, processing, and output should be performed by calls to Sub procedures.

27. Request a person's first name and last name as input and display the corresponding initials.

28. Request the amount of a restaurant bill as input and display the amount, the tip (15 percent), and the total amount.

29. Request the cost and selling price of an item of merchandise as input and display the percentage markup. Test the program with a cost of $4 and a selling price of $6. *Note:* The percentage markup is (selling price – cost) / cost.

30. Read the number of students in public colleges (12.1 million) and private colleges (3.7 million) from a file, and display the percentage of college students attending public colleges.

31. Read a baseball player's name (Sheffield), times at bat (557), and hits (184) from a file and display his name and batting average. *Note:* Batting average is calculated as (hits)/(times at bat).

32. Request three numbers as input and then calculate and display the average of the three numbers.

33. The Hat Rack is considering locating its new branch store in one of three malls. The following file gives the monthly rent per square foot and the total square feet available at each of the three locations. Write a program to display a table exhibiting this information along with the total monthly rent for each mall.

MALLS.TXT contains the following three lines:

"Green Mall", 6.50, 583
"Red Mall", 7.25, 426
"Blue Mall", 5.00, 823

34. Write a program that uses the data in the file CHARGES.TXT to display the end-of-month credit card balances of three people. (Each line gives a person's name, beginning balance, purchases during month, and payment for the month.) The end-of-month balance is calculated as [finance charges] + [beginning-of-month balance] + [purchases] – [payment], where the finance charge is 1.5 percent of the beginning-of-month balance.

CHARGES.TXT contains the following three lines:

"John Adams", 125.00, 60.00, 110.00
"Sue Jones", 0, 117.25, 117.25
"John Smith", 350.00, 200.50, 300.00

35. Write a program to produce a sales receipt. Each time the user clicks on a command button, an item and its price should be read from a pair of text boxes and displayed in a picture box. Use a form-level variable to track the sum of the prices. When the user clicks on a second command button (after all the entries have been made), the program should display the sum of the prices, the sales tax (5 percent of total), and the total amount to be paid. Figure 4.5 shows a sample output of the program.

```
Light bulbs   2.65
Soda          3.45
Soap          1.15
            --------
Sum           7.25
Tax           0.36
Total         7.61
```

Figure 4.5 Sales receipt for Exercise 35.

✔✔ Solutions to Practice Problems 4.2

1. 0 0 buckle my shoe.
      1 2

    This program illustrates the local nature of the variables in a Sub procedure. Notice that the variables *b* and *c* appearing in the Sub procedure have no relationship whatsoever to the variables of the same name in the event procedure. In a certain sense, the variables inside the Sub procedure can be thought of as having alternate names, such as *bRhyme* and *cRhyme*.

2. 1 2
    2 1
    2 1

    Both variables are passed by reference and so have their values changed by the Sub procedure.

3. 1 2
    2 1
    2 2

    Here *amt1* is passed by reference (the default method of passing) and *amt2* is passed by value. Therefore, only *amt1* has its value changed by the Sub procedure.

4. 1 2
    2 1
    1 2

    Both variables are passed by value and so their values are not changed by the Sub procedure.

4.3 FUNCTION PROCEDURES

Visual Basic has many built-in functions. In one respect, functions are like miniature programs. They use input, they process the input, and they have output. Some functions we encountered earlier are listed in Table 4.2.

Function	Example	Input	Output
Int	Int(2.6) is 2	number	number
Chr	Chr(65) is "A"	number	string
Len	Len("perhaps") is 7	string	number
Mid	Mid("perhaps",4,2) is "ha"	string,number,number	string
InStr	InStr("to be"," ") is 3	string,string	number

Table 4.2 Some Visual Basic built-in functions.

Although the input can involve several values, the output always consists of a single value. The items inside the parentheses can be constants (as in Table 4.2), variables, or expressions.

In addition to using built-in functions, we can define functions of our own. These new functions, called **Function procedures** or **user-defined functions**, are defined in much the same way as Sub procedures and are used in the same way as built-in functions. Like built-in functions, Function procedures have a single output that can be any data type. Function procedures can be used in expressions in exactly the same way as built-in functions. Programs refer to them as if they were constants, variables, or expressions. Function procedures are defined by function blocks of the form

```
Private Function FunctionName(var1 As Type1, var2 As Type2, ...) As DataType
    statement(s)
    FunctionName = expression
End Function
```

The variables appearing in the top line are called **parameters**. Variables declared inside the function block have local scope. Function names should be suggestive of the role performed and must conform to the rules for naming variables. The type *DataType*, which specifies the type of the output, will be one of String, Integer, Single, and so on. In the preceding general code, the next-to-last line assigns the output, which must be of type *DataType*, to the function name. Two examples of Function procedures are as follows:

```
Private Function FtoC(t As Single) As Single
    'Convert Fahrenheit temperature to Celsius
    FtoC = (5 / 9) * (t - 32)
End Function

Private Function FirstName(nom As String) As String
    Dim firstSpace As Integer
    'Extract the first name from the full name nom
    firstSpace = InStr(nom, " ")
    FirstName = Left(nom, firstSpace - 1)
End Function
```

The value of each of the preceding functions is assigned by a statement of the form *FunctionName = expression*. The variables *t* and *nom* appearing in the preceding functions are parameters. They can be replaced with any variable of the same type without affecting the function definition. For instance, the function FtoC could have been defined as

```
Private Function FtoC(temp As Single) As Single
    'Convert Fahrenheit temperature to Celsius
    FtoC = (5 / 9) * (temp - 32)
End Function
```

Like Sub procedures, Function procedures can be created from a Code window with Alt/T/P. The only difference is that the circle next to the word Function should be selected. After the name is typed and the OK button is clicked, the lines Private Function *FunctionName*( ) and End Function will be placed automatically (separated by a blank line) in the Code window. Functions also can be typed directly into the Code window.

EXAMPLE 1 | The following program uses the function FtoC.

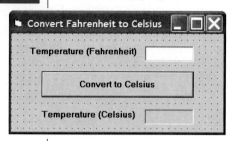

Object	Property	Setting
frm4_3_1	Caption	Convert Fahrenheit to Celsius
lblTempF	Caption	Temperature (Fahrenheit)
txtTempF	Text	(blank)
cmdConvert	Caption	Convert to Celsius
lblTempC	Caption	Temperature (Celsius)
picTempC		

```
Private Sub cmdConvert_Click()
  picTempC.Cls
  picTempC.Print FtoC(Val(txtTempF.Text))
End Sub

Private Function FtoC(t As Single) As Single
  'Convert Fahrenheit temperature to Celsius
  FtoC = (5 / 9) * (t - 32)
End Function
```

[Run, type 212 into the text box, and then click the command button.]

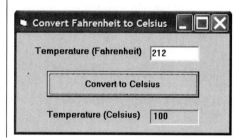

EXAMPLE 2 | The following program uses the function FirstName.

Object	Property	Setting
frm4_3_2	Caption	Extract First Name
lblName	Caption	Name
txtFullName	Text	(blank)
cmdDetermine	Caption	Determine First Name
picFirstName		

```
Private Sub cmdDetermine_Click()
  Dim nom As String
  'Determine a person's first name
  nom = txtFullName.Text
  picFirstName.Cls
  picFirstName.Print "The first name is "; FirstName(nom)
End Sub
```

```
Private Function FirstName(nom As String) As String
  Dim firstSpace As Integer
  'Extract the first name from a full name
  firstSpace = InStr(nom, " ")
  FirstName = Left(nom, firstSpace - 1)
End Function
```

[Run, type Thomas Woodrow Wilson into the text box, and then click the command button.]

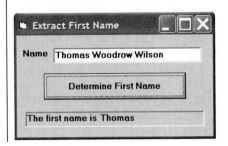

EXAMPLE 3   Some computer languages have a useful built-in function called Ceil that is similar to the function Int, except that it rounds noninteger numbers up to the next integer. For instance, Ceil(3.2) is 4 and Ceil(–1.6) is –1. The following program creates Ceil in Visual Basic as a user-defined function.

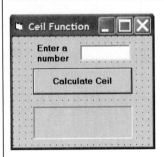

Object	Property	Setting
frm4_3_3	Caption	Ceil Function
lblNumber	Caption	Enter a number
txtNumber	Text	(blank)
cmdCalculate	Caption	Calculate Ceil
picResults		

```
Private Function Ceil(x As Single) As Single
  'Round nonintegers up
  Ceil = -Int(-x)
End Function

Private Sub cmdCalculate_Click()
  'Demonstrate the Ceil function
  picResults.Print "Ceil("; txtNumber.Text; ") ="; Ceil(Val(txtNumber.Text))
  txtNumber.Text = ""
  txtNumber.SetFocus
End Sub
```

[Run, type 4.3 into the text box, click the command button, type 4 into the text box, and then click the command button again.]

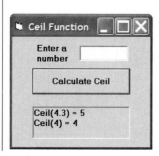

User-Defined Functions Having Several Parameters

The input to a user-defined function can consist of one or more values. Two examples of functions with several parameters follow. One-letter variable names have been used so that the mathematical formulas will look familiar and be readable. Because the names are not descriptive, the meanings of these variables are carefully spelled out in comment statements.

```
Private Function Hypotenuse(a As Single, b As Single) As Single
  'Calculate the hypotenuse of a right triangle
  'having sides of lengths a and b
  Hypotenuse = Sqr(a ^ 2 + b ^ 2)
End Function
```

```
Private Function FV(p As Single,r As Single,c As Single,n As Single) As Single
  Dim i As Single, m As Single
  'Find the future value of a bank savings account
  'p  principal, the amount deposited
  'r  annual rate of interest
  'c  number of times interest is compounded per year
  'n  number of years
  'i  interest rate per period
  'm  total number of times interest is compounded
  i = r / c
  m = c * n
  FV = p * ((1 + i) ^ m)
End Function
```

EXAMPLE 4 The following program uses the Hypotenuse function.

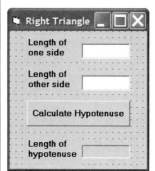

Object	Property	Setting
frm4_3_4	Caption	Right Triangle
lblSideOne	Caption	Length of one side
txtSideOne	Text	(blank)
lblSideTwo	Caption	Length of other side
txtSideTwo	Text	(blank)
cmdCalculate	Caption	Calculate Hypotenuse
lblHyp	Caption	Length of hypotenuse
picHyp		

```
Private Sub cmdCalculate_Click()
  Dim a As Single, b As Single
  'Calculate length of the hypotenuse of a right triangle
  a = Val(txtSideOne.Text)
  b = Val(txtSideTwo.Text)
  picHyp.Cls
  picHyp.Print Hypotenuse(a, b)
End Sub

Private Function Hypotenuse(a As Single, b As Single) As Single
  'Calculate the hypotenuse of a right triangle
  'having sides of lengths a and b
  Hypotenuse = Sqr(a ^ 2 + b ^ 2)
End Function
```

[Run, type 3 and 4 into the text boxes, and then click the command button.]

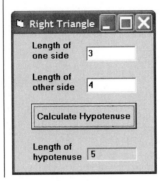

EXAMPLE 5   The following program uses the future value function. With the responses shown, the program computes the balance in a savings account when $100 is deposited for five years at 3% interest compounded quarterly. Interest is earned four times per year at the rate of 1% per interest period. There will be 4 * 5 or 20 interest periods.

Object	Property	Setting
frm4_3_5	Caption	Bank Deposit
lblAmount	Caption	Amount of bank deposit
txtAmount	Text	(blank)
lblRate	Caption	Annual rate of interest
txtRate	Text	(blank)
lblNumComp	Caption	Number of times interest is compounded per year
txtNumComp	Text	(blank)
lblNumYrs	Caption	Number of years
txtNumYrs	Text	(blank)
cmdCompute	Caption	Compute Balance
lblBalance	Caption	Balance
picBalance		

```
Private Sub cmdCompute_Click()
  Dim p As Single, r As Single, c As Single, n As Single
  'Find the future value of a bank deposit
  Call InputData(p, r, c, n)
  Call DisplayBalance(p, r, c, n)
End Sub

Private Sub InputData(p As Single, r As Single, c As Single, n As Single)
  'Get the four values from the text boxes
  p = Val(txtAmount.Text)
  r = Val(txtRate.Text)
  c = Val(txtNumComp.Text)
  n = Val(txtNumYrs.Text)
End Sub

Private Sub DisplayBalance(p As Single,r As Single,c As Single,n As Single)
  Dim balance As Single
  'Display the balance in the picture box
  picBalance.Cls
  balance = FV(p, r, c, n)
  picBalance.Print FormatCurrency(balance)
End Sub

Private Function FV(p As Single,r As Single,c As Single,n As Single) As Single
  Dim i As Single, m As Single
  'Find the future value of a bank savings account
  'p  principal, the amount deposited
  'r  annual rate of interest
  'c  number of times interest is compounded per year
  'n  number of years
  'i  interest rate per period
  'm  total number of times interest is compounded
  i = r / c
  m = c * n
  FV = p * ((1 + i) ^ m)
End Function
```

[Run, type 100, .03, 4, and 5 into the text boxes, then click the command button.]

There are many reasons for employing user-defined functions.

1. User-defined functions are consistent with the modular approach to program design. Once we realize a particular function is needed, we can give it a name but save the task of figuring out the computational details until later.

2. Sometimes a single formula must be used several times in a program. Specifying the formula as a function saves repeated typing of the same formula, improves readability, and simplifies debugging.

3. Functions written for one program can be used in other programs. Programmers maintain a collection, or library, of functions that might be needed.

Comments

1. By default, variables passed to a Function procedure are passed by reference; that is, their values are subject to being changed by the Function procedure. Variables also can be passed by value to Function procedures and thereby have their values persist. As with Sub procedures, a variable is passed by value if the variable is enclosed in an extra pair of parentheses when the function is invoked, or if the corresponding parameter in the Private Function statement is preceded with the word ByVal. Built-in functions have all their arguments passed by value. Some programmers feel that "by value" should have been the default for Function procedures, rather than "by reference."

2. Function procedures can perform the same tasks as Sub procedures. For instance, they can request input and display text. However, Function procedures are primarily used to calculate a single value. Normally, Sub procedures are used to carry out other tasks.

3. Function procedures differ from Sub procedures in the way they are accessed. Sub procedures are invoked with Call statements, whereas functions are invoked by placing them where you would otherwise expect to find a constant, variable, or expression. Unlike a Function procedure, a Sub procedure can't be used in an expression.

4. Function procedures can invoke other Function procedures or Sub procedures.

5. Function procedures, like Sub procedures, need not have any parameters. Unlike Sub procedures, when a parameterless function is used, the function name may be followed by an empty set of parentheses. The following program uses a "parameterless" function.

```
Private Sub cmdButton_Click()
  'Request and display a saying
  picBox.Cls
  picBox.Print Saying()        '() is optional
End Sub
```

```
Private Function Saying() As String
  'Retrieve a saying from the user
  Saying = InputBox("What is your favorite saying?")
End Function
```

[Run, click the command button, and then type *Less is more.* into the message box.]

The saying *Less is more.* is displayed in the picture box.

6. An alternative method of creating a Function procedure is to move the cursor to a blank line of the Code window outside of any procedure, type Private Function *FunctionName*, and press the Enter key.

PRACTICE PROBLEMS 4.3

1. Suppose a program contains the lines

```
Dim n As Single, x As String
picOutput.Print Arc(n, x)
```

What types of inputs and output (numeric or string) does the function Arc have?

2. What is displayed in the picture box when cmdCompute is clicked?

```
Private Sub cmdCompute_Click()
  Dim gallonsPerBushel As Single, apples As Single
  'How many gallons of apple cider can we make?
  Call GetData(gallonsPerBushel, apples)
  Call DisplayNumOfGallons(gallonsPerBushel, apples)
End Sub


Private Function Cider(g As Single, x As Single) As Single
  Cider = g * x
End Function


Private Sub DisplayNumOfGallons(galPerBu As Single, apples As Single)
  picOutput.Cls
  picOutput.Print "You can make"; Cider(galPerBu, apples);
  picOutput.Print "gallons of cider."
End Sub

Private Sub GetData(gallonsPerBushel As Single, apples As Single)
  'gallonsPerBushel     Number of gallons of cider one bushel
  '                     of apples makes
  'apples               Number of bushels of apples available
  gallonsPerBushel = 3
  apples = 9
End Sub
```

➤   **EXERCISES 4.3**

In Exercises 1 through 10, determine the output displayed in the picture box when the command button is clicked.

1.
```
Private Sub cmdConvert_Click()
    Dim temp As Single
    'Convert Celsius to Fahrenheit
    temp = 95
    picOutput.Print CtoF(temp)
End Sub

Private Function CtoF(t As Single) As Single
    CtoF = (9 / 5) * t + 32
End Function
```

2.
```
Private Sub cmdDisplay_Click()
    Dim acres As Single
    'acres      Number of acres in a parking lot
    acres = 5
    picOutput.Print "You can park about"; Cars(acres); "cars."
End Sub

Private Function Cars(x As Single) As Single
    'Parking cars
    Cars = 100 * x
End Function
```

3.
```
Private Sub cmdDisplay_Click()
    Dim p As Single
    'Rule of 72
    p = Val(txtPopGr.Text)        'Population growth as a percent
    picOutput.Print "The population will double in";
    picOutput.Print DoublingTime(p); "years."
End Sub

Private Function DoublingTime(x As Single) As Single
    'Estimate time required for a population to double
    'at a growth rate of x percent
    DoublingTime = 72 / x
End Function
```
(Assume that the text box contains the number *3*.)

4.
```
Private Sub cmdDisplay_Click()
    Dim initVel As Single, initHt As Single
    'Calculate max. ht. of a ball thrown straight up in the air
    initVel = Val(txtVel.Text)   'Initial velocity of ball
    initHt = Val(txtHt.Text)     'Initial height of ball
    picOutput.Print MaximumHeight(initVel, initHt)
End Sub

Private Function MaximumHeight(v As Single, h As Single) As Single
    MaximumHeight = h + v ^ 2 / 64
End Function
```
(Assume that the text boxes contain the values *96* and *256*.)

5.
```
Private Sub cmdDisplay_Click()
    Dim r As Single, h As Single
    'Compute volume of a cylinder
    r = 1
    h = 2
    Call DisplayVolume(r, h)
    r = 3
    h = 4
    Call DisplayVolume(r, h)
End Sub

Private Function Area(r As Single) As Single
    'Compute area of a circle of radius r
    Area = 3.14159 * r ^ 2
End Function

Private Sub DisplayVolume(r As Single, h As Single)
    picOutput.Print "Volume of cylinder having base area"; Area(r)
    picOutput.Print "and height"; h; "is"; h * Area(r)
End Sub
```

6.
```
Private Sub cmdDisplay_Click()
    Dim days As String, num As Integer
    'Determine the day of the week from its number
    days = "SunMonTueWedThuFriSat"
    num = Val(InputBox("Enter the number of the day"))
    picOutput.Print "The day is "; DayOfWeek(days, num)
End Sub

Private Function DayOfWeek(x As String, n As Integer) As String
    Dim position As Integer
    'x    string containing 3-letter abbreviations of days of the week
    'n    the number of the day
    position = 3 * n - 2
    DayOfWeek = Mid(x, position, 3)
End Function
```

(Assume that the response is 4.)

7.
```
Private Sub cmdDisplay_Click()
    Dim a As String
    'Demonstrate local variables
    a = "Choo "
    picOutput.Print TypeOfTrain()
End Sub

Private Function TypeOfTrain() As String
    Dim a As String
    a = a & a
    TypeOfTrain = a & "train"
End Function
```

8.
```
Private Sub cmdDisplay_Click()
    Dim num As Single
    'Triple a number
    num = 5
    picOutput.Print Triple(num);
    picOutput.Print num
End Sub

Private Function Triple(x As Single) As Single
    Dim num As Single
    num = 3
    Triple = num * x
End Function
```

9.
```
Private Sub cmdDisplay_Click()
    Dim word As String
    word = "moral"
    Call Negative(word)
    word = "political"
    Call Negative(word)
End Sub

Private Function AddA(word As String) As String
    AddA = "a" & word
End Function

Private Sub Negative(word As String)
    picOutput.Print word; " has the negative "; AddA(word)
End Sub
```

10.
```
Private Sub cmdDisplay_Click()
    Dim city As String, pop As Single, shrinks As Single
    Open "DOCS.TXT" For Input as #1
    Input #1, city, pop, shrinks
    Call DisplayData(city, pop, shrinks)
    Input #1, city, pop, shrinks
    Call DisplayData(city, pop, shrinks)
    Close #1
End Sub

Private Sub DisplayData(city As String, pop As Single, shrinks As Single)
    picOutput.Print city; " has"; ShrinkDensity(pop, shrinks);
    picOutput.Print "psychiatrists per 100,000 people."
End Sub

Private Function ShrinkDensity(pop As Single, shrinks As Single) As Integer
    ShrinkDensity = Int(100000 * (shrinks / pop))
End Function
```

(Assume that the file DOCS.TXT contains the following two lines.)

"Boston", 2824000, 8602
"Denver", 1633000, 3217

In Exercises 11 and 12, identify the errors.

```
11. Private Sub cmdDisplay_Click()
      Dim answer As Single
      'Select a greeting
      answer = Val(InputBox("Enter 1 or 2."))
      picOutput.Print Greeting(answer)
    End Sub

    Private Function Greeting(x As Single) As Single
      Greeting = Mid("hellohi ya", 5 * x - 4, 5)
    End Function
```

```
12. Private Sub cmdDisplay_Click()
      Dim word As String
      word = InputBox("What is your favorite word?")
      picOutput.Print "When the word is written twice,";
      picOutput.Print Twice(word); "letters are used."
    End Sub

    Private Function Twice(w As String) As Single
      'Compute twice the length of a string
      Twice(w) = 2 * Len(w)
    End Function
```

In Exercises 13 through 21, construct user-defined functions to carry out the primary task(s) of the program.

13. To determine the number of square centimeters of tin needed to make a tin can, add the square of the radius of the can to the product of the radius and height of the can, and then multiply this sum by 6.283. Write a program that requests the radius and height of a tin can in centimeters as input and displays the number of square centimeters required to make the can.

14. According to Plato, a man should marry a woman whose age is half his age plus seven years. Write a program that requests a man's age as input and gives the ideal age of his wife.

15. In 1998, the federal government developed the body mass index (BMI) to determine ideal weights. Body mass index is calculated as 703 times the weight in pounds, divided by the square of the height in inches, and then rounded to the nearest whole number. Write a program that accepts a person's weight and height as input and gives the person's body mass index. (*Note:* A BMI of 19 to 25 corresponds to a healthy weight.)

16. In order for exercise to be beneficial to the cardiovascular system, the heart rate (number of heart beats per minute) must exceed a value called the *training heart rate*, THR. A person's THR can be calculated from his age and resting heart rate (pulse when first awakening) as follows:

    (a) Calculate the maximum heart rate as 220 – age.
    (b) Subtract the resting heart rate from the maximum heart rate.
    (c) Multiply the result in step (b) by 60% and then add the resting heart rate.

Write a program to request a person's age and resting heart rate as input and display their THR. (Test the program with an age of 20 and a resting heart rate of 70, and then determine *your* training heart rate.)

17. The three ingredients for a serving of popcorn at a movie theater are popcorn, butter substitute, and a bucket. Write a program that requests the cost of these three items and the price of the serving as input and then displays the profit. (Test the program where popcorn costs 5 cents, butter substitute costs 2 cents, the bucket costs 25 cents, and the selling price is $5.)

18. Rewrite the population-density program from Example 4 of Section 4.1 using a function to calculate the population density.

19. The original cost of airmail letters was 5 cents for the first ounce and 10 cents for each additional ounce. Write a program to compute the cost of a letter whose weight is given by the user in a text box. **Hint:** Use the function Ceil discussed in Example 3. (Test the program with the weights 4, 1, 2.5, and .5 ounce.)

20. Suppose a fixed amount of money is deposited at the beginning of each month into a savings account paying 6% interest compounded monthly. After each deposit is made, [new balance] = 1.005 * [previous balance one month ago] + [fixed amount]. Write a program that requests the fixed amount of the deposits as input and displays the balance after each of the first four deposits. A sample outcome when 800 is typed into the text box for the amount deposited each month follows.

```
Month 1    800.00
Month 2    1604.00
Month 3    2412.02
Month 4    3224.08
```

21. Write a program to request the name of a United States senator as input and display the address and greeting for a letter to the senator. Assume the name has two parts and use a function to determine the senator's last name. A sample outcome when Robert Smith is typed into the text box holding the senator's name follows.

```
The Honorable Robert Smith
United States Senate
Washington, DC 20001

Dear Senator Smith,
```

✔✔ **Solutions to Practice Problems 4.3**

1. The first argument, *n*, takes numeric values and the second argument, *x*, takes string values; therefore, the input consists of a number and a string. From the two lines shown here, there is no way to determine the type of the output. This can be determined only by looking at the definition of the function.

2. You can make 27 gallons of cider. In this program, the function was used by a Sub procedure rather than by an event procedure.

4.4 MODULAR DESIGN

Top-Down Design

Full-featured software usually requires large programs. Writing the code for an event procedure in such a Visual Basic program might pose a complicated problem. One method programmers use to make a complicated problem more understandable is to divide it into smaller, less complex subproblems. Repeatedly using a "divide-and-conquer" approach to break up a large problem into smaller subproblems is called **stepwise refinement**. Stepwise refinement is part of a larger methodology of writing programs known as **top-down design**. The term top-down refers to the fact that the more general tasks occur near the top of the design and tasks representing their refinement occur below. Top-down design and structured programming emerged as techniques to enhance programming productivity. Their use leads to programs that are easier to read and maintain. They also produce programs containing fewer initial errors, with these errors being easier to find and correct. When such programs are later modified, there is a much smaller likelihood of introducing new errors.

The goal of top-down design is to break a problem into individual tasks, or modules, that can easily be transcribed into pseudocode, flowcharts, or a program. First, a problem is restated as several simpler problems depicted as modules. Any modules that remain too complex are broken down further. The process of refining modules continues until the smallest modules can be coded directly. Each stage of refinement adds a more complete specification of what tasks must be performed. The main idea in top-down design is to go from the general to the specific. This process of dividing and organizing a problem into tasks can be pictured using a hierarchy chart. When using top-down design, certain criteria should be met:

1. The design should be easily readable and emphasize small module size.

2. Modules proceed from general to specific as you read down the chart.

3. The modules, as much as possible, should be single-minded. That is, they should only perform a single well-defined task.

4. Modules should be as independent of each other as much as possible, and any relationships among modules should be specified.

This process is illustrated with the following example.

EXAMPLE 1 The chart in Figure 4.6 is a hierarchy chart for a program that gives certain information about a car loan. The inputs are the amount of the loan, the duration (in years), and the interest rate. The output consists of the monthly payment and the amount of interest paid during the first month. Figure 4.6 shows these tasks as the first row of a hierarchy chart.

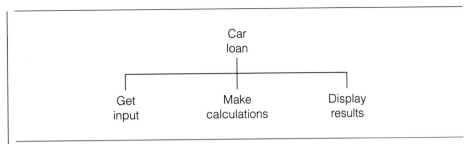

Figure 4.6 Beginning of a hierarchy chart for the car loan program.

Each of these tasks can be refined into more specific subtasks. (See Figure 4.7 for the final hierarchy chart.) Most of the subtasks in the second row are straightforward and so do not require further refinement. For instance, the first month's interest is computed by multiplying the amount of the loan by one-twelfth of the annual rate of interest. The most complicated subtask, the computation of the monthly payment, has been broken down further. This task is carried out by applying a standard formula found in finance books; however, the formula requires the number of payments.

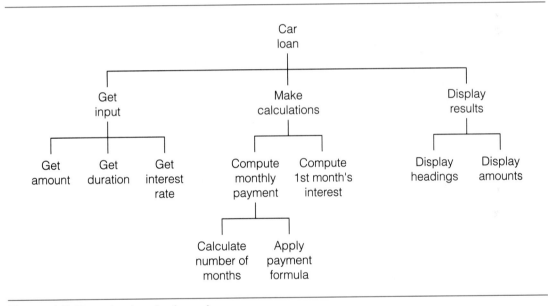

Figure 4.7 Hierarchy chart for the car loan program.

It is clear from the hierarchy chart that the top modules manipulate the modules beneath them. While the higher-level modules control the flow of the program, the lower-level modules do the actual work. By designing the top modules first, specific processing decisions can be delayed.

Structured Programming

A program is said to be **structured** if it meets modern standards of program design. Although there is no formal definition of the term **structured program**, computer scientists are in uniform agreement that such programs should have modular design and use only the three types of logical structures discussed in Chapter 2: sequences, decisions, and loops.

Sequences: Statements are executed one after another.

Decisions: One of several blocks of program code is executed based on a test for some condition.

Loops (iteration): One or more statements are executed repeatedly as long as a specified condition is true.

Chapters 5 and 6 are devoted to decisions and loops, respectively.

One major shortcoming of the earliest programming languages was their reliance on the GoTo statement. This statement was used to branch (that is, jump) from one line of a program to another. It was common for a program to be composed of a convoluted tangle of branchings that produced confusing code referred to as *spaghetti code*. At the heart of structured programming is the assertion of E. W. Dijkstra that GoTo statements should be eliminated entirely because they lead to complex and confusing programs. Two Italians, C. Bohm and G. Jacopini, were able to prove that GoTo statements are not needed and that any program can be written using only the three types of logic structures discussed before.

Structured programming requires that all programs be written using sequences, decisions, and loops. Nesting of such statements is allowed. All other logical constructs, such as GoTos, are not allowed. The logic of a structured program can be pictured using a flowchart that flows smoothly from top to bottom without unstructured branching (GoTos). The portion of a flowchart shown in Figure 4.8(a) contains the equivalent of a GoTo statement and, therefore, is not structured. A correctly structured version of the flowchart in which the logic flows from the top to the bottom appears in Figure 4.8(b).

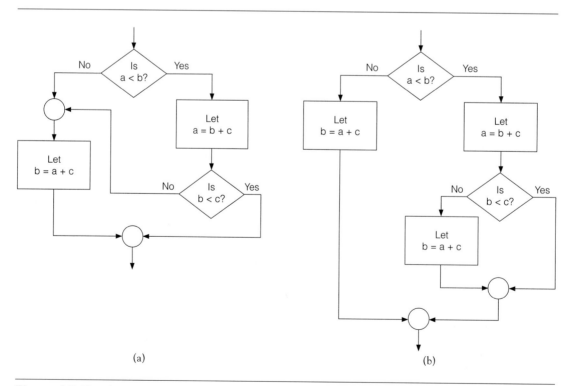

(a)

(b)

Figure 4.8 Flowcharts illustrating the removal of a GoTo statement.

Advantages of Structured Programming

The goal of structured programming is to create correct programs that are easy to write, understand, and change. Let us now take a closer look at the way modular design, along with a limited number of logical structures, contributes to attaining these goals.

1. *Easy to write.*

   Modular design increases the programmer's productivity by allowing him or her to look at the big picture first and focus on the details later. During the actual coding, the programmer works with a manageable chunk of the program and does not have to think about an entire complex program.

   Several programmers can work on a single large program, each taking responsibility for a specific module.

   Studies have shown structured programs require significantly less time to write than standard programs.

   Often, procedures written for one program can be reused in other programs requiring the same task. Not only is time saved in writing a program, but reliability is enhanced, because reused procedures will already be tested and debugged. A procedure that can be used in many programs is said to be **reusable**.

2. *Easy to debug.*

   Because each procedure is specialized to perform just one task, a procedure can be checked individually to determine its reliability. A dummy program, called a **driver**, is set up to test the procedure. The driver contains the minimum definitions needed to call the procedure to be tested. For instance, if the procedure to be tested is a function, the driver program assigns diverse values to the arguments and then examines the corresponding function value. The arguments should contain both typical and special-case values.

   The program can be tested and debugged as it is being designed with a technique known as **stub programming**. In this technique, the key event procedures and perhaps some of the smaller procedures are coded first. Dummy procedures, or stubs, are written for the remaining procedures. Initially, a stub procedure might consist of a Print method to indicate that the procedure has been called, and thereby confirm that the procedure was called at the right time. Later, a stub might simply display values passed to it in order to confirm not only that the procedure was called, but also that it received the correct values from the calling procedure. A stub also can assign new values to one or more of its parameters to simulate either input or computation. This provides greater control of the conditions being tested. The stub procedure is always simpler than the actual procedure it represents. Although the stub program is only a skeleton of the final program, the program's structure can still be debugged and tested. (The stub program consists of some coded procedures and the stub procedures.)

Old-fashioned unstructured programs consist of a sequence of instructions that are not grouped for specific tasks. The logic of such a program is cluttered with details and therefore difficult to follow. Needed tasks are easily left out and crucial details easily neglected. Tricky parts of the program cannot be isolated and examined. Bugs are difficult to locate because they might be present in any part of the program.

3. *Easy to understand.*

The interconnections of the procedures reveal the modular design of the program.

The meaningful procedure names, along with relevant comments, identify the tasks performed by the modules.

The meaningful variable names help the programmer to recall the purpose of each variable.

4. *Easy to change.*

Because a structured program is self-documenting, it can easily be deciphered by another programmer.

Modifying a structured program often amounts to inserting or altering a few procedures rather than revising an entire complex program. The programmer does not even have to look at most of the program. This is in sharp contrast to the situation with unstructured programs that require an understanding of the entire logic of the program before any changes can be made with confidence.

CHAPTER 4   SUMMARY

1. A *general procedure* is a portion of a program that is accessed by event procedures or other general procedures. The two types of general procedures are *Sub procedures* and *Function procedures*.

2. Sub procedures are defined in blocks beginning with Sub statements and ending with End Sub statements. They are accessed by Call statements.

3. Function procedures are defined in blocks beginning with Function statements and ending with End Function statements. A function is activated by a reference in an expression and returns a value.

4. In any procedure, the arguments appearing in the calling statement must match the parameters of the Sub or Function statement in number, type, and order. They need not match in name.

5. A variable declared in the (Declarations) section of (General) is *form-level*. Such a variable is available to every procedure in the form's code and retains its value from one procedure invocation to the next. Form-level variables are often initialized in the Form_Load event procedure.

6. Variables declared with a Dim statement inside a procedure are *local* to the procedure. The values of these variables are reinitialized each time the procedure is called. A variable with the same name appearing in another part of the program is treated as a different variable.

7. *Structured programming* uses modular design to refine large problems into smaller subproblems. Programs are coded using the three logical structures of sequences, decisions, and loops.

CHAPTER 4   PROGRAMMING PROJECTS

1. The numbers of calories per gram of carbohydrate, fat, and protein are 4, 9, and 4, respectively. Write a program that requests the nutritional content of a 1-ounce serving of food and displays the number of calories in the serving. The input and output should be handled by Sub procedures and the calories computed by a function. A sample run for a typical breakfast cereal is shown in Figure 4.9

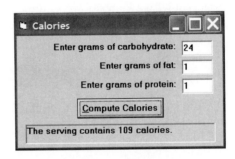

Figure 4.9 Sample run for Programming Project 1.

2. About twelve million notebook computers were sold during the year 2000. Table 4.3 gives the market share for the four largest vendors. Write a program that displays the number of computers sold by each of the Big Four. The input and output should be handled by Sub procedures and the number of computers calculated by a Function procedure.

Company	Market Share
Compaq	12%
Toshiba	12.5%
Dell	13%
IBM	13.5%

Table 4.3 2000 market shares of the top notebook vendors.
Source: CFO.com, January 21, 2001.

3. Table 4.4 gives the advertising expenditures (in millions of dollars) for the four most advertised soft drink brands during 1998 and 1999. Write a program that displays the percentage change in advertising for each brand. Sub procedures should be used for input and output, and the percentage change should be computed with a Function procedure. *Note:* The percentage change is 100 * ([1999 expenditure] – [1998 expenditure]) / [1998 expenditure].

Brand	1998 Expenditure	1999 Expenditure
Coca-Cola	115.5	138.7
Pepsi-Cola	82.7	88.8
Dr. Pepper	55.2	70.7
Sprite	56.5	68.2

Table 4.4 Most advertised soft drinks.
Source: CMR News, April 2000.

4. A fast-food vendor sells pizza slices ($1.25), fries ($1.00), and soft drinks ($.75). Write a program to compute a customer's bill. The program should request the quantity of each item ordered in a Sub procedure, calculate the total cost with a Function procedure, and use a Sub procedure to display an itemized bill. A sample output is shown in Figure 4.10.

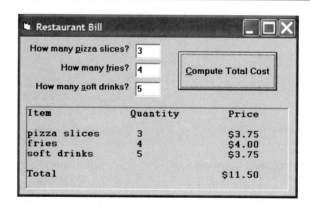

Figure 4.10 Sample run for Programming Project 4.

5. Write a program to generate a business travel expense attachment for an income tax return. The program should request as input the name of the organization visited, the date and location of the visit, and the expenses for meals and entertainment, airplane fare, lodging, and taxi fares. (Only 50% of the expenses for meals and entertainment are deductible.) A possible form layout and run are shown in Figures 4.11 and 4.12, respectively. Sub procedures should be used for the input and output.

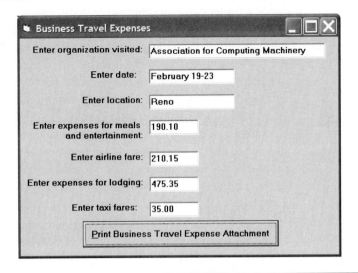

Figure 4.11 Form with sample data for Programming Project 5.

```
Business Travel Expense

Trip to attend meeting of
Association for Computing Machinery
February 19-23 in Reno

Meals and entertainment      $190.10
Airplane fare                $210.15
Lodging                      $475.35
Taxi fares                    $35.00

Total other than Meals and Entertainment: $720.50

50% of Meals and Entertainment: $95.05
```

Figure 4.12 Output on printer for sample run of Programming Project 5.

6. Rework Programming Project 8 of Chapter 3, Farecard Machine, using procedures. The program should contain a Sub procedure to display the farecard and another Sub procedure to display the change in the various denominations. Function procedures should be used to calculate the numbers of $1 bills, quarters, dimes, and nickels to be returned to the passenger. Each Function procedure should have a single parameter that is passed by value.

7. A furniture manufacturer makes two types of furniture—chairs and sofas. The file PRICE&TAXDATA.TXT contains three numbers giving the cost per chair, cost per sofa, and sales tax rate. Write a program to create an invoice form for an order. See Figure 4.13. After the data on the left side of Figure 4.13 is entered, you can display an invoice in a picture box by pressing the

Process Order command button and you can print a copy of the invoice by pressing the Print Invoice command button. You can press the Clear Form command button to clear all text boxes and the picture box and can press the Quit command button to exit the program. The invoice number consists of the capitalized first three letters of the customer's last name, followed by a randomly generated string of three characters consisting of a letter, a vowel, and a digit. The customer name is input with the last name first, followed by a comma, a space, and the first name. However, the name is displayed in the invoice in the proper order. The generation of the invoice number and the reorder of the first and last names should be carried out in Function procedures. The text file should be read as soon as the form is loaded.

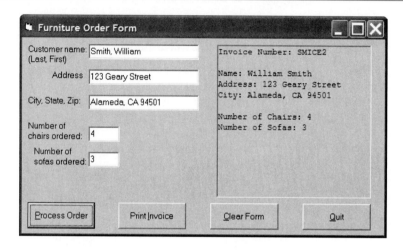

Figure 4.13 Sample run for Programming Project 7.

5 Decisions

5.1 RELATIONAL AND LOGICAL OPERATORS

A **condition** is an expression involving relational operators (such as < and =) that is either true or false. Conditions also may incorporate logical operators (such as And, Or, and Not).

The relational operator *less than* (<) can be applied to both numbers and strings. The number a is said to be less than the number b if a lies to the left of b on the number line. For instance, $2 < 5$, $-5 < -2$, and $0 < 3.5$.

The string a is said to be less than the string b if a precedes b alphabetically when using the ANSI (or ASCII) table to alphabetize their values. For instance, "cat" < "dog", "cart" < "cat", and "cat" < "catalog". Digits precede uppercase letters, which precede lowercase letters. Two strings are compared working from left to right, character by character, to determine which one should precede the other. Therefore, "9W" < "bat", "Dog" < "cat", and "Sales-99" < "Sales-retail".

Table 5.1 shows the different mathematical relational operators, their representations in Visual Basic, and their meanings.

Mathematical Notation	Visual Basic Notation	Numeric Meaning	String Meaning
=	=	equal to	identical to
≠	<>	unequal to	different from
<	<	less than	precedes alphabetically
>	>	greater than	follows alphabetically
≤	<=	less than or equal to	precedes alphabetically or is identical to
≥	>=	greater than or equal to	follows alphabetically or is identical to

Table 5.1 Relational operators.

EXAMPLE 1 Determine whether each of the following conditions is true or false.

(a) 1 <= 1

(b) 1 < 1

(c) "car" < "cat"

(d) "Dog" < "dog"

SOLUTION

(a) True. The notation <= means "less than *or* equal to." That is, the condition is true provided either of the two circumstances holds. The second one (equal to) holds.

(b) False. The notation < means "strictly less than" and no number can be strictly less than itself.

(c) True. The characters of the strings are compared one at a time working from left to right. Because the first two match, the third character decides the order.

(d) True. Because uppercase letters precede lowercase letters in the ANSI table, the first character of "Dog" precedes the first character of "dog."

Conditions also can involve variables, numeric operators, and functions. To determine whether a condition is true or false, first compute the numeric or string values and then decide if the resulting assertion is true or false.

EXAMPLE 2   Suppose the numeric variables *a* and *b* have values 4 and 3, and the string variables *c* and *d* have values "hello" and "bye". Are the following conditions true or false?

(a) (a + b) < 2 * a
(b) (Len(c) – b) = (a / 2)
(c) c < ("good" & d)

SOLUTION   (a) The value of a + b is 7 and the value of 2 * a is 8. Because 7 < 8, the condition is true.
(b) True, because the value of Len(c) – b is 2, the same as (a / 2).
(c) The condition "hello" < "goodbye" is false, because "h" follows "g" in the ANSI table.

Logical Operators

Programming situations often require more complex conditions than those considered so far. For instance, suppose we would like to state that the value of a numeric variable, *n*, is strictly between 2 and 5. The proper Visual Basic condition is

$$(2 < n) \text{ And } (n < 5)$$

The condition (2 < n) And (n < 5) is a combination of the two conditions 2 < n and n < 5 with the logical operator And.

The three main logical operators are And, Or, and Not. If *cond1* and *cond2* are conditions, then the condition

```
cond1 And cond2
```

is true if both *cond1* and *cond2* are true. Otherwise, it is false. The condition

```
cond1 Or cond2
```

is true if either *cond1* or *cond2* (or both) is true. Otherwise, it is false. The condition

```
Not cond1
```

is true if *cond1* is false, and is false if *cond1* is true.

EXAMPLE 3   Suppose the numeric variable *n* has value 4 and the string variable *answ* has value "Y". Determine whether each of the following conditions is true or false.

(a) (2 < n) And (n < 6)
(b) (2 < n) Or (n = 6)
(c) Not (n < 6)
(d) (answ = "Y") Or (answ = "y")
(e) (answ = "Y") And (answ = "y")
(f) Not (answ = "y")
(g) ((2 < n) And (n = 5 + 1)) Or (answ = "No")
(h) ((n = 2) And (n = 7)) Or (answ = "Y")
(i) (n = 2) And ((n = 7) Or (answ = "Y"))

SOLUTION

(a) True, because the conditions (2 < 4) and (4 < 6) are both true.

(b) True, because the condition (2 < 4) is true. The fact that the condition (4 = 6) is false does not affect the conclusion. The only requirement is that at least one of the two conditions be true.

(c) False, because (4 < 6) is true.

(d) True, because the first condition becomes ("Y" = "Y") when the value of *answ* is substituted for *answ*.

(e) False, because the second condition is false. Actually, this compound condition is false for every value of *answ*.

(f) True, because ("Y" = "y") is false.

(g) False. In this logical expression, the compound condition ((2 < n) And (n = 5 + 1)) and the simple condition (answ = "No") are joined by the logical operator Or. Because both of these conditions are false, the total condition is false.

(h) True, because the second Or clause is true.

(i) False. Comparing (h) and (i) shows the necessity of using parentheses to specify the intended grouping.

The use of parentheses with logical operators improves readability; however, they can be omitted sometimes. Visual Basic has an operator hierarchy for deciding how to evaluate logical expressions without parentheses. First, all arithmetic operations are carried out, and then all expressions involving >, <, and = are evaluated to true or false. The logical operators are next applied, in the order Not, then And, and finally Or. For instance, the logical expression in part (g) of Example 3 could have been written 2 < n And n = 5 + 1 Or answ = "No". In the event of a tie, the leftmost operator is applied first.

EXAMPLE 4

Place parentheses in the following condition to show how it would be evaluated by Visual Basic.

a < b + c Or d < e And Not f = g

SOLUTION

((a <(b + c)) Or ((d < e) And (Not (f = g))))

The step-by-step analysis of the order of operations is

```
 a < (b + c)   Or    d < e   And   Not  f = g        arithmetic operation
(a < (b + c))  Or   (d < e)  And   Not (f = g)        relational expressions
(a < (b + c))  Or   (d < e)  And  (Not (f = g))       Not
(a < (b + c))  Or  ((d < e)  And  (Not (f = g)))      And
((a < (b + c)) Or  ((d < e)  And  (Not (f = g))))     Or
```

Comments

1. A condition involving numeric variables is different from an algebraic truth. The assertion (a + b) < 2 * a, considered in Example 2, is not a valid algebraic truth because it isn't true for all values of *a* and *b*. When encountered in a Visual Basic program, however, it will be considered true if it is correct for the current values of the variables.

2. Conditions evaluate to either True or False. These two values often are called the possible **truth values** of the condition.

3. A condition such as 2 < n < 5 should never be used, because Visual Basic will not evaluate it as intended. The correct condition is (2 < n) And (n < 5).

4. A common error is to replace the condition Not (n < m) by the condition (n > m). The correct replacement is (n >= m).

✔ **PRACTICE PROBLEMS 5.1**

1. Is the condition "Hello " = "Hello" true or false?

2. Complete Table 5.2.

cond1	cond2	cond1 And cond2	cond1 Or cond2	Not cond2
True	True	True		
True	False		True	
False	True			False
False	False			

Table 5.2 Truth values of logical operators.

➤ **EXERCISES 5.1**

In Exercises 1 through 12, determine whether the condition is true or false. Assume a = 2 and b = 3.

1. 3 * a = 2 * b

2. (5 – a) * b < 7

3. b <= 3

4. a ^ b = b ^ a

5. a ^ (5 – 2) > 7

6. 3E–02 < .01 * a

7. (a < b) Or (b < a)

8. (a * a < b) Or Not (a * a < a)

9. Not ((a < b) And (a < (b + a)))

10. Not (a < b) Or Not (a < (b + a))

11. ((a = b) And (a * a < b * b)) Or ((b < a) And (2 * a < b))

12. ((a = b) Or Not (b < a)) And ((a < b) Or (b = a + 1))

In Exercises 13 through 24, determine whether the condition is true or false.

13. "9W" <> "9w"

14. "Inspector" < "gadget"

15. "Car" < "Train"

16. "J" >= "J"

17. "99" > "ninety-nine"

18. "B" > "?"

19. ("Duck" < "pig") And ("pig" < "big")

20. "Duck" < "Duck" & "Duck"

21. Not (("B" = "b") Or ("Big" < "big"))

22. Not ("B" = "b") And Not ("Big" < "big")

23. (("Ant" < "hill") And ("mole" > "hill")) Or Not
(Not ("Ant" < "hill") Or Not ("Mole" > "hill"))

24. (7 < 34) And ("7" > "34")

In Exercises 25 through 34, determine whether or not the two conditions are
equivalent—that is, whether they will be true or false for exactly the same
values of the variables appearing in them.

25. a <= b; (a < b) Or (a = b)

26. Not (a < b); a > b

27. (a = b) And (a < b); a <> b

28. Not ((a = b) Or (a = c)); (a <> b) And (a <> c)

29. (a < b) And ((a > d) Or (a > e));
((a < b) And (a > d)) Or ((a < b) And (a > e))

30. Not ((a = b + c) Or (a = b)); (a <> b) Or (a <> b + c)

31. (a < b + c) Or (a = b + c); Not ((a > b) Or (a > c))

32. Not (a >= b); (a <= b) Or Not (a = b)

33. Not (a >= b); (a <= b) And Not (a = b)

34. (a = b) And ((b = c) Or (a = c));
(a = b) Or ((b = c) And (a = c))

In Exercises 35 through 39, write a condition equivalent to the negation of
the given condition. (For example, a <> b is equivalent to the negation of
a = b.)

35. a > b

36. (a = b) Or (a = d)

37. (a < b) And (c <> d)

38. Not ((a = b) Or (a > b))

39. (a <> "") And (a < b) And (Len(a) < 5)

✔✔ **Solutions to Practice Problems 5.1**

1. False. The first string has six characters, whereas the second has five. Two strings must be
100% identical to be called equal.

2.

cond1	cond2	cond1 And cond2	cond1 Or cond2	Not cond2
True	True	True	True	False
True	False	False	True	True
False	True	False	True	False
False	False	False	False	True

5.2   IF BLOCKS

An **If block** allows a program to decide on a course of action based on whether a certain condition is true or false. A block of the form

```
If condition Then
    action1
  Else
    action2
End If
```

causes the program to take *action1* if *condition* is true and *action2* if *condition* is false. Each action consists of one or more Visual Basic statements. After an action is taken, execution continues with the line after the If block. Figure 5.1 contains the pseudocode and flowchart for an If block.

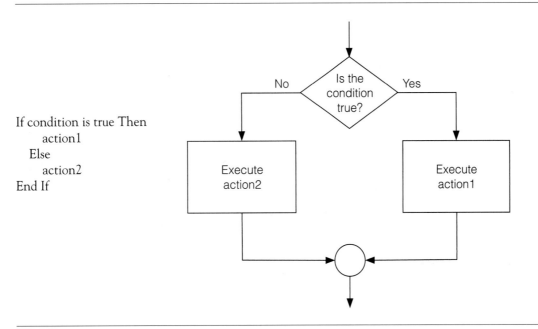

If condition is true Then
    action1
  Else
    action2
End If

Figure 5.1   Pseudocode and flowchart for an If block.

EXAMPLE 1   The following program finds the larger of two numbers input by the user. The condition is Val(txtFirstNum.Text) > Val(txtSecondNum.Text), and each action consists of a single assignment statement. With the input 3 and 7, the condition is false, and so the second action is taken.

Object	Property	Setting
frmMaximum	Caption	Maximum
lblFirstNum	Caption	First Number
txtFirstNum	Text	(blank)
lblSecondNum	Caption	Second Number
txtSecondNum	Text	(blank)
cmdFindLarger	Caption	Find Larger Number
picResult		

```
Private Sub cmdFindLarger_Click()
  Dim largerNum As Single
  picResult.Cls
  If Val(txtFirstNum.Text) > Val(txtSecondNum.Text) Then
      largerNum = Val(txtFirstNum.Text)
    Else
      largerNum = Val(txtSecondNum.Text)
  End If
  picResult.Print "The larger number is"; largerNum
End Sub
```

[Run, type 3 and 7 into the text boxes, and press the command button.]

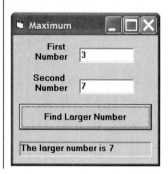

EXAMPLE 2   The following program requests the costs and revenue for a company and displays the message "Break even" if the costs and revenue are equal; otherwise it displays the profit or loss. The action following Else is another If block.

Object	Property	Setting
frm5_2_2	Caption	Profit/Loss
lblCosts	Caption	Costs
txtCosts	Text	(blank)
lblRev	Caption	Revenue
txtRev	Text	(blank)
cmdShow	Caption	Show Financial Status
picResult		

```
Private Sub cmdShow_Click()
  Dim costs As Single, revenue As Single, profit As Single, loss As Single
  costs = Val(txtCosts.Text)
  revenue = Val(txtRev.Text)
  picResult.Cls
  If costs = revenue Then
      picResult.Print "Break even"
    Else
      If costs < revenue Then
          profit = revenue - costs
          picResult.Print "Profit is "; FormatCurrency(profit)
        Else
          loss = costs - revenue
          picResult.Print "Loss is "; FormatCurrency(loss)
      End If
  End If
End Sub
```

[Run, type 9500 and 8000 into the text boxes, and press the command button.]

EXAMPLE 3

The If block in the following program has a logical operator in its condition.

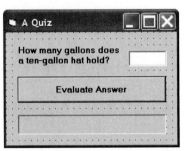

Object	Property	Setting
frmQuiz	Caption	A Quiz
lblQuestion	Caption	How many gallons does a ten-gallon hat hold?
txtAnswer	Text	(blank)
cmdEvaluate	Caption	Evaluate Answer
picSolution		

```
Private Sub cmdEvaluate_Click()
  Dim answer As Single
  'Evaluate answer
  picSolution.Cls
  answer = Val(txtAnswer.Text)
  If (answer >= .5) And (answer <= 1) Then
      picSolution.Print "Good, ";
    Else
      picSolution.Print "No, ";
  End If
  picSolution.Print "it holds about 3/4 of a gallon."
End Sub
```

[Run, type 10 into the text box, and press the command button.]

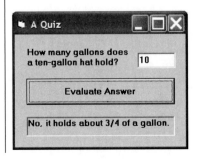

The Else part of an If block can be omitted. This important type of If block appears in the next example.

EXAMPLE 4 | The following program offers assistance to the user before presenting a quotation.

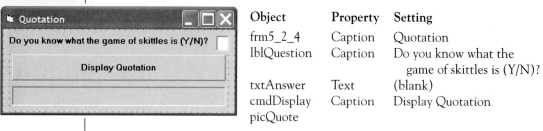

Object	Property	Setting
frm5_2_4	Caption	Quotation
lblQuestion	Caption	Do you know what the game of skittles is (Y/N)?
txtAnswer	Text	(blank)
cmdDisplay	Caption	Display Quotation
picQuote		

```
Private Sub cmdDisplay_Click()
  Dim message As String
  message = "Skittles is an old form of bowling in which a wooden" & _
            " disk is used to knock down nine pins arranged in a square."
  If UCase(txtAnswer.Text) = "N" Then
      MsgBox message, , ""
  End If
  picQuote.Cls
  picQuote.Print "Life ain't all beer and skittles. - Du Maurier (1894)"
End Sub
```

[Run, type N into the text box, and press the command button.]

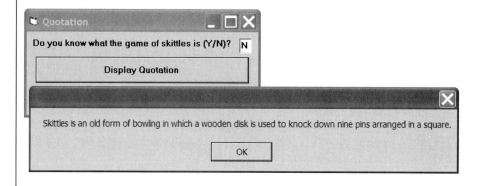

[Press OK.]

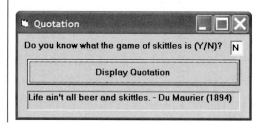

Note: Rerun the program, type Y into the text box, press the command button, and observe that the description of the game is skipped.

An extension of the If block allows for more than two possible alternatives with the inclusion of ElseIf clauses. A typical block of this type is

```
If condition1 Then
    action1
  ElseIf condition2 Then
    action2
  ElseIf condition3 Then
    action3
  Else
    action4
End If
```

This block searches for the first true condition, carries out its action, and then skips to the statement following End If. If none of the conditions is true, then Else's action is carried out. Execution then continues with the statement following the block. In general, an If block can contain any number of ElseIf clauses. As before, the Else clause is optional.

EXAMPLE 5   The following program redoes Example 1 so that if the two numbers are equal, the program so reports.

```
Private Sub cmdFindLarger_Click()
  picResult.Cls
  If Val(txtFirstNum.Text) > Val(txtSecondNum.Text) Then
      picResult.Print "The larger number is "; txtFirstNum.Text
    ElseIf Val(txtSecondNum.Text) > Val(txtFirstNum.Text) Then
      picResult.Print "The larger number is "; txtSecondNum.Text
    Else
      picResult.Print "The two numbers are equal."
  End If
End Sub
```

[Run, type 7 into both text boxes, and press the command button.]

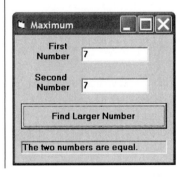

If blocks allow us to define functions whose values are not determined by a simple formula. The function in Example 6 uses an If block.

EXAMPLE 6 | The Social Security or FICA tax has two components—the Social Security benefits tax, which in 2003 is 6.2 percent on the first $87,000 of earnings for the year, and the Medicare tax, which is 1.45 percent of earnings. The following program calculates an employee's FICA tax for the current pay period.

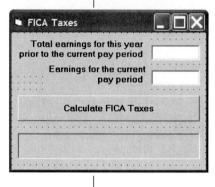

Object	Property	Setting
frmFICA	Caption	FICA Taxes
lblToDate	Caption	Total earnings for this year prior to the current pay period
txtToDate	Text	(blank)
lblCurrent	Caption	Earnings for the current pay period
txtCurrent	Text	(blank)
cmdCalculate	Caption	Calculate FICA Taxes
picTax		

```
Private Sub cmdCalculate_Click()
  Dim ficaTaxes As Single
  ficaTaxes = FICA(Val(txtToDate.Text), Val(txtCurrent.Text))
  picTax.Cls
  picTax.Print "Your FICA taxes for the current"
  picTax.Print "pay period are "; FormatCurrency(ficaTaxes)
End Sub

Private Function FICA(ytdEarnings As Single, curEarnings As Single) As Single
  Const wageBaseLimit03 As Single = 87000
  Dim socialSecurityBenTax As Single, medicare As Single
  'Calculate Social Security benefits tax and Medicare tax
  'for a single pay period in 2003
  socialSecurityBenTax = 0
  If (ytdEarnings + curEarnings) <= wageBaseLimit03 Then
      socialSecurityBenTax = .062 * curEarnings
    ElseIf ytdEarnings < wageBaseLimit03 Then
      socialSecurityBenTax = .062 * (wageBaseLimit03 - ytdEarnings)
  End If
  medicare = .0145 * curEarnings
  FICA = socialSecurityBenTax + medicare
End Function
```

[Run, type 12345.67 and 543.21 into the text boxes, and press the command button.]

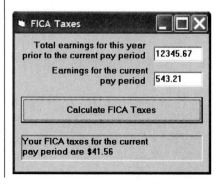

Comments

1. The actions of an If block and the words Else and ElseIf do not have to be indented. For instance, the If block of Example 1 can be written

```
If Val(txtFirstNum.Text) > Val(txtSecondNum.Text) Then
largerNum = Val(txtFirstNum.Text)
Else
largerNum = Val(txtSecondNum.Text)
End If
```

   However, because indenting improves the readability of the block, it is regarded as good programming style. As soon as you see the word If, your eyes can easily scan down the program to find the matching End If and the enclosed Else and ElseIf clauses. You then immediately have a good idea of the size and complexity of the block.

2. Constructs in which an If block is contained inside another If block are referred to as **nested** If blocks.

3. Care should be taken to make If blocks easy to understand. For instance, in Figure 5.2, the block on the left is difficult to follow and should be replaced by the clearer block on the right.

```
If cond1 Then              If cond1 And cond2 Then
    If cond2 Then              action
        action            End If
    End If
End If
```

Figure 5.2 A confusing If block and an improvement.

4. Some programs call for selecting among many possibilities. Although such tasks can be accomplished with complicated If blocks, the Select Case block (discussed in the next section) is often a better alternative.

5. In Appendix D, the section "Stepping Through Programs Containing Decision Structures: Chapter 5" uses the Visual Basic debugging tools to trace the flow through an If block.

6. Visual Basic also has a single-line If statement of the form

```
If condition Then action1 Else action2
```

   which is a holdover from earlier, unstructured versions of BASIC; it is seldom used in this text.

✔ **PRACTICE PROBLEMS 5.2**

1. Suppose the user is asked to input a number into txtNumber for which the square root is to be taken. Fill in the If block so that the lines of code below will display either the message "Number can't be negative." or the square root of the number.

```
Private Sub cmdTakeSquareRoot_Click()
  Dim num As Single
  'Check reasonableness of data
  num = Val(txtNumber.Text)
  If

  End If
End Sub
```

2. Improve the block

```
If a < b Then
    If c < 5 Then
        picBox.Print "hello"
    End If
End If
```

> ### EXERCISES 5.2

In Exercises 1 through 12, determine the output displayed in the picture box when the command button is clicked.

1.
```
Private Sub cmdDisplay_Click()
  Dim num As Single
  num = 4
  If num <= 9 Then
      picOutput.Print "Less than ten"
    Else
      If num = 4 Then
          picOutput.Print "Equal to four"
      End If
  End If
End Sub
```

2.
```
Private Sub cmdDisplay_Click()
  Dim gpa As Single
  gpa = 3.49
  If gpa >= 3.5 Then
      picOutput.Print "Honors ";
  End If
  picOutput.Print "Student"
End Sub
```

3.
```
Private Sub cmdDisplay_Click()
  Dim a As Single
  a = 5
  If (3 * a - 4) < 9 Then
      picOutput.Print "Remember, "
  End If
  picOutput.Print "tomorrow is another day."
End Sub
```

4.
```
Private Sub cmdDisplay_Click()
    Dim change As Single
    change = 356            'Amount of change in cents
    If change >= 100 Then
        picOutput.Print "Your change contains";
        picOutput.Print Int(change / 100); "dollars."
      Else
        picOutput.Print "Your change contains no dollars."
    End If
End Sub
```

5.
```
Private Sub cmdDisplay_Click()
    Dim a As Single, b As Single, c As Single
    a = 2
    b = 3
    c = 5
    If a * b < c Then
        b = 7
      Else
        b = c * a
    End If
    picOutput.Print b
End Sub
```

6.
```
Private Sub cmdDisplay_Click()
    Dim a As Single, b As Single
    a = Val(InputBox("Enter a number."))
    b = Val(InputBox("Enter another number."))
    If a > b Then
        a = a + 1
      Else
        b = b + 1
    End If
    picOutput.Print a; b
End Sub
```

(Assume that the responses are *7, 11*.)

7.
```
Private Sub cmdDisplay_Click()
    Dim length As Single
    'Cost of phone call from NY to Belgrade
    Call InputLength(length)
    Call DisplayCost(length)
End Sub

Private Function Cost(length As Single) As Single
    If length < 1 Then
        Cost = .46
      Else
        Cost = .46 + (length - 1) * .36
    End If
End Function

Private Sub DisplayCost(length As Single)
    'Display the cost of a call
    picOutput.Print "Cost of call: "; FormatCurrency(Cost(length))
End Sub
```

```
Private Sub InputLength(length As Single)
  'Request the length of a phone call
  length = Val(InputBox("Duration of the call in minutes?"))
End Sub
```

(Assume that the response is *31*.)

8.
```
Private Sub cmdDisplay_Click()
  Dim letter As String
  letter = InputBox("Enter A, B, or C.")
  If letter = "A" Then
      Call DisplayAmessage
    ElseIf letter = "B" Then
      Call DisplayBmessage
    ElseIf letter = "C" Then
      Call DisplayCmessage
    Else
      picOutput.Print "Not a valid letter"
  End If
End Sub

Private Sub DisplayAmessage()
  picOutput.Print "A, my name is Alice."
End Sub

Private Sub DisplayBmessage()
  picOutput.Print "To be or not to be."
End Sub

Private Sub DisplayCmessage()
  picOutput.Print "Oh, say, can you see."
End Sub
```

(Assume that the response is *B*.)

9.
```
Private Sub cmdDisplay_Click()
  Dim vowels As Integer
  vowels = 0     'Number of vowels
  Call ExamineLetter(vowels)
  Call ExamineLetter(vowels)
  Call ExamineLetter(vowels)
  picOutput.Print "The number of vowels is"; vowels
End Sub

Private Sub ExamineLetter(vowels As Integer)
  Dim ltr As String
  ltr = InputBox("Enter a letter.")
  ltr = UCase(ltr)
  If ltr = "A" Or ltr = "E" Or ltr = "I" Or ltr = "O" Or ltr = "U" Then
      vowels = vowels + 1
  End If
End Sub
```

(Assume that the three responses are *U*, *b*, and *a*.)

10.
```
Private Sub cmdDisplay_Click()
    Dim a As Single
    a = 5
    If (a > 2) And (a = 3 Or a < 7) Then
        picOutput.Print "Hi"
    End If
End Sub
```

11.
```
Private Sub cmdDisplay_Click()
    Dim num As Single
    num = 5
    If num < 0 Then
        picOutput.Print "neg"
      Else
        If num = 0 Then
            picOutput.Print "zero"
          Else
            picOutput.Print "positive"
        End If
    End If
End Sub
```

12.
```
Private Sub cmdDisplay_Click()
    Dim msg As String, age As Integer
    msg = "You are eligible to vote"
    age = Val(InputBox("Enter your age."))
    If age >= 18 Then
        picOutput.Print msg
      Else
        picOutput.Print msg & " in"; 18 - age; "years"
    End If
End Sub
```

(Assume that the response is *16*.)

In Exercises 13 through 20, identify the errors.

13.
```
Private Sub cmdDisplay_Click()
    Dim num As Single
    num = .5
    If 1 < num < 3 Then
        picOutput.Print "Number is between 1 and 3."
    End If
End Sub
```

14.
```
Private Sub cmdDisplay_Click()
    Dim num As Single
    num = 6
    If num > 5 And < 9 Then
        picOutput.Print "Yes"
      Else
        picOutput.Print "No"
    End If
End Sub
```

15.
```
Private Sub cmdDisplay_Click()
    If 2 <> 3
        picOutput.Print "Numbers are not equal"
    End If
End Sub
```

16.
```
Private Sub cmdDisplay_Click()
    Dim major As String
    If major = "Business" Or "Computer Science" Then
        picOutput.Print "Yes"
    End If
End Sub
```

17.
```
Private Sub cmdDisplay_Click()
    Dim numName As String, num As Single
    numName = "Seven"
    num = Val(InputBox("Enter a number."))
    If num < numName Then
        picOutput.Print "Less than"
      Else
        picOutput.Print "Greater than"
    End If
End Sub
```

18.
```
Private Sub cmdDisplay_Click()
    Dim switch As String
    'Change switch from "on" to "off", or from "off" to "on"
    switch = InputBox("Enter on or off.")
    If switch = "off" Then
        switch = "on"
    End If
    If switch = "on" Then
        switch = "off"
    End If
End Sub
```

19.
```
Private Sub cmdDisplay_Click()
    Dim j As Single, k As Single
    'Display "OK" if either j or k equals 4
    j = 2
    k = 3
    If j Or k = 4 Then
        picOutput.Print "OK"
    End If
End Sub
```

20.
```
Private Sub cmdDisplay_Click()
    Dim query As String, answer1 As String, answer2 As String
    'Is your program correct?
    query = "Are you certain everything in your program is correct?"
    answer1 = InputBox(query)
    answer1 = UCase(Left(answer1, 1))
    If answer1 = "N" Then
        picOutput.Print "Don't patch bad code, rewrite it."
```

```
        Else
          query = "Does your program run correctly?"
          answer2 = InputBox(query)
          answer2 = UCase(Left(answer2, 1))
          If answer2 = "Y" Then
              picOutput.Print "Congratulations"
            Else
              picOutput.Print "One of the things you are certain"
              picOutput.Print "about is wrong."
          End If
    End Sub
```

In Exercises 21 through 26, simplify the code.

21.
```
If a = 2 Then
      a = 3 + a
    Else
      a = 5
End If
```

22.
```
If Not (answer <> "y") Then
      picOutput.Print "YES"
    Else
      If (answer = "y") Or (answer = "Y") Then
          picOutput.Print "YES"
      End If
End If
```

23.
```
If j = 7 Then
      b = 1
    Else
      If j <> 7 Then
          b = 2
      End If
End If
```

24.
```
If a < b Then
      If b < c Then
          picOutput.Print b; "is between"; a; "and"; c
      End If
End If
```

25.
```
message = "Is Alaska bigger than Texas and California combined?"
answer = InputBox(message)
If Left(answer, 1) = "Y" Then
      answer = "YES"
End If
If Left(answer, 1) = "y" Then
      answer = "YES"
End If
If answer = "YES" Then
      picOutput.Print "Correct"
    Else
      picOutput.Print "Wrong"
End If
```

26.
```
message = "How tall (in feet) is the Statue of Liberty?"
feet = Val(InputBox(message))
If feet <= 141 Then
    picOutput.Print "Nope"
End If
If feet > 141 Then
    If feet < 161 Then
        picOutput.Print "Close"
    Else
        picOutput.Print "Nope"
    End If
End If
picOutput.Print "The Statue of Liberty is 151.08 feet"
picOutput.Print "from base to torch."
```

27. Write a program to determine how much to tip the server in a restaurant. The tip should be 15 percent of the check, with a minimum of $1.

28. Write a quiz program to ask "Who was the first Ronald McDonald?" The program should display "Correct." if the answer is Willard Scott and otherwise should display "Nice try."

29. A computer store sells diskettes at 25 cents each for small orders or at 20 cents each for orders of 100 diskettes or more. Write a program that requests the number of diskettes ordered and displays the total cost. (Test the program for purchases of 5 and 200 diskettes.)

30. A copying center charges 5 cents per copy for the first 100 copies and 3 cents per copy for each additional copy. Write a program that requests the number of copies as input and displays the total cost. (Test the program with the quantities 25 and 125.)

31. Write a txtBox_KeyPress event procedure that allows the user to type only digits into the text box.

32. Suppose a program has a command button with the caption "Quit." Suppose also that the Name property of this command button is cmdQuit. Write a cmdQuit_Click event procedure that gives the user a second chance before ending the program. The procedure should use an input dialog box to request that the user confirm that the program should be terminated, and then end the program only if the user responds in the affirmative.

33. Write a program to handle a savings account withdrawal. The program should request the current balance and the amount of the withdrawal as input and then display the new balance. If the withdrawal is greater than the original balance, the program should display "Withdrawal denied." If the new balance is less than $150, the message "Balance below $150" should be displayed.

34. Write a program that requests three scores as input and displays the average of the two highest scores. The input and output should be handled by Sub procedures, and the average should be determined by a user-defined function.

35. A lottery drawing produces three digits. Write a program that uses Rnd to generate three digits and then displays "Lucky seven." if two or more of the digits are 7.

36. Federal law requires hourly employees be paid "time-and-a-half" for work in excess of 40 hours in a week. For example, if a person's hourly wage is $8 and he works 60 hours in a week, his gross pay should be

$$(40 \times 8) + (1.5 \times 8 \times (60 - 40)) = \$560.$$

Write a program that requests as input the number of hours a person works in a given week and his hourly wage, and then displays his gross pay.

37. Write a program that requests a word (with lowercase letters) as input and translates the word into pig latin. The rules for translating a word into pig latin are as follows:

(a) If the word begins with a consonant, move the first letter to the end of the word and add *ay*. For instance, *chip* becomes *hipcay*.

(b) If the word begins with a vowel, add *way* to the end of the word. For instance, *else* becomes *elseway*.

38. The current calendar, called the Gregorian calendar, was introduced in 1582. Every year divisible by 4 was declared to be a leap year, with the exception of the years ending in 00 (that is, those divisible by 100) and not divisible by 400. For instance, the years 1600 and 2000 are leap years, but 1700, 1800, and 1900 are not. Write a program that requests a year as input and states whether or not it is a leap year. (Test the program on the years 1994, 1995, 1900, and 2000.)

39. Create a form with a picture box and two command buttons captioned Bogart and Raines. When Bogart is first pressed, the sentence "I came to Casablanca for the waters." is displayed in the picture box. The next time Bogart is pressed, the sentence "I was misinformed." is displayed. When Raines is pressed, the sentence "But we're in the middle of the desert." is displayed. Run the program and then press Bogart, Raines, Bogart to obtain a dialogue.

40. Write a program that allows the user to use one command button to toggle the appearance of the text in a text box between bold and italic and use another pair of command buttons to increase or decrease the size of the text to the next available point size. (Point sizes available in the default MS Sans Serif font are 8, 10, 12, 14, 18, and 24.)

41. Write a program that allows the user ten tries to answer the question "Which U.S. President was born on July 4?" After three incorrect guesses, the program should display the hint, "He once said, 'If you don't say anything, you won't be called upon to repeat it.'" in a message dialog box. After seven incorrect guesses, the program should give the hint, "His nickname was 'Silent Cal.'" The number of guesses should be displayed in a label. **Note:** Calvin Coolidge was born on July 4, 1872.

42. Write a program that reads a test score from a text box each time a command button is clicked, and then displays the two highest scores whenever a second command button is clicked. Use two form-level variables to track the two highest scores.

43. The flowchart in Figure 5.3 calculates New Jersey state income tax. Write a program corresponding to the flowchart. (Test the program with taxable incomes of $15,000, $30,000, and $60,000.)

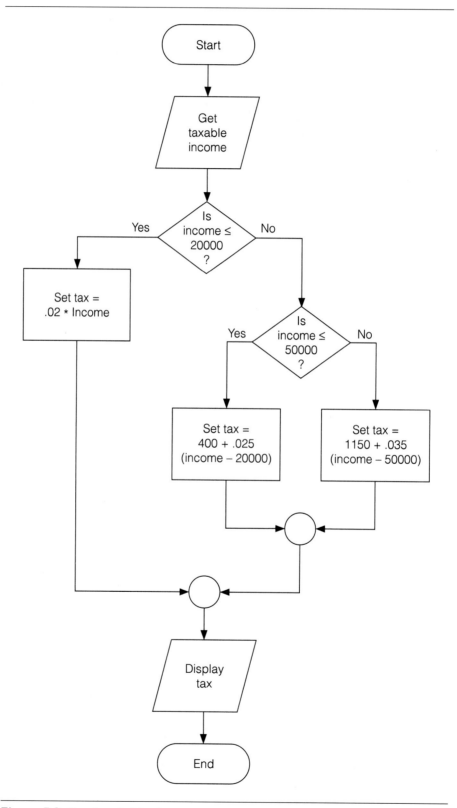

Figure 5.3 Flowchart for New Jersey state income tax program.

44. Write a program to play "Hide and Seek" with this picture of the treetops (in the file Trees.bmp in the Pictures folder of the CD accompanying this book) or with any other picture of your choosing. When the command button is pressed, the picture should disappear and the caption on the button should change to Show Picture. The next time the button is pressed, the picture should reappear and the caption revert to Hide Picture, and so on. (*Note:* This picture shows the autumn view from the author's office.)

Object	Property	Setting
frmHide	Caption	Hide and Seek
picTrees	Picture	Trees.bmp
cmdButton	Caption	Hide Picture

✔✔ **Solutions to Practice Problems 5.2**

1.
```
If num < 0 Then
    MsgBox "Number can't be negative.", , "Input Error"
    txtNumber.Text = ""
    txtNumber.SetFocus
  Else
    picSquareRoot.Print Sqr(num)
End If
```

2. The word "hello" will be displayed when (a < b) is true and (c < 5) is also true. That is, it will be displayed when both of these two conditions are true. The clearest way to write the block is

```
If (a < b) And (c < 5) Then
    picBox.Print "hello"
End If
```

5.3 SELECT CASE BLOCKS

A Select Case block is an efficient decision-making structure that simplifies choosing among several actions. It avoids complex If constructs. If blocks make decisions based on the truth value of a condition; Select Case choices are determined by the value of an expression called a **selector**. Each of the possible actions is preceded by a clause of the form

```
Case valueList
```

where *valueList* itemizes the values of the selector for which the action should be taken.

EXAMPLE I

The following program converts the finishing position in a horse race into a descriptive phrase. After the variable *position* is assigned a value from txtPosition, Visual Basic searches for the first Case clause whose value list contains that value and executes the succeeding statement. If the value of *position* is greater than 5, then the statement following Case Else is executed.

Object	Property	Setting
frmRace	Caption	Horse Race
lblPosition	Caption	Finishing position (1, 2, 3, . . .)
txtPosition	Text	(blank)
cmdDescribe	Caption	Describe Position
picOutcome		

```
Private Sub cmdDescribe_Click()
  Dim position As Integer    'selector
  position = Val(txtPosition.Text)
  picOutcome.Cls
  Select Case position
    Case 1
      picOutcome.Print "Win"
    Case 2
      picOutcome.Print "Place"
    Case 3
      picOutcome.Print "Show"
    Case 4, 5
      picOutcome.Print "You almost placed"
      picOutcome.Print "in the money."
    Case Else
      picOutcome.Print "Out of the money."
  End Select
End Sub
```

[Run, type 2 into the text box, and press the command button.]

EXAMPLE 2

In the following variation of Example 1, the value lists specify ranges of values. The first value list provides another way to specify the numbers 1, 2, and 3. The second value list covers all numbers from 4 on.

```
Private Sub cmdDescribe_Click()
  Dim position As Integer
  'Describe finishing positions in a horse race
```

```
    position = Val(txtPosition.Text)
    picOutcome.Cls
    Select Case position
      Case 1 To 3
        picOutcome.Print "In the money."
        picOutcome.Print "Congratulations."
      Case Is > 3
        picOutcome.Print "Not in the money."
    End Select
End Sub
```

[Run, type 2 into the text box, and press the command button.]

A typical form of the Select Case block is

```
Select Case selector
  Case valueList1
    action1
  Case valueList2
    action2
      .
      .
  Case Else
    action of last resort
End Select
```

where Case Else (and its action) is optional, and each value list contains one or more of the following types of items:

1. a constant

2. a variable

3. an expression

4. an inequality sign preceded by Is and followed by a constant, variable, or expression

5. a range expressed in the form *a* To *b*, where *a* and *b* are constants, variables, or expressions

Different items appearing in the same list must be separated by commas. Each action consists of one or more statements. After the selector is evaluated, Visual

Basic looks for the first value-list item including the value of the selector and carries out its associated action. (If the value of the selector appears in two different value lists, only the action associated with the first value list will be carried out.) If the value of the selector does not appear in any of the value lists and there is no Case Else clause, execution of the program will continue with the statement following the Select Case block. Figure 5.4 contains the flowchart for a Select Case block. The pseudocode for a Select Case block is the same as for the equivalent If block.

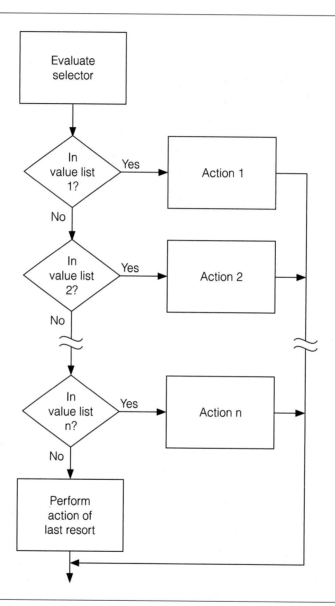

Figure 5.4 Flowchart for a Select Case block.

EXAMPLE 3 | The following program uses several different types of value lists. With the response shown, the second action was selected.

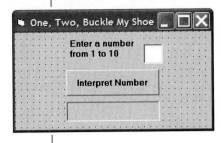

Object	Property	Setting
frm5_3_3	Caption	One, Two, Buckle My Shoe
lblEnterNum	Caption	Enter a number from 1 to 10
txtNumber	Text	(blank)
cmdInterpret	Caption	Interpret Number
picPhrase		

```
Private Sub cmdInterpret_Click()
  Dim x As Integer, y As Integer, num As Integer
  'One, Two, Buckle My Shoe
  picPhrase.Cls
  x = 2
  y = 3
  num = Val(txtNumber.Text)
  Select Case num
    Case y - x, x
      picPhrase.Print "Buckle my shoe."
    Case Is <= 4
      picPhrase.Print "Shut the door."
    Case x + y To x * y
      picPhrase.Print "Pick up sticks."
    Case 7, 8
      picPhrase.Print "Lay them straight."
    Case Else
      picPhrase.Print "Start all over again."
  End Select
End Sub
```

[Run, type 4 into the text box, and press the command button.]

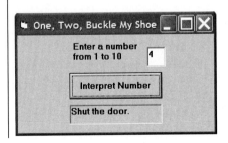

In each of the three preceding examples the selector was a numeric variable; however, the selector also can be a string variable or an expression.

EXAMPLE 4

The following program has the string variable *firstName* as a selector.

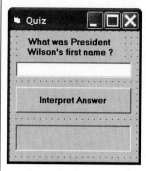

Object	Property	Setting
frmQuiz	Caption	Quiz
lblQuestion	Caption	What was President Wilson's first name?
txtName	Text	(blank)
cmdInterpret	Caption	Interpret Answer
picAnswer		

```
Private Sub cmdInterpret_Click()
  Dim firstName As String
  'Quiz
  picAnswer.Cls
  firstName = txtName.Text
  Select Case firstName
    Case "Thomas"
      picAnswer.Print "Correct."
    Case "Woodrow"
      picAnswer.Print "Sorry, his full name was"
      picAnswer.Print "Thomas Woodrow Wilson."
    Case "President"
      picAnswer.Print "Are you for real?"
    Case Else
      picAnswer.Print "Nice try, but no cigar."
  End Select
End Sub
```

[Run, type Woodrow into the text box, and press the command button.]

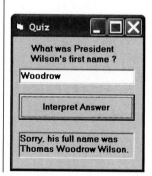

EXAMPLE 5

The following program has the selector Left(anyString, 1), a string expression. In the sample run, only the first action was carried out, even though the value of the selector was in both of the first two value lists. The computer stops looking as soon as it finds the value of the selector.

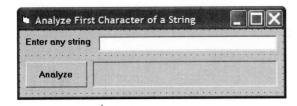

Object	Property	Setting
frm5_3_5	Caption	Analyze First Character of a String
lblEnter	Caption	Enter any string
txtString	Text	(blank)
cmdAnalyze	Caption	Analyze
picResult		

```
Private Sub cmdAnalyze_Click()
  Dim anyString As String
  'Analyze the first character of a string
  picResult.Cls
  anyString = UCase(txtString.Text)
  Select Case Left(anyString, 1)
    Case "S", "Z"
      picResult.Print "The string begins with a sibilant."
    Case "A" To "Z"
      picResult.Print "The string begins with a nonsibilant."
    Case "0" To "9"
      picResult.Print "The string begins with a digit."
    Case Is < "0"
      picResult.Print "The string begins with a character of ANSI"
      picResult.Print "value less than 48 (e.g. +, &, #, or %)."
    Case Else
      picResult.Print "The string begins with one of the following:"
      picResult.Print "       :  ;  <  =  >  ?  @  [  \  ]  ^  _  `"
  End Select
End Sub
```

[Run, type Sunday into the text box, and press the command button.]

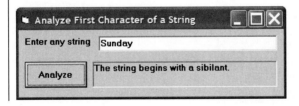

EXAMPLE 6   The color of the beacon light atop Boston's John Hancock Building forecasts the weather according to the rhyme below. The following program requests a color (blue or red) and a mode (steady or flashing) as input and displays the weather forecast. The program contains a Select Case block with a string expression as the selector.

Steady blue, clear view.
Flashing blue, clouds due.
Steady red, rain ahead.
Flashing red, snow instead.

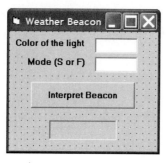

Object	Property	Setting
frmWeather	Caption	Weather Beacon
lblColor	Caption	Color of the light
txtColor	Text	(blank)
lblMode	Caption	Mode (S or F)
txtMode	Text	(blank)
cmdInterpret	Caption	Interpret Beacon
picForecast		

```
Private Sub cmdInterpret_Click()
   Dim color As String, mode As String
   'Interpret a weather beacon
   picForecast.Cls
   color = txtColor.Text
   mode = txtMode.Text
   Select Case UCase(mode) & UCase(color)
     Case "SBLUE"
       picForecast.Print "CLEAR VIEW"
     Case "FBLUE"
       picForecast.Print "CLOUDS DUE"
     Case "SRED"
       picForecast.Print "RAIN AHEAD"
     Case "FRED"
       picForecast.Print "SNOW AHEAD"
   End Select
End Sub
```

[Run, type *red* and *S* into the text boxes, and press the command button.]

EXAMPLE 7 Select Case is useful in defining functions that are not determined by a formula. The following program assumes the current year is not a leap year.

Object	Property	Setting
frm5_3_7	Caption	Seasons
lblSeason	Caption	Season
txtSeason	Text	(blank)
cmdNumber	Caption	Number of Days
picNumDays		

```
Private Sub cmdNumber_Click()
  Dim season As String
  'Determine the number of days in a season
  picNumDays.Cls
  season = txtSeason.Text
  picNumDays.Print season; " has"; NumDays(season); "days."
End Sub

Private Function NumDays(season As String) As Integer
  'Look up the number of days in a given season
  Select Case UCase(season)
    Case "WINTER"
      NumDays = 87
    Case "SPRING"
      NumDays = 92
    Case "SUMMER", "AUTUMN", "FALL"
      NumDays = 93
  End Select
End Function
```

[Run, type Summer into the text box, and press the command button.]

Comments

1. The Case statements and their actions do not have to be indented; however, because indenting improves the readability of the block, it is regarded as good programming style. As soon as you see the words Select Case, your eyes can easily scan down the block to find the matching End Select statement. You immediately know the number of different cases under consideration.

2. The items in the value list must evaluate to a constant of the same type, string or numeric, as the selector. For instance, if the selector evaluated to a string value, as in

```
Dim firstName As String
firstName = txtBox.Text
Select Case firstName
```

then the clause

```
Case Len(firstName)
```

would be meaningless.

3. If the word Is, which should precede an inequality sign in a value list, is accidentally omitted, the editor will automatically insert it when checking the line.

4. A Case clause of the form Case b To c selects values from *b* to *c* inclusive. However, the extreme values can be excluded by placing the action inside an If block beginning with If (*selector* <> b) And (*selector* <> c) Then.

5. In a Case clause of the form Case b To c, the value of *b* must be less than or equal to the value of *c*.

6. Every Select Case block can be replaced by an If block. Select Case is preferable to an If block when the possible choices have more or less the same importance.

7. In Appendix D, the section "Stepping Through Programs Containing Selection Structures: Chapter 5" uses the Visual Basic debugging tools to trace the flow through a Select Case block.

✔ **PRACTICE PROBLEMS 5.3**

1. Suppose the selector of a Select Case block is the numeric variable *num*. Determine whether each of the following Case clauses is valid.

   (a) `Case 1, 4, Is < 10`

   (b) `Case Is < 5, Is >= 5`

   (c) `Case num = 2`

2. Do the following two programs always produce the same output for a whole-number grade from 0 to 100?

```
grade = Val(txtBox.Text)              grade = Val(txtBox.Text)
Select Case grade                     Select Case grade
  Case Is >= 90                         Case Is >= 90
    picOutput.Print "A"                   picOutput.Print "A"
  Case Is >= 60                         Case 60 To 89
    picOutput.Print "Pass"                picOutput.Print "Pass"
  Case Else                             Case 0 To 59
    picOutput.Print "Fail"                picOutput.Print "Fail"
End Select                            End Select
```

➤ **EXERCISES 5.3**

In Exercises 1 through 8, for each of the responses shown in the parentheses, determine the output displayed in the picture box when the command button is clicked.

```
1. Private Sub cmdDisplay_Click()
     Dim age As Single, price As Single
     age = Val(InputBox("What is your age?"))
     Select Case age
```

```
        Case Is < 6
          price = 0
        Case 6 To 17
          price = 3.75
        Case Is >= 17
          price = 5
      End Select
      picOutput.Print "The price is "; FormatCurrency(price)
    End Sub
```

  (8.5, 17)

2.
```
Private Sub cmdDisplay_Click()
    Dim n As Single
    n = Val(InputBox("Enter a number from 5 to 12"))
    Select Case n
      Case 5
        picOutput.Print "case 1"
      Case 5 To 7
        picOutput.Print "case 2"
      Case 7 To 12
        picOutput.Print "case 3"
    End Select
  End Sub
```

  (7, 5, 11.2)

3.
```
Private Sub cmdDisplay_Click()
    Dim age As Integer
    age = Val(InputBox("Enter age (in millions of years)"))
    Select Case age
      Case Is < 70
        picOutput.Print "Cenozoic Era"
      Case Is < 225
        picOutput.Print "Mesozoic Era"
      Case Is <= 600
        picOutput.Print "Paleozoic Era"
      Case Else
        picOutput.Print "?"
    End Select
  End Sub
```

  (100, 600, 700)

4.
```
Private Sub cmdDisplay_Click()
    Dim yearENIAC As Integer
    Call AskQuestion(yearENIAC)
    Call ProcessAnswer(yearENIAC)
  End Sub

  Private Sub AskQuestion(yearENIAC As Integer)
    Dim message As String
    'Ask question and obtain answer
    message = "In what year was the ENIAC computer completed?"
    yearENIAC = Val(InputBox(message))
  End Sub
```

```
Private Sub ProcessAnswer(yearENIAC As Integer)
  'Respond to answer
  Select Case yearENIAC
    Case 1945
      picOutput.Print "Correct"
    Case 1943 To 1947
      picOutput.Print "Close, 1945."
    Case Is < 1943
      picOutput.Print "Sorry, 1945. Work on the ENIAC began ";
      picOutput.Print "in June 1943."
    Case Is > 1947
      picOutput.Print "No, 1945. By then IBM had built a stored-program ";
      picOutput.Print "computer."
  End Select
End Sub
```

(1940, 1945, 1950)

5.
```
Private Sub cmdDisplay_Click()
  Dim nom As String
  nom = InputBox("Who developed the stored program concept?")
  Select Case UCase(nom)
    Case "JOHN VON NEUMANN", "VON NEUMANN"
      picOutput.Print "Correct."
    Case "JOHN MAUCHLY", "MAUCHLY", "J. PRESPER ECKERT", "ECKERT"
      picOutput.Print "He worked with the developer, von Neumann, on the ENIAC."
    Case Else
      picOutput.Print "Nope."
  End Select
End Sub
```

(Grace Hopper, Eckert, John von Neumann)

6.
```
Private Sub cmdDisplay_Click()
  Dim message As String, a As Single, b As Single, c As Single
  message = "Analyzing solutions to the quadratic equation "
  message = message & "A*X^2 + B*X + C = 0.  Enter the value for "
  a = Val(InputBox(message & "A"))
  b = Val(InputBox(message & "B"))
  c = Val(InputBox(message & "C"))
  Select Case b * b - 4 * a * c
    Case Is < 0
      picOutput.Print "The equation has no real solutions."
    Case Is 0
      picOutput.Print "The equation has exactly one solution."
    Case Is > 0
      picOutput.Print "The equation has two solutions."
  End Select
End Sub
```

(1,2,3; 1,5,1; 1,2,1)

7.
```
Private Sub cmdDisplay_Click()
    Dim num1 As Single, word As String, num2 As Single
    'State a quotation
    num1 = 3
    word = "hello"
    num2 = Val(InputBox("Enter a number."))
    Select Case 2 * num2 - 1
      Case num1 * num1
        picOutput.Print "Less is more."
      Case Is > Len(word)
        picOutput.Print "Time keeps everything from happening at once."
      Case Else
        picOutput.Print "The less things change, the more they remain the same."
    End Select
End Sub
```

(2, 5, 6)

8.
```
Private Sub cmdDisplay_Click()
    Dim whatever As Single
    whatever = Val(InputBox("Enter a number."))
    Select Case whatever
      Case Else
        picOutput.Print "Hi"
    End Select
End Sub
```

(7, –1)

In Exercises 9 through 16, identify the errors.

9.
```
Private Sub cmdDisplay_Click()
    Dim num As Single
    num = 2
    Select Case num
      picOutput.Print "Two"
    End Select
End Sub
```

10.
```
Private Sub cmdDisplay_Click()
    Dim num1 As Single, num2 As Single
    num1 = 5
    num2 = 7
    Select Case num1
      Case 3 <= num1 <= 10
        picOutput.Print "between 3 and 10"
      Case num2 To 5; 4
        picOutput.Print "near 5"
    End Select
End Sub
```

11.
```
Private Sub cmdDisplay_Click()
    Dim a As String
    a = Inputbox("What is your name?")
    Select Case a
      Case a = "Bob"
        picOutput.Print "Hi Bob"
      Case Else
    End Select
End Sub
```

12. ```
    Private Sub cmdDisplay_Click()
        Dim word As String
        word = "hello"
        Select Case Left(word, 1)
          Case h
            picOutput.Print "begins with h"
        End Select
    End Sub
    ```

13. ```
    Private Sub cmdDisplay_Click()
        Dim word As String
        word = InputBox("Enter a word from the United States motto")
        Select Case UCase(word)
          Case "E"
            picOutput.Print "This is the first word of the motto."
          Case Left(word, 1) = "P"
            picOutput.Print "The second word is PLURIBUS."
          Case Else
            picOutput.Print "The third word is UNUM."
        End Select
    End Sub
    ```

14. ```
    Private Sub cmdDisplay_Click()
        Dim num As Single
        num = 5
        Select Case num
          Case 5, Is <> 5
            picOutput.Print "five"
          Case Is > 5
            picOutput.Print "greater than five"
    End Sub
    ```

15. ```
    Private Sub cmdDisplay_Click()
        Dim fruit As String
        fruit = "Peach"
        Select Case UCase(fruit)
          Case Is >= "Peach"
            picOutput.Print "Georgia"
          Case "ORANGE To PEACH"
            picOutput.Print "Ok"
        End Select
    End Sub
    ```

16. ```
    Private Sub cmdDisplay_Click()
        Dim purchase As Single
        purchase = Val(InputBox("Quantity purchased?"))
        Select Case purchase
          Case Is < 10000
            picOutput.Print "Five dollars per item."
          Case Is 10000 To 30000
            picOutput.Print "Four dollars per item."
          Case Is > 30000
            picOutput.Print "Three dollars per item."
        End Select
    End Sub
    ```
    ```

In Exercises 17 through 22, suppose the selector of a Select Case block, *word*, evaluates to a string value. Determine whether the Case clause is valid.

17. `Case "un" & "til"`

18. `Case "hello", Is < "goodbye"`

19. `Case 0 To 9`

20. `Case word <> "No"`

21. `Case Left("abc", 1)`

22. `Case word Then`

In Exercises 23 through 26, rewrite the code using a Select Case block.

23.
```
If a = 1 Then
    picOutput.Print "one"
  Else
    If a > 5 Then
        picOutput.Print "two"
    End If
End If
```

24.
```
If a = 1 Then
        picOutput.Print "lambs"
    End If
    If a <= 3 And a < 4 Then
        picOutput.Print "eat"
    End If
    If a = 5 Or a > 7 Then
        picOutput.Print "ivy"
    End If
```

25.
```
If a < 5 Then
    If a = 2 Then
        picOutput.Print "yes"
      Else
        picOutput.Print "no"
    End If
  Else
    If a = 2 Then
        picOutput.Print "maybe"
    End If
End If
```

26.
```
If a = 3 Then
    a = 1
End If
If a = 2 Then
    a = 3
End If
If a = 1 Then
    a = 2
End If
```

27. Table 5.3 gives the terms used by the National Weather Service to describe the degree of cloudiness. Write a program that requests the percentage of cloud cover as input and then displays the appropriate descriptor.

Percentage of Cloud Cover	Descriptor
0–30	clear
31–70	partly cloudy
71–99	cloudy
100	overcast

Table 5.3 Cloudiness descriptors.

28. Table 5.4 shows the location of books in the library stacks according to their call numbers. Write a program that requests the call number of a book as input and displays the location of the book.

Call Numbers	Location
100 to 199	basement
200 to 500 and over 900	main floor
501 to 900 except 700 to 750	upper floor
700 to 750	archives

Table 5.4 Location of library books.

29. Write a program that requests a month of the year and then gives the number of days in the month. If the month is February, the user should be asked whether or not the current year is a leap year.

30. Figure 5.5 shows some geometric shapes and formulas for their areas. Write a program that requests the user to select one of the shapes, requests the appropriate lengths, and then gives the area of the figure. The areas should be computed by Function procedures.

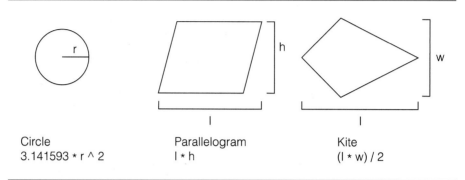

Circle
3.141593 * r ^ 2

Parallelogram
l * h

Kite
(l * w) / 2

Figure 5.5 Areas of geometric shapes.

31. Write a program that requests an exam score and assigns a letter grade with the scale 90–100 (A), 80–89 (B), 70–79 (C), 60–69 (D), 0–59 (F). The computation should be carried out in a Function procedure. (Test the program with the grades 84, 100, and 57.)

32. (Computerized quiz show.) Write a program that asks the contestant to select one of the numbers 1, 2, or 3 and then calls a Sub procedure that asks the question and requests the answer. The program should then tell the contestant if the answer is correct. Use the following three questions:

1. Who was the only living artist to have his work displayed in the Grand Gallery of the Louvre?
2. Who said, "Computers are useless. They can only give you answers."?
3. By what name is Pablo Blasio better known?

Note: These questions have the same answer, Pablo Picasso.

33. IRS informants are paid cash awards based on the value of the money recovered. If the information was specific enough to lead to a recovery, the informant receives 10 percent of the first $75,000, 5 percent of the next $25,000, and 1 percent of the remainder, up to a maximum award of $50,000. Write a program that requests the amount of the recovery as input and displays the award. (Test the program on the amounts $10,000, $125,000, and $10,000,000.) (*Note:* The source of this formula is *The Book of Inside Information*, Boardroom Books, 1993.)

34. Table 5.5 contains information on several states. Write a program that requests a state and category (flower, motto, and nickname) as input and displays the requested information. If the state or category requested is not in the table, the program should so inform the user.

State	Flower	Nickname	Motto
California	Golden poppy	Golden State	Eureka
Indiana	Peony	Hoosier State	Crossroads of America
Mississippi	Magnolia	Magnolia State	By valor and arms
New York	Rose	Empire State	Ever upward

Table 5.5 State flowers, nicknames, and mottoes.

35. Write a program that, given the last name of one of the five most recent presidents, displays his state and a colorful fact about him. *Hint:* The program might need to request further information.

Note: Carter: Georgia; The only soft drink served in the Carter White House was Coca-Cola. Reagan: California; His secret service code name was Rawhide. George P. Bush: Texas; He was the third left-handed president. Clinton: Arkansas; In college he did a good imitation of Elvis Presley. George W. Bush: Texas; He once owned the Texas Rangers baseball team.

36. Table 5.6 contains the meanings of some abbreviations doctors often use for prescriptions. Write a program that requests an abbreviation and gives its meaning. The user should be informed if the meaning is not in the table.

Abbreviation	Meaning
ac	before meals
ad lib	freely as needed
bid	twice daily
gtt	a drop
hs	at bedtime
qid	four times a day

Table 5.6 Physicians' abbreviations.

37. The user enters a number into a text box and then clicks on the appropriate command button to have either one of three pieces of humor or one of three insults displayed in the large label below the buttons. Place the humor and insults in Function procedures, with Select Case statements in each to return the appropriate phrase. Also, if the number entered is not between 1 and 3, the text box should be cleared.

Note: Some possible bits of humor are "I can resist everything except temptation.", "I just heard from Bill Bailey. He's not coming home.", and "I have enough money to last the rest of my life, unless I buy something." Some possible insults are "How much would you charge to haunt a house?", "I bet you have no more friends than an alarm clock.", and "When your IQ rises to 30, sell."

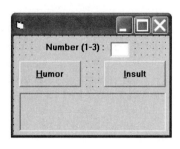

Object	Property	Setting
frmEx37	Caption	(blank)
lblNumber	Caption	Number (1–3):
txtNumber	Text	(blank)
cmdHumor	Caption	&Humor
cmdInsult	Caption	&Insult
lblSentence	BorderStyle	Fixed Single
	Caption	(blank)

Form for Exercise 37   Objects and Properties for Exercise 37

✔✔ **Solutions to Practice Problems 5.3**

1. (a) Valid. These items are redundant because 1 and 4 are just special cases of Is < 10. However, this makes no difference in Visual Basic.

   (b) Valid. These items are contradictory. However, Visual Basic looks at them one at a time until it finds an item containing the value of the selector. The action following this Case clause will always be carried out.

   (c) Not valid. It should be `Case 2`.

2. Yes. However, the program on the right is clearer and therefore preferable.

5.4 A CASE STUDY: WEEKLY PAYROLL

This case study processes a weekly payroll using the 2003 Employer's Tax Guide. Table 5.7 shows typical data used by a company's payroll office. These data are processed to produce the information in Table 5.8 that is supplied to each employee along with his or her paycheck. The program should request the data from Table 5.7 for an individual as input and produce output similar to that in Table 5.8.

The items in Table 5.8 should be calculated as follows:

Current Earnings: Hourly wage times hours worked (with time-and-a-half after 40 hours)

Year-to-Date Earnings: Previous year-to-date earnings plus current earnings

FICA Tax: Sum of 6.2 percent of first $87,000 of earnings (Social Security benefits tax) and 1.45 percent of total wages (Medicare tax)

Federal Income Tax Withheld: Subtract $58.65 from the current earnings for each withholding exemption and use Table 5.9 or Table 5.10, depending on marital status

Check Amount: [current earnings] – [FICA taxes] – [income tax withheld]

Name	Hourly Wage	Hours Worked	Withholding Exemptions	Marital Status	Previous Year-to-Date Earnings
Al Clark	$45.50	38	4	Married	$86,925.50
Ann Miller	$44.00	35	3	Married	$68,200.00
John Smith	$17.95	50	1	Single	$30,604.75
Sue Taylor	$25.50	43	2	Single	$36,295.50

Table 5.7 Employee data.

Name	Current Earnings	Yr. to Date Earnings	FICA Taxes	Income Tax Wh.	Check Amount
Al Clark	$1,729.00	$88,654.50	$29.69	$252.50	$1,446.81

Table 5.8 Payroll information.

Adjusted Weekly Income	Income Tax Withheld
$0 to $51	$0
Over $51 to $164	10% of amount over $51
Over $164 to $579	$11.30 + 15% of excess over $164
Over $579 to $1,268	$73.55 + 27% of excess over $579
Overt $1,268 to $2,792	$259.58 + 30% of excess over $1,268
Over $2,792 to $6,032	$716.78 + 35% of excess over $2,792
Over $6,032	$1,850.78 + 38.6% of excess over $6,032

Table 5.9 2003 Federal income tax withheld for a single person paid weekly.

Adjusted Weekly Income	Income Tax Withheld
$0 to $124	$0
Over $124 to $355	10% of excess over $124
Over $355 to $1,007	$23.10 + 15% of excess over $355
Over $1,007 to $2,150	$120.90 + 27% of excess over $1,007
Over $2,150 to $3,454	$429.51 + 30% of excess over $2,150
Over $3,454 to $6,093	$820.71 + 35% of excess over $3,454
Over $6,093	$1,744.36 + 38.6% of excess over $6,093

Table 5.10 2003 Federal income tax withheld for a married person paid weekly.

Designing the Weekly Payroll Program

After the data for an employee have been gathered from the text boxes, the program must compute the five items appearing in Table 5.8 and then display the payroll information. The five computations form the basic tasks of the program.

1. Compute current earnings.

2. Compute year-to-date earnings.

3. Compute FICA tax.

4. Compute federal income tax withheld.

5. Compute paycheck amount (that is, take-home pay).

Tasks 1, 2, 3, and 5 are fairly simple. Each involves applying a formula to given data. (For instance, if hours worked are at most 40, then [Current Earnings] = [Hourly Wage] times [Hours Worked].) Thus, we won't break down these tasks any further. Task 4 is more complicated, so we continue to divide it into smaller subtasks.

4. *Compute Federal Income Tax Withheld.* First, the employee's pay is adjusted for exemptions, and then the amount of income tax to be withheld is computed. The computation of the income tax withheld differs for married and single individuals. Task 4 is, therefore, divided into the following subtasks:

    4.1 Compute pay adjusted by exemptions.
    4.2 Compute income tax withheld for single employee.
    4.3 Compute income tax withheld for married employee.

The hierarchy chart in Figure 5.6 shows the stepwise refinement of the problem.

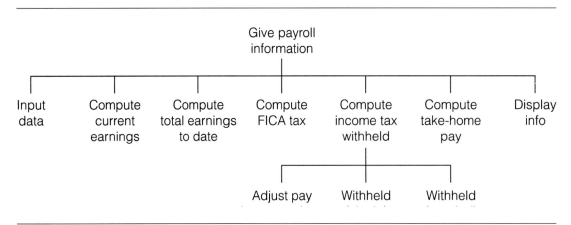

Figure 5.6 Hierarchy chart for the weekly payroll program.

Pseudocode for the Display Payroll Event

INPUT employee data (Sub procedure InputData)
COMPUTE CURRENT GROSS PAY (Function Gross_Pay)
COMPUTE TOTAL EARNINGS TO DATE (Function Total_Pay)
COMPUTE FICA TAX (Function FICA_Tax)
COMPUTE FEDERAL TAX (Function Fed_Tax)
   Adjust pay for exemptions
   If employee is single Then
      COMPUTE INCOME TAX WITHHELD from adjusted pay using tax
      brackets for single taxpayers (Function TaxSingle)
    Else
      COMPUTE INCOME TAX WITHHELD from adjusted pay using tax
      brackets for married taxpayers (Function TaxMarried)
   End If
COMPUTE PAYCHECK AMOUNT (Function Net_Check)
Display payroll information (Sub procedure ShowPayroll)

Writing the Weekly Payroll Program

The cmdDisplay_Click event procedure calls a sequence of seven procedures. Table 5.11 shows the tasks and the procedures that perform the tasks.

Task	Procedure
0. Input employee data.	InputData
1. Compute current earnings.	Gross_Pay
2. Compute year-to-date earnings.	Total_Pay
3. Compute FICA tax.	FICA_Tax
4. Compute federal income tax withheld.	Fed_Tax
4.1 Compute adjusted pay.	Fed_Tax
4.2 Compute amount withheld for single employee.	TaxSingle
4.3 Compute amount withheld for married employee.	TaxMarried
5. Compute paycheck amount.	Net_Check
6. Display payroll information.	ShowPayroll

Table 5.11 Tasks and their procedures.

The User Interface

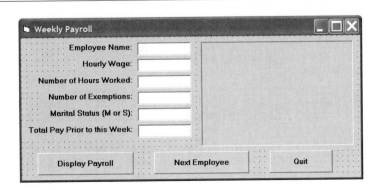

Figure 5.7 Template for entering payroll data.

Object	Property	Setting
frmPayroll	Caption	Weekly Payroll
lblName	Caption	Employee Name:
txtName	Text	(blank)
lblWage	Caption	Hourly Wage:
txtWage	Text	(blank)
lblHours	Caption	Number of Hours Worked:
txtHours	Text	(blank)
lblExempts	Caption	Number of Exemptions:
txtExempts	Text	(blank)
lblMarital	Caption	Marital Status (M or S):
txtMarital	Text	(blank)
lblPriorPay	Caption	Total Pay Prior to this Week:
txtPriorPay	Text	(blank)
cmdDisplay	Caption	Display Payroll
cmdNext	Caption	Next Employee
cmdQuit	Caption	Quit
picResults		

Table 5.12 Objects and initial properties for the weekly payroll program.

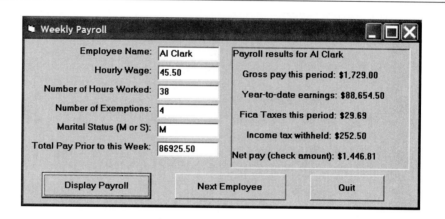

Figure 5.8 Sample run of weekly payroll program.

```
'Program to compute employees' weekly payroll
Const allowancePerExemption03 As Single = 58.65
Const wageBaseLimit03 As Single = 87000

Private Sub cmdDisplay_Click()
  Dim empName As String         'Name of employee
  Dim hrWage As Single          'Hourly wage
  Dim hrsWorked As Single       'Hours worked this week
  Dim exemptions As Integer     'Number of exemptions for employee
  Dim mStatus As String         'Marital status: S for Single; M for Married
  Dim prevPay As Single         'Total pay for year excluding this week
  Dim pay As Single             'This week's pay before taxes
  Dim totalPay As Single        'Total pay for year including this week
  Dim ficaTax As Single         'FICA taxes for this week
  Dim fedTax As Single          'Federal income tax withheld this week
```

```
    Dim check As Single          'Paycheck this week (take-home pay)
    'Obtain data, compute payroll, display results
    Call InputData(empName, hrWage, hrsWorked, exemptions, mStatus, prevPay) 'Task 0
    pay = Gross_Pay(hrWage, hrsWorked)                                        'Task 1
    totalPay = Total_Pay(prevPay, pay)                                       'Task 2
    ficaTax = FICA_Tax(pay, prevPay, totalPay)                              'Task 3
    fedTax = Fed_Tax(pay, exemptions, mStatus)                              'Task 4
    check = Net_Check(pay, ficaTax, fedTax)                                  'Task 5
    Call ShowPayroll(empName, pay, totalPay, ficaTax, fedTax, check)        'Task 6
End Sub

Private Sub cmdNext_Click()
  'Clear all text boxes for next employee's data
  txtName.Text = ""
  txtWage.Text = ""
  txtHours.Text = ""
  txtExempts.Text = ""
  txtMarital.Text = ""
  txtPriorPay.Text = ""
  picResults.Cls
End Sub

Private Sub cmdQuit_Click()
  End
End Sub

Private Sub InputData(empName As String, hrWage As Single, _
                      hrsWorked As Single, exemptions As Integer, _
                      mStatus As String, prevPay As Single)
  'Task 0: Get payroll data for employee
  empName = txtName.Text
  hrWage = Val(txtWage.Text)
  hrsWorked = Val(txtHours.Text)
  exemptions = Val(txtExempts.Text)
  mStatus = Left(UCase(txtMarital.Text), 1)    'M or S
  prevPay = Val(txtPriorPay.Text)
End Sub

Private Function Gross_Pay(hrWage As Single, hrsWorked As Single)
  'Task 1: Compute weekly pay before taxes
  If hrsWorked <= 40 Then
      Gross_Pay = hrsWorked * hrWage
    Else
      Gross_Pay = 40 * hrWage + (hrsWorked - 40) * 1.5 * hrWage
  End If
End Function

Private Function Total_Pay(prevPay As Single, pay As Single)
  'Task 2: Compute total pay before taxes
  Total_Pay = prevPay + pay
End Function
```

```
Private Function FICA_Tax(pay As Single, prevPay As Single, totalPay As Single)
   Dim socialSecurity As Single        'Social Security tax for this week
   Dim medicare As Single              'Medicare tax for this week
   'Task 3: Compute social security and medicare tax
   If totalPay <= wageBaseLimit03 Then
      socialSecurity = 0.062 * pay
   ElseIf prevPay < wageBaseLimit03 Then
      socialSecurity = 0.062 * (wageBaseLimit03 - prevPay)
   Else
      socialSecurity = 0
   End If
   medicare = 0.0145 * pay
   FICA_Tax = socialSecurity + medicare
   FICA_Tax = Round(FICA_Tax, 2)                'Round to nearest cent
End Function


Private Function Fed_Tax(pay As Single, exemptions As Integer, mStatus As String)
   Dim adjPay As Single
   'Task 4: Compute federal income tax
   adjPay = pay - (allowancePerExemption03 * exemptions) 'Task 4.1
   If adjPay < 0 Then
      adjPay = 0
   End If
   If mStatus = "S" Then
      Fed_Tax = TaxSingle(adjPay)                   'Task 4.2
   Else
      Fed_Tax = TaxMarried(adjPay)                  'Task 4.3
   End If
   Fed_Tax = Round(Fed_Tax, 2)                      'Round to nearest cent
End Function


Private Function Net_Check(pay As Single, ficaTax As Single, fedTax As Single)
   'Task 5: Compute amount of money given to employee
   Net_Check = pay - ficaTax - fedTax
End Function


Private Sub ShowPayroll(empName As String, pay As Single, _
      totalPay As Single, ficaTax As Single, fedTax As Single, check As Single)
   'Task 6: Display results of payroll computations
   picResults.Cls
   picResults.Print "Payroll results for "; empName
   picResults.Print
   picResults.Print "   Gross pay this period: "; FormatCurrency(pay)
   picResults.Print
   picResults.Print "    Year-to-date earnings: "; FormatCurrency(totalPay)
   picResults.Print
   picResults.Print "   Fica Taxes this period: "; FormatCurrency(ficaTax)
   picResults.Print
   picResults.Print "     Income tax withheld: "; FormatCurrency(fedTax)
   picResults.Print
   picResults.Print "Net pay (check amount): "; FormatCurrency(check)
End Sub
```

```
Private Function TaxSingle(adjPay As Single) As Single
  'Task 6.2: Compute federal tax for single person based on adjusted pay
  Select Case adjPay
    Case 0 To 51
      TaxSingle = 0
    Case 51 To 164
      TaxSingle = 0.1 * (adjPay - 51)
    Case 164 To 579
      TaxSingle = 11.3 + 0.15 * (adjPay - 164)
    Case 579 To 1268
      TaxSingle = 73.55 + 0.27 * (adjPay - 579)
    Case 1268 To 2792
      TaxSingle = 259.58 + 0.3 * (adjPay - 1268)
    Case 2792 To 6032
      TaxSingle = 716.78 + 0.35 * (adjPay - 2792)
    Case Is > 6032
      TaxSingle = 1850.78 + 0.386 * (adjPay - 6032)
  End Select
End Function

Private Function TaxMarried(adjPay As Single) As Single
  'Task 6.3: Compute federal tax for married person based on adjusted pay
  Select Case adjPay
    Case 0 To 124
      TaxMarried = 0
    Case 124 To 355
      TaxMarried = 0.1 * (adjPay - 124)
    Case 355 To 1007
      TaxMarried = 23.1 + 0.15 * (adjPay - 355)
    Case 1007 To 2150
      TaxMarried = 120.9 + 0.27 * (adjPay - 1007)
    Case 2150 To 3454
      TaxMarried = 429.51 + 0.3 * (adjPay - 2150)
    Case 3454 To 6093
      TaxMarried = 820.71 + 0.35 * (adjPay - 3454)
    Case Is > 6093
      TaxMarried = 1744.36 + 0.386 * (adjPay - 6093)
  End Select
End Function
```

Comments

1. In the function FICA_Tax, care has been taken to avoid computing Social Security benefits tax on income in excess of $87,000 per year. The logic of the program makes sure an employee whose income crosses the $87,000 threshold during a given week is taxed only on the difference between $87,000 and his previous year-to-date income.

2. The two functions TaxMarried and TaxSingle use Select Case to incorporate the tax brackets given in Tables 5.9 and 5.10 for the amount of federal income tax withheld. The upper limit of each Case clause is the same as the lower limit of the next Case clause. This ensures fractional values for adjPay, such as 51.50 in the TaxSingle function, will be properly treated as part of the higher salary range.

CHAPTER 5   SUMMARY

1. The *relational operators* are <, >, =, <>, <=, and >=.

2. The principal *logical operators* are And, Or, and Not.

3. A *condition* is an expression involving constants, variables, functions, and operators (arithmetic, relational, and/or logical) that can be evaluated as either True or False.

4. An If block decides what action to take depending on the truth values of one or more conditions. To allow several courses of action, the If and Else parts of an If statement can contain other If statements.

5. A Select Case block selects one of several actions depending on the value of an expression, called the *selector*. The entries in the *value lists* should have the same type (string or numeric) as the selector.

CHAPTER 5   PROGRAMMING PROJECTS

1. Table 5.13 gives the price schedule for Eddie's Equipment Rental. Full-day rentals cost one-and-a-half times half-day rentals. Write a program that displays Table 5.13 in a picture box when an appropriate command button is clicked and displays a bill in another picture box based on the item number and time period chosen by a customer. The bill should include a $30.00 deposit.

Piece of Equipment	Half-day	Full-day
1. Rug cleaner	$16.00	$24.00
2. Lawn mower	$12.00	$18.00
3. Paint sprayer	$20.00	$30.00

Table 5.13 Price schedule for Eddie's Equipment Rental.

A possible form layout and sample run is shown in Figure 5.9.

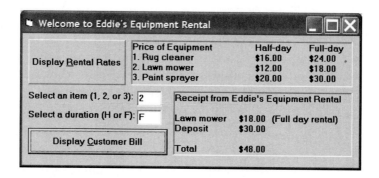

Figure 5.9 Form layout and sample run for Programming Project 1.

2. The American Heart Association suggests that at most 30 percent of the calories in our diet come from fat. Although food labels give the number of calories and amount of fat per serving, they often do not give the percentage of calories from fat. This percentage can be calculated by multiplying the number of grams of fat in one serving by 9, dividing that number by the total number of calories per serving, and multiplying the result by 100. Write a program that requests the name, number of calories per serving, and the grams of fat per serving as input, and tells us whether the food meets the American Heart Association recommendation. A sample run is as follows:

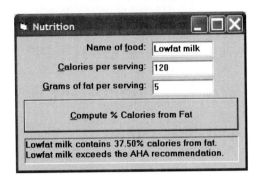

3. Table 5.14 gives the 2003 federal income tax rate schedule for single taxpayers. Write a program that requests taxable income and calculates the federal income tax. Use a Sub procedure for the input and a Function procedure to calculate the tax.

Taxable Income Over	But Not Over	Your Tax Is	Of Amount Over
$0	$6,000	10%	$0
$6,000	$28,400	$600 + 15%	$6,000
$28,400	$68,800	$3,960 + 27%	$28,400
$68,800	$143,500	$14,868 + 30%	$68,800
$143,500	$311,950	$37,278 + 35%	$143,500
$311,950		$96,235.50 + 38.6%	$311,950

Table 5.14 2003 federal income tax rates for single taxpayers.

4. Write a program to determine the real roots of the quadratic equation $ax^2 + bx + c = 0$ (where $a \neq 0$) after requesting the values of a, b, and c. Use a Sub procedure to ensure that a is nonzero. **Note:** The equation has 2, 1, or 0 solutions depending on whether the value of $b \wedge 2 - 4 * a * c$ is positive, zero, or negative. In the first two cases, the solutions are given by the quadratic formula $(-b \pm \text{Sqr}(b \wedge 2 - 4 * a * c)) / (2 * a)$. (Test the program with the following sets of coefficients.)

$a = 1$	$b = -11$	$c = 28$	Solutions are 4 and 7.
$a = 1$	$b = -6$	$c = 9$	Solution is 3.
$a = 1$	$b = 4$	$c = 5$	No solution.

5. Table 5.15 contains seven proverbs and their truth values. Write a program that presents these proverbs one at a time and asks the user to evaluate them as True or False. The program should then tell the user how many questions were answered correctly and display one of the following evaluations: Perfect (all correct), Excellent (5 or 6 correct), You might consider taking Psychology 101 (less than 5 correct).

Proverb	Truth Value
The squeaky wheel gets the grease.	True
Cry and you cry alone.	True
Opposites attract.	False
Spare the rod and spoil the child.	False
Actions speak louder than words.	True
Familiarity breeds contempt.	False
Marry in haste, repent at leisure.	True

Table 5.15 Seven proverbs.

Source: "You Know What They Say . . .," by Alfie Kohn, *Psychology Today*, April 1988.

6. Write a program to analyze a mortgage. The user should enter the amount of the loan, the annual rate of interest, and the duration of the loan in months. When the user clicks on the command button, the information that was entered should be checked to make sure it is reasonable. If bad data have been supplied, the user should be so advised. Otherwise, the monthly payment and the total amount of interest paid should be displayed. The formula for the monthly payment is

```
payment = p * r / (1 - (1 + r) ^ (-n))
```

where p is the amount of the loan, r is the monthly interest rate (annual rate divided by 12) given as a number between 0 (for 0 percent) and 1 (for 100 percent), and n is the duration of the loan. The formula for the total interest paid is

```
total interest = n * payment - p
```

(Test the program for a mortgage of $240,000 at 6% annual rate of interest, and duration 360 months. Such a mortgage will have a monthly payment of $1,438.92 and total interest of $278,011.65.)

7. Write a program using the form in Figure 5.10. Each time the command button is pressed, Rnd is used to simulate a coin toss and the values are updated. The figure shows the status after 35 coin tosses. **Note:** You can produce tosses quickly by just holding down the Enter key. Although the percentage of heads initially will fluctuate considerably, it should stay close to 50% after many (say, 1000) tosses.

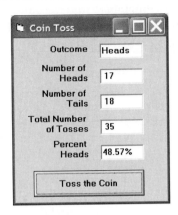

Figure 5.10 Form for Programming Project 7.

8. *Five, Six, Pick up Sticks* Write a program that allows the user to challenge the computer to a game of Pick-Up-Sticks. Here is how the game works. The user chooses the number of matchsticks (from 5 to 60) to place in a pile. Then, the computer chooses who will go first. At each turn, the contestant can remove one, two, or three matchsticks from the pile. The contestant who chooses the last matchstick loses. The computer should randomly select the contestant to go first. When the pile has four or fewer matchsticks remaining, the computer should make an intelligent choice. Until then, the computer should just randomly determine the number of matchsticks to select. After writing the program, play a few games with the computer. Hopefully you will win some of the time. Figure 5.11 shows a possible last move for the game.

Figure 5.11 A possible outcome of the program.

Write a second program that is similar to the one described above, but replace the random selections with intelligent selections. The computer should make the user always select from a pile where the number of matchsticks has a remainder of 1 when divided by 4. For instance, if the user initially chooses a number of matchsticks that has a remainder of 1 when divided by 4, then the computer should have the user go first. Otherwise, the computer should go first and remove the proper number of matchsticks. [**Note:** The remainder when n is divided by 4 is (n Mod 4).] After writing the program, play a few games with the computer and observe that the computer will always win.

9. Write a program to find the day of the week for any date after 1582, the year our current calendar was introduced. The program should

(a) Request the year and the number of the month as input.

(b) Determine the number of days in the month. *Note:* All years divisible by 4 are leap years, with the exception of those years divisible by 100 and not by 400. For instance, 1600 and 2000 are leap years, but 1700, 1800, and 1900 are not.

(c) Request the number of the day as input. The GotFocus event procedure for the day text box should cause the day label to list the possible range for the numbers of the day.

(d) Determine the day of the week with the following algorithm.

(1) Treat January as the 13th month and February as the 14th month of the previous year. For example, 1/23/2003 should be converted to 13/23/2002 and 2/6/2004 should be converted to 14/6/2003.

(2) Denote the number of the day, month, and year by d, m, and y, respectively. Compute

$$w = d + 2*m + Int(.6 * (m+1)) + y + Int(y/4) - Int(y/100) + Int(y/400) + 2$$

(3) The remainder when w is divided by 7 is the day of the week of the given date, with Saturday as the zeroth day of the week, Sunday the first day of the week, Monday the second, and so on.

A sample run of the program appears in Figure 5.12.

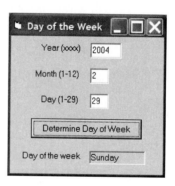

Figure 5.12 A possible run for Programming Project 8.

Test the program with the following memorable dates in the history of the U.S. space program.

On Tuesday, February 20, 1962, John Glenn became the first American to orbit the earth.

On Sunday, July 20, 1969, Neil Armstrong became the first person to set foot on the moon.

On Saturday, June 18, 1983, Sally Ride became the first American woman to travel in space.

6 Repetition

6.1 DO LOOPS

A **loop**, one of the most important structures in Visual Basic, is used to repeat a sequence of statements a number of times. At each repetition, or **pass**, the statements act upon variables whose values are changing.

The **Do loop** repeats a sequence of statements either as long as or until a certain condition is true. A Do statement precedes the sequence of statements, and a Loop statement follows the sequence of statements. The condition, preceded by either the word While or the word Until, follows the word Do or the word Loop. When Visual Basic executes a Do loop of the form

```
Do While condition
  statement(s)
Loop
```

it first checks the truth value of *condition*. If *condition* is false, then the statements inside the loop are not executed, and the program continues with the line after the Loop statement. If *condition* is true, then the statements inside the loop are executed. When the statement Loop is encountered, the entire process is repeated, beginning with the testing of *condition* in the Do While statement. In other words, the statements inside the loop are repeatedly executed only as long as (that is, while) the condition is true. Figure 6.1 contains the pseudocode and flowchart for this loop.

Do While condition is true
    Processing step(s)
Loop

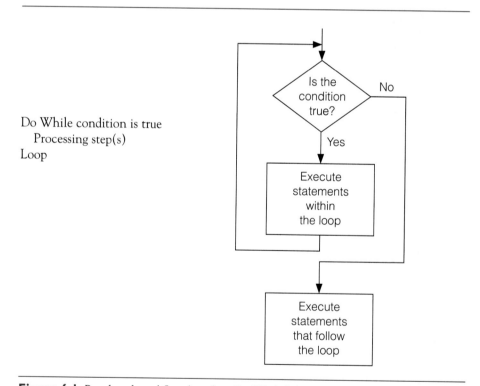

Figure 6.1 Pseudocode and flowchart for a Do While loop.

EXAMPLE 1 The following program, in which the condition in the Do loop is "num <= 10", displays the numbers from 1 through 10.

```
Private Sub cmdDisplay_Click()
  Dim num As Integer
  'Display the numbers from 1 to 10
  num = 1
  Do While num <= 10
    picNumbers.Print num;
    num = num + 1
  Loop
End Sub
```

[Run, and click the command button. The following is displayed in the picture box.]

```
1  2  3  4  5  6  7  8  9  10
```

Do loops are commonly used to ensure that a proper response is received from the InputBox function.

EXAMPLE 2 The following program requires the user to give a password before a secret file can be accessed.

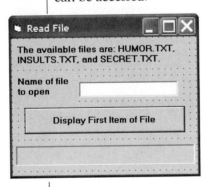

Object	Property	Setting
frm6_1_2	Caption	Read File
lblFiles	Caption	The available files are: HUMOR.TXT, INSULTS.TXT, and SECRET.TXT.
lblName	Caption	Name of file to open
txtName	Text	(blank)
cmdDisplay	Caption	Display First Item of File
picItem		

```
Private Sub cmdDisplay_Click()
  Dim passWord As String, info As String
  If UCase(txtName.Text) = "SECRET.TXT" Then
      passWord = ""
      Do While passWord <> "SHAZAM"
        passWord = InputBox("What is the password?")
        passWord = UCase(passWord)
      Loop
  End If
  Open txtName.Text For Input As #1
  Input #1, info
  picItem.Cls
  picItem.Print info
  Close #1
End Sub
```

[Run, type SECRET.TXT into the text box, and click the command button.]

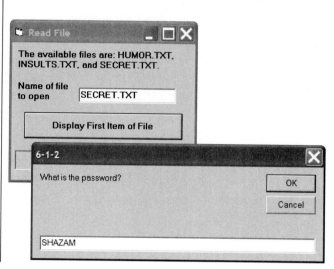

In Examples 1 and 2 the condition was checked at the top of the loop—that is, before the statements were executed. Alternatively, the condition can be checked at the bottom of the loop when the statement Loop is reached. When Visual Basic encounters a Do loop of the form

```
Do
    statement(s)
Loop Until condition
```

it executes the statements inside the loop and then checks the truth value of *condition*. If *condition* is true, then the program continues with the line after the Loop statement. If *condition* is false, then the entire process is repeated beginning with the Do statement. In other words, the statements inside the loop are executed once and then are repeatedly executed *until* the condition is true. Figure 6.2 shows the pseudocode and flowchart for this type of Do loop.

Do
    statement(s)
Loop Until condition is true

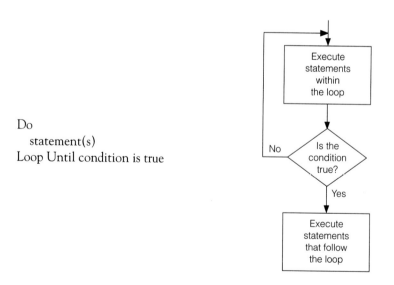

Figure 6.2 Pseudocode and flowchart for a Do loop with condition tested at the bottom.

EXAMPLE 3
The following program is equivalent to Example 2, except that the condition is tested at the bottom of the loop.

```
Private Sub cmdDisplay_Click()
  Dim passWord As String, info As String
  If UCase(txtName.Text) = "SECRET.TXT" Then
      Do
        passWord = InputBox("What is the password?")
        passWord = UCase(passWord)
      Loop Until passWord = "SHAZAM"
  End If
  Open txtName.Text For Input As #1
  Input #1, info
  picItem.Cls
  picItem.Print info
  Close #1
End Sub
```

Do loops allow us to calculate useful quantities for which we might not know a simple formula.

EXAMPLE 4
Suppose you deposit money into a savings account and let it accumulate at 7 percent interest compounded annually. The following program determines when you will be a millionaire.

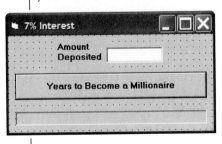

Object	Property	Setting
frmInterest	Caption	7% Interest
lblAmount	Caption	Amount Deposited
txtAmount	Text	(blank)
cmdYears	Caption	Years to Become a Millionaire
picWhen		

```
Private Sub cmdYears_Click()
  Dim balance As Single, numYears As Integer
  'Compute years required to become a millionaire
  picWhen.Cls
  balance = Val(txtAmount.Text)
  numYears = 0
  Do While balance < 1000000
    balance = balance + .07 * balance
    numYears = numYears + 1
  Loop
  picWhen.Print "In"; numYears; "years you will have a million dollars."
End Sub
```

[Run, type 10000 into the text box, and press the command button.]

Comments

1. Be careful to avoid infinite loops—that is, loops that are never exited. The following loop is infinite, because the condition "num < > 0" will always be true. *Note:* The loop can be terminated by pressing Ctrl+Break.

```
Private Sub cmdButton_Click()
    Dim num As Single
    'An infinite loop
    num = 7
    Do While num <> 0
        num = num - 2
    Loop
End Sub
```

Notice that this slip-up can be avoided by changing the condition to "num >= 0".

2. The statements between Do and Loop do not have to be indented. However, because indenting improves the readability of the program, it is regarded as good programming style. As soon as you see the word Do, your eyes can easily scan down the program to find the matching Loop statement. You know immediately the size of the loop.

3. Visual Basic allows the use of the words While and Until either at the top or bottom of a Do loop. In this text, the usage of these words is restricted for the following reasons.

   (a) Because any While statement can be easily converted to an Until statement and vice versa, the restriction produces no loss of capabilities and the programmer has one less matter to think about.
   (b) Restricting the use simplifies reading the program. The word While proclaims testing at the top, and the word Until proclaims testing at the bottom.
   (c) Certain other major structured languages only allow While at the top and Until at the bottom of a loop. Therefore, following this convention will make life easier for people already familiar with or planning to learn one of these languages.
   (d) Standard pseudocode uses the word While to denote testing a loop at the top and the word Until to denote testing at the bottom.

4. Good programming practice requires that all variables appearing in a Do loop be assigned values before the loop is entered rather than relying on

default values. For instance, the code at the left in what follows should be replaced with the code at the right.

```
'Add 1 through 10
Do While num < 10
  num = num + 1
  sum = sum + num
Loop
```

```
'Add 1 through 10
num = 0
sum = 0
Do While num < 10
    num = num + 1
    sum = sum + num
Loop
```

✔ **PRACTICE PROBLEMS 6.1**

1. How do you decide whether a condition should be checked at the top of a loop or at the bottom?

2. Change the following loop so it will be executed at least once.

```
Do While continue = "Yes"
  answer = InputBox("Do you want to continue? (Y or N)")
  If UCase(answer) = "Y" Then
      continue = "Yes"
    Else
      continue = "No"
  End If
Loop
```

➤ **EXERCISES 6.1**

In Exercises 1 through 6, determine the output displayed in the picture box when the command button is clicked.

1. ```
Private Sub cmdDisplay_Click()
  Dim q As Single
  q = 3
  Do While q < 15
    q = 2 * q - 1
  Loop
  picOutput.Print q
End Sub
```

2. ```
Private Sub cmdDisplay_Click()
  Dim balance As Single, interest As Single, n As Integer
  balance = 1000
  interest = .1
  n = 0                'Number of years
  Do
    picOutput.Print n; balance
    balance = (1 + interest) * balance
    n = n + 1
  Loop Until balance > 1200
  picOutput.Print n
End Sub
```

3.
```
Private Sub cmdDisplay_Click()
    Dim num As Single, message As String
    'Display a message
    num = 4
    Do
      Select Case num
        Case 1
          message = "grammer!"
          num = -1
        Case 2
          message = "re a su"
          num = (5 - num) * (3 - num)
        Case 3
          message = "per pro"
          num = 4 - num
        Case 4
          message = "You a"
          num = 2 * num - 6
      End Select
      picOutput.Print message;
    Loop Until num = -1
End Sub
```

4.
```
Private Sub cmdQuiz_Click()
    Dim prompt As String, firstYear As Integer
    'Computer-assisted instruction
    prompt = "In what year was the IBM PC first produced?"
    Do
      firstYear = Val(InputBox(prompt))
      Select Case firstYear
        Case 1981
          picQuiz.Print "Correct. The computer was an instant"
          picQuiz.Print "success. By the end of 1981, there was"
          picQuiz.Print "such a backlog of orders that customers"
          picQuiz.Print "had a three-month waiting period."
        Case Is < 1981
          picQuiz.Print "Later. The Apple II computer, which"
          picQuiz.Print "preceded the IBM PC, appeared in 1977."
        Case Is > 1981
          picQuiz.Print "Earlier. The first successful IBM PC clone,"
          picQuiz.Print "the Compaq Portable, appeared in 1983."
      End Select
      picQuiz.Print
    Loop Until firstYear = 1981
End Sub
```

(Assume that the first response is *1980* and the second response is *1981*.)

5.
```
Private Sub cmdDisplay_Click()
    'Calculate the remainder in long division
    picOutput.Print Remainder(3, 17)
End Sub
```

```
Private Function Remainder(divisor As Single, dividend As Single) As Single
  Dim sum As Single
  sum = 0
  Do While sum <= dividend
    sum = sum + divisor
  Loop
  Remainder = dividend - sum + divisor
End Function
```

6.
```
Private Sub cmdDisplay_Click()
  Dim info As String, counter As Integer, letter As String
  'Simulate InStr; search for the letter t
  info = "Potato"
  counter = 0
  letter = ""
  Do While (letter <> "t") And (counter < Len(info))
    counter = counter + 1
    letter = Mid(info, counter, 1)
    If letter = "t" Then
        picOutput.Print counter
    End If
  Loop
  If letter <> "t" Then
      picOutput.Print 0
  End If
End Sub
```

In Exercises 7 through 10, identify the errors.

7.
```
Private Sub cmdDisplay_Click()
  Dim q As Single
  q = 1
  Do While q > 0
    q = 3 * q - 1
    picOutput.Print q;
  Loop
End Sub
```

8.
```
Private Sub cmdDisplay_Click()
  Dim num As Integer
  'Display the numbers from 1 to 5
  Do While num <> 5
    num = 1
    picOutput.Print num;
    num = num + 1
  Loop
End Sub
```

9.
```
Private Sub cmdDisplay_Click()
  Dim answer As String
  'Repeat until a yes response is given
  Loop
    answer = InputBox("Did you chop down the cherry tree (Y/N)?")
  Do Until UCase(answer) = "Y"
End Sub
```

```
10. Private Sub cmdDisplay_Click()
      Dim n As Integer, answer As String
      'Repeat as long as desired
      Do
        n = n + 1
        picOutput.Print n
        answer = InputBox("Do you want to continue (Y/N)?")
      Until UCase(answer) = "Y"
    End Sub
```

In Exercises 11 through 20, replace each phrase containing Until with an equivalent phrase containing While, and vice versa. For instance, the phrase Until sum = 100 would be replaced by While sum < > 100.

11. Until num < 7

12. Until nom = "Bob"

13. While response = "Y"

14. While total = 10

15. While nom <> ""

16. Until balance >= 100

17. While (a > 1) And (a < 3)

18. Until (ans = "") Or (n = 0)

19. Until Not (n = 0)

20. While (ans = "Y") And (n < 7)

In Exercises 21 and 22, write simpler and clearer code that performs the same task as the given code.

```
21. Private Sub cmdDisplay_Click()
      Dim nom As String
      nom = InputBox("Enter a name:")
      picOutput.Print nom
      nom = InputBox("Enter a name:")
      picOutput.Print nom
      nom = InputBox("Enter a name:")
      picOutput.Print nom
    End Sub
```

```
22. Private Sub cmdDisplay_Click()
      Dim loopNum As Integer, answer As String
      loopNum = 0
      Do
        If loopNum >= 1 Then
            answer = InputBox("Do you want to continue (Y/N)?")
            answer = UCase(answer)
          Else
            answer = "Y"
        End If
        If (answer = "Y") Or (loopNum = 0) Then
            loopNum = loopNum + 1
            picOutput.Print loopNum
        End If
      Loop Until answer <> "Y"
    End Sub
```

23. Write a program that displays a Celsius-to-Fahrenheit conversion table. Entries in the table should range from −40 to 40 degrees Celsius in increments of 5 degrees. *Note:* The formula $f = (9/5) * c + 32$ converts Celsius to Fahrenheit.

24. World population doubled from 3 billion in 1959 to 6 billion in 1999. If we assume that the world population has been doubling every 40 years, write a program to determine in what year the world population would have been less than 6 million.

25. Recall that the function Rnd has a random value between 0 and 1 (excluding 1), and so the expression Int(6*Rnd)+1 has a random whole number value between 1 and 6. Write a program that repeatedly "throws" a pair of dice and tallies the number of tosses and the number of those tosses that total (lucky) seven. The program should stop when 100 lucky sevens have been tossed. The program should then report the approximate odds of tossing a lucky seven. (The odds will be "1 in" followed by the result of dividing the number of tosses by the number of tosses that came up lucky sevens.)

26. Write a program to display all the numbers between 1 and 100 that are perfect squares. (A perfect square is an integer that is the square of another integer; 1, 4, and 16 are examples of perfect squares.)

27. Write a program to display all the numbers between 1 and 100 that are part of the Fibonacci sequence. The Fibonacci sequence begins 1, 1, 2, 3, 5, 8, . . . , where each new number in the sequence is found by adding the previous two numbers in the sequence.

28. The world population reached 6.3 billion people in 2003 and is growing at the rate of 1.2 percent each year. Assuming that the population will continue to grow at the same rate, write a program to determine when the population will reach 10 billion.

29. An old grandfather clock reads 6:00 p.m. Sometime not too long after 6:30 p.m., the minute hand will pass directly over the hour hand. Write a program using a loop to make better and better guesses as to what time it is when the hands exactly overlap. Keep track of the positions of both hands using the minutes at which they are pointing. (At 6:00 p.m., the minute hand points at 0 while the hour hand points at 30.) You will need to use the fact that when the minute hand advances m minutes, the hour hand advances $m/12$ minutes. (For example, when the minute hand advances 60 minutes, the hour hand advances 5 minutes from one hour mark to the next.) To make an approximation, record how far the minute hand is behind the hour hand, then advance the minute hand by this much and the hour hand by $1/12$ this much. The loop should terminate when the resulting positions of the minute and hour hands differ by less than .0001 minute. (The exact answer is 32 and 8/11 minutes after 6.)

30. Write a program that requests a word containing the two letters r and n as input and determines which of the two letters appears first. If the word does not contain both of the letters, the program should so advise the user. (Test the program with the words *colonel* and *merriment*.)

31. The coefficient of restitution of a ball, a number between 0 and 1, specifies how much energy is conserved when a ball hits a rigid surface. A coefficient of .9, for instance, means a bouncing ball will rise to 90 percent of its previous height after each bounce. Write a program to input a coefficient of restitution and an initial height in meters, and report how many times a ball bounces when dropped from its initial height before it rises to a height of less than 10 centimeters. Also report the total distance traveled by the ball before this point. The coefficients of restitution of a tennis ball, basketball, super ball, and softball are .7, .75, .9, and .3, respectively.

In Exercises 32 through 35, write a program to solve the stated problem.

32. *Savings Account.* $15,000 is deposited into a savings account paying 5 percent interest and $1000 is withdrawn from the account at the end of each year. Approximately how many years are required for the savings account to be depleted? (**Note:** If at the end of a certain year the balance is $1000 or less, then the final withdrawal will consist of that balance and the account will be depleted.)

33. Rework Exercise 32 so that the amount of money deposited initially is input by the user and the program computes the number of years required to deplete the account. **Note:** Be careful to avoid infinite loops.

34. Consider an account in which $1000 is deposited upon opening the account and an additional $1000 is deposited at the end of each year. If the money earns interest at the rate of 5 percent, how long will it take before the account contains at least $1 million?

35. A person born in 1980 can claim, "I will be *x* years old in the year *x* squared." Write a program to determine the value of *x*.

36. Illustrate the growth of money in a savings account. When the user presses the command button, values for Amount and Interest Rate are obtained from text boxes and used to calculate the number of years until the money doubles and the number of years until the money reaches a million dollars. Use the form design shown below. **Note:** The balance at the end of each year is $(1 + r)$ times the previous balance, where r is the annual rate of interest in decimal form. Use Do loops to determine the number of years.

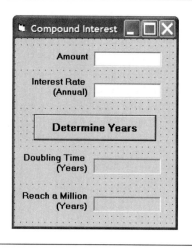

Object	Property	Setting
frmInterest	Caption	Compound Interest
lblAmount	Caption	Amount
txtAmount	Text	(blank)
lblRate	Caption	Interest Rate (Annual)
txtRate	Text	(blank)
cmdDetermine	Caption	Determine Years
lblDouble	Caption	Doubling Time (Years)
picDouble		
lblMillion	Caption	Reach a Million (Years)
picMillion		

Form for Exercise 36   Objects and Properties for Exercise 36

37. Allow the user to enter a sentence. Then, depending on which command button the user clicks, display the sentence entirely in capital letters or with just the first letter of each word capitalized.

In Exercises 38 and 39, write a program corresponding to the flowchart.

38. The flowchart in Figure 6.3 requests an integer greater than 1 as input and factors it into a product of prime numbers. (**Note:** A number is prime if its only factors are 1 and itself. Test the program with the numbers 660 and 139.)

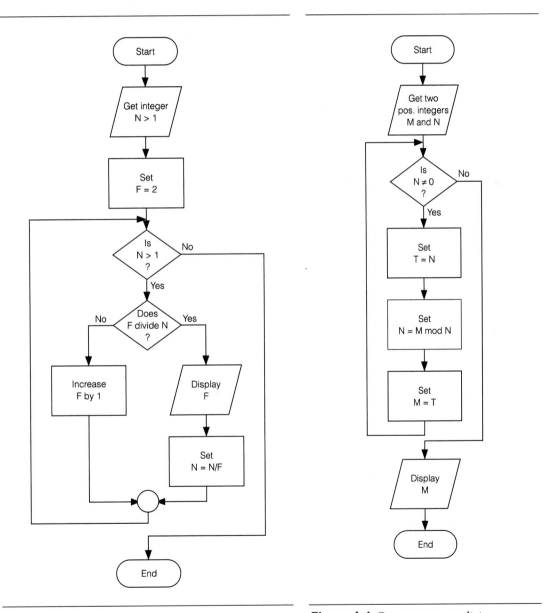

Figure 6.3 Prime factors.

Figure 6.4 Greatest common divisor.

39. The flowchart in Figure 6.4 finds the greatest common divisor (the largest integer that divides both) of two positive integers input by the user. Write a program that corresponds to the flowchart.

Solutions to Practice Problems 6.1

1. As a rule of thumb, the condition is checked at the bottom if the loop should be executed at least once.

2. Either precede the loop with the statement `continue = "Yes"`, or change the first line to `Do` and replace the Loop statement with `Loop Until continue <> "Yes"`.

6.2 PROCESSING LISTS OF DATA WITH DO LOOPS

One of the main applications of programming is the processing of lists of data. Do loops are used to display all or selected items from lists, search lists for specific items, and perform calculations on the numerical entries of a list. This section introduces several devices that facilitate working with lists. **Counters** calculate the number of elements in lists, **accumulators** sum numerical values in lists, **flags** record whether certain events have occurred, and the **EOF function** is used to determine when the end of a text file has been reached. **Nested loops** add yet another dimension to repetition.

EOF Function

Data to be processed are often retrieved from a file by a Do loop. Visual Basic has a useful function, EOF, that will tell us if we have reached the end of the file from which we are reading. Suppose a file has been opened with reference number n. At any time, the condition

`EOF(n)`

will be true if the end of the file has been reached, and false otherwise.

One of the programs I wrote when I got my first personal computer in 1982 stored a list of names and phone numbers and printed a phone directory. I first had the program display the directory on the screen and later changed the picNumbers.Print statements to Printer.Print statements to produce a printed copy. I stored the names in a file so I could easily add, change, or delete entries.

EXAMPLE 1   The following program displays the contents of a telephone directory. The names and phone numbers are contained in the file PHONE.TXT. The loop will repeat as long as the end of the file is not reached.

PHONE.TXT contains the following four lines:

"Bert", "123-4567"
"Ernie", "987-6543"
"Grover", "246-8321"
"Oscar", "135-7900"

Object	Property	Setting
frmPhone	Caption	Directory
cmdDisplay	Caption	Display Phone Numbers
picNumbers		

```
Private Sub cmdDisplay_Click()
  Dim nom As String, phoneNum As String
  picNumbers.Cls
  Open "PHONE.TXT" For Input As #1
  Do While Not EOF(1)
    Input #1, nom, phoneNum
    picNumbers.Print nom, phoneNum
  Loop
  Close #1
End Sub
```

[Run, and press the command button.]

The program in Example 1 illustrates the proper way to process a list of data contained in a file. The Do loop should be tested at the top with an end-of-file condition. (If the file is empty, no attempt is made to input data from the file.) The first set of data should be input *after* the Do statement, and then the data should be processed. Figure 6.5 contains the pseudocode and flowchart for this technique.

```
Do While there are still data in the file
   Get an item of data
   Process the item
Loop
```

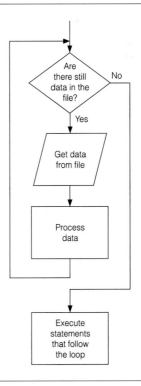

Figure 6.5 Pseudocode and flowchart for processing data from a file.

Text files can be quite large. Rather than list the entire contents, we typically search the file for a specific piece of information.

EXAMPLE 2 The following program modifies the program in Example 1 to search the telephone directory for a name specified by the user. If the name does not appear in the directory, the user is so notified. We want to keep searching as long as there is no match *and* we have not reached the end of the list. Therefore, the condition for the Do While statement is a compound logical expression with the operator And. After the last pass through the loop, we will know whether the name was found and be able to display the requested information.

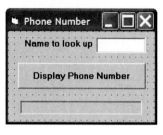

Object	Property	Setting
frmPhone	Caption	Phone Number
lblName	Caption	Name to look up
txtName	Text	(blank)
cmdDisplay	Caption	Display Phone Number
picNumber		

```
Private Sub cmdDisplay_Click()
  Dim nom As String, phoneNum As String
  Open "PHONE.TXT" For Input As #1
  nom = ""
  Do While (nom <> txtName.Text) And (Not EOF(1))
    Input #1, nom, phoneNum
  Loop
  Close #1
  picNumber.Cls
  If nom = txtName.Text Then
      picNumber.Print nom, phoneNum
    Else
      picNumber.Print "Name not found."
  End If
End Sub
```

[Run, type Grover into the text box, and press the command button.]

Counters and Accumulators

A **counter** is a numeric variable that keeps track of the number of items that have been processed. An **accumulator** is a numeric variable that totals numbers.

EXAMPLE 3   The following program counts and finds the value of coins listed in a file. The file COINS.TXT contains the following entries: 1, 1, 5, 10, 10, 25. The fourth and fifth lines of the event procedure are not needed since the counter *numCoins* and the accumulator *sum* have the initial value 0 by default. However, since these default values show the starting points for the two variables, the two assignment statements add clarity to the program.

Object	Property	Setting
frmCoins	Caption	Coins
cmdAnalyze	Caption	Analyze Change
picValue		

```
Private Sub cmdAnalyze_Click()
  Dim numCoins As Integer, sum As Single, value As Single
  Open "COINS.TXT" For Input As #1
  numCoins = 0
  sum = 0
  Do While Not EOF(1)
    Input #1, value
    numCoins = numCoins + 1
    sum = sum + value
  Loop
  picValue.Cls
  picValue.Print "The value of the"; numCoins; "coins is"; sum; "cents."
  Close #1
End Sub
```

[Run, and press the command button.]

The value of the counter, *numCoins*, was initially 0 and changed on each execution of the loop to 1, 2, 3, 4, 5, and finally 6. The accumulator, *sum*, initially had the value 0 and increased with each execution of the loop to 1, 2, 7, 17, 27, and finally 52.

Flags

A **flag** is a variable that keeps track of whether a certain situation has occurred. The data type most suited to flags is the **Boolean data type**. Variables of type Boolean can assume just two values—True and False. (As a default, Boolean variables are initialized to False.) Flags are used within loops to provide information that will be utilized after the loop terminates. Flags also provide an alternative method of terminating a loop.

EXAMPLE 4

The following program counts the number of words in the file WORDS.TXT and then reports whether the words are in alphabetical order. In each execution of the loop, a word is compared to the next word in the list. The flag variable, called *orderFlag*, is initially assigned the value True and is set to False if a pair of adjacent words is out of order. The technique used in this program will be used in Chapter 7 when we study sorting. **Note:** The first time through the loop, the value of *word1* is the empty string. Each word must first be read into the variable *word2*.

WORDS.TXT contains the following winning words from the U.S. National Spelling Bee:

"cambist", "croissant", "deification"
"hydrophyte", "incisor", "maculature"
"macerate", "narcolepsy", "shallon"

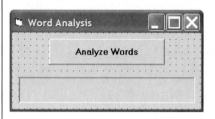

Object	Property	Setting
frmWords	Caption	Word Analysis
cmdAnalyze	Caption	Analyze Words
picReport		

```
Private Sub cmdAnalyze_Click()
  Dim orderFlag As Boolean, wordCounter As Integer
  Dim word1 As String, word2 As String
  'Count words.  Are they in alphabetical order?
  orderFlag = True
  wordCounter = 0
  word1 = ""
  Open "WORDS.TXT" For Input As #1
  Do While Not EOF(1)
    Input #1, word2
    wordCounter = wordCounter + 1
    If word1 > word2 Then     'Two words are out of order
        orderFlag = False
    End If
    word1 = word2
  Loop
  Close #1
  picReport.Print "The number of words is"; wordCounter
  If orderFlag = True Then
      picReport.Print "The words are in alphabetical order."
    Else
      picReport.Print "The words are not in alphabetical order."
  End If
End Sub
```

[Run, and press the command button.]

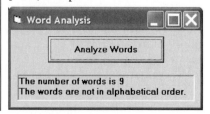

Nested Loops

The statements within a Do loop can contain another Do loop. Such a configuration is referred to as **nested loops** and is useful in repeating a single data-processing routine several times.

EXAMPLE 5 The following modification of the program in Example 2 allows the user to look through several lists of names. Suppose we have several different phone directories, the names of which are listed in the file LISTS.TXT. (For instance, the file LISTS.TXT might contain the entries CLIENTS.TXT, FRIENDS.TXT, and KINFOLK.TXT.) A sought-after name might be in any one of the files. The statements in the inner Do loop will be used to look up names as before. At least one pass through the outer Do loop is guaranteed and passes will continue as long as the name is not found and phone lists remain to be examined.

```
Private Sub cmdDisplay_Click()
  Dim foundFlag As Boolean, fileName As String
  Dim nom As String, phoneNum As String
  Open "LISTS.TXT" For Input As #1
  foundFlag = False
  nom = ""
  Do While (foundFlag = False) And (Not EOF(1))
    Input #1, fileName
    Open fileName For Input As #2
    Do While (nom <> txtName.Text) And (Not EOF(2))
      Input #2, nom, phoneNum
    Loop
    Close #2
    picNumber.Cls
    If nom = txtName.Text Then
        picNumber.Print nom, phoneNum
        foundFlag = True
    End If
  Loop
  Close #1
  If foundFlag = False Then
      picNumber.Print "Name not found."
  End If
End Sub
```

Comments

1. In Appendix D, the section "Stepping Through a Program Containing a Do Loop: Chapter 6" uses the Visual Basic debugging tools to trace the flow through a Do loop.

2. When *flagVar* is a variable of Boolean type, the statements

   ```
   If flagVar = True Then   and   If flagVar = False Then
   ```

   can be replaced by

   ```
   If flagVar Then   and   If Not flagVar Then
   ```

Similarly, the statements

```
Do While flagVar = True  and  Do While flagVar = False
```

can be replaced by

```
Do While flagVar  and  Do While Not flagVar
```

✔ **PRACTICE PROBLEMS 6.2**

1. Determine the output of the following program, where the file SCORES.TXT contains the scores 150, 200, and 300.

```
Private Sub cmdComputeTotal_Click()
  Dim sum As Single, score As Single
  'Find the sum of a collection of bowling scores
  sum = 0
  Open "SCORES.TXT" For Input As #1
  Input #1, score
  Do While Not EOF(1)
    sum = sum + score
    Input #1, score
  Loop
  Close #1
  picTotal.Print sum
End Sub
```

2. Why didn't the preceding program produce the intended output?

3. Correct the preceding program so it has the intended output.

➤ **EXERCISES 6.2**

In Exercises 1 through 10, determine the output displayed in the picture box when the command button is clicked.

```
1. Private Sub cmdDisplay_Click()
   Dim total As Single, num As Single
   total = 0
   Open "DATA.TXT" For Input As #1
   Do While Not EOF(1)
     Input #1, num
     total = total + num
   Loop
   Close #1
   picOutput.Print total
 End Sub
```

(Assume that the file DATA.TXT contains the following entries.)

5, 2, 6

2.
```
Private Sub cmdDisplay_Click()
    Dim nom As String
    Open "DATA.TXT" For Input As #1
    Do While Not EOF(1)
      Input #1, nom
      picOutput.Print nom
    Loop
    Close #1
End Sub
```

(Assume that the file DATA.TXT contains the following entries.)

"Roxie", "Velma"

3.
```
Private Sub cmdDisplay_Click()
    Dim dessert As String
    'Display list of desserts
    Open "DESSERTS.TXT" For Input As #1
    Do While Not EOF(1)
      Input #1, dessert
      picOutput.Print dessert
    Loop
    Close #1
End Sub
```

(Assume that the file DESSERTS.TXT contains the following entries.)

"pie", "cake", "melon"

4.
```
Private Sub cmdDisplay_Click()
    Dim city As String, pop As Single
    Open "CITYPOPS.TXT" For Input As #1
    Do While Not EOF(1)
      Input #1, city, pop
      If pop >= 7 Then
          picOutput.Print city, pop
      End If
    Loop
    Close #1
End Sub
```

(Assume that the file CITYPOPS.TXT contains the following four lines that give a metropolitan area and its population in millions.)

"San Francisco", 6.8
"Boston", 5.6
"Chicago", 8.8
"New York", 20.1

5.
```
Private Sub cmdDisplay_Click()
    Dim firstLetter As String, fruit As String
    firstLetter = ""
    Open "FRUITS.TXT" For Input As #1
    Do While Not EOF(1)
      Input #1, fruit
```

```
            If Left(fruit, 1) <> firstLetter Then
                If firstLetter <> "" Then
                    picOutput.Print
                End If
                firstLetter = Left(fruit, 1)
                picOutput.Print Tab(3); firstLetter
            End If
            picOutput.Print fruit
        Loop
        Close #1
    End Sub
```

(Assume that the file FRUITS.TXT contains the following entries.)

"Apple", "Apricot", "Avocado", "Banana", "Blueberry", "Grape", "Lemon", "Lime"

6.
```
Private Sub cmdDisplay_Click()
    Dim num As Single
    'Display list of numbers
    Open "DATA.TXT" For Input As #1
    Input #1, num
    Do While Not EOF(1)
        picOutput.Print num;
        Input #1, num
    Loop
    Close #1
End Sub
```

(Assume that the file DATA.TXT contains the following entries.)

2, 3, 8, 5

7.
```
Private Sub cmdDisplay_Click()
    Dim animal As String, groupName As String
    Call InputAnimal(animal)
    If animal <> "" Then
        Call SearchList(animal, groupName)
        Call DisplayResult(animal, groupName)
    End If
End Sub

Private Sub DisplayResult(anml As String, gName As String)
    If gName = "" Then
        picOutput.Print "Animal not found."
    Else
        picOutput.Print "A group of "; anml; "s is called a "; gName
    End If
End Sub

Private Sub InputAnimal(anml As String)
    'Request the name of an animal as input
    anml = InputBox("Please enter the name of an animal.")
End Sub

Private Sub SearchList(anml As String, gName As String)
    Dim creature As String, groupName As String
    creature = ""
```

```
      Open "ANIMALS.TXT" For Input As #1
      Do While (creature <> anml) And Not EOF(1)
        Input #1, creature, groupName
      Loop
      If EOF(1) Then
          gName = ""
        Else
          gName = groupName
      End If
      Close #1
    End Sub
```

(Assume that the file ANIMALS.TXT contains the following three lines that give an animal and the name of a group of those animals. Assume the response is *duck*.)

"lion", "pride"
"duck", "brace"
"bee", "swarm"

8.
```
    Private Sub cmdDisplay_Click()
      Dim excerpt As String
      excerpt = "I think I can. "
      Call Duplicate30(s)
      excerpt = "We're off to see the wizard, " & _
                "the wonderful wizard of Oz."
      Call Duplicate30(excerpt)
    End Sub


    Private Sub Duplicate30(sentence As String)
      Dim flag As Boolean
      flag = False      'Flag tells whether loop has been executed
      Do While Len(sentence) < 30
        flag = True
        sentence = sentence & sentence
      Loop
      If flag = True Then
          picOutput.Print sentence
        Else
          picOutput.Print "Loop not executed."
      End If
    End Sub
```

9.
```
    Private Sub cmdDisplay_Click()
      Dim word As String, cWord As String
      Open "WORDS.TXT" For Input As #1
      Do While Not EOF(1)
        Input #1, word
        If Left(word, 1) = "c" Then
            cWord = word
        End If
      Loop
      Close #1
      picOutput.Print cWord
    End Sub
```

(Assume that the file WORDS.TXT contains the following data.)

"time", "is", "a", "child", "idly", "moving", "counters", "in", "a", "game", "Heraclitus"

10.
```
Private Sub cmdDisplay_Click()
    Dim max As Single, value As Single, rowMax As Single
    max = 0
    Open "DATA.TXT" For Input As #1
    Do While Not EOF(1)
      Input #1, value
      rowMax = 0
      Do While value <> -2
        If value > rowMax Then
            rowMax = value
        End If
        Input #1, value
      Loop
      picOutput.Print rowMax
      If rowMax > max Then
          max = rowMax
      End If
    Loop
    Close #1
    picOutput.Print max
End Sub
```

(Assume that the file DATA.TXT contains the following entries.)

5, 7, 3, –2, 10, 12, 6, 4, –2, 1, 9, –2

In Exercises 11 through 14, identify the errors.

11.
```
Private Sub cmdDisplay_Click()
    Dim num As Single
    Open "DATA.TXT" For Input As #1
    Do While (Not EOF(1)) And (num > 0)
      Input #1, num
      picOutput.Print num
    Close #1
End Sub
```

(Assume that the file DATA.TXT contains the following entries.)

7, 6, 0, –1, 2

12.
```
Private Sub cmdDisplay_Click()
    Dim flag As Boolean, num As Single
    flag = False
    Do While flag = False
      num = Val(InputBox("Enter a number"))
      If num * num < 0 Then
          flag = True
      End If
    Loop
End Sub
```

13.
```
Private Sub cmdDisplay_Click()
    Dim president As String
    'Display names of some U.S. Presidents
    Open "PRES.TXT" For Input As #1
    Input #1, president
    Do
      picOutput.Print president
      Input #1, president
    Loop Until EOF(1)
    Close #1
End Sub
```

(Assume that the file PRES.TXT contains the following entries.)

"Lincoln", "Washington", "Kennedy", "Jefferson"

14.
```
Private Sub cmdDisplay_Click()
    Dim num As Single
    Open "DATA.TXT" For Input As #1
    If EOF(1) Then
        num = 0
      Else
        Input #1, num
    End If
    Do While 1 < num < 5
      picOutput.Print num
      If EOF(1) Then
          num = 0
        Else
          Input #1, num
      End If
    Loop
    Close #1
End Sub
```

(Assume that the file DATA.TXT contains the following entries)

3, 2, 4, 7, 2

15. Write a program to find and display the largest of a collection of positive numbers contained in a text file. (Test the program with the collection of numbers 89, 77, 95, and 86.)

16. Write a program to find and display those names that are repeated in a text file. Assume the file has already been sorted into alphabetical order. When a name is found to be repeated, display it only once.

17. Suppose the file FINAL.TXT contains student grades on a final exam. Write a program that displays the average grade on the exam and the percentage of grades that are above average.

18. Suppose the file BIDS.TXT contains a list of bids on a construction project. Write a program to analyze the list and report the two highest bids.

19. Suppose the file USPRES.TXT contains the names of the United States presidents in order from George Washington to George W. Bush. Write a program that asks the user to type a number from 1 to 43 into a text box, and then, when a command button is clicked, displays the name of the president corresponding to that number.

20. Table 6.1 shows the different grades of eggs and the minimum weight required for each classification. Write a program that processes the text file EGGS.TXT, a list of the weights of a sample of eggs. The program should report the number of eggs in each grade and the weight of the lightest and heaviest egg in the sample. (*Note:* Eggs weighing less than 1.5 ounces cannot be sold in supermarkets.) Figure 6.6 shows a sample output of the program.

Grade	Weight (in ounces)
Jumbo	2.5
Extra Large	2.25
Large	2
Medium	1.75
Small	1.5

Table 6.1 Grades of eggs.

57 Jumbo eggs
95 Extra Large eggs
76 Large eggs
96 Medium eggs
77 Small eggs
Lightest egg: 1.00 ounces
Heaviest egg: 2.70 ounces

Figure 6.6 Possible output for Exercise 20.

21. Write a program to request a positive integer as input and carry out the following algorithm. If the number is even, divide it by 2. Otherwise, multiply the number by 3 and add 1. Repeat this process with the resulting number and continue repeating the process until the number 1 is reached. After the number 1 is reached, the program should display how many iterations were required. *Note:* A number is even if Int(num / 2) = num / 2. (Test the program with the numbers 9, 21, and 27.)

22. Suppose the file USPRES.TXT contains the names of all United States Presidents, and the file USSENATE.TXT contains the names of all former and present U.S. Senators. Write a program with nested loops that uses these files to display the names of all Presidents who served in the Senate.

23. Suppose the file SONNET.TXT contains Shakespeare's Sonnet #18. Each entry in the file consists of a line of the sonnet enclosed in quotes. Write a program using nested loops to analyze this file line by line and report the average number of words in a line and the total number of words in the sonnet.

24. Suppose the file SALES.TXT contains information on the sales during the past week at a new car dealership. Assume the file begins as shown in Figure 6.7. The file contains the following information for each salesperson at the dealership: the name of the salesperson, pairs of numbers giving the final sales price and the dealer cost for each sale made by that salesperson, and a pair of zeros to indicate the end of data for that salesperson. Write a program to display the name of each salesperson and the commission earned for the week. Assume the commission is 15% of the profit on each sale.

"Tom Jones"
18100, 17655
22395, 21885
15520, 14895
0,0
"Bill Smith"
16725, 16080
.
.
.

Figure 6.7 Sales text file for Exercise 24.

25. Write a program that uses a flag and does the following.

    (a) Ask the user to input a sentence containing parentheses. [*Note:* The closing parenthesis should not directly precede the period.]
    (b) Display the sentence with the parentheses and their contents removed. Test the program with the following sentence as input: BASIC (Beginners All-purpose Symbolic Instruction Code) is the world's most widely known computer language.

26. The salespeople at a health club keep track of the members who have joined in the last month. Their names and types of membership (Bronze, Silver, or Gold), are stored in the text file NEWMEMBERS.TXT. Write a program that displays all the Bronze members, then the Silver members, and finally the Gold members.

27. Table 6.2 gives the prices of various liquids. Write a program that requests an amount of money as input and displays the names of all liquids for which a gallon could be purchased with that amount of money. The information from the table should be read from a file. As an example, if the user has $2.35, then the following should be displayed in the picture box:

    You can purchase one gallon of any of the following liquids.

    Bleach
    Gasoline
    Milk

Liquid	Price	Liquid	Price
Apple Cider	2.60	Milk	2.30
Beer	6.00	Gatorade	4.20
Bleach	1.40	Perrier	6.85
Coca-Cola	2.55	Pancake Syrup	15.50
Gasoline	1.30	Spring Water	4.10

Table 6.2 Some comparative prices per gallon of various liquids.

✔✔ **Solutions to Practice Problems 6.2**

1. 350

2. When the third score was read from the file, EOF(1) became true. With EOF(1) true, the loop terminated and the third score was never added to *sum*. In addition, if the text file had been empty or contained only one piece of data, then the error message "Input past end of file" would have been displayed.

3.
```
Private Sub cmdComputeTotal_Click()
  Dim sum As Single, score As Single
  'Find the sum of a collection of bowling scores
  sum = 0
  Open "SCORES.TXT" For Input As #1
  Do While Not EOF(1)
    Input #1, score
    sum = sum + score
  Loop
  Close #1
  picTotal.Print sum
End Sub
```

6.3 FOR...NEXT LOOPS

When we know exactly how many times a loop should be executed, a special type of loop, called a For...Next loop, can be used. For...Next loops are easy to read and write, and have features that make them ideal for certain common tasks. The following code uses a For...Next loop to display a table.

```
Private Sub cmdDisplayTable_Click()
  Dim i As Integer
  'Display a table of the first 5 numbers and their squares
  picTable.Cls
  For i = 1 To 5
    picTable.Print i; i ^ 2
  Next i
End Sub
```

[Run and click on cmdDisplayTable. The following is displayed in the picture box.]

```
1   1
2   4
3   9
4   16
5   25
```

The equivalent program written with a Do loop is as follows.

```
Private Sub cmdDisplayTable_Click()
  Dim i As Integer
  'Display a table of the first 5 numbers and their squares
  picTable.Cls
  i = 1
  Do While i <= 5
    picTable.Print i; i ^ 2
    i = i + 1
  Loop
End Sub
```

In general, a portion of a program of the form

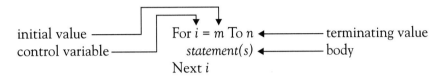

constitutes a For...Next loop. The pair of statements For and Next cause the statements between them to be repeated a specified number of times. The For statement designates a numeric variable, called the **control variable**, that is initialized and then automatically changes after each execution of the loop. Also, the For statement gives the range of values this variable will assume. The Next statement increments the control variable. If $m \leq n$, then i is assigned the values $m, m + 1, \ldots, n$ in order, and the body is executed once for each of these values. If $m > n$, then the body is skipped and execution continues with the statement after the For...Next loop.

When program execution reaches a For...Next loop, such as the one shown previously, the For statement assigns to the control variable i the initial value m and checks to see whether i is greater than the terminating value n. If so, then execution jumps to the line following the Next statement. If $i <= n$, the statements inside the loop are executed. Then, the Next statement increases the value of i by 1 and checks this new value to see if it exceeds n. If not, the entire process is repeated until the value of i exceeds n. When this happens, the program moves to the line following the loop. Figure 6.8 contains the pseudocode and flowchart of a For...Next loop.

The control variable can be *any* numeric variable. The most common single-letter names are i, j, and k; however, if appropriate, the name should suggest the purpose of the control variable.

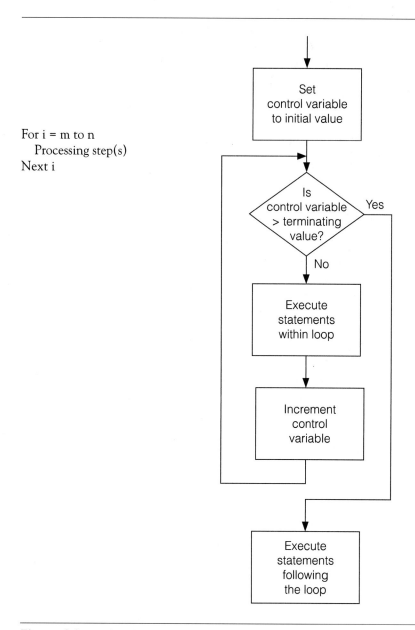

```
For i = m to n
    Processing step(s)
Next i
```

Figure 6.8 Pseudocode and flowchart of a For...Next loop.

Suppose the population of a city is 300,000 in the year 2002 and is growing at the rate of 3 percent per year. The following program displays a table showing the population each year until 2006.

Object	Property	Setting
frm6_3_1	Caption	POPULATION GROWTH
cmdDisplay	Caption	Display Population
picTable		

```
Private Sub cmdDisplay_Click()
  Const growthRate As Single = .03
  Dim pop As Single, yr As Integer
  'Display population from 2002 to 2006
  picTable.Cls
  pop = 300000
  For yr = 2002 To 2006
    picTable.Print yr, FormatNumber(pop, 0)
    pop = pop + growthRate * pop
  Next yr
End Sub
```

[Run, and click the command button.]

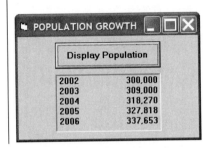

The initial and terminating values can be constants, variables, or expressions. For instance, the For statement in the preceding program can be replaced by

```
firstYr = 2002
lastYr = 2006
For yr = firstYr To lastYr
```

In Example 1, the control variable was increased by 1 after each pass through the loop. A variation of the For statement allows any number to be used as the increment. The statement

```
For i = m To n Step s
```

instructs the Next statement to add s to the control variable instead of 1. The numbers m, n, and s do not have to be whole numbers. The number s is called the **step value** of the loop. *Note:* If the control variable will assume values that are not whole numbers, then the variable must be of the type Single.

EXAMPLE 2

The following program displays the values of the index of a For...Next loop for terminating and step values input by the user.

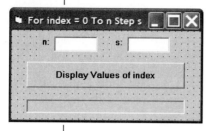

Object	Property	Setting
frm6_3_2	Caption	For index = 0 To n Step s
lblN	Caption	n:
txtEnd	Text	(blank)
lblS	Caption	s:
txtStep	Text	(blank)
cmdDisplay	Caption	Display Values of index
picValues		

```
Private Sub cmdDisplay_Click()
  Dim n As Single, s As Single, index As Single
  'Display values of index ranging from 0 to n Step s
  picValues.Cls
  n = Val(txtEnd.Text)
  s = Val(txtStep.Text)
  For index = 0 To n Step s
    picValues.Print index;
  Next index
End Sub
```

[Run, type 3.2 and .5 into the text boxes, and click the command button.]

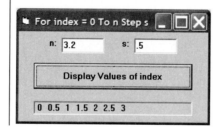

In the examples considered so far, the control variable was successively increased until it reached the terminating value. However, if a negative step value is used and the initial value is greater than the terminating value, then the control value is decreased until reaching the terminating value. In other words, the loop counts backward or downward.

EXAMPLE 3

The following program accepts a word as input and displays it backwards.

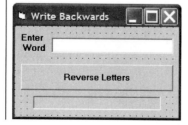

Object	Property	Setting
frm6_3_3	Caption	Write Backwards
lblWord	Caption	Enter Word
txtWord	Text	(blank)
cmdReverse	Caption	Reverse Letters
picTranspose		

```
Private Sub cmdReverse_Click()
  picTranspose.Cls
  picTranspose.Print Reverse(txtWord.Text)
End Sub

Private Function Reverse(info As String) As String
  Dim m As Integer, j As Integer, temp As String
  m = Len(info)
  temp = ""
  For j = m To 1 Step -1
    temp = temp + Mid(info, j, 1)
  Next j
  Reverse = temp
End Function
```

[Run, type SUEZ into the text box, and click the command button.]

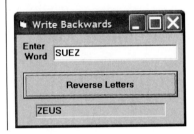

Note: The initial and terminating values of a For...Next loop can be expressions. For instance, the third and fifth lines of the function in Example 3 can be consolidated to

```
For j = Len(info) To 1 Step -1
```

The body of a For...Next loop can contain *any* sequence of Visual Basic statements. In particular, it can contain another For...Next loop. However, the second loop must be completely contained inside the first loop and must have a different control variable. Such a configuration is called **nested For...Next loops.** Figure 6.9 shows several examples of valid nested loops.

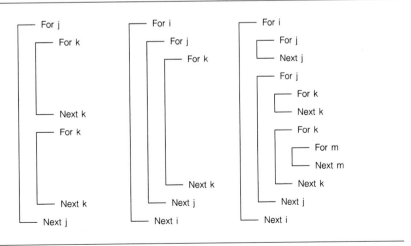

Figure 6.9 Nested For...Next loops.

EXAMPLE 4 The following program displays a multiplication table for the integers from 1 to 4. Here, *j* denotes the left factors of the products, and *k* denotes the right factors. Each factor takes on a value from 1 to 4. The values are assigned to *j* in the outer loop and to *k* in the inner loop. Initially, *j* is assigned the value 1, and then the inner loop is traversed four times to produce the first row of products. At the end of these four passes, the value of *j* will still be 1, and the value of *k* will have been incremented to 5. The `picTable.Print` statement just before `Next j` guarantees that no more products will be displayed in that row. The first execution of the outer loop is then complete. Following this, the statement `Next j` increments the value of *j* to 2. The statement beginning `For k` is then executed. It resets the value of *k* to 1. The second row of products is displayed during the next four executions of the inner loop and so on.

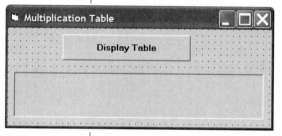

Object	Property	Setting
frmMultiply	Caption	Multiplication Table
cmdDisplay	Caption	Display Table
picTable		

```
Private Sub cmdDisplay_Click()
  Dim j As Integer, k As Integer
  picTable.Cls
  For j = 1 To 4
    For k = 1 To 4
      picTable.Print j; "x"; k; "="; j * k,
    Next k
    picTable.Print     'Move to next row
  Next j
End Sub
```

[Run and press the command button.]

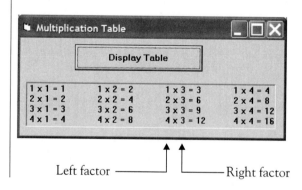

Left factor ⎯⎯⎯⎯⎯⎯ ⎿⎽ ⎽� Right factor

Comments

1. The body of a For...Next loop need not be indented. However, because indenting improves the readability of the program, it is good programming style. As soon as you see the word For, your eyes can easily scan down the program to find the matching Next statement. You then know two facts immediately: the number of statements in the body of the loop and the number of passes that will be made through the loop.

2. For and Next statements must be paired. If one is missing, the program will generate the error message "For without Next" or "Next without For."

3. Consider a loop beginning with For $i = m$ To n Step s. The loop will be executed exactly once if m equals n no matter what value s has. The loop will not be executed at all if m is greater than n and s is positive, or if m is less than n and s is negative.

4. The value of the control variable should not be altered within the body of the loop; doing so might cause the loop to repeat indefinitely or have an unpredictable number of repetitions.

5. Noninteger step values can lead to roundoff errors with the result that the loop is not executed the intended number of times. For instance, a loop beginning with For $i = 1$ To 2 Step $.1$ will be executed only 10 times instead of the intended 11 times. It should be replaced with For $i = 1$ To 2.01 Step $.1$.

✔ PRACTICE PROBLEMS 6.3

1. Why won't the following lines of code work as intended?

```
For i = 15 To 1
  picBox.Print i;
Next i
```

2. When is a For...Next loop more appropriate than a Do loop?

➤ EXERCISES 6.3

In Exercises 1 through 12, determine the output displayed in the picture box when the command button is clicked.

1.
```
Private Sub cmdDisplay_Click()
  Dim i As Integer
  For i = 1 To 4
    picOutput.Print "Pass #"; i
  Next i
End Sub
```

2.
```
Private Sub cmdDisplay_Click()
  Dim i As Integer
  For i = 3 To 6
    picOutput.Print 2 * i;
  Next i
End Sub
```

3.
```
Private Sub cmdDisplay_Click()
  Dim j As Integer
  For j = 2 To 8 Step 2
    picOutput.Print j;
  Next j
  picOutput.Print "Who do we appreciate?"
End Sub
```

4.
```
Private Sub cmdDisplay_Click()
  Dim countdown As Integer
  For countdown = 10 To 1 Step -1
    picOutput.Print countdown;
  Next countdown
  picOutput.Print "blastoff"
End Sub
```

5.
```
Private Sub cmdDisplay_Click()
   Dim num As Integer, i As Integer
   num = 5
   For i = num To 2 * num + 3
     picOutput.Print i;
   Next i
End Sub
```

6.
```
Private Sub cmdDisplay_Click()
   Dim i As Single
   For i = 3 To 5 Step .25
     picOutput.Print i;
   Next i
   picOutput.Print i
End Sub
```

7.
```
Private Sub cmdDisplay_Click()
   Dim recCount As Integer, miler As Integer
   Dim nom As String, mileTime As String
   'First entry in text file is number of records in file
   Open "MILER.TXT" For Input As #1
   Input #1, recCount
   For miler = 1 To recCount
     Input #1, nom, mileTime
     picOutput.Print nom, mileTime
   Next miler
   Close #1
End Sub
```

(Assume that the file MILER.TXT contains the following four lines.)

3
"Steve Cram", "3:46.31"
"Steve Scott", "3:51.6"
"Mary Slaney", "4:20.5"

8.
```
Private Sub cmdDisplay_Click()
   Dim recCount As Integer, total As Integer
   Dim i As Integer, score As Integer
   'First entry in text file is number of records in file
   Open "SCORES.TXT" For Input As #1
   Input #1, recCount
   total = 0
   For i = 1 To recCount
     Input #1, score
     total = total + score
   Next i
   Close #1
   picOutput.Print "Average ="; total / recCount
End Sub
```

(Assume that the file SCORES.TXT contains the following entries.)

4, 89, 85, 88, 98

9.
```
Private Sub cmdDisplay_Click()
   Dim i As Integer, j As Integer
   For i = 0 To 2
     For j = 0 To 3
       picOutput.Print i + 3 * j + 1; "  ";
     Next j
     picOutput.Print
   Next i
End Sub
```

10.
```
Private Sub cmdDisplay_Click()
    Dim i As Integer, j As Integer
    For i = 1 To 5
      For j = 1 To i
        picOutput.Print "*";
      Next j
      picOutput.Print
    Next i
End Sub
```

11.
```
Private Sub cmdDisplay_Click()
    Dim word As String, num1 As Integer, num2 As Integer
    word = InputBox("Please enter a word.")
    num1 = Int((20 - Len(word)) / 2)
    num2 = 20 - num1 - Len(word)
    Call Asterisks(num1)
    picOutput.Print word;
    Call Asterisks(num2)
End Sub

Private Sub Asterisks(num As Integer)
  Dim i As Integer
  'Display num asterisks
  For i = 1 To num
    picOutput.Print "*";
  Next i
End Sub
```

(Assume that the response is *Hooray.*)

12.
```
Private Sub cmdDisplay_Click()
    Dim info As String, i As Integer, letter As String
    'Display an array of letters
    info = "DATA"
    For i = 1 To Len(info)
      letter = Mid(info, i, 1)
      Call DisplayFive(letter)
      picOutput.Print        'Move to next line
    Next i
End Sub

Private Sub DisplayFive(letter As String)
  Dim i As Integer
  'Display letter five times
  For i = 1 To 5
    picOutput.Print letter;
  Next i
End Sub
```

In Exercises 13 through 16, identify the errors.

13.
```
Private Sub cmdDisplay_Click()
    Dim j As Single
    For j = 1 To 25.5 Step -1
        picOutput.Print j
    Next j
End Sub
```

14.
```
Private Sub cmdDisplay_Click()
    Dim i As Integer
    For i = 1 To 3
        picOutput.Print i; 2 ^ i
End Sub
```

15.
```
Private Sub cmdDisplay_Click()
    Dim i As Integer
    For i = 1 To 99
        If i Mod 2 = 0 Then
            Next i
        Else
            picOutput.Print i
        End If
    Next i
End Sub
```

16.
```
Private Sub cmdDisplay_Click()
    Dim i As Integer, j As Integer
    For i = 1 To 6
        For j = 1 To 3
            picOutput.Print i / j;
        Next i
    Next j
End Sub
```

In Exercises 17 and 18, rewrite the program using a For...Next loop.

17.
```
Private Sub cmdDisplay_Click()
    Dim num As Integer
    num = 1
    Do While num <= 10
        picOutput.Print num
        num = num + 2
    Loop
End Sub
```

18.
```
Private Sub cmdDisplay_Click()
    picOutput.Print "hello"
    picOutput.Print "hello"
    picOutput.Print "hello"
    picOutput.Print "hello"
End Sub
```

In Exercises 19 through 38, write a program to complete the stated task.

19. Display a row of 10 stars (asterisks).

20. Request a number from 1 to 20 and display a row of that many stars (asterisks).

21. Display a 10-by-10 array of stars.

22. Request a number and call a Sub procedure to display a square having that number of stars on each side.

23. Find the sum $1 + 1/2 + 1/3 + 1/4 + \ldots + 1/100$.

24. Find the sum of the odd numbers from 1 through 99.

25. You are offered two salary options for ten days of work. Option 1: $100 per day. Option 2: $1 the first day, $2 the second day, $4 the third day, and so on, with the amount doubling each day. Write a program to determine which option pays better.

26. When $1000 is deposited at 5 percent simple interest, the amount grows by $50 each year. When money is invested at 5 percent compound interest, then the amount at the end of each year is 1.05 times the amount at the beginning of that year. Write a program to display the amounts for 10 years

for a $1000 deposit at 5 percent simple and compound interest. The first few lines displayed in the picture box should appear as in Figure 6.10.

Year	Amount Simple Interest	Amount Compound Interest
1	$1,050.00	$1,050.00
2	$1,100.00	$1,102.50
3	$1,150.00	$1,157.63

Figure 6.10 Growth of $1000 at simple and compound interest.

27. According to researchers at Stanford Medical School (as cited in *Medical Self Care*), the ideal weight for a woman is found by multiplying her height in inches by 3.5 and subtracting 108. The ideal weight for a man is found by multiplying his height in inches by 4 and subtracting 128. Request a lower and upper bound for heights and then produce a table giving the ideal weights for women and men in that height range. For example, when a lower bound of 62 and an upper bound of 65 are specified, Figure 6.11 shows the output displayed in the picture box.

Height	Wt - Women	Wt - Men
62	109	120
63	112.5	124
64	116	128
65	119.5	132

Figure 6.11 Output for Exercise 27.

28. Table 6.3 gives data (in millions) on personal computer sales and revenues. Read the data from the file PC.TXT and generate an extended table with two additional columns, Pct Foreign (percent of personal computers sold outside the U.S.) and Avg Rev (average U.S. revenue per computer).

Year	US Sales	Worldwide Sales	US Revenues
1998	34.6	98.4	74,920
1999	40.1	116.2	80,200
2000	46.0	128.5	88,110
2001	43.5	132.0	77,000

Table 6.3 Personal computer sales and revenues (in millions).

29. Request a sentence, and display the number of sibilants (that is, letters S or Z) in the sentence. The counting should be carried out by a function.

30. Request a number, n, from 1 to 30 and one of the letters S or P. Then, depending upon whether S or P was selected, calculate the sum or product of the numbers from 1 to n. The calculations should be carried out in Function procedures.

31. Suppose $800 is deposited into a savings account earning 4 percent interest compounded annually, and $100 is added to the account at the end of each year. Calculate the amount of money in the account at the end of 10 years. (Determine a formula for computing the balance at the end of one year based on the balance at the beginning of the year. Then write a program that starts with a balance of $800 and makes 10 passes through a loop containing the formula to produce the final answer.)

32. A TV set is purchased with a loan of $563 to be paid off with five monthly payments of $116. The interest rate is 1 percent per month. Display a table giving the balance on the loan at the end of each month.

33. *Radioactive Decay.* Cobalt 60, a radioactive form of cobalt used in cancer therapy, decays or dissipates over a period of time. Each year, 12 percent of the amount present at the beginning of the year will have decayed. If a container of cobalt 60 initially contains 10 grams, determine the amount remaining after five years.

34. *Supply and Demand.* This year's level of production and price for most agricultural products greatly affects the level of production and price next year. Suppose the current crop of soybeans in a certain country is 80 million bushels and experience has shown that for each year,

[price this year] = 20 − .1 ∗ [quantity this year]

[quantity next year] = 5 ∗ [price this year] −10

where quantity is measured in units of millions of bushels. Generate a table to show the quantity and price for each of the next 12 years.

35. Request a number greater than 3, and display a hollow rectangle similar to the one in Figure 6.12(a) with each outer row and column having that many stars. Use a fixed-width font such as Courier New so that the spaces and asterisks will have the same width.

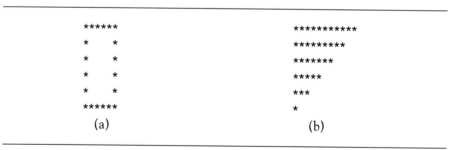

Figure 6.12 Outputs for Exercises 35 and 36.

36. Request an odd number, and display a triangle similar to the one in Figure 6.12(b) with the input number of stars in the top row.

37. Allow any two integers, *m* and *n*, between 2 and 12 to be specified and then generate an *m*-by-*n* multiplication table. Figure 6.13 shows the output when *m* is 5 and *n* is 7. To obtain a nicely lined up table, use a fixed-space font such as Courier together with the Format(var, "@@@@@@") function, which right-justifies a value in a field six spaces wide.

```
          1    2    3    4    5    6    7
          2    4    6    8   10   12   14
          3    6    9   12   15   18   21
          4    8   12   16   20   24   28
          5   10   15   20   25   30   35
```

Figure 6.13 Output for Exercise 37.

38. Create the histogram in Figure 6.14. A file should hold the years and values. The first entry in the file could be used to hold the title for the histogram.

```
1999   *****   5
2000   **********   11
2001   ***************   15
2002   ********************   21
2003   **************************   27

Worldwide PDA Sales in Millions
```

Figure 6.14 Histogram for Exercise 38.

39. A man pays $1 to get into a gambling casino. He loses half of his money there and then has to pay $1 to leave. He goes to a second casino, pays another $1 to get in, loses half of his money again and pays another $1 to leave. Then, he goes to a third casino, pays another $1 to get in, loses half of his money again, and pays another $1 to get out. After this, he's broke. Write a program to determine the amount of money he began with by testing $5, then $6, and so on.

40. Write a program to estimate how much a young worker will make before retiring at age 65. Request the worker's name, age, and starting salary as input. Assume the worker receives a 5 percent raise each year. For example, if the user enters Helen, 25, and 20000, then the picture box should display the following:

Helen will earn about $2,415,995

Exercises 41 through 44 require the Rnd function presented in Section 3.6.

41. Write a program that selects a word at random from among words in a file.

42. Write a program to simulate the tossing of a coin 100 times and display the numbers of "heads" and "tails" that occur.

43. A company has a text file containing the names of people who have qualified for a drawing to win an IBM Personal Computer. Write a program to select a name at random from the file. Test your program on a file consisting of five names.

44. A club has 20 members. Write a program to select two different people at random to serve as president and treasurer. (The names of the members should be contained in a file.)

✔✔ **Solutions to Practice Problems 6.3**

1. The loop will never be entered because 15 is greater than 1. The intended first line might have been

```
For i = 15 To 1 Step -1
```

or

```
For i = 1 To 15
```

2. If the exact number of times the loop will be executed is known before entering the loop, then a For...Next loop should be used. Otherwise, a Do loop is more appropriate.

6.4   A CASE STUDY: ANALYZE A LOAN

This case study develops a program to analyze a loan. Assume the loan is repaid in equal monthly payments and interest is compounded monthly. The program should request the amount (principal) of the loan, the annual rate of interest, and the number of years over which the loan is to be repaid. The four options to be provided by command buttons are as follows.

1. Calculate the monthly payment. The formula for the monthly payment is

$$\text{payment} = p * r / (1 - (1 + r) \wedge (-n))$$

where p is the principal of the loan, r is the monthly interest rate (annual rate divided by 12) given as a number between 0 (for 0 percent) and 1 (for 100 percent), and n is the number of months over which the loan is to be repaid. Because a payment computed in this manner can be expected to include fractions of a cent, the value should be rounded up to the next nearest cent. This corrected payment can be achieved using the formula

$$\text{correct payment} = \text{Round}(\text{payment} + .005, 2)$$

2. Display an amortization schedule, that is, a table showing the balance on the loan at the end of each month for any year over the duration of the loan. Also show how much of each monthly payment goes toward interest and how much is used to repay the principal. Finally, display the total interest paid over the duration of the loan. The balances for successive months are calculated with the formula

$$\text{balance} = (1 + r) * b - m$$

where r is the monthly interest rate (annual rate / 12, a fraction between 0 and 1), b is the balance for the preceding month (amount of loan left to be paid), and m is the monthly payment.

3. Show the effect of changes in the interest rate. Display a table giving the monthly payment for each interest rate from 1 percent below to 1 percent above the specified annual rate in steps of one-eighth of a percent.

4. Quit.

Designing the Analyze-a-Loan Program

For each of the tasks described in preceding options 1 to 4, the program must first look at the text boxes to obtain the particulars of the loan to be analyzed. Thus, the first division of the problem is into the following tasks:

1. Input the principal, interest, and duration.

2. Calculate the monthly payment.

3. Calculate the amortization schedule.

4. Display the effects of interest rate changes.

5. Quit.

Task 1 is a basic input operation and Task 2 involves applying the formula given in Option 1; therefore, these tasks need not be broken down any further. The demanding work of the program is done in Tasks 3 and 4, which can be divided into smaller subtasks.

3. *Calculate amortization schedule.* This task involves simulating the loan month by month. First, the monthly payment must be computed. Then, for each month, the new balance must be computed together with a decomposition of the monthly payment into the amount paid for interest and the amount going toward repaying the principal. That is, Task 3 is divided into the following subtasks:

3.1 Calculate monthly payment.
3.2 Calculate new balance.
3.3 Calculate amount of monthly payment for principal.
3.4 Calculate amount of monthly payment for interest.
3.5 Calculate total interest paid.

4. *Display the effects of interest-rate changes.* A table is needed to show the effects of changes in the interest rate on the size of the monthly payment. First, the interest rate is reduced by one percentage point and the new monthly payment is computed. Then the interest rate is increased by regular increments until it reaches one percentage point above the original rate, with new monthly payment amounts computed for each intermediate interest rate. The subtasks for this task are then:

4.1 Reduce the interest rate by 1 percent.
4.2 Calculate the monthly payment.
4.3 Increase the interest rate by 1/8 percent.
4.4 Repeat until a certain condition is met.

The hierarchy chart in Figure 6.15 shows the stepwise refinement of the problem.

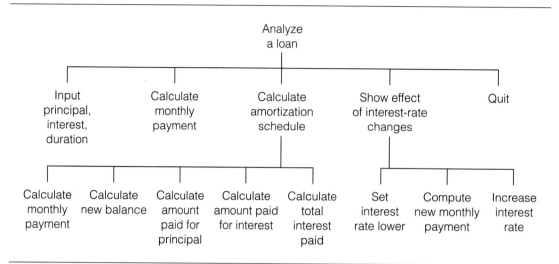

Figure 6.15 Hierarchy chart for the analyze-a-loan program.

The User Interface

Figure 6.16 shows a possible form design and Table 6.4 gives the initial settings for the form and its contents. Figures 6.17, 6.18, and 6.19 show possible runs of the program for each task available through the command buttons. The width and height of the picture box were adjusted by trial and error to handle the extensive output generated.

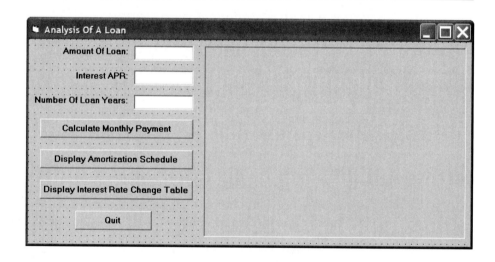

Figure 6.16 Template for the analyze-a-loan program.

Object	Property	Setting
frmLoan	Caption	Analysis Of A Loan
lblAmt	Caption	Amount Of Loan:
txtAmt	Text	(blank)
lblApr	Caption	Interest APR:
txtApr	Text	(blank)
lblYrs	Caption	Number Of Loan Years:
txtYrs	Text	(blank)
cmdPayment	Caption	Calculate Monthly Payment
cmdRateTable	Caption	Display Interest Rate Change Table
cmdAmort	Caption	Display Amortization Schedule
cmdQuit	Caption	Quit
picDisp		

Table 6.4 Objects and initial properties for the analyze-a-loan program.

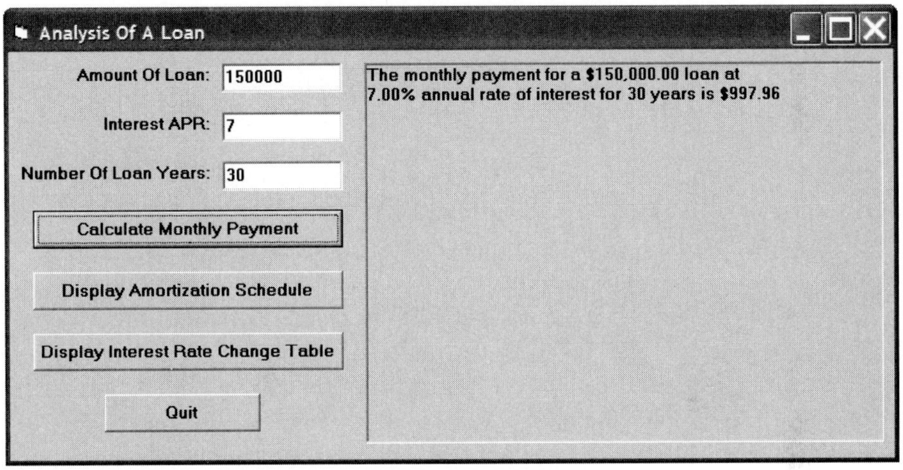

Figure 6.17 Monthly payment on a 30-year loan.

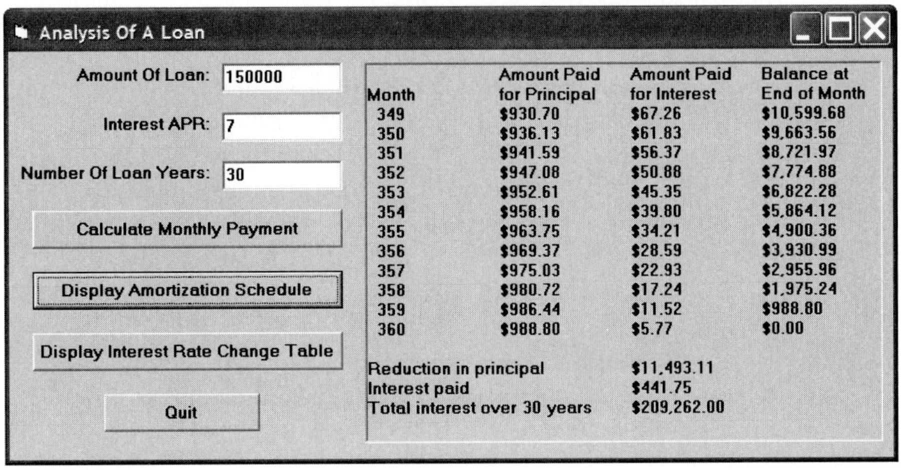

Figure 6.18 Amortization of year 30 of a loan.

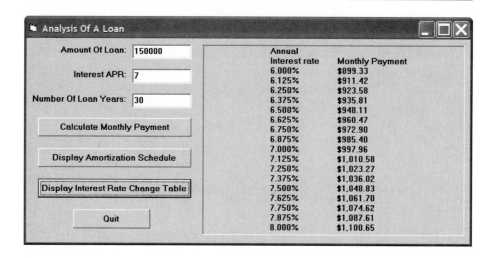

Figure 6.19 Interest-rate-change table for a 30-year loan.

Writing the Analyze-a-Loan Program

Table 6.5 shows each task discussed before and the procedure that carries out the task.

Pseudocode for the Analyze-a-Loan Program

Calculate Monthly Payment command button:
   INPUT LOAN DATA (Sub procedure InputData)
   COMPUTE MONTHLY PAYMENT (Function Payment)
   DISPLAY MONTHLY PAYMENT (Sub procedure ShowPayment)

Display Amortization Schedule command button:
   INPUT LOAN DATA (Sub procedure InputData)
   DISPLAY AMORTIZATION SCHEDULE (Sub procedure ShowAmortSched)
   Compute monthly interest rate
   COMPUTE MONTHLY PAYMENT (Function Payment)
   Calculate and display amortization table
   Display total interest paid

Display Interest Rate Change Table command button:
   INPUT LOAN DATA (Sub procedure InputData)
   DISPLAY INTEREST RATE CHANGE TABLE
      (Sub procedure ShowInterestChanges)
   Decrease annual rate by .01
   Do
      Display monthly interest rate
      COMPUTE AND DISPLAY MONTHLY PAYMENT (Function Payment)
      Increase annual rate by .00125
   Loop Until annual rate > original annual rate + .01

Task	Procedure
1. Input principal, interest, and duration.	InputData
2. Calculate monthly payment.	ShowPayment
3. Calculate amortization schedule.	ShowAmortSched
3.1 Calculate monthly payment.	Payment
3.2 Calculate new balance.	Balance
3.3 Calculate amount paid for principal.	ShowAmortSched
3.4 Calculate amount paid for interest.	ShowAmortSched
3.5 Calculate total interest paid.	ShowAmortSched
4. Show effect of interest rate changes.	ShowInterestChanges
4.1 Reduce interest rate.	ShowInterestChanges
4.2 Compute new monthly payment.	Payment
4.3 Increase interest rate.	ShowInterestChanges
4.4 Repeat until a condition is met.	ShowInterestChanges

Table 6.5 Tasks and their procedures.

```
'Analyze a loan

Private Sub cmdPayment_Click()
  Dim principal As Single    'Amount of loan
  Dim yearlyRate As Single   'Annual rate of interest
  Dim numMonths As Integer   'Number of months to repay loan
  Call InputData(principal, yearlyRate, numMonths)
  Call ShowPayment(principal, yearlyRate, numMonths)
End Sub

Private Sub cmdAmort_Click()
  Dim principal As Single    'Amount of loan
  Dim yearlyRate As Single   'Annual rate of interest
  Dim numMonths As Integer   'Number of months to repay loan
  Call InputData(principal, yearlyRate, numMonths)
  Call ShowAmortSched(principal, yearlyRate, numMonths)
End Sub

Private Sub cmdRateTable_Click()
  Dim principal As Single    'Amount of loan
  Dim yearlyRate As Single   'Annual rate of interest
  Dim numMonths As Integer   'Number of months to repay loan
  Call InputData(principal, yearlyRate, numMonths)
  Call ShowInterestChanges(principal, yearlyRate, numMonths)
End Sub

Private Sub cmdQuit_Click()
  End
End Sub

Private Sub InputData(prin As Single, yearlyRate As Single, numMs As Integer)
  Dim percentageRate As Single, numYears As Integer
  'Task 1: Input the loan amount, yearly rate of interest, and duration
  prin = Val(txtAmt.Text)
  percentageRate = Val(txtApr.Text)
  numYears = Val(txtYrs.Text)
  yearlyRate = percentageRate / 100
  numMs = numYears * 12
End Sub
```

```
Private Function Payment(prin As Single, mRate As Single, numMs As Integer) As Single
  Dim payEst As Single
  If numMs = 0 Then
     payEst = prin
    ElseIf mRate = 0 Then
      'If loan has no interest just repay the prinicpal over time
      payEst = prin / numMs
    Else
      'Otherwise use the formula for determining the monthly payment
      payEst = prin * mRate / (1 - (1 + mRate) ^ (-numMs))
  End If
  If payEst <> Round(payEst, 2) Then
     Payment = Round(payEst + .005, 2)   'round up to nearest cent
    Else
     Payment = payEst
  End If
End Function


Private Function Balance(mPayment As Single, prin As Single, mRate As Single) As Single
  Dim newBal As Single
  'Compute balance at end of month
  newBal = (1 + mRate) * prin
  If newBal <= mPayment Then
     mPayment = newBal
     Balance = 0
    Else
     Balance = newBal - mPayment
  End If
End Function


Private Sub ShowPayment(prin As Single, yearlyRate As Single, numMs As Integer)
  Dim mRate As Single, prn As String, apr As String
  Dim yrs As String, pay As Single, pymnt As String
  'Task 2: Display monthly payment amount
  mRate = yearlyRate / 12   'monthly rate
  prn = FormatCurrency(prin)
  apr = FormatNumber(yearlyRate * 100)
  yrs = FormatNumber(numMs / 12, 0)
  pay = Payment(prin, mRate, numMs)
  pymnt = FormatCurrency(pay)
  picDisp.Cls
  picDisp.Print "The monthly payment for a " & prn & " loan at "
  picDisp.Print apr & "% annual rate of interest for ";
  picDisp.Print yrs & " years is " & pymnt
End Sub


Private Sub ShowAmortSched(prin As Single, yearlyRate As Single, numMs As Integer)
  Dim msg As String, startMonth As Integer, mRate As Single
  Dim monthlyPayment As Single, totalInterest As Single
  Dim yearInterest As Single, oldBalance As Single
  Dim monthNum As Integer, newBalance As Single
  Dim principalPaid As Single, interestPaid As Single
  Dim reducPrin As Single, loanYears As Integer
  'Task 3: Display amortization schedule
```

```
    msg = "Please enter year (1-" & Str(numMs / 12)
    msg = msg & ") for which amorization is to be shown:"
    startMonth = 12 * Val(InputBox(msg)) - 11
    picDisp.Cls
    picDisp.Print "", "Amount Paid ",
    picDisp.Print "Amount Paid", "Balance at"
    picDisp.Print "Month", "for Principal",
    picDisp.Print "for Interest", "End of Month"
    mRate = yearlyRate / 12   'monthly rate
    monthlyPayment = Payment(prin, mRate, numMs)
    totalInterest = 0
    yearInterest = 0
    oldBalance = prin
    For monthNum = 1 To numMs
      newBalance = Balance(monthlyPayment, oldBalance, mRate)
      principalPaid = oldBalance - newBalance
      interestPaid = monthlyPayment - principalPaid
      totalInterest = totalInterest + interestPaid
      If (monthNum >= startMonth) And (monthNum <= startMonth + 11) Then
          picDisp.Print Tab(2); FormatNumber(monthNum, 0),
          picDisp.Print FormatCurrency(principalPaid),
          picDisp.Print FormatCurrency(interestPaid),
          picDisp.Print FormatCurrency(newBalance)
          yearInterest = yearInterest + interestPaid
      End If
      oldBalance = newBalance
    Next monthNum
    reducPrin = 12 * monthlyPayment - yearInterest
    loanYears = numMs / 12
    picDisp.Print
    picDisp.Print "Reduction in principal",
    picDisp.Print FormatCurrency(reducPrin)
    picDisp.Print "Interest paid", ,
    picDisp.Print FormatCurrency(yearInterest)
    picDisp.Print "Total interest over"; loanYears; "years",
    picDisp.Print FormatCurrency(totalInterest)
End Sub

Private Sub ShowInterestChanges(prin As Single, yearlyRate As Single, numMs As Integer)
    Dim newRate As Single, mRate As Single, py As Single
    Dim pymnt As String
    'Task 4: Display effect of interest changes
    picDisp.Cls
    picDisp.Print , "Annual"
    picDisp.Print , "Interest rate", "Monthly Payment"
    newRate = yearlyRate - .01
    Do
      mRate = newRate / 12   'monthly rate
      py = Payment(prin, mRate, numMs)
      pymnt = FormatCurrency(py)
      picDisp.Print , FormatPercent(newRate, 3), pymnt
      newRate = newRate + .00125
    Loop Until newRate > yearlyRate + .01
End Sub
```

Comments

1. Tasks 3.1 and 3.2 are performed by functions. Using functions to compute these quantities simplifies the computations in ShowAmortSched.

2. Because the payment was rounded up to the nearest cent, it is highly likely that the payment needed in the final month to pay off the loan will be less than the normal payment. For this reason, ShowAmortSched checks if the balance of the loan (including interest due) is less than the regular payment, and, if so, makes appropriate adjustments.

3. The standard formula for computing the monthly payment cannot be used if either the interest rate is zero percent or the loan duration is zero months. Although both of these situations do not represent reasonable loan parameters, provisions are made in the function Payment so that the program can handle these esoteric situations.

CHAPTER 6   SUMMARY

1. A *Do loop* repeatedly executes a block of statements either as long as or until a certain condition is true. The condition can be checked either at the top of the loop or at the bottom.

2. The EOF function tells us if we have read to the end of a file.

3. As various items of data are processed by a loop, a *counter* can be used to keep track of the number of items, and an *accumulator* can be used to sum numerical values.

4. A *flag* is a Boolean variable, used to indicate whether a certain event has occurred.

5. A *For…Next loop* repeats a block of statements a fixed number of times. The *control variable* assumes an initial value and increments by one after each pass through the loop until it reaches the terminating value. Alternative increment values can be specified with the Step keyword.

CHAPTER 6   **PROGRAMMING PROJECTS**

1. Write a program to display a company's payroll report in a picture box. The program should read each employee's name, hourly rate, and hours worked from a file and produce a report in the form of the sample run shown in Figure 6.20. Employees should be paid time-and-a-half for hours in excess of 40.

```
Payroll Report for Week ending 11/15/03

Employee      Hourly Rate    Hours Worked   Gross Pay

Al Adams        $6.50           38          $247.00
Bob Brown       $5.70           50          $313.50
Carol Coe       $7.00           40          $280.00

Final Total    $840.50
```

Figure 6.20 Sample output from Programming Project 1.

2. Table 6.6 shows the standard prices for items in a department store. Suppose prices will be reduced for the annual George Washington's Birthday Sale. The new price will be computed by reducing the old price by 10 percent, rounding up to the nearest dollar, and subtracting 1 cent. If the new price is greater than the old price, the old price is used as the sale price. Write a program to display in a picture box the output shown in Figure 6.21.

Item	Original Price
GumShoes	39.00
SnugFoot Sandals	21.00
T-Shirt	7.75
Maine Handbag	33.00
Maple Syrup	6.75
Flaked Vest	24.00
Nightshirt	26.00

Table 6.6 Washington's Birthday Sale.

```
                          Sale
Item                      Price
GumShoes                  35.99
SnugFoot Sandals          18.99
T-Shirt                    6.99
Maine Handbag             29.99
Maple Syrup                6.75
Flaked Vest               21.99
Nightshirt                23.99
```

Figure 6.21 Output of Project 2.

3. The Rule of 72 is used to make a quick estimate of the time required for prices to double due to inflation. If the inflation rate is r percent, then the Rule of 72 estimates that prices will double in $72/r$ years. For instance, at an inflation rate of 6 percent, prices double in about $72/6$ or 12 years. Write a program to test the accuracy of this rule. The program should display a table showing, for each value of r from 1 to 20, the rounded value of $72/r$ and the actual number of years required for prices to double at an r percent inflation rate. (Assume prices increase at the end of each year.) Figure 6.22 shows the first few rows of the output.

```
Interest      Rule
Rate (%)      of 72      Actual
   1           72          70
   2           36          36
   3           24          24
```

Figure 6.22 Rule of 72.

4. Table 6.7 shows the number of bachelor degrees conferred in 1980 and 1997 in certain fields of study. Tables 6.8 and 6.9 show the percentage change and a histogram of 1997 levels, respectively. Write a program that allows the user to display any one of these tables as an option and quit as a fourth option.

Field of Study	1980	1997
Business and management	184,867	226,633
Computer and info. science	11,154	24,768
Education	118,038	105,233
Engineering	68,893	75,157
Social sciences	103,662	124,891

Table 6.7 Bachelor degrees conferred in certain fields.
Source: U.S. National Center of Educational Statistics.

Field of Study	% Change (1980–1997)
Business and management	22.6
Computer and info. science	122.1
Education	−10.8
Engineering	9.1
Social sciences	20.5

Table 6.8 Percentage change in bachelor degrees conferred.

Business and management	********************** 226,633
Computer and info. science	** 24,768
Education	********** 105,233
Engineering	******** 75,157
Social sciences	*********** 124,891

Table 6.9 Bachelor degrees conferred in 1997 in certain fields.

5. *Least-Squares Approximation.* Table 6.10 shows the 1988 prices of a gallon of gasoline and the amounts of fuel consumed for several countries. Figure 6.23 displays the data as points in the *xy* plane. For instance, the point with coordinates (1, 1400) corresponds to the USA. Figure 6.23 also shows the straight line that best fits these data in the least-squares sense. (The sum of the squares of the distances of the 11 points from this line is as small as possible.) In general, if $(x_1, y_1), (x_2, y_2), \ldots, (x_n, y_n)$ are n points in the *xy* coordinate system, then the least-squares approximation to these points is the line $y = mx + b$, where

$$m = \frac{n * (\text{sum of } x_i * y_i) - (\text{sum of } x_i) * (\text{sum of } y_i)}{n * (\text{sum of } x_i * x_i) - (\text{sum of } x_i)^2}$$

and

$$b = ((\text{sum of } y_i) - m * (\text{sum of } x_i)) / n$$

Write a program that calculates and displays the equation of the least-squares line, and then allows the user to enter a fuel price and uses the equation of the line to predict the corresponding consumption of fuel. (Place the numeric data from the table in a text file.) A sample run is shown in Figure 6.24.

Country	Price per Gallon in U.S. Dollars	Tons of Oil per 1000 Persons	Country	Price per Gallon in U.S. Dollars	Tons of Oil per 1000 Persons
USA	$1.00	1400	France	$3.10	580
W. Ger.	$2.20	620	Norway	$3.15	600
England	$2.60	550	Japan	$3.60	410
Austria	$2.75	580	Denmark	$3.70	570
Sweden	$2.80	700	Italy	$3.85	430
Holland	$3.00	490			

Table 6.10 A comparison of 1988 fuel prices and per capita fuel use.

Source: World Resources Institute.

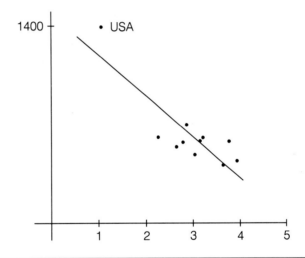

Figure 6.23 Least-squares fit to data from Table 6.10.

Figure 6.24 Sample run of Programming Project 5.

6. Write a program to provide information on the height of a ball thrown straight up into the air. The program should request the initial height, *h* feet, and the initial velocity, *v* feet per second, as input. The four options to be provided by command buttons are as follows:

(a) Determine the maximum height of the ball. *Note:* The ball will reach its maximum height after *v*/32 seconds.

(b) Determine approximately when the ball will hit the ground. *Hint:* Calculate the height after every .1 second and observe when the height is no longer a positive number.

(c) Display a table showing the height of the ball every quarter second for 5 seconds or until it hits the ground.

(d) Quit.

The formula for the height of the ball after *t* seconds, $h + v * t - 16 * t * t$, should be specified in a user-defined function. (Test the program with $v = 148$ and $h = 0$. This velocity is approximately the top speed clocked for a ball thrown by a professional baseball pitcher.)

7. *Depreciation to a Salvage Value of 0.* For tax purposes an item may be depreciated over a period of several years, *n*. With the *straight-line* method of depreciation, each year the item depreciates by 1/*n*th of its original value. With the *double-declining-balance* method of depreciation, each year the item depreciates by 2/*n*ths of its value at the *beginning* of that year. (In the last year it is depreciated by its value at the beginning of the year.) Write a program that

(a) requests a description of the item, the year of purchase, the cost of the item, the number of years to be depreciated (estimated life), and the method of depreciation. The method of depreciation should be chosen by clicking one of two command buttons.

(b) displays a depreciation schedule for the item similar to the schedule shown in Figure 6.25.

```
Description: Computer
Year of purchase: 2002
Cost: $2,000.00
Estimated life: 5
Method of depreciation: double-declining-balance


        Value at        Amount Deprec      Total Depreciation
Year    Beg of Yr       During Year        to End of Year

2002    2,000.00        800.00                  800.00
2003    1,200.00        480.00                1,280.00
2004      720.00        288.00                1,568.00
2005      432.00        172.80                1,740.80
2006      259.20        259.20                2,000.00
```

Figure 6.25 Depreciation schedule.

8. *The Twelve Days of Christmas.* Each year, Provident National Bank of Philadelphia publishes a Christmas price list. See Table 6.11. Write a program that requests an integer from 1 through 12 and then lists the gifts for that day along with that day's cost. On the *n*th day, the *n* gifts are 1 partridge in a pear tree, 2 turtle doves, . . . *n* of the *n*th item. The program also should give the total cost of all twelve days. As an example, Figure 6.26 shows the output in the picture box when the user enters 3.

Item	Cost	Item	Cost
partridge in a pear tree	102.50	swan-a-swimming	300.00
turtle dove	29.00	maid-a-milking	5.15
French hen	5.00	lady dancing	456.41
calling bird	79.00	lord-a-leaping	392.14
gold ring	76.50	piper piping	146.78
geese-a-laying	25.00	drummer drumming	145.76

Table 6.11 Christmas price index for 2002.

```
The gifts for day 3 are
 1 partridge in a pear tree
 2 turtle doves
 3 French hens
Cost:     175.50


Total cost for the twelve days: $54,951.23
```

Figure 6.26 Sample output for Programming Project 8.

9. A sentence is called a *chain-link* sentence if the last two letters of each word are the same as the first two letters of the next word. For instance, "The head administrator organized education on online networks." Write a program that accepts a sentence as input and determines whether or not it is a chain-link sentence. Test the program with the sentence "Broadcast station, once certified, educates estimable legions." (**Note:** Make sure that punctuation marks and mixed capitalization do not affect the outcome of the program.)

Programming projects 10 and 11 require that you can decide whether a year is a leap year. All years divisible by 4 are leap years, with the exception of those years divisible by 100 and not by 400. For instance, 1600 and 2000 are leap years, but 1700, 1800, and 1900 are not.

10. Compute the number of days between two dates input by the user.

11. Write a program that will display a calendar for any month specified by the user. See Figure 6.27. *Hint:* Use the FormatDateTime function to obtain the full date (including day of the week) for the first day of the month, and then apply appropriate string functions to strip out everything except the day of the week.

Figure 6.27 Sample run of Programming Project 11.

7 Arrays

7.1 CREATING AND ACCESSING ARRAYS

A **variable** (or simple variable) is a name to which Visual Basic can assign a single value. An **array variable** is a collection of simple variables of the same type to which Visual Basic can efficiently assign a list of values.

Consider the following situation. Suppose you want to evaluate the exam grades for 30 students. Not only do you want to compute the average score, but you also want to display the names of the students whose scores are above average. You might place the 30 pairs of student names and scores in a text file and run the program outlined.

```
Private Sub cmdButton_Click()
  Dim student1 As String, score1 As Single
  Dim student2 As String, score2 As Single
  Dim student3 As String, score3 As Single
    .
    .
    .
  Dim student30 As String, score30 As Single
  'Analyze exam grades
  Open "SCORES.TXT" For Input As #1
  Input #1, student1, score1
  Input #1, student2, score2
  Input #1, student3, score3
    .
    .
    .
  Input #1, student30, score30
  'Compute the average grade
    .
    .
    .
  'Display names of above average students
    .
    .
    .
End Sub
```

This program is going to be uncomfortably long. What's most frustrating is that the 30 Dim statements and 30 Input # statements are very similar and look as if they should be condensed into a short loop. A shorthand notation for the many related variables would be welcome. It would be nice if we could just write

```
For i = 1 To 30
  Input #1, studenti, scorei
Next i
```

Of course, this will not work. Visual Basic will treat *studenti* and *scorei* as two variables and keep reassigning new values to them. At the end of the loop, they will have the values of the thirtieth student.

Visual Basic provides a data structure called an **array** that lets us do what we tried to accomplish in the loop. The variable names, similar to those in the preceding program, will be

```
student(1), student(2), student(3), ..., student(30)
```

and

```
score(1), score(2), score(3), ..., score(30).
```

We refer to these collections of variables as the array variables *student*( ) and *score*( ). The numbers inside the parentheses of the individual variables are called **subscripts**, and each individual variable is called a **subscripted variable** or **element**. For instance, *student*(3) is the third subscripted variable of the array *student*( ), and *score*(20) is the 20th subscripted variable of the array *score*( ). The elements of an array are assigned successive memory locations. Figure 7.1 shows the memory locations for the array *score*( ).

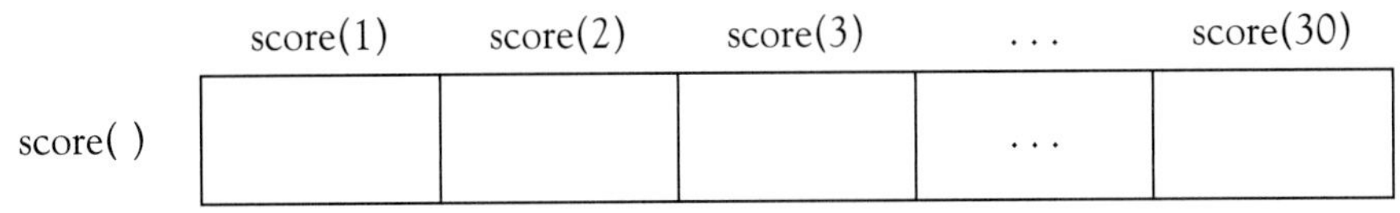

Figure 7.1 The array *score*( ).

Array variables have the same kinds of names as simple variables. If *array-Name* is the name of an array variable and *n* is a whole number, then the declaration statement

```
Dim arrayName(1 To n) As varType
```

placed in the (Declarations) section of (General) reserves space in memory to hold the values of the subscripted variables *arrayName*(1), *arrayName*(2), *arrayName*(3), . . . , *arrayName*(n). (Recall from Section 4.1 that the (Declarations) section of (General) is accessed from any Code window by selecting these values in the Object and Procedure boxes.) The spread of the subscripts specified by the Dim statement is called the **range** of the array, and the Dim statement is said to **dimension** the array. The subscripted variables will all have the same data type; namely, the type specified by *varType*. For instance, they could be all String variables or all Integer variables. In particular, the statements

```
Dim student(1 To 30) As String
Dim score(1 To 30) As Integer
```

dimension the arrays needed for the preceding program.

As with any variable created in the (Declarations) section of (General), these array variables are form-level as discussed in Chapter 4. Recall that form-level variables can be accessed from any procedure in the program and continue to exist and retain their values as long as the program is running.

Values can be assigned to individual subscripted variables with assignment statements and displayed in picture boxes just as values of ordinary variables. The default initial value of each subscripted variable is the same as with an ordinary variable—that is, the empty string for String types and 0 for numeric types. The statement

```
Dim score(1 To 30) As Integer
```

sets aside a portion of memory for the Integer array *score*( ) and assigns the default value 0 to each element.

score( )	score(1)	score(2)	score(3)	. . .	score(30)
	0	0	0	. . .	0

The statements

```
score(1) = 87
score(3) = 92
```

assign values to the first and third elements.

score( )	score(1)	score(2)	score(3)	. . .	score(30)
	87	0	92	. . .	0

The statements

```
For i = 1 To 4
  picBox.Print score(i);
Next i
```

then produce the output   87   0   92   0   in picBox.

EXAMPLE 1

The following program creates a string array consisting of the names of the first five World Series winners. Figure 7.2 shows the array created by the program.

```
'Create array for five strings
Dim teamName(1 To 5) As String    'in (Declarations) section of (General)

Private Sub cmdWhoWon_Click()
  Dim n As Integer
  'Fill array with World Series Winners
  teamName(1) = "Red Sox"
  teamName(2) = "Giants"
  teamName(3) = "White Sox"
  teamName(4) = "Cubs"
  teamName(5) = "Cubs"
  'Access array of five strings
  n = Val(txtNumber.Text)
  picWinner.Cls
  picWinner.Print "The "; teamName(n); " won World Series number"; n
End Sub
```

[Run, type 2 into the text box, and click the command button.]

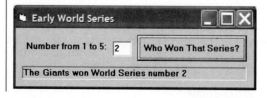

teamName( )	teamName(1)	teamName(2)	teamName(3)	teamName(4)	teamName(5)
	Red Sox	Giants	White Sox	Cubs	Cubs

Figure 7.2 The array *teamName*( ) of Example 1.

In Example 1, the array *teamName* was assigned values within the cmdWhoWon_Click event procedure. Every time the command button is clicked, the values are reassigned to the array. This manner of assigning values to an array can be very inefficient, especially in programs with large arrays where the task of the program (in Example 1, looking up a fact) may be repeated numerous times for different user input. When, as in Example 1, the data to be placed in an array are known at the time the program first begins to run, a more efficient location for the statements that fill the array is in Visual Basic's Form_Load event procedure. The Form_Load event procedure executes automatically as soon as the program is run, and this execution is guaranteed to occur before the execution of any other event or general procedure in the program. Example 2 uses the Form_Load procedure to improve on Example 1.

EXAMPLE 2 The following improvement on Example 1 assigns values to the elements of the array in the Form_Load procedure.

```
'Create array for five strings
Dim teamName(1 To 5) As String  'in (Declarations) section of (General)

Private Sub cmdDidTheyWin_Click()
  Dim team As String, foundFlag As Boolean, n As Integer
  'Search for an entry in a list of strings
  team = txtName.Text
  foundFlag = False
  n = 0
  Do
    n = n + 1
    If UCase(teamName(n)) = UCase(team) Then
        foundFlag = True
    End If
  Loop Until (foundFlag = True) Or (n = 5)
  'Above line can be replaced with Loop Until (foundFlag) or (n = 5)
  picWinner.Cls
  If foundFlag = False Then    'Can be replaced by If Not foundFlag Then
      picWinner.Print "The "; team; " did not win any";
      picWinner.Print " of the first five World Series."
  Else
      picWinner.Print "The "; teamName(n); " won World Series number"; n
  End If
End Sub
```

```
Private Sub Form_Load()
  'Fill array with World Series winners
  teamName(1) = "Red Sox"
  teamName(2) = "Giants"
  teamName(3) = "White Sox"
  teamName(4) = "Cubs"
  teamName(5) = "Cubs"
End Sub
```

[Run, type White Sox into the text box, and click the command button.]

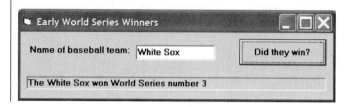

We could have written the program in Example 2 with a For...Next loop beginning For *n* = 1 To 5. However, such a loop would unnecessarily search the entire list when the sought-after item was found early. The wasted time could be significant for a large array.

In some applications, arrays are needed only temporarily to help a procedure complete a task. Visual Basic also allows us to create array variables that are local to a specific procedure and that exist temporarily while the procedure is executing. If the statement

```
Dim arrayName(1 To n) As varType
```

is placed inside an event procedure or general procedure, then space for *n* subscripted variables is set aside in memory each time the procedure is invoked and released when the procedure is exited.

In Example 1, values were assigned to the elements of the array with assignment statements. However, data for large arrays are more often stored in a text file and read with Input # statements. Example 3 uses this technique. Also, because the task of the program is likely to be performed only once during a run of the program, a local array is used.

EXAMPLE 3 The following program gives names and test scores from a mathematics contest given in 1953 (Table 7.1) and displays the names of the students scoring above the average for these eight students. The program creates a string array to hold the names of the contestants and a numeric array to hold the scores. The first element of each array holds data for the first contestant, the second element of each array holds data for the second contestant, and so on. See Figure 7.3. Note that the two arrays can be dimensioned in a single Dim statement by placing a comma between the array declarations.

Richard Dolen	135	Paul H. Monsky	150
Geraldine Ferraro	114	Max A. Plager	114
James B. Fraser	92	Robert A. Schade	91
John H. Maltby	91	Barbara M. White	124

Table 7.1 The top scores on the Fourth Annual Mathematics Contest Sponsored by the Metropolitan NY section of the MAA.

Source: The Mathematics Teacher, February 1953.

```
Private Sub cmdShow_Click()
  Dim total As Integer, student As Integer, average As Single
  'Create arrays for names and scores
  Dim nom(1 To 8) As String, score(1 To 8) As Integer
  'Assume the data has been placed in the file "SCORES.TXT"
  '(The first line of the file is "Richard Dolen", 135)
  Open "SCORES.TXT" For Input As #1
  For student = 1 To 8
    Input #1, nom(student), score(student)
  Next student
  Close #1
  'Analyze exam scores
  total = 0
  For student = 1 To 8
    total = total + score(student)
  Next student
  average = total / 8
  'Display all names with above-average grades
  picTopStudents.Cls
  For student = 1 To 8
    If score(student) > average Then
        picTopStudents.Print nom(student)
    End If
  Next student
End Sub
```

[Run, and click the command button.]

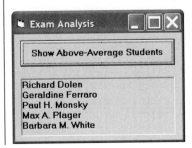

	nom(1)	nom(2)	. . .	nom(8)
nom( )	Richard Dolen	Geraldine Ferraro	. . .	Barbara M. White

	score(1)	score(2)	. . .	score(8)
score( )	135	114	. . .	124

Figure 7.3 Arrays created by Example 3.

In Example 3, the number of students to be processed had to be known at the time the program was written. In actual practice, the amount of data that a program will be processing is not known in advance. Programs should be flexible and incorporate a method for handling varying amounts of data. Visual Basic makes this possible with the statement

```
ReDim arrayName(1 to n) As varType
```

which can use variables or expressions when indicating the subscript range. However, ReDim statements can only be placed inside procedures.

EXAMPLE 4

The following program reworks Example 3 for the case when the amount of data is not known in advance.

```
Private Sub cmdShow_Click()
  Dim numStudents As Integer, nTemp As String, sTemp As Integer
  Dim student As Integer, total As Integer, average As Single
  'Determine amount of data to be processed
  numStudents = 0
  Open "SCORES.TXT" For Input As #1
  Do While Not EOF(1)
    Input #1, nTemp, sTemp
    numStudents = numStudents + 1
  Loop
  Close #1
  'Create arrays for names and scores
  ReDim nom(1 To numStudents) As String, score(1 To numStudents) As Integer
  Open "SCORES.TXT" For Input As #1
  For student = 1 To numStudents
    Input #1, nom(student), score(student)
  Next student
  Close #1
  'Analyze exam scores
  total = 0
  For student = 1 To numStudents
    total = total + score(student)
  Next student
```

```
    average = total / numStudents
    'Display all names with above-average grades
    picTopStudents.Cls
    For student = 1 To numStudents
      If score(student) > average Then
          picTopStudents.Print nom(student)
      End If
    Next student
End Sub
```

An alternative approach to program flexibility that does not require reading the text file twice is to require that the text file begin with a line that holds the number of records to be processed. If SCORES.TXT is modified by adding a new first line that gives the number of students, then the fifth through eighteenth lines of Example 4 can be replaced with

```
'Create arrays for names and scores
Open "SCORES.TXT" For Input As #1
Input #1, numStudents
ReDim nom(1 To numStudents) As String, score(1 To numStudents) As Integer
For student = 1 To numStudents
  Input #1, nom(student), score(student)
Next student
Close #1
```

In Example 4, the ReDim statement allowed us to create arrays whose size was not known before the program was run. On the other hand, the arrays that were created were local to the event procedure cmdShow_Click. Many applications require form-level arrays whose size is not known in advance. Unfortunately, Dim statements cannot use variables or expressions to specify the subscript range. The solution offered by Visual Basic is to allow the (Declarations) section of (General) to contain Dim statements of the form

```
Dim arrayName() As varType
```

where no range for the subscripts of the array is specified. An array created in this manner will be form-level but cannot be used until a ReDim statement is executed in a procedure to establish the range of subscripts. The "As *varType*" clause can be omitted from the ReDim statement.

EXAMPLE 5 Suppose the text file WINNERS.TXT contains the names of the teams who have won each of the World Series, with the first line of the file giving the number of World Series that have been played. The following program displays the years, if any, of the World Series that were won by a team specified by the user.

```
'Create form-level array
Dim teamName() As String
Dim seriesCount As Integer
```

```
Private Sub cmdDidTheyWin_Click()
  Dim teamToFind As String, numWon As Integer, series As Integer
  'Search for World Series won by user's team
  teamToFind = UCase(txtName.Text)
  numWon = 0
  picSeriesWon.Cls
  For series = 1 To seriesCount
    If UCase(teamName(series)) = teamToFind Then
        numWon = numWon + 1
        If numWon = 1 Then
            picSeriesWon.Print "The "; teamName(series);
            picSeriesWon.Print " won the following World Series: ";
          Else
            'Separate from previous
            picSeriesWon.Print ",";
            If (numWon = 5) Or (numWon = 16) Then
                'Start a new line at 5th and 16th win
                picSeriesWon.Print
            End If
        End If
        'First world series played in 1903
        picSeriesWon.Print Str(series + 1902);
    End If
  Next series
  If numWon = 0 Then
      picSeriesWon.Print "The "; teamToFind; " did not win any World Series."
  End If
End Sub

Private Sub Form_Load()
  Dim series As Integer
  'Fill array with World Series winners
  Open "WINNERS.TXT" For Input As #1
  Input #1, seriesCount
  ReDim teamName(1 To seriesCount) As String
  For series = 1 To seriesCount
    Input #1, teamName(series)
  Next series
  Close #1
End Sub
```

[Run, type Yankees into the text box, and click the command button.]

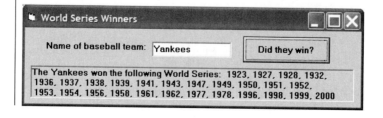

The range of an array need not just begin with 1. A statement of the form

```
Dim arrayName(m To n) As varType
```

where *m* is less than or equal to *n*, creates an array with elements *arrayName*(*m*), *arrayName*(*m* + 1), *arrayName*(*m* + 2), . . . , *arrayName*(*n*). The same holds for ReDim.

EXAMPLE 6   The following program segment stores the names of the 13th, 14th, and 15th Chief Justices of the U.S. Supreme Court in the array pictured in Figure 7.4.

```
'Place names of last three Chief Justices in an array
Dim chiefJustice(13 To 15) As String

Private Sub Form_Load()
  chiefJustice(13) = "Earl Warren"
  chiefJustice(14) = "Warren Burger"
  chiefJustice(15) = "William Rehnquist"
End Sub
```

	chiefJustice(13)	chiefJustice(14)	chiefJustice(15)
chiefJustice( )	Earl Warren	Warren Burger	William Rehnquist

Figure 7.4 The array created by Example 6.

An array can be used as either a checklist or a frequency table, as in the next example. The function Asc associates each character with its position in the ANSI table.

EXAMPLE 7   The following program requests a sentence as input and records the frequencies of the letters occurring in the sentence. The array *charCount*( ) has range Asc("A") To Asc("Z"), that is, 65 To 90. The number of occurrences of each letter is stored in the element whose subscript is the ANSI value of the uppercase letter.

```
Private Sub cmdAnalyze_Click()
  Dim index As Integer, letterNum As Integer, sentence As String
  Dim letter As String, column As Integer
  'Count occurrences of different letters in a sentence
  ReDim charCount(Asc("A") To Asc("Z")) As Integer
  For index = Asc("A") To Asc("Z")
    charCount(index) = 0
  Next index
  'Consider and tally each letter of sentence
  sentence = UCase(txtSentence.Text)
```

```
  For letterNum = 1 To Len(sentence)
    letter = Mid(sentence, letterNum, 1)
    If (letter >= "A") And (letter <= "Z") Then
        index = Asc(letter)
        charCount(index) = charCount(index) + 1
    End If
  Next letterNum
  'List the tally for each letter of alphabet
  picLetterCount.Font = "Courier New"
  picLetterCount.Cls
  column = 1    'Next column at which to display letter & count
  For letterNum = Asc("A") To Asc("Z")
    letter = Chr(letterNum)
    picLetterCount.Print Tab(column); letter;
    picLetterCount.Print Tab(column + 1); charCount(letterNum);
    column = column + 6
    If column > 42 Then    'only room for 7 sets of data in a line
        picLetterCount.Print
        column = 1
    End If
  Next letterNum
End Sub
```

[Run, type in the given sentence, and click the command button.]

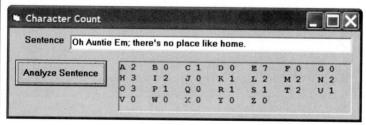

Comments

1. Arrays must be dimensioned in a Dim or ReDim statement before they are used. If a statement such as $a(6) = 3$ appears without a previous Dim or ReDim of the array $a(\ )$, then the error message "Sub or Function not defined" will be displayed when an attempt is made to run the program.

2. Subscripts in ReDim statements can be numeric expressions. Subscripts whose values are not whole numbers are rounded to the nearest whole number. Subscripts outside the range of the array produce an error dialog box during run time.

3. The two arrays in Example 3 are referred to as **parallel arrays** because subscripted variables having the same subscript are related.

4. The integers m and n in the statement Dim *arrayName*(m To n) As *varType* can be positive, negative, or zero. The only restriction is that m cannot be greater than n. The same holds true for ReDim statements.

5. The statement Dim *arrayName*(0 To n) As *varType* can be replaced by the statement Dim *arrayName*(n) As *varType*. The same holds for the ReDim statement.

6. An array whose range has been specified by a ReDim statement or by a Dim statement without a range is said to be **dynamic**. If *array1*( ) is a dynamic array, and *array2*( ) is another array of the same data type (such as String), then the line

```
array1 = array2
```

makes *array1*( ) an exact duplicate of *array2*( ). It will have the same size and contain the same information.

7. A dynamic array can be resized with another ReDim statement. However, the resized array loses all its information. If it is resized with the words **ReDim Preserve**, as much information as possible will be retained.

✔ **PRACTICE PROBLEMS 7.1**

1. When should arrays be used to hold data?

2. (a) Give an appropriate Dim statement to declare a string array to hold the names of the *Time* magazine "Man of the Year" awards for the years 1980 through 1989.
   (b) Write a statement to assign to the array element for 1982 the name of that year's winner, "The Computer".

➤ **EXERCISES 7.1**

In Exercises 1 through 6, determine the output displayed in the picture box when the command button is clicked. All Dim statements for arrays are in the (Declarations) section of (General).

1.
```
Dim a(1 To 20) As Integer

Private Sub cmdDisplay_Click()
  a(5) = 1
  a(10) = 2
  a(15) = 7
  picOutput.Print a(5) + a(10);
  picOutput.Print a(5 + 10);
  picOutput.Print a(20)
End Sub
```

2.
```
Dim sq(1 To 5) As Integer

Private Sub cmdDisplay_Click()
  Dim i As Integer, t As Integer
  For i = 1 To 5
    sq(i) = i * i
  Next i
  picOutput.Print sq(3)
  t = 3
  picOutput.Print sq(5 - t)
End Sub
```

3.
```
Dim fh(1 To 4) As String

Private Sub cmdDisplay_Click()
  Dim i As Integer, n As Integer
  Open "HORSEMEN.TXT" For Input As #1
  For i = 1 To 4
    Input #1, fh(i)
  Next i
  Close #1
  picOutput.Print fh(4)
  n = 1
  picOutput.Print fh(2 * n + 1)
End Sub
```

(Assume that the file HORSEMEN.TXT contains the following entries.)

"Miller", "Layden", "Crowley", "Stuhldreher"

4.
```
Dim s(1 To 4) As Integer

Private Sub cmdDisplay_Click()
  Dim t As Integer, k As Integer
  Open "DATA.TXT" For Input As #1
  t = 0
  For k = 1 To 4
    Input #1, s(k)
    t = t + s(k)
  Next k
  picOutput.Print t
  Close #1
End Sub
```

(Assume that the file DATA.TXT contains the following entries.)

3, 5, 2, 1

5.
```
Dim p(1 To 6) As Integer

Private Sub cmdDisplay_Click()
  Dim k As Integer
  Open "DATA.TXT" For Input As #1
  For k = 1 To 6
    Input #1, p(k)
  Next k
  Close #1
  For k = 6 To 1 Step -1
    picOutput.Print p(k);
  Next k
End Sub
```

(Assume that the file DATA.TXT contains the following entries.)

4, 3, 11, 9, 2, 6

6. ```
Dim a(1 To 4) As Integer
Dim b(1 To 4) As Integer
Dim c(1 To 4) As Integer

Private Sub cmdDisplay_Click()
  Dim i As Integer
  Open "DATA.TXT" For Input As #1
  For i = 1 To 4
    Input #1, a(i), b(i)
  Next i
  Close #1
  For i = 1 To 4
    c(i) = a(i) * b(i)
    picOutput.Print c(i);
  Next i
End Sub
```

(Assume that the file DATA.TXT contains the following entries.)

2, 5, 3, 4, 1, 3, 7, 2

**In Exercises 7 through 12, identify the errors.**

**7.** ```
Dim companies(1 To 100) As String

Private Sub Form_Load()
  Dim recCount As Integer, i As Integer
  Open "COMPLIST.TXT" For Input As #1
  Input #1, recCount
  ReDim companies(1 To recCount) As String
  For i = 1 To recCount
    Input #1, companies(i)
  Next i
  Close #1
End Sub
```

8. ```
Dim p(1 To 100) As Single

Private Sub cmdDisplay_Click()
  Dim i As Integer
  For i = 1 To 200
    p(i) = i / 2
  Next i
End Sub
```

**9.** ```
Dim a(1 To 10) As Integer

Private Sub cmdDisplay_Click()
  Dim i As Integer, k As Integer
  Open "DATA.TXT" For Input As #1
  For i = 1 To 9
    Input #1, a(i)
  Next i
  Close #1
```

```
    For k = 1 To 9
      a(k) = a(5 - k)
    Next k
  End Sub
```

(Assume that the file DATA.TXT contains the following entries.)

1, 2, 3, 4, 5, 6, 7, 8, 9

10.
```
maxRecords = 100
Dim patients(1 To maxRecords) As String

Private Sub cmdDisplay_Click()
  Dim recCount As Integer, i As Integer
  Open "PATIENTS.TXT" For Input As #1
  recCount = 0
  Do While (Not EOF(1)) And (recCount < maxRecords)
    recCount = recCount + 1
    Input #1, patients(recCount)
  Loop
  Close #1
  picOutput.Cls
  picOutput.Print recCount; "records were read."
End Sub
```

11.
```
Dim b(2 To 8 Step 2) As Integer

Private Sub cmdDisplay_Click()
  Dim t As Integer
  Open "DATA.TXT" For Input As #1
  For t = 2 To 8 Step 2
    Input #1, b(t)
  Next t
  Close #1
End Sub
```

(Assume that the file DATA.TXT contains the following entries.)

1, 4, 8, 19

12.
```
Dim names()

Private Sub Form_Load
  Dim i As Integer, recCount As Integer
  Open "DATA.TXT" For Input As #1
  Input #1, recCount
  ReDim names(1 to recCount) As String
  For i = 1 to recCount
    Input #1, names(i)
  Next i
  Close #1
End Sub
```

(Assume that the file DATA.TXT contains the following entries.)

3, "Tom", "Dick", "Harry"

13. Assuming that the array *river( )* is as shown below, fill in the empty rectangles to illustrate the progressing status of *river( )* after the execution of each program segment.

	river(1)	river(2)	river(3)	river(4)	river(5)
river( )	Nile	Ohio	Amazon	Volga	Thames

```
temp = river(1)
river(1) = river(5)
river(5) = temp
```

	river(1)	river(2)	river(3)	river(4)	river(5)
river( )					

```
temp = river(1)
For i = 1 To 4
  river(i) = river(i + 1)
Next i
river(5) = temp
```

	river(1)	river(2)	river(3)	river(4)	river(5)
river( )					

14. Assuming the array *cat( )* is as shown below, fill in the empty rectangles to show the final status of *cat( )* after executing the nested loops.

	cat(1)	cat(2)	cat(3)	cat(4)
cat( )	Morris	Garfield	Socks	Felix

```
For i = 1 To 3
  For j = 1 To 4 - i
    If cat(j) > cat(j + 1) Then
        temp = cat(j)
        cat(j) = cat(j + 1)
        cat(j + 1) = temp
    End If
  Next j
Next i
```

	cat(1)	cat(2)	cat(3)	cat(4)
cat( )				

15. The subscripted variables of the array a( ) have the following values: a(1) = 6, a(2) = 3, a(3) = 1, a(4) = 2, a(5) = 5, a(6) = 8, a(7) = 7. Suppose i = 2, j = 4, and k = 5. What values are assigned to n when the following assignment statements are executed?

(a) n = a(k) − a(i)

(c) n = a(k) * a(i + 2)

(b) n = a(k − i) + a(k − j)

(d) n = a(j − i) * a(i)

16. The array *monthName*( ) holds the following three-character strings.

   monthName(1)="Jan", monthName(2)="Feb", ..., monthName(12)="Dec"

   (a) What is displayed by the following statement?

   ```
   picMonth.Print monthName(4), monthName(9)
   ```

   (b) What value is assigned to *winter* by the following statement?

   ```
   winter = monthName(12) & "," & monthName(1) & "," & monthName(2)
   ```

17. Modify the program in Example 3 to display each student's name and the number of points by which his or her score differs from the average.

18. Modify the program in Example 3 to display only the name(s) of the student(s) with the highest score.

In Exercises 19 through 30, write a line of code or program segment to complete the stated task.

19. Inside a procedure, dimension the string array *bestPicture*( ) to have subscripts ranging from 1993 to 2003.

20. In the (Declarations) section of (General), dimension the string array *info*( ) to have subscripts ranging from 10 to 100.

21. Dimension the string array *marx*( ) with subscripts ranging from 1 to 4 so that the array is visible to all parts of the program. Assign the four values Chico, Harpo, Groucho, and Zeppo to the array as soon as the program is run.

22. Dimension the string array *stooges*( ) with subscripts ranging from 1 to 3 so that the array is local to the event procedure cmdStooges_Click. Assign the three values Moe, Larry, and Curly to the array as soon as the command button is clicked.

23. The arrays a( ) and b( ) have been dimensioned to have range 1 to 4, and values have been assigned to a(1) through a(4). Store these values in b( ) in reverse order.

24. Given two arrays, p( ) and q( ), each with range 1 to 20, compute the sum of the products of the corresponding array elements, that is,

   ```
   p(1)*q(1) + p(2)*q(2) + ... + p(20)*q(20)
   ```

25. Display the values of the array $a(\ )$ of range 1 to 30 in five columns as shown below.

```
a(1)     a(2)     a(3)     a(4)     a(5)
a(6)     a(7)     a(8)     a(9)     a(10)
  .        .        .        .        .
  .        .        .        .        .
a(26)    a(27)    a(28)    a(29)    a(30)
```

26. A list of 20 integers, all between 1 and 10, is contained in a text file. Determine how many times each integer appears and have the program display the frequency of each integer.

27. Compare two arrays $a(\ )$ and $b(\ )$ of range 1 to 10 to see if they hold identical values, that is, if $a(i) = b(i)$ for all i.

28. Calculate the sum of the entries with odd subscripts in an array $a(\ )$ of range 1 to 9.

29. Twelve exam grades are stored in the array *grades*$(\ )$. Curve the grades by adding 7 points to each grade.

30. Read 10 numbers contained in a text file into an array and then display three columns as follows: column 1 should contain the original 10 numbers, column 2 should contain these numbers in reverse order, and column 3 should contain the averages of the corresponding numbers in columns 1 and 2.

31. Thirty scores, each lying between 0 and 49, are given in a text file. Write a program that uses these scores to create an array *frequency*$(\ )$ as follows:

```
frequency(1) = # of scores < 10
frequency(2) = # of scores such that 10 <= score < 20
frequency(3) = # of scores such that 20 <= score < 30
frequency(4) = # of scores such that 30 <= score < 40
frequency(5) = # of scores such that 40 <= score < 50.
```

The program should then display the results in tabular form as follows:

Interval	Frequency
0 to 9	frequency(1)
10 to 19	frequency(2)
20 to 29	frequency(3)
30 to 39	frequency(4)
40 to 49	frequency(5)

32. Given the following flight schedule,

Flight #	Origin	Destination	Departure Time
117	Tucson	Dallas	8:45 a.m.
239	LA	Boston	10:15 a.m.
298	Albany	Reno	1:35 p.m.
326	Houston	New York	2:40 p.m.
445	New York	Tampa	4:20 p.m.

write a program to load this information into four arrays of range 1 to 5, *flightNum*( ), *orig*( ), *dest*( ), and *deptTime*( ), and ask the user to specify a flight number. Have the computer find the flight number and display the information corresponding to that flight. Account for the case where the user requests a nonexistent flight.

33. Table 7.2 contains the names and number of U.S. stores of the top 10 pizza chains in 2001. Write a program to place these data into a pair of parallel arrays, compute the total number of units for these 10 chains, and display a table giving the name and percentage of total units for each of the companies.

Name	Stores	Name	Stores
1. Pizza Hut	7,719	6. Piccadilly Circus	880
2. Domino's	4,813	7. Papa Murphy's	692
3. Little Caesar's	3,065	8. Godfather's	565
4. Papa John's	2,589	9. Round Table	508
5. Sbarro	816	10. Hungry Howie's	433

Table 7.2 Top 10 pizza chains and numbers of U.S. stores.
Source: Pizza Marketing Quarterly, Summer 2002.

34. A retail store has five bins, numbered 1 to 5, each containing a different commodity. At the beginning of a particular day, each bin contains 45 items. Table 7.3 shows the cost per item for each of the bins and the quantity sold during that day.

Bin	Cost per Item	Quantity Sold
1	3.00	10
2	12.25	30
3	37.45	9
4	7.49	42
5	24.95	17

Table 7.3 Costs of items and quantities sold for Exercise 34.

Write a program to

(a) Place the cost per item and the quantity sold from each bin into parallel arrays.
(b) Display a table giving the inventory at the end of the day and the amount of revenue obtained from each bin.
(c) Compute the total revenue for the day.
(d) List the number of each bin that contains fewer than 20 items at the end of the day.

35. Write a program that asks the user for a month by number and then displays the name of that month. For instance, if the user inputs 2, the program should display February. *Hint:* Create an array of 12 strings, one for each month of the year.

36. The file USPRES.TXT contains the names of the 43 U.S. Presidents in the order they served. Write a program that places the names in an array, supplies all presidents having a requested first name, and supplies all presidents for a requested range of numbers. A possible outcome is shown below.

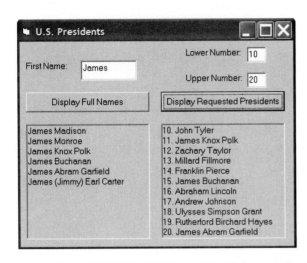

Sample run for Exercise 36

Sample run for Exercise 37

37. The file COLORS.TXT contains the names of the colors of Crayola®* crayons in alphabetical order. Write a program to read the colors into an array and then display the colors beginning with a specified letter. The program should declare an array with upper bound 50 and then increase the size of the array by 10 elements whenever it runs out of space to store the colors. A possible outcome is shown above.

38. An *anagram* of a word or phrase is another word or phrase that uses the same letters with the same frequency. Punctuation marks and spaces are ignored. Write a program that requests two words or phases as input and determines if they are anagrams of each other. (Test the program with the pair of anagrams DWIGHT DAVID EISENHOWER and HE DID VIEW THE WAR DOINGS.)

Exercises 39 and 40 require the Rnd function presented in Section 3.6.

39. Write a program to simulate 1000 rolls of a die and report the number of times each integer occurs.

40. Write a program to select the winning lottery numbers. The selection should consist of six randomly chosen whole numbers from 1 through 40 (with no repeats).

---

* Crayola® is a registered trademark of Binney & Smith.

✔✔ Solutions to Practice Problems 7.1

1. Arrays should be used when

   (a) Several pieces of data of the same type will be entered by the user.

   (b) Computations must be made on the items in a text file *after* all of the items have been read.

   (c) Lists of corresponding data are being analyzed.

2. (a) `Dim manOfTheYear(1980 To 1989) As String`

   (b) `manOfTheYear(1982) = "The Computer"`

7.2 USING ARRAYS

This section considers three aspects of the use of arrays: processing ordered arrays, reading part of an array, and passing arrays to procedures.

Ordered Arrays

An array is said to be **ordered** if its values are in either ascending or descending order. The following arrays illustrate the different types of ordered and unordered arrays. In an ascending ordered array, the value of each element is less than or equal to the value of the next element. That is,

$$[\text{each element}] \le [\text{next element}].$$

For string arrays, the ANSI table is used to evaluate the "less than or equal to" condition.

Ordered Ascending Numeric Array

dates( )	1492	1776	1812	1929	1969

Ordered Descending Numeric Array

discov( )	1610	1541	1513	1513	1492

Ordered Ascending String Array

king( )	Edward	Henry	James	John	Kong

Ordered Descending String Array

lake( )	Superior	Ontario	Michigan	Huron	Erie

Unordered Numeric Array

rates( )	8.25	5.00	7.85	8.00	6.50

Unordered String Array

char( )	G	R	E	A	T

Ordered arrays can be searched more efficiently than unordered arrays. In this section we use their order to shorten the search. The technique used here is applied to searching sequential files in Chapter 8.

EXAMPLE 1 The following program places an ordered list of names into an array, requests a name as input, and informs the user if the name is in the list. Because the list is ordered, the search of the array ends when an element is reached whose value is greater than or equal to the input name. On average, only half the ordered array will be searched. Figure 7.5 shows the flowchart for this search.

```
'Create array to hold 10 strings
Dim nom(1 To 10) As String

Private Sub cmdSearch_Click()
  Dim n As Integer, nameToFind As String
  'Search for a name in an ordered list
  nameToFind = UCase(Trim(txtName.Text))
  n = 0     'n is the subscript of the array
  Do
    n = n + 1
  Loop Until (nom(n) >= nameToFind) Or (n = 10)
  'Interpret result of search
  picResult.Cls
  If nom(n) = nameToFind Then
      picResult.Print "Found."
    Else
      picResult.Print "Not found."
  End If
End Sub

Private Sub Form_Load()
  'Place the names into the array
  'All names must be in uppercase
  nom(1) = "AL"
  nom(2) = "BOB"
  nom(3) = "CARL"
  nom(4) = "DON"
  nom(5) = "ERIC"
  nom(6) = "FRED"
  nom(7) = "GREG"
  nom(8) = "HERB"
  nom(9) = "IRA"
  nom(10) = "JUDY"
End Sub
```

[Run, type Don into the text box, and click the command button.]

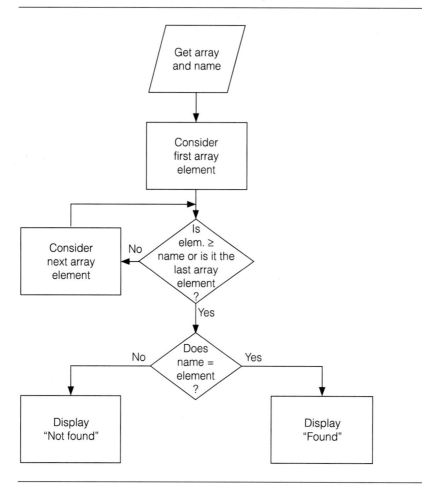

Figure 7.5 Flowchart for a search of an ordered array.

Using Part of an Array

In some programs, we must dimension an array before knowing how many pieces of data are to be placed into it. In these cases, we dimension the array large enough to handle all reasonable contingencies. For instance, if the array is to hold exam grades, and class sizes are at most 100 students, we use a statement such as `Dim grades(1 To 100) As Integer`. In such situations we must employ a **counter variable** to keep track of the number of values actually stored in the array. We create this counter variable using a Dim statement in the (Declarations) section of (General) so that all procedures will have access to it.

EXAMPLE 2 The following program requests a list of companies and then displays them along with a count.

```
'Demonstrate using only part of an array
Dim stock(1 To 100) As String
Dim counter As Integer
```

```
Private Sub cmdRecord_Click()
  If (counter < 100) Then
      counter = counter + 1
      stock(counter) = txtCompany.Text
      txtCompany.Text = ""
      txtCompany.SetFocus
    Else
      MsgBox "No space to record additional companies.", , ""
      txtCompany.Text = ""
      cmdSummarize.SetFocus
  End If
End Sub

Private Sub cmdSummarize_Click()
  Dim i As Integer
  'List stock companies that have been recorded
  picStocks.Cls
  picStocks.Print "You own the following"; counter; "stocks."
  For i = 1 To counter
    picStocks.Print stock(i) & "  ";
    'Move to new line after every 5 stocks
    If Int(i / 5) = i / 5 Then
        picStocks.Print
    End If
  Next i
End Sub

Private Sub Form_Load()
  'Initialize count of companies
  counter = 0
End Sub
```

[Run, type in the eleven companies shown below (press Record Name after each company), and press Summarize.]

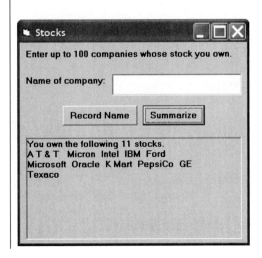

Merging Two Ordered Arrays

Suppose you have two ordered lists of customers (possibly with some customers on both lists) and you want to consolidate them into a single ordered list. The technique for creating the third list, called the **merge algorithm**, is as follows.

1. Compare the two names at the top of the first and second lists.

    (a) If one name alphabetically precedes the other, copy it onto the third list and cross it off its original list.

    (b) If the names are the same, copy the name onto the third list and cross out the name from the first and second lists.

2. Repeat Step 1 with the current top names until you reach the end of either list.

3. Copy the names from the remaining list onto the third list.

EXAMPLE 3   The following program stores two lists of names in arrays and merges them into a third list. At most 10 names will be placed into the third array; duplicates will reduce this number. Because the variable r identifies the next position to insert a name in the third array, $r - 1$ is the number of names in the array.

```
'Create arrays to hold list of names
Dim list1(1 To 5) As String, list2(1 To 5) As String
Dim newList(1 To 10) As String

Private Sub cmdMerge_Click()
  Dim m As Integer, n As Integer, r As Integer
  Dim numNames As Integer, i As Integer
  'Merge two lists of names
  m = 1    'Subscript for first array
  n = 1    'Subscript for second array
  r = 1    'Subscript and counter for third array
  Do While (m <= 5) And (n <= 5)
    Select Case list1(m)
      Case Is < list2(n)
        newList(r) = list1(m)
        m = m + 1
      Case Is > list2(n)
        newList(r) = list2(n)
        n = n + 1
      Case list2(n)
        newList(r) = list1(m)
        m = m + 1
        n = n + 1
    End Select
    r = r + 1
  Loop
  'If one of the lists has items left over, copy them into the third list
  'At most one of the following two loops will be executed
```

```
    Do While m <= 5        'Copy rest of first array into third
      newList(r) = list1(m)
      r = r + 1
      m = m + 1
    Loop
    Do While n <= 5        'Copy rest of second array into third
      newList(r) = list2(n)
      r = r + 1
      n = n + 1
    Loop
    numNames = r - 1
    'Show result of merging lists
    picMergedList.Cls
    For i = 1 To numNames
      picMergedList.Print newList(i) & "   ";
    Next i
End Sub

Private Sub Form_Load()
  'Fill list1 with names
  list1(1) = "Al"
  list1(2) = "Carl"
  list1(3) = "Don"
  list1(4) = "Greg"
  list1(5) = "Judy"
  'Fill list2 with names
  list2(1) = "Bob"
  list2(2) = "Carl"
  list2(3) = "Eric"
  list2(4) = "Greg"
  list2(5) = "Herb"
End Sub
```

[Run, and click the command button.]

Passing Arrays between Procedures

An array that is not dimensioned in the (Declarations) section of (General) but rather is declared in a procedure is local to that procedure and unknown in all other procedures. However, an entire local array can be passed to another procedure. The name of the array, followed by an empty set of parentheses, must appear as an argument in the calling statement, and an array variable name of the same type must appear as a corresponding parameter in the procedure definition of the procedure that is to receive the array.

| EXAMPLE 4 | The following program illustrates passing an array to both a Sub procedure and a Function procedure. |

```
Private Sub cmdDisplayAverage_Click()
  'Pass array to Sub procedure and Function procedure
  Dim score(1 To 10) As Integer
  Call FillArray(score())
  picAverage.Cls
  picAverage.Print "The average score is"; Sum(score()) / 10
End Sub

Private Sub FillArray(s() As Integer)
  'Fill array with scores
  s(1) = 85
  s(2) = 92
  s(3) = 75
  s(4) = 68
  s(5) = 84
  s(6) = 86
  s(7) = 94
  s(8) = 74
  s(9) = 79
  s(10) = 88
End Sub

Private Function Sum(s() As Integer) As Integer
  Dim total As Integer, index As Integer
  'Add up scores
  total = 0
  For index = 1 To 10
    total = total + s(index)
  Next index
  Sum = total
End Function
```

[Run, and click the command button.]

Sometimes it is also necessary to pass a form-level array from one procedure to another. For example, you might have a sorting procedure (discussed in Section 7.3) and three form-level arrays to be sorted. The sorting procedure would be called three times, each time passing a different form-level array. The method for passing a form-level array to another procedure is the same as the method for passing a local array.

EXAMPLE 5 The following program incorporates all three topics discussed in this section. It reads ordered lists of computer languages and spoken languages into form-level arrays, requests a new language as input, and inserts the language into its proper array position (avoiding duplication). The language arrays are dimensioned to hold up to 20 names; the variables *numCompLangs* and *numSpokLangs* record the actual number of languages in each of the ordered arrays. The contents of the text files are

COMPLANG.TXT: ADA, C, Cobol, Fortran, Pascal, Visual Basic
SPOKLANG.TXT: Cantonese, English, French, Mandarin, Russian, Spanish

Object	Property	Setting
frmAdding	Caption	Adding to an Ordered Array
lblNew	Caption	New language:
txtLang	Text	(blank)
cmdAddComp	Caption	Add to Computer List
cmdAddSpok	Caption	Add to Spoken List
picAllLang		

```
Dim compLang(1 To 20) As String
Dim spokLang(1 To 20) As String
Dim numCompLangs As Integer
Dim numSpokLangs As Integer

Private Sub AddALang(lang() As String, langCount As Integer)
  Dim language As String, n As Integer, i As Integer
  'Insert a language into an ordered array of languages
  language = Trim(txtLang.Text)
  n = 0
  Do
    n = n + 1
  Loop Until (UCase(lang(n)) >= UCase(language)) Or (n = langCount)
  If UCase(lang(n)) < UCase(language) Then      'Insert new language at end
      lang(langCount + 1) = language
      langCount = langCount + 1
    ElseIf UCase(lang(n)) > UCase(language) Then      'Insert before item n
      For i = langCount To n Step -1
        lang(i + 1) = lang(i)
      Next i
      lang(n) = language
      langCount = langCount + 1
  End If
End Sub

Private Sub cmdAddComp_Click()
  'Insert language into ordered array of computer languages
  Call AddALang(compLang(), numCompLangs)
```

```
    Call DisplayArray(compLang(), numCompLangs)
End Sub

Private Sub cmdAddSpok_Click()
  'Insert language into ordered array of spoken languages
  Call AddALang(spokLang(), numSpokLangs)
  Call DisplayArray(spokLang(), numSpokLangs)
End Sub

Private Sub DisplayArray(lang() As String, howMany As Integer)
  Dim i As Integer
  'Display the languages in the array
  picAllLang.Cls
  For i = 1 To howMany
    picAllLang.Print lang(i) & "  ";
  Next i
End Sub

Private Sub Form_Load()
  'Fill computer language array from COMPLANG.TXT
  numCompLangs = 0
  Open "COMPLANG.TXT" For Input As #1
  Do While (Not EOF(1)) And (numCompLangs < 20)
    numCompLangs = numCompLangs + 1
    Input #1, compLang(numCompLangs)
  Loop
  Close #1
  'Fill spoken language array from SPOKLANG.TXT
  numSpokLangs = 0
  Open "SPOKLANG.TXT" For Input As #1
  Do While (Not EOF(1)) And (numSpokLangs < 20)
    numSpokLangs = numSpokLangs + 1
    Input #1, spokLang(numSpokLangs)
  Loop
  Close #1
End Sub
```

[Run, type in German, and click Add to Spoken List.]

[Type in FORTRAN and click Add to Computer List.]

Comments

1. In Examples 1 and 5 we searched successive elements of an ordered list beginning with the first element. This is called a **sequential search**. An efficient alternative to the sequential search is the **binary search**, which is considered in the Section 7.4.

2. A single element of an array can be passed to a procedure just like any ordinary numeric or string variable.

```
Private Sub cmdButton_Click()
  Dim num(1 To 20) As Integer
  num(5) = 10
  picOutput.Print Triple(num(5))
End Sub

Private Function Triple(x As Integer) As Integer
  Triple = 3 * x
End Function
```

When the program is run and the command button clicked, 30 will be displayed.

3. Visual Basic provides two functions that simplify working with arrays that have been passed to a procedure. If an array has been dimensioned with the range m To n, then the values of the functions LBound(*arrayName*) and UBound(*arrayName*) are m and n, respectively.

```
Private Sub cmdButton_Click()
  Dim chiefJustice(13 To 15) As String
  chiefJustice(13) = "Warren"
  chiefJustice(14) = "Burger"
  chiefJustice(15) = "Rehnquist"
  Call Display(chiefJustice())
End Sub

Private Sub Display(a() As String)
  Dim i As Integer
  For i = LBound(a) To UBound(a)
    picOutput.Print a(i) & "  ";
  Next i
End Sub
```

When the program is run and the command button clicked, "Warren Burger Rehnquist" will be displayed.

✔ **PRACTICE PROBLEMS 7.2**

1. Can an array be in both ascending and descending order at the same time?

2. How can the Select Case block in Example 3 be changed so all entries of both arrays (including duplicates) are merged into the third array?

➤ **EXERCISES 7.2**

In Exercises 1 and 2, decide whether the array is ordered.

1. month()

January	February	March	April	May

2. pres()

Adams	Adams	Bush	Johnson	Johnson

In Exercises 3 through 8, determine the output displayed in the picture box when the command button is clicked.

3.
```
Private Sub cmdDisplay_Click()
    Dim lake(1 To 5) As String
    lake(3) = "Michigan"
    Call DisplayThird(lake())
End Sub

Private Sub DisplayThird(lake() As String)
  'Display the third element of an array
  picOutput.Print lake(3)
End Sub
```

4.
```
Private Sub cmdDisplay_Click()
   Dim i As Integer, num As Integer
   Dim square(1 To 20) As Integer
   num = Val(InputBox("Enter a number from 1 to 20:"))
   For i = 1 To num
     square(i) = i ^ 2
   Next i
   Call Total(square(), num)
End Sub

Private Sub Total(list() As Integer, n As Integer)
  Dim sum As Integer
  sum = 0
  For i = 1 To n
    sum = sum + list(i)
  Next i
  picOutput.Print "The sum of the first"; n; "elements is"; sum
End Sub
```

(Assume that the response is 4.)

5.
```
Private Sub cmdDisplay_Click()
   Dim i As Integer
   Dim value(1 To 5) As Integer
   Call FillArray(value())
   For i = 1 To 4
     Select Case value(i)
       Case Is < value(i + 1)
         picOutput.Print "less than"
       Case Is > value(i + 1)
         picOutput.Print "greater than"
```

```
         Case Else
            picOutput.Print "equals"
      End Select
   Next i
End Sub

Private Sub FillArray(list() As Integer)
   'Place values into an array of five elements
   Open "DATA.TXT" For Input As #1
   For i = 1 To 5
     Input #1, list(i)
   Next i
   Close #1
End Sub
```

(Assume that the file DATA.TXT contains the following entries.)

3, 7, 1, 1, 17

6.
```
Private Sub cmdDisplay_Click()
   Dim ocean(1 To 5) As String
   ocean(1) = "Pacific"
   Call Musical(ocean(1))
End Sub


Private Sub Musical(sea As String)
   picOutput.Print "South "; sea
End Sub
```

7.
```
Private Sub cmdDisplay_Click()
   Dim rainfall(1 To 12) As Single
   rainfall(1) = 2.4
   rainfall(2) = 3.6
   rainfall(3) = 4.0
   picOutput.Print "The total rainfall for the first quarter is";
   picOutput.Print Total(rainfall(), 3)
End Sub

Private Function Total(rainfall() As Single, n As Integer) As Single
   Dim sum As Single, i As Integer
   sum = 0
   For i = 1 To n
     sum = sum + rainfall(i)
   Next i
   Total = sum
End Function
```

8.
```
Private Sub cmdDisplay_Click()
   Dim i As Integer
   Dim num(1 To 8) As Integer
   Open "DATA.TXT" For Input As #1
   For i = 1 To 8
     Input #1, num(i)
   Next i
   Close #1
```

```
            picOutput.Print "The array has"; Nonzero(num()); "nonzero entries."
        End Sub

        Private Function Nonzero(digit() As Integer) As Integer
          Dim count As Integer, i As Integer
          count = 0
          For i = 1 To 8
            If digit(i) <> 0 Then
                count = count + 1
            End If
          Next i
          Nonzero = count
        End Function
```

(Assume that the file DATA.TXT contains the following entries.)

5, 0, 2, 1, 0, 0, 7, 7

In Exercises 9 through 12, identify the error.

9.
```
Private Sub cmdDisplay_Click()
    Dim city(1 To 3) As String
    Call Assign(city())
    picOutput.Print city
End Sub


Private Sub Assign(town() As String)
  town(1) = "Chicago"
End Sub
```

10.
```
Private Sub cmdDisplay_Click()
    Dim planet(1 To 9) As String
    Call Assign(planet)
    picOutput.Print planet(1)
End Sub


Private Sub Assign(planet As String)
  planet(1) = "Venus"
End Sub
```

11.
```
Private Sub cmdDisplay_Click()
    Dim prompt As String, n As Integer
    Dim number As Single, product As Single, i As Integer
    'Multiply several numbers together
    Dim num(1 To 5) As Single
    prompt = "Enter a positive number to multiply by, or, to see the "
    prompt = prompt & "product, press Enter without giving a number. "
    prompt = prompt & "(Five numbers maximum can be specified.)"
    n = 0
    Do
      n = n + 1
      number = Val(InputBox(prompt))
      If number > 0 Then
          num(n) = number
      End If
    Loop Until (number <= 0) Or (n = 5)
```

```
        product = 1
        For i = 1 To n
          product = product * num(i)
        Next i
        picOutput.Print "The product of the numbers entered is "; product
     End Sub

12.  Private Sub cmdDisplay_Click()
        Dim hue(0 To 15) As String
        hue(1) = "Blue"
        Call Favorite(hue())
     End Sub

     Private Sub Favorite(tone() As String)
        tone(1) = hue(1)
        picOutput.Print tone
     End Sub
```

In Exercises 13 and 14, find the error in the program and rewrite the program to correctly perform the intended task.

```
13.  Private Sub cmdDisplay_Click()
        Dim i As Integer
        Dim a(1 To 10) As Integer
        Dim b(1 To 10) As Integer
        For i = 1 To 10
          a(i) = i ^ 2
        Next i
        Call CopyArray(a(), b())
        picOutput.Print b(10)
     End Sub

     Private Sub CopyArray(a() As Integer, b() As Integer)
        'Place a's values in b
        b() = a()
     End Sub
```

```
14.  Private Sub cmdDisplay_Click()
        Dim a(1 To 3) As Integer
        a(1) = 42
        a(2) = 7
        a(3) = 11
        Call FlipFirstTwo(a())
        picOutput.Print a(1); a(2); a(3)
     End Sub

     Private Sub FlipFirstTwo(a() As Integer)
        'Swap first two elements
        a(2) = a(1)
        a(1) = a(2)
     End Sub
```

Suppose an array has been dimensioned in the (Declarations) section of (General) with the statement `Dim scores(1 To 50) As Single` and numbers assigned to each element by the Form_Load event procedure. In Exercises 15 through 18, write a procedure to perform the stated task.

15. Determine whether the array is in ascending order.

16. Determine whether the array is in descending order.

17. With a single loop, determine whether the array is in ascending order, descending order, both, or neither.

18. Assuming the array is in ascending order, determine how many numbers appear more than once in the array.

In Exercises 19 and 20, suppose arrays *a*( ), *b*( ), and *c*( ) are form-level and that arrays *a*( ) and *b*( ) have each been assigned 20 numbers in ascending order (duplications may occur) by a Form_Load event procedure. For instance, array *a*( ) might hold the numbers 1, 3, 3, 3, 9, 9, ...

19. Write a procedure to place all the 40 numbers from arrays *a*( ) and *b*( ) into *c*( ) so that *c*( ) is also ordered. The array *c*( ) could contain duplications.

20. Write a procedure to place the numbers from *a*( ) and *b*( ) into *c*( ) so that *c*( ) is ordered but contains no duplications.

21. Write a program to dimension an array with the statement `Dim state(1 To 50) As String` and maintain a list of certain states. The list of states should always be in alphabetical order and occupy consecutive elements of the array. The command buttons in the program should give the user the following options:

(a) Take the state specified by the user in a text box and insert it into its proper position in the array. (If the state is already in the array, so report.)
(b) Take the state specified by the user in a text box and delete it from the array. (If the state is not in the array, so report.)
(c) Display the states in the array.
(d) Quit.

22. Write a program that requests a sentence one word at a time from the user and then checks whether the sentence is a *word palindrome*. A word palindrome sentence reads the same, word by word, backward and forward (ignoring punctuation and capitalization). An example is "You can cage a swallow, can't you, but you can't swallow a cage, can you?" The program should hold the words of the sentence in an array and use procedures to obtain the input, analyze the sentence, and declare whether the sentence is a word palindrome. (Test the program with the sentences, "Monkey see, monkey do." and "I am; therefore, am I?")

23. Write a program to display the average score and the number of above-average scores on an exam. Each time the user clicks a "Record Score" command button, a grade should be read from a text box. The average score and the number of above-average scores should be displayed in a picture box whenever the user clicks on a "Show Average" command button. (Assume the class has at most 100 students.) Use a function to calculate the average and another function to determine the number of above-average scores.

Note: Pass the functions an array argument for the grades and a numeric argument for the number of elements of the array that have been assigned values.

24. Suppose an array of 100 names is in ascending order. Write a procedure to search for a name input by the user. If the first letter of the name is found in N through Z, then the search should begin with the 100th element of the array and proceed backward.

Exercises 25 and 26 require the Rnd function presented in Section 3.6.

25. Write a program to randomly select 40 different people from a group of 100 people whose names are contained in a text file. **Hint:** Use an array of 100 elements to keep track of whether or not a person has been selected.

26. *The Birthday Problem.* Given a random group of 23 people, how likely is it that two people have the same birthday? To answer this question, write a program that creates an array of range 1 To 23, randomly assigns to each subscripted variable one of the integers from 1 through 365, and checks to see if any of the subscripted variables have the same value. (Make the simplifying assumption that no birthdays occur on February 29.) Now expand the program to repeat the process 100 times and determine the percentage of the time that there is a match.

✔✔ Solutions to Practice Problems 7.2

1. Yes, provided each element of the array has the same value.

2. The third Case tests for duplicates and assigns only one array element to the third array if duplicates are found in the two arrays. Thus, we remove the third Case and change the first Case so it will process any duplicates. A situation where you would want to merge two lists while retaining duplications is the task of merging two ordered arrays of test scores.

```
Select Case list1(m)
  Case Is <= list2(n)
    newList(r) = list1(m)
    m = m + 1
  Case Is > list2(n)
    newList(r) = list2(n)
    n = n + 1
End Select
```

7.3 CONTROL ARRAYS

We have seen many examples of the usefulness of subscripted variables. They are essential for writing concise solutions to many programming problems. Because of the great utility that subscripts provide, Visual Basic also provides for arrays of text boxes, labels, command buttons, and so on. Because text boxes, labels, and command buttons are referred to generically in Visual Basic as controls, arrays of these objects are called **control arrays**.

Unlike variable arrays, which can only be created by Dim and ReDim statements once a program is running, at least one element of a control array must be created when the form is designed. The remaining elements can be created either during form design, or, perhaps more typically, with the Load statement when the program is run.

To create the first element of an array of text boxes, create an ordinary text box, then access the Properties window, and select the property called Index. By default this property is blank. Change the Index property to 0 (zero). Your text box is now the first element in a subscripted control array. If the name of a text box is *txtBox* and its Index property is 0, then assigning a value to the text box during run time requires a statement of the form

```
txtBox(0).Text = value
```

Arrays are not of much use if they contain only a single element. To create additional elements of the *txtBox*( ) control array during form design, make sure that the element you just created is active by clicking on it. Next, press Ctrl+C (or open the Edit menu and select Copy). Visual Basic has now recorded all the properties associated with *txtBox*(0) and is ready to reproduce as many copies as you desire. To create a copy, press Ctrl+V (or open the Edit menu and select Paste). The copy of *txtBox*(0) appears in the upper-left corner of the form. The value of the Index property for this new text box is 1; thus the text box is referred to as *txtBox*(1). Move this text box to the desired position. Press Ctrl+V again and another copy of *txtBox*(0) appears in the upper left corner of the form. Its Index property is 2. Move *txtBox*(2) to an appropriate position. Continue copying *txtBox*(0) in this manner until all desired controls have been created.

It is important to note that all property settings of *txtBox*(0) are being passed (as default settings) to the other elements of the *txtBox*( ) control array, with the exception of the Index, Top, and Left settings. Thus, as a matter of efficiency, before you begin copying *txtBox*(0), set all properties that you want carried over to all elements of *txtBox*( ). For example, if you desire to have the Text property blank for all *txtBox*( ) elements, set the Text property of *txtBox*(0) to (blank) before starting the copying process.

The preceding discussion gave a process for creating an array of text boxes. This same process applies to creating arrays of labels or any other control. In summary, the following steps create an array of controls while designing a form:

1. Add one instance of the desired control to the form.

2. Set the Index property of this control to 0.

3. Set any other properties of the control that will be common to all elements of the array.

4. Click on the control and then press Ctrl+C to prepare to make a copy of the control.

5. Press Ctrl+V to create a copy of the control. Position this control as desired.

6. Repeat Step 5 until all desired elements of the control array have been created.

EXAMPLE 1

A department store has five departments. The following program requests the amount of sales for each department and displays the total sales for the store. The five labels identifying the departments are grouped into an array of labels and the five text boxes for the individual amounts are grouped into an array of text boxes. For the label captions we use "Department 1", "Department 2", and so on. Because these labels are the same except for the number, we wait until run time and use a For...Next loop inside the Form_Load ( ) event procedure to assign the captions to each element of the *lblDepart*( ) control array. At design time, before making copies of *lblDepart*(0), we set the Alignment property to "1 – Right Justify" so that all elements of the array inherit this property. Similarly, the Text property of *txtSales*(0) is set to (blank) before copying.

Object	Property	Setting
frm7_3_1	Caption	(blank)
lblDepart()	Index	0 to 4
	Alignment	1 – Right Justify
txtSales( )	Index	0 to 4
	Text	(blank)
cmdCompute	Caption	Compute Total Sales
picTotal		

```
Private Sub Form_Load()
  Dim depNum As Integer
  For depNum = 0 To 4
    lblDepart(depNum).Caption = "Department" & Str(depNum + 1)
  Next depNum
End Sub

Private Sub cmdCompute_Click()
  Dim depNum As Integer, sales As Single
  sales = 0
  For depNum = 0 To 4
    sales = sales + Val(txtSales(depNum).Text)
  Next depNum
  picTotal.Cls
  picTotal.Print "Total sales were "; FormatCurrency(sales)
End Sub
```

[Run, type data into the text boxes, and click the command button.]

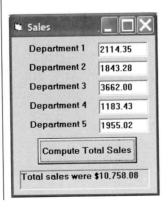

Control Array Event Procedures

In Chapter 3 we discussed several events related to text boxes. One example was the GotFocus event procedure. If *txtBox* is an ordinary text box, then the GotFocus event procedure begins with the statement

```
Private Sub txtBox_GotFocus()
```

If, on the other hand, we make *txtBox* a control array, the GotFocus event procedure begins with the statement

```
Private Sub txtBox_GotFocus(Index As Integer)
```

Two points should be noted. First, even though we may have a dozen or more elements in the *txtBox( )* control array, we will have just one txtBox_GotFocus event procedure to deal with. Second, Visual Basic passes to this one event procedure the value of the Index property for the element of the control array that has just received the focus. We may wish to respond in the same manner whenever any element of *txtBox( )* has the focus, in which case we simply ignore the value of *Index*. If, on the other hand, we wish to respond in different ways, depending on which element has the focus, then we write the GotFocus event procedure in the form

```
Private Sub txtBox_GotFocus(Index As Integer)
  Select Case Index
    Case 0
      action when txtBox(0) gets the focus
    Case 1
      action when txtBox(1) gets the focus
      .
      .
      .
  End Select
End Sub
```

All event procedures for a control array have the additional parameter Index As Integer. This additional parameter can be used, if desired, to base the action taken by the event procedure on which element of the control array underwent the event.

EXAMPLE 2 The following program creates an electronic dialing pad. The form contains a control array of 10 command buttons. Each time a command button is clicked, the Index parameter conveys the digit to be added onto the phone number. This program illustrates using the Index parameter without employing a Select Case statement.

Object	Property	Setting
frm7_3_2	Caption	(blank)
cmdDigit( )	Index	0 to 9
	Caption	(same as Index)
lblPhoneNum	BorderStyle	1 – Fixed Single
	Caption	(blank)

```
Private Sub cmdDigit_Click(Index As Integer)
    lblPhoneNum.Caption = lblPhoneNum.Caption & Right(Str(index), 1)
    If Len(lblPhoneNum.Caption) = 3 Then
        lblPhoneNum.Caption = lblPhoneNum.Caption & "-"
      ElseIf Len(lblPhoneNum.Caption) = 8 Then
        MsgBox "Dialing ...", , ""
        lblPhoneNum.Caption = ""
    End If
End Sub
```

Creating Control Arrays at Run Time

We have discussed the process for creating an entire control array while designing a form—that is, at design time. However, copying and positioning control array elements can become tedious if the number of elements is large. Also, the actual number of elements needed in a control array may not be known until a response from the user is processed at run time. In light of these concerns, Visual Basic provides a solution via the Load statement that only requires us to create the first element of a control array during design time. The remaining elements are then created as needed at run time. Before we discuss creating arrays at run time, we must consider a preliminary topic—the Left, Top, Width, and Height properties of controls. These properties specify the location and size of controls.

The standard unit of measurement in Visual Basic is called a **twip**. There are about 1440 twips to the inch. At design time, when a control is active the two panels on the right side of the Toolbar give the location and size of the control, respectively. Figure 7.6(a) shows an active text box, named Text1. The first panel says that the left side of the text box is 960 twips from the left side of the form, and the top of the text box is 720 twips down from the title bar of the form. In terms of properties, Text1.Left is 960, and Text1.Top is 720. Similarly, the numbers 1935 and 975 in the second panel give the width and height of the text box in twips. In terms of properties, Text1.Width is 1935 and Text1.Height is 975. Figure 7.6(b) shows the meanings of these four properties.

The location and size properties of a control can be altered at run time with statements such as

```
Text1.Left = 480
```

which moves the text box to the left or

```
Text2.Top = Text1.Top + 1.5 * Text1.Height
```

which places Text2 a comfortable distance below Text1. As a result of the second statement, the distance between the two text boxes will be half the height of Text1.

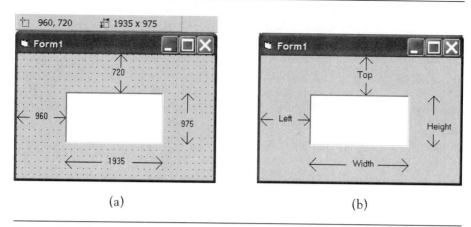

Figure 7.6 The location and size of a control.

If *controlName* is the name of a control whose Index property was assigned a value during form design (thus creating the beginnings of a control array) and *num* is a whole number that has not yet been used as an index for the *controlName*( ) array, then the statement

```
Load controlName(num)
```

copies all the properties of *controlName*(0), including the Top and Left properties, and creates the element *controlName*(*num*) of the *controlName*( ) array. The only property of *controlName*(*num*) that may differ from that of *controlName*(0) is the Visible property. The Load statement always sets the Visible property of the created element to False. After creating a new element of a control array, you will want to adjust the Top and Left properties so that the new element has its own unique location on the form, and then set the Visible property of the new element to True.

EXAMPLE 3   Write a program to create a control array of 12 labels and a control array of 12 text boxes. Position the labels and text boxes so that they form two columns, with the labels to the left of the text boxes and the text boxes one immediately below the other. Use text boxes whose height is as small as possible. Use labels whose height is just large enough to display a single line. Assign the captions Jan, Feb, and so on, to the labels.

SOLUTION   When designing the form, we place the first label to the left of the first text box and set the Index property of both controls to 0. The height of the shortest text box is 288 units and the height of a label just tall enough for a single line is 252 units. We use the text box's Height property as the unit of vertical spacing for both the new text box elements and the new label elements. The following is the form at design time and at run time.

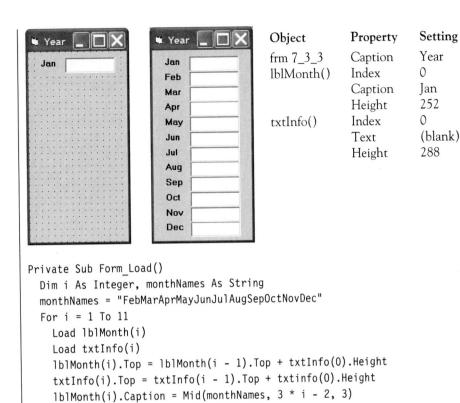

Object	Property	Setting
frm 7_3_3	Caption	Year
lblMonth()	Index	0
	Caption	Jan
	Height	252
txtInfo()	Index	0
	Text	(blank)
	Height	288

```
Private Sub Form_Load()
  Dim i As Integer, monthNames As String
  monthNames = "FebMarAprMayJunJulAugSepOctNovDec"
  For i = 1 To 11
    Load lblMonth(i)
    Load txtInfo(i)
    lblMonth(i).Top = lblMonth(i - 1).Top + txtInfo(0).Height
    txtInfo(i).Top = txtInfo(i - 1).Top + txtinfo(0).Height
    lblMonth(i).Caption = Mid(monthNames, 3 * i - 2, 3)
    lblMonth(i).Visible = True
    txtInfo(i).Visible = True
  Next i
End Sub
```

Comments

1. In the discussion and examples of control arrays, the initial index was always 0. For a particular application it may be more natural to have the lowest index of a control array be 1 or even 2000. To achieve this when creating just the first element at design time and the remaining controls at run time, set the Index property of the first element to the desired lowest index value at design time, then Load the other elements using the desired indexes at run time. (The Load statement copies the properties of the element with the lowest index, whatever that lowest index may be.) For example, at design time you might create *txtSales*(2000) and then at run time execute the statements

```
For yearNum = 2001 to 2010
  Load txtSales(yearNum)
Next yearNum
```

To create an entire control array at design time with indexes starting at a value other than 0, first create the control array using an initial index of 0. Once all elements have been created, use the Properties window to adjust the index of each element of the control array, starting with the element having the highest index.

✔ **PRACTICE PROBLEMS 7.3**

1. Suppose an event procedure has the first line

```
Private Sub txtBox_GotFocus()
```

How do you know whether txtBox is the name of an ordinary control or a control array?

2. Assume element 0 of the txtBox control array was created during design time. What is the shortcoming of the following event procedure?

```
Private Sub Form_Load()
  Load txtBox(1)
  txtBox(1).Visible = True
End Sub
```

3. What is the effect of adding the following line to the event procedure in Problem 2?

```
txtBox(1).Top = txtBox(0).Top + 2 * txtBox(0).Height
```

➤ **EXERCISES 7.3**

In Exercises 1 to 4, design the given form using the indicated number and type of controls.

1. A control array of four text boxes, a command button, and a picture box.

2. A control array of three command buttons and a picture box.

3. A control array of six labels, a control array of six text boxes, and a command button.

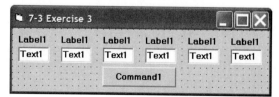

4. Two control arrays of four text boxes each and a control array of four command buttons.

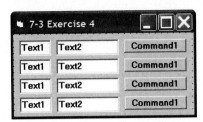

In Exercises 5 to 10, give the effect of the statement.

5. `txtBox.Width = .5 * txtBox.Width`

6. `txtBox.Top = .5 * txtBox.Height`

7. `txtBox.Left = txtBox.Top`

8. `txtBox.Width = txtBox.Height`

9. `txtBox.Width = Form1.Width`

10. `txtBox.Width = .5 * Form1.Width`

In Exercises 11 through 18, suppose the control array cmdButton( ) consists of the two command buttons cmdButton(0) and cmdButton(1) placed vertically, and write an event procedure to carry out the indicated task.

11. When a button is clicked, it disappears.

12. When a button is clicked, it moves 100 twips to the right.

13. When the button is clicked, its caption turns italic and the caption of the other button turns nonitalic.

14. When a button is clicked, the other button assumes the caption of the clicked-on button, but with the letters reversed.

15. When a button is clicked, it moves 100 twips to the right of the other button.

16. When a button is clicked, it moves 100 twips below the other button.

17. When a button is clicked, it doubles in width.

18. When a button is clicked, it becomes twice the width of the other button.

In Exercises 19 and 20, write lines of code to carry out the given tasks.

19. Suppose the text box txtBox with index 0 was created at design time. Create a new text box at run time and place it 100 twips below the original text box.

20. Suppose the text box txtBox with index 0 was created at design time. Create two additional text boxes at run time and place them below the original text box. Then italicize the contents of a text box when the text box gets the focus.

In Exercises 21 through 24, identify the error.

21.
```
Private Sub cmdButton(1)_Click
    cmdButton(1).Caption = "Push Me"
End Sub
```

22.
```
Load cmdButton(Index As Integer)
```

23.
```
Private Sub Form_Load()
    Dim i As Integer
    For i = 0 To 5
      Load lblID(i)
      lblID(i).Caption = Str(1995 + i)
      lblID(i).Top = lblID(i - 1).Top + lblID(i - 1).Height
      lblID(i).Visible = True
    Next i
End Sub
```

24.
```
Private Sub Form_Load()
    Dim i As Integer
    For i = 1 To 12
      Load txtBox(i)
      txtBox.Text(i) = ""
      txtBox.Left(i) = txtBox.Left(i - 1) + txtBox.TextWidth(i - 1)
    Next i
    txtBox.Visible(i - 1) = True
End Sub
```

In Exercises 25 through 28, use the following form (already filled in by the user) to determine the output displayed in the picture box when the command button is clicked. The text boxes on the form consist of four control arrays— *txtWinter( )*, *txtSpring( )*, *txtSummer( )*, **and** *txtFall( )*—**with each control array having indexes ranging from 1 to 4.**

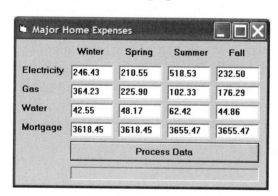

25.
```
Private Sub cmdProcessData_Click()
    Dim itemNum As Integer, total As Single
    total = 0
    For itemNum = 1 to 4
      total = total + Val(txtWinter(itemNum).Text)
    Next itemNum
    picBox.Print "Home expenses for winter were ";
    picBox.Print FormatCurrency(total)
End Sub
```

26.
```
Private Sub cmdProcessData_Click()
    Dim total As Single
    total = 0
    total = total + Val(txtWinter(3).Text)
    total = total + Val(txtSpring(3).Text)
    total = total + Val(txtSummer(3).Text)
    total = total + Val(txtFall(3).Text)
    picBox.Print "Annual water bill was ";
    picBox.Print FormatCurrency(total)
End Sub
```

27.
```
Private Sub cmdProcessData_Click()
    Dim itemNum As Integer, diff As Single, total As Single
    total = 0
    For itemNum = 1 To 4
      diff = Val(txtSummer(itemNum).Text) - Val(txtWinter(itemNum).Text)
      total = total + diff
    Next itemNum
    picBox.Print "Summer bills exceeded winter by ";
    picBox.Print FormatCurrency(total)
End Sub
```

28.
```
Private Sub cmdProcessData_Click()
    Dim itemNum As Integer, total As Single
    total = 0
    For itemNum = 1 To 4
      total = total + TotalCateg(itemNum)
    Next itemNum
    picBox.Print "Total major expenses were ";
    picBox.Print FormatCurrency(total)
End Sub

Private Function TotalCateg(itemNum As Integer) As Single
    Dim total As Single
    total = 0
    total = total + Val(txtWinter(itemNum).Text)
    total = total + Val(txtSpring(itemNum).Text)
    total = total + Val(txtSummer(itemNum).Text)
    total = total + Val(txtFall(itemNum).Text)
    TotalCateg = total
End Function
```

For Exercises 29 through 32, the design-time appearance of a form follows along with the properties assigned to the controls. Determine the appearance of the form after the given program segment is executed.

Object	Property	Setting
frmExer	Caption	7-3 Exercise 29
lblSide	Index	1
	Caption	Row 1
lblTop	Index	1
	Caption	Col 1
txtInfo	Index	1
	Text	(blank)

29.
```
Dim itemNum As Integer
For itemNum = 2 To 4
    Load lblSide(itemNum)
    Load txtInfo(itemNum)
    lblSide(itemNum).Top=lblSide(itemNum-1).Top + 1.5*txtInfo(1).Height
    txtInfo(itemNum).Top=txtInfo(itemNum-1).Top + 1.5*txtInfo(1).Height
    lblSide(itemNum).Caption = "Row" & Str(itemNum)
    lblSide(itemNum).Visible = True
    txtInfo(itemNum).Visible = True
Next itemNum
```

30.
```
Dim itemNum As Integer
For itemNum = 2 To 4
    Load lblTop(itemNum)
    Load txtInfo(itemNum)
    lblTop(itemNum).Left=lblTop(itemNum-1).Left + 1.5*txtInfo(1).Width
    txtInfo(itemNum).Left=txtInfo(itemNum-1).Left + 1.5*txtInfo(1).Width
    lblTop(itemNum).Caption = "Col" & Str(itemNum)
    lblTop(itemNum).Visible = True
    txtInfo(itemNum).Visible = True
Next itemNum
```

31.
```
Dim itemNum As Integer
For itemNum = 2 To 4
    Load lblTop(itemNum)
    Load txtInfo(itemNum)
    lblTop(itemNum).Left = lblTop(itemNum - 1).Left + txtInfo(1).Width
    txtInfo(itemNum).Left = txtInfo(itemNum - 1).Left + txtInfo(1).Width
    lblTop(itemNum).Caption = "Col" & Str(itemNum)
    lblTop(itemNum).Visible = True
    txtInfo(itemNum).Visible = True
Next itemNum
```

32.
```
Dim itemNum As Integer
For itemNum = 2 To 4
    Load lblTop(itemNum)
    Load lblSide(itemNum)
    Load txtInfo(itemNum)
    lblTop(itemNum).Left = lblTop(itemNum - 1).Left + txtInfo(1).Width
    lblSide(itemNum).Top = lblSide(itemNum - 1).Top + txtInfo(1).Height
    txtInfo(itemNum).Left = txtInfo(itemNum - 1).Left + txtInfo(1).Width
    txtInfo(itemNum).Top = txtInfo(itemNum - 1).Top + txtInfo(1).Height
    lblTop(itemNum).Caption = "Col" & Str(itemNum)
    lblSide(itemNum).Caption = "Row" & Str(itemNum)
    lblTop(itemNum).Visible = True
    lblSide(itemNum).Visible = True
    txtInfo(itemNum).Visible = True
Next itemNum
```

33. Modify the form given for Exercises 25 through 28 by deleting the command button and picture box and adding a row of labels below the row of Mortgage text boxes (use a control array named *lblQuarterTot*) and a column of labels to the right of the Fall text boxes (use a control array named *lblCategTot*). The purpose of these new labels is to hold the totals of each column and each row. Write an event procedure that updates the totals displayed on these new labels whenever the cursor is moved from one text box to another.

34. Write a program to compute a student's grade-point average. The program should use InputBox in the Form_Load event procedure to request the number of courses to be averaged and then create elements in two text box control arrays to hold the grade and semester hours credit for each course. After the student fills in these text boxes and clicks on a command button, the program should use a Function procedure to compute the GPA. Then a Sub procedure should display the GPA along with one of two messages. A student with a GPA of 3 or more should be informed that he or she has made the honor roll. Otherwise, the student should be congratulated on having completed the semester. In either case, the student should be wished a merry vacation.

35. Simulate a traffic light with a control array consisting of three small square picture boxes placed vertically on a form. Initially, the bottom picture box is solid green and the other picture boxes are white. When the Tab key is pressed, the middle picture box turns yellow and the bottom picture box turns white. The next time Tab is pressed, the top picture box turns red and the middle picture box turns white. Subsequent pressing of the Tab key cycles through the three colors. **Hint:** First, place the bottom picture box on the form, then the middle picture box, and finally the top picture box.

36. A *Primitive Typewriter*. Create a form containing a picture box and a control array of 26 small command buttons, each having one of the letters of the alphabet as its caption. Add a command button with the caption "Space Bar". When a command button is pressed, its letter (or a space) should be added to the text in the picture box.

37. *Multiple-Choice Quiz*. Write a program to ask multiple-choice questions with four possible answers. Figure 7.7 shows a typical question. The user selects an answer by clicking on a command button and is informed of the correctness of the answer by a message box. When the user gives a correct answer, a new question is presented. The program ends when all questions have been presented or when the user clicks on the Quit command button. Questions and correct answers should be read from a text file. The numbered command buttons should be elements of a command button control array. The question and answers should be displayed using a five-element control array of labels.

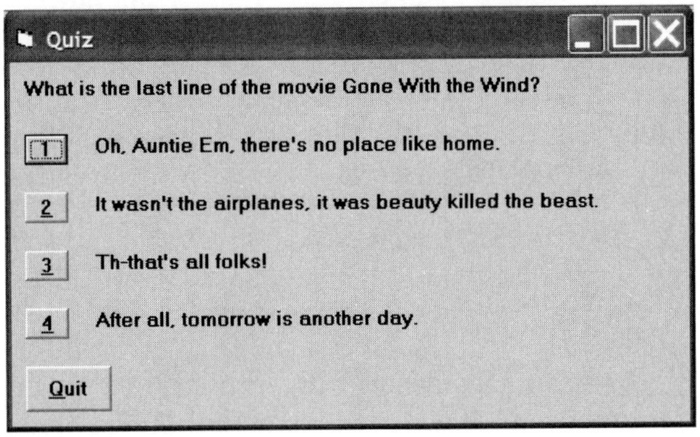

Figure 7.7 A typical question for Exercise 37.

38. Table 7.4 gives the U.S. Census Bureau projections for the populations (in millions) of the states predicted to be the most populous in the year 2025. Write a program that stores the 2025 data in an array and provides a control array of text boxes for the input of the current population of each of these states. When a command button is clicked, the population growths for the states should be displayed in a control array of labels. In a picture box below these five values, the program should display the percentage growth for the collection of five states. (Figure 7.8 shows a possible form design and run with sample data for 2000.) The growth is calculated using the formula

growth = (projected pop. − current pop.) / current pop.

Percentage growth can be obtained using FormatPercent(growth). Test the program with the current populations shown in Figure 7.8.

State	Population in 2025
California	46.3
Texas	34.9
New York	21.8
Illinois	15.3
Florida	27.4

Table 7.4 State populations in the year 2025.

Figure 7.8 Sample run for Exercise 38.

✔✔ **Solutions to Practice Problems 7.3**

1. It is an ordinary control. If it were a control array, the parentheses at the end of the line would contain the words "Index As Integer."

2. The new text box will be placed in the exact same location as the original text box. An additional line, like the one in Practice Problem 3, is needed.

3. The new text box will be placed below the original text box, with space between them equal to the height of the text boxes.

7.4 SORTING AND SEARCHING

A **sort** is an algorithm for ordering an array. Of the many different techniques for sorting an array we discuss two, the **bubble sort** and the **Shell sort**. Both require the interchange of values stored in a pair of variables. If *var1*, *var2*, and *temp* are all variables of the same data type (such as all String), then the statements

```
    temp = var1
    var1 = var2
    var2 = temp
```

assign *var1*'s value to *var2* and *var2*'s value to *var1*.

EXAMPLE I   The following program alphabetizes two words supplied in text boxes.

```
Private Sub cmdAlphabetize_Click()
  Dim firstWord As String, secondWord As String, temp As String
  'Alphabetize two words
  firstWord = txtFirstWord.Text
  secondWord = txtSecondWord.Text
  If firstWord > secondWord Then
      temp = firstWord
      firstWord = secondWord
      secondWord = temp
  End If
  picResult.Cls
  picResult.Print firstWord; " before "; secondWord
End Sub
```

[Run, type "beauty" and "age" into the text boxes, and click the command button.]

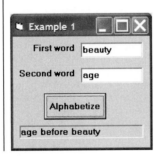

Bubble Sort

The bubble sort is an algorithm that compares adjacent items and swaps those that are out of order. If this process is repeated enough times, the list will be ordered. Let's carry out this process on the list Pebbles, Barney, Wilma, Fred, and Dino. The steps for each pass through the list are as follows:

1. Compare the first and second items. If they are out of order, swap them.

2. Compare the second and third items. If they are out of order, swap them.

3. Repeat this pattern for all remaining pairs. The final comparison and possible swap are between the next-to-last and last elements.

The first time through the list, this process is repeated to the end of the list. This is called the first pass. After the first pass, the last item (Wilma) will be in its proper position. Therefore, the second pass does not have to consider it and so requires one less comparison. At the end of the second pass, the last two items will be in their proper position. (The items that must have reached their proper position have been underlined.) Each successive pass requires one less comparison. After four passes, the last four items will be in their proper positions, and hence, the first will be also.

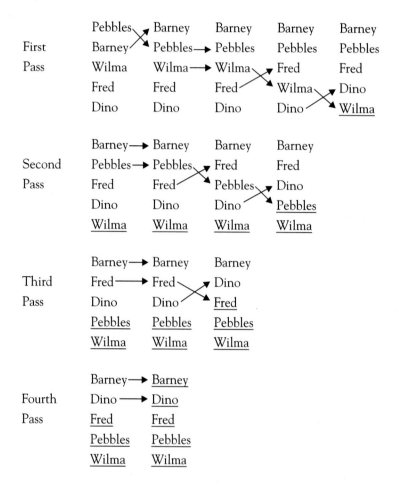

EXAMPLE 2 The following program alphabetizes the names Pebbles, Barney, Wilma, Fred, and Dino. Sorting the list requires a pair of nested loops. The inner loop performs a single pass, and the outer loop controls the number of passes.

```
Dim nom(1 To 5) As String

Private Sub cmdSort_Click()
  Dim passNum As Integer, i As Integer, temp As String
  'Bubble sort names
  For passNum = 1 To 4      'Number of passes is 1 less than number of items
    For i = 1 To 5 - passNum           'Each pass needs 1 less comparison
      If nom(i) > nom(i + 1) Then
          temp = nom(i)
          nom(i) = nom(i + 1)
          nom(i + 1) = temp
      End If
    Next i
  Next passNum
```

```
      'Display alphabetized list
      picNames.Cls
      For i = 1 To 5
        picNames.Print nom(i),
      Next i
    End Sub

    Private Sub Form_Load()
      'Fill array with names
      nom(1) = "Pebbles"
      nom(2) = "Barney"
      nom(3) = "Wilma"
      nom(4) = "Fred"
      nom(5) = "Dino"
    End Sub
```

[Run, and click the command button.]

EXAMPLE 3   Table 7.5 contains facts about the 10 most populous metropolitan areas with listings in ascending order by city name. The following program sorts the table in descending order by population. Data are read from a file into parallel arrays by the Form_Load event procedure. When cmdDisplayStats is clicked, the collection of parallel arrays is sorted based on the array *pop*( ). Each time two items are interchanged in the array *pop*( ), the corresponding items are interchanged in each of the other arrays. This way, for each city, the items of information remain linked by a common subscript.

Metro Area	Population in Millions	Median Income per Household	% Native to State	% Advanced Degree
Boston	4.2	$40,666	73	12
Chicago	8.1	$35,918	73	8
Dallas	3.9	$32,825	64	8
Detroit	4.7	$34,729	76	7
Houston	3.7	$31,488	67	8
Los Angeles	14.5	$36,711	59	8
New York	18.1	$38,445	73	11
Philadelphia	5.9	$35,797	70	8
San Francisco	6.3	$41,459	60	11
Washington	3.9	$47,254	32	17

Note: Column 4 gives the percentage of residents who were born in their current state of residence. Column 5 gives the percentage of residents age 25 or older with a graduate or professional degree.

Table 7.5 The 10 most populous metropolitan areas.

Source: The 1990 Census.

```
Dim city(1 To 10) As String, pop(1 To 10) As Single, income(1 To 10) As Single
Dim natives(1 To 10) As Single, advDeg(1 To 10) As Single

Private Sub cmdDisplayStats_Click()
  Call SortData
  Call ShowData
End Sub

Private Sub Form_Load()
  Dim i As Integer
  'Assume the data for city name, population, medium income, % native,
  'and % advanced degree have been placed in the file "CITYSTAT.TXT"
  '(First line of file is "Boston", 4.2, 40666, 73, 12)
  Open "CITYSTAT.TXT" For Input As #1
  For i = 1 To 10
    Input #1, city(i), pop(i), income(i), natives(i), advDeg(i)
  Next i
  Close #1
End Sub

Private Sub ShowData()
  Dim i As Integer
  'Display ordered table
  picTable.Cls
  picTable.Print , "Pop. in", "Med. income", "% Native", "% Advanced"
  picTable.Print "Metro Area", "millions", "per hsd", "to State", "Degree"
  picTable.Print
  For i = 1 To 10
    picTable.Print city(i); Tab(16); pop(i), income(i), natives(i), advDeg(i)
  Next i
End Sub

Private Sub SortData()
  Dim passNum As Integer, index As Integer
  'Bubble sort table in descending order by population
  For passNum = 1 To 9
    For index = 1 To 10 - passNum
      If pop(index) < pop(index + 1) Then
          Call SwapData(index)
      End If
    Next index
  Next passNum
End Sub

Private Sub SwapData(index As Integer)
  'Swap entries
  Call SwapStr(city(index), city(index + 1))
  Call SwapNum(pop(index), pop(index + 1))
  Call SwapNum(income(index), income(index + 1))
  Call SwapNum(natives(index), natives(index + 1))
  Call SwapNum(advDeg(index), advDeg(index + 1))
End Sub
```

```
Private Sub SwapNum(a As Single, b As Single)
  Dim temp As Single
  'Interchange values of a and b
  temp = a
  a = b
  b = temp
End Sub

Private Sub SwapStr(a As String, b As String)
  Dim temp As String
  'Interchange values of a and b
  temp = a
  a = b
  b = temp
End Sub
```

[Run, and click the command button.]

Shell Sort

The bubble sort is easy to understand and program. However, it is too slow for really long lists. The Shell sort, named for its inventor, Donald L. Shell, is much more efficient in such cases. It compares distant items first and works its way down to nearby items. The interval separating the compared items is called the **gap**. The gap begins at one-half the length of the list and is successively halved until eventually each item is compared with its neighbor as in the bubble sort. The algorithm for a list of n items is as follows.

1. Begin with a gap of $g = \text{Int}(n / 2)$.

2. Compare items 1 and $1 + g$, 2 and $2 + g$, ..., $n - g$ and n. Swap any pairs that are out of order.

3. Repeat Step 2 until no swaps are made for gap g.

4. Halve the value of g.

5. Repeat Steps 2, 3, and 4 until the value of g is 0.

The Shell sort is illustrated in what follows, in which crossing arrows indicate that a swap occurred.

Initial Gap = Int([Number of Items] / 2) = Int(5 / 2) = 2

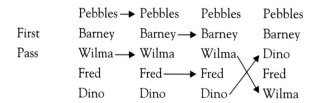

Because there was a swap, use the same gap for the second pass.

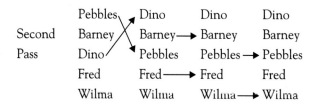

Again, there was a swap, so keep the current gap.

Third Pass
```
Dino ———▶ Dino      Dino      Dino
Barney    Barney—▶ Barney    Barney
Pebbles—▶ Pebbles  Pebbles —▶ Pebbles
Fred      Fred———▶ Fred      Fred
Wilma     Wilma    Wilma ——▶ Wilma
```

There were no swaps for the current gap of 2, so

Next Gap = Int([Previous Gap] / 2) = Int(2 / 2) = 1

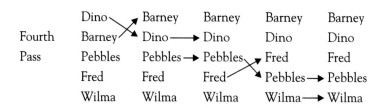

Because there was a swap (actually two swaps), keep the same gap.

Fifth Pass
```
Barney—▶ Barney    Barney    Barney    Barney
Dino ——▶ Dino ——▶ Dino      Dino      Dino
Fred      Fred———▶ Fred ———▶ Fred      Fred
Pebbles   Pebbles  Pebbles —▶ Pebbles —▶ Pebbles
Wilma     Wilma    Wilma    Wilma—▶ Wilma
```

Because there were no swaps for the current gap, then

Next Gap = Int([Previous Gap] / 2) = Int(1 / 2) = 0

and the Shell sort is complete.

Notice that the Shell sort required 17 comparisons to sort the list, whereas the bubble sort required only 10 comparisons for the same list. This illustrates the fact that for very short lists, the bubble sort is preferable; however, for lists of 30 items or more, the Shell sort will consistently outperform the bubble sort. Table 7.6 shows the average number of comparisons required to sort arrays of varying sizes.

Array Elements	Bubble Sort Comparisons	Shell Sort Comparisons
5	10	15
10	45	57
15	105	115
20	190	192
25	300	302
30	435	364
50	1225	926
100	4950	2638
500	124,750	22,517
1000	499,500	58,460

Table 7.6 Efficiency of bubble and Shell sorts.

EXAMPLE 4 The following program uses the Shell sort to alphabetize the parts of a running shoe (see Figure 7.9). The data are read into an array whose size is large enough to guarantee sufficient space. In the event procedure Form_Load, the variable *numParts* provides the subscripts for the array and serves as a counter. The final value of *numParts* is available to all procedures because the variable was created in the (Declarations) section of (General). The Sub procedure SortData uses a flag to indicate if a swap has been made during a pass.

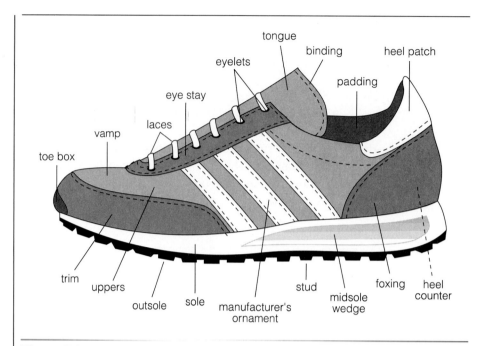

Figure 7.9 Running shoe.

```
Dim part(1 To 50) As String
Dim numParts As Integer

Private Sub cmdDisplayParts_Click()
  'Sort and display parts of running shoe
  Call SortData
  Call ShowData
End Sub

Private Sub Form_Load()
  'Read part names
  numParts = 0     'Number of parts
  Open "SHOEPART.TXT" For Input As #1
  Do While (Not EOF(1)) And (numParts < UBound(part))
    numParts = numParts + 1
    Input #1, part(numParts)
  Loop
  Close #1
End Sub

Private Sub ShowData()
  Dim i As Integer
  'Display sorted list of parts
  picParts.Cls
  For i = 1 To numParts
    picParts.Print part(i),
    If i Mod 5 = 0 Then   'only put 5 items per line
        picParts.Print
    End If
  Next i
End Sub
```

```
Private Sub SortData()
  Dim gap As Integer, doneFlag As Boolean
  Dim index As Integer, temp As String
  'Shell sort shoe parts
  gap = Int(numParts / 2)
  Do While gap >= 1
    Do
      doneFlag = True
      For index = 1 To numParts - gap
        If part(index) > part(index + gap) Then
            temp = part(index)
            part(index) = part(index + gap)
            part(index + gap) = temp
            doneFlag = False
        End If
      Next index
    Loop Until doneFlag = True    'Can also be written Loop Until doneFlag
    gap = Int(gap / 2)            'Halve the length of the gap
  Loop
End Sub
```

[Run, and click the command button.]

Parts of a Running Shoe

Display Shoe Parts in Alphabetical Order

binding	eye stay	eyelets	foxing	heel counter
heel patch	laces	mfg's ornmt	midsle wdge	outsole
padding	sole	stud	toe box	tongue
trim	uppers	vamp		

Searching

Suppose we had an array of 1000 names in alphabetical order and wanted to locate a specific person in the list. One approach would be to start with the first name and consider each name until a match was found. This process is called a **sequential search**. We would find a person whose name begins with "A" rather quickly, but 1000 comparisons might be necessary to find a person whose name begins with "Z." For much longer lists, searching could be a time-consuming matter. However, there is a method, called a **binary search**, that shortens the task considerably.

Let us refer to the sought item as *quarry*. The binary search looks for *quarry* by determining in which half of the list it lies. The other half is then discarded, and the retained half is temporarily regarded as the entire list. The process is repeated until the item is found. A flag can indicate if *quarry* has been found.

The algorithm for a binary search of an ascending list is as follows (Figure 7.10 shows the flowchart for a binary search):

1. At each stage, denote the subscript of the first item in the retained list by *first* and the subscript of the last item by *last*. Initially, the value of *first* is 1, the value of *last* is the number of items in the list, and the value of *flag* is False.

2. Look at the middle item of the current list, the item having the subscript $middle = Int((first + last) / 2)$.

3. If the middle item is *quarry*, then *flag* is set to True and the search is over.

4. If the middle item is greater than *quarry*, then *quarry* should be in the first half of the list. So the subscript of *quarry* lies between *first* and *middle* − 1. That is, the new value of *last* is *middle* − 1.

5. If the middle item is less than *quarry*, then *quarry* should be in the second half of the list of possible items. So the subscript of *quarry* lies between *middle* + 1 and *last*. That is, the new value of *first* is *middle* + 1.

6. Repeat Steps 2 through 5 until *quarry* is found or until the halving process uses up the entire list. (When the entire list has been used up, *first* > *last*.) In the second case, *quarry* was not in the original list.

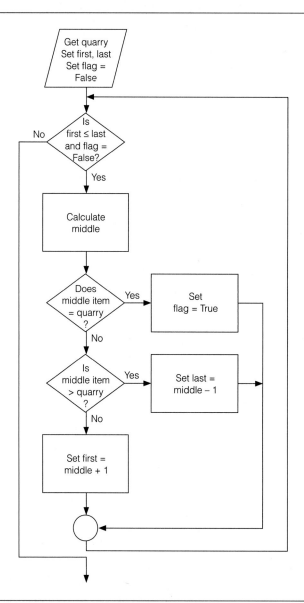

Figure 7.10 Flowchart for a binary search.

EXAMPLE 5   In the following program the array *firm*( ) contains the alphabetized names of up to 100 corporations. The program requests the name of a corporation as input and uses a binary search to determine whether the corporation is in the array.

```
Dim firm(1 TO 100) As String
Dim numFirms As Integer

Private Sub BinarySearch(corp As String, result As String)
  Dim foundFlag As Boolean
  Dim first As Integer, middle As Integer, last As Integer
  'Array firm() assumed already ordered alphabetically
  'Binary search of firm() for corp
  foundFlag = False
  first = 1
  last = numFirms
  Do While (first <= last) And (Not foundFlag)
    middle = Int((first + last) / 2)
    Select Case UCase(firm(middle))
      Case corp
        foundFlag = True
      Case Is > corp
        last = middle - 1
      Case Is < corp
        first = middle + 1
    End Select
  Loop
  If foundFlag Then
      result = "found"
    Else
      result = "not found"
  End If
End Sub

Private Sub cmdSearch_Click()
  Dim corp As String, result As String
  corp = UCase(Trim(txtCorporation.Text))
  Call BinarySearch(corp, result)
  'Display results of search
  picResult.Cls
  picResult.Print corp; " "; result
End Sub

Private Sub Form_Load()
  'Fill array with data from FIRMS.TXT
  Open "FIRMS.TXT" For Input As #1      'Contains up to 100 companies
  numFirms = 0
  Do While (Not EOF(1)) And (numFirms < UBound(firm))
    numFirms = numFirms + 1
    Input #1, firm(numFirms)
  Loop
  Close #1
End Sub
```

[Run, type IBM into the text box, and click the command button.]

Suppose the array contains 100 corporations and the corporation input in Example 5 is in the second half of the array. On the first pass, *middle* would be assigned Int$((1 + 100)/2)$ = Int(50.5) = 50 and then *first* would be altered to $50 + 1 = 51$. On the second pass, *middle* would be assigned Int$((51 + 100)/2)$ = Int(75.5) = 75. If the corporation is not the array element with subscript 75, then either *last* would be assigned 74 or *first* would be assigned 76, depending on whether the corporation appears before or after the 75th element. Each pass through the loop halves the range of subscripts containing the corporation until the corporation is located.

In Example 5, the binary search merely reported whether an array contained a certain item. After finding the item, its array subscript was not needed. However, if related data are stored in parallel arrays (as in Table 7.5), the subscript of the found item can be used to retrieve the related information in the other arrays. This process, called a **table lookup**, is used in the following example.

EXAMPLE 6

The following program uses a binary search procedure to locate the data for a city from Example 3 requested by the user. The program does not include a sort of the text file CITYSTAT.TXT because the file is already ordered alphabetically by city name.

```
Dim city(1 To 10) As String, pop(1 To 10) As Single, income(1 To 10) As Single
Dim natives(1 To 10) As Single, advDeg(1 To 10) As Single

Private Sub cmdDisplayStats_Click()
  Dim searchCity As String, result As Integer
  'Search for city in the metropolitan areas table
  Call GetCityName(searchCity)
  Call FindCity(searchCity, result)
  picResult.Cls
  If result > 0 Then
      Call ShowData(result)
    Else
      picResult.Print searchCity & " not in file"
  End If
End Sub

Private Sub FindCity(searchCity As String, result As Integer)
  Dim first As Integer, middle As Integer, last As Integer
  Dim foundFlag As Boolean
  'Binary search table for city name
  first = 1
  last = 10
  foundFlag = False
```

```
      Do While (first <= last) And (Not foundFlag)
        middle = Int((first + last) / 2)
         Select Case UCase(city(middle))
           Case searchCity
             foundFlag = True
           Case Is > searchCity
             last = middle - 1
           Case Is < searchCity
              first = middle + 1
         End Select
      Loop
      If foundFlag Then
          result = middle
        Else
          result = 0
      End If
    End Sub

    Private Sub Form_Load()
      Dim i As Integer
      'Assume that the data for city name, population, medium income, % native,
      'and % advanced degree have been placed in the file "CITYSTAT.TXT"
      '(First line of file is "Boston", 4.2, 4066, 73, 12)
      Open "CITYSTAT.TXT" For Input As #1
      For i = 1 To 10
        Input #1, city(i), pop(i), income(i), natives(i), advDeg(i)
      Next i
      Close #1
    End Sub

    Private Sub GetCityName(searchCity As String)
      'Request name of city as input
      searchCity = UCase(Trim(txtCity.Text))
    End Sub

    Private Sub ShowData(index As Integer)
      'Display city and associated information
      picResult.Print , "Pop. in", "Med. income", "% Native", "% Advanced"
      picResult.Print "Metro Area", "millions", "per hsd", "to State", "Degree"
      picResult.Print
      picResult.Print city(index), pop(index), income(index),
      picResult.Print natives(index), advDeg(index)
    End Sub
```

[Run, type San Francisco into the text box, and click the command button.]

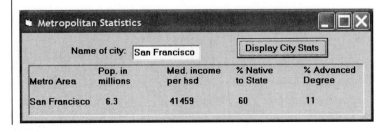

Comments

1. Suppose our bubble sort algorithm is applied to an ordered list. The algorithm will still make $n - 1$ passes through the list. The process could be shortened for some lists by flagging the presence of out-of-order items as in the Shell sort.

2. In Example 3, parallel arrays already ordered by one field were sorted by another field. Usually, parallel arrays are sorted by the field to be searched when accessing the file. This field is called the **key field**.

3. Suppose an array of 2000 items is searched sequentially—that is, one item after another—in order to locate a specific item. The number of comparisons would vary from 1 to 2000, with an average of 1000. With a binary search, the number of comparisons would be at most 11, because $2^{11} > 2000$.

4. The built-in function UCase converts all the characters in a string to uppercase. UCase is useful in sorting and searching arrays of strings when the alphabetic case (upper or lower) is unimportant. For instance, Example 5 includes UCase in the Select Case comparisons, and so the binary search will locate "Mobil" in the array even if the user entered "MOBIL".

5. The Visual Basic function Timer can be used to determine the speed of a sort. Precede the sort with the statement t = Timer. After the sort has executed, the statement picOutput.Print Timer − t will display the duration of the sort in seconds.

PRACTICE PROBLEMS 7.4

1. The pseudocode for a bubble sort of an array of n items follows. Why is the terminating value of the outer loop $n - 1$ and the terminating value of the inner loop $n - j$?

```
For j = 1 To n - 1
  For k = 1 To n - j
    If [kth and (k+1)st items are out of order] Then [interchange them]
  Next k
Next j
```

2. Complete the table below by filling in the values of each variable after successive passes of a binary search of a list of 20 items, where the sought item is in the 13th position.

First	Last	Middle
1	20	10
11	20	

EXERCISES 7.4

In Exercises 1 through 4, determine the output displayed in the picture box when the command button is clicked.

1.
```
Private Sub cmdDisplay_Click()
    Dim p As Integer, q As Integer, temp As Integer
    p = 100
    q = 200
    temp = p
    p = q
    q = temp
    picOutput.Print p; q
End Sub
```

2.
```
Dim gag(1 To 2) As String

Private Sub cmdDisplay_Click()
  If gag(2) < gag(1) Then
      Dim temp As String
      temp = gag(2)
      gag(2) = gag(1)
      gag(1) = temp
  End If
  picOutput.Print gag(1), gag(2)
End Sub

Private Sub Form_Load()
  gag1 = "Stan"
  gag2 = "Oliver"
End Sub
```

3.
```
Private Sub cmdDisplay_Click()
    Dim x As Single, y As Single, temp As Single
    Dim swappedFlag As Boolean
    x = 7
    y = 11
    swappedFlag = False
    If y > x Then
        temp = x
        x = y
        y = temp
        swappedFlag = True
    End If
    picOutput.Print x; y;
    If swappedFlag = True Then
        picOutput.Print "Numbers interchanged."
    End If
End Sub
```

4.
```
Dim a(1 To 3) As Integer

Private Sub cmdDisplay_Click()
  Dim j As Integer, k As Integer, temp As Integer
  For j = 1 To 2
    For k = 1 To 3 - j
      If a(k) > a(k + 1) Then
          temp = a(k)
          a(k) = a(k + 1)
          a(k + 1) = temp
      End If
```

```
      Next k
    Next j
    For j = 1 To 3
      picOutput.Print a(j);
    Next j
End Sub

Private Sub Form_Load()
  Dim j As Integer
  Open "DATA.TXT" For Input As #1
  For j = 1 To 3
    Input #1, a(j)
  Next j
  Close #1
End Sub
```

(Assume that the file DATA.TXT contains the following entries.)

7, 4, 3

In Exercises 5 and 6, identify the errors.

5. `Dim c(1 To 4) As Integer, d(1 To 4) As Integer`

```
Private Sub cmdDisplay_Click()
  'swap two items
  c(4) = d(4)
  d(4) = c(4)
  picOutput.Print c(4), d(4)
End Sub

Private Sub Form_Load()
  Dim i As Integer
  Open "DATA.TXT" For Input As #1
  For i = 1 To 4
    Input #1, c(i), d(i)
  Next i
  Close #1
End Sub
```

(Assume that the file DATA.TXT contains the following entries.)

1, 2, 3, 4, 5, 6, 7, 8

6. `Dim a(1 To 3) As Integer, b(1 To 3) As Integer`

```
Private Sub cmdDisplay_Click()
  Dim temp(1 To 3) As Integer
  temp() = a()
  a() = b()
  b() = temp()
End Sub

Private Sub Form_Load()
  Dim i As Integer
  Open "DATA.TXT" For Input As #1
```

```
      For i = 1 To 3
        Input #1, a(i), b(i)
      Next i
      Close #1
  End Sub
```

(Assume that the file DATA.TXT contains the following entries.)

1, 3, 5, 7, 9, 11

7. Which type of search would be best for the following array?

1	2	3	4	5
Paul	Ringo	John	George	Pete

8. Which type of search would be best for the following array?

1	2	3	4	5
Beloit	Green Bay	Madison	Milwaukee	Oshkosh

9. Consider the items Tin Man, Dorothy, Scarecrow, and Lion in that order. After how many swaps in a bubble sort will the list be in alphabetical order?

10. How many comparisons will be made in a bubble sort of six items?

11. How many comparisons will be made in a bubble sort of n items?

12. Modify the program in Example 2 so that it will keep track of the number of swaps and comparisons and display these numbers before ending.

13. Rework Exercise 9 using the Shell sort.

14. How many comparisons would be made in a Shell sort of six items if the items were originally in descending order and were sorted in ascending order?

15. If a list of six items is already in the proper order, how many comparisons will be made by a Shell sort?

16. The following Sub procedure fills an array of 2000 integers with values between 0 and 63 that are in need of sorting. Write a program that uses the Sub procedure and sorts the array *nums*( ) with a bubble sort. Run the program and time the execution. Do the same for the Shell sort.

```
Private Sub FillArray(nums() As Integer)
  'Generate numbers from 0 to 63 and place in array
  nums(1) = 5
  For i = 2 To 2000
    nums(i) = (9 * nums(i - 1) + 7) Mod 64
  Next i
End Sub
```

17. Suppose a list of 5000 numbers is to be sorted, but the numbers consist of only 1, 2, 3, and 4. Describe a method of sorting the list that would be much faster than either the bubble or Shell sort.

18. The bubble sort gets its name because in an ascending sort successive passes cause "lighter" items to rise to the top like bubbles in water. How did the Shell sort get its name?

19. What is the maximum number of comparisons required to find an item in a sequential search of 16 items? What is the average number of comparisons? What is the maximum number of comparisons required to find an item in a binary search of 16 items?

20. Redo Exercise 19 with 2^n items, where n is any positive integer.

In Exercises 21 through 28, write a program (or procedure) to complete the stated task.

21. Exchange the values of the variables x, y, and z so that x has y's value, y has z's value, and z has x's value.

22. Display the names of the seven dwarfs in alphabetical order. For the contents of a text file use

    Doc, Grumpy, Sleepy, Happy, Bashful, Sneezy, Dopey

23. The nation's capital has long been a popular staging area for political, religious and other large public rallies, protest marches, and demonstrations. The events in Table 7.7 have drawn the largest crowds, according to estimates from D.C., U.S. Park, or Capitol police. Read the data into a pair of parallel arrays and display a similar table with the event names in alphabetical order.

Event	Crowd Estimate (in thousands)
LBJ inauguration (1/23/65)	1,200
Bicentennial fireworks (7/4/76)	1,000
Desert Storm rally (6/8/91)	800
Bill Clinton inauguration (1/20/93)	800
Beach Boys concert (7/4/85)	625
Washington Redskins victory parade (2/3/88)	600
Vietnam moratorium rally (11/15/69)	600
Ronald Reagan inauguration (1/20/81)	500
U.S. Iran hostage motorcade (1/28/81)	500

Table 7.7 Largest Public Displays of Emotion in Washington, D.C.

24. Table 7.8 presents statistics on the five leading athletic footwear brands. Read the data into three parallel arrays and display a similar table with market share in descending order.

Brand	Revenue (in $ millions)	Percentage Share of U.S. Market
Adidas USA	3,536	15.1
K-Swiss	222	3.6
New Balance	2,201	9.4
Nike	9,489	39.2
Reebok	2,865	10.9

Table 7.8 2000 U.S. market share in athletic footwear.

Source: Business Wire.

25. Accept 10 words to be input in alphabetical order and store them in an array. Then accept an 11th word as input and store it in the array in its correct alphabetical position.

26. An airline has a list of 200 flight numbers (between 1 and 1000) in ascending order in the file FLIGHTS.TXT. Accept a number as input and do a binary search of the list to determine if the flight number is valid.

27. Modify the program in Exercise 16 to compute and display the number of times each of the numbers from 0 through 63 appears.

28. Allow a number n to be input by the user. Then accept as input a list of n numbers. Place the numbers into an array and apply a bubble sort.

29. Write a program that accepts a word as input and converts it into Morse code. The dots and dashes corresponding to each letter of the alphabet are as follows:

A · –	H · · · ·	O – – –	V · · · –
B – · · ·	I · ·	P · – – ·	W · – –
C – · – ·	J · – – –	Q – – · –	X – · · –
D – · ·	K – · –	R · – ·	Y – · – –
E ·	L · – · ·	S · · ·	Z – – · ·
F · · – ·	M – –	T –	
G – – ·	N – ·	U · · –	

30. Write a program that accepts an American word as input and performs a binary search to translate it into its British equivalent. Use the following list of words for data, and account for the case when the word requested is not in the list.

American	British	American	British
attic	loft	ice cream	ice
business suit	lounge suit	megaphone	loud hailer
elevator	lift	radio	wireless
flashlight	torch	sneakers	plimsolls
french fries	chips	truck	lorry
gasoline	petrol	zero	nought

31. Write a program that accepts a student's name and seven test scores as input and calculates the average score after dropping the two lowest grades.

32. Suppose letter grades are assigned as follows:

97 and above	A+	74–76	C
94–96	A	70–73	C–
90–93	A–	67–69	D+
87–89	B+	64–66	D
84–86	B	60–63	D–
80–83	B–	0–59	F
77–79	C+		

Write a program that accepts a grade as input and displays the corresponding letter. *Hint:* This problem shows that when you search an array, you don't always look for equality. Set up an array *range*( ) containing the values 97, 94, 90, 87, 84, . . . , 0 and the parallel array *letter*( ) containing A+, A, A–, B+, . . . , F. Next, perform a sequential search to find the first *i* such that *range*(i) is less than or equal to the input grade.

33. The *median* of a set of n measurements is a number such that half the n measurements fall below the median, and half fall above. If the number of measurements n is odd, the median is the middle number when the measurements are arranged in ascending or descending order. If the number of measurements n is even, the median is the average of the two middle measurements when the measurements are arranged in ascending or descending order. Write a program that requests a number n and a set of n measurements as input and then displays the median.

34. Write a program with two command buttons labeled Ascending Order and Descending Order that displays the eight vegetables in V8® in either ascending or descending alphabetic order. The vegetables (tomato, carrot, celery, beet, parsley, lettuce, watercress, and spinach) should be stored in a form-level array.

✔✔ **Solutions to Practice Problems 7.4**

1. The outer loop controls the number of passes, one less than the number of items in the list. The inner loop performs a single pass, and the jth pass consists of $n - j$ comparisons.

2.

First	Last	Middle
1	20	10
11	20	15
11	14	12
13	14	13

7.5 TWO-DIMENSIONAL ARRAYS

Each array discussed so far held a single list of items. Such array variables are called **single-subscripted variables**. An array can also hold the contents of a table with several rows and columns. Such arrays are called **two-dimensional arrays** or **double-subscripted variables**. Two tables follow. Table 7.9 gives the road mileage between certain cities. It has four rows and four columns. Table 7.10 shows the leading universities in three disciplines. It has three rows and five columns.

	Chicago	Los Angeles	New York	Philadelphia
Chicago	0	2054	802	738
Los Angeles	2054	0	2786	2706
New York	802	2786	0	100
Philadelphia	738	2706	100	0

Table 7.9 Road mileage between selected U.S. cities.

	1	2	3	4	5
Business	U of PA	U of IN	U of MI	UC Berk	U of VA
Comp Sci.	MIT	Cng-Mellon	UC Berk	Cornell	U of IL
Engr/Gen.	U of IL	U of OK	U of MD	Cng-Mellon	CO Sch. of Mines

Table 7.10 University rankings.

Source: A Rating of Undergraduate Programs in American and International Universities, Dr. Jack Gourman, 1998.

Two-dimensional array variables store the contents of tables. They have the same types of names as other array variables. The only difference is that they have two subscripts, each with its own range. The range of the first subscript is determined by the number of rows in the table, and the range of the second subscript is determined by the number of columns. The statement

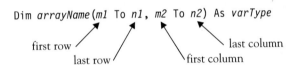

```
Dim arrayName(m1 To n1, m2 To n2) As varType
```
first row
last row
first column
last column

declares an array of type *varType* corresponding to a table with rows labeled from *m1* To *n1* and columns labeled from *m2* to *n2*. The entry in the *j*th row, *k*th column is *arrayName(j,k)*. For instance, the data in Table 7.9 can be stored in an array named *rm( )*. The statement

```
Dim rm(1 To 4, 1 To 4) As Single
```

will declare the array. Each element of the array has the form *rm(row, column)*. The entries of the array are

rm(1,1)=0	rm(1,2)=2054	rm(1,3)=802	rm(1,4)=738
rm(2,1)=2054	rm(2,2)=0	rm(2,3)=2786	rm(2,4)=2706
rm(3,1)=802	rm(3,2)=2786	rm(3,3)=0	rm(3,4)=100
rm(4,1)=738	rm(4,2)=2706	rm(4,3)=100	rm(4,4)=0

As with one-dimensional arrays, when a two-dimensional array is declared using Dim in the (Declarations) section of (General), it is accessible in all event procedures and general procedures and retains whatever values are assigned until the program is terminated. Two-dimensional arrays also can be declared with Dim that are local to a procedure and cease to exist once the procedure is exited. When the range of the subscripts is given by one or more variables, the proper statement to use is

```
ReDim arrayName(m1 To n1, m2 To n2) As varType
```

The data in Table 7.10 can be stored in a two-dimensional string array named *univ*( ). The appropriate array is declared with the statement

```
Dim univ(1 To 3, 1 To 5) As String
```

Some of the entries of the array are

univ(1,1) = "U of PA"
univ(2,3) = "UC Berk"
univ(3,5) = "CO Sch. of Mines"

EXAMPLE 1 The following program stores and accesses the data from Table 7.9. Data are read from the file DISTANCE.TXT into a two-dimensional form-level array using a pair of nested loops. The outer loop controls the rows, and the inner loop controls the columns.

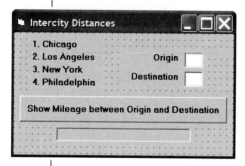

Object	Property	Setting
frmDist	Caption	Intercity Distances
lblCh	Caption	1. Chicago
lblLA	Caption	2. Los Angeles
lblNY	Caption	3. New York
lblPh	Caption	4. Philadelphia
lblOrig	Caption	Origin
txtOrig	Text	(blank)
lblDest	Caption	Destination
txtDest	Text	(blank)
cmdShow	Caption	Show Mileage between Origin and Destination
picMiles		

```
Dim rm(1 To 4, 1 To 4) As Single  'In (Declarations) section of (General)

Private Sub cmdShow_Click()
  Dim row As Integer, col As Integer
  'Determine road mileage between cities
  row = Val(txtOrig.Text)
  col = Val(txtDest.Text)
  If (row >= 1 And row <= 4) And (col >= 1 And col <= 4) Then
      Call ShowMileage(rm(), row, col)
    Else
      MsgBox "Origin and Destination must be numbers from 1 to 4", , "Error"
  End If
  txtOrig.SetFocus
End Sub

Private Sub Form_Load()
  Dim row As Integer, col As Integer
  'Fill two-dimensional array with intercity mileages
  'Assume the data have been placed in the file "DISTANCE.TXT"
  '(First line of the file is 0,2054,802,738)
```

```
    Open "DISTANCE.TXT" For Input As #1
    For row = 1 To 4
      For col = 1 To 4
        Input #1, rm(row, col)
      Next col
    Next row
    Close #1
End Sub

Private Sub ShowMileage(rm() As Single, row As Integer, col As Integer)
    'Display mileage between cities
    picMiles.Cls
    picMiles.Print "The road mileage is"; rm(row, col)
End Sub
```

[Run, type 3 into the Origin box, type 1 into the Destination box, and click the command button.]

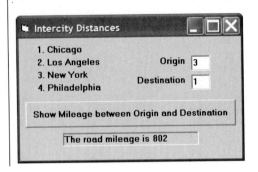

So far, two-dimensional arrays have been used only to store data for convenient lookup. In the next example, an array is used to make a valuable computation.

EXAMPLE 2   The Center for Science in the Public Interest publishes *The Nutrition Scorebook*, a highly respected rating of foods. The top two foods in each of five categories are shown in Table 7.11 along with some information on their composition. The following program computes the nutritional content of a meal. The table is read into an array, and then the program requests the quantities of each food item that is part of the meal. The program then computes the amounts of each nutritional component consumed by summing each column with each entry weighted by the quantity of the food item. Coding is simplified by using a control array of labels to hold the food names and a control array of text boxes to hold the amounts input by the user. In the following template, the label captions have been assigned an initial value "(food name)" so that the labels can be seen. The five nutrients of interest and the actual names and nutrient values of the foods to be used in building a meal are read from the file NUTTABLE.TXT.

	Calories	Protein (grams)	Fat (grams)	Vit A (IU)	Calcium (mg)
spinach (1 cup)	23	3	0.3	8100	93
sweet potato (1 med.)	160	2	1	9230	46
yogurt (8 oz.)	230	10	3	120	343
skim milk (1 cup)	85	8	0	500	302
whole wheat bread (1 slice)	65	3	1	0	24
brown rice (1 cup)	178	3.8	0.9	0	18
watermelon (1 wedge)	110	2	1	2510	30
papaya (1 lg.)	156	2.4	0.4	7000	80
tuna in water (1 lb)	575	126.8	3.6	0	73
lobster (1 med.)	405	28.8	26.6	984	190

Table 7.11 Composition of 10 top-rated foods.

Object	Property	Setting
frmMeal	Caption	Nutrition in a Meal
lblFood()	Caption	(food name)
	Index	0 – 9
lblQnty	Caption	Quantity in Meal
txtQnty()	Text	(blank)
	Index	0 – 9
cmdAnalyze	Caption	Analyze Meal Nutrition
picAnalysis		

```
Dim nutName(1 To 5) As String              'nutrient names
Dim nutTable(1 To 10, 1 To 5) As Single 'nutrient values for each food

Private Sub cmdAnalyze_Click()
  'Determine the nutritional content of a meal
  Dim quantity(1 To 10) As Single 'amount of food in meal
  Call GetAmounts(quantity())
  Call ShowData(quantity())
End Sub

Private Sub Form_Load()
  Dim i As Integer, j As Integer, foodName As String
  'Fill arrays; assign label captions
  Open "NUTTABLE.TXT" For Input As #1
  For i = 1 To 5
    Input #1, nutName(i)
  Next i
  For i = 1 To 10
    Input #1, foodName
    lblFood(i - 1).Caption = foodName
```

```
      For j = 1 To 5
        Input #1, nutTable(i, j)
      Next j
    Next i
    Close #1
End Sub

Private Sub GetAmounts(quantity() As Single)
  Dim i As Integer
  'Obtain quantities of foods consumed
  For i = 1 To 10
    quantity(i) = Val(txtQnty(i - 1).Text)
  Next i
End Sub

Private Sub ShowData(quantity() As Single)
  Dim col As Integer, row As Integer
  Dim amount As Single
  'Display amount of each component
  picAnalysis.Cls
  picAnalysis.Print "This meal contains the"
  picAnalysis.Print "following quantities"
  picAnalysis.Print "of these nutritional"
  picAnalysis.Print "components:"
  picAnalysis.Print
  For col = 1 To 5
    amount = 0
    For row = 1 To 10
      amount = amount + quantity(row) * nutTable(row, col)
    Next row
    picAnalysis.Print nutName(col) & ":"; Tab(16); amount
  Next col
End Sub
```

[Run, type the following quantities into each text box, and click the command button.]

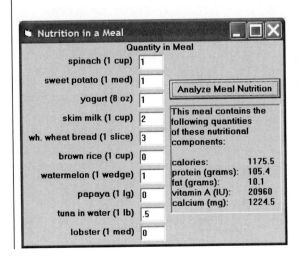

Comments

1. The lower bound of the first coordinate of a two-dimensional array is given by LBound(*arrayName*, 1) and the lower bound of the second coordinate is given by LBound(*arrayName*, 2). The corresponding upper bounds are given by UBound(*arrayName*, 1) and UBound(*arrayName*, 2).

2. A dynamic two-dimensional array (that is, an array previously declared by a Dim statement without any ranges or by a ReDim statement) can be resized with ReDim *arrayName*(r, s) which loses the current contents, or with ReDim Preserve *arrayName*(m, s) which keeps the current values. However, when the keyword Preserve is used, only the last coordinate can be resized.

3. A ReDim statement cannot change the number of dimensions of an array. For instance, it cannot change a one-dimensional array into a two-dimensional array.

4. We can define three- (or higher-) dimensional arrays much as we do two-dimensional arrays. A three-dimensional array uses three subscripts, and the assignment of values requires a triple-nested loop. As an example, a meteorologist might use a three-dimensional array to record temperatures for various dates, times, and elevations. The array might be created by the statement

```
Dim temps(1 To 31, 1 To 24, 0 To 14) As Single
```

✔ PRACTICE PROBLEMS 7.5

1. Consider the road-mileage program in Example 1. How can the program be modified so the actual names of the cities can be supplied by the user?

2. In what types of problems are two-dimensional arrays superior to parallel arrays?

➤ EXERCISES 7.5

In Exercises 1 through 8, determine the output displayed in the picture box when the command button is clicked. All Dim statements for arrays are in the (Declarations) section of (General).

1. ```
Dim a(1 To 20, 1 To 30) As Single

Private Sub cmdDisplay_Click()
  a(3, 5) = 6
  a(5, 3) = 2 * a(3, 5)
  picOutput.Print a(5, 3)
End Sub
```
```

2. `Dim years(1 To 100, 1 To 50) As Single`

```
Private Sub cmdDisplay_Click()
  Dim x As Single, y As Single
  x = 7
  y = 8
  years(x, y) = 1937
  picOutput.Print years(7, 8) + 50
End Sub
```

3. `Dim w(1 To 10, 1 To 15) As String`

```
Private Sub cmdDisplay_Click()
  Dim d As String, n As Integer
  d = "Dorothy"
  w(1, 1) = d
  n = 1
  picOutput.Print w(n, n)
End Sub
```

4. `Dim actor(1 To 5, 1 To 5) As String`

```
Private Sub cmdDisplay_Click()
  Dim a As Integer, b As Integer, temp As Integer
  a = 2
  b = 3
  actor(a, b) = "Bogart"
  temp = a
  a = b
  b = temp
  picOutput.Print "1. "; actor(a, b)
  picOutput.Print "2. "; actor(b, a)
End Sub
```

5. `Dim a() As Single`

```
Private Sub cmdDisplay_Click()
  Dim p As Integer, q As Integer
  Dim j As Integer, k As Integer
  Open "DATA.TXT" For Input As #1
  Input #1, p, q
  ReDim a(1 To p, 1 To q) As Single
  For j = 1 To p
    For k = 1 To q
      Input #1, a(j, k)
      picOutput.Print a(j, k);
    Next k
    picOutput.Print
  Next j
  Close #1
End Sub
```

(Assume that the file DATA.TXT contains the following entries.)

2, 3, 4, 1, 6, 5, 8, 2

6. `Dim a(1 To 4, 1 To 5) As Integer`

```
Private Sub cmdDisplay_Click()
  Dim j As Integer, k As Integer
  For j = 1 To 4
    For k = 1 To 5
      a(j, k) = (j - k) * j
        picOutput.Print a(j, k);
    Next k
      picOutput.Print
  Next j
End Sub
```

7. `Dim s(1 To 3, 1 To 3) As Single`

```
Private Sub cmdDisplay_Click()
  Dim j As Integer, k As Integer
  Open "DATA.TXT" For Input As #1
  For j = 1 To 3
    For k = 1 To 3
      Input #1, s(j, k)
    Next k
  Next j
  Close #1
  For j = 1 To 3
    picOutput.Print s(j, j);
  Next j
End Sub
```

(Assume that the file DATA.TXT contains the following entries.)

1, 2, 3, 4, 3, 2, 3, 4, 5

8. `Dim m() As Integer`

```
Private Sub cmdDisplay_Click()
  Dim x As Integer, y As Integer
  Dim j As Integer, k As Integer
  Open "DATA.TXT" For Input As #1
  Input #1, x, y
  ReDim m(1 To x, 1 To y) As Integer
  For j = 1 To x
    For k = 1 To y - j
      Input #1, m(j, k)
      picOutput.Print m(j, k) - k;
    Next k
    picOutput.Print
  Next j
  Close #1
End Sub
```

(Assume that the file DATA.TXT contains the following entries.)

2, 3, 6, 3, 2, 1, 3, 4, 9, 8

In Exercises 9 and 10, identify the errors.

9.
```
Dim a(1 To 3, 1 To 4) As Integer

Private Sub cmdDisplay_Click()
  Dim j As Integer, k As Integer
  'Fill an array
  Open "DATA.TXT" For Input As #1
  For j = 1 To 4
    For k = 1 To 3
      Input #1, a(j, k)
    Next k
  Next j
  Close #1
End Sub
```

(Assume that the file DATA.TXT contains the following entries.)

1, 2, 3, 4, 5, 6, 7, 8, 9, 0, 1, 2

10.
```
Dim score(1 To 3, 1 To 3) As Integer

Private Sub Form_Load()
  Dim j As Integer, k As Integer, student As Integer
  'Fill array from text file
  Open "SCORES.TXT" For Input As #1
  For j = 1 To 3
    Input #1, student
    For k = 1 To 3
      Input #1, score(k, j)
    Next k
  Next j
End Sub

Private Sub cmdDisplay_Click()
  Dim student As Integer, exam As Integer
  'Report individual scores
  student = Val(txtStudent.Text)
  exam = Val(txtExam.Text)
  If (student >= 1 And student <= 3) And (exam >= 1 And exam <= 3) Then
    picOutput.Print score(student, exam)
  End If
End Sub
```

(Assume that the file SCORES.TXT contains the following three lines.)

1, 80, 85, 90
2, 72, 80, 88
3, 87, 93, 90

In Exercises 11 through 14, write a procedure to perform the stated task.

11. Given an array declared with the statement Dim a(1 To 10, 1 To 10) As Single, set the entries in the jth column to j (for $j = 1, \ldots, 10$).

12. Given an array declared with the statement Dim a(1 To 10, 1 To 10) As Single, and values assigned to each entry, compute the sum of the values in the 10th row.

13. Given an array declared with the statement `Dim a(1 To 10, 1 To 10) As Single`, and values assigned to each entry, interchange the values in the second and third rows.

14. Given an array declared with the statement `Dim a(1 To 3, 1 To 45) As Single`, and values assigned to each entry, find the greatest value and the locations (possibly more than one) at which it occurs.

In Exercises 15 through 24, write a program to perform the stated task.

15. A company has two stores (1 and 2), and each store sells three items (1, 2, and 3). The following tables give the inventory at the beginning of the day and the amount of each item sold during that day.

	Item		
	1	2	3
Store 1	25	64	23
Store 2	12	82	19

Beginning Inventory

	Item		
	1	2	3
Store 1	7	45	11
Store 2	4	24	8

Sales for Day

(a) Record the values of each table in an array.

(b) Adjust the values in the first array to hold the inventories at the end of the day and display these new inventories.

(c) Calculate and display the total number of items in each store at the end of the day.

16. Table 7.12 gives the results of a survey on the uses of computers in the workplace. Each entry shows the percentage of respondents from the age category that use the computer for the indicated purpose.

(a) Place the data from the table in an array.

(b) Determine the average of the percentages in the Databases column.

Age	Word Processing	Spread-sheets	Databases	Communications	Desktop Publishing
18–24	43.1	28.2	23.4	35.3	18.4
25–29	58.3	41.7	35.0	46.6	25.8
30–39	58.5	44.0	35.4	49.1	28.3
40–49	58.9	43.6	36.9	48.6	27.1
50–59	58.8	39.1	33.5	49.0	26.1
60 and older	54.1	33.5	28.8	42.2	21.6

Table 7.12 Workers using computers on the job.
Source: U.S. Center of Educational Statistics, *Digest of Educational Statistics, 1998.*

17. A university offers 10 courses at each of three campuses. The number of students enrolled in each is presented in Table 7.13.

(a) Find the total number of course enrollments on each campus.

(b) Find the total number of students taking each course.

		Course									
		1	2	3	4	5	6	7	8	9	10
	1	5	15	22	21	12	25	16	11	17	23
Campus	2	11	23	51	25	32	35	32	52	25	21
	3	2	12	32	32	25	26	29	12	15	11

Table 7.13 Number of students enrolled in courses.

18. Table 7.14 gives the 2000 and 2001 U.S. sales for the five largest restaurant chains.

    (a) Place the data into an array.
    (b) Calculate the total change in sales for these five restaurant chains.

	2000 sales $MM	2001 sales $MM
1. McDonald's	19.6	20.1
2. Burger King	8.7	8.5
3. Wendy's	6.4	6.8
4. Taco Bell	5.1	5.1
5. Pizza Hut	5.0	4.7

Table 7.14 Top restaurant chains.

Source: QSR Online, January 2003.

19. The scores for the top three golfers at the 2003 Buick International are shown in Table 7.15.

    (a) Place the data into an array.
    (b) Compute the total score for each player.
    (c) Compute the average score for each round.

	Round			
	1	2	3	4
Tiger Woods	70	66	68	68
Carl Pettersson	69	68	70	69
Brad Faxon	70	64	71	72

Table 7.15 2003 Buick Invitational.

20. Table 7.16 contains part of the pay schedule for federal employees in Washington, D.C. Table 7.17 gives the number of employees of each classification in a certain division. Place the data from each table into an array and compute the amount of money this division pays for salaries during the year.

	Step			
	1	**2**	**3**	**4**
GS–1	15,214	15,722	16,228	16,731
GS–2	17,106	17,512	18,079	18,559
GS–3	18,664	19,286	19,908	20,530
GS–4	20,952	21,650	22,348	23,046
GS–5	23,442	24,223	25,004	25,785
GS–6	26,130	27,001	27,872	28,743
GS–7	29,037	30,005	30,973	31,941

Table 7.16 2003 pay schedule for federal workers.

	1	**2**	**3**	**4**
GS–1	0	0	2	1
GS–2	2	3	0	1
GS–3	4	2	5	7
GS–4	12	13	8	3
GS–5	4	5	0	1
GS–6	6	2	4	3
GS–7	8	1	9	2

Table 7.17 Number of employees in each category.

21. Consider Table 7.10, the rankings of three university departments. Write a program that places the data into an array, allows the name of a college to be input, and gives the categories in which it appears. Of course, a college might appear more than once or not at all.

22. Table 7.18 gives the monthly precipitation for a typical Nebraska city during a 5-year period.

	Jan.	Feb.	Mar.	Apr.	May	June	July	Aug.	Sept.	Oct.	Nov.	Dec.
1986	0.88	1.11	2.01	3.64	6.44	5.58	4.23	4.34	4.00	2.05	1.48	0.77
1987	0.76	0.94	2.09	3.29	4.68	3.52	3.52	4.82	3.72	2.21	1.24	0.80
1988	0.67	0.80	1.75	2.70	4.01	3.88	3.72	3.78	3.55	1.88	1.21	0.61
1989	0.82	0.80	1.99	3.05	4.19	4.44	3.98	4.57	3.43	2.32	1.61	0.75
1990	0.72	0.90	1.71	2.02	2.33	2.98	2.65	2.99	2.55	1.99	1.05	0.92

Table 7.18 Monthly precipitation (in inches) for a typical Nebraska city.

Write a program that reads the table from a text file into an array and then displays in a picture box the following output.

```
Total precipitation for each year
1986  36.53
1987  31.59
1988  28.56
1989  31.96
1990  22.81

Average precipitation for each month
Jan   Feb   Mar   Apr   May   Jun   Jul   Aug   Sep   Oct   Nov   Dec
0.77  0.91  1.91  2.94  4.33  4.08  3.62  4.10  3.50  2.09  1.32  0.77
```

23. Suppose a course has 15 students enrolled and five exams are given during the semester. Write a program that accepts each student's name and grades as input and places the names in a one-dimensional array and the grades in a two-dimensional array. The program should then display each student's name and semester average. Also, the program should display the median for each exam. (For an odd number of grades, the median is the middle grade. For an even number of grades, it is the average of the two middle grades.)

24. An *n*-by-*n* array is called a magic square if the sums of each row, each column, and each diagonal are equal. Write a program to determine if an array is a magic square and use it to determine if either of the following arrays is a magic square. **Hint:** If, at any time, one of the sums is not equal to the others, the search is complete.

(a)

1	15	15	4
12	6	7	9
8	10	11	5
13	3	2	16

(b)

11	10	4	23	17
18	12	6	5	24
25	19	13	7	1
2	21	20	14	8
9	3	22	16	15

25. A company has three stores (1, 2, and 3), and each store sells five items (1, 2, 3, 4, and 5). The following tables give the number of items sold by each store and category on a particular day, and the cost of each item.

(a) Place the data from the left-hand table in a two-dimensional array and the data from the right-hand table in a one-dimensional array.

(b) Compute and display the total dollar amount of sales for each store and for the entire company.

		Item				
		1	**2**	**3**	**4**	**5**
	1	25	64	23	45	14
Store	2	12	82	19	34	63
	3	54	22	17	43	35

Number of Items Sold During Day

Item	Cost
1	$12.00
2	$17.95
3	$95.00
4	$86.50
5	$78.00

Cost per Item

✔✔ Solutions to Practice Problems 7.5

1. Enlarge the text boxes so that they can hold city names. The function FindCityNum can be used to determine the subscript associated with each city. This function and the modified event procedure cmdShow_Click are as follows:

```
Private Function FindCityNum(city As String) As Integer
  Select Case UCase(city)
    Case "CHICAGO"
      FindCityNum = 1
    Case "LOS ANGELES"
      FindCityNum = 2
    Case "NEW YORK"
      FindCityNum = 3
    Case "PHILADELPHIA"
      FindCityNum = 4
    Case Else
      FindCityNum = 0
  End Select
End Function
```

```
Private Sub cmdShow_Click()
  Dim orig As String, dest As String
  Dim row As Integer, col As Integer
  'Determine road mileage between cities
  orig = txtOrig.Text
  dest = txtDest.Text
  row = FindCityNum(orig)
  col = FindCityNum(dest)
  If (row < 1) Or (row > 4) Then
      MsgBox "City of origin not available", , "Error"
    ElseIf (col < 1) Or (col > 4) Then
      MsgBox "Destination city not available", , "Error"
    Else
      Call ShowMileage(rm(), row, col)
  End If
  txtOrig.SetFocus
End Sub
```

2. Both parallel arrays and two-dimensional arrays are used to hold related data. If some of the data are numeric and some are string, then parallel arrays must be used because all entries of an array must be of the same type. Parallel arrays should also be used if the data will be sorted. Two-dimensional arrays are best suited to tabular data.

7.6 A CASE STUDY: CALCULATING WITH A SPREADSHEET

Spreadsheets are one of the most popular types of software used on personal computers. A spreadsheet is a financial planning tool in which data are analyzed in a table of rows and columns. Some of the items are entered by the user. Other items, often totals and balances, are calculated using the entered data. The outstanding feature of electronic spreadsheets is their ability to recalculate an entire table after changes are made in some of the entered data, thereby allowing the user to determine the financial implications of various alternatives. This is called "What if?" analysis.

The Design of the Program

Figure 7.11 contains an example of a spreadsheet used to analyze a student's financial projections for the four quarters of a year. Column F holds the sum of the entries in columns B through E, rows 6 and 14 hold sums of the entries in rows 3 through 5 and 9 through 13, respectively, and row 16 holds the differences of the entries in rows 6 and 14. Because the total balance is negative, some of the amounts in the spreadsheet must be changed and the totals and balances recalculated.

	A	B	C	D	E	F
1		Fall	Winter	Spring	Summer	Total
2	**Income**					
3	Job	1000	1300	1000	2000	5300
4	Parents	200	200	200	0	600
5	Scholarship	150	150	150	0	450
6	**Total**	1350	1650	1350	2000	6350
7						
8	**Expenses**					
9	Tuition	400	0	400	0	800
10	Food	650	650	650	650	2600
11	Rent	600	600	600	400	2200
12	Books	110	0	120	0	230
13	Misc	230	210	300	120	860
14	**Total**	1990	1460	2070	1170	6690
15						
16	**Balance**	−640	190	−720	830	−340

Figure 7.11 Spreadsheet for a student's financial projections.

The 96 locations in the spreadsheet that hold information are called **cells**. Each cell is identified by its row number and column letter. For instance, the cell 14, C contains the amount 1460. For programming purposes, each column is identified by a number, starting with 1 for the leftmost column. Thus cell 14, C will be cell 14, 3 in our program.

This case study develops a program to produce a spreadsheet with the five columns of numbers shown in Figure 7.11, three user-specified categories of income, and five user-specified categories of expenses. The following tasks are to be selected by command buttons:

1. Start a new spreadsheet. All current category names and values are erased and the cursor is placed in the text box of the first income category.

2. Quit.

Three additional tasks need to be performed as the result of other events:

1. Create the spreadsheet when the form is loaded.

2. Limit the user to editing category names and quarterly values.

3. Display totals after a change is made in the spreadsheet.

The User Interface

Each cell in the spreadsheet will be an element of a text box control array. A control array of labels is needed for the numeric labels to the left of each row and another control array of labels for the alphabetic labels at the top of each column. Finally, two command buttons are required. The task of controlling which cells the user can edit will be handled by a GotFocus event. The task of updating the totals will be handled by a LostFocus event. Figure 7.12 shows one possible form design with all control elements loaded. For this application of a spreadsheet, the headings that have been assigned to cells in rows 1, 2, 6, 8, 14, and 16 are fixed; the user will not be allowed to edit them. The other entries in column A, the category names, may be edited by the user, but we have provided the set from Figure 7.11 as the default.

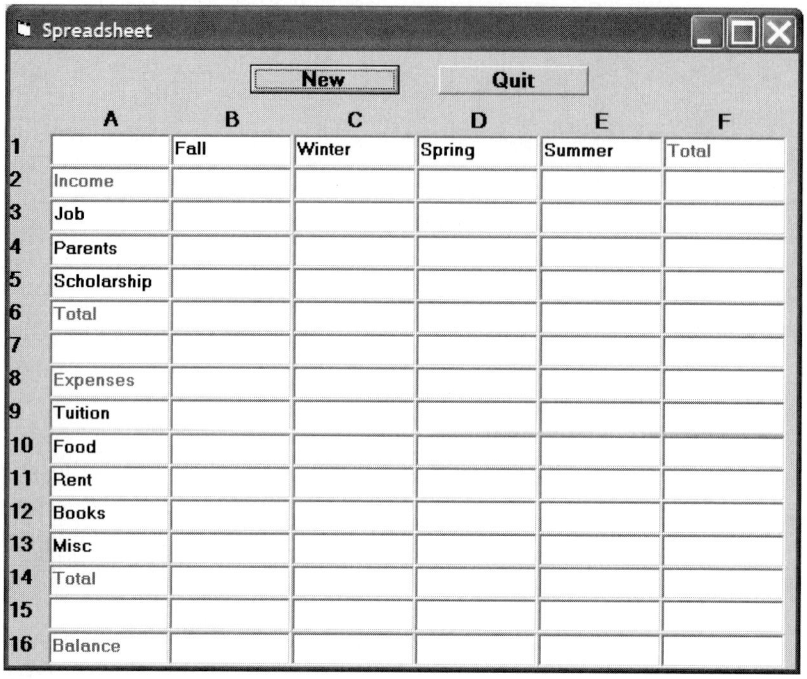

Figure 7.12 Template for spreadsheet.

Because processing the totals for the spreadsheet involves adding columns and rows of cells, coding is simplified by using a control array of text boxes, so that an index in a For...Next loop can step through a set of cells. A two-dimensional array of text boxes seems natural for the spreadsheet. Unfortunately, only a single index is available for control arrays in Visual Basic. However, a single dimensional array of text boxes can be used without much difficulty if we define a function Indx that connects a pair of row (1 to 16) and column (1 to 6) values to a unique index (1 to 96) value. An example of such a rule would be Indx(row,column)=(row−1)*6+column. Successive values of this function are generated by going from left to right across row 1, then left to right across row 2, and so on.

A solution to the spreadsheet problem that uses one control array of text boxes and uses two control arrays of labels follows. The text box control array *txtCell*( ) provides the 96 text boxes needed for the spreadsheet cells. Because the proposed Indx function advances by one as we move from left to right across a row of cells, the cells must be positioned in this order as they are loaded. The label control array *lblRowLab*( ) provides a label for each of the rows of cells, while label control array *lblColLab*( ) provides a label for each column of cells. Figure 7.13 shows the layout of the form at design time. The properties for the controls are given in Table 7.19. The Height and Width properties given for the text box will assure enough room on the screen for all 96 cells. These dimensions can be obtained by creating a normal size text box, then reducing its width by one set of grid marks and its height by two sets of grid marks.

Figure 7.13 Controls at design time.

Object	Property	Setting
frmSpreadsheet	Caption	Spreadsheet
cmdNew	Caption	New
cmdQuit	Caption	Quit
lblRowLab()	Caption	1
	Index	1
lblColLab()	Caption	A
	Index	1
txtCell()	Text	(blank)
	Index	1
	Height	1095
	Width	285

Table 7.19 Objects and their properties.

Coding the Program

The top row of Figure 7.14 shows the different events to which the program must respond. Table 7.20 identifies the corresponding event procedures and the general procedures they call. Let's examine each event procedure.

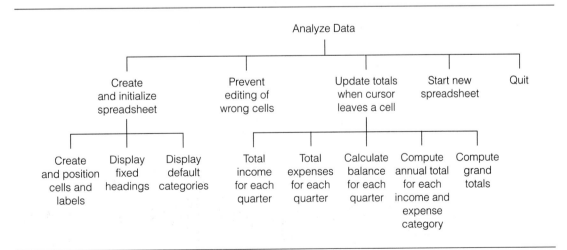

Figure 7.14 Hierarchy chart for spreadsheet program.

1. Create & Initialize spreadsheet	Form_Load
1.1 Create & position cells & labels	CreateSpreadsheet
1.2 Display fixed headings	SetStructure
1.3 Display default categories	SetDefaults
2. Prevent editing of wrong cells	txtCell_GotFocus
3. Update totals when cursor leaves a cell	txtCell_LostFocus/DisplayTotals
3.1 Total income for each quarter	TotalIncome
3.2 Total expenses for each quarter	TotalExpenses
3.3 Calculate balances for each quarter	ShowBalances
3.4 Total each income & expense category	TotalRows
3.5 Compute grand totals	ShowGrandTotals
4. Start a new spreadsheet	cmdNew_Click
5. End program	cmdQuit_Click

Table 7.20 Tasks and their procedures.

1. Form_Load assigns the number of rows (16) and columns (6) in our spreadsheet to the form-level variables *maxRow* and *maxCol*. Form_Load then calls three general procedures to create and initialize the spreadsheet.

The procedure CreateSpreadsheet loads each element of the *txtCell*( ) control array in order from left to right, top to bottom. Cell 1, which is to be the first cell in the first row, is not loaded because it was created at design time. The Top property of a new cell is set so that the top edge of the new cell overlaps the bottom edge of the previous cell in the column. The Top property of the first cell in a column is not modified, and so the value of the Top property is the same as cell 1. Similarly, the Left property of a new cell is set so that the left edge of the new cell overlaps the right edge of the previous cell in the row. The Left property of the first cell in a row is not modified, and so the value of the Left property is the same as cell 1. CreateSpreadsheet also loads the additional row and column label elements and assigns an appropriate caption. CreateSpreadsheet's final task is to set the Height and Width properties of frmSpreadSheet to accommodate all the objects that have been loaded. The numbers 500 and 200, which appear in these statements, were obtained by trial and error and are necessary to account for the space used by the form caption and borders.

The procedure SetStructure assigns heading values to various cells of the spreadsheet in accordance with the specific application we were asked to program. The user will not be able to alter the value in these cells, because the rules for which cells are to be totaled and where these totals are to be placed are "hard wired" into the program and cannot be changed by the user. SetStructure also assigns values to a set of form-level variables so that other procedures in the program can be coded using meaningful names rather than possibly obscure numbers. Besides Form_Load, SetStructure is also called by the cmdNew_Click event procedure.

The procedure SetDefaults assigns the income and expense category headings shown in Figure 7.11 to the appropriate cells. The user may change these headings at any time, and must supply them if the "New" command is issued.

2. txtCell_GotFocus checks to see if the cell that has received the focus may, according to the rules of this application, be edited by the user. The row and column numbers for the cell are computed from the cell's index. If the cell that has received the focus is in a column after *stopCol*, the last editable column, then the column to be edited is changed to *startCol*, the first editable column, and the row to be edited is advanced by one. If the row to be edited does not contain any editable cells, then the row to be edited is advanced to the next row containing editable cells. (When the focus goes past the last row of editable cells, the next editable row is the first editable row, that is, *incStartRow*.) Finally, focus is set to the adjusted row and column, but only if an adjustment has been made. If the test Indx(row,col)<>Index were not made and focus were reset to a cell that already had the focus, then the GotFocus event procedure would be invoked again as a result of the SetFocus, and then again as a result of the SetFocus performed by this invocation of GotFocus, and so on, resulting in an infinite loop.

3. txtCell_LostFocus invokes the general procedure DisplayTotals when the cursor leaves one of the spreadsheet cells. DisplayTotals in turn invokes five general procedures that each compute one set of needed totals and display the results by assigning values to appropriate text boxes. TotalIncome adds up the income for each quarter and saves the results in the array *iTot*( ). Similarly, TotalExpenses adds up the expenses for each quarter and saves the results in the array *eTot*( ). ComputeBalances takes the results stored in *iTot*( ) and *eTot*( ) and subtracts them to determine the balance for each quarter. TotalRows adds the four quarters for each category and assigns the results to the text boxes at the right end of each row. Finally, DetermineGrandTotals adds the values in *iTot*( ) and *eTot*( ) to determine the values for the right end of the "balance" row and each "total" row.

4. cmdNew_Click prepares for the entry of a new spreadsheet by setting the Text property of each element of the control array *txtCell*( ) to the null string and then setting focus to the first cell in the spreadsheet.

5. cmdQuit_Click ends the program.

```
Dim maxCol As Integer          'Number of columns in spreadsheet
Dim maxRow As Integer          'Number of rows in spreadsheet
Dim incStartRow As Integer     'Row where income categories begin
Dim incStopRow As Integer      'Row where income categories end
Dim incTotRow As Integer       'Row where income total is displayed
Dim expStartRow As Integer     'Row where expense categories begin
Dim expStopRow As Integer      'Row where expense categories end
Dim expTotRow As Integer       'Row where expense total is displayed
Dim balRow As Integer          'Row where balance is displayed
Dim startCol As Integer        'Column where numeric data begins
Dim stopCol As Integer         'Column where numeric data ends
Dim totCol As Integer          'Column where total for each row is displayed
```

```
'Control Arrays
'txtCell()                      Control array for data cells
'lblRowLab()                    Control array for numeric row labels
'lblColLab()                    Control array for alphabetic column labels

Private Sub Form_Load()
  'Task 1: Create and initialize spreadsheet
  'Establish number of rows and columns. Trial and error show
  'that a maximum of 20 rows and 8 columns will fit the screen.
  'For this particular application, 16 rows and 6 columns are adequate.
  maxRow = 16
  maxCol = 6
  Call CreateSpreadsheet
  Call SetStructure
  Call SetDefaults
End Sub

Private Sub CreateSpreadsheet()
  Dim row As Integer, col As Integer, i As Integer
  Dim cellHeight As Single, cellWidth As Single
  Dim cellTop As Single, cellLeft As Single
  cellHeight = txtCell(1).Height
  cellWidth = txtCell(1).Width
  'Create cells
  For row = 1 To maxRow
    For col = 1 To maxCol
      i = Indx(row, col)
      If Not (col = 1 And row = 1) Then
          Load txtCell(i)
      End If
      If row > 1 Then
          cellTop = txtCell(Indx(row - 1, col)).Top
          txtCell(i).Top = cellTop + cellHeight
      End If
      If col > 1 Then
          cellLeft = txtCell(Indx(row, col - 1)).Left
          txtCell(i).Left = cellLeft + cellWidth
      End If
      txtCell(i).Visible = True
    Next col
  Next row
  'Create Row Labels
  For row = 2 To maxRow
    Load lblRowLab(row)
    lblRowLab(row).Top = lblRowLab(row - 1).Top + cellHeight
    lblRowLab(row).Caption = LTrim(Str(row))
    lblRowLab(row).Visible = True
  Next row
  'Create Column Labels
  For col = 2 To maxCol
    Load lblColLab(col)
    lblColLab(col).Left = lblColLab(col - 1).Left + cellWidth
    lblColLab(col).Caption = Chr(col + 64)
    lblColLab(col).Visible = True
  Next col
```

```
    'Set form height and width to accommodate all objects
    i = Indx(maxRow, maxCol)
    frmSpreadsheet.Height = txtCell(i).Top + cellHeight + 500
    frmSpreadsheet.Width = txtCell(i).Left + cellWidth + 200
End Sub

Private Sub SetStructure()
  txtCell(Indx(1, 2)).Text = "Fall"
  txtCell(Indx(1, 3)).Text = "Winter"
  txtCell(Indx(1, 4)).Text = "Spring"
  txtCell(Indx(1, 5)).Text = "Summer"
  txtCell(Indx(1, 6)).Text = "Total"
  txtCell(Indx(1, 6)).ForeColor = vbGreen
  txtCell(Indx(2, 1)).Text = "Income"
  txtCell(Indx(2, 1)).ForeColor = vbMagenta
  txtCell(Indx(6, 1)).Text = "Total"
  txtCell(Indx(6, 1)).ForeColor = vbGreen
  txtCell(Indx(8, 1)).Text = "Expenses"
  txtCell(Indx(8, 1)).ForeColor = vbMagenta
  txtCell(Indx(14, 1)).Text = "Total"
  txtCell(Indx(14, 1)).ForeColor = vbGreen
  txtCell(Indx(16, 1)).Text = "Balance"
  txtCell(Indx(16, 1)).ForeColor = vbGreen
  incStartRow = 3
  incStopRow = 5
  incTotRow = 6
  expStartRow = 9
  expStopRow = 13
  expTotRow = 14
  balRow = 16
  startCol = 2
  stopCol = 5
  totCol = 6
End Sub

Private Sub SetDefaults()
  'Set default values specific to this application
  txtCell(Indx(3, 1)).Text = "Job"
  txtCell(Indx(4, 1)).Text = "Parents"
  txtCell(Indx(5, 1)).Text = "Scholarship"
  txtCell(Indx(9, 1)).Text = "Tuition"
  txtCell(Indx(10, 1)).Text = "Food"
  txtCell(Indx(11, 1)).Text = "Rent"
  txtCell(Indx(12, 1)).Text = "Books"
  txtCell(Indx(13, 1)).Text = "Misc"
End Sub

Private Sub txtCell_GotFocus(Index As Integer)
  'Task 2: Prevent editing of wrong cells
  Dim row As Integer, col As Integer
  'Force focus into a data txtCell for this application
  row = Int((Index - 1) / maxCol) + 1
  col = ((Index - 1) Mod maxCol) + 1
```

```
        If col > stopCol Then
            row = row + 1
            col = startCol
        End If
        If row < incStartRow Then
            row = incStartRow
          ElseIf (row > incStopRow) And (row < expStartRow) Then
            row = expStartRow
          ElseIf row > expStopRow Then
            row = incStartRow
        End If
        If Indx(row, col) <> Index Then
            txtCell(Indx(row, col)).SetFocus
        End If
End Sub

Private Sub txtCell_LostFocus(Indx As Integer)
  'Task 3: Update totals when cursor leaves a cell
  Call DisplayTotals
End Sub

Private Sub DisplayTotals()
  ReDim itot(startCol To stopCal) As Single
  ReDim etot(startCol To stopCal)  As Single
  'Calculate and show totals for Income each quarter
  Call TotalIncome(itot())
  'Calculate and show totals for Expenses each quarter
  Call TotalExpenses(etot())
  'Calculate and show Balances for each quarter
  Call ShowBalances(itot(), etot())
  'Calculate and show the Total of each Income & Expense category
  Call TotalRows
  'Calculate and show grand totals of quarter totals and balances
  Call ShowGrandTotals(itot(), etot())
End Sub

Private Sub TotalIncome(itot() As Single)
  Dim row As Integer, col As Integer
  'Total income for each of four quarters
  For col = startCol To stopCol
    itot(col) = 0
    For row = incStartRow To incStopRow
      itot(col) = itot(col) + Val(txtCell(Indx(row, col)).Text)
    Next row
    txtCell(Indx(incTotRow, col)).Text = FormatNumber(itot(col), 0)
  Next col
End Sub

Private Sub TotalExpenses(etot() As Single)
  Dim row As Integer, col As Integer
  'Total expenses for each of four quarters
  For col = startCol To stopCol
    etot(col) = 0
```

```
      For row = expStartRow To expStopRow
        etot(col) = etot(col) + Val(txtCell(Indx(row, col)).Text)
      Next row
      txtCell(Indx(expTotRow, col)).Text = FormatNumber(etot(col), 0)
   Next col
End Sub

Private Sub ShowBalances(itot() As Single, etot() As Single)
   Dim col As Integer
   For col = startCol To stopCol
     txtCell(Indx(balRow, col)).Text = FormatNumber(itot(col) - etot(col), 0)
   Next col
End Sub

Private Sub TotalRows()
   Dim row As Integer, col As Integer, rowTot As Single
   'Total each income category
   For row = incStartRow To incStopRow
     rowTot = 0
     For col = startCol To stopCol
       rowTot = rowTot + Val(txtCell(Indx(row, col)).Text)
     Next col
     txtCell(Indx(row, totCol)).Text = FormatNumber(rowTot, 0)
   Next row
   'Total each expense category
   For row = expStartRow To expStopRow
     rowTot = 0
     For col = startCol To stopCal
       rowTot = rowTot + Val(txtCell(Indx(row, col)).Text)
     Next col
     txtCell(Indx(row, totCol)).Text = FormatNumber(rowTot, 0)
   Next row
End Sub

Private Sub ShowGrandTotals(itot() As Single, etot() As Single)
   Dim col As Integer, iTotal As Single, eTotal As Single
   'Compute and display grand totals for income, expenses, and balance
   iTotal = 0
   eTotal = 0
   For col = startCol To stopCol
     iTotal = iTotal + itot(col)
     eTotal = eTotal + etot(col)
   Next col
   txtCell(Indx(incTotRow, totCol)) = FormatNumber(iTotal, 0)
   txtCell(Indx(expTotRow, totCol)) = FormatNumber(eTotal, 0)
   txtCell(Indx(balRow, totCol)) = FormatNumber(iTotal - eTotal, 0)
End Sub

Private Sub cmdNew_Click()
   'Task 4: Start a new spreadsheet
   Dim row As Integer, col As Integer
   'Clear all text boxes
```

```
      For col = 1 To maxCol
        For row = 1 To maxRow
          txtCell(Indx(row, col)).Text = ""
        Next row
      Next col
      Call SetStructure
      Call SetDefaults
      'Place cursor in first data txtCell
      txtCell(Indx(1, 1)).SetFocus
    End Sub

    Private Sub cmdQuit_Click()
      'Task 5: End program
      End
    End Sub

    Private Function Indx(row As Integer, col As Integer) As Integer
      Indx = (row - 1) * maxCol + col
    End Function
```

CHAPTER 7   SUMMARY

1. For programming purposes, tabular data are most efficiently processed if stored in an *array*. The *ranges* of arrays are specified by Dim or ReDim statements.

2. An array of labels, text boxes, or command buttons, referred to as a *control array*, can be created by assigning a value (usually zero) to the *Index* property of the control at design time. Additional elements of the control array are created either at design time by using Ctrl+C and Ctrl+V to copy the first element in the array or at run time by using the Load statement. New elements created in either way inherit all the properties of the first element except the Index, Visible (if created with Load), Top (when copied at design time), and Left (when copied at design time) properties.

3. Two of the best-known methods for ordering (or *sorting*) arrays are the *bubble sort* and the *Shell sort*.

4. Any array can be searched *sequentially* to find the subscript associated with a sought-after value. Ordered arrays can be searched most efficiently by a *binary search*.

5. A table can be effectively stored in a *two-dimensional array*.

CHAPTER 7   PROGRAMMING PROJECTS

1. Table 7.21 contains some lengths in terms of feet. Write a program that displays the nine different units of measure, requests the unit to convert from, the unit to convert to, and the quantity to be converted, and then displays the converted quantity. A typical outcome is shown in Figure 7.15.

1 inch = .0833 foot	1 rod = 16.5 feet
1 yard = 3 feet	1 furlong = 660 feet
1 meter = 3.2815 feet	1 kilometer = 3281.5 feet
1 fathom = 6 feet	1 mile = 5280 feet

Table 7.21 Equivalent lengths.

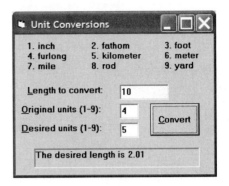

Figure 7.15 Possible outcome of Programming Project 1.

2. Statisticians use the concepts of **mean** and **standard deviation** to describe a collection of data. The mean is the average value of the items, and the standard deviation measures the spread or dispersal of the numbers about the mean. Formally, if $x_1, x_2, x_3, \ldots, x_n$ is a collection of data, then

$$\text{mean} = m = \frac{x_1 + x_2 + x_3 + \cdots + x_n}{n}$$

$$\text{standard deviation} = s = \sqrt{\frac{(x_1 - m)^2 + (x_2 - m)^2 + (x_3 - m)^2 + \cdots + (x_n - m)^2}{n - 1}}$$

Write a computer program to

(a) Place the exam scores 59, 60, 65, 75, 56, 90, 66, 62, 98, 72, 95, 71, 63, 77, 65, 77, 65, 50, 85, and 62 into an array.

(b) Calculate the mean and standard deviation of the exam scores.

(c) Assign letter grades to each exam score, ES, as follows:

$ES \geq m + 1.5s$	A
$m + .5s \leq ES < m + 1.5s$	B
$m - .5s \leq ES < m + .5s$	C
$m - 1.5s \leq ES < m - .5s$	D
$ES < m - 1.5s$	F

For instance, if m were 70 and s were 12, then grades of 88 or above would receive A's, grades between 76 and 87 would receive B's, and so on. A process of this type is referred to as *curving grades*.

(d) Display a list of the exam scores along with their corresponding grades as shown in Figure 7.16.

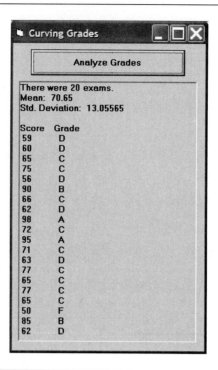

Figure 7.16 Output of Programming Project 2.

3. *Rudimentary Translator.* Table 7.22 gives English words and their French and German equivalents. Store these words in a text file and read them into three parallel arrays, one for each language. Write a program that sorts all three arrays according to the array of English words. The program should then request an English sentence as input from the keyboard and translate it into French and German. For example, if the English sentence given is MY PENCIL IS ON THE TABLE, then the French translation will be MON CRAYON EST SUR LA TABLE, and the German translation will be MEIN BLEISTIFT IST AUF DEM TISCH.

English	French	German	English	French	German
YES	OUI	JA	LARGE	GROS	GROSS
TABLE	TABLE	TISCH	NO	NON	NEIN
THE	LA	DEM	HAT	CHAPEAU	HUT
IS	EST	IST	PENCIL	CRAYON	BLEISTIFT
YELLOW	JAUNE	GELB	RED	ROUGE	ROT
FRIEND	AMI	FREUND	ON	SUR	AUF
SICK	MALADE	KRANK	AUTO	AUTO	AUTO
MY	MON	MEIN	OFTEN	SOUVENT	OFT

Table 7.22 English words and their French and German equivalents.

4. Write a program that allows a list of no more than 50 soft drinks and their percent changes in sales volume for a particular year to be input and displays the information in two lists titled *gainers* and *losers*. Each list should be sorted by the *amount* of the percent change. Try your program on the data for the eight soft drinks in Table 7.23. **Note:** You will need to store the data initially in an array to determine the number of gainers and losers.

Brand	% Change in Volume	Brand	% Change in Volume
Coke Classic	−2	Sprite	−1.8
Pepsi-Cola	−2.8	Dr. Pepper	−1.7
Diet Coke	1.7	Diet Pepsi	2
Mt. Dew	−3.9	7-Up	−7

Table 7.23 Changes in sales volume from 2000 to 2001 of leading soft-drink brands.
Source: Beverage Digest Online, 2003.

5. Each team in a six-team soccer league played each other team once. Table 7.24 shows the winners. Write a program to

(a) Place the team names in a one-dimensional array.
(b) Place the data from Table 7.24 in a two-dimensional array.
(c) Place the number of games won by each team in a one-dimensional array.
(d) Display a listing of the teams giving each team's name and number of games won. The list should be in decreasing order by the number of wins.

	Jazz	Jets	Owls	Rams	Cubs	Zips
Jazz	—	Jazz	Jazz	Rams	Cubs	Jazz
Jets	Jazz	—	Jets	Jets	Cubs	Zips
Owls	Jazz	Jets	—	Rams	Owls	Owls
Rams	Rams	Jets	Rams	—	Rams	Rams
Cubs	Cubs	Cubs	Owls	Rams	—	Cubs
Zips	Jazz	Zips	Owls	Rams	Cubs	—

Table 7.24 Soccer league winners.

6. A poker hand can be stored in a two-dimensional array. The statement

```
Dim hand(1 To 4, 1 To 13) As Integer
```

declares a 52-element array, where the first subscript ranges over the four suits and the second subscript ranges over the thirteen denominations. A poker hand is specified by placing ones in the elements corresponding to the cards in the hand. See Figure 7.17.

Write a program that requests the five cards as input from the user, creates the related array, and passes the array to procedures to determine the type of the hand: flush (all cards have the same suit), straight (cards have consecutive denominations—ace can come either before 2 or after King), straight flush, four-of-a-kind, full house (three cards of one denomination, two cards of another denomination), three-of-a-kind, two pairs, one pair, or none of the above.

	A	2	3	4	5	6	7	8	9	10	J	Q	K
Club ♣	0	0	0	0	0	0	0	0	1	0	0	0	0
Diamond ♦	1	0	0	0	0	0	0	0	0	0	0	0	0
Heart ♥	1	0	0	0	0	0	0	0	0	0	0	1	0
Spade ♠	0	0	0	0	1	0	0	0	0	0	0	0	0

Figure 7.17 Array for the poker hand A♥ A♦ 5♠ 9♣ Q♥.

7. *Airline Reservations.* Write a reservation system for an airline flight. Assume the airplane has 10 rows with 4 seats in each row. Use a two-dimensional array of strings to maintain a seating chart. In addition, create an array to be used as a waiting list in case the plane is full. The waiting list should be "first come, first served," that is, people who are added early to the list get priority over those added later. Allow the user the following three options:

(1) Add a passenger to the flight or waiting list.
   (a) Request the passenger's name.
   (b) Display a chart of the seats in the airplane in tabular form.
   (c) If seats are available, let the passenger choose a seat. Add the passenger to the seating chart.
   (d) If no seats are available, place the passenger on the waiting list.
(2) Remove a passenger from the flight.
   (a) Request the passenger's name.
   (b) Search the seating chart for the passenger's name and delete it.
   (c) If the waiting list is empty, update the array so the seat is available.
   (d) If the waiting list is not empty, remove the first person from the list, and give him or her the newly vacated seat.
(3) Quit.

8. The Game of Life was invented by John H. Conway to model some genetic laws for birth, death, and survival. Consider a checkerboard consisting of an *n*-by-*n* array of squares. Each square can contain one individual (denoted by 1) or be empty (denoted by –). Figure 7.18(a) shows a 6-by-6 board with four of the squares occupied. The future of each individual depends on the number of his neighbors. After each period of time, called a *generation*, certain individuals will survive, others will die due to either loneliness or over-

crowding, and new individuals will be born. Each nonborder square has eight neighboring squares. After each generation, the status of the squares change as follows:

(a) An individual *survives* if there are two or three individuals in neighboring squares.

(b) An individual *dies* if he has more than three individuals or less than two in neighboring squares.

(c) A new individual is *born* into each empty square with exactly three individuals as neighbors.

Figure 7.18(b) shows the status after one generation. Write a program to do the following:

(1) Declare an *n*-by-*n* array, where *n* is input by the user, to hold the status of each square in the current generation. To specify the initial configuration, have the user input each row as a string of length *n*, and break the row into 1's or dashes with Mid.

(2) Declare an *n*-by-*n* array to hold the status of each square in the next generation. Compute the status for each square and produce the display in Figure 7.18(b). **Note:** The generation changes all at once. Only current cells are used to determine which cells will contain individuals in the next generation.

(3) Assign the next-generation values to the current generation and repeat as often as desired.

(4) Display the number of individuals in each generation.

Hint: The hardest part of the program is determining the number of neighbors a cell has. In general, you must check a 3-by-3 square around the cell in question. Exceptions must be made when the cell is on the edge of the array. Don't forget that a cell is not a neighbor of itself.

(Test the program with the initial configuration shown in Figure 7.19. It is known as the figure-eight configuration and repeats after eight generations.)

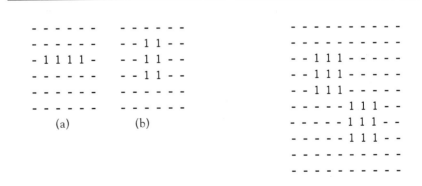

Figure 7.18 Two generations. **Figure 7.19** The figure eight.

9. Simulate the game Concentration. The Form_Load routine should create an array of 20 command buttons placed vertically on a form. A list of 10 words should be randomly assigned as potential captions for the buttons, with each word assigned to two command buttons. Initially, none of the but-

tons should show their words. However, when a button is clicked on, its word is revealed as its caption. After two words have been revealed, either both of the command buttons should become invisible (if their words match) or their captions should again become blank (if the two words do not match). When all matches have been found, a message box should display the number of tries (pairs of words exposed) and an appropriate remark about the user's concentration ability. Possible remarks might be, "You must have ESP" (less than 14 tries), "Amazing concentration" (14 to 20 tries), "Can't hide anything from you" (21 to 28 tries), "Perhaps a nap would recharge your concentration" (29 to 37 tries), and "Better find a designated driver" (more than 37 tries).

10. Every book is identified by a ten-character International Standard Book Number (ISBN) that is usually printed on the back cover of the book. The first nine characters are digits and the last character is either a digit or the letter X (which stands for ten). Three examples of ISBN numbers are 0-13-030657-6, 0-32-108599-X, and 0-471-58719-2. The hyphens separate the characters into four blocks. The first block usually consists of a single digit, and identifies the language (0 for English, 2 for French, 3 for German, . . .). The second block identifies the publisher (for example, 13 for Prentice Hall, 23 for Addison-Wesley-Longman, and 471 for Wiley). The third block is the number the publisher has chosen for the book. The fourth block, which always consists of a single character, called the check digit, is used to test for errors. Let's refer to the ten characters of the ISBN as $d_1, d_2, d_3, d_4, d_5, d_6, d_7, d_8, d_9$, and d_{10}. The check digit is chosen so that the sum

$$10 \cdot d_1 + 9 \cdot d_2 + 8 \cdot d_3 + 7 \cdot d_4 + 6 \cdot d_5 + 5 \cdot d_6 + 4 \cdot d_7 + 3 \cdot d_8 + 2 \cdot d_9 + 1 \cdot d_{10} \qquad (*)$$

is a multiple of 11 (**Note:** A number is multiple of 11 if it is exactly divisible by 11). If the last character of the ISBN is an X, then in the sum (*), d_{10} is replaced with 10. For example, with the ISBN 0-32-108599-X, the sum would be

$$10 \cdot 0 + 9 \cdot 3 + 8 \cdot 2 + 7 \cdot 1 + 6 \cdot 0 + 5 \cdot 8 + 4 \cdot 5 + 3 \cdot 9 + 2 \cdot 9 + 1 \cdot 10 = 165$$

Since 165/11 is 15, the sum is a multiple of 11. This checking scheme will detect every single-digit and transposition-of-adjacent-digits error. That is, if while coping an IBSN number you miscopy a single character or transpose two adjacent characters, then the sum (*) will no longer be a multiple of 11.

(a) Write a program to accept an ISBN type number (including the hyphens) as input, calculate the sum (*), and tell if it is a valid ISBN number. (**Hint:** The number n is divisible by 11 if n Mod 11 is 0.) Before calculating the sum, the program should check that each of the first nine characters is a digit and that the last character is either a digit or an X.

(b) Write a program that begins with a valid ISBN number, such as 0-13-030657-6, and then confirms that the checking scheme described above detects every single-digit and transposition-of-adjacent-digits error by testing every possible error. [**Hint:** If d is a digit to be replaced, then the nine possibilities for the replacements are $(d + 1)$ Mod 10, $(d + 2)$ Mod 10, $(d + 3)$ Mod 10, . . . , $(d + 9)$ Mod 10.]

11. *User-Operated Directory Assistance* Have you ever tried to call a person at their business and been told to type in some of the letters of their name on your telephone's keypad in order to obtain their extension? Write a program to simulate this type of directory assistance. Suppose the names and telephone extensions of all the employees of a company are contained in the text file EMPLOYEES.TXT. Each line of the file has four pieces of information: last name, first name, middle name(s), and telephone extension. (We have filled the file with the names of the U.S. Presidents so that the names will be familiar.) The user should be asked to type in the first three letters of the person's last name followed by the first letter of the first name. For instance, if the person's name is Gary Land, the user would type in 5264. The number 5264 is referred to as the "push-button encoding" of the name. **Note:** People with different names can have the same push-button encoding—for instance, Herb James and Gary Land.

The program should declare three parallel arrays to hold full names, extensions, and push-button encodings. The arrays should be filled while making a single pass through the file, and then sorted by push-button encoding. After the user presses four keys on the keypad, the program should display the names and extensions of all the employees having the specified push-button encoding. See Figure 7.20.

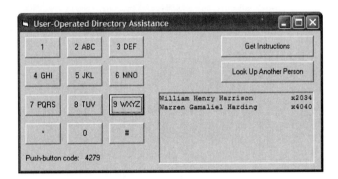

Figure 7.20 Sample run of Programming Project 11.

8 Sequential Files

8.1 SEQUENTIAL FILES

Throughout this text we have processed data from files created with Windows Notepad and saved on a disk. Such files are stored on disk as a sequence of characters. (Two special characters, called "carriage return" and "line feed," are inserted at the end of each line to indicate where new lines should be started.) These files are called **sequential files** or **text files**. In this section, we create sequential files with Visual Basic programs and develop techniques for using sequential files.

Creating a Sequential File

There are many ways to organize data in a sequential file. The technique presented here is easy to implement. The following steps create a new sequential file and write data to it.

1. Choose a file name. A file name can contain up to 215 characters consisting of letters, digits, and a few other assorted characters (including spaces and periods).

2. Choose a number from 1 through 511 to be the **reference number** of the file. While the file is in use, it will be identified by this number.

3. Execute the statement

    ```
    Open "filespec" For Output As #n
    ```

    where *n* is the reference number. This process is referred to as **opening a file for output**. It establishes a communications link between the computer and the disk drive for storing data *onto* the disk. It allows data to be output from the computer and recorded in the specified file.

4. Place data into the file with the Write # statement. If *a* is a string, then the statement

    ```
    Write #n, a
    ```

    writes the string *a* surrounded by quotation marks into the file. If *c* is a number, then the statement

    ```
    Write #n, c
    ```

    writes the number *c*, without any leading or trailing spaces, into file number *n*. The statement

    ```
    Write #n, a, c
    ```

    writes *a* and *c* as before, but with a comma separating them. Similarly, if the statement Write #*n* is followed by a list of several strings and/or numbers separated by commas, then all the strings and numbers appear as before, separated by commas. After each Write # statement is executed, "carriage return" and "line feed" characters are placed into the file.

5. After all the data have been recorded in the file, execute

```
Close #n
```

where *n* is the reference number. This statement breaks the communications link with the file and dissociates the number *n* from the file.

EXAMPLE I The following program illustrates the different aspects of the Write # statement. Notice the absence of leading and trailing spaces for numbers and the presence of quotation marks surrounding strings.

```
Private Sub cmdCreateFile_Click()
  Dim name1 As String, name2 As String
  'Demonstrate use of Write # statements
  Open "PIONEER.TXT" For Output As #1
  Write #1, "ENIAC"
  Write #1, 1946
  Write #1, "ENIAC", 1946
  name1 = "Eckert"
  name2 = "Mauchly"
  Write #1, 14 * 139, "J.P. " & name1, name2, "John"
  Close #1
End Sub
```

[Run, click the command button, and then load the file PIONEER.TXT into Windows' Notepad. The following will appear.]

"ENIAC"
1946
"ENIAC",1946
1946,"J.P. Eckert","Mauchly","John"

Caution: If an existing sequential file is opened for output, the computer will erase the existing data and create a new empty file.

Write # statements allow us to create files just like the Notepad files that appear throughout this text. We already know how to read such files with Input # statements. The remaining major task is adding data to the end of sequential files.

Adding Items to a Sequential File

Data can be added to the end of an existing sequential file with the following steps.

1. Choose a number from 1 through 511 to be the reference number for the file. It need not be the number that was used when the file was created.

2. Execute the statement

```
Open "filespec" For Append As #n
```

where *n* is the reference number. This procedure is called **opening a file for append**. It allows data to be output and recorded at the end of the specified file.

3. Place data into the file with Write # statements.

4. After all the data have been recorded into the file, close the file with the statement Close #*n*.

The Append option is used to add data to an existing file. However, it also can be used to create a new file. If the file does not exist, then the Append option acts just like the Output option and creates the file.

The three options, Output, Input, and Append, are referred to as **modes**. A file should not be open in two modes at the same time. For instance, after a file has been opened for output and data have been written to the file, the file should be closed before being opened for input.

An attempt to open a nonexistent file for input terminates the program with the "File not found" error message. There is a function that tells us whether a certain file already exists. If the value of

```
Dir("filespec")
```

is the empty string "", then the specified file does not exist. (If the file exists, the value will be the file name.) Therefore, prudence dictates that files be opened for input with code such as

```
If Dir("filespec") <> "" Then
    Open "filespec" For Input As #1
  Else
    message = "Either no file has yet been created or "
    message = message & "the file is not where expected."
    MsgBox message, , "File Not Found"
End If
```

There is one file-management operation that we have yet to discuss—changing or deleting an item of information from a file. An individual item of a file cannot be changed or deleted directly. A new file must be created by reading each item from the original file and recording it, with the single item changed or deleted, into the new file. The old file is then erased, and the new file renamed with the name of the original file. Regarding these last two tasks, the Visual Basic statement

```
Kill "filespec"
```

removes the specified file from the disk and the statement

```
Name "oldfilespec" As "newfilespec"
```

changes the filespec of a file. (**Note:** The Kill and Name statements cannot be used with open files. So doing generates a "File already open" message.)

EXAMPLE 2 The following program manages a file of names and years of birth.

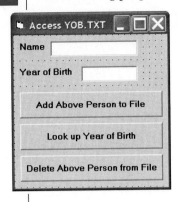

Object	Property	Setting
frm8_1_2	Caption	Access YOB.TXT
lblName	Caption	Name
txtName	Text	(blank)
lblYOB	Caption	Year of Birth
txtYOB	Text	(blank)
cmdAdd	Caption	Add Above Person to File
cmdLookUp	Caption	Look up Year of Birth
cmdDelete	Caption	Delete Above Person from File

```
Private Sub cmdAdd_Click()
  Dim message As String
  'Add a person's name and year of birth to file
  If (txtName.Text <> "") And (txtYOB.Text <> "") Then
      Open "YOB.TXT" For Append As #1
      Write #1, txtName.Text, Val(txtYOB.Text)
      Close #1
      txtName.Text = ""
      txtYOB.Text = ""
      txtName.SetFocus
    Else
      message = "You must enter a name and year of birth."
      MsgBox message, , "Information Incomplete"
  End If
End Sub

Private Sub cmdLookUp_Click()
  Dim message As String
  'Determine a person's year of birth
  If txtName.Text <> "" Then
      If Dir("YOB.TXT") <> "" Then
          Call DisplayYearOfBirth
        Else
          message = "Either no file has yet been created or "
          message = message & "the file is not where expected."
          MsgBox message, , "File Not Found"
      End If
    Else
      MsgBox "You must enter a name.", , "Information Incomplete"
  End If
  txtName.SetFocus
End Sub

Private Sub cmdDelete_Click()
  Dim message As String
  'Remove a person from the file
  If txtName.Text <> "" Then
      If Dir("YOB.TXT") <> "" Then
          Call DeletePerson
```

```
            Else
              message = "Either no file has yet been created or "
              message = message & "the file is not where expected."
              MsgBox message, , "File Not Found."
          End If
        Else
          MsgBox "You must enter a name.", , "Information Incomplete"
      End If
    txtName.SetFocus
End Sub

Private Sub DeletePerson()
  Dim nom As String, yob As Integer, foundFlag As Boolean
  foundFlag = False
  Open "YOB.TXT" For Input As #1
  Open "TEMP" For Output As #2
  Do While Not EOF(1)
    Input #1, nom, yob
    If nom <> txtName.Text Then
        Write #2, nom, yob
      Else
        foundFlag = True
    End If
  Loop
  Close #1
  Close #2
  Kill "YOB.TXT"
  Name "TEMP" As "YOB.TXT"
  If Not foundFlag Then
      MsgBox "The name was not found.", , ""
    Else
      txtName.Text = ""
      txtYOB.Text = ""
  End If
End Sub

Private Sub DisplayYearOfBirth()
  Dim nom As String, yob As Integer
  'Find the year of birth for the name in txtName
  txtYOB.Text = ""
  Open "YOB.TXT" For Input As #1
  nom = ""
  Do While (nom <> txtName.Text) And (Not EOF(1))
    Input #1, nom, yob
  Loop
  If nom = txtName.Text Then
      txtYOB.Text = Str(yob)
    Else
      MsgBox "Person is not in file.", , ""
      txtName.Text = ""
  End If
  Close #1
End Sub
```

[Run. After several names have been added, the file might look as shown in Figure 8.1.]

```
"Barbra",1942
"Ringo",1940
"Sylvester",1946
```

Figure 8.1 Sample contents of YOB.TXT.

Error Trapping

If you try to Open a file on a diskette in drive A and there is no diskette in drive A, the program will crash with the error message "Disk not ready." Visual Basic has a device, called **error-trapping**, for handling this and many other types of errors. If an error occurs while error-trapping is active, two things happen. An identifying number is assigned to the Number property of an object called Err, and the program jumps to some lines of code called an **error-handling routine**, which takes corrective measures based on the value of Err.Number. Some errors and the values they generate are as follows:

Type of error	Value of Err.Number
Subscript out of range	9
Division by zero	11
File not found	53
File already open	55
File already exists	58
Disk full	61
Disk not ready	71

To set up error-trapping inside a procedure, do the following:

1. Make the first line inside the procedure

```
On Error GoTo ErrorHandler
```

2. Type in the lines that carry out the error-handling routine.

3. Make the last lines of the procedure

```
Exit Sub
ErrorHandler:
  error-handling routine
Resume
```

The statement "On Error GoTo ErrorHandler" activates error-trapping. If an error occurs during the execution of a line of the procedure, the program will jump to the error-handling routine. The Resume statement causes the program to jump back to the line causing the error. The Exit Sub statement, which causes an early exit from the procedure, prevents the error-handling routine from being entered when no error occurs. For instance, the following procedure has an error-handling routine that is called when a file cannot be found.

```
Private Sub OpenFile()
  On Error GoTo ErrorHandler
```

```
      Dim fileName As String
      fileName = InputBox("Enter the name of the file to be opened.")
      Open fileName For Input As #1
      Exit Sub
  ErrorHandler:
    Select Case Err.Number
      Case 53  'File not found
        MsgBox "File not found. Try Again."
        fileName = InputBox("Enter the name of the file to be opened.")
      Case 71  'Disk not ready
         MsgBox "The disk might not be in the drive - please check."
    End Select
    Resume
  End Sub
```

The word "ErrorHandler", which is called a **line label**, can be replaced by any word of at most 40 letters. The line, which is placed just before the error-handling routine, must start at the left margin and must end with a colon. If Resume is replaced by Resume Next, then the program will jump to the line following the line causing the error.

The line label must be in the same procedure as the On Error statement. However, the error-handling routine can call another procedure.

There are two variations of the On Error statement. The statement "On Error GoTo 0" turns off error-trapping. The statement "On Error Resume Next" specifies that when a run-time error occurs, execution continues with the statement following the statement where the error occurred.

Comments

1. Sequential files make efficient use of disk space and are easy to create and use. Their disadvantages are as follows:

   (a) Often a large portion of the file must be read in order to find one specific item.
   (b) An individual item of the file cannot be changed or deleted easily.

   Another type of file, known as a **random-access file**, has neither of the disadvantages of sequential files; however, random-access files typically use more disk space, require greater effort to program, and are not flexible in the variety and format of the stored data. Random-access files are discussed in Chapter 9.

2. Consider the sequential file shown in Figure 8.1 at the end of Example 2. This file is said to consist of three records of two fields each. A **record** holds all the data about a single individual. Each item of data is called a **field**. The three records are

   "Barbra", 1942
   "Ringo", 1940
   "Sylvester", 1946

   and the two fields are

   name field, year of birth field

PRACTICE PROBLEMS 8.1

1. Compose a Sub procedure RemoveDups that could be used in Example 2 to delete from YOB.TXT all repeated records except the first instance of a name matching the name in txtName. (Assume that the existence of YOB.TXT is checked prior to the execution of this Sub procedure.)

2. Compose a Sub procedure AddNoDuplicate to add a name and year of birth to the end of the file YOB.TXT only if the name to be added is not already present in the file. (Assume that the existence of YOB.TXT is checked prior to the execution of this Sub procedure.)

EXERCISES 8.1

In Exercises 1 through 4, determine the output displayed in the picture box when the command button is clicked.

1.
```
Private Sub cmdDisplay_Click()
  Dim salutation As String
  Open "GREETING.TXT" For Output As #1
  Write #1, "Hello"
  Write #1, "Aloha"
  Close #1
  Open "GREETING.TXT" For Input As #1
  Input #1, salutation
  picOutput.Print salutation
  Close #1
End Sub
```

2.
```
Private Sub cmdDisplay_Click()
  Dim salutation As String, welcome As String
  Open "GREETING.TXT" For Output As #2
  Write #2, "Hello", "Aloha"
  Close #2
  Open "GREETING.TXT" For Input As #1
  Input #1, salutation, welcome
  picOutput.Print welcome
  Close #1
End Sub
```

3.
```
Private Sub cmdDisplay_Click()
  Dim salutation As String
  Open "GREETING.TXT" For Output As #2
  Write #2, "Hello"
  Write #2, "Aloha"
  Write #2, "Bon Jour"
  Close #2
  Open "GREETING.TXT" For Input As #1
  Do While Not EOF(1)
    Input #1, salutation
    picOutput.Print salutation
  Loop
  Close #1
End Sub
```

4. Assume the contents of the file GREETING.TXT are as shown in Figure 8.2.

```
Private Sub cmdDisplay_Click()
  Dim file As String, salutation As Integer, g As String
  file = "GREETING.TXT"
  Open file For Append As #3
  Write #3, "Buenos Dias"
  Close #3
  Open file For Input As #3
  For salutation = 1 To 4
    Input #3, g
    picOutput.Print g
  Next salutation
  Close #3
End Sub
```

"Hello"
"Aloha"
"Bon Jour"

Figure 8.2 Contents of the file GREETING.TXT.

5. Assume that the contents of the file GREETING.TXT are as shown in Figure 8.2. What is the effect of the following program?

```
Private Sub cmdDisplay_Click()
  Dim g As String
  Open "GREETING.TXT" For Input As #1
  Open "WELCOME.TXT" For Output As #2
  Do While Not EOF(1)
    Input #1, g
    If g <> "Aloha" Then
        Write #2, g
    End If
  Loop
  Close
End Sub
```

6. Assume that the contents of the file YOB.TXT are as shown in Figure 8.1. What is the effect of the following program?

```
Private Sub cmdDisplay_Click()
  Dim flag As Boolean, nom As String, year As Integer
  Open "YOB.TXT" For Input As #1
  Open "YOB2.TXT" For Output As #2
  flag = False
  nom = ""
  Do While (nom < "Clint") And (Not EOF(1))
    Input #1, nom, year
    If nom >= "Clint" Then
        Write #2, "Clint", 1930
        flag = True
    End If
    Write #2, nom, year
  Loop
```

```
      Do While Not EOF(1)
        Input #1, nom, year
        Write #2, nom, year
      Loop
      If Not flag Then
         Write #2, "Clint", 1930
      End If
      Close
    End Sub
```

In Exercises 7 through 12, identify any errors. Assume that the contents of the files YOB.TXT and GREETING.TXT are as shown in Figures 8.1 and 8.2.

7.
```
Private Sub cmdDisplay_Click()
    Open YOB.TXT For Append As #1
    Write #1, "Michael", 1965
    Close #1
End Sub
```

8.
```
Private Sub cmdDisplay_Click()
    Dim nom As String, yr As Integer
    Open "YOB.TXT" For Output As #2
    Input #2, nom, yr
    picOutput.Print yr
    Close #2
End Sub
```

9.
```
Private Sub cmdDisplay_Click()
    Dim i As Integer, g As String
    Open "GREETING.TXT" For Input As #1
    For i = 1 To EOF(1)
      Input #1, g
      picOutput.Print g
    Next i
    Close #1
End Sub
```

10.
```
Private Sub cmdDisplay_Click()
    Dim g As String
    Open "GREETING.TXT" For Input As #1
    Do While Not EOF
      Input #1, g
      picOutput.Print g
    Loop
    Close #1
End Sub
```

11.
```
Private Sub cmdDisplay_Click()
    Dim nom As String, g As String
    Open "GREETING.TXT" For Input As #1
    nom = "NEWGREET.TXT"
    Open "nom" For Output As #2
    Do While Not EOF(1)
      Input #1, g
      Write #2, g
    Loop
    Close
End Sub
```

12.
```
Private Sub cmdDisplay_Click()
    Open "GREETING.TXT" For Input As #1
    Close "GREETING.TXT"
End Sub
```

Exercises 13 through 20 are related and use the data in Table 8.1. The file created in Exercise 13 should be used in Exercises 14 through 20.

13. Write a program to create the sequential file COWBOY.TXT containing the information in Table 8.1.

Colt Peacemaker	12.20
Holster	2.00
Levi Strauss Jeans	1.35
Saddle	40.00
Stetson	10.00

Table 8.1 Prices paid by cowboys for certain items in mid-1800s.

14. Write a program to display all items in the file COWBOY.TXT that cost more than $10.

15. Write a program to add the data *Winchester rifle, 20.50* to the end of the file COWBOY.TXT.

16. Suppose an order is placed for 3 Colt Peacemakers, 2 Holsters, 10 pairs of Levi Strauss Jeans, 1 saddle, and 4 Stetsons. Write a program to perform the following tasks.

   (a) Create the sequential file ORDER.TXT to hold the numbers 3, 2, 10, 1, 4.
   (b) Use the files COWBOY.TXT and ORDER.TXT to display a sales receipt with three columns giving the name of each item, the quantity ordered, and the cost for that quantity.
   (c) Compute the total cost of the items and display it at the end of the sales receipt.

17. Write a program to request an additional item and price from the user. Then create a sequential file called COWBOY2.TXT containing all the information in the file COWBOY.TXT with the additional item (and price) inserted in its proper alphabetical sequence. Run the program for both of the following data items: *Boots, 20* and *Horse, 35*.

18. Suppose the price of saddles is reduced by 20%. Use the file COWBOY.TXT to create a sequential file, COWBOY3.TXT, containing the new price list.

19. Write a program to create a sequential file called COWBOY4.TXT containing all the information in the file COWBOY.TXT except for the data *Holster, 2*.

20. Write a program to allow additional items and prices to be input by the user and added to the end of the file COWBOY.TXT. Include a method to terminate the process.

21. Suppose the file YOB2.TXT contains many names and years and that the names are in alphabetical order. Write a program that requests a name as input and either gives the person's age or reports that the person is not in the file. *Note:* Because the names are in alphabetical order, usually there is no need to search to the end of the file.

22. Suppose the file YOB2.TXT contains many names and years. Write a program that creates two files, called SENIORS.TXT and JUNIORS.TXT, and copies all the data on people born before 1948 into the file SENIORS and the data on the others into the file JUNIORS.TXT.

23. A publisher maintains two sequential files, HARDBACK.TXT and PAPERBCK.TXT. Each record consists of the name of a book and the quantity in stock. Write a program to access these files. (The program should allow for the case when the book is not in the file.) A run of the program might look as follows:

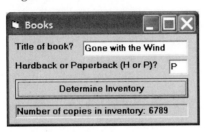

24. Fill in the missing code for the error-handling routine to handle a "division by zero" error.

Object	Property	Setting
frm8_1_E24	Caption	Exercise 24
picResult		
cmdDivide	Caption	Divide Two Numbers

```
Private Sub cmdDivide_Click()
  On Error GoTo ErrorHandler
  Dim a As Single, b As Single, c As Single
  picResult.Cls
  a = Val(InputBox("Enter the numerator."))
  b = Val(InputBox("Enter the denominator."))
  c = a / b
  picResult.Print "The quotient of"
  picResult.Print a; "and"; b
  picResult.Print "is"; c
  Exit Sub
ErrorHandler:
  missing code
End Sub
```

25. Visual Basic cannot Kill a file that is open. Attempting to do so generates a "File already open" error. Write a short program that uses error-trapping to handle such an error.

✔✔ **Solutions to Practice Problems 8.1**

1. A record in YOB.TXT is kept if the name in the record does not match the search name, or if the name in the record matches the search name and a flag indicates that the search name has not been found previously.

```
Private Sub RemoveDups()
  Dim nom As String, yob As Integer, foundFlag As Boolean
  foundFlag = False
  Open "YOB.TXT" For Input As #1
  Open "TEMP" For Output As #2
  Do While Not EOF(1)
    Input #1, nom, yob
    If nom <> txtName.Text Then
        Write #2, nom, yob
      Else
        If Not foundFlag Then
            Write #2, nom, yob
        End If
        foundFlag = True
    End If
  Loop
  Close #1
  Close #2
  Kill "YOB.TXT"
  Name "TEMP" As "YOB.TXT"
  If foundFlag = False Then
      MsgBox "The name was not found.", , ""
    Else
      txtName.Text = ""
      txtYOB.Text = ""
  End If
End Sub
```

2. The file YOB.TXT is first opened for Input and scanned for the new name. If the name is not found, YOB.TXT is reopened for Append and the name and year of birth are added to the end of the file.

```
Private Sub AddNoDuplicate()
  Dim nom As String, yob As Integer, foundFlag As Boolean
  Open "YOB.TXT" For Input As #1
  foundFlag = False
  Do While (Not(EOF(1))) And (Not foundFlag)
    Input #1, nom, yob
    If nom = txtName.Text Then
        foundFlag = True
    End If
  Loop
  Close #1
  If Not foundFlag Then
      Open "YOB.TXT" For Append As #1
      Write #1, txtName.Text, Val(txtYOB.Text)
      Close #1
  End If
End Sub
```

8.2 USING SEQUENTIAL FILES

In addition to being accessed for information, sequential files are regularly updated by modifying certain pieces of data, removing some records, and adding new records. These tasks can be performed most efficiently if the files are first sorted.

Sorting Sequential Files

The records of a sequential file can be sorted on any field by first reading the data into parallel arrays and then sorting on a specific array.

EXAMPLE 1 The following program sorts the sequential file YOB.TXT of the previous section by year of birth.

```
Private Sub cmdSort_Click()
  Dim numPeople As Integer
  'Sort data from YOB.TXT file by year of birth
  numPeople = NumberOfRecords("YOB.TXT")
  ReDim nom(1 To numPeople) As String
  ReDim yearBorn(1 To numPeople) As Integer
  Call ReadData(nom(), yearBorn(), numPeople)
  Call SortData(nom(), yearBorn(), numPeople)
  Call ShowData(nom(), yearBorn(), numPeople)
  Call WriteData(nom(), yearBorn(), numPeople)
End Sub

Private Function NumberOfRecords(filespec As String) As Integer
  Dim nom As String, yearBorn As Integer
  Dim n As Integer     'Used to count records
  n = 0
  Open filespec For Input As #1
  Do While Not EOF(1)
    Input #1, nom, yearBorn
    n = n + 1
  Loop
  Close #1
  NumberOfRecords = n
End Function

Private Sub ReadData(nom() As String, yearBorn() As Integer, numPeople As _
        Integer)
  Dim index As Integer
  'Read data from file into arrays
  Open "YOB.TXT" For Input As #1
  For index = 1 To numPeople
    Input #1, nom(index), yearBorn(index)
  Next index
  Close #1
End Sub
```

```
Private Sub ShowData(nom() As String, yearBorn() As Integer, numPeople As _
        Integer)
  Dim index As Integer
  'Display the sorted list
  picShowData.Cls
  For index = 1 To numPeople
    picShowData.Print nom(index), yearBorn(index)
  Next index
End Sub

Private Sub SortData(nom() As String, yearBorn() As Integer, numPeople As Integer)
  Dim passNum As Integer, index As Integer
  'Bubble sort arrays by year of birth
  For passNum = 1 To numPeople - 1
    For index = 1 To numPeople - passNum
      If yearBorn(index) > yearBorn(index + 1) Then
          Call SwapData(nom(), yearBorn(), index)
      End If
    Next index
  Next passNum
End Sub

Private Sub SwapData(nom() As String, yearBorn() As Integer, index As Integer)
  Dim stemp As String, ntemp As Integer
  'Swap names and years
  stemp = nom(index)
  nom(index) = nom(index + 1)
  nom(index + 1) = stemp
  ntemp = yearBorn(index)
  yearBorn(index) = yearBorn(index + 1)
  yearBorn(index + 1) = ntemp
End Sub

Private Sub WriteData(nom() As String, yearBorn() As Integer, numPeople As Integer)
  Dim index As Integer
  'Write data back into file
  Open "YOB.TXT" For Output As #1
  For index = 1 To numPeople
    Write #1, nom(index), yearBorn(index)
  Next index
  Close #1
End Sub
```

[Run, and then click on the command button. The following is displayed in the picture box.]

```
Ringo        1940
Barbra       1942
Sylvester    1946
```

Merging Sequential Files

In Section 7.2, we considered an algorithm for merging two arrays. This same algorithm can be applied to merging two ordered files.

Suppose you have two ordered files (possibly with certain items appearing in both files), and you want to merge them into a third ordered file (without duplications). The technique for creating the third file is as follows.

1. Open the two ordered files For Input and open a third file For Output.

2. Try to get an item of data from each file.

3. Repeat steps (a) and (b) below until an item of data is not available in one of the files.

    (a) If one item precedes the other, write it into the third file and try to get another item of data from its file.
    (b) If the two items are identical, write one into the third file and try to get another item of data from each of the two ordered files.

4. At this point, an item of data has most likely been retrieved from one of the files and not yet written to the third file. In this case, write that item and all remaining items in that file to the third file.

5. Close the three files.

EXAMPLE 2 The following program merges two ordered files of numbers into a third ordered file.

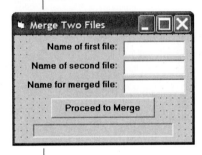

Object	Property	Setting
frmMerge	Caption	Merge Two Files
lblNameFirst	Caption	Name of first file:
txtNameFirst	Text	(blank)
lblNameSecond	Caption	Name of second file:
txtNameSecond	Text	(blank)
lblNameMerged	Caption	Name for merged file:
txtNameMerged	Text	(blank)
cmdProceed	Caption	Proceed to Merge
picProgress		

```
Private Sub cmdProceed_Click()
    Dim file1 As String, file2 As String, file3 As String
    Dim have1data As Boolean, have2data As Boolean
    Dim num1 As Single, num2 As Single
    Dim recCount As Integer      'Number of records in merged file
    'Merge two ordered files
    picProgress.Cls
    file1 = txtNameFirst.Text
    file2 = txtNameSecond.Text
    file3 = txtNameMerged.Text
    Open file1 For Input As #1
    Open file2 For Input As #2
    Open file3 For Output As #3
    have1data = Get1data(num1)
    have2data = Get2data(num2)
    recCount = 0
```

```
     Do While (have1data And have2data)
       Select Case num1
         Case Is < num2
           Write #3, num1
           have1data = Get1data(num1)
         Case Is > num2
           Write #3, num2
           have2data = Get2data(num2)
         Case num2
           Write #3, num1
           have1data = Get1data(num1)
           have2data = Get2data(num2)
       End Select
       recCount = recCount + 1
     Loop
     Do While have1data
       Write #3, num1
       recCount = recCount + 1
       have1data = Get1data(num1)
     Loop
     Do While have2data
       Write #3, num2
       recCount = recCount + 1
       have2data = Get2data(num2)
     Loop
     Close #1, #2, #3
     picProgress.Print recCount; "records written to "; file3
End Sub

Private Function Get1data(num1 As Single) As Boolean
   'If possible, read next value from file 1
   'Return value of True when new data are read; False if data not available
   If Not EOF(1) Then
       Input #1, num1
       Get1data = True
     Else
       Get1data = False
   End If
End Function

Private Function Get2data(num2 As Single) As Boolean
   'If possible, read next value from file 2
   'Return value True when new data are read; False if data not available
   If Not EOF(2) Then
       Input #2, num2
       Get2data = True
     Else
       Get2data = False
   End If
End Function
```

Control Break Processing

Suppose a small real estate company stores its sales data for a year in a sequential file in which each record contains four fields: month of sale, day of sale (1 through 31), address, and price. Typical data for the sales of the first quarter of a year are shown in Figure 8.3. The records are ordered by date of sale.

Month	Day	Address	Price
January	9	102 Elm Street	$203,000
January	20	1 Main Street	$315,200
January	25	5 Maple Street	$123,450
February	15	1 Center Street	$100,000
February	23	2 Vista Drive	$145,320
March	15	205 Rodeo Circle	$389,100

Figure 8.3 Real estate sales for first quarter of year.

Figure 8.4 shows the output of a program that displays the total sales for the quarter year, with a subtotal for each month.

```
January    9     102 Elm Street        $203,000.00
January   20     1 Main Street         $315,200.00
January   25     5 Maple Street        $123,450.00

               Subtotal for January:   $641,650.00

February  15     1 Center Street       $100,000.00
February  23     2 Vista Drive         $145,320.00

               Subtotal for February:  $245,320.00

March     15     205 Rodeo Circle      $389,100.00

               Subtotal for March:     $389,100.00

Total for First Quarter: $1,276,070.00
```

Figure 8.4 Output of Example 3.

A program to produce the output of Figure 8.4 must calculate a subtotal at the end of each month. The variable holding the month triggers a subtotal whenever its value changes. Such a variable is called a **control variable**, and each change of its value is called a **break**.

EXAMPLE 3   The following program produces the output of Figure 8.4. The data of Figure 8.3 are stored in the sequential file HOMESALE.TXT. The program allows for months with no sales. Because monthly subtotals will be printed, the month-of-sale field is an appropriate control variable.

```
Private Sub cmdCreateReport_Click()
  Dim currentMonth As String, newMonth As String
  Dim dayNum As Integer, address As String
  Dim price As Single, monthTotal As Single
  Dim yearTotal As Single, doneFlag As Boolean
```

```
                    'Display home sales by month
                    picReport.Cls
                    Open "HOMESALE.TXT" For Input As #1
                    currentMonth = ""                       'Name of month being subtotaled
                    monthTotal = 0
                    yearTotal = 0
                    doneFlag = False                        'Flag to indicate end of list
                    Do While Not doneFlag
                      If Not EOF(1) Then
                          Input #1, newMonth, dayNum, address, price
                        Else
                          doneFlag = True                   'End of list
                      End If
                      If (newMonth <> currentMonth) Or (doneFlag) Then 'Control break processing
                          If currentMonth <> "" Then    'Don't print subtotal before 1st month
                              picReport.Print
                              picReport.Print Tab(15); "Subtotal for "; currentMonth; ":";
                              picReport.Print Tab(38); FormatCurrency(monthTotal)
                              picReport.Print
                          End If
                          currentMonth = newMonth
                          monthTotal = 0
                      End If
                      If Not doneFlag Then
                          picReport.Print newMonth;
                          picReport.Print Tab(11); FormatNumber(dayNum, 0);
                          picReport.Print Tab(18); address;
                          picReport.Print Tab(38); FormatCurrency(price)
                          yearTotal = yearTotal + price
                      End If
                      monthTotal = monthTotal + price
                    Loop
                    Close #1
                    picReport.Print "Total for First Quarter: "; FormatCurrency(yearTotal)
                End Sub
```

Comments

1. In the examples of this and the previous section, the files to be processed have been opened and closed within a single procedure. However, the solution to some programming problems requires that a file be opened just once the instant the program is run and stay open until the program is terminated. This is easily accomplished by placing the Open statement in the Form_Load event procedure and the Close and End statements in the click event procedure for a command button labeled "Quit."

✔ **PRACTICE PROBLEMS 8.2**

1. The program in Example 2 contains three Do loops. Explain why at most one of the last two loops will be executed. Under what circumstances will neither of the last two loops be executed?

2. Modify the program in Example 2 so that duplicate items will be repeated in the merged file.

> **EXERCISES 8.2**

Exercises 1 through 4 are related. They create and maintain the sequential file AVERAGE.TXT to hold batting averages of baseball players.

1. Suppose the season is about to begin. Compose a program to create the sequential file containing the name of each player, his times at bat, and his number of hits. The program should allow the user to type a name into a text box and then click a command button to add a record to the file. The times at bat and number of hits initially should be set to 0. (*Hint:* Open the file for Output in the Form_Load event procedure and Close the file when a "Quit" command button is clicked.)

2. Each day, the statistics from the previous day's games should be used to update the file. Write a program to read the records one at a time and allow the user to enter the number of times at bat and the number of hits in yesterday's game for each player in appropriate text boxes on a form. When a command button is clicked, the program should update the file by adding these numbers to the previous figures. (*Hint:* Open files in the Form_Load event procedure. Close the files and end the program when all data have been processed.)

3. Several players are added to the league. Compose a program to update the file.

4. Compose a program to sort the file AVERAGE.TXT with respect to batting averages and display the players with the top 10 batting averages. *Hints:* The file must be read once to determine the number of players and again to load the players into an array. A batting average can be displayed in standard form with `FormatNumber(ave, 3, vbFalse)`.

Exercises 5 and 6 refer to the ordered file BLOCK.TXT containing the names of people on your block and the ordered file TIMES.TXT containing the names of all people who subscribe to the *New York Times*.

5. Write a program that creates a file consisting of the names of all people on your block who subscribe to the *New York Times*.

6. Write a program that creates a file consisting of the names of all *New York Times* subscribers who do not live on your block.

7. Suppose a file of positive integers is in ascending order. Write a program to determine the maximum number of times any integer is repeated in the file. (For instance, if the entries in the file are 5, 5, 6, 6, 6, and 10, then the output is 3.)

8. Suppose each record of the file SALES.TXT contains a salesperson's name and the dollar amount of a sale, and the records are ordered by the names. Write a program to display the name, number of sales, and average sale amount for each salesperson. For instance, if the first four records of the file are

"Adams", 123.45
"Adams", 432.15
"Brown", 89.95
"Cook", 500.00

then the first two entries of the output would be

```
Salesperson    Number of Sales    Average Sale Amount
Adams          2                  $277.80
Brown          1                  $89.95
```

9. An elementary school holds a raffle to raise funds. Suppose each record of the file RAFFLE.TXT contains a student's grade (1 through 6), name, and the number of raffle tickets sold, and that the records are ordered by grade. Write a program using a control break to display the number of tickets sold by each grade and the total number of tickets sold.

10. *Multiple Control Breaks.* Suppose the sorted sequential file CENSUS.TXT contains names of all residents of a state, where each record has the form "lastName","firstName". Write a program to determine, in one pass through the file, the most common last name and most common full name. (**Note:** In the unlikely event of a tie, the program should display the first occurring name.) For instance, the output in the picture box might be as follows.

```
The most common last name is Brown
The most common full name is John Smith
```

In Exercises 11 and 12, suppose the file MASTER.TXT contains the names and phone numbers of all members of an organization, where the records are ordered by name.

11. Suppose the ordered file MOVED.TXT contains the names and new phone numbers of all members who have changed their phone numbers. Write a program to update the file MASTER.TXT.

12. Suppose the ordered file QUIT.TXT contains the names of all members who have left the organization. Write a program to update the file MASTER.TXT.

13. What are some advantages of files over arrays?

✔✔ Solutions to Practice Problems 8.2

1. Execution proceeds beyond the first Do loop only when EOF becomes True for one of the input files. Because each of the last two Do loops executes only if EOF is not True, at most one loop can execute.

Neither of the last two loops will be executed if each input file is empty or if the last entries of the files are the same.

2. Change the Select Case block to the following:

```
Select Case num1
  Case Is <= num2
    Write #3, num1
    have1data = Get1data(num1)
  Case Is > num2
    Write #3, num2
    have2data = Get2data(num2)
End Select
```

8.3   A CASE STUDY: RECORDING CHECKS AND DEPOSITS

The purpose of this section is to take you through the design and implementation of a quality program for personal checkbook management. Nothing in this chapter shows off the power of Visual Basic better than the program in this section. That a user-friendly checkbook management program can be written in less than five pages of code clearly shows Visual Basic's ability to improve the productivity of programmers. It is easy to imagine an entire finance program, similar to programs that have generated millions of dollars of sales, being written in only a few weeks by using Visual Basic!

Design of the Program

Though there are many commercial programs available for personal financial management, they include so many bells and whistles that their original purposes—keeping track of transactions and reporting balances—have become obscured. The program in this section was designed specifically as a checkbook program. It keeps track of expenditures and deposits and produces a printed report. Adding a reconciliation feature would be easy enough, although we did not include one.

The program is supposed to be user-friendly. Therefore, it showcases many of the techniques and tools available in Visual Basic.

The general design goals for the program included the abilities to

- Automatically enter the user's name on each check and deposit slip.
- Automatically provide the next consecutive check or deposit slip number. (The user can override this feature if necessary.)
- Automatically provide the date. (Again, this feature can be overridden.)
- For each check, record the payee, the amount, and optionally a memo.
- For each deposit slip, record the source, the amount, and optionally a memo.
- Display the current balance at all times.
- Produce a printout detailing all transactions.

User Interface

With Visual Basic we can place a replica of a check or deposit slip on the screen and let the user supply the information as if actually filling out a check or deposit slip. Figure 8.5 shows the form in its check mode. A picture box forms the boundary of the check. Below the picture box are two labels for the current balance and four command buttons.

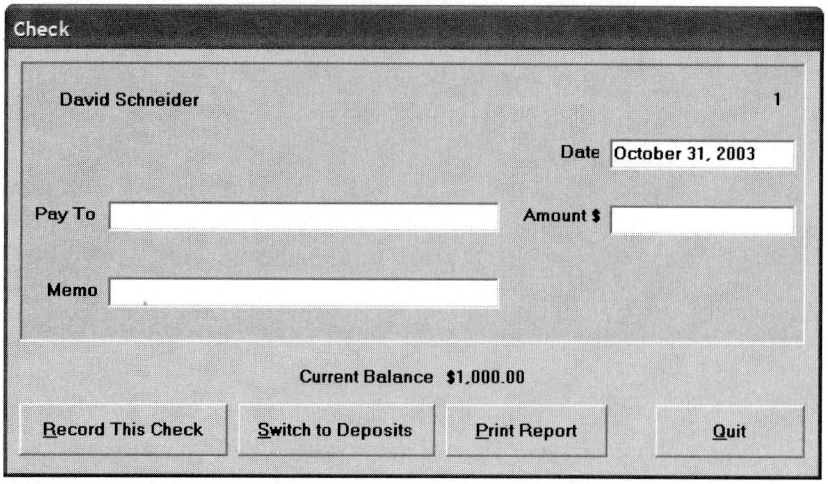

Figure 8.5 Template for entering a check.

The first time the program is run, the user is asked for his or her name, the starting balance, and the numbers of the first check and deposit slip. Suppose the user's name is David Schneider, the first check has number 1, the starting balance is $1000, and the first deposit slip is also number 1. Figure 8.5 shows the form after the three pieces of input. The upper part of the form looks like a check. The check has a color of light turquoise blue (or cyan). The Date box is automatically set to today's date, but can be altered by the user. The user fills in the payee, amount, and optionally a memo. When the user pushes the Record This Check button, the information is written to a file, the balance is updated, and check number 2 appears.

To record a deposit, the user pushes the Switch to Deposits button. The form then appears as in Figure 8.6. The form's title bar now reads Deposit Slip, the words Pay To changes to Source, and the color of the slip changes to yellow. Also, in the buttons at the bottom of the form, the words Check and Deposit are interchanged. A deposit is recorded in much the same way as a check. When the Print Report button is pushed, a printout similar to the one in Figure 8.7 is printed on the printer.

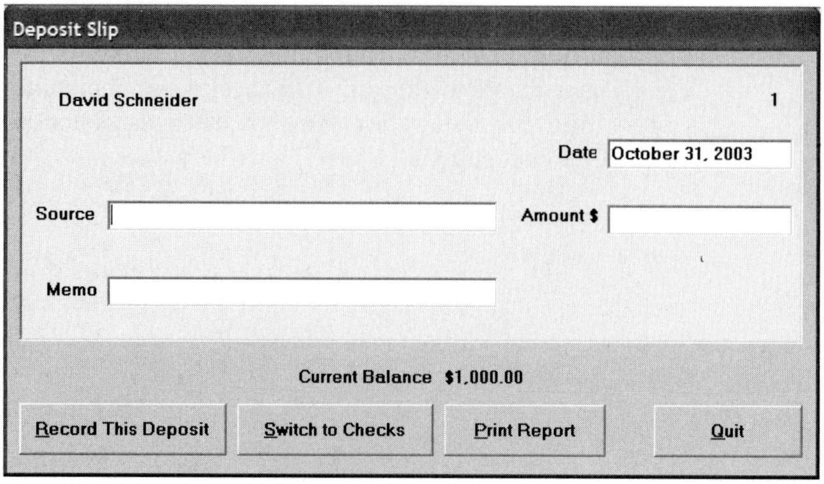

Figure 8.6 Template for entering a deposit.

Name: David Schneider   Monday, May 5, 2003

Starting balance: $1,000.00

Date	Transaction	Amount	Balance
April 21, 2003	Check #: 1 Paid to: Land's End Memo: shirts	$75.95	$924.05
April 29, 2003	Check #: 2 Paid to: Bethesda Coop Memo: groceries	$125.00	$799.05
May 5, 2003	Deposit #: 1 Source: Prentice Hall Memo: typing expenses	$245.00	$1,044.05

Ending Balance: $1,044.05

Figure 8.7 Sample printout of transactions.

The common design for the check and deposit slip allows one set of controls to be used for both items. Figure 8.8 shows the controls and their suggestive names. The caption of the label lblName is set to the user's name, while the caption of the label lblToFrom will change back and forth between Pay To and Source.

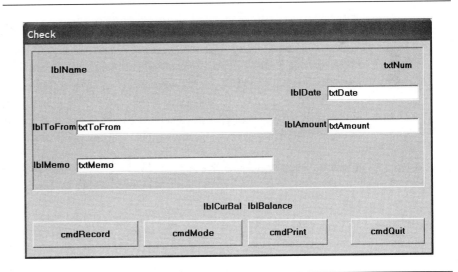

Figure 8.8 Control names for checkbook management program.

Table 8.2 lists the objects and their initial property settings. Because the program will always begin by displaying the next check, all the captions for the labels and the BackColor property of the picture box could have been set at design time. We chose instead to leave these assignments to the SetupCheck Sub procedure, which is normally used to switch from deposit entry to check entry, but also can be called by the Form_Load event procedure to prepare the initial mode (check or deposit) for the form.

Object	Property	Setting
frmCheckbook		
picBox		
lblName	BackStyle	0 – Transparent
txtNum	BorderStyle	0 – None
lblDate	BackStyle	0 – Transparent
	Caption	Date
txtDate		
lblToFrom	BackStyle	0 – Transparent
txtToFrom		
lblAmount	BackStyle	0 – Transparent
	Caption	Amount $
txtAmount		
lblMemo	BackStyle	0 – Transparent
	Caption	Memo
txtMemo		
lblCurBal	Caption	Current Balance
lblBalance		
cmdRecord		
cmdMode		
cmdPrint	Caption	&Print Report
cmdQuit	Caption	&Quit

Table 8.2 Objects and initial properties for the checkbook management program.

The transactions are stored in a text file named CHECKBOOK.TXT. The first four entries of the file are the name to appear on the check or deposit slip, the starting balance, the number of the first check, and the number of the first deposit slip. After that, each transaction is recorded as a sequence of eight items—the type of transaction, the contents of txtToFrom, the current balance, the number of the last check, the number of the last deposit slip, the amount of money, the memo, and the date.

Coding the Program

The top row of Figure 8.9 shows the different events to which the program must respond. Table 8.3 identifies the corresponding event procedures and the general procedures they call.

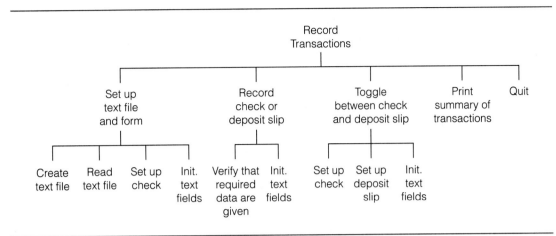

Figure 8.9 Hierarchy chart for checkbook management program.

Task	Procedure
1. Set up text file and form	Form_Load
1.1 Create text file	CreateTextFile
1.2 Read text file	ReadTextFile
1.3 Set up check	SetupCheck
1.4 Initialize text fields	InitializeFields
2. Record check or deposit slip	cmdRecord_Click
2.1 Verify that required data are given	AllDataGiven
2.2 Initialize text fields	InitializeFields
3. Toggle between check & deposit slip	cmdMode_Click
3.1 Set up check	SetupCheck
3.2 Set up deposit slip	SetupDeposit
3.3 Initialize text fields	InitializeFields
4. Print summary of transaction	cmdPrint_Click
5. Quit	cmdQuit_Click

Table 8.3 Tasks and their procedures.

Let's examine each event procedure.

1. Form_Load first looks to see if the file CHECKBOOK.TXT has been created. The function Dir returns "CHECKBOOK.TXT" if the file exists and
otherwise returns the empty string. If CHECKBOOK.TXT does not exist,
the routine CreateTextFile is called. CreateTextFile prompts the user for the
name to appear on the checks and deposit slips, the starting balance, and the
numbers of the first check and deposit slip, and then writes these items to
the text file. If CHECKBOOK.TXT does exist, the routine ReadTextFile is
called to read through the entire file to determine all information needed to
proceed. The event procedure calls SetupCheck to set the transaction type
to Check and set the appropriate captions and background colors for a
check. The event procedure then calls InitializeFields, which initializes all
the text boxes.

In the first assignment statement of the procedure, the drive is specified as the A drive. Therefore, the text file will be written to and read from a diskette on the A drive. Feel free to change the letter A to whatever drive you prefer. You may even want to specify an entire path.

2. **cmdRecord_Click** first confirms that the required fields contain entries. This is accomplished by calling the function AllDataGiven. If the value returned is True, then cmdRecord_Click opens the text file for output as Append, sends eight pieces of data to the file, and then closes the file. When AllDataGiven returns False, the function itself pops up a message box to tell the user where information is needed. The user must type in the information and then press the Record button again.

3. **cmdMode_Click** toggles back and forth from a check to a deposit slip. It calls SetupCheck, or its analog SetupDeposit, and then calls InitializeFields.

4. **cmdPrint_Click** prints out a complete history of all transactions, as shown in Figure 8.7.

5. **cmdQuit_Click** ends the program.

```
Dim fileName As String    'Name of text file
Dim nameOnChk As String   'Name to appear on checks
Dim lastCkNum As Integer  'Number of last check written
Dim lastDpNum As Integer  'Number of last deposit slip processed
Dim curBal As Single      'Current balance in account
Dim transType As String   'Type of transaction, check or deposit


Private Sub Form_Load()
  Dim drive As String, today As String
  'If no text file exists, create one. Otherwise, open the
  'text file and get the user's name, last used check and
  'deposit slip numbers, and current balance.
  'In next line adjust drive as necessary
  drive = "A:"                      'Drive (or path) for text file
  fileName = drive & "CHECKBOOK.TXT" 'Program uses one text file
  If Dir(fileName) = "" Then
      'Text file does not exist, so create it and obtain initial data
      Call CreateTextFile
    Else
      Call ReadTextFile
  End If
  'Set name and balance labels
  lblName.Caption = nameOnChk
  lblBalance.Caption = FormatCurrency(curBal)
  'Set the date field to the current date
  today = FormatDateTime(Now, vbLongDate)
  txtDate.Text = Mid(today, 2 + InStr(today, ","))
  Call SetupCheck                   'Always start session with checks
  Call InitializeFields
End Sub
```

```
Private Sub cmdRecord_Click()
  Dim amt As String, amount As Single, itemNum As Integer
  'Check to ensure all required fields are filled
  If AllDataGiven Then
      amt = txtAmount.Text 'Amount of transaction as string
      amount = Val(amt)     'Amount of transaction as number
      amt = FormatCurrency(amt)
      itemNum = Val(txtNum.Text)
      If transType = "Check" Then
          curBal = curBal - amount
          lastCkNum = itemNum
        Else                'transType = "Deposit"
          curBal = curBal + amount
          lastDpNum = itemNum
      End If
      lblBalance.Caption = FormatCurrency(curBal)
      Open fileName For Append As #1
      Write #1, transType, txtToFrom.Text, curBal, lastCkNum, lastDpNum, amt, _
              txtMemo.Text, txtDate.Text
      Close #1
      Call InitializeFields
      txtToFrom.SetFocus
  End If
End Sub


Private Sub cmdMode_Click()
  'Toggle from Check to/from Deposit Slip
  If transType = "Check" Then
      Call SetupDeposit
    Else   'transType = "Deposit"
      Call SetupCheck
  End If
  Call InitializeFields
  txtToFrom.SetFocus
End Sub


Private Sub cmdPrint_Click()
  Dim temp As String, lineNo As Integer
  Dim nameOnChk As String, balance As Single, ck As Integer, dp As Integer
  Dim toFrom As String, amount As String, memo As String, theDate As String
  'Print out a detailed list of all transactions.
  temp = frmCheckbook.Caption              'Save the current form caption
  frmCheckbook.Caption = "Printing..."     'Set form caption to indicate printing
  lineNo = 1                               'Line number being printed
  Open fileName For Input As #1            'Open the file
  Input #1, nameOnChk, balance, ck, dp     'Read in the file header
  'Print the details of the individual transactions.
  Do Until EOF(1)
    If lineNo >= 57 Then
        '57 or more lines have been printed; start a new page
        Printer.NewPage
        lineNo = 1
    End If
```

```
      If lineNo = 1 Then
          'Print the report header
          Printer.Print
          Printer.Print "Name: "; nameOnChk; Tab(65); FormatDateTime(Now, vbLongDate)
          Printer.Print
          Printer.Print , , "Starting balance: "; FormatCurrency(balance)
          Printer.Print
          Printer.Print "Date", , "Transaction"; Tab(60); "Amount";
          Printer.Print Tab(75); "Balance"
          Printer.Print "____", , "_____"; Tab(60); "_____";
          Printer.Print Tab(75); "_____"
          Printer.Print
          Printer.Print
          lineNo = 10
      End If
      Input #1, transType, toFrom, balance, ck, dp, amount, memo, theDate
      If transType = "Check" Then
          Printer.Print theDate; Tab(29); "Check #: "; ck; Tab(60); amount;
          Printer.Print Tab(75); FormatCurrency(balance)
          Printer.Print , , "Paid to: "; toFrom
        Else              'Transaction was a deposit
          Printer.Print theDate; Tab(29); "Deposit #: "; dp; Tab(60); amount;
          Printer.Print Tab(75); FormatCurrency(balance)
          Printer.Print , , "Source: "; toFrom
      End If
      lineNo = lineNo + 2
      'If there was a memo, then print it.
      If memo <> "" Then
          Printer.Print , "Memo: "; memo
          lineNo = lineNo + 1
      End If
      Printer.Print
      lineNo = lineNo + 1
    Loop
    Close #1                    'Close the file
    'Print the ending balance
    Printer.Print
    Printer.Print , "Ending Balance: "; FormatCurrency(balance)
    Printer.EndDoc                       'Send the output to the Printer
    frmCheckbook.Caption = temp          'Restore the form caption
    txtToFrom.SetFocus                   'Set focus for the next entry
End Sub

Private Sub cmdQuit_Click()
  'Exit the program
  End
End Sub

Private Sub CreateTextFile()
  Dim startBal As Single, ckNum As integer
  'The first time the program is run, create a text file
  Open fileName For Output As #1
  nameOnChk = InputBox("Name to appear on checks:")
  startBal = Val(InputBox("Starting balance:"))
```

```
  ckNum = Val(InputBox("Number of the first check:"))
  lastCkNum = ckNum - 1    'Number of "last" check written
  ckNum = Val(InputBox("Number of the first deposit slip:"))
  lastDpNum = ckNum - 1    'Number of "last" deposit slip processed
  curBal = startBal        'Set current balance
  'First record in text file records name to appear on checks
  'plus initial data for account
  Write #1, nameOnChk, startBal, lastCkNum, lastDpNum
  Close #1
End Sub


Private Sub ReadTextFile()
  Dim t As String, s As String, n As String, m As String, d As String
  'Recover name to appear on checks, current balance,
  'number of last check written, and number of last deposit slip processed
  Open fileName For Input As #1
  Input #1, nameOnChk, curBal, lastCkNum, lastDpNum
  Do Until EOF(1)
    'Read to the end of the file to recover the current balance and the
    'last values recorded for ckNum and dpNum.
    't, s, n, m and d are dummy variables and are not used at this point
    Input #1, t, s, curBal, lastCkNum, lastDpNum, n, m, d
  Loop
  Close #1
End Sub


Private Sub SetupCheck()
  'Prepare form for the entry of a check
  transType = "Check"
  frmCheckbook.Caption = "Check"
  lblToFrom.Caption = "Pay To"
  cmdRecord.Caption = "&Record This Check"
  cmdMode.Caption = "&Switch to Deposits"
  picBox.BackColor = vbCyan   'color of check is light turquoise blue
  txtNum.BackColor = vbCyan
End Sub


Private Sub InitializeFields()
  'Initialize all text entry fields except date
  txtToFrom.Text = ""
  txtAmount.Text = ""
  txtMemo.Text = ""
  If transType = "Check" Then
      'Make txtNum text box reflect next check number
      txtNum.Text = Str(lastCkNum + 1)
    Else              'transType = "Deposit"
      'Make txtNum text box reflect next deposit slip number
      txtNum.Text = Str(lastDpNum + 1)
  End If
End Sub
```

```
Private Function AllDataGiven() As Boolean
   Dim message As String
   'If one of the four required pieces of information
   'is missing, assign its name to message
   message = ""
   If txtDate.Text = "" Then
       message = "Date"
       txtDate.SetFocus
     ElseIf txtToFrom.Text = "" Then
       If transType = "Check" Then
           message = "Pay To"
         Else
           message = "Source"
       End If
       txtToFrom.SetFocus
     ElseIf txtAmount.Text = "" Then
       message = "Amount"
       txtAmount.SetFocus
     ElseIf txtNum.Text = "" Then
       If transType = "Check" Then
           message - "Check Number"
         Else
           message = "Deposit Number"
       End If
       txtNum.SetFocus
   End If

   If message = "" Then
       'All required data fields have been filled; recording can proceed
       AllDataGiven = True
     Else
       'Advise user of required data that are missing
       MsgBox "The '" & message & " 'field must be filled", , "Error"
       AllDataGiven = False
   End If
End Function

Private Sub SetupDeposit()
   'Prepare form for the entry of a deposit
   transType = "Deposit"
   frmCheckbook.Caption = "Deposit Slip"
   lblToFrom.Caption = "Source"
   cmdRecord.Caption = "&Record This Deposit"
   cmdMode.Caption = "&Switch to Checks"
   picBox.BackColor = vbYellow   'color of deposit slip is yellow
   txtNum.BackColor = vbYellow
End Sub
```

CHAPTER 8   SUMMARY

1. When sequential files are opened, we must specify whether they will be created and written to, added to, or read from by use of the terms Output, Append, or Input. The file must be *closed* before the operation is changed. Data are written to the file with Write # statements and retrieved with Input # statements. The EOF function tells if we have read to the end of the file.

2. Error-trapping can reduce the likelihood that a program crashes. If an error occurs after an `On Error GoTo ErrorHandler` statement has been executed, execution branches to the code in an error-handling routine and then branches back to the statement that caused the error (or the next statement).

3. A sequential file can be ordered by placing its data in arrays, sorting the arrays, and then writing the ordered data into a file.

CHAPTER 8   PROGRAMMING PROJECTS

1. Table 8.4 gives the leading eight soft drinks in 2003 and their percentage share of the market. Write and execute a program to place these data into a sequential file. Then write a second program to use the file to

   (a) display the eight brands and their gross sales in billions. (The entire soft drink industry grosses about $50 billion.)
   (b) calculate the total percentage market share of the leading eight soft drinks.

Coke Classic	19.9	Sprite	6.5
Pepsi-Cola	13.2	Dr. Pepper	6.2
Diet Coke	8.8	Diet Pepsi	5.3
Mountain Dew	6.9	7 Up	1.9

Table 8.4 Leading soft drinks and percentages of 2001 market share.
Source: Beverage Digest, 1/22/03.

2. Suppose the sequential file ALE.TXT contains the information shown in Table 8.5. Write a program to use the file to produce Table 8.6 in which the baseball teams are in descending order by the percentage of games won. **Note:** A batting average can be displayed in standard form with `FormatNumber(ave, 3, vbFalse)`.

Team	Won	Lost
Baltimore	67	95
Boston	93	69
New York	103	58
Tampa Bay	55	106
Toronto	78	84

Table 8.5 American League East games won and lost in 2002.

American League East			
	W	**L**	**Pct**
New York	103	58	0.640
Boston	93	69	0.574
Toronto	78	84	0.481
Baltimore	67	95	0.414
Tampa Bay	55	106	0.342

Table 8.6 Final 2002 American League East standings.

3. Write a rudimentary word processing program. The program should do the following:

(a) Use InputBox to request the name of the sequential file to hold the document being created.

(b) Set the label for a text box to "Enter Line1," and allow the user to enter the first line of the document into a text box.

(c) When the Enter key is pressed or a "Record Line" command button is clicked, determine if the line is acceptable. Blank lines are acceptable input, but lines exceeding 60 characters in length should not be accepted. Advise the user of the problem with a message dialog box, and then set the focus back to the text box so that the user can edit the line to an acceptable length. When an acceptable line is entered, write this line to the file and display it in a picture box.

(d) Change the label to "Enter Line 2", clear the text box, allow the user to enter the second line of the document into the text box, and carry out (c) for this line using the same picture box. (Determine in advance how many lines the picture box can display and only clear the picture box when the lines already displayed do not leave room for a new line.)

(e) Continue as in (d) with appropriate labels for subsequent lines until the user clicks on a "Finished" command button.

(f) Clear the picture box, and display the number of lines written and the name of the text file created.

4. Write a program that counts the number of times a word occurs in the sequential file created in Programming Project 3. The file name and word should be read from text boxes. The search should not be sensitive to the case of the letters. For instance, opening a file that contained the first three sentences of the directions to this problem and searching for "the" would produce the output: "the" occurs six times.

5. *Create and Maintain Telephone Directories.* Write a program to create and maintain telephone directories. Each directory will be a separate sequential file. The following command buttons should be available:

(a) Select a directory to access. A list of directories that have been created should be stored in a separate sequential file. When a request is made to open a directory, the list of available directories should be displayed as part of an InputBox prompt requesting the name of the directory to be accessed. If the user responds with a directory name not listed, the desire

to create a new directory should be confirmed, and then the new directory created and added to the list of existing directories.
(b) Add name and phone number (as given in the text boxes) to the end of the current directory.
(c) Delete name (as given in the text box) from the current directory.
(d) Sort the current directory into name order.
(e) Print out the names and phone numbers contained in the current directory.
(f) Terminate the program.

6. Table 8.7 contains the statistics for a stock portfolio. (The current prices are given for January 23, 2003.)

Stock	Number of Shares	Date Purchased	Purchase Price/Share	Current Price/Share
Amgen	200	8/19/97	50.750	53.51
Delta Airlines	100	12/3/97	111.750	10.75
Novell	500	8/27/97	10.375	3.52
PPG	100	12/18/97	56.750	50.93
Timken	300	3/13/98	34.625	19.10

Table 8.7 Stock portfolio.

(a) Compose a program to create the sequential file STOCKS.TXT containing the information in Table 8.7.
(b) Compose a program to perform the following tasks. A possible form design is shown in Figure 8.10.
  (1) Display the information in the file STOCKS.TXT as in Table 8.7 when the user clicks on a "Display Stocks" command button.
  (2) Add an additional stock onto the end of the file STOCKS.TXT when the user clicks on an "Add Stock" command button. The data for the new stock should be read from appropriately labeled text boxes.
  (3) Update the Current Price/Share of a stock in the file STOCKS.TXT when the user clicks on an "Update Price" command button. The name of the stock to be updated and the new price should be read from the appropriate text boxes. The file STOCKS.TXT should then be copied to a temp file until the specified stock is found. The update record for this stock should then be written to the temp file, followed by all remaining records in STOCKS.TXT. Finally, the original STOCKS.TXT file should be erased and the temp file renamed to STOCKS.TXT.
  (4) Process the data in the file STOCKS.TXT and produce the display shown in Figure 8.11 when a "Show Profit/Loss" command button is clicked.
  (5) Quit.

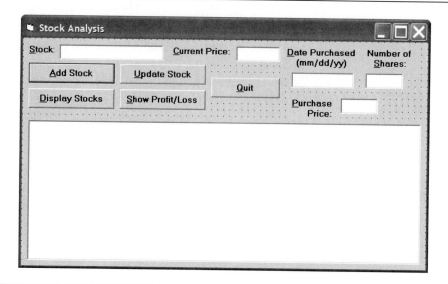

Figure 8.10 Possible form design for Programming Project 6.

Stock	Cost	Current Value	Profit (or Loss)
========	===========	===========	===========
Amgen	$10,150.00	$10,702.00	$552.00
Delta Airlines	$11,175.00	$1,075.00	($10,100.00)
Novell	$5,187.50	$1,760.00	($3,427.50)
PPG	$5,675.00	$5,093.00	($582.00)
Timken	$10,387.50	$5,730.00	($4,657.50)

Figure 8.11 Output of Project 6.

7. A department store has a file containing all sales transacted for a year. Each record contains a customer's name, zip code, and amount of the sale. The file is ordered first by zip code and then by name. Write a program to display the total sales for each customer, the total sales for each zip code, and the total sales for the store. For instance, if the first six records of the file are

```
"Adams, John", 10023, 34.50
"Adams, John", 10023, 60.00
"Jones, Bob", 10023, 62.45
"Green, Mary", 12345, 54.00
"Howard, Sue", 12345, 79.25
"Smith, George", 20001, 25.10
```

then the output in the picture box will begin as shown in Figure 8.12.

Customer	Total Sales
Adams, John	$94.50
Jones, Bob	$62.45
Total sales of zip code 10023: $156.95	
Green, Mary	$54.00

Figure 8.12 Sample output for Programming Project 7.

8. *Savings Account.* ACCOUNTS.TXT is a sequential file containing the name, account number, and beginning-of-month balance for each depositor. TRANS.TXT is a sequential file containing all the transactions (deposits and withdrawals) for the month. Use TRANS.TXT to update the file ACCOUNTS. For each customer, print a statement similar to the one received from banks that shows all transactions and the end-of-month balance. Also, record all overdrawn accounts in a file. (As an optional embellishment, deduct a penalty if the balance fell below a certain level any time during the month. The penalty could include a fixed fee of $10 plus a charge of $1 for each check and deposit.) **Hint:** Assume that no more than 500 transactions have occurred.

9. A fuel economy study was carried out for five models of cars. Each car was driven for 100 miles of city driving, and then the model of the car and the number of gallons used were placed in the sequential file MILEAGE.TXT with the statement

```
Write #1, modelName, gallons
```

Table 8.8 shows the first entries of the file. Write a program to display the models and their average miles per gallon in decreasing order with respect to mileage. The program should utilize three parallel arrays of range 1 to 5. The first array should record the name of each model of car. This array is initially empty; each car model name is added when first encountered in reading the file. The second array should record the number of test vehicles for each model. The third array should record the total number of gallons used by that model. **Note:** The first array must be searched each time a record is read to determine the appropriate index to use with the other two arrays.

Model	Gal	Model	Gal	Model	Gal
LeBaron	4.9	Cutlass	4.5	Cutlass	4.6
Escort	4.1	Escort	3.8	LeBaron	5.1
Beretta	4.3	Escort	3.9	Escort	3.8
Skylark	4.5	Skylark	4.6	Cutlass	4.4

Table 8.8 Gallons of gasoline used in 100 miles of city driving.

10. Each item in a supermarket is identified by its Universal Product Code (UPC), which consists of a sequence of 12 digits appearing below a rectangle of bars. See Figure 8.13. The bars have these digits encoded in them so that the UPC can be read by an optical scanner. Let's refer to the UPC as d_1- d_2 d_3 d_4 d_5 d_6- d_7 d_8 d_9 d_{10} d_{11}- d_{12}. The single digit on the left, d_1, identifies the type of product (for instance, 0 for general groceries, 1 for meat and produce, 3 for drug and health products, and 4 for non-food items). The first set of five digits, d_2 d_3 d_4 d_5 d_6, identifies the manufacturer, and the second set of five digits, d_7 d_8 d_9 d_{10} d_{11}, identifies the product. The twelfth digit on the right, d_{12}, is a check digit. It is chosen so that

$$3 \cdot d_1 + d_2 + 3 \cdot d_3 + d_4 + 3 \cdot d_5 + d_6 + 3 \cdot d_7 + d_8 + 3 \cdot d_9 + d_{10} + 3 \cdot d_{11} + d_{12}. \quad (*)$$

is a multiple of 10. For instance, for the UPC in Figure 8.13,

$$3 \cdot 0 + 7 + 3 \cdot 0 + 7 + 3 \cdot 3 + 4 + 3 \cdot 0 + 0 + 3 \cdot 0 + 0 \cdot 0 + 3 \cdot 3 + 4 = 40.$$

Since $40 = 4 \cdot 10$, 40 is a multiple of 10. In the event that the cashier has to enter the UPC manually and mistypes a digit, the above sum will usually not add up to a multiple of 10.

Figure 8.13 A Universal Product Code.

Write a program to simulate an automated checkout counter at a supermarket. A master sequential file called, UPC.TXT, should have a record for each item consisting of the fields for the UPC, name of the item, and the price of the item. For instance, the file might contain the following three records:

```
"070734000034", "Celestial Seasons Sleepytime Tea", 2.59
```

The file should be ordered with respect to the UPCs. The program should allow the cashier to enter UPCs one at a time, should keep a running total of the number of items processed, and should place the UPCs in an array. Each UPC should be checked with the sum (*) as soon as it is entered, and should be reentered if the sum is not a multiple of 10. After all items have been processed, the program should sort the array of UPCs and then produce a receipt similar to the one in Figure 8.14 after making just one pass through the master sequential file.

```
22-oz Jif Peanut Butter          2.29
Celestial Seasons Sleepytime Tea  2.59
365 Soda Root Beer                 .55
Total ============================> $5.43
```

Figure 8.14 Sample output of Programming Project 10.

11. At the beginning of 1990, a complete box of Crayola crayons had 72 colors (in the file PRE1990.TXT). During the 1990s, 8 colors were retired (in the file RETIRED.TXT) and 56 new colors were added (in the file ADDED.TXT). Each of the three files is in alphabetical order. Write a program that uses the three sequential files to create a fourth sequential file named COLORS.TXT containing the current 120 colors. The most efficient solution to this problem does not use arrays and simultaneously makes one pass through the files.

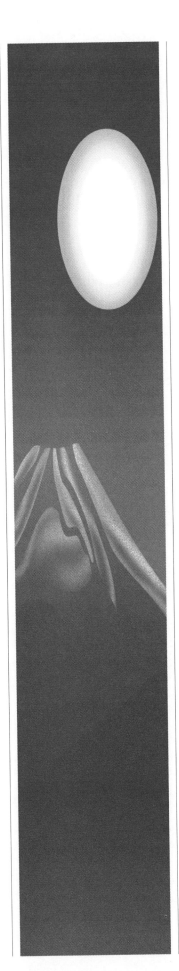

9 Random-Access Files

9.1 USER-DEFINED DATA TYPES

Records provide a convenient way of packaging as a single unit several related variables of different types. Before we can explore this powerful variable type, we must first explore a new category of variable, the fixed-length string.

Fixed-Length Strings

Fixed-length string variables are named following the same rules as other variable types. They are declared with statements of the form

```
Dim var As String * n
```

where n is a positive integer. After such a declaration, the value of *var* will always be a string of length n. Suppose *info* is an ordinary string and a statement of the form

```
var = info
```

is executed. If *info* has more than n characters, then only the first n characters will be assigned to *var*. If *info* has less than n characters, then spaces will be added to the end of the string to guarantee that *var* has length n.

EXAMPLE 1
The following program uses fixed-length strings. In the output, San Francisco is truncated to a string of length 9 and Detroit is padded on the right with two blank spaces.

```
Private Sub cmdGo_Click()
  Dim city As String * 9
  'Illustrate fixed-length strings
  picOutput.Cls
  picOutput.Print "123456789"
  city = "San Francisco"
  picOutput.Print city
  city = "Detroit"
  picOutput.Print city; "MI"
  picOutput.Print Len(city)
End Sub
```

[Set picOutput's Font property to Courier New. Run, and click the command button.]

Care must be taken when comparing an ordinary (variable-length) string with a fixed-length string or comparing two fixed-length strings of different lengths.

EXAMPLE 2 In the following program, the strings assigned to the variables *town*, *city*, and *municipality* have lengths 7, 9, and 12, respectively, and therefore are all different.

```
Private Sub cmdGo_Click()
  Dim town As String * 7
  Dim city As String * 9
  Dim municipality As String * 12
  'Illustrate fixed-length strings
  town = "Chicago"
  city = "Chicago"
  municipality = "Chicago"
  picOutput.Cls
  If (city = town) Or (city = municipality) Then
      picOutput.Print "same"
    Else
      picOutput.Print "different"
  End If
  picOutput.Print "123456789012345"
  picOutput.Print city & "***"
  picOutput.Print town & "***"
  picOutput.Print municipality & "***"
End Sub
```

[Set picOutput's Font property to Courier New. Run, and click the command button.]

There are times when we want to consider the values assigned to variables of different types as being the same, such as *city* and *town* in Example 2. In this situation, the function RTrim comes to the rescue. If *info* is an ordinary string or a fixed-length string, then the value of

```
RTrim(info)
```

is the (variable-length) string consisting of *info* with all trailing spaces removed. For instance, the value of RTrim("hello   ") is the string "hello". In Example 2, if the If block is changed to

```
If (RTrim(city) = town) And (RTrim(city) = RTrim(municipality)) Then
    picOutput.Print "same"
  Else
    picOutput.Print "different"
  End If
```

then the first line of the output will be "same".

Records

In this text, we have worked with numbers, strings, arrays, and now fixed-length strings. Strings and numbers are built-in data types that can be used without being declared, although we have always elected to declare numeric and string variables using Dim statements. On the other hand, arrays and fixed-length strings are user-defined data types that must be declared with a Dim statement before being used. A record is a user-defined data type that provides a convenient way of packaging as a single unit several related variables of different types.

Figure 9.1 shows an index card that can be used to hold data about colleges. The three pieces of data—name, state, and year founded—are called **fields**. Each field functions like a variable in which information can be stored and retrieved. The **length** of a field is the number of spaces allocated to it. In the case of the index card, we see that there are three fields having lengths 30, 2, and 4, respectively. The layout of the index card can be identified by a name, such as collegeData, called a record type.

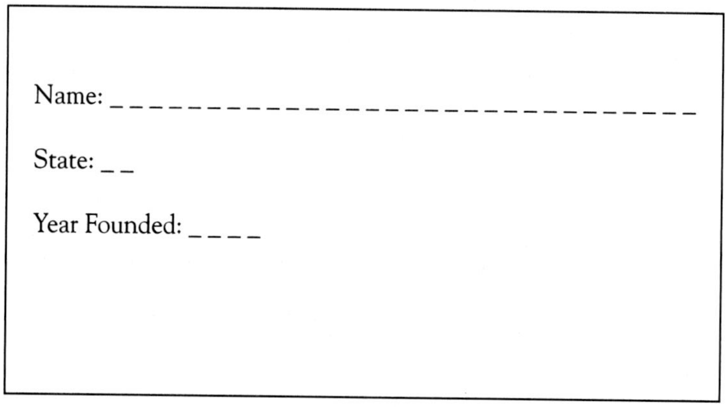

Figure 9.1 An index card having three fields.

For programming purposes, the layout of the record is declared by a block of statements similar to

```
Type collegeData
  nom As String * 30
  state As String * 2
  yearFounded As Integer
End Type
```

Each character of a string is stored in a piece of memory known as a byte. Therefore, a field of type String * *n* requires *n* bytes of memory. However, numbers (that is, the integer or single-precision numbers we use in this text) are stored in a different manner than strings. Integer numbers *always* use two bytes of memory, whereas single-precision numbers *always* use four bytes of memory.

Visual Basic requires that Type declarations, such as the preceding record structure *collegeData*, be placed in either the (Declarations) section of (General) or in a special module, referred to as a BAS module (or a standard code module).

When placed in the (Declarations) section of (General) portion of a form, the word "Type" must be preceded by "Private" and the record type is only valid for that form. When placed in a BAS module, the word "Type" may be preceded by either "Private" (valid for the current BAS module) or "Public" (valid throughout the entire program). In this text, we primarily place our declarations inside BAS modules and make them Public.

To create a BAS module for the program currently being designed, press Alt/ P/M and double-click on Module. A window like the one in Figure 9.2 will appear. This window is where our Type declarations will be entered. To switch between this BAS module window and the form(s), press Ctrl+R to activate the Project Explorer and double-click on a form or module. (When the program is saved, the information in the BAS module will be saved in a separate file with the extension *bas*.) You can also switch between the BAS module and form windows by clicking on any portion of the desired window.

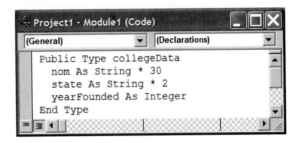

Figure 9.2 BAS module window for type declarations.

A record variable capable of holding the data for a specific college is declared in the form code by a statement such as

```
Dim college As collegeData
```

Each field is accessed by giving the name of the record variable and the field, separated by a period. For instance, the three fields of the record variable college are accessed as *college.nom*, *college.state*, and *college.yearFounded*. Figure 9.3 shows a representation of the way the record variable is organized.

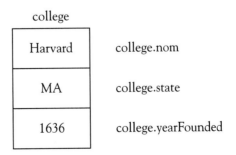

Figure 9.3 Record variable with values assigned to the fields.

In general, a record type is created in a BAS module by a Type block of the form

```
Public Type recordType
  fieldName1 As fieldType1
  fieldname2 As fieldType2
    .
    .
    .
End Type
```

where *recordType* is the name of the user-defined data type; *fieldName1*, *fieldName2*, . . . , are the names of the fields of the record variable; and *fieldType1*, *fieldType2*, . . . , are the corresponding field types, either String * *n* (for some *n*), Integer, Single, or Boolean in this text. In the form code, a record variable *recordVar* is declared to be of the user-defined type by a statement of the form

```
Dim recordVar As recordType
```

EXAMPLE 3 The following program processes records.

```
'In BAS module
Public Type collegeData
  nom As String * 30
  state As String * 2
  yearFounded As Integer
End Type

'In Form code
Private Sub cmdProcess_Click()
  Dim century As Integer, when As String
  'Demonstrate use of records
  picResult.Cls
  Dim college As collegeData
  college.nom = txtCollege.Text
  college.state = txtState.Text
  college.yearFounded = Val(txtYear.Text)
  century = 1 + Int(college.yearFounded / 100)
  picResult.Print RTrim(college.nom); " was founded in the" & Str(century);
  picResult.Print "th century in "; college.state
  Dim university As collegeData
  university.nom = "M.I.T."
  university.state = "MA"
  university.yearFounded = 1878
  If college.yearFounded < university.yearFounded Then
      when = "before "
    Else
      when = "same year or after "
  End If
  picResult.Print RTrim(college.nom); " was founded ";
  picResult.Print when; RTrim(university.nom)
End Sub
```

[Run, type the following data into text boxes, and press the command button.]

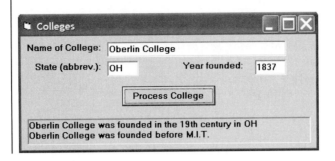

Dim statements can be used in procedures to declare a local record variable. When records are passed to and from procedures, the parameter in the Private Sub or Function statement must have the form

parameter As *recordType*

EXAMPLE 4   The following program uses Sub procedures to perform the same tasks as the program in Example 3.

```
'In BAS module
Public Type collegeData
  nom As String * 30
  state As String * 2
  yearFounded As Integer
End Type

'In Form code
Private Sub cmdProcess_Click()
  'Demonstrate use of records
  picBox.Cls
  Dim college As collegeData
  Call GetDat(college)
  Call DisplayStatement(college)
End Sub

Private Sub DisplayStatement(school As collegeData)
  Dim century As Integer, when As String
  century = 1 + Int(school.yearFounded / 100)
  picBox.Print RTrim(school.nom); " was founded in the" & Str(century);
  picBox.Print "th century in "; school.state
  Dim university As collegeData
  university.nom = "M.I.T."
  university.state = "MA"
  university.yearFounded = 1878
  If school.yearFounded < university.yearFounded Then
      when = "before "
    Else
      when = "same year or after "
  End If
```

```
   picBox.Print RTrim(school.nom); " was founded ";
   picBox.Print when; RTrim(university.nom)
End Sub

Private Sub GetDat(school As collegeData)
   school.nom = txtCollege.Text
   school.state = txtState.Text
   school.yearFounded = Val(txtYear.Text)
End Sub
```

Comments

1. Record variables are similar to arrays in that they both store and access data items using a common name. However, the elements in an array must be of the same data type, whereas the fields in a record variable can be a mixture of different data types. Also, the different elements of an array are identified by their indices, whereas the fields of a record are identified by a name following a period.

2. If the record variables *recVar1* and *recVar2* have the same type, then all the field values of *recVar2* can be assigned simultaneously to *recVar1* by the statement

   ```
   recVar1 = recVar2
   ```

3. Statements of the form

   ```
   picBox.Print recVar
   ```

   are invalid, where *recVar* is a record variable. Each field of a record must appear separately in a picBox.Print statement. Also, comparisons involving records using the relational operators <, >, =, <>, <=, and >= are valid only with the record fields, and not with the records themselves.

4. In addition to being declared as numeric, Boolean, or fixed-length string data types, the elements of a user-defined variable type can also be declared as other types of records. However, we do not use such structures in this text.

5. An array of fixed-length strings is declared by a statement of the form

   ```
   Dim arrayName(a To b) As String * n
   ```

6. An array of records is declared with a statement such as

   ```
   Dim colleges(1 To 8) As collegeData
   ```

   and information is accessed with statements such as

   ```
   picBox.Print colleges(1).nom
   ```

7. When fixed-length strings are passed to and from procedures, the corresponding parameter in the Sub or Function statement must be an ordinary (variable-length) string.

8. Any data types can be used as field types appearing in a Type block, including (variable-length) strings. However, the String data type is not allowed in Type blocks that will be used with random-access files.

PRACTICE PROBLEMS 9.1

1. Find the errors in the following event procedure. Assume that the record variable *squad* will be used to place information into a random-access file.

```
Private Sub cmdDisplay_Click()
  Public Type Team
    school As String
    mascot As String
  End Type
  Dim squad As Team
  squad.school = "Rice"
  squad.mascot = "Owls"
  picOutput.Print squad.school & " " & squad.mascot
End Sub
```

2. Correct the code in Practice Problem 1.

EXERCISES 9.1

In Exercises 1 through 4, determine the output displayed in the picture box when the command button is clicked.

1.
```
Private Sub cmdDisplay_Click()
  Dim ocean As String * 10
  Dim river As String * 10
  ocean = "Pacific"
  river = "Mississippi"
  picOutput.Print ocean; river
End Sub
```

2.
```
Private Sub cmdDisplay_Click()
  Dim color As String
  Dim colour as String * 6
  colour = "Blue"
  color = "Red"
  picOutput.Print colour; color; colour
End Sub
```

3.
```
'In BAS module
Public Type appearance
  height As Single
  weight As Single
  eyeColor As String * 5
End Type

'In Form code
Private Sub cmdDisplay_Click()
  Dim person1 As appearance
  Dim person2 As appearance
  person1.height = 72
  person1.weight = 170
  person1.eyeColor = "brown"
  person2.height = 12 * 6
```

```
        person2.weight = person1.weight
        person2.eyeColor = "brownish green"
        If person1.height = person2.height Then
            picOutput.Print "heights are same"
        End If
        picOutput.Print person2.weight
        If person1.eyeColor = person2.eyeColor Then
            picOutput.Print "eye colors are same"
        End If
    End Sub
```

4.
```
'In BAS module
Public Type testData
  nom As String * 5
  score As Single
End Type

'In Form code
Private Sub cmdDisplay_Click()
  Dim i As Integer
  Dim student As testData
  Open "SCORES.TXT" For Input As #1
  picOutput.Cls
  For i = 1 to 3
    Call GetScore(student)
    Call PrintScore(student)
  Next i
  Close #1
End Sub

Private Sub GetScore(student As testData)
  Input #1, student.nom, student.score
End Sub

Private Sub PrintScore(student As testData)
  picOutput.Print student.nom; student.score
End Sub
```

(Assume that the file SCORES.TXT contains the following three lines.)

"Joe", 18
"Moe", 20
"Albert", 25

In Exercises 5 through 10, determine the errors.

5.
```
'In BAS module
Public Type zodiac
  nom As String * 15
  sign As String * 11
End Type

'In Form code
Private Sub cmdDisplay_Click()
  Dim astrology As zodiac
  nom = "Michael"
  sign = "Sagittarius"
End Sub
```

6.
```
Private Sub cmdDisplay_Click()
   Public Type address
     street As String * 30
     city As String * 20
     state As String * 2
     zip As String * 10
   End Type
   Dim whiteHouse As address
   whiteHouse.street = "1600 Pennsylvania Avenue"
   whiteHouse.city = "Washington"
   whiteHouse.state = "DC"
   whiteHouse.zip = "20500"
End Sub
```

7.
```
'In BAS module
Public Type employee
  name As String * 15
  socSecNum As String * 11
  payRate As Single
  exemptions As Integer
  maritalStat As String * 1


'In Form code
Private Sub cmdDisplay_Click()
  employee.name = "Bob"
End Sub
```

8.
```
Public Type print
   firstWord As String * 5
   secondWord As String * 5
End Type
```

9.
```
Public Type values
   label As String * 5
   var2 As Number
End Type
```

10.
```
'In BAS module
Public Type vitamins
  a As Single
  b As Single
End Type


'In Form code
Private Sub cmdDisplay_Click()
  Dim minimum As vitamins
  minimum.b = 200
  minimum.a = 500
  picOutput.Print minimum
End Sub
```

In Exercises 11 through 14, write à Type block to declare a user-defined data type of the given name and types of elements.

11. Name: planet; Elements: planetName, distanceFromSun

12. Name: taxData; Elements: SSN, grossIncome, taxableIncome

13. Name: car; Elements: make, model, yr, mileage

14. Name: party; Elements: numberOfGuests, address

15. Write a program that reads words from three text boxes and then displays them in a picture box in the first three zones without using any commas in the picOutput.Print statement. Do this by declaring the variables used to hold the words as fixed-length strings of the appropriate length, and setting the Font property of the picture box to Courier New.

16. Write a program to look up data on notable tall buildings. The program should declare a user-defined data type named "building" with the elements "nom", "city", "height", and "stories". This interactive program should allow the user to type the name of a building into a text box and then search through a text file to determine the city, height, and number of stories of the building when a command button is pressed. If the building is not in the text file, then the program should so report. Use the information in Table 9.1 for the text file.

Building	City	Height (ft)	Stories
Empire State	New York	1250	102
Sears Tower	Chicago	1454	110
Texas Commerce Tower	Houston	1002	75
Transamerica Pyramid	San Francisco	853	48

Table 9.1 Tallest buildings.

✔✔ **Solutions to Practice Problems 9.1**

1. The event procedure contains two errors, both related to the Type declaration. First, the Type declaration cannot be inside a procedure. Instead, we enter the Type declaration in a BAS module. Second, strings in a Type declaration to be used with a random-access file must be of fixed length; an asterisk and a whole number must follow String in defining the elements *school* and *mascot*.

2. In addition to correcting the errors that Visual Basic notices, we also need to keep the output looking as intended, thus the addition of the RTrim functions that follow.

```
'In BAS module
Public Type Team
  school As String * 20
  mascot As String * 20
End Type

'In Form code
Private Sub cmdDisplay_Click()
  Dim squad As Team
  squad.school = "Rice"
  squad.mascot = "Owls"
  picOutput.Print RTrim(squad.school) & " " & RTrim(squad.mascot)
End Sub
```

9.2 RANDOM-ACCESS FILES

A random-access file is like an array of records stored on a disk. The records are numbered 1, 2, 3, and so on, and can be referred to by their numbers. Therefore, a random-access file resembles a box of index cards, each having a numbered tab. Any card can be selected from the box without first reading every index card preceding it; similarly, any record of a random-access file can be read without having to read every record preceding it.

One statement suffices to open a random-access file for all purposes: creating, appending, writing, and reading. Suppose a record type has been defined with a Type block and a record variable, called *recVar*, has been declared with a Dim statement. Then after the statement

```
Open "filespec" For Random As #n Len = Len(recVar)
```

is executed, records may be written, read, added, and changed. The file is referred to by the number *n*. Each record will have as many characters as allotted to each value of *recVar*.

Suppose appropriate Type, Dim, and Open statements have been executed. The two-step procedure for entering a record into the file is as follows.

1. Assign a value to each field of a record variable.

2. Place the data into record *r* of file *#n* with the statement

```
Put #n, r, recVar
```

where *recVar* is the record variable from Step 1.

EXAMPLE 1 The following program creates and writes records to the random-access file COLLEGES.DAT.

```
'In BAS module
Public Type collegeData
  nom As String * 30    'Name of college
  state As String * 2   'State where college is located
  yrFounded As Integer  'Year college was founded
End Type

'In Form code
Dim recordNum As Integer

Private Sub cmdAddCollege_Click()
  'Write a record into the file COLLEGES.DAT
  Dim college As collegeData
  college.nom = txtCollege.Text
  college.state = txtState.Text
  college.yrFounded = Val(txtYear.Text)
  recordNum = recordNum + 1
  Put #1, recordNum, college
  txtCollege.Text = ""
  txtState.Text = ""
  txtYear.Text = ""
  txtCollege.SetFocus
End Sub

Private Sub cmdDone_Click()
  Close #1
  End
End Sub
```

```
Private Sub Form_Load()
  'Create COLLEGES.DAT
  Dim college As collegeData
  Open "COLLEGES.DAT" For Random As #1 Len = Len(college)
  recordNum = 0
End Sub
```

[Run, and type into the text boxes the data shown in the following first window. Click the "Add College to File" command button. Record number 1 is added to COLLEGES.DAT and the text boxes are cleared. Proceed to record the data shown for the other two colleges and then click the "Done" command button.]

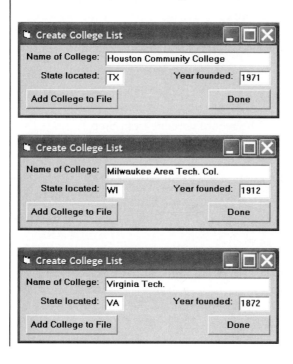

The two-step procedure for reading data from a record is as follows:

1. Execute the statement

   ```
   Get #n, r, recVar
   ```

   to assign record *r* of file *#n* to the record variable *recVar*.

2. Use the field variables of the record variable to either display values with picBox.Print or to transfer values to other variables with assignment statements.

EXAMPLE 2　The following program displays the entire contents of the random-access file COLLEGES.DAT.

```
'In BAS module
Public Type collegeData
  nom As String * 30      'Name of college
  state As String * 2     'State where college is located
  yrFounded As Integer    'Year college was founded
End Type
```

```
'In Form code
Private Sub cmdDisplay_Click()
  Call DisplayFile
End Sub

Private Sub DisplayFile()
  Dim recordNum As Integer
  'Access the random-access file COLLEGES.DAT
  Dim college As collegeData
  Open "COLLEGES.DAT" For Random As #1 Len = Len(college)
  picOutput.Cls
  picOutput.Print "College"; Tab(30); "State"; Tab(45); "Year founded"
  For recordNum = 1 To 3
    Get #1, recordNum, college
    picOutput.Print college.nom; Tab(30); college.state; _
                    Tab(45); college.yrFounded
  Next recordNum
  Close #1
End Sub
```

[Run, and click the command button.]

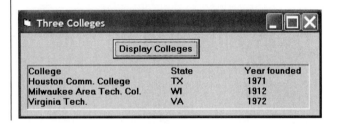

The total number of characters in the file with reference number *n* is given by the value of the function

```
LOF(n)
```

The number of the last record in the file can be calculated by dividing this value by the record length. The LOF function, rather than the EOF function, should be used to determine when the end of the file has been reached. For instance, in Example 2, the For statement in the Sub procedure DisplayFile can be written as

```
For recordNum = 1 To LOF(1) / Len(college)
```

Also, the pair of statements

```
lastRecord = LOF(1) / Len(college)
Put #1, lastRecord + 1, college
```

can be used to add a record to the end of the file.

Comments

1. Random-access files are also known as **direct-access** or **relative** files. Because each record has the same number of characters, the computer can calculate where to find a specified record and, therefore, does not have to search for it sequentially.

2. Unlike sequential files, random-access files needn't be closed between placing information into them and reading from them.

3. Random-access files do not have to be filled in order. For instance, a file can be opened and the first Put statement can be Put #n, 9, recVar. In this case, space is allocated for the preceding eight records.

4. If the record number r is omitted from a Put or Get statement, then the record number used will be the one following the number most recently used in a Put or Get statement. For instance, if the line

```
Put #1, , college
```

is added to the program in Example 1 after the existing Put statement, then the information on Virginia Tech will occupy records 3 and 4 of the file COLLEGES.DAT.

5. Users often enter records into a random-access file without keeping track of the record numbers. If file #n is open, then the value of the function

```
Loc(n)
```

is the number of the record most recently written to or read from file n with a Put or Get statement.

6. Each record in a random-access file has the same length. This length can be any number from 1 to 32767.

7. When the statement Open "COLLEGES.DAT" For Random As #1 Len = Len(college) is typed, the words "For Random" can be omitted. The editor will insert them automatically.

8. The decision of whether to store data in a sequential file or in a random-access file depends on how the data are to be processed. If processing requires a pass through all the data in the file, then sequential files are probably desirable. If processing involves seeking out one item of data, however, random-access files are the better choice.

✔ **PRACTICE PROBLEM 9.2**

1. In Example 2, suppose the font for the picture box is Courier New and the two picOutput.Print statements are changed to

```
picOutput.Print "College", , "State", "Year founded"
picOutput.Print college.nom; college.state, college.yrFounded
```

The first picOutput.Print statement clearly displays "State" in the third print zone. Why will the second picOutput.Print statement also display the value of college.state in the third print zone?

In Exercises 1 through 8, determine the output displayed in the picture box when the command button is clicked. For each problem, assume that the file COLLEGES.DAT was just created by Example 1 and that the given code replaces the ????? in the following program.

```
'In BAS module
Public Type collegeData
  nom As String * 30     'Name of college
  state As String * 2    'State where college is located
  yrFounded As Integer   'Year college was founded
End Type

'In Form code
Private Sub cmdDisplay_Click()
  Dim i As Integer
  Dim college As collegeData
  picOutput.Cls
  Open "COLLEGES.DAT" For Random As #1 Len = Len(college)
  ?????
  Close #1
End Sub
```

1. Get #1, 3, college
   picOutput.Print college.state

2. Get #1, 3, college
   picOutput.Print LOF(1); Loc(1)

3. For i = 1 To LOF(1) / Len(college)
       Get #1, i, college
         picOutput.Print college.state
     Next i
     picOutput.Print Loc(1)

4. college.yrFounded = 1876
   Put #1, 2, college
   Get #1, 2, college
   picOutput.Print college.nom; college.yrFounded

5. college.nom = "Harvard"
   college.state = "MA"
   college.yrFounded = 1636
   Put #1, 4, college
   For i = 3 To 4
     Get #1, i, college
       picOutput.Print college.nom, college.state, college.yrFounded
   Next i

6.
```
college.nom = "Michigan State"
college.state = "MI"
college.yrFounded = 1855
Put #1, 1, college
For i = 1 To 3
  Get #1, i, college
  picOutput.Print college.nom
Next i
```

7.
```
Get #1, 1, college
Get #1, , college
picOutput.Print college.nom, college.state, college.yrFounded
```

8.
```
lastRec = LOF(1) / Len(college)
Get #1, lastRec, college
picOutput.Print college.nom, college.state, college.yrFounded
```

In Exercises 9 through 12, identify the errors. Assume the given code replaces the ????? in the following program.

```
'In BAS module
Public Type filmCredits
  nom As String * 25      'Name of actor or actress
  film As String * 35     'Name of film
End Type

'In Form code
Private Sub cmdDisplay_Click()
  Dim lastRec As Integer
  Dim actor As filmCredits
  ?????
End Sub
```

9.
```
Open "ACTORS.DAT" For Random As #2 Len = Len(filmCredits)
actor.nom = "Bogart"
actor.film = "Casablanca"
Put #2, 3, actor
Close #2
```

10.
```
Open ACTRESS.DAT For Random As #3 Len = Len(actor)
actor.nom = "Garland"
actor.film = "Wizard of Oz"
lastRec = LOF(3) / Len(actor)
Put #3, lastRec + 1, actor
Close #3
```

11.
```
Open "ACTORS.DAT" For Random As #1 Len = Len(actor)
actor.nom = "Stallone"
actor.film = "Rocky"
Put #1, 1, actor
Get #1, 1, actor
Close #1
picBox.Print actor
```

12.
```
Open "ACTRESS.DAT" For Random As #3 Len = Len(actor)
Put #1, 1, actor
Close #1
```

13. Give an Open statement and Type block for a random-access file named NUMBERS.DAT in which each record consists of three numbers.

14. Give an Open statement and Type block for a random-access file named ACCOUNTS.DAT in which each record consists of a person's name (up to 25 characters) and the balance in their savings account.

15. Consider the sequential file YOB.TXT discussed in Section 8.1 and assume the file contains many names. Write a program to place all the information into a random-access file.

16. Write a program that uses the random-access file created in Exercise 15 and displays the names of all people born before 1970.

17. Write a program that uses the random-access file created in Exercise 15 to determine a person's year of birth. The program should request that the name be typed into a text box, then search for the proper record when the command button is pressed, and either give the year of birth or report that the person is not in the file.

18. Write a program that uses the random-access file created in Exercise 15 and adds the data *Joan, 1934* to the end of the file.

Exercises 19 through 23 refer to the file COLLEGES.DAT. Assume many colleges have been added to the file in no particular order.

19. Write a program to allow additional colleges to be added to the end of the file using the same user interface as shown in Example 1.

20. Modify the program in Exercise 19 to issue an error message rather than record the data if the name of the college input has more than 30 characters.

21. Write a program to find the two oldest colleges.

22. Write a program to display the data on any college whose name is typed into a text box by the user. The college should be identified by name and located by a sequential search of the records. **Note:** Remember to take into account that each college name retrieved from the file will contain 30 characters.

23. Extend the program in Exercise 22 in the following way: After the information on a college is displayed, exchange its record with the previous record, unless, of course, the displayed record is the first record. (A familiar rule of thumb for office filing is, 80 percent of the action involves 20 percent of the records. After the program has been used many times, the most frequently requested records will tend to be near the top of the file and the average time required for searches should decrease.)

✔✔ **Solution to Practice Problem 9.2**

1. The value of college.nom will have length 30 for each college. Therefore, it will extend beyond the second print zone and force the value of college.state into the third print zone.

CHAPTER 9   SUMMARY

1. A *fixed-length string* is a variable declared with a statement of the form Dim *var* As String * *n*. The value of *var* is always a string of *n* characters.

2. A *record* is a composite user-defined data type with a fixed number of fields each of which can be any data type. Type statements [in this text appearing in the (Declarations) section of a BAS module] define record types and Dim statements are used to declare a variable to be of that type.

3. After a record type has been specified, the associated *random-access file* is an ordered collection of record values numbered 1, 2, 3, and so on. Record values are placed into the file with Put statements and read from the file with Get statements. At any time, the value of LOF(n) / Len(*recordVar*) is the number of the highest record value in the file and the value of Loc is the number of the record value most recently accessed by a Put or Get statement.

CHAPTER 9   PROGRAMMING PROJECTS

1. *Balance a Checkbook.* Write an interactive program to request information (payee, check number, amount, and whether or not the check has cleared) for each check written during a month and store this information in a random-access file. The program should then request the balance at the beginning of the month and display the current balance and the payee and amount for every check still outstanding.

2. A teacher maintains a random-access file containing the following information for each student: name, social security number, grades on each of two hourly exams, and the final exam grade. Assume the random-access file GRADES.DAT has been created with string fields of lengths 25 and 11 and three numeric fields, and all the names and social security numbers have been entered. The numeric fields have been initialized with zeros. Write a program with the five command buttons "Display First Student," "Record Grade(s) & Display Next Student," "Locate Student," "Print Grade List," and "Done" to allow the teacher to do the following.

   (a) Enter all the grades for a specific exam.
   (b) Locate and display the record for a specific student so that one or more grades may be changed.
   (c) Print a list of final grades that can be posted. The list should show the last four digits of the social security number, the grade on the final exam, and the semester average of each student. The semester average is determined by the formula (exam1 + exam2 + 2 * finalExam) / 4.

3. *Speed Dialing.* Many telephones have a feature called *speed dialing* (also known as *speed calling* or *abbreviated calling*) that allows you to assign one- or two-digit numbers to your most frequently called telephone numbers. This feature saves time looking up and dialing telephone numbers.

Suppose that your telephone can store speed dialing numbers from 1 through 99. Let the random-access file PHONEBOOK.DAT be a telephone directory consisting of up to 99 records, where each record holds a name and a telephone number. A person's record number will serve as their speed dialing code. Each record should have three fields: name field, phone-number field, and a single-character "active/deleted" field. Initially each "active/deleted" field will contain the letter A. However, this letter will be changed to a *D* to indicate that a person has been removed from the telephone directory.

Write a program that simulates speed dialing. The program should allow you to add new listings, delete existing listings, or dial someone. When you dial a person or delete a listing, you should be able to input either their name or their speed dialing code. The program should use the Asc function to distinguish between names and speed dialing codes, and should then take the appropriate action. Upon loading, the program should create an array (with indices ranging from 1 through 99) containing the names of the active people in the phone directory. The person in record *n* should be stored in the *n*th array element. Empty array entries correspond to either deleted or unused records.

The program should delete a record from the file by changing the entry in its "active/deleted" field to the letter *D*. The program should add a record by overwriting the first record containing the letter *D* in its "active/deleted" field. If no such record exists, the added record should be placed at the end of the file if possible. The number of records should not be allowed to exceed 99.

Suppose the information for George is located in record 2 of the random file. The outcome in Figure 9.4 can be produced by pressing the "Call a Person" button, entering 2 or George into the input dialog box that appears, and clicking on OK in the input dialog box.

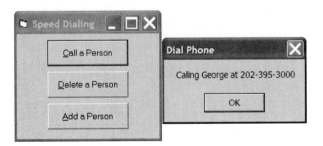

Figure 9.4 Possible run of Programming Project 3.

4. The CD accompanying this textbook contains the sequential file STATES.TXT which provides data on the 50 states. Each line of the file contains five pieces of information about a single state: name, abbreviation, year it entered the union, area (in square miles), and population in the year 2000. The records are ordered by the date of entry into the union. The first line of the file is

```
Delaware","DE",1787,2489,783600
```

(a) Write a program that transfers this information into the random-access file STATES.DAT.

(b) Write a second program that uses the file STATES.DAT to carry out the following tasks:

(1) Given two years input by the user, display the names of all the states admitted into the union during the time period spanned by those years. Also, display the total area added to the United States during that time period and the total population of those states in the year 2000.

(2) Allow the user to navigate through the states and display the five pieces of information about a state along with the state's ranking in terms of entering the union in text boxes. Initially, the text boxes should display the information about Delaware. The form should contain four command buttons captioned First, Previous, Next, and Last that navigate through the states as suggested by the captions.

10 The Graphical Display of Data

10.1 INTRODUCTION TO GRAPHICS

Visual Basic has impressive graphics capabilities. Figure 10.1 shows four types of charts that can be displayed in a picture box and printed by the printer.

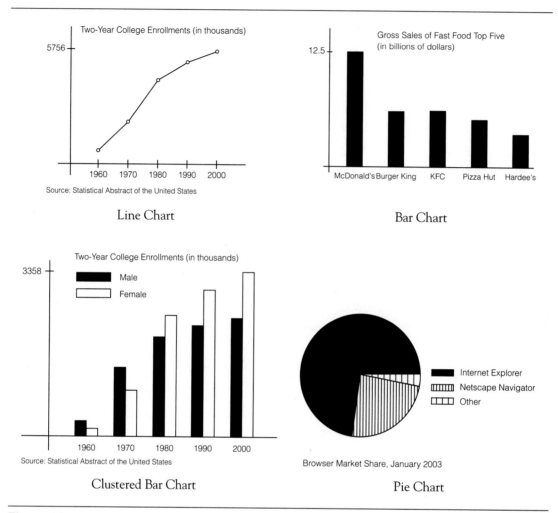

Figure 10.1 Four types of charts.

The construction of each of these charts involves three basic steps: (1) define a coordinate system; (2) use graphics methods to draw the appropriate lines, rectangles, and circles; and (3) place text at appropriate points on the chart. The basic tools for accomplishing each of these steps follow.

Specifying a Coordinate System

Suppose we have a piece of paper, a pencil, and a ruler and we want to graph a line extending from (2, 40) to (5, 60). We would most likely use the following three-step procedure:

1. Use the ruler to draw an *x*-axis and a *y*-axis. Focus on the first quadrant because both points are in that quadrant.

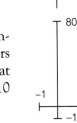

2. Select scales for the two axes. For instance, we might decide that the numbers on the *x*-axis range from –1 to 6 and that the numbers on the *y*-axis range from –10 to 80.

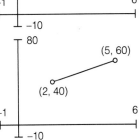

3. Plot the two points and use the ruler to draw the straight-line segment joining them.

EXAMPLE I   (a) Draw a coordinate system with the numbers on the *x*-axis ranging from –2 to 10, and the numbers on the *y*-axis ranging from –3 to 18.
(b) Draw the straight line from (1, 15) to (8, 6).
(c) Draw the straight line from (–2, 0) to (10, 0).

SOLUTION   (a)

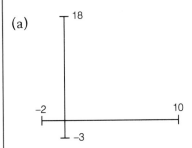

(b)

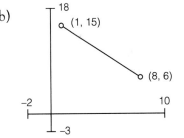

(c) The point (–2, 0) is the left-hand end point of the *x*-axis and the point (10, 0) is the right-hand end point; therefore, the line joining them is just the portion of the *x*-axis we have already drawn.

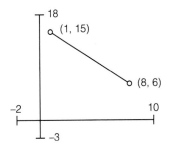

We draw these graphs on the screen with the same three steps we use with paper, pencil, and ruler. The only difference is that we first do Step 2 and then Steps 1 and 3. The Visual Basic method Scale is used to specify the range of values for the axes and the method Line serves as the ruler.

The statement

```
picBox.Scale (a, d)-(b, c)
```

specifies that numbers on the x-axis range from a to b and that numbers on the y-axis range from c to d. See Figure 10.2. The ordered pair (a, d) gives the coordinates of the top left corner of the picture box, and the ordered pair (b, c) gives the coordinates of the bottom right corner of the picture box.

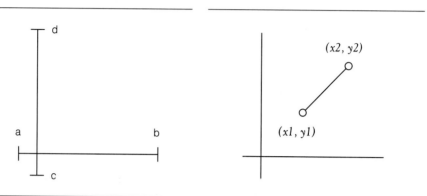

Figure 10.2 Result of the Scale method.   **Figure 10.3** Result of the Line method.

Graphics Methods for Drawing Lines, Points, and Circles

After an appropriate coordinate system has been specified by a picBox.Scale statement, graphics can be drawn in the picture box using the Line and Circle methods. The statement

```
picBox.Line (x1, y1)-(x2, y2)
```

draws the line segment from the point with coordinates (x1, y1) to the point with coordinates (x2, y2) in the picture box (see Figure 10.3). In particular, the statement picBox.Line (a, 0)–(b, 0) draws the x-axis and the statement picBox. Line (0, c)–(0, d) draws the y-axis.

The following event procedure produces the graph of Example 1, part (b):

```
Private Sub cmdDraw_Click()
  picOutput.Cls
  picOutput.Scale (-2, 18)-(10, -3)    'Specify coordinate system
  picOutput.Line (-2, 0)-(10, 0)       'Draw x-axis
  picOutput.Line (0, -3)-(0, 18)       'Draw y-axis
  picOutput.Line (1, 15)-(8, 6)        'Draw the straight line
End Sub
```

EXAMPLE 2   Consider Figure 10.4.

(a) Give the statement that specifies the range for the numbers on the axes.
(b) Give the statements that will draw the axes.
(c) Give the statement that will draw the line.

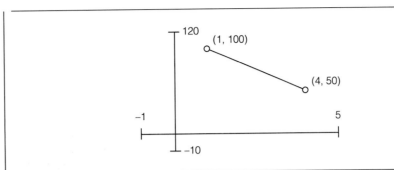

Figure 10.4 Graph for Example 2.

SOLUTION
(a) `picOutput.Scale (-1, 120)-(5, -10)`

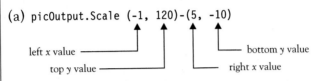

(b) x-axis: `picOutput.Line (-1, 0)-(5, 0)`

y-axis: `picOutput.Line (0, -10)-(0, 120)`

(c) `picOutput.Line (1, 100)-(4, 50)`

There are two other graphics methods that are just as useful as the Line method. The statement

`picOutput.PSet (x, y)`

plots the point with coordinates (x, y). The statement

`picOutput.Circle (x, y), r`

draws the circle with center (x, y) and radius r.

EXAMPLE 3 The following event procedure plots the point $(7, 6)$ in a picture box and draws a circle of radius 3 about the point. The rightmost point to be drawn will have x coordinate 10; therefore the numbers on the x-axis must range beyond 10. In the following event procedure, we allow the numbers to range from –2 to 12. See Figure 10.5.

```
Private Sub cmdDraw_Click()
  'Draw circle with center (7, 6) and radius 3
  picOutput.Cls                        'Clear picture box
  picOutput.Scale (-2, 12)-(12, -2)    'Specify coordinate system
  picOutput.Line (-2, 0)-(12, 0)       'Draw x-axis
  picOutput.Line (0, -2)-(0, 12)       'Draw y-axis
  picOutput.PSet (7, 6)                'Draw center of circle
  picOutput.Circle (7, 6), 3           'Draw the circle
End Sub
```

[Run, and then click the command button. The contents of the picture box is shown in Figure 10.5.]

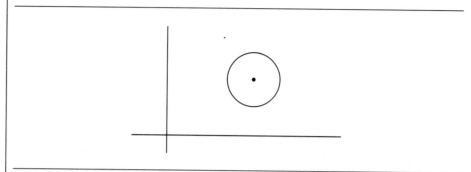

Figure 10.5 Graph for Example 3.

The numbers appearing in the Scale, Line, PSet, and Circle methods can be replaced by variables or expressions. The following example demonstrates this feature.

EXAMPLE 4

The following event procedure draws a graph of the square root function. The function is graphed for values of x from 0 to 100. See Figure 10.6.

```
Private Sub cmdDraw_Click()
  Dim x As Single
  'Graph the Square Root Function
  picOutput.Cls
  picOutput.Scale (-20, 12)-(120, -2)    'Specify coordinate system
  picOutput.Line (-5, 0)-(100, 0)        'Draw x-axis
  picOutput.Line (0, -1)-(0, 10)         'Draw y-axis
  For x = 0 To 100 Step 0.2              'Plot about 500 points
    picOutput.PSet (x, Sqr(x))           'Plot point on graph
  Next x
End Sub
```

[Run, and then click the command button. The resulting picture box is shown in Figure 10.6.]

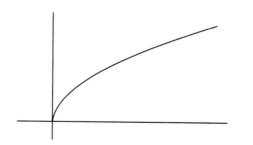

Figure 10.6 Graph of the square root function.

Positioning Text

There are times when text is placed on the screen in conjunction with graphics. This would be the case if a graph were to be titled or a tick mark needed a label. The ability to position such text appropriately in the picture box is essential to good-looking graphs. A picture box has two properties, CurrentX and CurrentY, and two methods, TextHeight and TextWidth, that allow us to precisely position text alongside graphics.

The properties CurrentX and CurrentY record the precise horizontal and vertical location at which the next character of text will be printed. By assigning appropriate values to these properties before executing a Print method, we can position text very precisely in the picture box. In the following event procedure, the coordinates of the right end of the tick mark are $(x, y) = (.3, 3)$. As a first attempt at labeling a tick mark on the y-axis, the CurrentX and CurrentY properties are set to these coordinates. The results are shown in Figure 10.7(a).

```
Private Sub cmdDraw_Click()
  picOutput.Cls
  picOutput.Scale (-4, 4)-(4, -4)
  picOutput.Line (-4, 0)-(4, 0)       'Draw x-axis
  picOutput.Line (0, -4)-(0, 4)       'Draw y-axis
  picOutput.Line (-.3, 3)-(.3, 3)     'Draw tick mark
  picOutput.CurrentX = .3             'Right end of tick mark
  picOutput.CurrentY = 3              'Same vertical position as tick mark
  picOutput.Print "y=3"               'Label for tick mark
End Sub
```

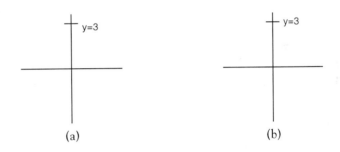

(a)   (b)

Figure 10.7 Placing labels: (a) first attempt and (b) second attempt.

Note that the top of the text is even with the tick mark. This reflects the fact that the value of the CurrentY property used by Visual Basic is the location for the **top** of the character cursor. Ideally, the text should be moved up so that the tick mark aligns with the middle of the text. To do this, the value of the CurrentY property needs to be increased by one-half the height of the text. The following statement assigns a corrected value to the CurrentY property by using the TextHeight method to obtain the height of the text being used as the tick mark label. (Since $c < d$ in the scale method, TextHeight returns $(-1) \times$ [height of text].)

```
picOutput.CurrentY = 3 - picOutput.TextHeight("y=3") / 2
```

The result of using this corrected value for CurrentY is shown in Figure 10.7(b).

When the TextHeight method is used, all characters have the same height. Thus the height of a string can be obtained by asking for the height of any single character. The following procedure uses the TextHeight method with a space character to center the text cursor at the requested graphic point.

```
Private Sub PositionText(x As Single, y As Single)
  'Center text cursor at the point (x, y)
  picOutput.CurrentX = x
  picOutput.CurrentY = y - picOutput.TextHeight(" ") / 2
End Sub
```

Another useful picture box method is TextWidth. Whereas the Len function returns the number of characters in a string, the TextWidth method considers the varying widths of characters and returns the physical width of the entire string in the units of the current scale for the picture box. The TextWidth method is essential when centering text, as illustrated in the following example.

EXAMPLE 5   The following event procedure displays the phrase "Th-that's all Folks!" centered and double underlined in a picture box with x values ranging from 0 to 6 and y values ranging from 0 to 4. Centering text requires knowing the coordinates of the center of the picture box, which for the given ranges will be the point (3, 2). Next, we need the width and height of the text being centered. These values are available using the TextWidth and TextHeight methods. The text cursor needs to start with a CurrentX that is half the text's width to the left of center and a CurrentY that is half the text's height above center. The first underline can be placed at half the text's height below center. The additional distance down to the second underline should be in proportion to the height of the text. We decided after some experimenting to use a proportion of 1/6th.

```
Private Sub cmdDraw_Click()
  Dim xCenter As Single, yCenter As Single, phrase as String
  Dim w As Single, h As Single, leftEdge As Single, rightEdge As Single
  Dim ul1Pos As Single, ul2Pos As Single
  'Center and double underline a phrase
  picOutput.Scale (0, 4)-(6, 0)
  picOutput.Cls
  xCenter = 3
  yCenter = 2
  phrase = "Th-that's all Folks!"
  w = picOutput.TextWidth(phrase)
  h = picOutput.TextHeight(" ")
  picOutput.CurrentX = xCenter - w / 2
  picOutput.CurrentY = yCenter - h / 2
  picOutput.Print phrase
  leftEdge = xCenter - w / 2
  rightEdge = xCenter + w / 2
  ul1Pos = yCenter + h / 2
  ul2Pos = ul1Pos + h / 6
  picOutput.Line (leftEdge, ul1Pos)-(rightEdge, ul1Pos)
  picOutput.Line (leftEdge, ul2Pos)-(rightEdge, ul2Pos)
End Sub
```

[Run, and then click the command button. The resulting picture box follows.]

Th-that's all Folks!

Comments

1. In Examples 1 through 4, examples that produce graphs, the range of numbers on the axes extended from a negative number to a positive number. Actually, any value of *a*, *b*, *c*, and *d* can be used in a Scale method. In certain cases, however, you will not be able to display one or both of the axes on the screen. (For instance, after picOutput.Scale (1, 10)–(10, –1) has been executed, the *y*-axis cannot be displayed.)

2. The following technique can be used to determine a good range of values for a Scale method when graphs with only positive values are to be drawn.
   (a) Let *r* be the *x* coordinate of the rightmost point that will be drawn by any Line, PSet, or Circle method.
   (b) Let *h* be the *y* coordinate of the highest point that will be drawn by any Line, PSet, or Circle method.
   (c) Let the numbers on the *x*-axis range from about –[20% of *r*] to about *r* + [20% of *r*]. Let the numbers on the *y*-axis range from about –[20% of *h*] to about *h* + [20% of *h*]. That is, use

   ```
   picOutput.Scale (-.2 * r, 1.2 * h)-(1.2 * r, -.2 * h)
   ```

3. Usually one unit on the *x*-axis is a different length than one unit on the *y*-axis. The statement `picBox.Circle (x,y), r,` draws a circle whose radius is *r* *x*-axis units.

4. If one or both of the points used in the Line method fall outside the picture box, the computer only draws the portion of the line that lies in the picture box. This behavior is referred to as **line clipping** and is used for the Circle method also.

5. A program can execute a picOutput.Scale statement more than once. Executing a new picOutput.Scale statement has no effect on the text and graphics already drawn; however, future graphics statements will use the new coordinate system. This technique can be used to produce the same graphics figure in different sizes and/or locations within the picture box. The output from the following event procedure is shown in Figure 10.8.

```
Private Sub cmdDraw_Click()
  Dim i As Integer
  picOutput.Cls
  For i = 0 To 3
    picOutput.Scale (0, 2 ^ i)-(2 ^ i, 0)
    picOutput.Line (0, 0)-(.5, 1)
    picOutput.Line (.5, 1)-(.8, 0)
    picOutput.Line (.8, 0)-(0, .8)
    picOutput.Line (0, .8)-(1, .5)
    picOutput.Line (1, .5)-(0, 0)
  Next i
End Sub
```

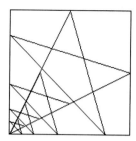

Figure 10.8 Output from Comment 5.

6. The programs in this section can be modified to produce colorful displays.

Lines, points, and circles can be drawn in color through use of the vb*Color* constants. To use color, place "*, vbColor*" at the end of the corresponding graphics statement. For instance, the statement

```
picBox.Line (x1, y1)-(x2, y2), vbRed
```

draws a red line.

✔ **PRACTICE PROBLEMS 10.1**

Suppose you want to write a program to draw a line from (3, 45) to (5, 80).

1. Use the technique of Comment 2 to select appropriate values for the Scale method.

2. Write an event procedure to draw the axes, the line, and a small circle around each end point of the line.

3. Write the statements that draw a tick mark on the y-axis at height 80 and label it with the number 80.

➤ **EXERCISES 10.1**

1. Determine the Scale method corresponding to the coordinate system of Figure 10.9.

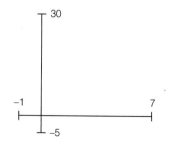

Figure 10.9 Coordinate system for Exercise 1.

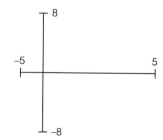

Figure 10.10 Coordinate system for Exercise 2.

2. Determine the Scale method corresponding to the coordinate system of Figure 10.10.

3. Suppose the statement picBox.Scale (–1, 40)–(4, –8) has been executed. Write down the statements that draw the x-axis and the y-axis.

4. Suppose the statement picBox.Scale (–3, 1)–(18, –.2) has been executed. Write down the statements that draw the x-axis and the y-axis.

In Exercises 5 through 8, write an event procedure to draw a line between the given points. Select an appropriate Scale method, draw the axes, and draw a small circle around each end point of the line.

5. (3, 200), (10, 150)

6. (4, 4), (9, 9)

7. (2, .5), (4, .3)

8. (5, 30), (6, 30)

In Exercises 9 through 20, write an event procedure to draw the given figures in a picture box. Draw the axes only when necessary.

9. Draw a circle whose center is located at the center of the picture box.

10. Draw a tick mark on the x-axis at a distance of 5 from the origin.

11. Draw a tick mark on the y-axis at a distance of 70 from the origin.

12. Draw a circle whose leftmost point is at the center of the picture box.

13. Draw four small quarter-circles, one in each corner of the picture box.

14. Draw a triangle with two sides of the same length.

15. Draw a rectangle.

16. Draw a square.

17. Draw five concentric circles, that is, five circles with the same center.

18. Draw a point in the center of the picture box.

19. Draw a circle and a line that is tangent to the circle.

20. Draw two circles that touch at a single point.

In Exercises 21 through 24, consider the following event procedure. What would be the effect on the circle if the picOutput.Scale statement were replaced by the given picOutput.Scale statement?

```
Private Sub cmdDraw_Click()
  picOutput.Cls
  picOutput.Scale (-5, 5)-(5, -5)    'Specify coordinate system
  picOutput.Circle (0, 0), 3         'Draw circle centered at origin
End Sub
```

21. picOutput.Scale (-8, 8)-(8, -8)

22. picOutput.Scale (-5, 8)-(5, -8)

23. picOutput.Scale (-8, 5)-(8, -5)

24. picOutput.Scale (-4, 4)-(4, -4)

In Exercises 25 through 27, write an event procedure to perform the given task.

25. Draw a graph of the function $y = x^2$ for x between 0 and 10.

26. Draw a graph of the function $200 / (x + 5)^2$ for x between 0 and 20.

27. Draw displays such as the one in Figure 10.11. Let the user specify the maximum number (in this display, 8).

Figure 10.11 Display for Exercise 27.

In Exercises 28 through 30, use the statement picOutput.Scale (0, 50)–(100, 0).

28. Write a program to produce Figure 10.12. Let the maximum number of lines (in this display, 3) be specified by the user.

—————— LINE 1

—————— LINE 2

—————— LINE 3

Figure 10.12 Display for Exercise 28.

29. Write a program to produce a sheet of graph paper.

30. Write a program to produce a form for a course schedule. See Figure 10.13.

COURSE SCHEDULE						
Time	Mon.	Tues.	Wed.	Thurs.	Fri.	Sat./Sun.

Figure 10.13 Course schedule.

✔✔ Solutions to Practice Problems 10.1

1. The largest value of any x coordinate is 5. Because 20% of 5 is 1, the numbers on the x-axis should range from -1 to 6 ($= 5 + 1$). Similarly, the numbers on the y-axis should range from -16 to 96 ($= 80 + 16$). Therefore, an appropriate scaling statement is

   ```
   picOutput.Scale (-1, 96)-(6, -16)
   ```

2.
   ```
   Private Sub cmdDraw_Click()
       picOutput.Scale (-1, 96)-(6, -16)   'Specify coordinate system
       picOutput.Line (-1, 0)-(6, 0)        'Draw x-axis
       picOutput.Line (0, -16)-(0, 96)      'Draw y-axis
       picOutput.Line (3, 45)-(5, 80)       'Draw the line
       picOutput.Circle (3, 45), .1         'Draw small circle about left end point
       picOutput.Circle (5, 80), .1         'Draw small circle about right end point
   End Sub
   ```

   The radius for the small circles about the end points was determined by trial and error. As a rule of thumb, it should be about 2 percent of the length of the x-axis.

3. Add the following lines before the End Sub statement of the preceding event procedure. The length of the tick mark was taken to be the diameter of the circle. See Figure 10.14 for the output of the entire program.

   ```
   picOutput.Line (-.1, 80)-(.1, 80)   'Draw tick mark
   picOutput.CurrentX = -.5             'Prepare cursor position for label
   picOutput.CurrentY = 80 - picOutput.TextHeight(" ") / 2
   picOutput.Print "80"                 'Display label
   ```

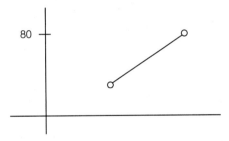

Figure 10.14 Final output from practice problems.

10.2 LINE CHARTS

A line chart displays the change in a certain quantity in relation to another quantity (often time). The following steps produce a line chart.

1. Look over the data to be displayed. A typical line chart displays between 3 and 20 items of data corresponding to evenly spaced units of time: years, months, or days. The positions on the x-axis will contain labels such as "Jan Feb Mar Apr..." or "1996 1997 1998 1999...". These labels can be placed at the locations 1, 2, 3, ... on the x-axis.

2. Choose a coordinate system based on the number of data items and the size of the quantities. A convenient scale for the x-axis is from -1 to one more than the number of data items. The scale for the y-axis is determined by the largest quantity to be displayed.

3. Draw the line segments. It is a good idea to draw a small circle around the end points of the line segments.

4. Draw and label tick marks on the coordinate axes. The x-axis should have a tick mark for each time period. The y-axis should have at least one tick mark to indicate the magnitude of the quantities displayed.

5. Title the chart, and give the source of the data.

Table 10.1 gives enrollment data for 2-year colleges taken from the *Statistical Abstract of the United States*. The program presented below displays the total enrollments for the given years in a line chart.

Year	1960	1970	1980	1990	2000
Male	283	1375	2047	2233	2398
Female	170	945	2479	3007	3358
Total	453	2320	4526	5240	5756

Table 10.1 Two-year college enrollments (in thousands).

Figure 10.15 shows the graph that results from executing the following program. The data in ENROLL.TXT are taken from the first and fourth lines of Table 10.1. For example, the first line in the file is "1960", 453. (Explanatory remarks follow the program.)

```
'In (Declarations) section of (General)
Dim numYears As Integer, maxEnroll As Single

Private Sub cmdDraw_Click()
  'Line Chart of Total Two-Year College Enrollments
  numYears = 5
  ReDim label(1 To numYears) As String
  ReDim total(1 To numYears) As Single
  Call ReadData(label(), total())
  Call DrawAxes
  Call DrawData(total())
  Call ShowTitle
  Call ShowLabels(label())
End Sub

Private Sub DrawAxes()
  'Draw axes
  picEnroll.Scale (-1, 1.2 * maxEnroll) - (numYears + 1, -.2 * maxEnroll)
  picEnroll.Line (-1, 0)-(numYears + 1, 0)
  picEnroll.Line (0, -.1 * maxEnroll)-(0, 1.1 * maxEnroll)
End Sub

Private Sub DrawData(total() As Single)
  Dim i As Integer
  'Draw lines connecting data and circle data points
  For i = 1 To numYears
    If i < numYears Then
        picEnroll.Line (i, total(i))-(i + 1, total(i + 1))
    End If
```

```
        picEnroll.Circle (i, total(i)), .01 * numYears
   Next i
End Sub

Private Sub Locate(x As Single, y As Single)
  picEnroll.CurrentX = x
  picEnroll.CurrentY = y
End Sub

Private Sub ReadData(label() As String, total() As Single)
  Dim i As Integer
  'Assume the data have been placed in the file "ENROLL.TXT"
  '(First line of the file is "1960",453)
  'Read data into arrays, find highest enrollment
  maxEnroll = 0
  Open "ENROLL.TXT" For Input As #1
  For i = 1 To numYears
    Input #1, label(i), total(i)
    If total(i) > maxEnroll Then
        maxEnroll = total(i)
    End If
  Next i
  Close #1
End Sub

Private Sub ShowLabels(label() As String)
  Dim i As Integer, lbl As String, lblWid As Single
  Dim lblHght As Single, tickFactor As Single
  'Draw tick marks and label them
  For i = 1 To numYears
    lbl = Right(label(i), 2)
    lblWid = picEnroll.TextWidth(lbl)
    tickFactor = .02 * maxEnroll
    picEnroll.Line (i, -tickFactor)-(i, tickFactor)
    Call Locate(i - lblWid / 2, -tickFactor)
    picEnroll.Print lbl
  Next i
  lbl = Str(maxEnroll)
  lblWid = picEnroll.TextWidth(lbl)
  lblHght = picEnroll.TextHeight(lbl)
  tickFactor = .02 * numYears
  picEnroll.Line (-tickFactor, maxEnroll)-(tickFactor, maxEnroll)
  Call Locate(-tickFactor - lblWid, maxEnroll - lblHght / 2)
  picEnroll.Print lbl
End Sub

Private Sub ShowTitle()
  'Display source and title
  Call Locate(-.5, -.1 * maxEnroll)
  picEnroll.Print "Source: Statistical Abstract of the United States"
  Call Locate(.5, 1.2 * maxEnroll)
  picEnroll.Print "Two-Year College Enrollments (in thousands)"
End Sub
```

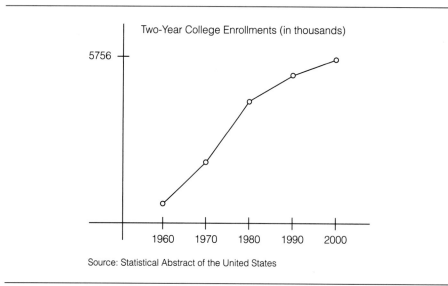

Figure 10.15 Chart for Example 1.

Remarks on the Program in Example 1

1. The value of *tickFactor* in the Sub procedure ShowLabels was set to 2 percent of the scale determiners (*numYears* and *maxEnroll*) for the *x* and *y* axes. This percentage is appropriate for picture boxes that occupy 1/4th to 1/3rd of the screen. Smaller picture boxes might require a factor of 3 percent or 4 percent for good-looking tick marks. Picture boxes that almost fill the screen might have good results with a factor as small as 1 percent.

2. In the Sub procedure ShowLabels, the TextWidth and TextHeight methods were used to obtain the width and height of each label. These values were used together with the coordinates of the appropriate end of the tick mark to assign values to CurrentX and CurrentY for proper placement of the label relative to the graphics.

3. In the event procedure cmdDraw_Click, the number of data points (5) was assigned to the variable *numYears*, and then *numYears* was used as a parameter to all other Sub procedures. This feature makes it easy to add additional data to the line chart. For instance, if we decide to include the data for one additional year, we will only have to change the value of *numYears* and add one more line to the text file.

Line Styling

Patterned, or "styled," lines can be drawn between two points. Some available line styles are shown in Figure 10.16. Each line has an associated number identifying its style. If *s* is one of the numbers in the figure, then the statements

```
picBox.DrawStyle = s
picBox.Line (a, b)-(c, d)
```

draw the line from (a, b) to (c, d) in the style corresponding to the number *s*.

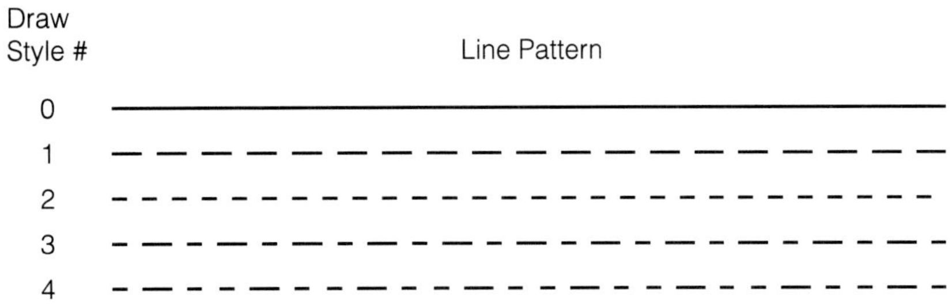

Draw
Style #   Line Pattern

  0 ────────────────────────────────────

  1 ─ ─ ─ ─ ─ ─ ─ ─ ─ ─ ─ ─ ─ ─ ─ ─ ─ ─

  2 -

  3 - ─ - ─ - ─ - ─ - ─ - ─ - ─ - ─ - ─ - ─ -

  4 - ─ - - ─ - - ─ - - ─ - - ─ - - ─ - - ─ -

Figure 10.16 Line patterns.

Styling is useful when displaying several line charts on the same coordinate system.

EXAMPLE 2   The following program is a modification of Example 1 that draws a line chart displaying the male, female, and total enrollments of 2-year colleges. The text file must be changed to contain the enrollment figures for males and females, and arrays must be created to hold this information. The totals can be computed from the other numbers. The styled lines for male and female enrollments must be drawn. Finally, legends must be given to identify the different line charts. Figure 10.17 shows the picture box that results from the modified program.

```
'In (Declarations) section of (General)
Dim numYears As Integer, maxEnroll As Single

Private Sub cmdDraw_Click()
  'Line Charts of Two-Year College Enrollments
  numYears = 5
  ReDim label(1 To numYears) As String
  ReDim male(1 To numYears) As Single
  ReDim female(1 To numYears) As Single
  ReDim total(1 To numYears) As Single
  Call ReadData(label(),male(),female(),total())
  Call DrawAxes
  Call DrawData(male(), female(), total())
  Call ShowTitle
  Call ShowLabels(label())
  Call ShowLegend
End Sub

Private Sub DrawAxes()
  'Draw axes
  picEnroll.Scale (-1, 1.2 * maxEnroll) - (numYears + 1, -.2 * maxEnroll)
  picEnroll.Line (-1, 0)-(numYears + 1, 0)
  picEnroll.Line (0, -.1 * maxEnroll)-(0, 1.1 * maxEnroll)
End Sub
```

```
Private Sub DrawData(male() As Single, female() As Single, total() As Single)
  Dim i As Integer
  For i = 1 To numYears
    If i < numYears Then
        'Draw lines connecting data points
        picEnroll.DrawStyle = 2
        picEnroll.Line (i, male(i))-(i + 1, male(i + 1))
        picEnroll.DrawStyle = 1
        picEnroll.Line (i, female(i))-(i + 1, female(i + 1))
        picEnroll.DrawStyle = 0
        picEnroll.Line (i, total(i))-(i + 1, total(i + 1))
    End If
    'Draw small circles around data points
    picEnroll.Circle (i, male(i)), .01 * numYears
    picEnroll.Circle (i, female(i)), .01 * numYears
    picEnroll.Circle (i, total(i)), .01 * numYears
  Next i
End Sub

Private Sub Locate(x As Single, y As Single)
  picEnroll.CurrentX = x
  picEnroll.CurrentY = y
End Sub

Private Sub ReadData(label() As String, male() As Single, _
                     female() As Single, total() As Single)
  'The two lines above should be enter as one line
  Dim i As Integer
  'Assume the data has been placed in the file "ENROLLMF.TXT"
  'as Year, male, female
  '(First line of file is "1960",283,170)
  'Read data into arrays, find highest enrollment
  Open "ENROLLMF.TXT" For Input As #1
  maxEnroll = 0
  For i = 1 To numYears
    Input #1, label(i), male(i), female(i)
    total(i) = male(i) + female(i)
    If maxEnroll < total(i) Then
        maxEnroll = total(i)
    End If
  Next i
  Close #1
End Sub

Private Sub ShowLabels(label() As String)
  Dim i As Integer, lbl As String, lblWid As Single
  Dim lblHght As Single, tickFactor As Single
  'Draw tick marks and label them
  For i = 1 To numYears
    lbl = Right(label(i), 2)
    lblWid = picEnroll.TextWidth(lbl)
    tickFactor = .02 * maxEnroll
    picEnroll.Line (i, -tickFactor)-(i, tickFactor)
    Call Locate(i - lblWid / 2, -tickFactor)
    picEnroll.Print lbl
  Next i
```

```
    lbl = Str(maxEnroll)
    lblWid = picEnroll.TextWidth(lbl)
    lblHght = picEnroll.TextHeight(lbl)
    tickFactor = .02 * numYears
    picEnroll.Line (-tickFactor, maxEnroll)-(tickFactor, maxEnroll)
    Call Locate(-tickFactor - lblWid, maxEnroll - lblHght / 2)
    picEnroll.Print lbl
End Sub

Private Sub ShowLegend()
    'Show legend
    picEnroll.DrawStyle = 2
    picEnroll.Line (.1, 1.05 * maxEnroll)-(.9, 1.05 * maxEnroll)
    Call Locate(1, 1.1 * maxEnroll)
    picEnroll.Print "Male"
    picEnroll.DrawStyle = 1
    picEnroll.Line (.1, .95 * maxEnroll)-(.9, .95 * maxEnroll)
    Call Locate(1, maxEnroll)
    picEnroll.Print "Female"
    picEnroll.DrawStyle = 0
    picEnroll.Line (.1, .85 * maxEnroll)-(.9, .85 * maxEnroll)
    Call Locate(1, .9 * maxEnroll)
    picEnroll.Print "Total"
End Sub

Private Sub ShowTitle()
    'Display source and title
    Call Locate(-.5, -.1 * maxEnroll)
    picEnroll.Print "Source: Statistical Abstract of the United States"
    Call Locate(.5, 1.2 * maxEnroll)
    picEnroll.Print "Two-Year College Enrollments (in thousands)"
End Sub
```

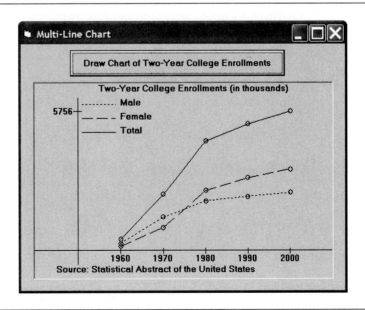

Figure 10.17 Chart for Example 2.

Comment

1. The line charts drawn in Examples 1 and 2 can be printed on the printer instead of displayed in a picture box. Just replace each occurrence of picOutput with Printer, and add

   Printer.EndDoc

   as the last statement of the cmdDraw_Click event procedure. Also, the charts will look best in landscape orientation which is invoked with the statement

   Printer.Orientation = 2

   placed before the Scale method is executed.

 PRACTICE PROBLEMS 10.2

Consider the program of Example 2 that draws the three-line chart of two-year college enrollments.

1. The enrollments for 1950 were Males—140, Females—78, Total—218. Change the program to include these data.

2. Suppose the enrollment data were given in units of millions instead of thousands. How would this affect the appearance of the three-line chart?

3. Why wasn't 2000 used in the picEnroll.Scale statement to determine the scale for the x-axis? It is the largest value of x.

EXERCISES 10.2

In Exercises 1 and 2, determine a picOutput.Scale statement that could have been used to obtain the chart.

1.

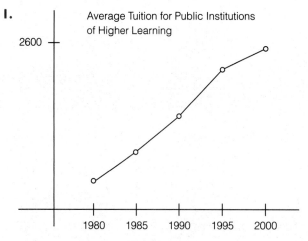

Source: National Center for Educational Statistics

2.

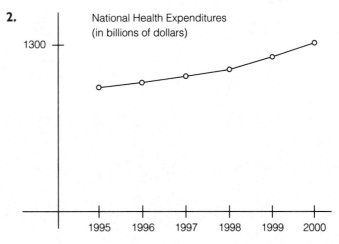

National Health Expenditures
(in billions of dollars)

1300

1995 1996 1997 1998 1999 2000

Source: Centers for Medicare & Medicaid Services

In Exercises 3 through 7, write a program to display the given information in a line chart.

3. The Consumer Price Index is a measure of living costs based on changes in retail prices, with 1972 taken as the base year.

Year	1972	1977	1982	1987	1992	1997	2002
CPI	100.0	145.0	230.9	291.8	335.7	384.0	430.4

Source: Bureau of Labor Statistics

4. Percentage of College Freshmen Who Smoke

Year	1991	1993	1995	1997	1999	2001
Percent	11.4	11.7	14.6	16.1	14.2	8.6

Source: Higher Education Research Institute

5. Freshman Life Goals (% of students committed to goal)

	1968	1976	1984	1992	2000
Be very well off financially	45	57	70	73	73
Develop a meaningful philosophy of life	80	57	45	46	42

Source: Higher Education Research Institute

6. Normal Monthly Precipitation (in inches)

	Jan	Apr	July	Oct
Mobile, AL	4.6	5.35	7.7	2.6
Phoenix, AZ	.7	.3	.7	.6
Portland, OR	6.2	2.3	.5	3.0
Washington, DC	2.8	2.9	3.9	2.9

Source: Statistical Abstract of the United States

7. Age Distribution (%) of the Labor Force

	16–24	25–39	Over 39
1990	18	42	40
2000	16	36	48
2010	17	32	51

Source: Bureau of Labor Statistics.

✔✔ **Solutions to Practice Problems 10.2**

1. Change *numYears* to 6 in the cmdDraw_Click event procedure and add the following line to the beginning of the text file.

   `"1950", 140, 78`

2. Not at all. The value of *maxEnroll*, 5756, would change to 5.756 but the picEnroll.Scale statement would scale the y-axis with respect to this new value of *maxEnroll* and the line charts would look exactly the same as before.

3. If 2000 had been used, the line charts would have been unreadable. Line charts are used to illustrate from about 3 to 15 pieces of data. These are best placed at the numbers 1, 2, 3, ... on the x-axis. In many cases the classifications given below the tick marks are words (such as Jan, Feb, ...) instead of numbers.

10.3   BAR CHARTS

Drawing bar charts requires a variation of the line statement. If $(x1, y1)$ and $(x2, y2)$ are two points on the screen, then the statement

```
picBox.Line (x1, y1)-(x2, y2), , B
```

draws a rectangle with the two points as opposite corners. If B is replaced by BF, a solid rectangle will be drawn (see Figure 10.18).

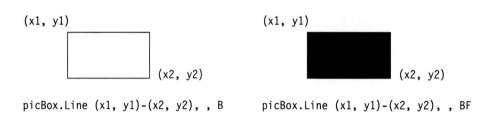

Figure 10.18 Line method with B and BF options.

EXAMPLE 1

The 2002 populations of California and New York are 35 and 19 million, respectively. The following program produces the chart shown in Figure 10.19. The first five lines are the same as those of a line chart with two pieces of data. The base of the rectangle for California is centered above the point $(1, 0)$ on the x-axis and extends .3 unit to the left and right. (The number .3 was chosen arbitrarily; it had to be less than .5 so that the rectangles would not touch.) Therefore, the upper-left corner of the rectangle has coordinates $(.7, 35)$ and the lower-right corner has coordinates $(1.3, 0)$. Figure 10.20 shows the coordinates of the principal points of the rectangles.

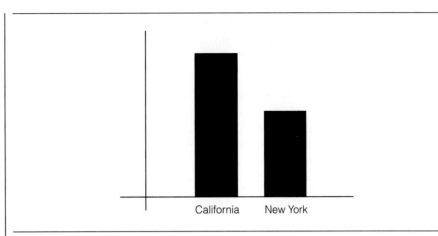

Figure 10.19 Bar chart for Example 1.

```
Private Sub cmdDisplayPop_Click()
  'Populations of California and New York
  picPop.Scale (-1, 40)-(3, -5)        'Specify coordinates
  picPop.Line (-1, 0)-(3, 0)           'Draw x-axis
  picPop.Line (0, -5)-(0, 40)          'Draw y-axis
  picPop.Line (.7, 35)-(1.3, 0),,BF    'Draw solid rectangle for CA
  picPop.Line (1.7, 19)-(2.3, 0),,BF   'Draw solid rectangle for NY
  picPop.CurrentY = -1                 'Vertical position of labels
  picPop.CurrentX = .7        'Beginning horizontal position of label for CA
  picPop.Print "California";  'Beginning horizontal position of label for NY
  picPop.CurrentX = 1.7
  picPop.Print "New York";
End Sub
```

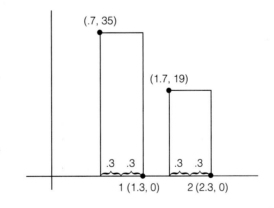

Figure 10.20 Coordinates of principal points of Example 1.

Any program that draws a line chart can be easily modified to produce a bar chart. Multiple line charts are converted into so-called **clustered bar charts**.

EXAMPLE 2   Display the 2-year college enrollments for males and females in a clustered bar chart. Use the data in Table 10.2 of Section 10.2.

SOLUTION   The output of the following program appears in Figure 10.21. This program is very similar to the program that produced Figure 10.17 of Section 10.2.

```
Private Sub cmdDraw_Click()
  Dim numYears As Integer, maxEnroll As Single
  'Bar Chart of Total Two-Year College Enrollments
  numYears = 5
  ReDim label(1 To numYears) As String
  ReDim male(1 To numYears) As Single
  ReDim female(1 To numYears) As Single
  Call ReadData(label(), male(), female(), numYears, maxEnroll)
  Call DrawAxes(numYears, maxEnroll)
  Call DrawData(male(), female(), numYears)
  Call ShowTitle(maxEnroll)
  Call ShowLabels(label(), numYears, maxEnroll)
  Call ShowLegend(maxEnroll)
End Sub

Private Sub DrawAxes(numYears As Integer, maxEnroll As Single)
  'Draw axes
  picEnroll.Scale (-1, 1.2 * maxEnroll)-(numYears + 1, -.2 * maxEnroll)
  picEnroll.Line (-1, 0)-(numYears + 1, 0)
  picEnroll.Line (0, -.1 * maxEnroll)-(0, 1.1 * maxEnroll)
End Sub

Private Sub DrawData(male() As Single, female() As Single, _
                     numYears As Integer)
  Dim i As Integer
  'Draw rectangles
  For i = 1 To numYears
    picEnroll.Line (i - .3, male(i))-(i, 0), , BF
    picEnroll.Line (i, female(i))-(i + .3, 0), , B
  Next i
End Sub

Private Sub Locate(x As Single, y As Single)
  picEnroll.CurrentX = x
  picEnroll.CurrentY = y
End Sub

Private Sub ReadData(label() As String, male() As Single, _
            female() As Single, numYears As Integer, maxEnroll As Single)
  Dim i As Integer
  'Assume the data have been placed in the file ENROLLMF.TXT
  '(First line is file is "1960",283,170)
  'Read data into arrays, find highest enrollment
  Open "ENROLLMF.TXT" For Input As #1
  maxEnroll = 0
```

```
    For i = 1 To numYears
      Input #1, label(i), male(i), female(i)
      If male(i) > maxEnroll Then
          maxEnroll = male(i)
      End If
      If female(i) > maxEnroll Then
          maxEnroll = female(i)
      End If
    Next i
    Close #1
End Sub

Private Sub ShowLabels(label() As String, numYears As Integer, _
                       maxEnroll As Single)
  Dim i As Integer, lbl As String, lblWid As Single
  Dim lblHght As Single, tickFactor As Single
  'Draw tick marks and label them
  For i = 1 To numYears
    lbl = label(i)
    lblWid = picEnroll.TextWidth(lbl)
    tickFactor = .02 * maxEnroll
    picEnroll.Line (i, -tickFactor)-(i, tickFactor)
    Call Locate(i - lblWid / 2, -tickFactor)
    picEnroll.Print lbl
  Next i
  lbl = Str(maxEnroll)
  lblWid = picEnroll.TextWidth(lbl)
  lblHght = picEnroll.TextHeight(lbl)
  tickFactor = .01 * numYears
  picEnroll.Line (-tickFactor, maxEnroll)-(tickFactor, maxEnroll)
  Call Locate(-tickFactor - lblWid, maxEnroll - lblHght / 2)
  picEnroll.Print lbl
End Sub

Private Sub ShowLegend(maxEnroll As Single)
  'Show legend
  picEnroll.Line (.1, 1.05 * maxEnroll)-(.9, .95 * maxEnroll), , BF
  Call Locate(1, 1.05 * maxEnroll)
  picEnroll.Print "Male"
  picEnroll.Line (.1, .9 * maxEnroll)-(.9, .8 * maxEnroll), , B
  Call Locate(1, .9 * maxEnroll)
  picEnroll.Print "Female"
End Sub

Private Sub ShowTitle(maxEnroll As Single)
  'Display source and title
  Call Locate(-.5, -.1 * maxEnroll)
  picEnroll.Print "Source: Statistical Abstract of the United States"
  Call Locate(.5, 1.2 * maxEnroll)
  picEnroll.Print "Two-Year College Enrollments (in thousands)"
End Sub
```

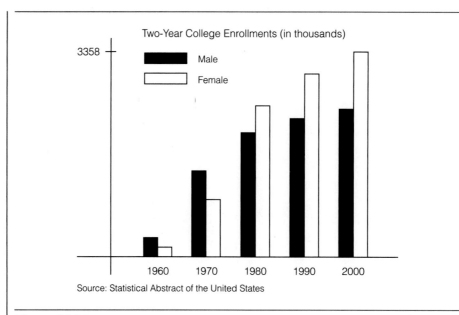

Figure 10.21 Chart for Example 2.

Comments

1. Any line chart can be converted to a bar chart and vice versa. Line charts are best suited for displaying quantities that vary with time. The slopes of the individual line segments clearly portray the rates at which the quantity is changing. Bar charts excel in contrasting the magnitudes of different entities.

2. The Line method can produce colored rectangles. If vb*Color* is one of the 8 color constants, then the statement picBox.Line $(x1, y1)–(x2, y2)$, vb*Color*, B draws a rectangle in color. A colored solid rectangle will be produced if B is replaced by BF. The use of color permits clustered bar charts with three bars per cluster.

3. In Section 10.4, we discuss a method to fill in rectangles using various patterns, such as horizontal lines and crosshatches. Using this technique, we can create black-and-white clustered bar charts having three or more bars per cluster.

✔ **PRACTICE PROBLEMS 10.3**

Consider the bar chart in Figure 10.22.

1. How does this bar chart differ from the other charts considered so far?

2. Outline methods to achieve the effects referred to in the solution to Practice Problem 1.

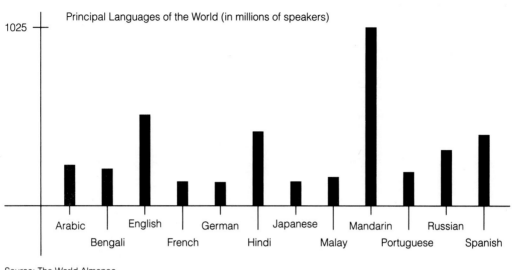

Source: The World Almanac

Figure 10.22 Bar chart for practice problems.

➤ **EXERCISES 10.3**

1. Suppose data for a few more years are added to the data of Example 2. What changes will have to be made in the program?

In Exercises 2 through 9, write a program to display the given information in a bar chart.

2. United States Minimum Wage

1958	1.00
1968	1.15
1978	2.65
1988	3.35
1998	5.15

3. Number of Computers in U.S. Public Schools, K–12 (in millions)

1991	2.2
1993	4.1
1995	5.7
1997	7.4
1999	9.8

Source: Statistical Abstract of the United States

4. Most Popular Majors for College Freshmen in Fall 2002

Field	Percent
Elementary Education	5.2
Psychology	4.8
Predent, Premed, Prevet	4.2
Biology (general)	4.1
Business Administration	3.8

Source: "The American Freshman: National Norms for Fall 2002."

5. Average Tuition and Required Fees at Four-Year Colleges

	1975	1980	1985	1990	1995	2000
Public	599	840	1388	2035	2977	3506
Private	2614	3811	6843	10348	14527	15531

Source: National Center for Educational Statistics

6. Educational Attainment of Persons 25 years Old and Older (in %)

	1975	1985	1995
High School Graduate	62.5	73.9	81.7
College Graduate	13.9	19.4	23.0

Source: U.S. Bureau of the Census

7. Motor Vehicles in Use (in millions)

	1980	1985	1990	1995
Cars	104.6	114.7	123.3	123.2
Trucks	35.2	42.4	56.0	70.2

Source: Statistical Abstract of the United States, 2000

8. Principal Languages of the World (in millions of "first language" speakers)

Arabic	199	Japanese	125
Bengali	207	Javanese	75
English	341	Mandarin	874
French	77	Portuguese	176
German	100	Russian	167
Hindi	366	Spanish	340

Source: The World Almanac, 2003

9. 2000 Federal Funding for Research and Development to Universities and Colleges (in millions of dollars)

Johns Hopkins Univ.	933	Univ. of Michigan	378
Univ. of Washington	445	Univ. of Pennsylvania	374
UC, Los Angeles	399	UC, San Diego	358
Stanford Univ.	378	Harvard Univ.	331

Source: National Science Foundation

The program that follows draws a circle in the center of the picture box. In Exercises 10 through 12, rewrite the picOutput.Scale statement in order to achieve the stated result.

```
Private Sub cmdDraw_Click ()
  picOutput.Cls
  picOutput.Scale (-5, 5)-(5, -5)
  picOutput.Circle (0, 0), 2
End Sub
```

10. Draw the circle in the left half of the picture box.

11. Draw the circle in the right half of the picture box.

12. Draw the circle in the upper-left corner of the picture box.

13. Clustered bar charts are sometimes drawn with overlapping rectangles. See Figure 10.23. What changes would have to be made to do this in the program of Example 2?

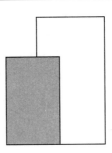

Figure 10.23 Clustered Bar Chart

✔✔ **Solutions to Practice Problems 10.3**

1. (a) The number of characters in the labels is so large the labels must be placed in two rows.

   (b) Every other label had to be lowered.

   (c) Short vertical lines extend from the bars to the legends.

2. (a) A slight change in the picOutput.Scale statement will produce extra room at the bottom of the screen. The negative number that specifies the lower range of the y-axis should be increased in magnitude.

   (b) The For...Next loop that places the label should be replaced by two loops that increment by 2 and place the labels on two rows.

   (c) The For...Next loops in step (b) should each draw vertical lines at the same spots where tick marks usually appear. The lines should extend from the x-axis to the appropriate label. The length of these lines can be determined by experimentation.

10.4   PIE CHARTS

Drawing pie charts requires the Circle method and the FillStyle property. The Circle method draws not only circles, but also sectors (formed by an arc and two radius lines). The FillStyle property determines what pattern, if any, is used to fill a sector. The FillColor property can be used, if desired, to lend color to the fill patterns.

Figure 10.24 shows a circle with several radius lines drawn. The radius line extending to the right from the center of the circle is called the **horizontal radius line**. Every other radius line is assigned a number between 0 and 1 according to the percentage of the circle that must be swept out in the counterclockwise direction in order to reach that radius line. For instance, beginning at the horizontal radius line and rotating 1/4 of the way around the circle counterclockwise, we reach the radius line labeled .25.

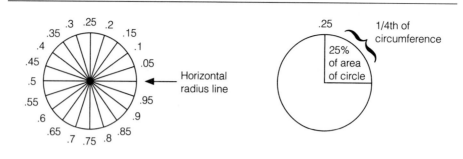

Figure 10.24 Numbers assigned to radius lines.

EXAMPLE 1

In Figure 10.25, what percentage of the area of the circle lies in the shaded sector?

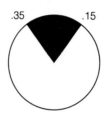

Figure 10.25 Circle for Example 1.

SOLUTION

The percentage of the circle contained between the radius lines labeled .15 and .35 is 35% − 15%, or 20%.

The statement

```
picBox.Circle (x, y), r
```

draws the circle with center (x, y) and radius r. More precisely, the length of the horizontal radius line will be r units in the scale for the x-axis determined by the picBox.Scale statement. If $0 < a < b < 1$ and c is the circumference of the unit circle ($2*\pi$), then the statement

```
picBox.Circle (x, y), r, , a * c, b * c
```

draws an arc from the end of radius line a to the end of radius line b. See Figure 10.26(a). The statement

```
picBox.Circle (x, y), r, , -a * c, -b * c
```

draws the sector corresponding to that arc. See Figure 10.26(b).

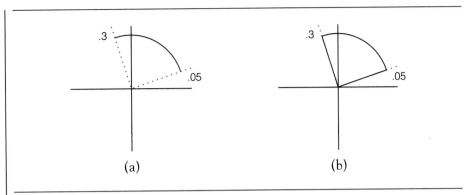

Figure 10.26 (a) Arc of a circle and (b) sector of a circle.

A special case occurs when a is 0. The expression $-a * c$ will be zero rather than a negative number. As a result, Visual Basic does not draw the horizontal radius line associated with $a = 0$. In order to create a sector that has the horizontal radius line as one of its edges, use a small number such as .0000001 for a.

EXAMPLE 2 Write a program to draw a sector whose sides are a horizontal radius line and the radius line that is 40 percent of the way around the circle.

SOLUTION The following program draws the sector with its center at the center of the picture box. The radius was arbitrarily chosen to be 2 and the picOutput.Scale statement was chosen so that the circle would be fairly large. The output displayed in the picture box is shown in Figure 10.27.

```
Private Sub cmdDraw_Click()
  Dim c As Single, a As Single, b As Single
  picOutput.Cls
  picOutput.Scale (-3, 3)-(3, -3)    'Specify coordinate system
  c = 2 * 3.14159
  a = .0000001
  b = .4
  'Draw sector with radius lines corresponding to 0 and .4
  picOutput.Circle (0, 0), 2, , -a * c, -b * c
End Sub
```

Figure 10.27 Display from Example 2.

A sector can be "painted" using any of the patterns shown in Figure 10.28. Which pattern is used to fill a sector is determined by the value of the FillStyle property. The default value of this property is 1 for transparent. Thus, by default, the interior of a sector is not painted.

Fill Style #	Fill Pattern	Fill Style #	Fill Pattern
0		4	
1		5	
2		6	
3		7	

Figure 10.28 Fill patterns.

EXAMPLE 3

Write a program to draw the sector consisting of the bottom half of a circle and fill it with vertical lines.

SOLUTION

Vertical lines correspond to a FillStyle of 3. See Figure 10.29 for the output of the following program.

```
Private Sub cmdDraw_Click()
  Dim c As Single
  'Draw bottom half of circle filled with vertical lines
  c = 2 * 3.14159
  picSector.Cls
  picSector.Scale (-3, 3)-(3, -3)        'Specify coordinate system
  picSector.FillStyle = 3                'Vertical lines
  picSector.Circle (0, 0), 2, , -.5 * c, -1 * c
End Sub
```

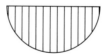

Figure 10.29 Display from Example 3.

The color used to fill the interior of a sector is determined by the value of the FillColor property. If the FillStyle of a picture box is any value except 1, then the statement

```
picBox.FillColor = vbColor
```

where vb*Color* is a color constant, will cause new circles and sectors drawn in the picture box to be filled with a colored pattern.

EXAMPLE 4

The following program subdivides a circle into four quadrants and fills in the second quadrant, that is, the quadrant extending from radius line .25 to radius line .5, with magenta crosshatched lines. Crosshatched lines correspond to a FillStyle of 6. See Figure 10.30 for the output of the following program.

```
Private Sub cmdDraw_Click()
  Dim c As Single
  'Draw quarters of circle and paint upper-left quadrant
  c = 2 * 3.14159
  picBox.Cls
  picBox.Scale (-3, 3)-(3, -3)        'Specify coordinate system
  picBox.Circle (0, 0), 2, , -.0000001 * c, -.25 * c
  picBox.FillStyle = 6                'Crosshatched
  picBox.FillColor = vbMagenta
  picBox.Circle (0, 0), 2, , -.25 * c, -.5 * c
  picBox.FillStyle = 1               'Transparent
  picBox.Circle (0, 0), 2, , -.5 * c, -.75 * c
  picBox.Circle (0, 0), 2, , -.75 * c, -1 * c
End Sub
```

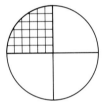

Figure 10.30 Display from Example 4.

The FillStyle and FillColor properties can be used when creating rectangles. The statements

```
picBox.FillStyle = s
picBox.FillColor = vbColor
picBox.Line (x1, y1)-(x2, y2), , B
```

draw a rectangle filled with the pattern specified by s in the color specified by vbColor. This capability is often used when creating the legend to accompany a graph.

The procedure for drawing a pie chart is as follows:

1. Read the categories and the quantities into arrays, such as *category*() and *quantity*().

2. Determine the radius lines. The number associated with the *i*th radius line is *cumPercent*(*i*). This number is a total of *quantity*(*i*) and the preceding percentages.

3. Draw and fill each sector with a pattern. The first sector extends from the horizontal radius line to radius line 1, the second sector from radius line 1 to radius line 2, and so on.

4. Draw rectangular legends to associate each sector with its category.

EXAMPLE 5 Table 10.2 gives the market share of Internet browsers for January 2003. The following program constructs a pie chart that displays the market share. Figure 10.31 shows the output displayed by the program.

	Percent of Total Market
Internet Explorer	73
Netscape Navigator	24
Other	3

Table 10.2 Browser Market Share, January 2003.

```
Private Sub cmdDraw_Click()
  Dim numItems As Integer, radius As Single
  'Draw pie chart of Browser Market Share
  numItems = 3
  ReDim category(1 To numItems) As String
  ReDim quantity(1 To numItems) As Single
  Call ReadData(category(), quantity(), numItems)
  Call DrawData(quantity(), numItems, radius)
  Call ShowLegend(category(), numItems, radius)
  Call ShowTitle(radius)
End Sub

Private Sub DrawData(quantity() As Single, numItems As Integer, _
                radius As Single)
  Dim circumf As Single, leftEdge As Single, rightEdge As Single
  Dim topEdge As Single, bottomEdge As Single, i As Integer
  Dim startAngle As Single, stopAngle As Single
  'Draw and fill each sector of pie chart
  'All scaling and text positioning done as a percentage of radius
  radius = 1  'actual value used is not important
  'Make picture 4 radii wide to provide plenty of space for
  'circle and legends. Place origin 1.25 radii from left edge;
  'space of 1.75 radii will remain on right for legends.
  leftEdge = -1.25 * radius
  rightEdge = 2.75 * radius
  'Force vertical scale to match horizontal scale;
  'center origin vertically
  topEdge = 2 * radius * (picShare.Height / picShare.Width)
  bottomEdge = -topEdge
  picShare.Cls
  picShare.Scale (leftEdge, topEdge)-(rightEdge, bottomEdge)
  circumf = 2 * 3.14159
  ReDim cumPercent(0 To numItems) As Single
```

```
    cumPercent(0) = .0000001 'a value of "zero" that can be made negative
  For i = 1 To numItems
    cumPercent(i) = cumPercent(i - 1) + quantity(i)
    startAngle = cumPercent(i - 1) * circumf
    stopAngle = cumPercent(i) * circumf
    picShare.FillStyle = (8 - i) 'use fill patterns 7, 6, and 5
    picShare.Circle (0, 0), radius, , -startAngle, -stopAngle
  Next i
End Sub

Private Sub Locate (x As Single, y As Single)
  picShare.CurrentX = x
  picShare.CurrentY = y
End Sub

Private Sub ReadData(category() As String, quantity() As Single, _
                     numItems As Integer)
  Dim i As Integer
  'Load categories and percentages of market share
  'Assume the data have been placed in the file BROWSERS.TXT
  '(First line in file is "Internet Explorer", .73)
  Open "BROWSERS.TXT" For Input As #1
  For i = 1 To numItems
    Input #1, category(i), quantity(i)
  Next i
  Close #1
End Sub

Private Sub ShowLegend(category() As String, numItems As Integer, _
                       radius As Single)
  Dim lblHght As Single, legendSize As Single
  Dim i As Integer, vertPos As Single
  'Place legend centered to right of pie chart
  'Make separation between items equal to one line of text
  '"Text lines" needed for legends is thus (2*numItems-1)
  lblHght = picShare.TextHeight(" ")
  legendSize = lblHght * (2 * numItems - 1)
  For i = 1 To numItems
    picShare.FillStyle = (8 - i)
    vertPos = (legendSize / 2) - (3 - i) * (2 * lblHght)
    picShare.Line (1.1 * radius, vertPos)-(1.4 * radius, _
                   vertPos + lblHght), ,B
    Call Locate(1.5 * radius, vertPos)
    picShare.Print category(i)
  Next i
End Sub

Private Sub ShowTitle(radius As Single)
  Dim lbl As String, lblWid As Single
  'Display title right below circle
  lbl = "Browser Market Share, January 2003"
  lblWid = picShare.TextWidth(lbl)
  Call Locate(-lblWid / 2, -(radius + .05))
  picShare.Print lbl
End Sub
```

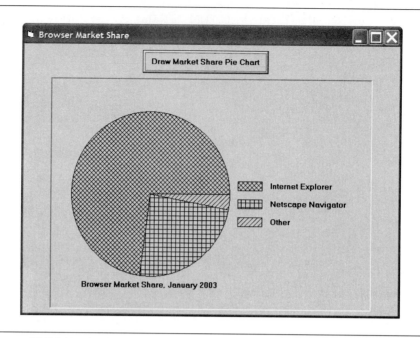

Figure 10.31 Display from Example 5.

✔ PRACTICE PROBLEMS 10.4

1. Label each of the radius lines in Figure 10.32 with a number from 0 to 1.

Figure 10.32 Circle for Practice Problem 1.

2. Write a program to draw the circle and radius lines in Problem 1 and to fill in the sector consisting of 30 percent of the area of the circle.

➤ EXERCISES 10.4

1. Label each of the radius lines in Figure 10.33(a) with a number from 0 to 1.

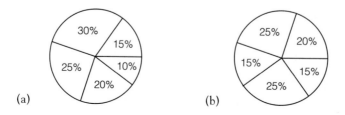

Figure 10.33 Circles for Exercises 1 and 2.

2. Label each of the radius lines in Figure 10.33(b) with a number from 0 to 1.

3. Write a program to draw the circle and radius lines of Figure 10.33(a) and to fill in the sector consisting of 10 percent of the circle.

4. Write a program to draw the circle and radius lines of Figure 10.33(b) and to fill in the sector consisting of 25 percent of the circle.

In Exercises 5 and 6, draw a pie chart to display the given data.

5. United States Recreational Beverage Consumption

Soft Drinks	52.9%
Beer	14.7%
Bottled Water	11.1%
Other	21.3%

Source: International Bottle Water Association

6. Average Number of Miles from College to Home for College Freshmen

5 or less	10%	51 to 100	15%
6 to 10	8%	101 to 500	28%
11 to 50	30%	more than 500	9%

Source: Higher Education Research Institute

7. Construct a general pie-chart program that prompts the user for the title, the number of sectors (2 through 8), and legends. Try the program with the following data.

Share of Bagel Market

Supermarkets	54%
Bagel stores	20%
Bakeries	20%
Other	6%

Source: Bakery Production and Marketing magazine, Food Marketing Institute

8. Modify the program in Exercise 7 to accept raw data and convert them to percentages. Try the program with the following data.

Fiscal Year 2003 Operating Budget for Montgomery County, Maryland (in millions of dollars)

Education	1600	Park & Planning	91
Public Safety	323	Arts, Culture, & Recreation	62
Public Works and Transportation	244	Other	113
Health and Human Services	202		

Source: Montgomery County Government Department of Finance

9. Write a program that produces the drawing in Figure 10.34.

Figure 10.34 Drawing for Exercise 9.

10. Write a program that draws a Smiley face. See Figure 10.35.

Figure 10.35 Drawing for Exercise 10.

✔✔ **Solutions to Practice Problems 10.4**

1. Each number was obtained by summing the percentages for each of the sectors from the horizontal radius line to the radius line under consideration.

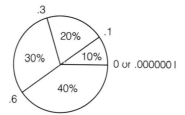

2. The 30 percent sector is the third sector, extending from radius line .3 to radius line .6.

```
Private Sub cmdDraw_Click()
  Dim perc(0 To 4) As Single, c As Single, i As Integer
  perc(0) = .0000001
  perc(1) = .1
  perc(2) = .3
  perc(3) = .6
  perc(4) = 1
  picOutput.Cls
  picOutput.Scale (-3, 3)-(3, -3)   'Specify coordinate system
  c = 2 * 3.14159
  For i = 1 To 4
    If i = 3 Then
        picOutput.FillStyle = 0    'Solid fill
      Else
        picOutput.FillStyle = 1    'Transparent fill
    End If
    picOutput.Circle (0, 0), 2, , -perc(i - 1) * c, -perc(i) * c    'Draw sector
  Next i
End Sub
```

CHAPTER 10   SUMMARY

1. Data can be vividly displayed in *line*, *bar*, *clustered bar*, and *pie charts*.

2. The programmer can select his or her own coordinate system with the Scale method.

3. The Line method draws lines, rectangles, and solid rectangles. Styled lines can be drawn by assigning appropriate values to the DrawStyle property.

4. The Circle method is used to draw circles, radius lines, and sectors. Each radius line is specified by a number between 0 and 1. The number $2 * \pi$ (or 6.283185) is used by the Circle method when drawing radii and sectors.

5. The PSet method turns on a single point and is useful in graphing functions.

6. The FillStyle property allows circles, sectors, and rectangles to be filled with one of eight patterns, and the FillColor property allows them to appear in assorted colors.

CHAPTER 10   PROGRAMMING PROJECTS

1. Look in magazines and newspapers for four sets of data, one suited to each type of chart discussed in this chapter. Write programs to display the data in chart form.

2. Figure 10.36 is called a *horizontal bar chart*. Write a program to produce this chart.

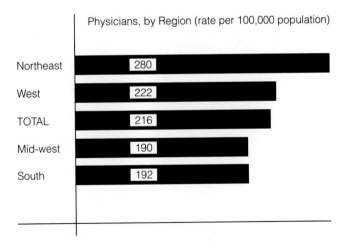

Source: Statistical Abstract of the United States

Figure 10.36 Horizontal bar chart.

3. Figure 10.37 is called a segmented bar chart. Write a program to construct this chart.

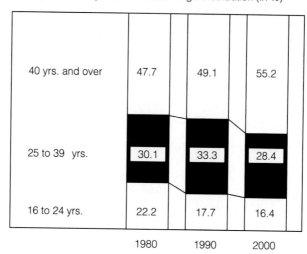

Population 16 years and Older—Age Distribution (in %)

Source: Statistical Abstract of the United States

Figure 10.37 Segmented bar chart.

4. Figure 10.38 is called a *range chart*. Using the data in Table 10.3, write a program to produce this chart.

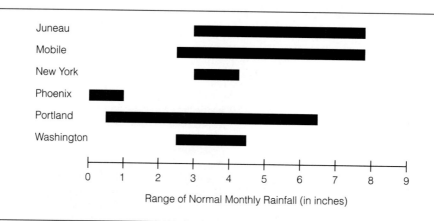

Range of Normal Monthly Rainfall (in inches)

Figure 10.38 Range chart.

	Lowest NMR	Highest NMR
Mobile	2.6	7.7
Portland	.5	6.4
Phoenix	.1	1.0
Washington	2.6	4.4
Juneau	2.9	7.7
New York	3.1	4.2

Table 10.3 Range of normal monthly rainfall for selected cities (in inches).

5. A community of 10,000 individuals is exposed to a flu epidemic in which infected individuals are sick for two days and then are immune from the illness. When we first start to observe the epidemic (that is, on day 0), 200 people have had the illness for one day, and 100 people have had the illness for two days. At any time, the rate at which the epidemic is spreading is proportional to the product of the number currently ill and the number susceptible. Specifically, each day

[# of individuals in the first day of the illness] =
    Int(0.0001735 * [# sick the previous day] * [# susceptible the previous day])

Write a program that displays successive bar graphs illustrating the progress of the epidemic. Initially, the bar graph should show the distribution for day 0 (Figure 10.39). Each time the command button is pressed, a bar graph showing the distribution for the next day should appear. Figure 10.40 shows the bar graph after the command button has been pressed three times.

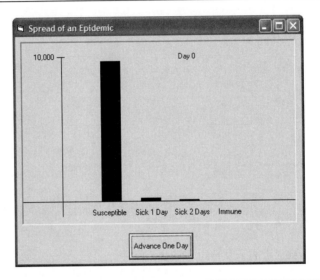

Figure 10.39 Initial distribution.

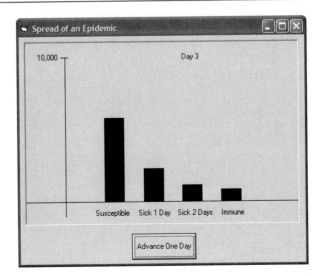

Figure 10.40 Distribution on day 3 of epidemic.

6. *Mini Vector Graphics.* Write a program that can produce drawings involving points, lines, and circles by reading the contents of a sequential file. Of course, you must also design a flexible format for the sequential file. For instance, a pair of lines in the file of the form

```
"Circle"
2, 3, 5
```

might tell the program to draw a circle of center (2, 3) and radius 5. A pair of lines in the file of the form

```
"LineBF"
2, 3, 5, 6
```

might tell the program to draw the filled rectangle defined by the points (2, 3) and (5, 6), Use the complete syntax of the PSet, Line, and Circle commands found in Appendix C to make the program as thorough as possible.

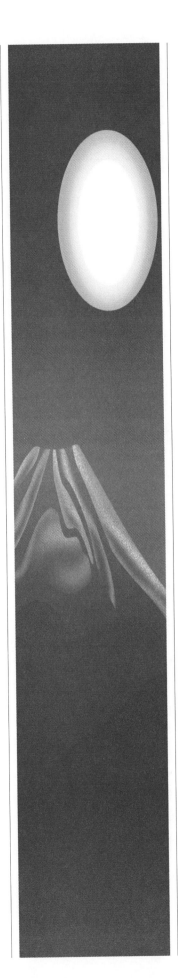

11 Additional Controls and Objects

11.1 LIST BOXES AND COMBO BOXES

The dialog box in Figure 11.1 contains one **list box**, one text box, and two **combo boxes**. The list box displays a list of program files. You click on a program file to highlight it and double-click on it to open the program. A combo box combines the features of a text box and a list box. With the two combo boxes (known as dropdown combo boxes), only the text box part is showing. The associated list drops down when you click on the arrow to the right of the text box part.

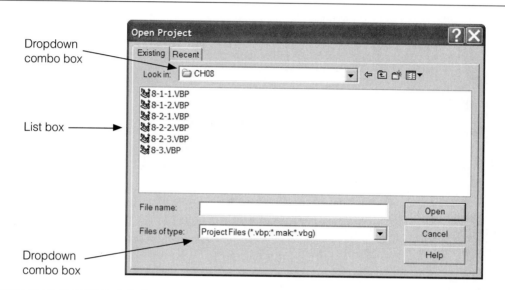

Dropdown combo box

List box

Dropdown combo box

Figure 11.1 Open Project dialog box.

The List Box Control

The fifth row of the standard Toolbox (in most editions of Visual Basic) contains the combo box icon on the left and the list box icon on the right. The list boxes discussed in this text will display a single column of strings, referred to as **items**. The items to appear initially can either be specified at design time with the List property or set with code in a procedure. Code is then used to access, add, or delete items from the list. We will first carry out all tasks with code and then show how the initial items can be specified at design time. The standard prefix for the name of a list box is *lst*.

The Sorted property is perhaps the most interesting list box property. When it is set to True, the items will automatically be displayed in alphabetical (that is, ANSI) order. The default value of the Sorted property is False.

If *item* is a string or number, then the statement

```
lstBox.AddItem item
```

adds *item* to the list. The item is added at the proper sorted position if the Sorted property is True, and otherwise is added to the end of the list. At any time, the value of

```
lstBox.ListCount
```

is the number of items in the list box.

Each item in lstBox is identified by an index number ranging from 0 through lstBox.ListCount – 1. The value of

```
lstBox.NewIndex
```

is the index number of the item most recently added to lstBox by the AddItem method. During run time you can highlight an item from a list by clicking on it with the mouse or by moving to it with the up- and down-arrow keys when the list box has the focus. (The second method triggers the Click event each time an arrow key causes the highlight to move.) The value of

```
lstBox.ListIndex
```

is the index number of the item currently highlighted in lstBox. (If no item is highlighted, the value of lstBox.ListIndex is –1.)

The string array lstBox.List( ) holds the list of items stored in the list box. In particular, the value of

```
lstBox.List(n)
```

is the item of lstBox having index n. For instance, the statement `picBox.Print lstBox.List(0)` displays the first item of the list box lstBox. The value of

```
lstBox.List(lstBox.ListIndex)
```

is the item (string) currently highlighted in lstBox. Alternatively, the value of

```
lstBox.Text
```

is also the currently highlighted item. Unlike the Text property of a text box, you may not assign a value to lstBox.Text.

The statement

```
lstBox.RemoveItem n
```

deletes the item of index n from lstBox, the statement

```
lstBox.RemoveItem lstBox.ListIndex
```

deletes the item currently highlighted in lstBox, and the statement

```
lstBox.Clear
```

deletes every item of lstBox.

EXAMPLE 1   An oxymoron is a pairing of contradictory or incongruous words. The following program displays a sorted list of oxymorons. When you click an item (or highlight it with the up- and down-arrow keys), it is displayed in a picture box. A command button allows you to add an additional item with an input dialog box. You can delete an item by double-clicking on it with the mouse. (**Note:** When you double-click the mouse, two events are processed—the Click event and the DblClick event.) After running the program, click on different items, add an item or two (such as "same difference" or "liquid gas"), and delete an item.

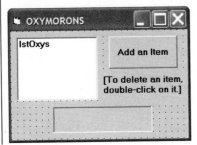

Object	Property	Setting
frmOxyMor	Caption	OXYMORONS
lstOxys	Sorted	True
cmdAdd	Caption	Add an Item
lblDelete	Caption	[To delete an item, double-click on it.]
picSelected		

```
Private Sub Form_Load()
  lstOxys.AddItem "jumbo shrimp"
  lstOxys.AddItem "definite maybe"
  lstOxys.AddItem "old news"
  lstOxys.AddItem "good grief"
End Sub

Private Sub lstOxys_Click()
  Dim quoteMark As String
  quoteMark = Chr(34)
  picSelected.Cls
  picSelected.Print "The selected item is"
  picSelected.Print quoteMark & lstOxys.Text & quoteMark & "."
End Sub

Private Sub lstOxys_DblClick()
  lstOxys.RemoveItem lstOxys.ListIndex
End Sub

Private Sub cmdAdd_Click()
  Dim item As String
  item = InputBox("Item to Add:")
  lstOxys.AddItem item
End Sub
```

[Run, and then click on the second item of the list box.]

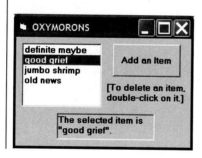

The following steps show how to fill a list box at design time. (This method is used in Example 3.)

1. Select the List property of the list box.

2. Click on the down arrow of the Settings box. (A small box will be displayed.)

3. Type in the first item, and press Ctrl+Enter. (The cursor will move to the next line.)

4. Repeat Step 3 for each of the other items.

5. When you are finished entering items, press the Enter key.

When the Sorted property of a list box is True, the index associated with an item will change when a "lesser" item is added to or removed from the list. In many applications it is important to have a fixed number associated with each item in a list box. Visual Basic makes this possible using the ItemData property. The statement

```
lstBox.ItemData(n) = m
```

associates the number *m* with the item of index *n*, and the statement

```
lstBox.ItemData(lstBox.NewIndex) = m
```

associates the number *m* with the item most recently added to the list box. Thus, lstBox can be thought of as consisting of two arrays, lstBox.List( ) and lstBox.ItemData( ). The contents of lstBox.List( ) are displayed in the list box, allowing the user to make a selection, while the hidden contents of lstBox.Item-Data( ) can be used by the programmer to index records. As illustrated in Example 2, they can also be used to set up parallel arrays that hold other data associated with each item displayed in the list box.

EXAMPLE 2 The following program uses NewIndex and ItemData to provide data about inventions. When an item is highlighted, its ItemData value is used to locate the appropriate entries in the inventor( ) and yr( ) arrays. Assume the file INVENTOR.TXT contains the following three lines:

"Ball-point pen", "Lazlo and George Biro", 1938
"Frozen food", "Robert Birdseye", 1929
"Bifocal lenses", "Ben Franklin", 1784

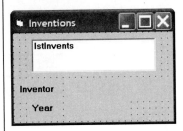

Object	Property	Setting
frmInvent	Caption	Inventions
lstInvents	Sorted	True
lblInventor	Caption	Inventor
lblWho	Caption	(none)
lblYear	Caption	Year
lblWhen	Caption	(none)

```
'In the (Declarations) section of (General)
Dim inventor(0 To 10) As String
Dim yr(0 To 10) As Integer

Private Sub Form_Load()
  Dim what As String, who As String, when As Integer, index As Integer
  Open "INVENTOR.TXT" For Input As #1
  index = 0
  Do While (index < UBound(inventor)) And (Not EOF(1))
    Input #1, what, who, when
    index = index + 1
    lstInvents.AddItem what
```

```
        lstInvents.ItemData(lstInvents.NewIndex) = index
        inventor(index) = who
        yr(index) = when
    Loop
    Close #1
End Sub

Private Sub lstInvents_Click()
    lblWho.Caption = inventor(lstInvents.ItemData(lstInvents.ListIndex))
    lblWhen.Caption = Str(yr(lstInvents.ItemData(lstInvents.ListIndex)))
End Sub
```

[Run, and then highlight the second entry in the list.]

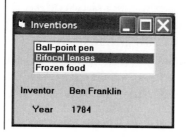

The Combo Box Control

A combo box is best thought of as a text box with a helping list box attached. With an ordinary text box, the user must type information into the box. With a combo box, the user has the option of either typing in information or just selecting the appropriate piece of information from a list. The two most useful types of combo box are denoted as style 0 (Dropdown) and style 1 (Simple) combo boxes. See Figure 11.2. The standard prefix for the name of a combo box is *cbo*.

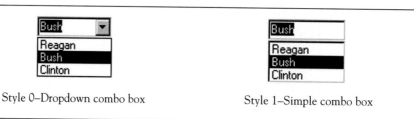

Style 0–Dropdown combo box   Style 1–Simple combo box

Figure 11.2 Styles of combo boxes.

With a Simple combo box, the list is always visible. With a Dropdown combo box, the list drops down when the user clicks on the arrow, and then disappears after a selection is made. In either case, when an item from the list is highlighted, the item automatically appears in the text box at the top and its value is assigned to the Text property of the combo box.

Combo boxes have essentially the same properties, events, and methods as list boxes. In particular, all the statements discussed for list boxes also hold for combo boxes. The Text property determines what appears at the top of the combo box before the user accesses the combo box. The Style property of a combo box must be specified at design time.

EXAMPLE 3 The following program uses a simple combo box to obtain a person's title for the first line of the address of a letter. (**Note:** At design time, first set the combo box's Style property to 1 – Simple Combo, and then lengthen the height of the combo box.)

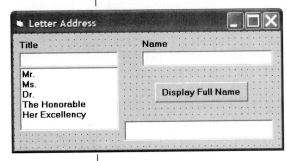

Object	Property	Setting
frmTitle	Caption	Letter Address
lblTitle	Caption	Title
cboTitle	List	Mr.
		Ms.
		Dr.
		The Honorable
		Her Excellency
	Style	1 – Simple Combo
	Text	(blank)
lblName	Caption	Name
txtName	Text	(blank)
cmdDisplay	Caption	Display Full Name
txtDisplay	Text	(blank)

```
Private Sub cmdDisplay_Click()
  txtDisplay.Text = cboTitle.Text & " " & txtName.Text
End Sub
```

[Run, select an item from the combo box, type a name into the Name text box, and click the command button.]

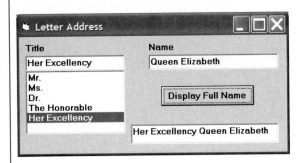

The same program with a style 0 – Dropdown Combo box produces the output shown below.

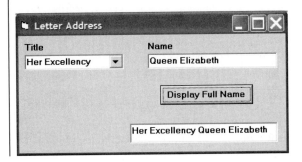

⬚ Drive, ⬚ Directory, and ⬚ File List Box Controls

Boxes similar to those inside the Open Project dialog box of Figure 11.1 are available to any Visual Basic program via icons from the Toolbox. Visual Basic does much of the work of providing the appropriate lists for the three boxes. Windows determines the contents of the drive box. The programmer determines the contents of directory list boxes and file list boxes with Path properties.

Most of the properties, methods, and events of list boxes are also valid for the three file-related list boxes. For instance, in the file list box File1, File1.ListCount is the number of files and File1.List(n) is the name of the nth file, where counting begins with 0. The selected items for the three controls are identified by the Drive, Path, and FileName properties, respectively. For instance, in the drive list box Drive1, the selected drive is given by the string Drive1.Drive.

Suppose a form contains a drive list box named Drive1, a directory list box named Dir1, and a file list box named File1. (These names are the default names supplied by Visual Basic.) When the user selects a new drive from the Drive1 list box, the directories in Dir1 should reflect this change. The proper event procedure to effect the change is

```
Private Sub Drive1_Change()
   Dir1.Path = Drive1.Drive
End Sub
```

This event is triggered by clicking on the drive name or using the arrow keys to highlight the drive name and then pressing Enter. When the user selects a new directory in Dir1, the files in File1 can be changed with the event procedure

```
Private Sub Dir1_Change()
   File1.Path = Dir1.Path
End Sub
```

This event procedure is triggered by double-clicking on a directory name. If the preceding two event procedures are in place, a change of the drive will trigger a change of the directory, which in turn will trigger a change in the list of files. The standard prefixes for the names of the drive, directory, and file list box controls are *drv*, *dir*, and *fil*, respectively.

EXAMPLE 4

The following program can be used to display the full name of any file on any drive.

Object	Property	Setting
frmFiles	Caption	Select a File
drvList		
dirList		
filList		
cmdDisplay	Caption	Display Complete Name of File
picFileSpec		

```
Private Sub cmdDisplay_Click()
  picFileSpec.Cls
  picFileSpec.Print dirList.Path;
  If Right(dirList.Path, 1) <> "\" Then
      picFileSpec.Print "\";
  End If
  picFileSpec.Print filList.FileName
End Sub

Private Sub dirList_Change()
  filList.Path = dirList.Path
End Sub

Private Sub drvList_Change()
  dirList.Path = drvList.Drive
End Sub
```

[Run, select a drive, double-click on a directory, select a file, and then click the command button.]

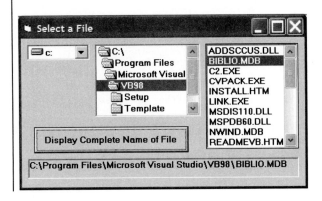

Comments

1. If a list or combo box is too short to display all the items that have been added to it, Visual Basic automatically places a vertical scroll bar on the right side of the list box. The user can then scroll to see the remaining items of the list.

2. When the Style property of a combo box is set to 2, the combo box becomes a dropdown list box. The Drive list box is an example of a dropdown list box.

3. Dropdown combo boxes (Style 0) are used in Windows applications as a text box with a "history list" (list of past entries) from which you can either type a new entry or select an old entry.

4. The standard Windows convention for opening a file is to double-click on a name in a file list box. The program must contain code for a DblClick event procedure to carry out this task.

5. File list boxes can be made to display selective lists based on wildcard characters by setting the Pattern property. For instance, setting File1.Pattern equal to "*.TXT" dictates that only files with the extension TXT will be displayed.

PRACTICE PROBLEMS 11.1

1. Write code to copy the contents of a list box into a file.

2. Give a statement that will display the last item in the combo box cboBox.

➤ EXERCISES 11.1

For Exercises 1 through 12, suppose that the list box lstBox is as shown and determine the effect of the code. (Assume the Sorted property is set to True.)

```
Bach
Beethoven
Chopin
Mozart
Tchaikovsky
```

1. `picOutput.Print lstBox.Text`

2. `picOutput.Print lstBox.List(2)`

3. `picOutput.Print lstBox.List(lstBox.ListCount - 1)`

4. `lstBox.AddItem "Haydn"`

5. `lstBox.AddItem "Brahms"`
    `picOutput.Print lstBox.List(lstBox.NewIndex)`

6. `lstBox.RemoveItem 0`

7. `lstBox.RemoveItem lstBox.ListIndex`

8. `lstBox.RemoveItem lstBox.ListCount - 1`

9. `lstBox.Clear`

10.
```
Open "COMPOSER.TXT" For Output As #1
For n = 0 To lstBox.ListCount - 1
  Write #1, lstBox.List(n)
Next n
Close #1
```

11.
```
For n = 0 To lstBox.ListCount - 1
    If Len(lstBox.List(n)) = 6 Then
        lstBox.RemoveItem n
    End If
Next n
```

12.
```
For n = 0 To lstBox.ListCount - 1
   Composer(n) = lstBox.List(n)   'Composer() is a string array
Next n
lstBox.Clear
For n = lstBox.ListCount - 1 To 0 Step -1
  lstBox.AddItem Composer(n)
Next n
```

In Exercises 13 through 24, assume that the simple combo box cboBox appears as shown and that the Sorted property is set to True. Give a statement or statements that will carry out the stated task.

13. Display the string "Dante".

14. Display the string "Goethe".

15. Display the first item of the list. (The statement should do the job even if additional items were added to the list.)

16. Delete the string "Shakespeare".

17. Delete the string "Goethe".

18. Delete the last item of the list. (The statement should do the job even if additional items were added to the list.)

19. Insert the string "Cervantes". Where will it be inserted?

20. Display every other item of the list in a picture box.

21. Delete every item beginning with the letter "M". (The code should do the job even if additional items were added to the list.)

22. Determine if "Cervantes" is in the list. (The statement should do the job even if additional items were added to the list.)

23. Display the item most recently added to the list.

24. Store the items in the file AUTHOR.TXT.

In Exercises 25 through 30, suppose the form contains a list box containing positive single-digit numbers, a command button, and a picture box. Write a Click event procedure for the command button that displays the requested information in the picture box.

25. The average of the numbers in the list.

26. The largest number in the list.

27. Every other number in the list.

28. All numbers greater than the average.

29. The *spread* of the list, that is, the difference between the largest and smallest numbers in the list.

30. The median of the numbers in the list.

31. Assume the data in Table 11.1 are contained in the sequential file STATEINF.TXT. Write a program that shows the states in a sorted list box and displays a state's nickname and motto when the state is double-clicked.

State	Nickname	Motto
Wisconsin	Badger State	Forward
Rhode Island	Ocean State	Hope
Texas	Lone Star State	Friendship
Utah	Beehive State	Industry

Table 11.1 State nicknames and mottos.

32. Table 11.2 contains the five U.S. presidents rated highest by history professors. Create a form with a list box and two command buttons captioned "Order by Year Inaugurated" and "Order by Age at Inaugural". Write a program that shows the presidents in the list box. When one of the command buttons is clicked, the list box should display the presidents in the requested order.

President	Year Inaugurated	Age at Inaugural
Abraham Lincoln	1861	52
Franklin Roosevelt	1933	51
George Washington	1789	57
Thomas Jefferson	1801	58
Theodore Roosevelt	1901	42

Table 11.2 Highest-rated U.S. presidents.

33. Table 11.3 contains wind-chill factors for several temperatures (in degrees Fahrenheit) and wind speeds (in miles per hour). Write a program containing the temperatures in one list box and the wind speeds in another. When the user selects an item from each list box and clicks on a command button, the program should display the corresponding wind-chill factor.

		Wind Speed		
	5	**10**	**15**	**20**
0	−5	−22	−31	−39
Temperature **5**	0	−15	−25	−31
10	7	−9	−18	−24
15	12	−3	−11	−17

Table 11.3 Wind-chill factors.

34. Suppose a form contains a list box (with Sorted = False), a label, and two command buttons captioned "Add an Item" and "Delete an Item". When the Add an Item button is clicked, the program should request an item with an input dialog box and then insert the item above the currently highlighted item. When the Delete an Item button is clicked, the program should remove the highlighted item from the list. At all times, the label should display the number of items in the list.

35. Consider the Length Converter in Figure 11.3. Write a program to place the items in the list and carry out the conversion. (See the first programming project in Chapter 7 for a table of equivalent lengths.)

Figure 11.3 Sample output for Exercise 35.

36. Write a program to ask a person which Monopoly® space he or she has landed on and then display the result in a picture box. The response should be obtained with a combo box listing the squares most commonly landed on— Illinois Avenue, Go, B&O Railroad, and Free Parking. (One possible outcome to be displayed in the picture box is "You have landed on Park Place.")

37. Write a program to question a person about his or her IBM-compatible computer and then display a descriptive sentence in a picture box. The form should contain combo boxes for brand, amount of memory, and size of screen. The lists should contain the most common responses for each category. The most common PCs are Compaq, Dell, Hewlett-Packard, IBM, and Gateway. The most common amounts of memory are 128MB, 256MB, 512MB and 1GB. The most common screen sizes are 15 inch, 17 inch, and 21 inch. (One possible outcome to be displayed in the picture box is "You have a Gateway computer with 256MB of memory and a 17-inch monitor.")

38. Modify the program in Example 4 so that the names of all the files with extension .frm in the files list box are printed on the printer.

39. Write a program to display a picture (contained in a *.bmp* file in the Windows directory) in a picture box. A file should be selected with drive, directory, and file list boxes and the picture displayed with a statement of the form picBox.Picture = LoadPicture(*full name of file*).

✔✔ **Solutions to Practice Problems 11.1**

```
1. Private Sub SaveListBox()
     Dim i As Integer
     Open "LISTDATA.TXT" For Output As #1
     For i = 0 to lstBox.ListCount - 1
       Write #1, lstBox.List(i)
     Next i
     Close #1
   End Sub
```

```
2. picBox.Print cboBox.List(cboBox.ListCount - 1)
```

11.2 NINE ELEMENTARY CONTROLS

In this section, we discuss the nine controls indicated on the Toolbox in Figure 11.4.

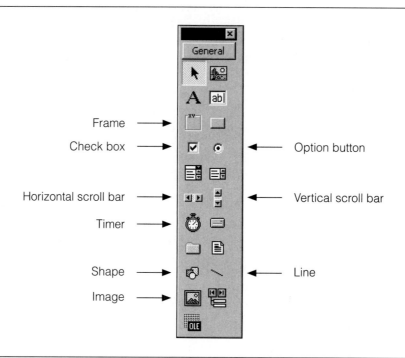

Figure 11.4 Nine elementary controls.

 The Frame Control

Frames are passive objects used to group related sets of controls for visual effect. You rarely write event procedures for frames. The preceding frame has a group of three text boxes attached to it. When you drag the frame, the attached controls follow as a unit. If you hide the frame, the attached controls will be hidden as well.

A control must be attached to a frame in a special way. You cannot just double-click to create the control and then drag it into a frame. To attach a control to a frame, first create the frame. Next, single-click on the control icon to activate it, then move the mouse pointer inside the frame to the point where you want to place the upper-left corner of the control. Finally, drag the mouse to the right and down, and then release the mouse button when you are satisfied with the size of the control. This is referred to as the **single-click-draw technique**.

A group of controls also can be attached to a picture box. The advantages of using frames are that they have a title sunk into their borders that can be set with the Caption property and that they cannot receive the focus. As shown later in this section, the frame control is particularly important when working with groups of option button controls. The standard prefix for the name of a frame is fra.

☑ The Check Box Control

A check box, which consists of a small square and a caption, presents the user with a yes/no choice. The form in Example 1 uses four check box controls. The Value property of a check box is 0 when the square is empty and is 1 when the square is checked. At run time, the user clicks on the square to toggle between the unchecked and checked states. So doing also triggers the Click event.

EXAMPLE 1 The following program allows an employee to compute the monthly cost of various benefit packages.

Object	Property	Setting
frmBenefits	Caption	Benefits Menu
chkDrugs	Caption	Prescription Drug Plan ($12.51)
chkDental	Caption	Dental Plan ($9.68)
chkVision	Caption	Vision Plan ($1.50)
chkMedical	Caption	Medical Plan ($25.25)
lblTotal	Caption	Total monthly payment:
lblAmount	Caption	$0.00

```
Private Sub chkDrugs_Click()
  Call Tally
End Sub

Private Sub chkDental_Click()
  Call Tally
End Sub

Private Sub chkVision_Click()
  Call Tally
End Sub

Private Sub chkMedical_Click()
  Call Tally
End Sub

Private Sub Tally()
  Dim sum As Single
  If chkDrugs.Value = 1 Then
      sum = sum + 12.51
  End If
  If chkDental.Value = 1 Then
      sum = sum + 9.68
  End If
```

```
        If chkVision.Value = 1 Then
            sum = sum + 1.5
        End If
        If chkMedical.Value = 1 Then
            sum = sum + 25.25
        End If
        lblAmount.Caption = FormatCurrency(sum)
End Sub
```

[Run, and then click on the desired options.]

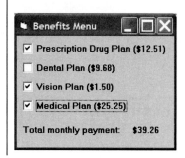

When a check box has the focus, the spacebar can be used to check (or uncheck) the box and invoke the Click event. In addition, the state of a check box can be toggled from the keyboard without first setting the focus to the check box, if you create an access key for the check box by including an ampersand in the Caption property. (Access keys appear underlined at run time.) For instance, if the Caption property for the Dental Plan in Example 1 is set as "&Dental Plan", then the user can check (or uncheck) the box by pressing Alt+D.

Notice that the program code for the solution to Example 1 involved four identical click event procedures. This is a good indication that a control array of check boxes will simplify the program, as shown in Example 2.

EXAMPLE 2   The following program reworks Example 1 using a control array of check boxes, with an access key for each check box. The program has been made more general and easy to update by placing the name and cost of each benefit plan in the data file BENEFITS.TXT. Each line of the file consists of the name of the plan followed by the cost of the plan, as illustrated by the first line of the file:

"&Prescription Drug Plan", 12.51

Object	Property	Setting
frmBenefits	Caption	Benefits Menu
chkPlan( )	Index	0 through 3
lblTotal	Caption	Total monthly payment:
lblAmount	Caption	$0.00

```
Dim price(0 To 3) As Single 'In (Declarations) section of (General)
Dim sum As Single
```

```
Private Sub Form_Load()
  Dim i As Integer, plan As String, cost As Single
  Open "BENEFITS.TXT" For Input As #1
  For i = 0 To 3
    Input #1, plan, cost
    price(i) = cost
    chkPlan(i).Caption = plan & " (" & FormatCurrency(cost) & ")"
  Next i
  Close #1
  sum = 0
End Sub

Private Sub chkPlan_Click(Index As Integer)
  If chkPlan(Index).Value = 1 Then
      sum = sum + price(Index)
    Else
      sum = sum - price(Index)
  End If
  lblAmount.Caption = FormatCurrency(sum)
End Sub
```

The Value property of a check box also can be set to "2-Grayed". When a grayed square is clicked, it becomes unchecked. When clicked again, it becomes checked.

◉ The Option Button Control

Option buttons are used to give the user a single choice from several options. Normally, a group of several option buttons is attached to a frame or picture box with the single-click-draw technique. Each button consists of a small circle accompanied by text that is set with the Caption property. When a circle or its accompanying text is clicked, a solid dot appears in the circle and the button is said to be "on." At most one option button in a group can be on at the same time. Therefore, if one button is on and another button in the group is clicked, the first button will turn off. By convention, the names of option buttons have the prefix *opt*.

The Value property of an option button tells if the button is on or off. The property

```
optButton.Value
```

is True when optButton is on and False when optButton is off. The statement

```
optButton.Value = True
```

turns on optButton and turns off all other buttons in its group. The statement

```
optButton.Value = False
```

turns off optButton and has no effect on the other buttons in its group.

The Click event for an option button is triggered only when an off button is turned on. It is not triggered when an on button is clicked.

EXAMPLE 3 The following program tells you if an option button is on.

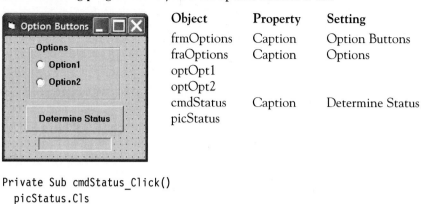

Object	Property	Setting
frmOptions	Caption	Option Buttons
fraOptions	Caption	Options
optOpt1		
optOpt2		
cmdStatus	Caption	Determine Status
picStatus		

```
Private Sub cmdStatus_Click()
  picStatus.Cls
  If optOpt1.Value Then
      picStatus.Print "Option1 is on."
    ElseIf optOpt2.Value Then
      picStatus.Print "Option2 is on."
    Else
      picStatus.Print "Neither is on."
  End If
End Sub

Private Sub Form_Load()
  optOpt1.Value = False    'Turn off optOpt1
  optOpt2.Value = False    'Turn off optOpt2
End Sub
```

[Run, click on one of the option buttons, and then click the command button.]

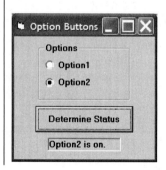

The text alongside an option button is specified with the Caption property. As with a command button and a check box, an ampersand can be used to create an access key for an option button.

EXAMPLE 4 The following program allows the user to select the text size in a text box. The three option buttons have been attached to the frame with the single-click-draw technique.

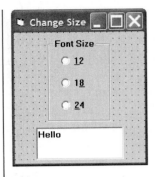

Object	Property	Setting
frmSize	Caption	Change Size
fraFontSize	Caption	Font Size
opt12pt	Caption	&12
opt18pt	Caption	1&8
opt24pt	Caption	&24
txtInfo	Text	Hello

```
Private Sub opt12pt_Click()
  txtInfo.Font.Size = 12
End Sub

Private Sub opt18pt_Click()
  txtInfo.Font.Size = 18
End Sub

Private Sub opt24pt_Click()
  txtInfo.Font.Size = 24
End Sub
```

[Run, and click on the last option button (or press Alt+2).]

A single form can have several groups of option buttons. However, each group must be attached to its own frame or picture box, or to the form itself.

The Horizontal and Vertical Scroll Bar Controls

Figure 11.5 shows the two types of scroll bars. When the user clicks on one of the arrow buttons, the scroll box moves a small amount toward that arrow. When the user clicks between the scroll box and one of the arrow buttons, the scroll box moves a large amount toward that arrow. The user can also move the scroll box by dragging it. The main properties of a scroll bar control are Min, Max, Value, SmallChange, and LargeChange, which are set to integers. At any time, hsbBar.Value is a number between hsbBar.Min and hsbBar.Max determined by the position of the scroll box. If the scroll box is halfway between the two arrows, then hsbBar.Value is a number halfway between hsbBar.Min and hsbBar.Max. If the scroll box is near the left arrow button, then hsbBar.Value is an appropriately proportioned value near hsbBar.Min. When an arrow button is clicked, hsbBar.Value changes by hsbBar.SmallChange and the scroll box moves accordingly. When the bar between the scroll box and one of the arrows is clicked, hsbBar.Value changes by hsbBar.LargeChange and the scroll box moves accordingly. When the scroll box is dragged, hsbBar.Value changes accordingly. The default values of Min, Max, SmallChange, and LargeChange are 0, 32767, 1, and 1, respectively. However, these values are usually reset at design time. Vertical scroll bars behave similarly. **Note:** The setting for the Min property can be a number greater than the setting for the Max property. The Min property determines the values for the left and top arrows. The Max property determines the values for the right and bottom arrows.

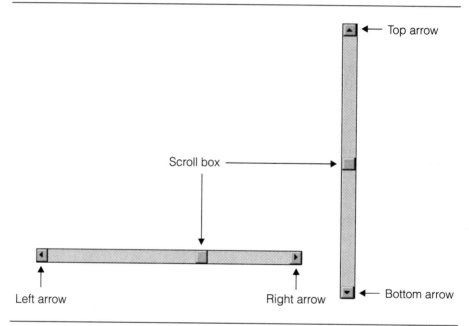

Figure 11.5 Horizontal and vertical scroll bars.

The Change event is triggered whenever an arrow or bar is clicked, or after the scroll box has been dragged. The Scroll event is triggered whenever the scroll box is being dragged.

EXAMPLE 5   The following program uses scroll bars to move a smiling face around the form. The face is a large Wingdings character J inside a label. The values lblFace.Left and lblFace.Top are the distances in twips of the label from the left side and top of the form. (When printing, 1440 twips equal one inch; on the screen, 1440 twips are more or less an inch.)

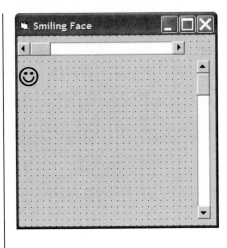

Object	Property	Setting
frmFace	Caption	Smiling Face
hsbXPos	Min	0
	Max	3000
	SmallChange	100
	LargeChange	500
	Value	0
vsbYPos	Min	500
	Max	3000
	SmallChange	100
	LargeChange	500
	Value	500
lblFace	Caption	J
	Font	Wingdings
	Font Size	24
	Left	0
	Top	500

```
Private Sub hsbXPos_Change()
  lblFace.Left = hsbXPos.Value
End Sub

Private Sub vsbYPos_Change()
  lblFace.Top = vsbYPos.Value
End Sub
```

[Run and move the scroll boxes on the scroll bars.]

In Example 5, when you drag the scroll box, the face does not move until the dragging is completed. This can be corrected by adding the following two event procedures.

```
Private Sub hsbXPos_Scroll()
  lblFace.Left = hsbXPos.Value
End Sub

Private Sub vsbYPos_Scroll()
  lblFace.Top = vsbYPos.Value
End Sub
```

⏱ The Timer Control

The timer control, which is invisible during run time, triggers an event after a specified amount of time has passed. The length of time, measured in milliseconds, is set with the Interval property to be any number from 0 to 65,535 (about 1 minute and 5 seconds). The event triggered each time Timer1.Interval milliseconds elapses is called Timer1_Timer( ). In order to begin timing, a timer must first be turned on by setting its Enabled property to True. A timer is turned off either by setting its Enabled property to False or by setting its Interval property to 0. The standard prefix for the name of a timer control is *tmr*.

EXAMPLE 6 The following program creates a stopwatch that updates the time every tenth of a second.

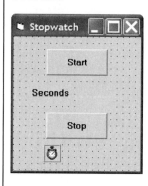

Object	Property	Setting
frmWatch	Caption	Stopwatch
cmdStart	Caption	Start
lblSeconds	Caption	Seconds
lblTime	Caption	(blank)
cmdStop	Caption	Stop
tmrWatch	Interval	100
	Enabled	False

```
Private Sub cmdStart_Click()
  lblTime.Caption = "0"     'Reset watch
  tmrWatch.Enabled = True
End Sub

Private Sub cmdStop_Click()
  tmrWatch.Enabled = False
End Sub

Private Sub tmrWatch_Timer()
  lblTime.Caption = Str(Val(lblTime.Caption) + .1)
End Sub
```

[Run, click on the Start button, wait 10.6 seconds, and click on the Stop button.]

⬚ The Shape Control

The shape control assumes one of six possible predefined shapes depending on the value of its Shape property. Figure 11.6 shows the six shapes and the values of their corresponding Shape properties. Shapes are usually placed on a form at design time for decoration or to highlight certain parts of the form. By convention, names of shape controls have the prefix *shp*.

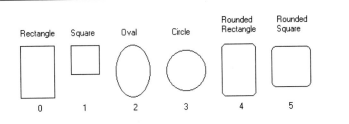

Figure 11.6 The six possible shapes for a shape control.

The most useful properties of shapes are BackStyle (transparent vs. opaque; see Figure 11.7), BorderWidth (thickness of border), BorderStyle (solid, dashed, dotted, etc.), BackColor (background color), FillStyle (fill-in pattern: horizontal lines, upward diagonal lines, etc., as in Figure 10.28), FillColor (color used by FillStyle), and Visible.

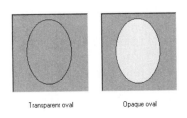

Figure 11.7 Effect of the value of the BackStyle property.

Figure 11.8 shows several effects that can be achieved with shapes. In the first effect, a command button is set off by placing it on top of a rounded rectangle shape whose BackStyle is opaque, BackColor is blue, FillStyle is downward diagonal, and FillColor is yellow. In the second effect, the icon (displayed in an appropriately sized, borderless picture box) is "framed" by placing it on top of an oval shape whose BackStyle is opaque and BackColor is the same as the background color of the icon. In the last effect, two command buttons are tied together by surrounding them with a circle shape whose FillStyle is transparent, BorderWidth is 8, and BorderColor is green, and by placing behind the command buttons an oval shape whose FillStyle is transparent, BorderWidth is 3, and BorderColor is blue.

Figure 11.8 Several effects achieved with shape controls.

 The Line Control

The line control, which produces lines of various thickness, styles, and colors, is primarily used to enhance the visual appearance of forms. The most useful properties of lines are BorderColor (color of the line), BorderWidth (thickness of the line), BorderStyle (solid, dashed, dotted, etc.), and Visible. Figure 11.9 shows several effects that can be achieved with lines. By convention, names of line controls have the prefix *lin*.

Figure 11.9 Several effects achieved with line controls.

The Image Control

The image control is designed to hold pictures stored in graphics files such as .BMP files created with Windows' Paint, ICO files of icons that come with Visual Basic, or GIF and JPEG images used on the World Wide Web. Pictures are placed in image controls with the Picture property. If you double-click on the Picture property during design time, a file-selection dialog box appears and assists you in selecting an appropriate file. However, prior to setting the Picture property, you should set the Stretch property. If the Stretch property is set to False (the default value), the image control will be resized to fit the picture. If the Stretch property is set to True, the picture will be resized to fit the image control. Therefore, with the Stretch property set to True, pictures can be reduced (by placing them into a small image control) or enlarged (by placing them into an image control bigger than the picture). Figure 11.10 shows a picture created with Paint and reduced to several different sizes. By convention, names of image controls have the prefix *img*.

A picture can be assigned to an image control at run time. However, a statement such as

```
imgBox.Picture = "filespec"
```

will not do the job. Instead, we must use the LoadPicture function in a statement such as

```
imgBox.Picture = LoadPicture("filespec")
```

Image controls enhance the visual appeal of programs. Also, because image controls respond to the Click event and can receive the focus, they can serve as pictorial command buttons.

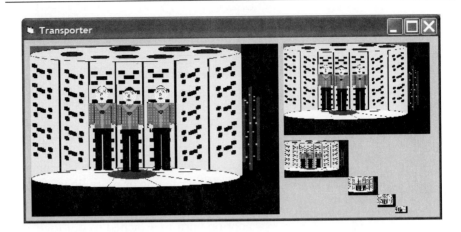

Figure 11.10 A picture created with Paint and reduced several times.

Comments

1. When placing line and shape controls on a form, greater precision can be achieved by first turning off the "Align Controls to Grid" option in the General tab of the Options submenu of the Tools menu.

2. Although frames cannot receive the focus, they can have an access key that sends the focus to the first control inside the frame that can receive the focus.

3. You can paste a picture into an image control by copying it from your paint program and pressing Crl+V with the image control selected.

✔ PRACTICE PROBLEMS 11.2

1. Suppose you create a frame and then drag a preexisting text box into the frame. How will this text box differ from a text box that was attached to the frame by the single-click-draw method?

2. What is the difference between a group of check boxes attached to a frame and a group of option buttons attached to a frame?

➤ EXERCISES 11.2

In Exercises 1 through 18, determine the effect of setting the property to the value shown.

1. `Frame1.Caption = "Income"`

2. `Check1.Value = 1`

3. `Check1.Value = 0`

4. `Check1.Caption = "&Vanilla"`

5. `Option1.Value = False`

6. `Option1.Caption = "Punt"`

7. `HScroll2.Value = HScroll2.Max`

8. `HScroll2.Value = (HScroll2.Max + HScroll2.Min) / 2`

9. `VScroll2.SmallChange = VScroll2.LargeChange`

10. `Timer1.Interval = 5000`   **11.** `Timer1.Interval = 0`

12. `Timer1.Enabled = False`   **13.** `Shape1.Shape = 2`

14. `Shape2.BackColor = Shape1.BackColor`

15. `Shape1.FillStyle = 6`   **16.** `Line1.Visible = False`

17. `Line1.BorderWidth = 2 * Line1.BorderWidth`

18. `Image1.Stretch = True`

In Exercises 19 through 28, write one or more lines of code to carry out the task.

19. A frame has two option buttons attached to it. Move all three objects 100 twips to the right.

20. Clear the small rectangular box of Check1.

21. Turn off Option2.

22. Move the scroll box of VScroll2 as high as possible.

23. Move the scroll box of HScroll2 one-third of the way between the left arrow and the right arrow.

24. Specify that Timer1 trigger an event every half second.

25. Specify that Timer1 trigger an event every 2 minutes and 10 seconds. **Hint:** Use a form-level variable called *flag*.

26. Make Shape1 a circle.

27. Fill Shape1 with vertical lines.

28. Make Image1 vanish.

In Exercises 29 and 30, determine the state of the two option buttons after the command button is clicked.

29.
```
Private Sub Command1_Click()
    Option1.Value = True
    Option2.Value = True
End Sub
```

30.
```
Private Sub Command1_Click()
    Option1.Value = False
    Option2.Value = False
End Sub
```

31. Which of the controls presented in this section can receive the focus? Design a form containing all of the controls, and repeatedly press the Tab key to confirm your answer.

32. Create a form with two frames, each having two option buttons attached to it. Run the program and confirm that the two pairs of option buttons operate independently of each other.

33. Suppose a frame has two option buttons attached to it. If the statement Frame1.Visible = False is executed, will the option buttons also vanish? Test your answer.

34. Why are option buttons also called "radio buttons"?

A form contains a command button, a small picture box, and a frame with three check boxes (Check1, Check2, and Check3) attached to it. In Exercises 35 and 36, write a Click event procedure for the command button that displays the stated information in the picture box when the command button is clicked.

35. The number of boxes checked.

36. The captions of the checked boxes.

37. A computer dealer offers two basic computers, the Deluxe ($1500) and the Super ($1700). The customer can order any of the following additional options: multimedia kit ($300), internal modem ($100), or 256MB of added memory ($50). Write a program that computes the cost of the computer system selected.

38. Item 37a of Form 1040 for the U.S. Individual Income Tax Return reads as follows:

37a Check if: ☐ **You** were 65 or older, ☐ Blind; ☐ **Spouse** was 65 or older, ☐ Blind
Add the number of boxes checked above and enter the total here → 37a ☐

Write a program that looks at the checked boxes and displays the value for the large square.

39. Write a program for the Font Style form in Figure 11.11. The style of the words in the text box should be determined by the settings in the two frames.

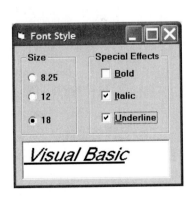

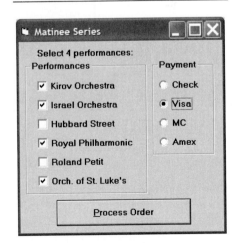

Figure 11.11 Form for Exercise 39.   **Figure 11.12** Form for Exercise 40.

40. Subscribers to the Matinee Series for a recent season at the Kennedy Center for the Performing Arts had to select four performances out of the six shown in the Matinee Series form in Figure 11.12 and had to indicate the method of payment. Write the Click event procedure for the command button. The procedure should first determine whether exactly four performances have been checked. If not, the user should be so informed with a message dialog box. Then the method of payment should be examined. If no method has been indicated, the user must be reminded to select one. Depending on the method of payment, the user should be told with a message dialog box to either mail in the check with the order form or give the credit card number with an input dialog box request. At the end of the process, the caption on the command button should change to "Thank You".

41. Create a form with a line, an oval, and a horizontal scroll bar. Write a program that uses the scroll bar to alter the thickness of the line and the oval from 1 through 12. At any time, the number for the thickness should be displayed in a label.

42. *Simulation of Times Square Ball.* Create a form with a vertical scroll bar and a timer control. When the program is run, the scroll box should be at the top of the scroll bar. Each second the scroll box should descend one-tenth of the way down. When the scroll box reaches the bottom after 10 seconds, a message box displaying HAPPY NEW YEAR should appear.

43. Write a program to synchronize the two thermometers shown in the Temperatures form in Figure 11.13. When the scroll box of either thermometer is moved, the other thermometer moves to the corresponding temperature and each temperature is displayed above the thermometer.

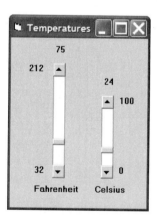

Figure 11.13 Form for Exercise 43.

Figure 11.14 Form for Exercise 44.

44. Write a program to create a decorative digital clock. The clock in the Digital Clock form in Figure 11.14 is inserted in an image control containing any .BMP picture. The values for hour, minute, and second can be obtained as Hour(Now), Minute(Now), and Second(Now) and can be formatted with the FormatNumber function.

45. The Pictures directory of the CD accompanying this text contains files named MOON1.BMP, MOON2.BMP, . . . , MOON8.BMP, which show eight phases of the moon. Create a form consisting of an image control, a timer control, and a file list box. Set the Path property of the file list box to the directory containing the moon icons (such as "D:\PICTURES"), set the Pattern property to MOON?.BMP, and set the Visible property to False. Every two seconds assign another file from the file list box to the Picture property of the Image control to see the moon cycle through its phases every 16 seconds. One phase is shown in Figure 11.15.

Figure 11.15 Form for Exercise 45.

✔✔ **Solutions to Practice Problems 11.2**

1. The text box attached by the single-click-draw method will move with the frame, whereas the other text box will not.

2. With option buttons, at most one button can be on at any given time, whereas several check boxes can be checked simultaneously.

11.3 FIVE ADDITIONAL OBJECTS

In this section we discuss three controls and two objects that are not controls. The three controls are the Microsoft FlexGrid control (a custom control), the menu control (not accessed through the Toolbox), and the common dialog box control (a custom control). The two objects are the clipboard and the form. The discussion of the form deals with the use of multiple forms.

▦ The Microsoft FlexGrid Control

The FlexGrid control does not initially appear in your Toolbox. To add the control, click on Components in the Project menu, click the Controls tab, and click on the check box to the left of "Microsoft FlexGrid Control 6.0." Then press the OK button. By convention, names of Microsoft FlexGrids have the prefix *msg*.

A grid is a rectangular array used to display tables or to create spreadsheet-like applications. The grid in Figure 11.16 has 6 rows and 7 columns. The number of rows and columns can be specified at design time with the Rows and Cols properties or at run time with statements such as `msgFlex.Rows = 6` and `msgFlex.Cols = 7`. Rows and columns are numbered beginning with 0. For instance, the rows in Figure 11.16 are numbered (from top to bottom) as 0, 1, 2, 3, 4, and 5.

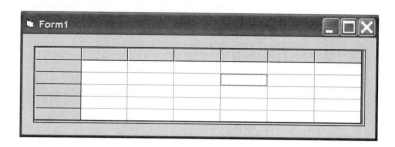

Figure 11.16 A simple FlexGrid control.

The width, measured in twips (there are about 1440 twips to an inch), of each column can be specified only at run-time with the ColWidth property. A typical statement is `msgFlex.ColWidth(3) = 1200`, which sets the width of column 3 to 1200 twips. (The default column width is 555 twips.) Similarly, the RowHeight property specifies the height of each row. The width and height of the entire grid can be specified at design time by dragging the mouse or by setting the Width and Height properties.

The grayed row and column in Figure 11.16 are referred to as **fixed**. Fixed rows and columns must be at the top and left sides of the grid. The number of fixed rows and columns is specified by the FixedRows and FixedCols properties. The grid in Figure 11.16 has the default settings FixedRows = 1 and FixedCols = 1.

If the width of the grid is too small to show all the columns, a horizontal scroll bar will automatically appear across the bottom of the grid. Then, during run-time, the nonfixed columns can be scrolled to reveal the hidden columns. Similarly, a vertical scroll bar appears when the height of the grid is too small to show all the rows. Scroll bars can be suppressed by setting the ScrollBars property of the grid to 0 – flexScrollBarNone. (The default value of the ScrollBars property is 3 – flexScrollBarBoth.)

The individual small rectangles are called **cells.** Each cell is identified by its row and column numbers. At any time, one cell is singled out as the **current cell.** Initially, the cell in row 1, column 1 is the current cell. The pair of statements `msgFlex.Row = m`, `msgFlex.Col = n` set the current cell to the cell in the mth row and nth column. When the user clicks on a nonfixed cell, it becomes the current cell. The cell's border becomes dotted, its row number is assigned to the Row property, and its column number is assigned to the Col property. (In Figure 11.16, the cell in row 2, column 4 is the current cell.) The horizontal and vertical lines forming the cells can be turned off by setting the GridLines property to 0 – flexGridNone.

Unfortunately, you can't just place text into a cell by clicking on the cell and typing, as you would with a text box. The statement `msgFlex.Text = str` places the value of str into the current cell and the statement str = `msgFlex.Text` reads the contents of the current cell. The text inside all the nonfixed cells of column n can be displayed left-aligned, right-aligned, or centered with a statement of the form `msgFlex.ColAlignment(n) = r`, where r is 1 for left-alignment, 7 for right-alignment, and 4 for centered. The fixed cells of column n can be justified with a statement of the form `msgFlex.FixedAlignment(n) = r`.

EXAMPLE I

The following program uses a grid to display an improved version of the table of student expenses from Example 5 of Section 3.5. The five expense categories and numeric data for the table are stored in the file COLLEGECOSTS.TXT. Each record of the file consists of a string followed by four numbers.

Object	Property	Setting
frmCosts	Caption	Average Expenses of Commuter Students (2002–2003)
msgCosts	BorderStyle	0 – flexBorderNone
	Cols	5
	FixedCols	0
	FixedRows	0
	Font	Courier New
	GridLines	0 – flexGridNone
	Rows	9
	ScrollBars	0 – flexScrollBarNone

```
Private Sub Form_Load()
  Dim rowNum As Integer, colNum As Integer
  Dim strData As String, numData As Single
  'Column headings
  msgCosts.Row = 0
  msgCosts.Col = 1
  msgCosts.Text = "Pb 2-yr"
  msgCosts.Col = 2
  msgCosts.Text = "Pr 2-yr"
  msgCosts.Col = 3
  msgCosts.Text = "Pb 4-yr"
  msgCosts.Col = 4
  msgCosts.Text = "Pr 4-yr"
  'Read data from text file and obtain column totals
  Dim total(1 To 4) As Single
  Open "COLLEGECOSTS.TXT" For Input As #1
  For rowNum = 2 To 6    'row 0 holds headings, row 1 is blank
    For colNum = 0 To 4
      msgCosts.Row = rowNum
      msgCosts.Col = colNum
      If colNum = 0 Then
          Input #1, strData
          msgCosts.Text = strData
        Else
          Input #1, numData
          msgCosts.Text = FormatCurrency(numData, 0)
          total(colNum) = total(colNum) + numData
      End If
    Next colNum
  Next rowNum
  'Display totals
  msgCosts.Row = 8
  msgCosts.Col = 0
  msgCosts.Text = "Total"
```

```
  For colNum = 1 To 4
    msgCosts.Col = colNum
    msgCosts.Row = 7
    msgCosts.Text = "-------"
    msgCosts.Row = 8
    msgCosts.Text = FormatCurrency(total(colNum), 0)
  Next colNum
  'Set column widths to accommodate data; right-justify dollar amounts
  msgCosts.ColWidth(0) = 2000            'Space for category names
  msgCosts.ColAlignment(0) = 1           'Left alignment
  For colNum = 1 To 4
    msgCosts.ColWidth(colNum) = 1200     'Space for dollar amounts
    msgCosts.ColAlignment(colNum) = 7    'Right alignment
  Next colNum
  'Set overall grid size to minimum needed for the data
  msgCosts.Width = 2000 + 4 * 1200
  msgCosts.Height = 9 * msgCosts.RowHeight(0)
End Sub
```

[Run]

Average Expenses of College Students (2002-2003)	Pb 2-yr	Pr 2-yr	Pb 4-yr	Pr 4-yr
Tuition & Fees	$1,735	$9,890	$4,081	$18,273
Books & Supplies	$727	$766	$786	$807
Room & Board	$5,430	$5,327	$5,582	$6,779
Transportation	$1,104	$1,086	$1,013	$957
Other Expenses	$1,462	$1,476	$1,643	$1,419
	-------	-------	-------	-------
Total	$10,458	$18,545	$13,105	$28,235

EXAMPLE 2 The following program creates a simplified spreadsheet. The user places a number into the active cell by typing the number into an input dialog box. The program keeps a running total of the sum of the numbers.

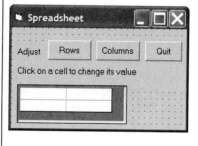

Object	Property	Setting
frmSprdSht	Caption	Spreadsheet
lblAdjust	Caption	Adjust
cmdRows	Caption	Rows
cmdCols	Caption	Columns
cmdQuit	Caption	Quit
lblMsg	Caption	Click on a cell to change its value
msgSprdSht	ScrollBars	0 – flexScrollBarNone
	FixedRows	0
	FixedCols	0
	Font	Courier New

```
'In (Declarations) section of (General)
Dim numRows As Integer        'number of rows
Dim numCols As Integer        'number of columns
```

```
Private Sub cmdRows_Click()
  Dim temp As String
  'Adjust the number of rows in the spreadsheet
  temp = InputBox("Enter new number of rows (4-24):")
  If (Val(temp) >= 4) And (Val(temp) <= 24) Then
      numRows = Val(temp)
      Call SetUpGrid
      Call ShowValues
      Call ShowTotals
  End If
End Sub

Private Sub cmdCols_Click()
  Dim temp As String
  'Adjust number of columns in the spreadsheet
  temp = InputBox("Enter new number of columns (2-7):")
  If (Val(temp) >= 2) And (Val(temp) <= 7) Then
      numCols = Val(temp)
      Call SetUpGrid
      Call ShowValues
      Call ShowTotals
  End If
End Sub

Private Sub cmdQuit_Click()
  End
End Sub

Private Sub Form_Load()
   'Set default number of rows and columns
  numRows = 8 'row 0 is for headings, last 2 rows are for totals
  numCols = 2 'column 0 is for category names
  Call SetUpGrid
  Call ShowValues
  Call ShowTotals
End Sub

Private Sub msgSprdSht_Click()
  Dim temp As String, message As String
  'Obtain new value for cell if it is not in the "total" row
  If messageSprdSht.Row < numRows - 2 Then
      message = "Enter new value for the row "
      message = message & Str(msgSprdSht.Row + 1) & " column "
      message = message & Str(msgSprdSht.Col + 1) & " cell:"
      temp = InputBox(message,,msgSprdSht.Text) 'Propose old value as default
      If (msgSprdSht.Col = 0) Or (msg SprdSht.Row = 0) Then
         msgSprdSht.Text = temp
       Else
         msgSprdsht.Text = FormatNumber(Val(temp), , , , vbFalse)
         Call ShowTotals
      End If
    End If
  End If
End Sub
```

```
Private Sub SetUpGrid()
  Dim colNum As Integer
  'Set up grid
  msgSprdSht.Col = 0
  msgSprdSht.Row = msgSprdSht.Rows - 1
  msgSprdSht.Text = ""              'erase "Total" in case increasing rows
  msgSprdSht.Rows = numRows
  msgSprdSht.Cols = numCols
  'Set column widths; right-justify columns with numeric data
  msgSprdSht.ColWidth(0) = 2000   'space for category names
  msgSprdSht.ColAlignment(0) = 1  'show data left-justified
  For colNum = 1 To numCols - 1
    msgSprdSht.ColWidth(colNum) = 1200   'space for dollar amounts
    msgSprdSht.ColAlignment(colNum) = 7 'show data right-justified
  Next colNum
  'Set overall grid size to minimum needed for the data
  msgSprdSht.Width = 2000 + (numCols - 1) * 1200 + 15 * (numCols + 1) + 8
  msgSprdSht.Height = numRows*msgSprdSht.RowHeight(0)+15*(numRows + 1)+8
  'Adjust form to accommodate grid and other controls
  frmSprdSht.Width = msgSprdSht.Left + msgSprdSht.Width + 200
  frmSprdSht.Height = msgSprdSht.Top + msgSprdSht.Height + 500
  frmSprdSht.Top = 0
  frmSprdSht.Left = 0
End Sub

Private Sub ShowTotals()
  Dim colNum As Integer, rowNum As Integer, total As Single
  'Compute and display total of each numeric column
  msgSprdSht.Row = numRows - 1
  msgSprdSht.Col = 0
  msgSprdSht.Text = "Total"
  For colNum = 1 To numCols - 1
    total = 0
    For rowNum = 1 To numRows - 3
      msgSprdSht.Row = rowNum
      msgSprdSht.Col = colNum
      total = total + Val(msgSprdSht.Text)
    Next rowNum
    msgSprdSht.Row = numRows - 2
    msgSprdSht.Text = "----------------"
    msgSprdSht.Row = numRows - 1
    msgSprdSht.Text = FormatCurrency(total)
  Next colNum
End Sub

Private Sub ShowValues()
  Dim rowNum As Integer, colNum As Integer
  'Refresh values displayed in cells
  For rowNum = 1 To numRows - 1
    For colNum = 1 To numCols - 1
      msgSprdSht.Row = rowNum
      msgSprdSht.Col = colNum
      msgSprdSht.Text = FormatNumber(Val(msgSprdSht.Text), , , , vbFalse)
    Next colNum
  Next rowNum
End Sub
```

[A possible run of the program is shown.]

So far we have used the Text property of grids to place strings into cells. Grids also have a Picture property. A picture (such as a .BMP file created with Paint or an .ICO file from Visual Basic's icon directory) can be placed into the current cell with a statement of the form

```
Set msgFlex.CellPicture = LoadPicture("filespec")
```

If both text and a picture are assigned to a cell, then the picture appears in the upper left portion of the cell, and the text appears to the right of the picture.

The Menu Control

Visual Basic forms can have menu bars similar to those in most Windows applications. Figure 11.17 shows a typical menu, with the Font menu revealed. Here, the menu bar contains two menu items (Font and Size), referred to as **top-level** menu items. When the Font menu item is clicked, a dropdown list of two second-level menu items (Courier and TimesRm) appears. Although not visible here, the dropdown list under Size contains the two second-level menu items "12" and "24". Each menu item is treated as a distinct control that responds to only one event—the click event. The click event is triggered not only by the click of the mouse button, but also for top-level items by pressing Alt+*accessKey* and for second-level items by just pressing the access key. The click event for the Courier menu item in Figure 11.17 can be activated directly by pressing the shortcut key F1.

Figure 11.17 A simple menu.

Menus are created with the Menu Editor window available from the Tools menu on the Visual Basic main menu bar. Figure 11.18 shows the Menu Design window used to create the menu in Figure 11.17. Each menu item has a Caption property (what the user sees) and a Name property (used to refer to the item in the code.) For instance, the last menu item in Figure 11.18 has Caption property "24" and Name property "mnu24". The following steps are used to create the Font-Size menu:

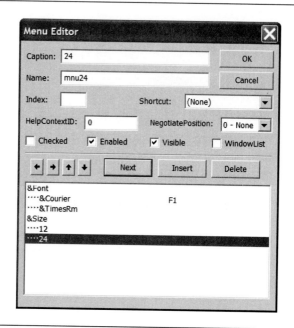

Figure 11.18 The Menu Editor window used to create the menu in Figure 11.17.

1. Type &Font into the Caption box and type mnuFont into the Name box.

2. Click on the Next button.

3. Click on the Right Arrow button. (This creates the ellipses and indents the next menu item, which will be a second-level item.)

4. Type &Courier into the Caption box and type mnuCourier into the Name box.

5. Click on the arrow to the right of the Shortcut box and select F1 from the dropdown list.

6. Click on the Next button.

7. Type &TimesRm into the Caption box and type mnuTimesRm into the Name box.

8. Click on the Next button

9. Click on the Left Arrow button. (This causes the next item to appear flush left to indicate that it is a top-level menu item.)

10. Type &Size into the Caption box and type mnuSize into the Name box.

11. Click on the Next button and then click on the Right Arrow button.

12. Type 12 into the Caption box and type mnu12 into the Name box.

13. Click on the Next button.

14. Type 24 into the Caption box and type mnu24 into the Name box. Your Menu Editor window should now appear as in Figure 11.18.

15. Click the OK button to close the Menu Editor window.

Three of the check boxes on the Menu Editor window are especially useful. When the Checked box is checked, a checkmark appears in front of the menu item. This checkmark can be altered in code with statements such as `mnuItem.Checked = False` and `mnuItem.Checked = True`. When the Enable box is unchecked, the menu item appears gray and does not respond to the click event. The enabled state can be altered in code with statements such as `mnuItem.Enabled = False` and `mnuItem.Enabled = True`. When the Visible property is unchecked, the menu item is invisible.

EXAMPLE 3 The following program creates the application in Figure 11.17, in which the menu is used to alter the appearance of the contents of a text box. The form has the caption "Alter Font & Size" and the properties of the menu items are as created before.

```
Private Sub mnu12_Click()
  txtInfo.Font.Size = 12
End Sub

Private Sub mnu24_Click()
  txtInfo.Font.Size = 24
End Sub

Private Sub mnuCourier_Click()
  txtInfo.Font.Name = "Courier"
End Sub

Private Sub mnuTimesRm_Click()
  txtInfo.Font.Name = "Times New Roman"
End Sub
```

The Clipboard Object

The clipboard object is used to copy or move information from one location to another. It is maintained by Windows and therefore even can be used to transfer information from one Windows application to another. It is actually a portion of memory that holds information and has no properties or events.

If *str* is a string, then the statement

```
Clipboard.SetText str
```

replaces any text currently in the clipboard with *str*. The statement

```
strVar = Clipboard.GetText()
```

assigns the text in the clipboard to the string variable *strVar*.
The statement

```
Clipboard.Clear
```

deletes the contents of the clipboard.

A portion of the text in a text box or combo box can be **selected** by dragging the mouse across it or by moving the cursor across it while holding down the Shift key. After you select text, you can place it into the clipboard by pressing Ctrl+C. Also, if the cursor is in a text box and you press Ctrl+V, the contents of the clipboard will be inserted at the cursor position. These tasks also can be carried out in code. The SelText property of a text box holds the selected string from the text box and a statement such as

```
Clipboard.SetText txtBox.SelText
```

copies this selected string into the clipboard. The statement

```
txtBox.SelText = Clipboard.GetText()
```

replaces the selected portion of txtBox with the contents of the clipboard. If nothing has been selected, the statement inserts the contents of the clipboard into txtBox at the cursor position. The clipboard can actually hold any type of data, including graphics. Any time you use the Copy menu item, you are putting information into the clipboard. The Paste menu item sends that data to your program.

Multiple Forms

A Visual Basic program can contain more than one form. Additional forms are created from the Project menu with Add Form (Alt/P/F/Enter), which brings up an Add Form dialog box. To add a new form select the "New" tab, click on the "Form" icon, and click on "Open." The second form has the default name Form2, the third form has the default name Form3, and so on. The name of each form appears in the Project Explorer window, and any form can be made the active form by double-clicking on its name in this window. Forms are hidden or activated with statements such as

```
Form1.Hide
```

or

```
Form2.Show
```

When a program is run, the first form created is the only one visible. After that, the Hide and Show methods can be used to determine what forms appear.

Often, additional forms, such as message and dialog boxes, are displayed to present a special message or request specific information. When a message or dialog box appears, the user cannot shift the focus to another form without first hiding the message or dialog box by clicking an OK or Cancel command button. If a form is displayed with a statement of the type *formName*.Show 1   or   *formName*.Show vbModal

then the form will exhibit this same behavior. The user will not be allowed to shift the focus back to the calling form until *formName* is hidden. Such a form is said to be **modal**. It is customary to set the BorderStyle property of modal forms to "3-Fixed Dialog".

Each form has its own controls and code. However, code from one form can refer to a control in another form. If so, the control must be prefixed with the name of the other form, followed by a period. For instance, the statement

```
Form2.txtBox.Text = "Hello"
```

in Form1 causes text to be displayed in a text box on Form2. (**Note:** Two forms can have a text box named txtBox. Code using the name txtBox refers to the text box in its own form unless prefixed with the name of another form.)

EXAMPLE 4   The following program uses a second form as a dialog box to total the different sources of income. Initially, only frmIncome is visible. The user types in his or her name and then either can type in the income or click on the command button for assistance in totaling the different sources of income. Clicking on the command button in frmIncome causes frmSources to appear and be active. The user fills in the three text boxes and then clicks on the command button to have the amounts totaled and displayed in the Total Income text box of the first form.

Object	Property	Setting
frmIncome	Caption	Income
lblName	Caption	Name
txtName	Text	(blank)
lblTotal	Caption	Total Income
txtTotal	Text	(blank)
cmdShowTot	Caption	Determine Total Income

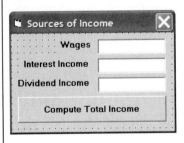

Object	Property	Setting
frmSources	Caption	Sources of Income
	BorderStyle	3 – Fixed Dialog
lblWages	Caption	Wages
txtWages	Text	(blank)
lblInterest	Caption	Interest Income
txtInterest	Text	(blank)
lblDividend	Caption	Dividend Income
txtDividend	Text	(blank)
cmdCompute	Caption	Compute Total Income

```
'frmSources code
Private Sub cmdShowTot_Click()
  frmSources.Show vbModal
End Sub
```

```
'frmIncome code
Private Sub cmdCompute_Click()
  Dim sum As Single
  sum = Val(txtWages.Text) + Val(txtInterest.Text) + Val(txtDividend.Text)
  frmIncome.txtTotal.Text = FormatCurrency(Str(sum))
  frmSources.Hide
End Sub
```

[Run, enter name, click the command button, and fill in the sources of income.] *Note:* After the Compute Total Income button is pressed, frmSources will disappear and the sum of the three numbers will be displayed in the Total Income text box of frmIncome.

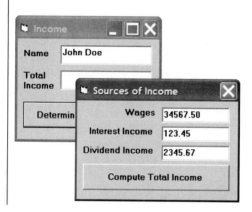

All variables declared and general procedures created in the (General) object of a form are local to that form; that is, they are not available to any other form. Such variables and procedures are said to be of **form level**. However, you can declare global variables and procedures that are available to all forms. To do so, select Add Module from the Project menu and then double-click on the Module icon. A code window will appear with Module1 in the title bar. Procedures created in this window with the Public keyword will be available to all forms. To declare a variable that is available to all forms, declare it in the Module1 window, but use the word Public instead of Dim. For instance, if the statement

```
Public person As String
```

appears in the Module1 code window, the variable *person* can be accessed anywhere in the program.

The contents of this code window are said to form a (Standard) code module. Project Explorer shows the names of all forms and code modules and gives you access to the code from any form or module. When a code module is selected, you can save it by choosing Save Module As from the File menu. You add an existing code module to a program by choosing Add File from the Project menu.

The Common Dialog Control

The common dialog control does not initially appear in your Toolbox. To add the control, select Components from the Project menu, click the Controls tab, and click on the check box to the left of "Microsoft Common Dialog Control 6.0." Then press the OK button. By convention, names of common dialog boxes have the prefix dlg.

The common dialog control can produce each of the useful dialog boxes in Figures 11.19 through 11.23, thereby saving the programmer the trouble of designing custom dialog boxes for these purposes. The common dialog control has no events, only methods and properties. Actually, like the Timer control, the common dialog box control is invisible. However, when you execute a statement of the form

```
CommonDialog1.Show_____
```

where the blank line is filled with Open, Save, Color, Font, or Printer, the specified dialog box is produced. Table 11.4 gives the purposes of the various dialog boxes.

Type of Dialog box	Purpose of Dialog Box
Open	Determine what file to open
Save As	Determine where and with what name to save a file
Color	Select any available color
Font	Select a font for the screen or printer
Print	Help control the printer

Table 11.4 The different types of dialog boxes.

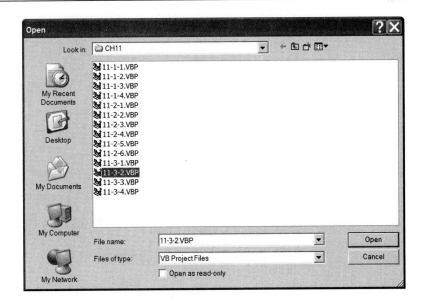

Figure 11.19 An Open common dialog box.

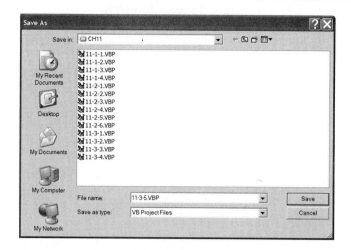

Figure 11.20 A Save As common dialog box.

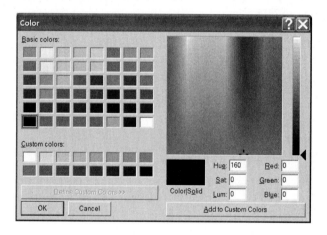

Figure 11.21 A Color common dialog box.

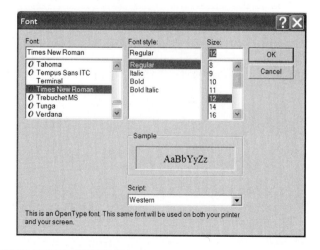

Figure 11.22 A Font common dialog box.

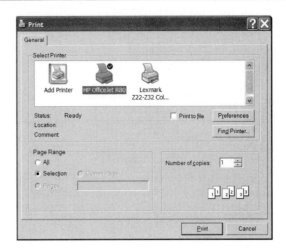

Figure 11.23 A Print common dialog box.

The Flags property influences certain features of the dialog box and should be set prior to setting the Show method. A complete discussion of the Flags property would be too great a digression. For our purposes, we will be well served by always setting the Flags property to 3 with the statement

```
dlgBox.Flags = 3
```

After selections are made from a common dialog box and the OK button is clicked, the values of the selections are stored in properties such as FileName, Color, FontName, FontItalic, FontSize and Copies. For instance, the following event procedure specifies the font for the contents of a text box.

```
Private Sub cmdButton_Click()
  dlgFont.Flags = 3
  dlgFont.ShowFont                'invoke Font common dialog box
  'Select Font, Font style, and Size and then click on OK
  txtBox.Font.Name = dlgFont.FontName
  txtBox.Font.Bold = dlgFont.FontBold
  txtBox.Font.Italic = dlgFont.FontItalic
  txtBox.Font.Size = dlgFont.FontSize
End Sub
```

Table 11.5 gives the principal properties whose setting are garnered from the common dialog boxes.

Type of Common Dialog Box	Principal Properties
Open	FileName
Save As	FileName
Color	Color
Font	FontName, FontSize, FontBold, FontItalic
Print	Copies, FromPage, ToPage

Table 11.5 Principal properties of the common dialog boxes.

With Open and Save As common dialog boxes, a property is needed to specify what types of files should be displayed. A statement of the form

```
dlgFile.Filter = "dscrpt1|filter1|dscrpt2|filter2|dscrpt3|filter3"
```

provides verbal descriptions for the Type box and strings using wildcard characters (filters) to identify the files. A specific statement might be

```
dlgFile.Filter = "Text Files|*.TXT|FRM Files|*.FRM|All Files|*.*"
```

After the filter property is set, the FilterIndex property can be used to set the default filter. For instance, if the preceding statement is followed with

```
dlgFile.FilterIndex = 1
```

the default will be the first pair of filter items. That is, when the dialog box pops up, the Files of type box will display Text Files, and the large box will show only files with the extension TXT.

Comment

1. In the Properties window of a FlexGrid control, one setting of the GridLines property is "0 – flexGridNone." In code, this setting can be invoked with either

```
msgFlex.GridLines = 0
```

or

```
msgFlex.GridLines = flexGridNone
```

✔ **PRACTICE PROBLEMS 11.3**

1. What is the difference between the Row property and the Rows property of a FlexGrid control?

2. What is the effect of the statement `txtBox.SelText = ""`?

➤ **EXERCISES 11.3**

In Exercises 1 through 32, describe the effect of executing the statement.

1. `msgFlex.Cols = 5`   **2.** `msgFlex.Rows = 3`

3. `msgFlex.RowHeight(3) = 400`   **4.** `msgFlex.ColWidth(2) = 2000`

5. `msgFlex.FixedCols = 2`   **6.** `msgFlex.FixedRows = 2`

7. `msgFlex.Row = 3`   **8.** `msgFlex.Col = 4`

9. `msgFlex.Text = "Income"`   **10.** `amount = Val(msgFlex.Text)`

11. `msgFlex.ColAlignment(3) = 4`   **12.** `msgFlex.ColAlignment(2) = 1`

13. `msgFlex.GridLines = 0`   **14.** `msgFlex.GridLines = 3`

15. `msgFlex.ScrollBars = 0`

16. `mnuCopy.Enabled = False`

17. `mnuCut.Enabled = True`

18. `mnuPaste.Checked = True`

19. `mnuSave.Checked = False`

20. `phrase = Clipboard.GetText()`

21. `Clipboard.Clear`

22. `Clipboard.SetText "Hello"`

23. `Clipboard.SetText txtBox.SelText`

24. `txtBox.SelText = Clipboard.GetText()`

25. `frmTwo.Show`

26. `frmTwo.Show 1`

27. `frmOne.Hide`

28. `Public amount As Single`

29. `dlgBox.ShowColor`

30. `dlgBox.ShowFont`

31. `dlgBox.Filter = "All Files|*.*|Text Files|*.TXT|"`

32. `dlgBox.FilterIndex = 2`

In Exercises 33 through 64, write one or more lines of code to carry out the task.

33. Set the number of rows in msgFlex to 7.

34. Set the number of columns in msgFlex to 5.

35. Set the width of the first column of msgFlex to 3000 twips.

36. Set the height of the first row of msgFlex to 300 twips.

37. Fix the top two rows of msgFlex.

38. Fix the leftmost column of msgFlex.

39. Specify that the current cell of msgFlex be in the third column (that is, column number 2).

40. Specify that the current cell of msgFlex be in the fourth row (that is, row number 3).

41. Display the contents of the current cell of msgFlex in picBox.

42. Place the number 76 into the current cell of msgFlex.

43. Right-align the contents of the cells in the second column of msgFlex.

44. Center the contents of the nonfixed cells in the third column of msgFlex.

45. Show grid lines in msgFlex.

46. Delete grid lines from msgFlex.

47. Disable the menu item mnuExit and make it appear gray.

48. Ungray the menu item mnuExit.

49. Place a check mark to the left of the menu item mnuNormal.

50. Remove a check mark from the left of the menu item mnuBold.

51. Assign the contents of the clipboard to the variable *street*.

52. Clear out the contents of the clipboard.

53. Place the word "Happy" into the clipboard.

54. Copy the selected text in txtBox into the clipboard.

55. Insert the contents of the clipboard at the cursor position in txtBox.

56. Replace the selected portion of txtBox by the contents of the clipboard.

57. Delete the selected portion of txtBox.

58. Display frmTwo as a nonmodal form.

59. Display frmTwo as a modal form.

60. Declare the variable *wholeNumber* as an Integer variable recognized by every form.

61. Remove frmTwo from the screen.

62. Specify that a Save As dialog box be displayed in a common dialog box.

63. Specify that an Open dialog box be displayed in a common dialog box.

64. Specify that the types of files listed in a Save As or Open dialog box's Type list box be of the types "*.vbp" or "*.frm".

In Exercises 65 and 66, determine what happens to msgFlex when the command button is clicked.

65.
```
Private Sub cmdButton_Click()
    msgFlex.Row = 4
    msgFlex.Col = 5
    msgFlex.Text = Str(32)
End Sub
```

66.
```
Private Sub cmdButton_Click()
    Dim i As Integer, j As Integer
    For i = 0 To 5
      msgFlex.Row = i
      For j = 0 To 5
        msgFlex.Col = j
        msgFlex.Text = Str(i) & "," & Str(j)
      Next j
    Next i
End Sub
```

67. Write a program to create the powers-of-two table shown in Figure 11.24.

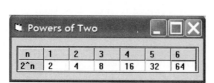

Figure 11.24 Table for Exercise 67.

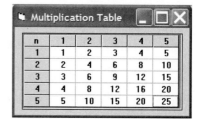

Figure 11.25 Table for Exercise 68.

68. Write a program to create the multiplication table shown in Figure 11.25.

69. Write a program to produce a spreadsheet that serves as an order form. The grid should have three columns headed "Description," "Qty.," and "Price Each". The user should be able to fill in an entry by clicking on it and then responding to an input dialog box. When the command button is clicked, the total cost of the order should appear in a picture box. A sample run is shown in Figure 11.26.

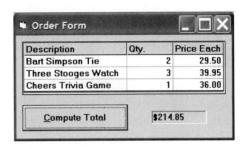

Figure 11.26 Sample run of Exercise 69.

70. The Colleges form in Figure 11.27 contains information about five colleges where the author of this book either attended or taught. Write a program to place the data into a grid as shown. When a nonfixed cell is clicked, the program should sort the entire grid by the heading of the cell's column. For instance, if a year is clicked, the colleges should reappear in order of their age.

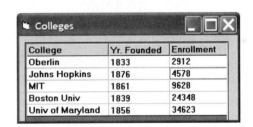

Figure 11.27 Form with data in grid for Exercise 70.

71. Redo Exercise 70 with a menu and include a search capability. The top-level items should be Sort (with second-level items College, Year Founded, Enrollment) and Search (with second-level items College and Year Founded). The sort should be the same as in Exercise 70. The search options should allow the user to enter a college or a year into an input dialog box and should display the relevant information about the row containing the college or year. If the college or year cannot be found, the user should be so informed.

72. Modify the spreadsheet program in Example 2 to add an additional column on the right to hold the sums of the rows. Also, a thin column should be added before the final sums column to set it off.

73. Modify the spreadsheet program in Example 2 to sum only the changed column when the msgSprdSht_Click event is called.

74. Write a program with a single text box and a menu with the single top-level item Edit and the four second-level items Copy, Paste, Cut, and Exit. Copy should place a copy of the selected portion of txtBox into the clipboard, Paste should duplicate the contents of the clipboard at the cursor position, Cut should delete a selected portion of the text box and place it in the clipboard, and Exit should terminate the program.

75. Write a program containing the two forms shown in Figure 11.28. Initially, the Number to Dial form appears. When the Show Push Buttons command button is clicked, the Push Button form appears. The user enters a number by clicking on successive push buttons and then clicks on Enter to have the number transferred to the label at the bottom of the first form.

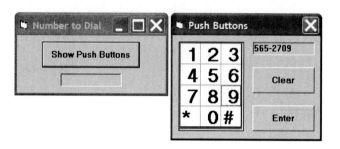

Figure 11.28 Sample run of Exercise 75.

76. Consider the Select Style form shown in Figure 11.29. Write a program to select the color and the font for the text box. When the user clicks on a command button, the corresponding custom dialog box should appear to expedite the choice.

Figure 11.29 Form for Exercise 76.

✔✔ **Solutions to Practice Problems 11.3**

1. The Rows property determines how many rows a grid contains, and the Row property specifies which row in the grid contains the current cell.

2. If part of the contents of txtBox has been selected, the selected text will be deleted. Otherwise, nothing happens.

CHAPTER 11   SUMMARY

1. *List boxes* provide easy access to lists of strings. The array List( ) holds the items stored in the list. Each item is identified by an index number (0, 1, 2, . . .). The lists can be automatically sorted (Sorted property = True) or altered (AddItem, RemoveItem, and Clear methods), the currently highlighted item identified (Text property), and the number of items determined (List-Count property). The most recently inserted item can be determined with the NewIndex property. The ItemData property associates a number with each item of text.

2. *Combo boxes* are enhanced text boxes. They not only allow the user to enter information by typing it into a text box (read with the Text property), but also allow the user to select the information from a list of items.

3. *Drive, directory,* and *file list boxes* are specialized list boxes managed largely by Windows. The selected items are identified by the Drive, Path, and File-Name properties, respectively. A directory list box always displays the subdirectories of the directory identified by its Path property, and a files list box displays the files in the directory identified by its Path property.

4. Selections are made with *check boxes* (allow several) and *option buttons* (allow at most one). The state of the control (*checked* vs. *unchecked* or *on* vs. *off*) is stored in the Value property. Clicking on a check box toggles its state. Clicking on an option button gives it the *on* state and turns *off* the other option buttons in its group.

5. *Frames* are used to group controls, especially option buttons, as a unit.

6. *Horizontal* and *vertical scroll bars* permit the user to select from among a range of numbers by clicking or dragging with the mouse. The range is specified by the Min and Max properties, and new settings trigger the Click and Change events.

7. The *timer control* triggers an event repeatedly after the duration of a specified time interval.

8. The *shape* and *line controls* enhance the visual look of a form with rectangles, ovals, circles, and lines of different size, thickness, and color.

9. The *image control*, which displays pictures or icons, can either expand to accommodate the size of the drawing or have the drawing alter its size to fit the image control.

10. A Microsoft FlexGrid control is a rectangular array of cells, each identified by a row and column number. The numbers of rows and columns are specified by the Rows and Cols properties. If the size of the grid is larger than provided by the control, scroll bars can be used to look at different parts of the grid. The FixedRows and FixedCols properties fix a certain number of the top rows and leftmost columns so that they will not scroll. The Row and Col properties are used to designate one cell as *current*. The Text property is used to read or place text into the current cell.

11. *Menus,* similar to the menus of Visual Basic itself, can be created with the Menu Design window.

12. The *clipboard* is filled with the SetText method or by pressing Ctrl+C, and is copied with the GetText function or with Ctrl+V.

13. *Additional forms* serve as new windows or dialog boxes. They are revealed with the Show method and concealed with the Hide method.

14. *Common dialog boxes* provide a standard way of specifying files, colors, and fonts, and of communicating with the printer.

CHAPTER 11   PROGRAMMING PROJECTS

1. *Membership List.* Write a menu-driven program to manage a membership list. (See the following Membership List form.) Assume that the names and phone numbers of all members are stored in the sequential file MEMBERS.TXT. The names should be read into the list box when the form is loaded, and the phone numbers should be read into an array. When a name is highlighted, both the name and phone number of the person should appear in the text boxes at the bottom of the screen. To delete a person, highlight his or her name and click on the Delete menu item. To change either the phone number or the spelling of the person's name, make the corrections in the text boxes, and click on the menu item Modify. To add a new member, type his or her name and phone number into the text boxes, and click on the menu item Add. When Exit is clicked, the new membership list should be written to a file, and the program should terminate.

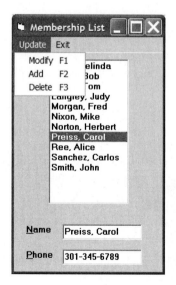

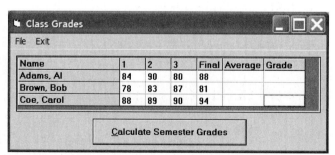

2. *Grade Book.* Write a comprehensive program that a professor could use to record student grades for several classes and save the records in sequential files. (See the preceding Class Grades form.) Each class has three hourly exams and a final exam. The file for a single class should consist of the number of students in the class, call it *n*, and a record of five fields (name, grade1, grade2, grade3, final) for each student, with the records ordered alphabetically by the student's name. (A typical name might appear as "Doe, John".)

Initially, the four grade fields should contain zeros. The program should contain a top-level menu item, File, with second-level subitems for Open, Save, Add Student, Remove Student. When a file is opened (via a file list directory or common dialog box), the data for the students should be loaded into a grid of n + 1 rows and 7 columns. (The last two columns should remain blank.) The professor should be able to enter (or alter) exam data by clicking on the cell and responding to an input dialog box. When a student is added, the grid should be enlarged by one row and the student inserted in proper alphabetical position. When a student is deleted, the grid should be reduced by one row. When the Calculate Semester Grades button is clicked, the last two columns should be filled in by the program. (Assume that the final exam counts as two hour exams.) If a grade is changed after the last two columns have been filled in, the corresponding average and grade should be recomputed.

3. *Tic-Tac-Toe.* Write a program that "officiates" a game of tic-tac-toe. That is, the program should allow two players to alternate entering X's and O's into a tic-tac-toe board until either someone wins or a draw is reached. If one of the players wins, the program should announce the winner immediately; in case of a draw, the program should display "Cat's game". The players should enter their plays by clicking on the desired cell in the tic-tac-toe grid, and the program should check that each play is valid. **Optional Enhancement:** Allow the players to enter a number n. The program should officiate a best-of-n tournament, keeping track of the number of games won by each player until one of them wins more than half of the games. Ignore draws.

4. *Hangman.* Write a program to play Hangman. (See the following Hangman form.) A list of 20 words should be placed in a sequential file and one selected at random with Rnd. The program should do the following:

   (a) Draw a gallows on the screen with three line controls.
   (b) Create a grid having 1 row and 26 columns, and fill the grid with the 26 letters of the alphabet.
   (c) Create a second grid of one row and the number of columns equal to the length of the word selected.
   (d) Each time the user clicks on one of the letters of the alphabet, that letter should be removed. If the letter is in the selected word, its location(s) should be revealed in the second grid. If the letter is not in the word, another piece of the man should be drawn with a shape control.

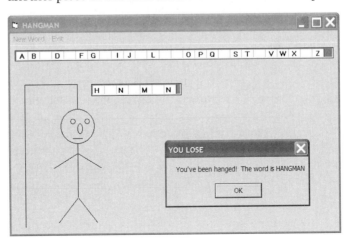

5. *Inventory Control.* Write an inventory program for a book store, and save the information in a sequential file. Each record should consist of five fields—title, author, category, wholesale price, and number in stock. (The two categories are fiction and nonfiction.) At any time, the program should display the titles of the books in stock in a list box, for which the user should have the option of displaying either all titles or just those in one of the two categories. When a book is selected from the list, its title, author, category, wholesale price, and number in stock should be displayed in a picture box. The user should be able to add a new book, delete a book, or change the inventory level of a book in stock. At any time, the user should be able to calculate the total value of all books, or the total value of the books in either category.

6. *Voting Machine.* The members of the local Gilligan's Island fan club bring a computer to their annual meeting to use in the election of a new president. Write a program to handle the election. The program should add each candidate to a list box as he or she is nominated. After the nomination process is complete, club members should be able to approach the computer one at a time and double-click on the candidate of their choice. When a "Tally Votes" command button is clicked, a second list box, showing the number of votes received by each candidate, should appear alongside the first list box. Also, the name(s) of the candidate(s) with the highest number of votes should be displayed in a picture box.

7. *Airplane Seating Chart.* An airplane has 30 rows (numbered 1 through 30), with 6 seats (labeled A, B, C, D, E, and F) in each row. Write a program to display a 7-by-31 grid with a cell for each seat. As each passenger selects a seat and a meal (regular, low-calorie, or vegetarian), the ticket agent clicks on the cell corresponding to the seat. A dialog box requests the type of meal and then one of the letters R, L, or V is placed in the cell clicked. At any time, the agent can request the number of seats filled, the number of window seats vacant, and the numbers of each type of meal ordered.

8. *The Underdog and the World Series.* What is the probability that the underdog will win the World Series of Baseball? What is the average number of games for a World Series? Write an animated program to answer these questions. For instance, suppose that the underdog is expected to win 40% of the time. We say that the probability of the underdog winning a game is .40. (**Note:** In order for a team to be the underdog, the probability that the team wins a game must be less than .50.) Figure 11.30 shows that the probability that the underdog wins the World Series is about 28.13% and that such a series should be expected to last an average of about 5.68 games. The program should simulate the playing of 10,000 World Series where the underdog has the probability of winning input in the text box. The values of the horizontal scroll bars should extend from 0 to 10000 and should be calculated after each series so that the scroll boxes steadily move across the bars. **Note 1:** In order for the label to the right of the scroll bars to display data as the program progresses (and not just at the end of the program), execute a statement such as lblUnderdogTotal.Refresh in each of the 10,000 passes through the loop. **Note 2:** A condition that will be true 40% of the time is (Rnd < .40).

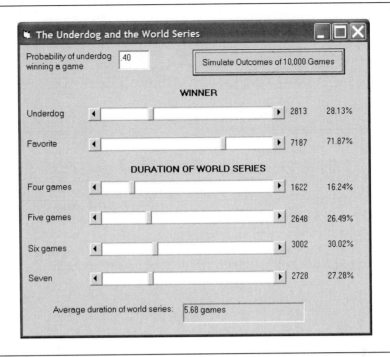

Figure 11.30 A sample run of Programming Project 8.

9. The admissions offices of large colleges often rely on a point system. A point system similar to the one in Figure 11.31 is used by a large state university. Write a program that displays the information in Figure 11.31 and allows an admissions officer to determine whether an applicant should be admitted. The numbers in brackets give the point count for each response. The GPA score displayed in the label to the right of the horizontal scroll bar should change (from 2.0 to 4.0 in steps of .1) as the user clicks on the bar's right arrow. The point value in the brackets to the right of the label is 20 times the GPA. A total of at most 40 points can be earned for the responses below the line. The program should calculate the total score and then accept every applicant whose score is at least 100.

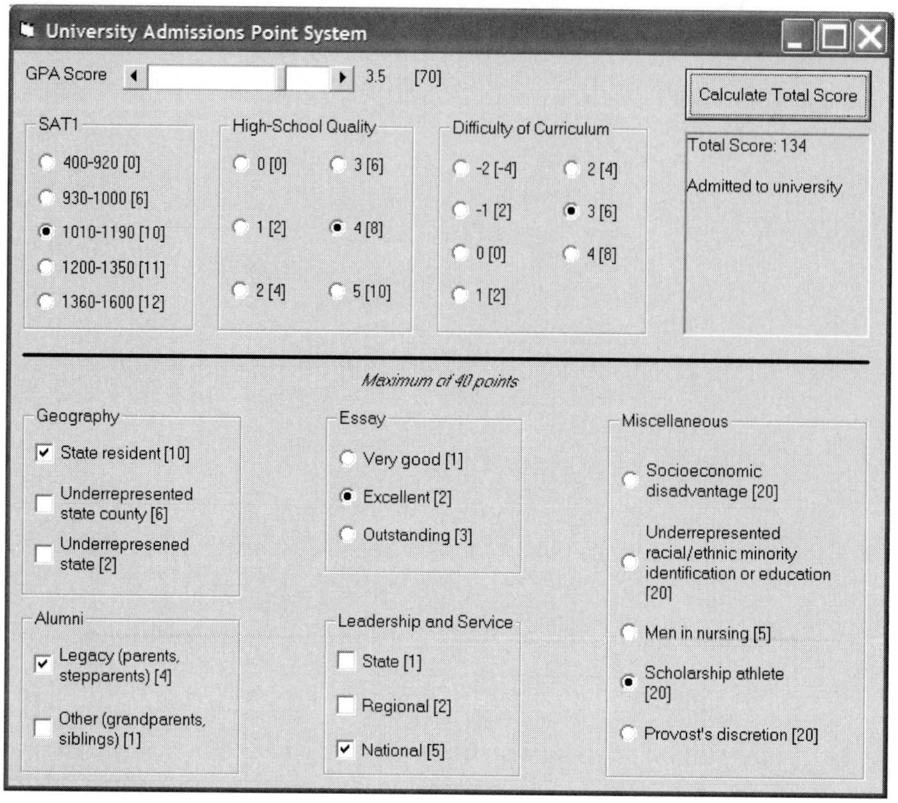

Figure 11.31 Sample run of Programming Project 9.

12 Database Management

12.1 AN INTRODUCTION TO DATABASES

The management of databases is the number one use of computers today. Airlines use databases to handle nearly 1.5 billion passenger reservations per year. The 6,500 hospitals in the United States use databases to document the care of over 30 million patients per year. Banks in the United States utilize databases to monitor the use of 350 million credit cards. Although databases vary considerably in size and complexity, most of them adhere to the fundamental principles of design discussed in this chapter. That is, they are composed of a collection of interrelated tables.

A **table** is a two-dimensional array of data. Table 12.1 provides information about large cities. Each column of the table is called a **field**. (The third column gives the 1995 population in millions and the fourth column gives the projected 2015 population in millions.) The names of the fields are *city, country, pop1995,* and *pop2015.* Each row, called a **record**, contains the same type of information as every other row. Also, the pieces of information in each row are related; they all apply to a specific city. Table 12.2, Countries, has three fields and nine records.

city	country	pop1995	pop2015
Beijing	China	12.4	19.4
Bombay	India	15.1	27.4
Calcutta	India	11.7	17.6
Los Angeles	USA	12.4	14.3
Mexico City	Mexico	15.6	18.8
New York	USA	16.3	17.6
Sao Paulo	Brazil	16.4	20.8
Shanghai	China	15.1	23.4
Tianjin	China	10.7	17.0
Tokyo	Japan	26.8	28.7

Table 12.1 Cities.

country	pop1995	currency
Brazil	155.8	real
China	1185.2	yuan
India	846.3	rupee
Indonesia	195.3	rupiah
Japan	125.0	yen
Mexico	85.6	peso
Nigeria	95.4	naira
Russia	148.2	ruble
USA	263.4	dollar

Table 12.2 Countries.

Source: An Urbanized World—Global Report on Human Settlements 1996, a report presented at Habitat II, a UN conference on the world's cities held in Istanbul in June 1996.

A **database** (or **relational database**) is a collection of one or more (usually related) tables that has been created with **database-management software**. The best known dedicated database management products are Oracle, SQL Server, and DB2. Every version of Visual Basic 6.0 can manage, revise, and analyze a database that has been created with one of these products. Section 12.3 shows how to create a database with Visual Data Manager, a mini-version of Access that is supplied with Visual Basic.

The databases used in this chapter can be found in the collection of files accompanying this text. The database files have the extension .MDB. For instance, the file MEGACITIES1.MDB is a database file containing the two tables presented here as Tables 12.1 and 12.2. (**Note:** MDB files should be copied from the CD onto a hard drive and accessed from the hard drive. In Windows Explorer, after copying the file, you should right-click on it, click on Properties, and delete the check mark from the Read-only box.)

The ADO Data Control

Visual Basic can communicate with databases through data controls. Data controls can read, modify, delete, and add records to databases. Two types of data controls are available with Visual Basic. The first type is found on the Toolbox and is known as the **DAO data control** or the **intrinsic data control.** (DAO stands for Data Access Objects.) The second type of control is the **ADO data control.** (ADO stands for ActiveX Data Objects.) The ADO data control is a custom control that must be added to the Toolbox using the Components dialog box that is invoked from the Project menu. (In the Toolbox, the name of the control is Adodc.)

ADO is a technology developed by Microsoft for interacting with databases. It makes use of the same database engine that powers Access, the popular database management software that is packaged with the Professional Edition of Microsoft Office. According to Microsoft, "the ADO model strives to expose everything that the underlying data provider can do, while still adding value by giving you shortcuts for common operations." It was intended to replace the older DAO technology. In this section, we use the ADO data control exclusively. The following walkthrough uses an ADO data control to connect Visual Basic to the database MEGACITIES1.MDB.

An ADO Data Control Walkthrough

1. Press Alt/File/New Project and double-click on Standard EXE.

2. Press Alt/P/O to invoke the Components dialog box from the Projects menu.

3. Scroll down the list of controls and click on the small square to the left of "Microsoft ADO Data Control 6.0." This will cause a check mark to appear in the square.

4. Click the OK button to place the ADO data control icon on the Toolbox.

5. Double-click on the ADO data control icon to place an ADO data control in the center of the form.

6. Set its Name property to adoCities and its Caption property to Cities.

7. Stretch the control horizontally to see the caption Cities.

8. Select the ConnectionString property from the ADO Data Control's Property window, and click on the ellipsis (…) button at the right side of the settings box to bring up the Property Pages dialog box shown in Figure 12.1.

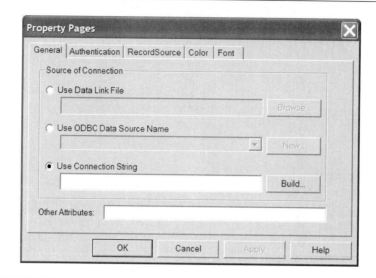

Figure 12.1 The Property Pages dialog box.

9. Click on the Build button to bring up the Data Link Properties window shown in Figure 12.2.

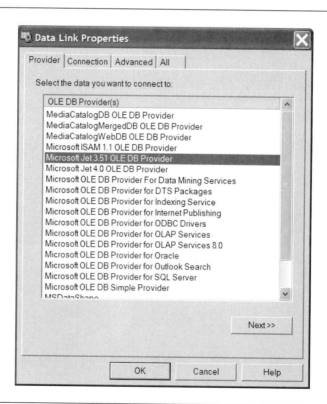

Figure 12.2 The Data Link Properties window.

10. In the Data Link Properties window, select Microsoft Jet 3.51 OLE DB Provider and push the Next button. This has the effect of selecting the Connection tab on the Data Link Properties window. See Figure 12.3.

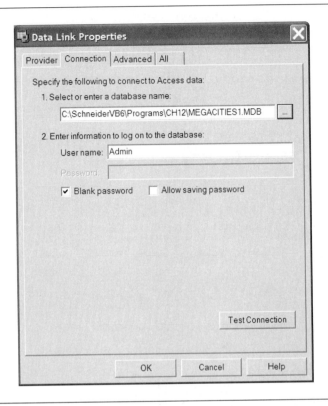

Figure 12.3 The Data Link Properties window with the Connection tab active.

11. Click on the ellipsis (. . .) button to the right of the first text box, browse through the folders on your computer, and select the database that you would like to connect to. In Figure 12.3 we have selected the database MEGACITIES1.MDB.

12. Click on the Test Connection button. A message dialog box displaying the message "Test connection succeeded" should appear.

13. Click on the message dialog box's OK button. Then close the Data Link Properties and the Property Pages windows by pressing on their OK buttons. This concludes setting the ConnectionString[1] property.

14. Select the RecordSource property from the ADO data control's Property window, but do not click on the ellipsis (. . .) button at the right side of the settings box. Instead, just type Cities into the settings box and press the Enter key. The ADO data control is now connected to the Cities table of the database MEGACITIES1.MDB.

---

1. The setting for the ConnectionString property will actually read something like "Provider=Microsoft.Jet.OLEDB.3.51; Persist Security Info = False;Data Source=C:\PROGRAMS\CH12\Megacities1.mdb." However, we will just write MEGACITIES1.MDB as the setting in the Object-Property-Setting chart.

Caution: Steps 8 through 14 of the walkthrough above are said to **build a connection** to the database. When you copy a program from the CD accompanying this book, you most likely will have to rebuild the connection for the ADO Data Control. Otherwise, you will get the error message "Could not find file 'C:. . . . MDB'."

15. Place a text box, txtCity, on the form.

   Text boxes are said to be **data-aware** because they can be bound to a data control and access its data.

16. In the Properties window, select the DataSource property of txtCity.

17. Click on the down arrow to the right of the Settings box and select adoCities.

18. Select the DataField property and click on the down arrow at the right of the Settings box.

   You will see the names of the different fields in the table.

19. Select the field *city*.

   The text box now is said to be **bound** to the data control. It can now display data from the *city* field of the Cities table.

20. Place another text box, txtPop1995, on the form.

21. Select txtPop1995's DataSource property.

22. Click on the down arrow to the right of the Settings box and select adoCities.

23. Select the DataField property, click on the down arrow at the right of the Settings box, and select *pop1995*.

24. Run the program.

   The form will appear as in Figure 12.4. The arrows on the data control, called **navigation arrows**, look and act like VCR buttons. The arrows have been identified by the tasks they perform.

25. Click on the various navigation arrows on the data control to see the different cities and their populations in the Cities table displayed in the text boxes.

26. Change the name of a city or change its population and then move to another record.

   If you look back through the records, you will see that the data have been permanently changed.

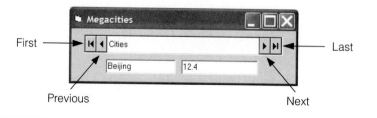

Figure 12.4 An ADO data control with two text boxes bound to it.

Using Code with an ADO Data Control

Only one record can be accessed at a time; this record is called the **current record**. In this walkthrough, the text boxes bound to the data control showed the contents of the *city* and *pop1995* fields of the current record. The user clicked on the navigation arrows of the data control to select a new current record.

Code can be used to designate another record as the current record. The methods MoveNext, MovePrevious, MoveLast, and MoveFirst select a new current record, as suggested by their names. For instance, the statement

```
Adodc1.Recordset.MoveLast
```

specifies the last record of the table to be the current record. (The word Recordset is inserted in most data-control statements that manipulate records for reasons that needn't concern us now.)

The entry of the field *fieldName* of the current record is

```
Adodc1.Recordset.Fields("fieldName").Value
```

For instance, with the status as in Figure 12.4, the statement

```
strVar = adoCities.Recordset.Fields("city").Value
```

assigns "Beijing" to the variable *strVar* and the statements

```
adoCities.Recordset.Fields("city").Value = "Peking"
adoCities.Recordset.Update
```

change the *city* field of the current record to "Peking".

The number of records in the table is given by the RecordCount property. The EOF (End Of File) and BOF (Beginning Of File) run-time properties indicate whether the end or beginning of the file has been reached. For instance, the following two sets of statements each place the cities into a list box.

```
adoCities.Recordset.MoveFirst
For i = 1 to adoCities.Recordset.RecordCount
  lstBox.AddItem adoCities.Recordset.Fields("city").Value
  adoCities.Recordset.MoveNext
Next i

adoCities.Recordset.MoveFirst
Do While Not adoCities.Recordset.EOF
  lstBox.AddItem adoCities.Recordset.Fields("city").Value
  adoCities.Recordset.MoveNext
Loop
```

The current record can be marked for removal with the statement

```
Adodc1.Recordset.Delete
```

The record will be removed when a data control navigation arrow is clicked or a Move method is executed. A new record can be added to the end of the table with the statement

```
Adodc1.Recordset.AddNew
```

followed by

```
Adodc1.Recordset.Fields("fieldName").Value = entryForField
```

statements for each field and an

```
Adodc1.Recordset.Update
```

statement. Alternately, the AddNew method can be followed by the user typing the information into text boxes bound to the data control and then moving to another record. (**Note:** When you add a record and then click on the Move-Previous arrow, you will not see the next-to-last record, but rather will see the record preceding the record that was current when AddNew was executed.)

EXAMPLE 1   The following program is a general database manager for the Cities table in the MEGACITIES1.MDB database. It allows the user to edit the Cities table as needed and to locate information based on the city name.

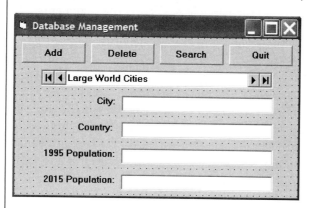

Object	Property	Setting
frmDBMan	Caption	Database Management
cmdAdd	Caption	Add
cmdDelete	Caption	Delete
cmdSearch	Caption	Search
cmdQuit	Caption	Quit
adoCities	Caption	Large World Cities
	ConnectionString	MEGACITIES1.MDB
	RecordSource	Cities
lblCity	Caption	City:
txtCity	Text	(blank)
	DataSource	adoCities
	DataField	city
lblCountry	Caption	Country:
txtCountry	Text	(blank)

	DataSource	adoCities
	DataField	country
lblPop1995	Caption	1995 Population:
txtPop1995	Text	(blank)
	DataSource	adoCities
	DataField	pop1995
lblPop2015	Caption	2015 Population:
txtPop2015	Text	(blank)
	DataSource	adoCities
	DataField	pop2015

```
Private Sub cmdAdd_Click()
  'Add a new record
  adoCities.Recordset.AddNew
  txtCity.SetFocus     'Data must be entered and a new record moved to
End Sub

Private Sub cmdDelete_Click ()
  'Delete the currently displayed record
  adoCities.Recordset.Delete
  'Move so that user sees deleted record disappear
  adoCities.Recordset.MoveNext
  If adoCities.Recordset.EOF Then
      adoCities.Recordset.MovePrevious
  End If
End Sub

Private Sub cmdSearch_Click()
  Dim strSearchFor As String, foundFlag As Boolean
  'Search for the city specified by the user
  strSearchFor = UCase(InputBox("Name of city to find:"))
  If Len(strSearchFor) > 0 Then
      adoCities.Recordset.MoveFirst
      foundFlag = False
      Do While (Not foundFlag) And (Not adoCities.Recordset.EOF)
        If UCase(adoCities.Recordset.Fields("City").Value) = strSearchFor Then
            foundFlag = True
          Else
            adoCities.Recordset.MoveNext
        End If
      Loop
      If Not foundFlag Then
          MsgBox "Unable to locate requested city.", , "Not Found"
          adoCities.Recordset.MoveLast  'move so that EOF is no longer true
      End If
    Else
      MsgBox "Must enter a city.", , ""
  End If
End Sub

Private Sub cmdQuit_Click()
  End
End Sub
```

[Run, click the Search button, and enter New York.]

```
┌─────────────────────────────────────────────────┐
│ ▪ Database Management              [_][□][X]      │
├─────────────────────────────────────────────────┤
│  ┌────────┐ ┌────────┐ ┌────────┐ ┌────────┐     │
│  │  Add   │ │ Delete │ │ Search │ │  Quit  │     │
│  └────────┘ └────────┘ └────────┘ └────────┘     │
│                                                   │
│   │◄ ◄│Large World Cities          ► ►│           │
│                                                   │
│         City:  │New York              │           │
│                                                   │
│      Country:  │USA                   │           │
│                                                   │
│  1995 Population:  │16.3              │           │
│                                                   │
│  2015 Population:  │17.6              │           │
│                                                   │
└─────────────────────────────────────────────────┘
```

Binding Data List and Data Combo Controls to an ADO Data Control

The **data list** and **data combo** controls can be bound to an ADO data control and automatically populated with items in a field of the table that is the record source for the ADO data control. Like the ADO data control, the data list and data combo controls are custom controls that must be added to the Toolbox. To add them, select "Microsoft DataList Controls 6.0" from the Components dialog box that is invoked from the Project menu and then press the OK button. (In the Toolbox, the names of these controls are DataList and ComboList.)

Two properties must be set to bind a data list or data combo control to an ADO data control:

1. Set the **RowSource** property of the data list or data combo control to the name of the ADO data control.

2. Set the **ListField** property of the data list or data combo control to a field of the ADO data control's table that will be used to fill the list.

The data list and data combo controls look like the standard list box and combo box controls. They are often used with data-entry forms to speed data entry and ensure that valid data is entered. Since these controls automatically fill with a column from a table after the above two properties are set, three methods (AddItem, Clear, and RemoveItem) and two properties (ListCount and Sorted) used with the regular list box and combo box are not available with the data list and data combo controls. The number of items displayed in these controls is determined by the RecordCount property of the table specified by the ADO data control (that is, it is the value of Adodc1.Recordset.RecordCount).

EXAMPLE 2

The data list control in the following example displays the countries in the Countries table of MEGACITIES1.MDB. When a item in the list box is clicked, the list box's Text property is used to display the name of the country's unit of currency in a label. (Recall that the value of the Text property is the currently highlighted item.) The ADO data control is made invisible, since it is not needed by the user.

Object	Property	Setting
frmCountries	Caption	Large Countries
adoCountries	ConnectionString	MEGACITIES1.MDB
	RecordSource	Countries
	Visible	False
dlCountries	RowSource	adoCountries
	ListField	country
lblCurrency	Caption	Currency:
lblUnit	Caption	(blank)
	BorderStyle	1-Fixed Single

```
Private Sub dlCountries_Click()
  adoCountries.Recordset.MoveFirst
  'Advance the current record until the record whose country
  'field contains the name of the selected country
  Do While adoCountries.Recordset.Fields("country") <> dlCountries.Text
    adoCountries.Recordset.MoveNext
  Loop
  'Display the name of the currency for the current record
  lblUnit.Caption = adoCountries.Recordset.Fields("currency")
End Sub
```

[Run, and then click on Japan.]

Data Validation

Programmers customarily take precautions to guarantee that proper data is entered into a database. Three helpful tools are the Validate event procedure, the Locked property of text boxes, and the use of list and combo boxes to provide suitable data items.

The Validate event for a text box is triggered whenever the text box is about to lose the focus. One possible general type of procedure is

```
Private Sub txtBox_Validate(Cancel As Boolean)
  'Prevent improper data from being entered into the text box
  If data is improper Then
    Cancel = True
  End If
End Sub
```

The parameter Cancel has the default value False. If the parameter is set to True, the focus will be returned to the text box. As an example, suppose the user is asked to enter Y or N into a text box. The following event procedure prevents the user from leaving the text box until he or she has complied.

```
Private Sub txtBox_Validate(Cancel As Boolean)
  'Guarantee that Y or N be entered into the text box
  If (UCase(txtBox.Text) <> "Y") And (UCase(txtBox.Text) <> "N") Then
      Cancel = True
    Else
      txtBox.Text = UCase(txtBox.Text)
  End If
End Sub
```

When the Locked property of a text box is set to True, the user will not be able to type into the text box. Thus, data can be entered into the text box only with code. Therefore, the programmer has power over the text that will be entered into the text box. One technique is to display the possibilities in a list box and require the user to make a selection. This same functionality can be achieved with a Style 2 combo box. (A Style 2 combo box has a dropdown list, and only items in the list can be placed into the top part of the combo box.)

EXAMPLE 3

The following enhancement to Example 1 only allows countries appearing in the Countries table of MEGACITIES1.MDB to appear in the Country text box. The program also will not allow a city to be added if the 1995 population is less than one million. The Object-Property-Setting chart below gives the additions to the settings listed in Example 1. The controls lblCountryList and dlCountries become visible only after the Add button is clicked, and they stay visible until a country is selected from the list. The code listing shows only the new procedures and the altered procedures from the code for Example 1.

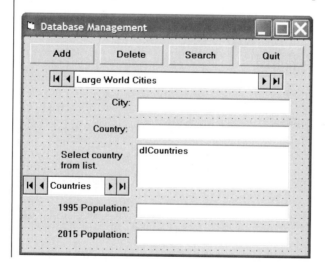

Object	Property	Setting
txtCountry	Locked	True
lblCountryList	Caption	Select country from list.
	Visible	False
adoCountries	ConnectionString	MEGACITIES1.MDB
	RecordSource	Countries
	Visible	False
dlCountries	RowSource	adoCountries
	ListField	country
	Visible	False

```
Private Sub cmdAdd_Click()
  'Add a new record
  dlCountries.Visible = True
  lblCountryList.Visible = True
  adoCities.Recordset.AddNew
  txtCity.SetFocus 'Data must be entered and a new record moved to
End Sub

Private Sub dlCountries_Click()
  txtCountry.Text = dlCountries.Text
  dlCountries.Visible = False
  lblCountryList.Visible = False
End Sub

Private Sub txtPop1995_Validate(Cancel As Boolean)
  'Prevent a user from adding a city of population under 1 million
  Dim strMsg As String
  If (Val(txtPop1995.Text) < 1) Then
    strMsg = "We only allow cities having a population of " & _
             "at least one million."
    MsgBox strMsg, , "Population too small!"
    Cancel = True
  End If
End Sub
```

[Run, click the Add button, enter the city Lagos, and scroll down the list. The screen appears as shown below. (The country can be entered by clicking on Nigeria in the list box.)]

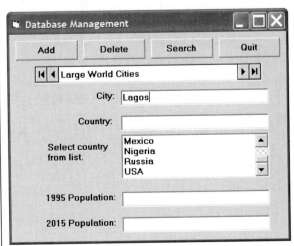

[Run, click on Add, and attempt to enter the data for San Jose. The Validate event procedure prevents .84 from being entered as the 1995 population. The user will be forced to enter data for a more populous city.]

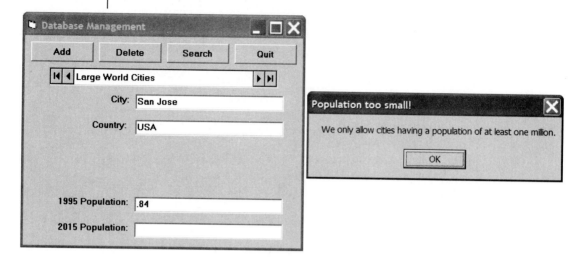

Comments

1. App.Path cannot be used when you set the ConnectionString property of a data control in the Properties window at design time. However, App.Path can be used in the Form_Load event procedure. If so, all the settings to connect the ADO data control to the database and the settings to bind controls to the ADO data control should be made in the Form_Load event procedure. For instance, if you add the lines

```
Private Sub Form_Load()
    adoCities.ConnectionString = "Provider=Microsoft.Jet.OLEDB.3.51;" & _
                            "Persist Security Info=False;" & _
                            "Data Source=" & App.Path & "\MEGACITIES1.MDB"
    adoCities.RecordSource = "Cities"
    txtCity.DataField = "city"
    txtCountry.DataField = "country"
    txtPop1995.DataField = "pop1995"
    txtPop2015.DataField = "pop2015"
End Sub
```

to Example 1, the program will find the database when it is located in the same folder as the program. **Caution:** At design time, be sure to set the Data-Source property of each text box to adoCities, but do not set the DataField property.

2. The property CommandType also affects connecting an ADO data control to a database. We have left the setting at its default, "8 – adCmdUnknown." This setting gives us some flexibility that we will appreciate after reading Section 12.2. Another useful setting for CommandType is "2 –

adCmdTable." After this setting has been made, you can have Visual Basic display a list of the tables in the database. To do so, click on the ellipses (...) button on the right side of the RecordSource property's Settings box. A Property Pages dialog box will appear. After you click on the down-arrow button of the second dropdown combo box, you will be able to select a table from a list. (**Note:** The list might contain some extraneous tables with strange names such as MsyslMEXColumns. Ignore them.)

3. You will most likely alter the file MEGACITIES1.MDB while experimenting with the data control or running the program in Example 1. You can always obtain a fresh copy of MEGACITIES1.MDB by recopying it from the CD (Don't forget to deselect the file's Read-only property.).

4. Some entries in a table can be empty. For instance, in the Cities table, if the 2015 projected value is not known for a particular city, it can be omitted.

5. Field names can be up to 64 characters in length and can consist of letters, numbers, and spaces. If spaces are used in a name, then the name must be enclosed in brackets when used in Visual Basic.

6. Both tables in the database MEGACITIES1.MDB have fields called *country*. If there is ever any question about which is being referred to, we can distinguish them by using the two (full) names Cities.country and Countries.country.

7. In the MEGACITIES1.MDB database, the values in the field *city* are all of data type String and the values in the field *pop1995* are all of data type Single. We say that field *city* has type String (also known as Text) and the field *pop1995* has type Single. Two other common data types are Date/Time and Boolean (also known as Yes/No).

8. When a field is first created, a type must be specified. When that type is String (or Text), a maximum length can also be specified. In the MEGACITIES1.MDB database, the fields *city* and *country* have maximum length 20 and the field *currency* has maximum length 10.

✔ **PRACTICE PROBLEMS 12.1**

The Access database BIBLIO.MDB is supplied with Visual Basic 6.0 and is usually stored in the folder PROGRAM FILES\MICROSOFT VISUAL STUDIO\VB98. How might you determine each of the following quantities?

1. The number of tables in this database

2. The names of the fields in the table Titles

3. The number of records in the table Titles

➤ **EXERCISES 12.1**

Exercises 1 through 14 refer to the database MEGACITIES1.MDB. In Exercises 1 through 10, use an ordering (non-bound) list box.

1. Write a program to place in a list box the names of the countries in the Countries table in the order they appear in the table.

2. Write a program to place in a list box the names of the countries in the Countries table in the reverse order that they appear in the table.

3. Write a program to place in a list box the names of the cities in the Cities table whose populations are projected to exceed 20 million in the year 2015.

4. Write a program to place in a list box the names of the cities in the Cities table whose 1995 populations are between 12 and 16 million.

5. Write a program to place in a list box the names of the countries in the Countries table, where each name is followed by a hyphen and the name of its currency.

6. Write a program to find and display the city in the Cities table that will experience the greatest percentage growth from 1995 to 2015. [**Note:** The percentage growth is (pop2015 – pop1995) / pop1995.]

7. Write a program to place the countries from the Countries table in a list box in descending order of their 1995 populations. (**Hint:** Place the countries and their 1995 populations in a pair of parallel arrays and sort the pair of arrays in descending order based on the populations.)

8. Write a program to place the cities from the Cities table in a list box in descending order of their percentage population growth from 1995 to 2015.

9. Write a program to display the name and currency of each city in the table Cities. (**Hint:** Use two ADO data controls.)

10. Write a program to display the names of each country in the table Countries, followed by the cities in that country that are listed in the Cities table.

11. Write a program to back up the contents of the Cities table in one sequential file and the Countries table in another sequential file. Run the program and compare the sizes of these two sequential files with the size of the file MEGACITIES1.MDB.

12. Suppose the sequential file ADDCOUNTRY.TXT contains several records for countries not in MEGACITIES1.MDB, where each record consists of the name of a country, its 1995 population (in millions), and the name of its currency. Write a program to add the contents of this file into the Countries table.

13. Suppose the sequential file UPDATE.TXT contains several records, where each record consists of the name of a country, its 1995 population (in millions), and the name of its currency. Write a program to use the information in UPDATE.TXT to update the Countries table. If a record in UPDATE.TXT contains the same country as a record in the Countries table, then the population in 1995 and the name of the currency in the Countries table

should be replaced with the corresponding values from UPDATE.TXT. If a record in UPDATE.TXT contains a country that does not appear in the Countries table, a new record should be added to the table.

14. Write a program that allows the user to specify a city and then displays the percentage of its country's population that lives in that city.

Exercises 15 through 17 refer to the BIBLIO.MDB database supplied with Visual Basic.

15. Give the names of the fields in the table Publishers.

16. How many records are in the table Publishers?

17. Write a program that requests the name of a publisher (such as Prentice Hall or Microsoft Press) and gives the publisher's address.

18. The database STATEABBR.MDB contains one table, States, having two fields, *abbreviation* and *state*. Each record consists of a two-letter abbreviation and the name of a state. Some records are (AZ, Arizona) and (MD, Maryland). Write a program that allows the user to enter a two-letter abbreviation and obtain the name of the state. Of course, if the two-letter abbreviation does not correspond to any state, the user should be so informed.

19. In a table, a *row* is to a *record* as a *column* is to a _____ .

In Exercises 20 through 22, describe the effect of executing the statement(s).

20. `Msgbox Adodc1.Recordset.RecordCount`

21. ```
Adodc1.Recordset.MoveNext
If Adodc1.Recordset.EOF Then
    Adodc1.Recordset.MoveFirst
End If
```

22. ```
Adodc1.Recordset.MovePrevious
If Adodc1.Recordset.BOF Then
    Adodc1.Recordset.MoveLast
End If
```

23. Write an additional event procedure for Example 3 which guarantees that, when a new city is added to the Cities table, the 2015 population is greater than the 1995 population.

24. Write an additional event procedure for Example 3 which guarantees that, when adding a city to the Cities table, the name of the city in the text box is different from the names already in the table.

Exercises 25 through 28 use the database EXCHANGERATES.MDB found on the CD accompanying this book. It gives the exchange rates (in terms of American dollars) for 41 currencies of major countries on January 1, 2003. Figure 12.5 shows the first eight records in the database. The dollar-Rate column gives the number of units of the currency that can be purchased for one American dollar. For instance, one American dollar purchases 1.579 Canadian dollars.

name	dollarRate
American Dollars	1
Argentine Pesos	3.35
Australian Dollars	1.775
Brazilian Reals	3.535
British Pounds	0.621
Canadian Dollars	1.579
Chilean Pesos	720
Cyprus Pounds	0.547

Figure 12.5 Exchange rates.

25. Write a program that displays the names of the currencies in a data list box. When the user clicks on one of the names, the exchange rate should be displayed.

26. Write a program that displays the names of the currencies in a data list box. Run the program, click on one of the currencies, and then press the letter S several times. Describe what happens.

27. Write a program that displays the names of the currencies in a data list box. Set the MatchEntry property of the list box to 1 – dblExtendedMatching. Run the program, click on one of the currencies, and then press then type the letters SPA. Describe what happens.

28. Write a program containing two data list boxes as shown in Figure 12.6. When the user selects two currencies and an amount of money, and clicks on the command button, the program should convert the amount from one currency to the other.

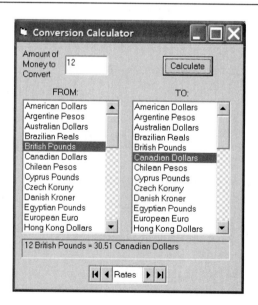

Figure 12.6 A possible output for Exercise 28.

29. Suppose a form contains a text box labeled Phone Number. Write an event procedure that prevents a user from entering any data into the text box other than a string of the form ddd-ddd-dddd, where each *d* is a digit.

30. Suppose a form contains a text box labeled "Enter your six-digit password:". (Assume that each password must begin with a vowel and contain exactly one digit.) Write an event procedure that prevents a user from entering any data into the text box other than an acceptable password.

The CD accompanying this textbook contains the database BASEBALL. MDB that has the two tables Players and Teams. The fields for the Players table are *name, team, atBats,* and *hits*. The fields for the Teams table are *name, city* (or *state*), *league, stadium, atBats,* and *hits*. Suppose the database has been filled with information from the 2002 baseball season for the major leagues. Three sample records from each table are as follows.

Barry Bonds, Giants, 403, 149
Junior Spivey, Diamondbacks, 538, 162
Manny Ramirez, Red Sox, 436, 152

Giants, San Francisco, National, Pacific Bell Park, 5497, 1465
Diamondbacks, Arizona, National, Bank One Ballpark, 5508, 1471
Red Sox, Boston, American, Fenway Park, 5640, 1560

The BASEBALL.MDB database should be used in Exercises 31 through 38.

31. Write a program to determine the player in the Players table with the highest batting average. (**Note:** In the case of a tie, the program should list all players having that batting average.)

32. Write a program to determine the American League player in the Players table with the highest batting average for that league. (**Note:** In the case of a tie, the program should list all players having that batting average.)

33. Write a program to count the number of players in the Players table who play for a National League team.

34. Write a program to count the number of players in the Players table who play for a team based in New York.

35. Write a program that displays all the players in a data list box bound to the Players table, asks the user to click on one of the players, and then displays the name of his home stadium.

36. Write a program that displays all the teams in a data list box bound to the Teams table, asks the user to click on one of the teams, and then displays all the players in the database from that team.

37. Write a program that allows new records to be added to the Players table. Each player's team should be selected from one of the teams listed in the Teams table. Also, after an entry has been made for the number of times at bat text box, the entry for the number of hits text box should not be larger than the number of times at bat.

38. Write a program that requests a batting average and a league (American or National) and then displays in a list box the names of all the players in the league whose batting average is above the given batting average. The program should not permit the given batting average to be greater than 1 or less than 0.

✔✔ Solutions to Practice Problems 12.1

Place an ADO data control, call it adoBooks, on a form and set its ConnectString property to the file BIBLIO.MDB.

1. First, set the CommandType property to "2 – adCmdTable." Then, select the RecordSource property and click on the ellipses button at the right of its Settings box. When the Property Pages dialog box appears, click on the down-arrow box on the second combo box, and use it to determine the number of tables.

2. Set the RecordSource property of adoBooks to the table Titles. Place a text box, call it txtBook, on the form and bind it to the data control by setting its DataSource property to adoBooks. Select the DataField property of txtBook and click on the down-arrow button at the right of its settings box. Count the number of entries in the dropdown list of fields that appears.

3. Place a picture box and a command button on the screen. Place the statement

   ```
   picBox.Print adoBooks.Recordset.RecordCount
   ```

   in the cmdDisplay_Click event procedure. Run the program and then click on the command button.

12.2 RELATIONAL DATABASES AND SQL

Primary and Foreign Keys

A well-designed table should have a field (or set of fields) that can be used to uniquely identify each record. Such a field (or set of fields) is called a **primary key**. For instance, in the Countries table of Section 12.1, the *country* field is a primary key. In the Cities table, because we are only considering very large cities (of over 1 million population), the *city* field is a primary key. Databases of student enrollments in a college usually use a field of social security numbers as the primary key. Names would not be a good choice, because there could easily be two students having the same name.

When a database is created, a field can be specified as a primary key. If so, Visual Basic will insist that every record have an entry in the primary key field and that the same entry does not appear in two different records. If the user tries to enter a record with no data in the primary key, the error message "Index or primary key can't contain a null record." will be generated. If the user tries to enter a record with the same primary key data as another record, the error message "Duplicate value in index, primary key, or relationship. Changes were unsuccessful." will be displayed.

When a database contains two or more tables, the tables are usually related. For instance, the two tables Cities and Countries are related by their *country* field. Let's refer to these two fields as Cities.country and Countries.country. Notice that every entry in Cities.country appears uniquely in Countries.country and that Countries.country is a primary key . We say that Cities.country is a **foreign key** of Countries.country. Foreign keys can be specified when a table is first created. If so, Visual Basic will insist on the **Rule of Referential Integrity**, namely, that each value in the foreign key must also appear in the primary key of the other table.

The CD accompanying this book contains a database named MEGA-CITIES2. MDB. It has the same information as MEGACITIES1.MDB except that Cities.city and Countries.country have been specified as primary keys for their respective tables, and Cities.country has been specified as a foreign key of Countries.country. If the user tries to add a city to the Cities table whose country does not appear in the Countries table, then the error message "Can't add or change record. Referential integrity rules require a related record in table 'Countries'." will be displayed. The message will also be generated if the user tries to delete a country from the Countries.country field that appears in the Cities.country field. Due to the interdependence of the two tables in MEGACITIES2.MDB, this database is called a **relational database**.

A foreign key allows Visual Basic to link (or **join**) together two tables from a relational database in a meaningful way. For instance, when the two tables Cities and Countries from MEGACITIES2.MDB are joined based on the foreign key Cities.country, the result is Table 12.3. The record for each city is expanded to show its country's population and its currency. This joined table is very handy if, say, we want to navigate through a table with buttons as in Example 1 of Section 12.1, but display a city's name and currency. We only have to create the original two tables; Visual Basic creates the joined table as needed. The request for a joined table is made in a language called SQL.

city	Cities. country	Cities. pop1995	Cities. pop2015	Countries. country	Countries. pop1995	Countries. currency
Tokyo	Japan	26.8	28.7	Japan	125.0	yen
Sao Paulo	Brazil	16.4	20.8	Brazil	155.8	real
New York	USA	16.3	17.6	USA	263.4	dollar
Mexico City	Mexico	15.6	18.8	Mexico	85.6	peso
Bombay	India	15.1	27.4	India	846.3	rupee
Shanghai	China	15.1	23.4	China	1185.2	yuan
Los Angeles	USA	12.4	14.3	USA	263.4	dollar
Beijing	China	12.4	19.4	China	1185.2	yuan
Calcutta	India	11.7	17.6	India	846.3	rupee
Tianjin	China	10.7	17.0	China	1185.2	yuan

Table 12.3 A join of two tables.

SQL

Structured Query Language (SQL) was developed in the early 1970s at IBM for use with relational databases. The language was standardized in 1986 by ANSI (American National Standards Institute). Visual Basic uses a version of SQL that is compliant with ANSI-89 SQL. There are some minor variations that are of no concern in this book.

SQL is a very powerful language. One use of SQL is to request specialized information from an existing database and to have the information presented in a specified order.

Four SQL Requests

We will focus on four basic types of requests that can be made with SQL.

Request I: Show the records of a table in a specified order.

Some variations of ordering with MEGACITIES2.MDB are

(a) Alphabetical order based on the name of the city.
(b) Alphabetical order based on the name of the country, and within each country group, the name of the city.
(c) In descending order based on the projected 2015 population.

Request II: Show just the records that meet certain criteria.

Some examples of criteria with MEGACITIES2.MDB are

(a) Cities that are in China.
(b) Cities whose 2015 population is projected to be at least 20 million.
(c) Cities whose name begins with the letter S.

Request III: Join the tables together, connected by a foreign key, and present the records as in Requests I and II.

Some examples with MEGACITIES2.MDB are

(a) Show the cities in descending order of the populations of their countries.
(b) Show the cities whose currency has "u" as its second letter.

Request IV: Make available just *some* of the fields of either the basic tables or the joined table. (For now, this type of request just conserves space and effort by Visual Basic. However, it will be very useful in Section 12.3 when used with a data grid control.)

Some examples with MEGACITIES2.MDB are

(a) Make available just the city and country fields of the table Cities.
(b) Make available just the city and currency fields of the joined table.

Normally, we set the RecordSource property of a data control to an entire table. Also, the records of the table are normally presented in the order they are physically stored in the table. We make the requests just discussed by specifying the RecordSource property as one of the following kinds of settings.

Request I: SELECT * FROM *Table1* ORDER BY *field1* ASC

        or SELECT * FROM *Table1* ORDER BY *field1* DESC

Request II: SELECT * FROM *Table1* WHERE *criteria*

Request III: SELECT * FROM *Table1* INNER JOIN *Table2* ON *foreign field =
primary field* WHERE *criteria*

Request IV: SELECT *field1, field2, . . . fieldN* FROM *Table1* WHERE *criteria*

ASC and DESC specify ASCending and DESCending orders, respectively. A *criteria* clause is a string containing a condition of the type used with If blocks. In addition to the standard operators <, >, and =, *criteria* strings frequently contain the operator Like. Essentially, Like uses the wildcard characters ? and * to compare a string to a pattern. A question mark stands for a single character in the same position as the question mark. For instance, the pattern "B?d" is matched by "Bid", "Bud", and "Bad". An asterisk stands for any number of characters in the same position as the asterisk. For instance, the pattern "C*r" is matched by "Computer", "Chair", and "Car". See Comments 3 through 5 for further information about Like.

In the sentence

```
SELECT fields FROM clause
```

fields is either * (to indicate all fields) or a sequence of the fields to be available (separated by commas), and *clause* is either a single table or a join of two tables. A join of two tables is indicated by a *clause* of the form

```
table1 INNER JOIN table2 ON foreign key of table1=primary key of table2
```

Appending

```
WHERE criteria
```

to the end of the sentence restricts the records to those satisfying *criteria*. Appending

```
ORDER BY field(s) ASC (or DESC)
```

presents the records ordered by the specified *field* or *fields*.

In general, the SQL statements we consider will look like

```
SELECT www FROM xxx WHERE yyy ORDER BY zzz
```

where SELECT *www* FROM *xxx* is always present and accompanied by one or both of WHERE *yyy* and ORDER BY *zzz*. In addition, the *xxx* portion might contain an INNER JOIN phrase.

The settings for the examples mentioned earlier are as follows:

1 (a) Show the records from Cities in alphabetical order based on the name of the city.

```
SELECT * FROM Cities ORDER BY city ASC
```

I (b) Show the records from Cities in alphabetical order based first on the name of the country and, within each country group, the name of the city.

```
SELECT * FROM Cities ORDER BY country, city ASC
```

I (c) Show the records from Cities in descending order based on the projected 2015 population.

```
SELECT * FROM Cities ORDER BY pop2015 DESC
```

II (a) Show the records for the Cities in China.

```
SELECT * FROM Cities WHERE country = 'China'
```

II (b) Show the records from Cities whose 2015 population is projected to be at least 20 million.

```
SELECT * FROM Cities WHERE pop2015 >= 20
```

II (c) Show the records from Cities whose name begins with the letter S.

```
SELECT * FROM Cities WHERE city Like 'S*'
```

III (a) Show the records from the joined table in descending order of the populations of their countries.

```
SELECT * FROM Cities INNER JOIN Countries ON Cities.country =
Countries.country ORDER BY Countries.pop1995 DESC
```

III (b) Show the records from the joined table whose currency has "u" as its second letter.

```
SELECT * FROM Cities INNER JOIN Countries ON Cities.country =
Countries.country WHERE currency Like '?u*'
```

IV (a) Make available just the city and country fields of the table Cities.

```
SELECT city, country FROM Cities
```

IV (b) Make available just the city and currency fields of the joined table.

```
SELECT city, currency FROM Cities INNER JOIN Countries ON
Cities.country = Countries.country
```

Note: In several of the statements the single quote, rather than the normal double quote, was used to surround strings. This is standard practice with SQL statements.

We can think of an SQL statement as creating in essence a new "virtual" table from existing tables. For instance, we might regard the statement

```
SELECT city, pop2015 FROM Cities WHERE pop2015>=20
```

as creating the "virtual" table

city	pop2015
Tokyo	28.7
Sao Paulo	20.8
Bombay	27.4
Shanghai	23.4

This table is a subtable of the original table Cities—that is, it consists of what is left after certain columns and rows are deleted.

As another example, the statement

```
SELECT Cities.city, Cities.Country, Country.currency FROM Cities INNER JOIN
Countries ON Cities.country = Countries.country WHERE Countries.country>'K'
```

creates in essence the "virtual" table

Cities.city	Cities.country	Countries.currency
New York	USA	dollar
Mexico City	Mexico	peso
Los Angeles	USA	dollar

which is a subtable of a join of the two tables Cities and Countries.

These "virtual" tables don't exist in the database. However, for all practical purposes, Visual Basic acts as if they did. In Visual Basic terminology, a "virtual" table is called a **recordset** and SQL statements are said to create a recordset. In standard relational database books, a "virtual" table is called a **view**.

SQL also can be used in code with a statement of the form

```
Adodc1.RecordSource = "SELECT ... FROM ..."
```

to alter the order and kinds of records presented from a database. However, such a statement must be followed by the statement

```
Adodc1.Refresh
```

to reset the information processed by the data control.

EXAMPLE 1   The following program allows the user to alter the order and kinds of information displayed from a database. When the first command button is pressed, the cities are presented in ascending order based on their 1995 populations. When the second command button is pressed, the cities are presented in alphabetical order along with their currencies. (*Caution:* Be sure that the CommandType property of adoCities has its default setting "8 – adCmdUnknown." This setting allows the RecordSource property to be set to either a table or an SQL statement.)

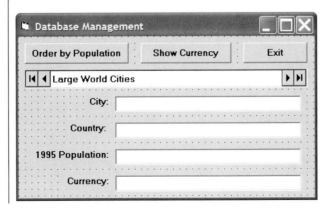

Object	Property	Setting
frmDBMan	Caption	Database Management
cmdOrderByPop	Caption	Order by Population
cmdShowCurrency	Caption	Show Currency
cmdExit	Caption	Exit
adoCities	Caption	Large World Cities
	ConnectionString	MEGACITIES2.MDB
	RecordSource	Cities
lblCity	Caption	City:
txtCity	DataSource	adoCities
	DataField	city
	Text	(blank)
lblCountry	Caption	Country:
txtCountry	DataSource	adoCities
	DataField	country
	Text	(blank)
lblPopulation	Caption	1995 Population:
txtPopulation	DataSource	adoCities
	DataField	pop1995
	Text	(blank)
lblCurrency	Caption	Currency:
txtCurrency	DataSource	adoCities
	Text	(blank)

```
Private Sub cmdOrderByPop_Click()
  Dim strSQL As String
  txtCurrency.DataField = ""
  txtCurrency.Text = ""
  strSQL = "SELECT * FROM Cities ORDER BY pop1995 ASC"
  adoCities.RecordSource = strSQL
  adoCities.Refresh
End Sub

Private Sub cmdShowCurrency_Click()
  Dim strSQL As String
  strSQL = "SELECT city, Cities.country, Cities.pop1995, currency " & _
           "FROM Cities INNER JOIN Countries " & _
           "ON Cities.country=Countries.country " & _
           "ORDER BY city ASC"
  adoCities.RecordSource = strSQL
  adoCities.Refresh
  txtCurrency.DataField = "currency"
End Sub

Private Sub cmdExit_Click()
  End
End Sub
```

[Run, and click on Order by Population.]

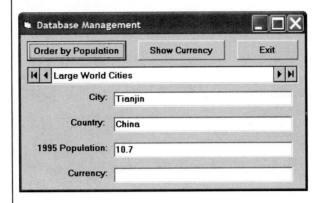

[Click on Show Currency, and then click on the Next navigator arrow six times.]

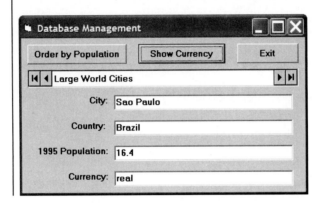

The program in Example 1 of Section 12.1 searched a table for a specific record by looping through all the records. Whereas this technique is fine for small tables, it is not efficient for searches of large tables. Visual Basic provides a better way with Find methods.

Find Method

Suppose a table has been attached to the ADO data control Adodc1, and an SQL statement has been used to create and order a recordset. Then a statement of the form

```
Adodc1.RecordSet.Find criteria
```

starts with the current record, searches for the first record that satisfies the criteria, and makes that record the new current record. Here, *criteria* is a string similar to a *criteria* phrase that follows WHERE in an SQL statement. (**Note:** If the original current record satisfies the criteria, it will remain the current record.) A statement of the form

```
dodc1.RecordSet.Find criteria, 1
```

starts at the current record, searches for the first record *after* the current record that satisfies the criteria, and makes that record the new current record. (**Note:** If the original current record satisfies the criteria, it only will remain the current record if it is the last record.)

The Find method also can search backward. The statement

```
Adodc1.RecordSet.Find criteria, 1, adSearchBackward
```

searches backward for the first record *before* the current record that satisfies the criteria, and makes that record the new current record. The statement

```
Adodc1.RecordSet.Find criteria, , adSearchBackward
```

searches backward for the first record *before* and *including* the current record that satisfies the criteria, and makes that record the new current record.

In forward and backward searches, the search stops at the end or start of the recordset. That is, after the search, the value of `Adodc1.Recordset.BOF` or `Adodc1.Recordset.EOF` will be True, depending on the direction searched. The BookMark property is helpful when a Find method fails to locate a suitable record. If *bkmk* is a variable of type Variant,[2] then the statement

```
bkmk = Adodc1.RecordSet.BookMark
```

tags the current record for quick access at a later time. When the statement

```
Adodc1.RecordSet.BookMark = bkmk
```

is executed at a later time, the tagged record will again become the current record.

Note: The Find method can be used only if a control (such as a text box, list box, or combo box) has been bound to the ADO data control.

EXAMPLE 2

The following program displays the large cities in a country specified by the user. Due to the SQL statement in the setting for adoCities.RecordSource, the cities will be presented alphabetically. Notice the handling of the string variable *criteria*. Had the Find statement been

```
adoCities.Recordset.Find "country = nom"
```

a run-time error message would have been generated. Also, the DataSource property of txtCountry was set to adoCities since an ADO data control will not function unless a control is bound to it.

---

2. A variable of type Variant can hold any type of data. When values are assigned to a variable of type Variant, Visual Basic keeps track of the "type" of data that has been stored in the Variant variable and handles it accordingly.

Object	Property	Setting
frmDBMan	Caption	EXAMPLE 12-2-2
lstCities		
cmdFind	Caption	Find Cities
lblCountry	Caption	Country
txtCountry	Text	(blank)
	DataSource	adoCities
adoCities	Caption	Large World Cities
	Connection-String	MEGACITIES2.MDB
	RecordSource	SELECT * FROM Cities ORDER BY city ASC

```
Private Sub cmdFind_Click()
  Dim nom As String, criteria As String
  lstCities.Clear
  If txtCountry.Text <> "" Then
      nom = txtCountry.Text
      criteria = "country = " & "'" & nom & "'"
      adoCities.Recordset.MoveFirst
      adoCities.Recordset.Find criteria
      Do While Not adoCities.Recordset.EOF
        lstCities.AddItem adoCities.Recordset.Fields("city").Value
        adoCities.Recordset.Find criteria, 1
      Loop
      If lstCities.ListCount = 0 Then
          lstCities.AddItem "None"
      End If
    Else
      MsgBox "You must enter a country.", , ""
      txtCountry.SetFocus
  End If
End Sub
```

[Run, type China into the text box, and press the command button.]

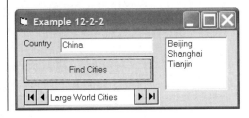

Comments

1. Each record of the Countries table is related to one or more records of the Cities table, but each record of the Cities table is related to only one record of the Countries table. Therefore, we say that there is a **one-to-many relationship** from the Countries table to the Cities table.

2. SQL statements and the Find method are insensitive to case. For instance, the following choices for *criteria* have the same effect: City='Tokyo', city='tokyo', CITY='tokyo', CiTy='TOKYO'.

3. When the Like operator is used, the "pattern" must appear on the right of the operator. For instance, the SQL statement

   ```
   SELECT * FROM Cities WHERE city Like 'S*'
   ```

   cannot be replaced by

   ```
   SELECT * FROM Cities WHERE 'S*' Like city
   ```

4. The operator Like permits a refinement of the wildcard character "?". Whereas "?" is a placeholder for any letter, an expression of the form "[*letter1-letter2*]" is a placeholder for any letter from *letter1* to *letter2*. For instance, the pattern "[A-F]ad" is matched by Bad and Dad, but not Sad.

5. The Like operator can be used in If blocks in much the same way as the operators >, =, and <. In this situation, the operator is case-sensitive. For instance, the condition ("bad" Like "[A-F]ad") is False. However, when Like is used in SQL statements, it is case-insensitive. That is, ('bad' Like '[A-F]ad') is True.

6. Sometimes a pair of fields is specified as a primary key. For instance, in a table of college courses, a single course might have several sections—a course might be identified as CMSC 102, Section 3. In this case, the pair of fields *course, section* would serve as a primary key for the table.

7. The requirement that no record may have a null primary key and that entries for primary keys be unique is called the **Rule of Entity Integrity**.

8. If there is no field with unique entries, database designers usually add a "counter field" containing the numbers 1, 2, 3, and so on. This field then can serve as a primary key.

 PRACTICE PROBLEMS 12.2

Consider the procedure cmdSearch_Click( ) of Example 1 in Section 12.1.

1. Rewrite the procedure using an SQL statement to display the requested record.

2. Rewrite the procedure using a Find method to display the requested record.

> **EXERCISES 12.2**

Exercises 1 and 4 refer to the database MEGACITIES2.MDB, where the primary keys of Cities and Countries are *city* and *country*, respectively, and *Cities.country* is a foreign key to *Countries.country*. Determine whether the stated action could ever cause a problem. Explain.

1. Add a new record to the Cities table.

2. Delete a record from the Countries table.

3. Delete a record from the Cities table.

4. Add a new record to the Countries table.

In Exercises 5 through 10, use the database BIBLIO.MDB that is provided with Visual Basic. By experimentation, determine the primary keys for each of the tables in Exercises 5 through 8.

5. Authors   6. Publishers

7. Titles   8. Title Author

Determine the foreign keys for the pairs of tables in Exercises 9 and 10.

9. Authors, Titles   10. Publishers, Titles

The following tables are "virtual" tables derived from the MEGACITIES2. MDB database. In Exercises 11 through 14, identify the "virtual" table associated with the SQL statement.

(A)

country	pop1995	currency
Russia	148.2	ruble
Indonesia	195.3	rupiah
India	846.3	rupee
Brazil	155.8	real

(B)

country	pop1995	currency
China	1185.2	yuan

(C)

country	pop1995	currency
China	1185.2	yuan
India	846.3	rupee

(D)

country	pop1995	currency
China	1185.2	yuan
Brazil	155.8	real

11. `SELECT * FROM Countries WHERE pop1995>1000 ORDER BY pop1995 ASC`

12. `SELECT * FROM Countries WHERE country<'E' ORDER BY pop1995 DESC`

13. `SELECT * FROM Countries WHERE currency Like 'r*' ORDER BY country DESC`

14. `SELECT * FROM Countries WHERE pop1995>700 ORDER BY country ASC`

The following tables are "virtual" tables derived from the MEGACITIES2.
MDB database. In Exercises 15 through 18, identify the "virtual" table associated with the SQL statement.

(A)

city	currency
Sao Paulo	real
Shanghai	yuan

(B)

city	currency
Tokyo	yen
Bombay	rupee
Shanghai	yuan

(C)

city	currency
Bombay	rupee
Calcutta	rupee

(D)

city	currency
Tokyo	yen

15. `SELECT city, currency FROM Cities INNER JOIN Countries ON Cities.country = Countries.country WHERE city='Tokyo'`

16. `SELECT city, currency FROM Cities INNER JOIN Countries ON Cities.country= Countries.country WHERE pop2015>22 ORDER BY pop2015 DESC`

17. `SELECT city, currency FROM Cities INNER JOIN Countries ON Cities.country = Countries.country WHERE Cities.country='India' ORDER BY Cities.pop1995 DESC`

18. `SELECT city, currency FROM Cities INNER JOIN Countries ON Cities.country = Countries.country WHERE city Like 'S*' ORDER BY Countries.pop1995 ASC`

Exercises 19 through 22 refer to the database MEGACITIES2.MDB. Identify the city in the current record after the following lines of code are executed.

19.
```
adoCities.RecordSource = "SELECT * FROM Cities"
adoCities.Refresh
adoCities.Recordset.MoveFirst
adoCities.Recordset.Find "pop2015 < 20"
```

20.
```
adoCities.RecordSource = "SELECT * FROM Cities ORDER BY city ASC"
adoCities.Refresh
adoCities.Recordset.MoveLast
adoCities.Recordset.Find "pop2015 < 20", , adSearchBackward
```

21.
```
adoCities.RecordSource = "SELECT * FROM Cities ORDER BY pop2015 ASC"
adoCities.Refresh
adoCities.Recordset.MoveFirst
adoCities.Recordset.Find "pop2015 < 20"
```

22.
```
adoCities.RecordSource = "SELECT * FROM Cities WHERE country = 'India'"
adoCities.Refresh
adoCities.Recordset.MoveLast
adoCities.Recordset.Find "pop2015 < 20", , adSearchBackward
```

Write a set of statements as in Exercises 19 through 22 to accomplish the following task.

23. Find the city in China that will have the largest population in 2015.

24. Find the city that has the smallest population in 1995.

25. Consider the database MEGACITIES2.MDB. Write a program with a single list box and four command buttons captioned "Alphabetical Order", "Order by 1995 Population", "Order by 2015 Population", and "Alphabetical Order by Country and City". Each time one of the command buttons is pressed, the cities from the Cities table should be displayed in the list box as described by the command button.

26. Consider the database BIBLIO.MDB. Write a program that requests a year as input and then displays in a list box the titles and authors of all books published in that year. The program should use the Find method to locate the books.

Exercises 27 and 28 refer to the database PHONEBOOK.MDB, which holds all the information for the residence listings of a telephone book for a city. Assume the database consists of one table, Entries, with the six fields: lastName, firstName, middleInitial, streetNumber, street, and phoneNumber.

27. Write a program that will display the contents of the phone book in the standard form shown in Figure 12.7(a).

28. Write a program that will display a "criss-cross" directory that gives phone numbers with the entries organized by street as in Figure 12.7(b).

AAKER Larry	3 Main St	874-2345	APPLE ST	3	Carl Aaron	405-2345
AARON Alex	23 Park Ave	924-3456		5	John Smith	862-1934
Bob R	17 Elm St	347-3456		7	Ted T Jones	405-1843
Carl	3 Apple St	405-2345	ARROW RD	1	Ben Rob	865-2345
(a)				(b)		

Figure 12.7 (a) Standard phone directory and **(b)** criss-cross directory.

The following exercises use the database BASEBALL.MDB discussed in Exercises 12.1. In Exercises 29 through 32, write an event procedure for a command button that can be used with the database to display the stated information in a data list box bound to the database. The procedure should make extensive use of SQL statements.

29. The names of the players who play for a team based in New York.

30. The city (or location) of a team input by the user in txtTeam.

31. The name(s) of the player(s) in the American League having the most hits.

32. The names of the three players in the Players table having the greatest number of hits.

✔✔ **Solutions to Practice Problems 12.2**

```
1. Private Sub cmdSearch_Click ()
      Dim strSearchFor As String, strSQL As String
      'Search for the city specified by the user
      strSearchFor = InputBox("Name of city to find:")
      If Len(strSearchFor) > 0 Then
          strSQL = "SELECT * FROM Cities " & _
                      "WHERE city=" & "'" & strSearchFor & "'"
          adoCities.RecordSource = strSQL
          adoCities.Refresh
          If txtCity.Text = "" Then
              MsgBox "Unable to locate requested city.", ,"Not Found"
              adoCities.RecordSource = "SELECT * FROM Cities"
              adoCities.Refresh
          End If
        Else
          Msgbox "Must enter a city.", ,""
      End If
   End Sub

2. Private Sub cmdSearch_Click ()
      Dim strSearchFor As String
      'Search for the city specified by the user
      strSearchFor = InputBox("Name of city to find:")
      If Len(strSearchFor) > 0 Then
          adoCities.Recordset.MoveFirst
          adoCities.Recordset.Find "city= " & "'" & strSearchFor & "'"
          If adoCities.Recordset.EOF = True Then
              MsgBox "Unable to locate requested city.", ,"Not Found"
          End If
        Else
          Msgbox "Must enter a city.", ,""
      End If
   End Sub
```

12.3 THE DATA GRID CONTROL; CREATING AND DESIGNING DATABASES

The Data Grid Control

The FlexGrid control discussed in Chapter 11 is based on DAO (Data Access Objects) technology, and therefore cannot be bound to the ADO data control. Microsoft has provided a substitute with the more powerful data grid control that *is* based on ADO technology. The data grid control must be added to the Toolbar using the Components dialog box that is invoked from the Project menu. The following steps add the data grid control to the Toolbox.

1. Press Alt/P/O to invoke the Components dialog box.

2. Scroll down the list of controls and click on the check box to the left of Microsoft DataGrid Control 6.0.

3. Click the OK button to place the DataGrid icon on the Toolbox.

A data grid's DataSource property is used to bind the data grid to an ADO data control. The ADO data control in turn is connected to a (virtual) table of a database. The bound data grid control will automatically display the table's records (including the field names) in a spreadsheet-like array with an arrow pointing to the current record. See Figure 12.8. Each time you press the down- or up-arrow key, the pointer moves accordingly. The rows and columns display the records and fields. The intersection of a row and column is called a **cell**. You can specify the current cell in code or can change it at run time using the mouse or the arrow keys. You can read and edit the contents of each cell either directly or with code. The standard prefix for the name of a data grid is *dg*.

city	country	pop1995	pop2015
▶ Beijing	China	12.4	19.4
Bombay	India	15.1	27.4
Calcutta	India	11.7	17.6
Los Angeles	USA	12.4	14.3
Mexico City	Mexico	15.6	18.8
New York	USA	16.3	17.6
Sao Paulo	Brazil	16.4	20.8
Shanghai	China	15.1	23.4
Tianjin	China	10.7	17
Tokyo	Japan	26.8	28.7

Figure 12.8 The Microsoft data grid control.

Two properties of the data grid, AllowAddNew and AllowDelete, let you decide whether the user can add new records and delete existing records directly in the control. The default values for both properties are False. When the AllowAddNew property is set to True, the last row displayed in the data grid control is left blank to permit users to enter new records. An asterisk appears to the left of the row. See Figure 12.9. When the AllowDelete property is set to True, the user can remove a record by clicking on the (gray) rectangle to the left of the record and then pressing the Delete key. Of course, with any property setting, records can always be added or deleted programmatically. You can prevent the user from making changes directly to an individual cell by setting the AllowUpdate property of the data grid to False. The default value is True.

city	country	pop1995	pop2015
▶ Beijing	China	12.4	19.4
Bombay	India	15.1	27.4
Calcutta	India	11.7	17.6
Los Angeles	USA	12.4	14.3
Mexico City	Mexico	15.6	18.8
New York	USA	16.3	17.6
Sao Paulo	Brazil	16.4	20.8
Shanghai	China	15.1	23.4
Tianjin	China	10.7	17
Tokyo	Japan	26.8	28.7
*			

Figure 12.9 The Microsoft data grid control with the AllowAddNew property set to True.

You can use an SQL statement in code to specify the fields displayed in a data grid. For instance, if the data grid control has adoCities as its DataSource and the ConnectionString setting for adoCities is MEGACITIES2.MDB, then the statements

```
adoCities.CommandType = adCmdText  'This line is not needed if the
'property was set to 8-adCmdUnknown or 1-adCmdText at design time.
adoCities.RecordSource = "SELECT city, country FROM Cities"
adoCities.Refresh
```

cause the data grid to display only the first two columns of the Cities table. The same effect can be achieved at design time (provided that the CommandType for adoCities was set to "1-adCmdText" or "8-adCmdUnknown.") by setting the RecordSource property of adoCities to

```
SELECT city, country FROM Cities
```

EXAMPLE 1 The following program displays the contents of the Cities table of the MEGACITIES2.MDB database. When you click on the command button, the data grid displays the cities, their countries, and currency. Also, the caption of the command button changes to "Show City, Country, Populations". The next time you click the command button, the contents of the data grid returns to its original state.

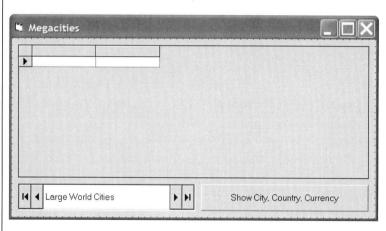

Object	Property	Setting
frm12_3_1	Caption	Megacities
adoCities	Caption	Large World Cities
	ConnectionString	MEGACITIES2.MDB
	RecordSource	Cities
dgCities	DataSource	adoCities
cmdShow	Caption	Show City, Country, Currency

```
Private Sub cmdShow_Click()
  If cmdShow.Caption = "Show City, Country, Currency" Then
      'Join the two tables and display cities, countries, and currency
      adoCities.RecordSource = "SELECT city, Cities.country, currency FROM " & _
        "Cities INNER JOIN Countries ON Countries.country = Cities.country " & _
        "ORDER BY city"
      adoCities.Refresh
      cmdShow.Caption = "Show City, Country, Populations"
    Else
      adoCities.RecordSource = "Cities"
      adoCities.Refresh
      cmdShow.Caption = "Show City, Country, Currency"
  End If
End Sub
```

[Run]

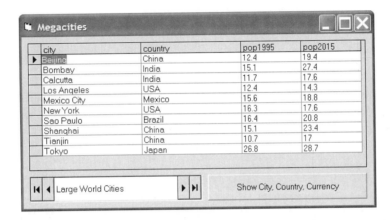

[Click on the command button.]

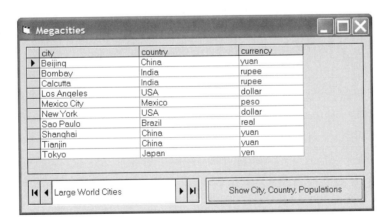

Creating a Database with Visual Data Manager

You invoke Visual Data Manager (VisData) from Visual Basic by pressing Alt/ Add-Ins/Visual Data Manager. The first two entries of the File menu of VisData are Open Database, used to view and alter an existing database, and New, used to create a new database. See Figure 12.10.

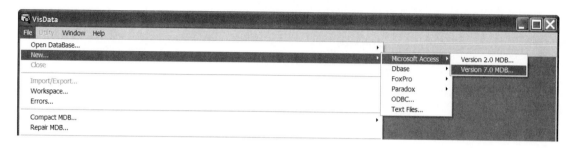

Figure 12.10 Visual Data Manager's File menu.

Let's focus on creating a new database. After you select New, you are presented with a dropdown menu used to choose the type of database as shown in Figure 12.10. Choose Microsoft Access and then specify a version. (Version 7.0 is the later version of Access, the one that came with the Professional Edition of Office 95.) Then a standard file-naming dialog box titled "Select Microsoft Access Database to Create" appears. See Figure 12.11.

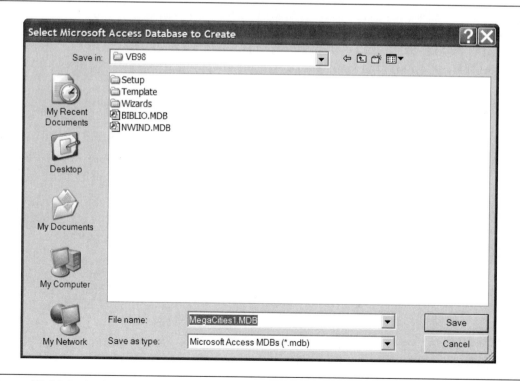

Figure 12.11 Dialog box used to name the database.

After you name the database, say as MEGACITIES1.MDB, and click Save, the Database window and SQL Statement box appear. We will work solely with the Database window.

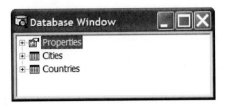

Figure 12.12 Database window. (Appears after the database is named. Initially the window will contain only the Properties line. Additional lines will appear as tables are created.)

Suppose you want to create a database with two tables. Starting from the Database window, the basic steps are as follows:

1. Create the database and the two tables.

   (a) Click on the right mouse button within the Database window. Click on New Table and use the Table Structure window (Figure 12.13) to name the first table and to specify the fields and their data types. The steps listed after Figure 12.13 show how to carry out these tasks.

   (b) Repeat Step 1 for the second table.

2. (Optional) Specify a primary key for a table.

   (a) Highlight the table name in the Database window.

   (b) Press the right mouse button and choose Design to invoke the Table Structure window (Figure 12.13).

   (c) Press the Add Index button to invoke the Add Index window (Figure 12.14) and follow the steps listed after the figure.

3. Place records into a table.

   (**Note:** The VisData Toolbar contains three sets of icons. This discussion assumes that the left icon of each of the first two sets has been selected. These are the "Table type Recordset" and "Use Data Control on New Form" icons.)

   (a) Double-click on the table in the Database window to invoke the Table window (Figure 12.15).

   (b) Follow the directions listed after Figure 12.15.

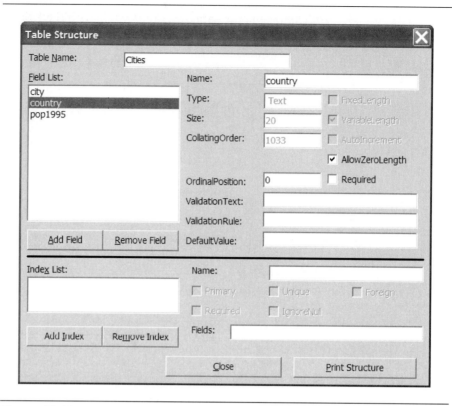

Figure 12.13 Table Structure window. (Invoked from the Database window with the right mouse button by choosing New or Design.)

How to use the Table Structure window

1. Type the name of the table in the Table Name text box.

2. Click on the Add Field button. (An Add Field window will be displayed.)

3. Type the name of a field in the Name text box.

4. Click on the down arrow of the Type combo box and select a type from the dropdown list. (We use primarily the type "Text" for strings, and "Single" or "Integer" for numbers.)

5. If the data type is "Text," type the length of the largest possible string needed in the Size box. (For instance, length 20 should suffice for names of cities. The length must be no longer than 255 characters.)

6. Press OK to add the field to the table.

7. Repeat Steps 3 through 6 until you have added all the fields to the table. When you are through, click on the Close button to return to the Database window.

8. To delete a field, highlight the field by clicking on it in the list box and then press the Remove Field button.

9. When all fields have been specified, press the "Build the Table" button to save the table and return to the Database window. (If we later decide to add a new field or delete an existing field, we can return to the Table Structure

window by highlighting the table in the Database window, clicking the right mouse button, and choosing Design.)

(**Note:** The "Build the Table" button appears only for new tables, otherwise, use the Close button return to the Database window.)

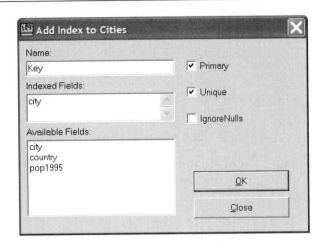

Figure 12.14 Add Index window (Invoked from the Table Structure window by pressing Add Index.)

How to use the Add Index window to specify a primary key

1. Type in a name for an index, such as Principal, click on the field which is to be the primary field, and place check marks in the Primary and Unique check boxes.

2. Click OK and then click Close.

   Note: To specify an ordinary index, follow all steps except turning on the Primary check box.

3. Press "Build the Table" or Close to return to the Database window.

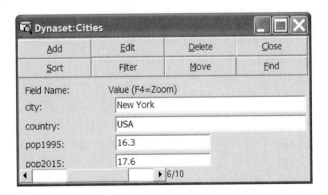

Figure 12.15 Table window (Invoked from the Database window by double-clicking on the table name. Or, choose the table, click on the right mouse button, and click on Open.)

How to use the Table window

1. If the table has no records, the Value text boxes will be blank. To add a record, type data into the fields and press the Update button.

2. To add a new record to the end of a table that already contains records, click the Add button, type data into the fields, and press the Update button. If you make a mistake entering the data, click on the Cancel button.

3. To view an existing record, use the navigator buttons (identical to those of the data control) or the Find button to move to a record of a specified value.

4. To remove the current record from the table, click the Delete button. The record is immediately deleted and cannot be recovered.

5. To edit an existing record, make changes in the data and click on the Update button.

6. Press the Close button to return to the Database window.

At any time, the main section of the Database window contains a list of the tables you have specified. Initially the main section is blank except for Properties. (This is a list of properties pertaining to the database.) If you click the right mouse button while highlighting a table, a menu will appear with the following options:

Menu Item	Use
Open	Open the table to allow records to be added.
Design	Specify the design (number and types of fields).
Rename	Rename the given table.
Delete	Remove the given table from the database.
Copy Structure	Copies the structure of the given database with or without the data currently contained in the database.
Refresh List	Redisplay the list in the Database window.
New Table	Open the Table Structure window.
New Query	Open the Query Builder window.

Principles of Database Design

In order to design a database, you must decide how many tables to use, what fields to include in each table, what fields to make primary or foreign keys, and what validation criteria to specify. The programming paradigm "Plan first, code later" also applies to databases. Before you design a database, you first must understand how the database will be used. For instance, you must know in what way and how often the user will update the data, and what types of reports the user will want to be generated from the database. Failure to plan ahead can be very costly.

You have no doubt read about the "year 2000 crisis." Databases designed in the 1960s and 1970s saved space by using just two digits to refer to each year. As a result, they could not distinguish between the year 2000 and the year 1900. Correcting this oversight has cost government and industry billions of dollars.

Good relational database design is more an art than a science. However, there are certain fundamental guidelines that the designer should keep in mind.

Include the necessary data.

After you have a clear picture of the types of reports the user must generate, you will know what fields and relationships to include. On the other hand, some data that seem relevant do not have to be kept.

Be aware that data should often be stored in their smallest parts.

For instance, city, state, and zip code are usually best stored in three fields. Doing so will allow you to sort a mailing by zip code or target a mailing to the residents of a specific city.

Avoid redundancy.

The process of avoiding redundancy by splitting a table into two or more related tables is called **data normalization**. For instance, the excessive duplication in Table 12.4(a) can be avoided by replacing the table with the two related tables, Tables 12.4(b) and 12.4(c).

course	section	name	time	credits	prerequisite
CS102	1001	Intro to Databases	MWF 8–9	3	CS101
CS102	1002	Intro to Databases	MWF 1–2	3	CS101
CS102	1003	Intro to Databases	MWF 2–3	3	CS101
CS102	1004	Intro to Databases	MWF 3–4	3	CS101
CS105	1001	Visual Basic	MWF 1–2	4	CS100

Table 12.4(a) A table with redundant data.

course	section	time
CS102	1001	MWF 8–9
CS102	1002	MWF 1–2
CS102	1003	MWF 2–3
CS102	1004	MWF 3–4
CS105	1001	MWF 1–2

Table 12.4(b)

course	name	credits	prerequisite
CS102	Intro to Databases	3	CS101
CS105	Visual Basic	4	CS100

Table 12.4(c)

Avoid tables with intentionally blank entries.

Tables with entries that are intentionally left blank waste space and are inefficient to use. Table 12.5, which serves as a directory of faculty and students, has an excessive number of blank entries. The table should be split into two tables, each dealing with just one of the groups.

name	ssn	classifi- cation	date hired	dept	office number	gpa	credits earned
Sarah Brown	816-34-9012	student				3.7	78
Pat Riley	409-22-1234	faculty	9/1/90	biology	Y-3014		
Joe Russo	690-32-1108	faculty	9/1/88	math	T-2008		
Juan Lopez	509-43-4110	student				3.2	42

Table 12.5 A table with an excessive number of blank entries

Strive for table clarity.

Each table should have a basic topic and all the data in the table should be connected to that topic.

Don't let a table get unnecessarily large.

A bookstore might keep a permanent record of each purchase for the purpose of targeting mailings. A better solution is to add a couple of extra fields to the customer table that identify the types of books of interest to the customer.

Avoid fields whose values can be calculated from existing fields.

A calculated field is one whose value can be determined from other fields. For instance, if a table has fields for both the population and area of a state, then there is no need to include a field for the population density.

Calculated Columns with SQL

Suppose we want to display in a data grid the cities in the MEGACITIES2.MDB database along with their expected population growth from 1995 to 2015. We could add a fifth field to the Cities table and fill it with the population growth. That is, for each record the entry in the new field would be the difference between its pop2015 and pop1995 fields. However, this would violate our last principle of database design—*avoid fields whose values can be calculated from existing fields*. SQL provides a way to display a population growth column without creating a new field for the Cities table.

If dgCities is a data grid connected to the Cities table of MEGACITIES2. MDB via the ADO data control adoCities, then the statements

```
sqlStr = "SELECT city, (pop2015 - pop1995) FROM Cities"
adoCities.RecordSource = sqlStr
adoCities.Refresh
```

will cause the data grid to display two columns as shown in Figure 12.16, where the second column shows the population growth for each city. This column is called a **calculated column**.

city	Expr1001
▸ Beijing	7
Bombay	12.2999992370605
Calcutta	5.90000057220459
Los Angeles	1.90000057220459
Mexico City	3.19999885559082
New York	1.30000114440918
Sao Paulo	4.39999961853027
Shanghai	8.29999923706055
Tianjin	6.30000019073486
Tokyo	1.90000152587891

Figure 12.16

The display in Figure 12.16 has two flaws—the second column does not have a meaningful name and the numbers in the second column are not rounded to one decimal place. The first flaw can be corrected by adding the clause AS popGrowth after (pop2015 – pop1995). This will give the column the heading *popGrowth*. The second flaw should be correctable by replacing (pop2015 – pop1995) with Round(pop2015 – pop1995, 1). Unfortunately, the version of SQL used by Visual Basic does not support the Round function. However, it does support the Int function, which can be used to round numbers. If x is a number, then the value of

$$\text{Int}(10 * x + .5) / 10$$

will be x rounded to one decimal place. (For instance, if $x = 1.267$, then $10 * x$ is 12.67, $10 * x + .5$ is 13.17, $\text{Int}(10 * x + .5)$ is 13, and finally $\text{Int}(10 * x + .5)/10$ is 1.3. In general, to round x to n decimal places, replace 10 by 10^n.) Therefore, the statements

```
sqlStr = "SELECT city, Int(10*(pop2015–pop1995)+.5)/10 AS popGrowth " & _
         "FROM Cities"
adoCities.RecordSource = sqlStr
adoCities.Refresh
```

produce the output shown in Figure 12.17.

city	popGrowth
▸ Beijing	7
Bombay	12.3
Calcutta	5.9
Los Angeles	1.9
Mexico City	3.2
New York	1.3
Sao Paulo	4.4
Shanghai	8.3
Tianjin	6.3
Tokyo	1.9

Figure 12.17

Note: The column title following the AS keyword can contain spaces. If so, the title should be surrounded by brackets. For instance, if the clause is AS [Population Growth], then the column title will be Population Growth.

Calculated values can be used in an ORDER clause to sort the displayed data. For instance, if the first statement in the lines of code above is changed to

```
sqlStr = "SELECT city, Int(10*(pop2015-pop1995)+.5)/10 As popGrowth" & _
         "FROM Cities ORDER BY (pop2015-pop1995) DESC"
```

then the cities will be sorted by their population growth.

Comments

1. Visual Data Manager can not create foreign keys.

2. Be careful if you create a database with empty tables. If you pull it into a program and try to move through it with the navigator arrows, an error will be generated. You must add at least one record before starting to navigate.

PRACTICE PROBLEMS 12.3

1. What would be some benefits of storing people names in two fields instead of one?

2. Give an SQL string that can be used with the MEGACITIES2.MDB database to display a data grid having two columns in which each row contains the name of a country and the percent of the world's population living in that country. (**Note:** The World population in 1995 was about 5.7 billion people.) The first line of the data grid should contain the information Brazil, 2.7.

EXERCISES 12.3

For each grid in Exercises 1 through 10, give an SQL statement that can be used to create the grid from the MEGACITIES2.MDB database. Then test your answer with a data grid attached to an ADO data control having the SQL statement as its RecordSource. (**Note:** Several of the exercises here have more than one correct answer.)

1.

country	pop1995	currency
Indonesia	195.3	rupiah
India	846.3	rupee

2.

country
Mexico
Brazil

3.

country	currency
Japan	yen
Russia	ruble
Brazil	real
Indonesia	rupiah

4.

country	pop1995	currency
India	846.3	rupee
Indonesia	195.3	rupiah
Brazil	155.8	real
Russia	148.2	ruble

5.

city	country	pop1995	pop2015
Shanghai	China	15.1	23.4
Beijing	China	12.4	19.4
Tianjin	China	10.7	17

6.

city	country	pop1995	pop2015
Sao Paulo	Brazil	16.4	20.8
Shanghai	China	15.1	23.4
Bombay	India	15.1	27.4
Tokyo	Japan	26.8	28.7

7.

city	country	pop1995	pop2015
Shanghai	China	15.1	23.4
Bombay	India	15.1	27.4
Mexico City	Mexico	15.6	18.8

8.

city	country	pop1995	pop2015
Sao Paulo	Brazil	16.4	20.8
Mexico City	Mexico	15.6	18.8

9.

city	pop2015	currency
Bombay	27.4	rupee
Calcutta	17.6	rupee

10.

city	Cities.pop1995	Countries.pop1995
Tokyo	26.8	125
Sao Paulo	16.4	155.8
New York	16.3	263.4

11. Consider the database EXCHANGERATES.MDB discussed in Exercises 12.1. Write a program that displays in a data grid a table similar to the one in Figure 12.5. However, the second column should show the number of American dollars that can be purchased with one unit of the country's currency.

12. Create the following table of leading restaurant chains for a database. Make the rank2001 field the primary key. Write a program to display the table in a DataGrid.

rank2001	name	segment
1	McDonald's	quick service burgers
2	Burger King	quick service burgers
3	Wendy's	quick service burgers
4	Taco Bell	quick service tacos
5	Pizza Hut	full service pizza

13. Create the following table of U.S. presidents for a database. Make the number field the primary key. Write a program to display the table in a DataGrid.

number	name	ageAtInauguration
1	George Washington	57
2	John Adams	61
3	Thomas Jefferson	58

14. Create a database having the following two tables. The left table contains famous novels along with their authors. The right table contains a list of important authors along with their country and year of birth. The field *author* in the right table should be a primary key. Use this database in a codeless program that displays a grid of three columns, where the first column contains a famous novel, the second column contains the country in which it was written, and the third column contains the author's year of birth.

novel	author
War and Peace	Tolstoy
My Antonia	Cather
Anna Karenina	Tolstoy
Les Miserables	Hugo
O Pioneers!	Cather

author	country	yrOfBirth
Tolstoy	Russia	1828
Cather	USA	1873
Hugo	France	1802
Cervantes	Spain	1547

15. Create a database having the following two tables. The left table contains famous lines from films that were spoken by the leading male actor. The field *film* in the second table should be a primary key. Use this database in a codeless program that displays a grid of two columns, where the first column contains a famous line and the second column contains the name of the actor who spoke the line.

famousLine	film
Rosebud.	Citizen Kane
We'll always have Paris.	Casablanca
You're going to need a bigger boat.	Jaws
The name is Bond. James Bond.	Goldfinger
I stick my neck out for nobody.	Casablanca

film	maleLead
Citizen Kane	Orson Wells
Casablanca	Humphrey Bogart
Jaws	Roy Scheider
Goldfinger	Sean Connery

16. The database BIBLIO.MDB is provided with Visual Basic and is usually found in the directory C:\Program Files\Microsoft Visual Studio\VB98. Use either Visual Data Manager or any other database management program to determine the names of the tables, the primary keys, and the foreign keys in the database.

17. The first Summer Olympic Games were held in Athens, Greece, in 1896. The database OLYMPICS.MDB has a single table called Summer, part of which is displayed in Table 12.6. The *year* field has been designated as the primary key. Unfortunately, the designer of the table Summer used a string of length 2 for the year and we are therefore unable to enter the data for the 1996 summer olympics. Create a new database with an integer field to display the year in Summer, and write a program to transfer the information from the old table into the new table. Then add the records "1996, Atlanta, USA" and "2000, Sydney, USA". (**Note:** The Summer Olympic Games were canceled in 1916, 1940, and 1944 due to war.)

year	site	mostMedals
96	Athens	Greece
00	Paris	France
04	St. Louis	USA
.		
.		
.		
88	Seoul	USSR
92	Barcelona	Unified Team

Table 12.6 Summer Olympics.

18. Specify all tables, fields, primary keys, foreign keys, validation rules, and validation text for a database to hold the student registrations for all the courses at a college. The registrar will use the database to print out a course schedule for each student and a class list for each course. Each course schedule should contain the student's name, address, social security number, and the list of courses currently registered for (with course name, section number, time, room, instructor, and number of credits). Each class list should contain the course name, section number, instructor, and list of students (with social security number, name, major, and rank).

19. Specify all tables, fields, primary keys, foreign keys, and validation rules and text for a database to be used by a bank to keep track of all checking account transactions for a month. At the end of the month, the bank will use the database to send out statements for each account. Each statement will contain a name, address, account number, opening balance, closing balance, and a detailed listing of all checks written and deposits made.

20. Reduce redundancy in the following table.

name	address	city	state	zip
R. Myers	3 Maple St.	Seattle	WA	98109
T. Murphy	25 Main St.	Seattle	WA	98109
L. Scott	14 Park Ave.	New York	NY	10199
B. Jones	106 5th St.	Seattle	WA	98109
W. Smith	29 7th Ave	New York	NY	10199
V. Miller	4 Flower Ave	Chicago	IL	60607

21. Reduce redundancy in the following table of members of the U.S. House of Representatives.

name	state	party	statePop	numColleges
J. Dingell	MI	D	9.6	106
W. Gilcrest	MD	R	5.1	57
J. Conyers	MI	D	9.6	106
R. Bartlett	MD	R	5.1	57
B. Frank	MA	D	6.1	117
A. Wynn	MD	D	5.1	57

22. Why use a field for a person's birth date rather than a field for his or her age?

In Exercises 23 and 24, use either Visual Data Manager or code to make the following changes in the Countries table of MEGACITIES2.MDB.

23. Add the record "Canada, 29.5, dollar".

24. Add a new field, *area*, and fill in the entries with the area of the country in millions of square miles. The areas are: Brazil, 3.3; China, 3.7; India, 1.3; Indonesia, .7; Japan, .2; Mexico, .8; Nigeria, .4; Russia, 6.6; USA, 3.7.

25. Suppose the database USSTATES.MDB contains the table States consisting of the three fields *name, population,* and *area,* with one record for each of the 50 U.S. states. Give an SQL string that can be used to display a data grid having two columns, the first column containing the names of the states and the second column containing their population densities. The states should appear in decreasing order of their population densities.

26. Suppose the database EMPLOYEES.MDB contains the table Payroll consisting of the four fields *name*, *phoneNumber*, *hoursWorked*, and *hourlyPayRate*. Assume that each entry *phoneNumber* field has the form xxx-xxx-xxxx, and the *hoursWorked* field is filled with the number of hours the person worked during a week. Give an SQL string that can be used to display a data grid having two columns with the first column containing the names of the people whose area code is 301 and the second column containing their wages for the week. The names should appear in increasing order of their earnings for the week.

The following exercises use the database BASEBALL.MDB discussed in Exercises 12.1. In Exercises 27 and 32, give an SQL string that can be used with the database to display a data grid in which each row contains the stated information. A sample row is shown in parentheses below each description.

27. player name, batting average
(Barry Bonds, 0.370)
Records should be sorted in descending order by batting average.

28. team name, stadium, team batting average
(Diamondbacks, Bank One Ballpark, 0.267)
Records should be sorted in ascending order by team batting average.

29. player name, stadium, batting average
(Manny Ramirez, Fenway Park, 0.349)
Display only players in the American League.

30. player name, league, team's batting average
(Barry Bonds, National, 0.267)

31. player name, batting average
(Junior Spivey, 0.301)
Records should be sorted in descending order by batting average and should only show the players whose batting average exceeded their team's batting average.

32. player name, difference between player's batting average and team's batting average
(Junior Spivey, Bank One Ballpark, 0.034)

✔✔ **Solutions to Practice Problems 12.3**

1. You can order the records by the last name. Also, you can use the record in a mailing and refer to each person in the salutation by his or her first name; as in "Dear Mabel."

2.
```
sqlStr = "SELECT country, Int(1000*(pop1995/5700)+.5)/10 AS percentPop " & _
         "FROM Countries"
```

1. A *table* is a group of data items arranged in a two-dimensional array, each row containing the same categories of information. Each data item (row) is called a *record*. Each category (column) is called a *field*. Two tables with a common field are said to be *related*. A *database* is a collection of one or more tables that are usually related.

2. The ADO *data control* is used to access a database. When a text box is bound to a data control through its DataSource and DataField properties, the user can read and edit a field of the database. At any time, one record is specified as the *current record*. The user can change the current record with the data control's *navigator arrows* or with *Move* statements. The property *Record-Count* counts records, the property *BOF* indicates whether the beginning of the recordset has been reached, and the property *EOF* indicates whether the end of the recordset has been reached. The *Value* property of Fields("*fieldName*") reads the contents of a field of the current record.

3. The *TextBox control* and the custom controls *DataList*, *DataCombo*, and *DataGrid* can be bound to a "virtual" table generated by an SQL statement, and filled automatically with one or more of the table's fields.

4. The *Validate event* for a text box, which is triggered whenever the text box is about to lose the focus, is used to require that the text box contains valid data. If not, the focus will remain on the text box, and the user can be informed of the problem. Also, in some situations the *Locked property* of a text box can be set to True to prevent the user from making any changes to the text.

5. A *primary key* is a field or set of fields that uniquely identifies each row of a table. The *rule of entity integrity* states that no record can have a null entry in a primary key. A *foreign key* is a field or set of fields in one table that refers to a primary key in another table. The *rule of referential integrity* states that each value in the foreign key must also appear in the primary key.

6. Structured Query Language (SQL) is used to create a "virtual" table consisting of a subtable of a table or of a join of two tables and imposes an order on the records. The subtable or join is specified with the reserved words SELECT, FROM, WHERE, ORDER BY, and INNER JOIN . . . ON. The WHERE clause of an SQL statement commonly uses the Like operator in addition to the standard operators. SQL statements are either employed at design time or run time as the setting of the RecordSource property. During run time, the Refresh method for the data control should be executed after the Record-Source property is set.

7. *Visual Data Manager*, a database management program supplied with most versions of Visual Basic, can be used to create a database and specify primary keys and validation criteria.

8. Although good database design is an art, there are several fundamental principles that usually should be followed.

9. A *computed column* of a data grid does not contain values from a field in a database table, but rather contains values that are computed from one or more fields.

1. The database MICROLAND.MDB (on the accompanying CD) is maintained by the Microland Computer Warehouse, a mail order computer supply company. Tables 12.7 through 12.9 show parts of three tables in the database. The table Customers identifies each customer by an ID number and gives, in addition to the name and address, the total amount of purchases during the current year prior to today. The table Inventory identifies each product in stock by an ID number and gives, in addition to its description and price (per unit), the quantity in stock at the beginning of the day. The table Orders gives the orders received today. Suppose that it is now the end of the day. Write a program that uses the three tables to do the following.

   (a) Update the *quantity* field of the Inventory table.
   (b) Display in a list box the items that are out of stock and therefore must be reordered.
   (c) Update the *amtPurchases* field of the Customers table.
   (d) Print bills to all customers who ordered during the day. (You can assume that each customer only calls once during a particular day and therefore that all items ordered by a single customer are grouped together. The bill should indicate if an item is currently out of stock. You can just display the bills one at a time in a picture box instead of actually printing them.)

custID	name	street	city	amtPurchases
1	Michael Smith	2 Park St.	Dallas, TX 75201	234.50
2	Brittany Jones	5 Second Ave	Tampa, FL 33602	121.90
3	Warren Pease	7 Maple St	Boston, MA 02101	387.20

Table 12.7 First three records of the Customers table.

itemID	description	price	quantity
PL208	Visual Basic – Standard	89.50	12
SW109	MS Office Upgrade	195.95	2
HW913	Scanner	49.95	8

Table 12.8 First three records of the Inventory table.

custID	itemID	quantity
3	SW109	1
1	PL208	3
1	HW913	2
2	PL208	1

Table 12.9 First four records of the Orders table.

2. Most college libraries have a computerized online catalog that allows you to look up books by author or title. Use the database BIBLIO.MDB to design such a catalog. You should create a new database with the necessary tables and fields and copy all needed information from BIBLIO.MDB into the new

database. (One field should hold the number of copies that the library owns and another field should hold the number of copies currently on the shelf. Use the Rnd function to fill the first field with numbers from 1 to 3.) The user should be able to do the following.

(a) View the books by author in either alphabetical or chronological order and then obtain relevant information (publisher, ISBN, copyright year, number of copies available and owned) on a specific book.
(b) Determine if a book with a specified title is owned by the library.
(c) Search for all books containing a certain word in its title.
(d) Check out a book that is on the shelf.
(e) Reserve a book that is currently not on the shelf. (A number can be assigned to each reservation to determine priority.)

The librarian should be able to generate a listing of all books for which there is a waiting list.

3. *Baseball Statistics* Suppose you are in charge of maintaining statistics for an intramural baseball league. Develop a database and write a program that will help you maintain statistics for the league players and teams. The database that you create should be similar to BASEBALL.MDB, having a table for Players and a table for Teams. The Players table should have fields for *playerName*, *teamName*, *atBats*, and *hits*. The Teams database should have the fields *teamName*, *wins*, and *losses*. Your program should accept input from text files to initialize the database for the season, and to update the database after each round of games.

The initialization file consists of lines of the form:

"John Doe", "Hawks"

which will cause an entry for player John Doe to be added to the Players table (with the numbers set to 0, and team set to Hawks), and an entry for the Hawks in the Teams table if one does not already exist. (**Note:** Don't forget to clear out existing entries in the database first before initializing for a new season.)

An update file consists of lines having one of the following two formats:

"John Doe", 4 ,1

causing the player entry for John Doe to have 4 at bats and 1 hit added to his current statistics, and

"Win", "Eagles", "Hawks"

causing a win to be added to the Eagles record in the Teams table, and a loss added to the Hawks record.

In addition to this functionality, the program should be capable of carrying out at least two of the following statistical tasks. [**Note:** Display the output of parts (a) and (b) in data grids using SQL. Display the output to parts (c) and (d) in picture boxes.]

(a) Display the team rankings in order of decreasing winning percentages (calculated by the formula *wins / number of games played*).
(b) Display the top 5 player batting averages

(c) Display the top 5 team batting averages

(d) Display the player name, batting average, and team name for the top player from each team, ordered by descending batting average.

4. *Grade Book* A teacher maintains a database containing two tables—Students and Grades. The Students table has the six fields *socSecNumber, lastName, firstName, streetAddress, cityAndState, zipCode*. The Grades table has the four fields *socSecNumber, firstExam, secondExam, finalExam*. At the beginning of the semester, the Students table is completely filled in with a record for each student in a class, and the Grades table has no records. (The database is contained in the file GRADEBOOK.MDB on the CD accompanying this textbook.) Write a program that allows the instructor to record and process the grades for the semester. The program should do the following.

(a) Use the Students table to add a record to the Grades table for each student that contains the student's social security number.

(b) Create a data grid that can be used to fill in the grades for each student after each exam.

(c) At the end of the semester, display a data grid showing the name of each student and his or her semester average. The semester average should be calculated as (firstExam + secondExam + 2 * finalExam) / 4.

(d) Print a list of semester grades that the instructor can post on his or her office door. The list should contain the last four digits of each student's social security number and the student's semester grade. (The semester grade should be determined by the semester average with an A for 90 – 100, a B for 80 – 89, and so on.) The list should be ordered by semester average. (You can just display the list in a picture box instead of actually printing it.)

(e) Print a letter for each student similar to the one shown below. (You can just display the letters one at a time in a picture box instead of actually printing them.)

George Jackson
123 Main Street
Washington, DC 20015

Dear George,

Your grades for CMSC 100 are as follows:

Final Exam: 87
Semester Grade: B

Best wishes for a good summer,
Professor Jones

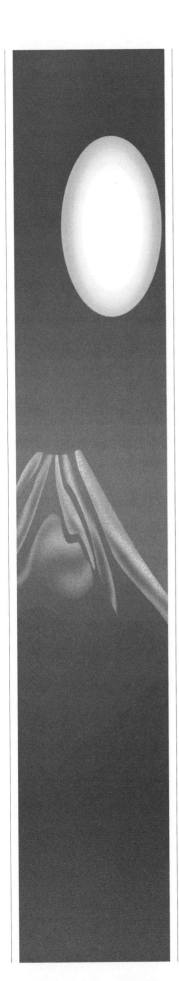

13 Object-Oriented Programming

13.1   CLASSES AND OBJECTS

noun A word used to denote or name a person, place, thing, quality, or act.

verb That part of speech that expresses existence, action, or occurrence.

adjective Any of a class of words used to modify a noun or other substantive by limiting, qualifying, or specifying.

The American Heritage Dictionary of the English Language

"A good rule of thumb for object-oriented programming is that classes are the nouns in your analysis of the problem. The methods in your object correspond to verbs that the noun does. The properties are the adjectives that describe the noun."

Gary Cornell & David Jezak[1]

Practical experience in the financial, scientific, engineering, and software design industries has revealed some difficulties with traditional program design methodologies. As programs grow in size and become more complex, and as the number of programmers working on the same project increases, the number of dependencies and interrelationships throughout the code increases exponentially. A small change made by one programmer in one place may have many effects, both intended and unintended, in many other places. The effects of this change may ripple throughout the entire program, requiring the rewriting of a great deal of code along the way.

A partial solution to this problem is "data hiding" where, within a unit, as much implementation detail as possible is hidden. Data hiding is an important principle underlying object-oriented programming. An object is an encapsulation of data and procedures that act on the data. The only thing of concern to a programmer using an object is the tasks that the object can perform and the parameters used by these tasks. The details of the data structures and procedures are hidden within the object.

Two types of objects will be of concern to us, **control objects** and **code objects**. Examples of control objects are text boxes, picture boxes, command buttons and all the other controls that can be created from the Visual Basic Toolbox. Code objects are specific instances of user-defined types that are defined similarly to record types in a separate module. Both types of objects have properties and respond to methods. The main differences are that control objects are predefined and have physical manifestations, whereas code objects must be created by the programmer and exist solely in a portion of memory. In this section, when we use the word "object" without a qualifier, we mean "code object."

Whenever you double-click on the TextBox icon in the Toolbox, a new text box is created. Although each text box is a separate entity, they all have the same properties and methods. Each text box is said to be an **instance** of the class TextBox. In some sense, the TextBox icon in the Toolbox is a template for creating text boxes. (When you look at the Properties window for a text box, the dropdown list box at the top of the window reads something like "Text1 TextBox". "Text1" is the name of the control object, and "TextBox" is the name

---

1. *ActiveX Visual Basic 5 Control Creation Edition*, Prentice-Hall, 1997.

of its class.) You can't set properties or invoke methods of the TextBox icon, you can only set properties or invoke methods of the specific text boxes that are instances of the class. The analogy is often made between the TextBox icon and a cookie cutter. The cookie cutter is used to create cookies that you can eat, but you can't eat the cookie cutter.

Object-oriented programs are populated with objects that hold data, have properties, respond to methods, and raise events. (The generation of events will be discussed in the next section.) Six examples are as follows.

1. In a professor's program to assign and display semester grades, a student object might hold a single student's name, social security number, midterm grade, and final exam grade. A CalcSemGrade method might calculate the student's semester grade. Events might be raised when improper data are passed to the object.

2. In a payroll program, an employee object might hold an employee's name, hourly wage, and hours worked. A CalculatePay method would tell the object to calculate the wages for the current pay period.

3. In a checking account program, a check register object might record and total the checks written during a certain month, a deposit slip object might have methods that record and total the deposits made during a certain month, and an account object might keep a running total of the balance in the account. The account object would raise an event to alert the bank when the balance gets too low.

4. In a bookstore inventory program, a textbook object might hold the name, author, quantity in stock, and wholesale price of an individual textbook. A CalcRetailPrice method might instruct the book object to calculate the selling price of the textbook. An event could be triggered when the book goes out of stock.

5. In a game program, an airplane object might hold the location of an airplane. At any time, the program could tell the object to display the airplane at its current location or to drop a bomb. An event can be triggered each time a bomb is released or moved so that the program can determine if anything was hit.

6. In a card game program, a card object might hold the denomination and suit of a specific card. An IdentifyCard method might return a string such as "Ace of Spades." A deck of cards object might consist of an array of card objects and a ShuffleDeck method that thoroughly shuffles the deck. A Shuffling event might indicate the progress of the shuffle.

The most important object-oriented term is **class**. A class is a template from which objects are created. The class specifies the properties and methods that will be common to all objects that are instances of that class. Classes are formulated in class modules. An object, which is an instance of a class, can be created in a program with a pair of statements of the form

```
Dim objectName As className
Set objectName = New className
```

The first of these two statements declares what type of object the variable will refer to, but does not create the object. The second creates a new object of the type *className* and then sets the variable to refer to that object. (In essence, the phrase "New *className*" creates the new object, and the Set keyword causes the variable *objectName* to refer to that object.) The second statement can only appear inside a procedure. The first statement can appear either in the general declarations section of a program (to declare a form-level variable) or inside a procedure (to declare a local variable). An object variable can be declared and assigned to a new instance of a class at the same time by use of the single statement

```
Dim objectName As New className
```

which may appear either in the general declarations section of a program or inside a procedure.

In a program, properties, methods, and events of the object are accessed with statements of the form shown in the following table.

Task	Statement
Assign a value to a property	`objectName.propertyName ‑ value`
Display the value of a property	`picBox.Print objectName.propertyName`
Carry out a method	`objectName.methodName(arg1, ...)`
Raise an event	`RaiseEvent eventName`

The following walkthrough creates a student class and a program that uses that class. The data stored by an object of this class are name, social security number, and grades on two exams (midterm and final).

1. Start a new program.

2. From the Project menu on the menu bar, click on Add Class Module.

3. Double-click on Class Module in the Add Class Module dialog box. (The window that appears looks like an ordinary Code window.)

4. If the Properties window is not visible, press F4 to display it. (Notice that the class has the default name Class1.)

5. Change the setting of the Name property to CStudent. (We will follow the common convention of beginning each class name with the uppercase letter C.)

6. Type the following lines into the class module.

```
Private m_name As String      'Name
Private m_ssn As String       'Social security number
Private m_midterm As Single   'Numerical grade on midterm exam
Private m_final As Single     'Numerical grade on final exam
```

(These lines of code declare four variables that will be used to hold data. The word Private guarantees that the variables cannot be accessed directly from outside the object. In object-oriented programming terminology, these variables are called **member variables** (or **instance variables**). We will follow the common convention of beginning the name of each member variable with the prefix "m_".)

7. From the Tools menu on the menu bar, click on Add Procedure. (As before, an Add Procedure dialog box will appear.)

8. Type "Name" into the Name text box, click on Property in the Type frame, and click on OK. The following lines will appear in the class module window.

```
Public Property Get Name() As Variant

End Property

Public Property Let Name(ByVal vNewValue As Variant)

End Property
```

9. Change the words Variant to String, the word vNewValue to vName, and type code into the two property procedures as shown below.

```
Public Property Get Name() As String
   Name = m_name
End Property

Public Property Let Name(ByVal vName As String)
   m_name = vName
End Property
```

Our program will call the first procedure to retrieve the value of the variable *m_name* and the second to assign a value to the variable *m_name*.

10. In the same manner as in Steps 7–9, create the following pair of property procedures that will be used to retrieve and assign values to the variable *m_ssn*.

```
Public Property Get SocSecNum() As String
   SocSecNum = m_ssn
End Property

Public Property Let SocSecNum(ByVal vNum As String)
   m_ssn = vNum
End Property
```

11. Property procedures can be typed directly into the class module without the use of Add Procedure. Also, property procedures needn't come in pairs. For instance, if we wanted the value of a member variable to be "write only," we would use a Property Let procedure and have no Property Get procedure. Type the following two property procedures into the class module. The inclusion of the word Public is optional.

```
Property Let midGrade(ByVal vGrade As Single)
   m_midterm = vGrade
End Property

Property Let finGrade(ByVal vGrade As Single)
   m_final = vGrade
End Property
```

12. Create the following ordinary Public function with the name CalcSem-Grade.

```
Public Function CalcSemGrade() As String
  Dim grade As Single
  grade = (m_midterm + m_final) / 2
  grade = Round(grade)    'Round the grade
  Select Case grade
    Case Is >= 90
      CalcSemGrade = "A"
    Case Is >= 80
      CalcSemGrade = "B"
    Case Is >= 70
      CalcSemGrade = "C"
    Case Is >= 60
      CalcSemGrade = "D"
    Case Else
      CalcSemGrade = "F"
  End Select
End Function
```

(This function will be used by our program when we invoke a method requesting an object to calculate a student's semester grade.)

13. From the File menu, click on Save CStudent As and save the class module with the name 13-1-1S.cls. (We chose this name since the class will be used in Example 1. Another good choice of name would have been Student.cls. The extension *cls* is normally given to files holding class modules.)

14. Click on the form window to activate it. We can now write a program that creates an object, call it *pupil*, that is an instance of the class and uses the object to calculate a student's semester grade. The object variable is declared (in the general declarations section of the form code) and an instance of the class is created with the statement

```
Dim pupil As New CStudent
```

The Property Let procedures are used to assign values to the member variables, and the Property Get procedures are used to retrieve values. The function CalcSemGrade becomes a method for obtaining the student's grade.

Some examples are

```
pupil.Name = "Adams, Al"       'Assign a value to m_name
picBox.Print pupil.Name         'Display the student's name
picBox.Print pupil.CalcSemGrade 'Display the student's semester grade
```

The first statement calls the Property Let Name procedure, the second calls the Property Get Name procedure, and the third calls the method CalcSemGrade.

EXAMPLE 1 The following program uses the class CStudent to calculate and display a student's semester grade.

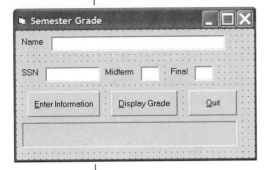

Object	Property	Setting
frm13_1_1	Caption	Semester Grade
lblName	Caption	Name
txtName	Text	(blank)
lblSSN	Caption	SSN
txtSSN	Text	(blank)
lblMidterm	Caption	Midterm
txtMidterm	Text	(blank)
lblFinal	Caption	Final
txtFinal	Text	(blank)
cmdEnter	Caption	&Enter Information
cmdDisplay	Caption	&Display Grade
cmdQuit	Caption	&Quit
picGrade		

```
'Student Class (CStudent)
Private m_name As String
Private m_ssn As String
Private m_midterm As Single
Private m_final As Single

Property Get Name() As String
  Name = m_name
End Property

Property Let Name(ByVal vName As String)
  m_name = vName
End Property

Property Get SocSecNum() As String
  SocSecNum = m_ssn
End Property

Property Let SocSecNum(ByVal vNum As String)
  m_ssn = vNum
End Property

Property Let midGrade(ByVal vGrade As Single)
  m_midterm = vGrade
End Property

Property Let finGrade(ByVal vGrade As Single)
  m_final = vGrade
End Property

Public Function CalcSemGrade() As String
  Dim grade As Single
  grade = (m_midterm + m_final) / 2
  grade = Round(grade)    'Round the grade
```

```
    Select Case grade
      Case Is >= 90
        CalcSemGrade = "A"
      Case Is >= 80
        CalcSemGrade = "B"
      Case Is >= 70
        CalcSemGrade = "C"
      Case Is >= 60
        CalcSemGrade = "D"
      Case Else
        CalcSemGrade = "F"
    End Select
End Function


'Form Code
Dim pupil As New CStudent          'pupil is an object of class CStudent

Private Sub cmdEnter_Click()
  'Read the values stored in the text boxes
  pupil.Name = txtName.Text
  pupil.SocSecNum = txtSSN.Text
  pupil.midGrade = Val(txtMidterm.Text)
  pupil.finGrade = Val(txtFinal.Text)
  'Clear Text Boxes
  txtName.Text = ""
  txtSSN.Text = ""
  txtMidterm.Text = ""
  txtFinal.Text = ""
  picGrade.Cls
  picGrade.Print "Student recorded."
End Sub


Private Sub cmdDisplay_Click()
  picGrade.Cls
  picGrade.Print pupil.Name; Tab(28); pupil.SocSecNum; _
                       Tab(48); pupil.CalcSemGrade
End Sub


Private Sub cmdQuit_Click()
  End
End Sub
```

[Run, enter the data for a student (such as "Adams, Al", "123-45-6789", "82", "87"), press the Enter Information button to send the data to the object, and press the Display Grade button to display the student's name, social security number, and semester grade.]

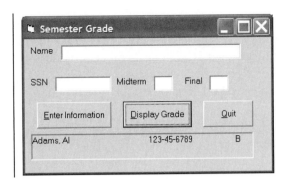

In summary, the following seven steps are used to create a class.

1. Identify a *thing* in your program that is to become an object.

2. Determine the properties and methods that you would like the object to have.

3. A class will serve as a template for the object. Add a class module from the Project menu.

4. Set the Name property of the class. (A common convention is to begin the name with the letter C.)

5. For each of the properties in Step 2, declare a private member variable with a statement of the form

   ```
   Private m_variableName As dataType
   ```

6. For each of the member variables in Step 5, create one or two public property procedures to retrieve and assign values of the variable. The general forms of the procedures are

   ```
   Public Property Get ProcedureName() As DataType
     ProcedureName = m_variableName
     (Possibly additional code.)
   End Property
   ```

   ```
   Public Property Let Procedurename(ByVal vNewValue As DataType)
     m_variableName = vNewValue
     (Possibly additional code.)
   End Property
   ```

   Note: Since the member variables were declared as Private, they cannot be accessed directly from outside an object. They can only be accessed through property procedures which allow values to be checked and perhaps modified. Also, a property procedure is able to take other steps necessitated by a change in a member variable.

7. For each method in Step 2, create a Sub procedure or Function procedure to carry out the task.

EXAMPLE 2 The following program modifies Example 1 and calculates semester grades for students who have registered on a "Pass/Fail" basis. The program creates a new class, named CPFStudent, with the same member variables and property procedures as the class CStudent. The only change needed in the class module occurs in the CalcSemGrade method. The new code for this method is

```
Public Function CalcSemGrade() As String
  Dim grade As Single
  grade = (m_midterm + m_final) / 2
  grade = Round(grade)   'Round the grade
  If grade >= 60 Then
      CalcSemGrade = "Pass"
    Else
      CalcSemGrade = "Fail"
  End If
End Function
```

The only change needed in the form code is to replace the two occurrences of CStudent with CPFStudent. When the program is run with the same input as in Example 1, the output will be

```
Adams, Al        123-45-6789     Pass
```

The Initialize Event Procedure

The Object dropdown combo box in a class module window displays two items, General and Class. When you click on Class, the following template appears.

```
Private Sub Class_Initialize()

End Sub
```

This event procedure is automatically invoked when an object is created from the class. Any code you type into the procedure is then executed. This procedure is used to set default values for member variables and to create other objects associated with this object.

Since methods are created with ordinary Function or Sub procedures, arguments can be passed to them when they are called. The graphical program in Example 3 makes use of arguments. The program involves "twips," which are a unit of screen measurement. (One inch is about 1440 twips.) The settings for the Top, Left, Height, and Width properties of a control are given in twips. For instance, the statements

```
Image1.Width = 1440      '1 inch
Image1.Height = 2160     '1.5 inch
Image1.Top = 2880        '2 inches
Image1.Left = 7200       '5 inches
```

set the size of the image control as 1" by 1.5", and place the control 2 inches from the top of the form and 5 inches from the left side of the form. (See Figure 7.6 in Section 7.3.) Programs using the Height property of the form should have the

BorderStyle property of the form set to "0-None" since otherwise the height of the border is included in the height of the form.

EXAMPLE 3 The following program contains a circle object. The object should keep track of the center and radius of the circle. (The center is specified by two numbers, called the coordinates, giving the distance from the left side and top of the form. Distances and the radius are measured in twips.) A Show method displays the circle on the form and a Move method adds 500 twips to each coordinate of the center of the circle. Initially, the (unseen) circle has its center at (0, 0) and radius 500. The form has a command button captioned "Move and Show Circle" that invokes both methods.

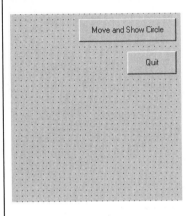

Object	Property	Setting
frmCircles	BorderStyle	0-None
cmdMove	Caption	Move and Show Circle
cmdQuit	Caption	Quit

```
'Class module for CCircle
Private m_x As Integer  'Dist from center of circle to left side of form
Private m_y As Integer  'Distance from center of circle to top of form
Private m_r As Integer  'Radius of circle

Private Sub Class_Initialize()
  'Set the initial center of the circle to the upper
  'left corner of the form and set its radius to 500.
  m_x = 0
  m_y = 0
  m_r = 500
End Sub

Public Property Get Xcoord() As Integer
  Xcoord = m_x
End Property

Public Property Let Xcoord(ByVal vNewValue As Integer)
  m_x = vNewValue
End Property

Public Property Get Ycoord() As Integer
  Ycoord = m_y
End Property
```

```
Public Property Let Ycoord(ByVal vNewValue As Integer)
  m_y = vNewValue
End Property

Public Sub Show()
  'Display the circle.
  'See discussion of Circle method in Section 10.4.
  frmCircles.Circle (m_x, m_y), m_r
End Sub

Public Sub Move(Dist As Integer)
  'Move the center of the circle Dist twips to the right
  'and Dist twips down. Then display the circle.
  m_x = m_x + Dist
  m_y = m_y + Dist
  Call Show
End Sub

'Form code
Dim round As New CCircle

Private Sub cmdMove_Click()
  round.Move(500)
End Sub

Private Sub cmdQuit_Click()
  End
End Sub
```

[Run, and press the command button five times.]

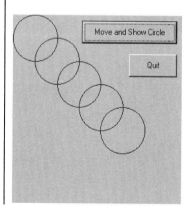

Comments

1. The statement

   ```
   Set objectVar = Nothing
   ```

   dissociates the object variable from the actual object and frees up the memory used by the object.

2. An object created inside a procedure without a declaration statement in the general declarations section of the form code ceases to exist when the procedure is exited. (We say that the object falls out of scope.) The effect is the same as when the variable is set to Nothing.

3. The counterpart to the Initialize event is the Terminate event procedure which has the template

```
Private Sub Class_Terminate()

End Sub
```

and is automatically invoked when all references to the object are Set to Nothing or when the object falls out of scope. This procedure is often used to set any objects you may have created inside the class module to Nothing.

4. Methods can be either Function or Sub procedures. A method that returns a value must be a Function procedure; otherwise it can be a Sub procedure.

5. A program with a class module has at least three components: a form, form code, and class module code. Although the View menu gives you access to the form (Alt/V/B) and the form code (Alt/V/C), only the Project Explorer gives access to all three. To view the code for a class module, double-click on the name of the class in the Project Explorer.

6. A class module is saved in a file whose file name has the extension .cls. Therefore, classes have both a name (C*something*) and a file name (*something*.cls).

7. To insert an existing (saved) class module into a program, click on Add Class Module in the Project menu, click on the Existing tab, and enter the filespec for the class module.

8. To delete a class from a program, right click on the class name in the Project Explorer and click on Remove *className*.

9. If *objVar1* and *objVar2* are both object variables of the same type, then the statement

```
Set objVar2 = objVar1
```

makes *objVar2* refer to the object that is referred to by *objVar1*. For example, after the code

```
Dim objVar1 As className
Dim objVar2 As className
Set objVar1 = New className
Set objVar2 = objVar1
```

has been executed, both variables will refer to the object created with the New keyword in the third statement.

10. An object variable also can be declared with a statement of the form

```
Dim pupil As Object
```

Later, *pupil* can be assigned to any type of object.

11. The set of properties, methods, and events for a class is called the class **interface**. The classes CStudent and CPFStudent have the same interface, even though they carry out the task of computing a grade differently. The programmer need only be aware of the CalcSemGrade method and needn't be concerned about its implementation. The feature that two classes can have behaviors that are named the same and have essentially the same purpose but different implementations is called **polymorphism**.

12. Sometimes you will have difficulty deciding whether an interface item should be a property or a method. As a rule of thumb, properties should access data and methods should perform operations.

13. The ByVal (which stands for "by value") keyword is automatically inserted before parameters in Property Let statements invoked from the Tools menu. However, this keyword is optional. The default way of passing an argument to a parameter is ByRef (which stands for "by reference"). Usually, passing by reference is more efficient than passing by value.

14. The default parameter name in a Property Let procedure is vNewValue. Although we usually substitute a meaningful name, we retain the convention of beginning the name with the prefix v.

15. We could have preceded our member variables with the keyword Public and allowed direct access to the variables. However, this is considered poor programming practice. By using Property Let procedures to update the data, we can enforce constraints and carry out validation.

16. In a class module, a property is implemented by two procedures, one to set and the other to retrieve the property value. These procedures that access properties are sometimes referred to as **accessor** methods.

PRACTICE PROBLEMS 13.1

1. Which of the following analogies is out of place?

   (a) class : object
   (b) sewing pattern : garment
   (c) blueprint : house
   (d) programmer : program
   (e) cookie cutter : cookie

2. What is the main difference between an object and a user-defined record?

EXERCISES 13.1

Exercises 1 through 12 refer to the class CStudent. When applicable, assume that *pupil* is an instance of the class.

1. What will be the effect if the Property Let midGrade procedure is changed to the following?

```
Property Let midGrade(ByVal vGrade As Single)
  Select Case vGrade
    Case Is < 0
      m_midterm = 0
    Case Is > 100
      m_midterm = 100
    Case Else
      m_midterm = vGrade
  End Select
End Property
```

2. What will be the effect if the `Property Let midGrade` procedure is changed to the following?

```
Property Let midGrade(ByVal vGrade As Single)
  m_midterm = vGrade + 10
End Property
```

3. Modify the class module for CStudent so that the following statement will display the student's midterm grade.

```
picBox.Print pupil.midGrade
```

4. Modify the class module for CStudent so that the student's semester average can be displayed with a statement of the form

```
picBox.Print pupil.Average
```

5. Find the error in the following form code.

```
Dim scholar As CStudent

Private Sub cmdGo_Click()
  Dim nom as String
  scholar.Name = "Peace, Warren"
  nom = scholar.Name
End Sub
```

6. Find the error in the following form code.

```
Dim scholar As CStudent

Private Sub cmdGo_Click()
  Dim nom as String
  Set scholar = CStudent
  scholar.Name = "Peace, Warren"
  nom = scholar.Name
End Sub
```

7. Find the error in the following form code.

```
Dim scholar As CStudent

Private Sub cmdGo_Click()
  Dim nom as String
  Set scholar = New CStudent
  m_Name = "Peace, Warren"
  nom = scholar.Name
End Sub
```

8. Find the error in the following form code.

```
Dim scholar As CStudent

Private Sub cmdGo_Click()
  Set scholar = New CStudent
  scholar.Name = "Peace, Warren"
  nom = m_Name
End Sub
```

9. Find the error in the following form code.

```
Dim scholar As CStudent

Private Sub cmdGo_Click()
  Dim grade As String
  Set scholar = New CStudent
  scholar.CalcSemGrade = "A"
  grade = scholar.CalcSemGrade
End Sub
```

10. Write code for the class module that sets the two grades to 10 whenever an instance of the class is created.

11. What is the effect of adding the following code to the class module.

```
Private Sub Class_Initialize()
  m_ssn = "999-99-9999"
End Sub
```

12. What is the output of the following form code?

```
Dim pupil As CStudent
Dim scholar As CStudent

Private Sub cmdGo_Click()
  Set scholar = New CStudent
  Set pupil = New CStudent
  scholar.midGrade = 89
  pupil.midGrade = scholar.midGrade
  picBox.Print pupil.midGrade
End Sub
```

Exercises 13 through 16 refer to the class CCircle.

13. Consider the program in Example 3. What would be the effect of removing the four property procedures from the class module?

14. Modify the program in Example 3 so that the four property procedures are used.

15. Modify Example 3 so that the circle originally has its center at the lower-right corner of the form and moves diagonally upward each time cmdMove is pressed.

16. Modify the form code of Example 3 so that each time cmdMove is pressed, the distance moved (in twips) is a randomly selected number from 0 to 999.

17. Write the class module for a class called CSquare. The class should have three properties, Length, Perimeter, and Area, with their obvious meanings. When a value is assigned to one of the properties, the values of the other two should be recalculated automatically. When the following form code is executed, the numbers 5 and 20 should be displayed in the picture box.

```
Dim poly As CSquare

Private Sub cmdGo_Click()
  Set poly = New CSquare
  poly.Area = 25
  picBox.Print poly.Length; poly.Perimeter
End Sub
```

18. Modify the class CSquare in the previous exercise so that all squares will have lengths between 1 and 10. For instance, the statement poly.Area = .5 should result in a square of length 1, and the statement poly.Area = 200 should result in a square of length 10.

19. Write the class module for a class called CPairOfDice. The function Rnd should be used to obtain the value for each die. (**Note:** The value of Int(6 * Rnd) + 1 will be a randomly chosen whole number between 1 and 6.) When the following form code is executed, three numbers (such as 3, 4, and 7) should be displayed in the picture box.

```
Dim cubes As New CPairOfDice

Private Sub cmdGo_Click()
  cubes.Roll
  picBox.Print cubes.Die1; cubes.Die2; cubes.SumOfFaces
End Sub
```

20. Write a program to toss a pair of dice 1000 times, and display the number of times that the sum of the two faces is 7. The program should use an instance of the class CPairOfDice discussed in the previous exercise.

21. Write the class module for a class called CStopWatch. The class should have the methods Start, Halt, and TimeElapsed. The time elapsed should be given in seconds. (**Note:** The function Timer gives the number of seconds that have elapsed since midnight.) When the following form code is executed, a number (such as 4.8) should be displayed in the picture box.

```
Dim timekeeper As CStopWatch

Private Sub cmdGo_Click()
  'Time the execution of a loop
  Dim i As Integer, j As Integer, value As Single
  Set timekeeper = New CStopWatch
  timekeeper.Start
```

```
    For i = 1 to 2000
      For j = 1 to 2000
        value = Sqr(j)
      Next j
    Next i
    timekeeper.Halt
    picBox.Print FormatNumber(timekeeper.TimeElapsed, 1)
  End Sub
```

22. Write the class module for a class called CCollege. The class should have properties Name, NumStudents, and NumFaculty. The method SFRatio should compute the student-faculty ratio. When the following form code is executed, the number 18.7 should be displayed in the picture box.

```
Dim school As CCollege

Private Sub cmdGo_Click()
  Set school = New CCollege
  school.Name = "University of Maryland, College Park"
  school.NumStudents = 30648
  school.NumFaculty = 1638
  picBox.Print FormatNumber(school.SFRatio, 1)
End Sub
```

23. Write a program that calculates an employee's pay for a week based on the hourly wage and the number of hours worked. All computations should be performed by an instance of the class CWages.

24. Write a program that a college bookstore can use to keep track of and determine the retail prices of textbooks. All computations should be performed by an instance of the class CTextbooks. The class should have properties Title, Author, Cost (wholesale cost), Quantity (number of copies in stock), and the method Price, that is, the retail price. Assuming that the bookstore marks up books by 25%, the Price should be 1.25 times the Cost.

25. Write a program that calculates an employee's FICA tax, with all computations performed by an instance of a class CFICA. The FICA tax has two components: the Social Security benefits tax, which in 2003 is 6.2 percent of the first $87,000 of earnings for the year, and the Medicare tax, which is 1.45 percent of earnings.

26. Write a program that adds two fractions and displays their sum in reduced form. The program should use a CFraction class that stores the numerator and denominator of a fraction and has a Reduce method that divides each by their greatest common divisor. Exercise 39 of Section 6.1 contains an algorithm for calculating the greatest common divisor of two numbers.

✔✔ Solutions to Practice Problems 13.1

1. (d) A programmer is not a template for creating a program.

2. Whereas both hold data, only an object has methods. Also, as we will see in the next section, objects can have events.

13.2 COLLECTIONS AND EVENTS

"An object without an event is like a telephone without a ringer."

Anonymous

A collection is an entity, similar to an array, that is especially well suited to working with sets of objects. This section discusses collections of objects and user-defined events for classes.

Collections

A collection of objects is an ordered set of objects where the objects are identified by the numbers 1, 2, 3, ... A collection is declared with a statement of the form

```
Dim collectionName As New Collection
```

and initially contains no objects. (We say that the variable *collectionName* is of the type Collection.) The statement

```
collectionName.Add objectName
```

adds the named object to the collection and automatically assigns it the next available number. The numbers for the different objects will reflect the order they were added to the collection. The statement

```
collectionName.Remove n
```

deletes the nth object from the collection and automatically reduces the object numbers from n + 1 on by 1 so that there will be no gap in the numbers. At any time, the value of

```
collectionName.Count
```

is the number of objects in the collection. The value of

```
collectionName.Item(n).propertyName
```

is the value of the named property in the nth object of the collection. The statement

```
collectionName.Item(n).methodName
```

runs the named method of the nth object of the collection.

EXAMPLE 1 In the following program, the user enters four pieces of data about a student into text boxes and selects a type of registration. When the AddStudent button is pressed, the data is used to create and initialize an appropriate object (either from class CStudent or class CPFStudent) and the object is added to a collection.

When the Calculate Grades button is pressed, the name, social security number, and semester grade for each student in the collection is displayed in the picture box.

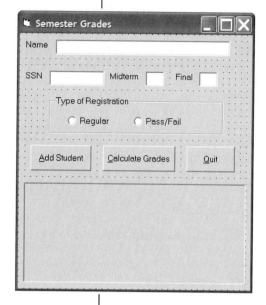

Object	Property	Setting
frm13_2_1	Caption	Semester Grades
lblName	Caption	Name
txtName	Text	(blank)
lblSSN	Caption	SSN
txtSSN	Text	(blank)
lblMidterm	Caption	Midterm
txtMidterm	Text	(blank)
lblFinal	Caption	Final
txtFinal	Text	(blank)
fraType	Caption	Type of Registration
optReg	Caption	Regular
optPF	Caption	Pass/Fail
cmdAdd	Caption	&Add Student
cmdCalculate	Caption	&Calculate Grades
cmdQuit	Caption	&Quit
picGrades		

```
'Student Class (CStudent)
Private m_name As String
Private m_ssn As String
Private m_midterm As Single
Private m_final As Single

Property Get Name() As String
  Name = m_name
End Property

Property Let Name(ByVal vName As String)
  m_name = vName
End Property

Property Get SocSecNum() As String
  SocSecNum = m_ssn
End Property

Property Let SocSecNum(ByVal vNum As String)
  m_ssn = vNum
End Property

Property Let midGrade(ByVal vGrade As Single)
  m_midterm = vGrade
End Property

Property Let finGrade(ByVal vGrade As Single)
  m_final = vGrade
End Property
```

```vb
Public Function CalcSemGrade() As String
  Dim grade As Single
  grade = (m_midterm + m_final) / 2
  grade = Round(grade)    'Round the grade
  Select Case grade
    Case Is >= 90
      CalcSemGrade = "A"
    Case Is >= 80
      CalcSemGrade = "B"
    Case Is >= 70
      CalcSemGrade = "C"
    Case Is >= 60
      CalcSemGrade = "D"
    Case Else
      CalcSemGrade = "F"
  End Select
End Function

'Pass/Fail Student Class (CPFStudent)
Private m_name As String
Private m_ssn As String
Private m_midterm As Single
Private m_final As Single

Property Get Name() As String
  Name = m_name
End Property

Property Let Name(ByVal vName As String)
  m_name = vName
End Property

Property Get SocSecNum() As String
  SocSecNum = m_ssn
End Property

Property Let SocSecNum(ByVal vNum As String)
  m_ssn = vNum
End Property

Property Let midGrade(ByVal vGrade As Single)
  m_midterm = vGrade
End Property

Property Let finGrade(ByVal vGrade As Single)
  m_final = vGrade
End Property

Public Function CalcSemGrade() As String
  Dim grade As Single
  grade = (m_midterm + m_final) / 2
  grade = Round(grade)    'Round the grade
```

```
      If grade >= 60 Then
          CalcSemGrade = "Pass"
        Else
          CalcSemGrade = "Fail"
      End If
  End Function

  'Form code
  Dim section As New Collection

  Private Sub cmdAdd_Click()
    Dim pupil As Object
    If optReg.Value Then
        Set pupil = New CStudent
      Else
        Set pupil = New CPFStudent
    End If
    'Read the Values stored in the Text boxes
    pupil.Name = txtName.Text
    pupil.SocSecNum = txtSSN.Text
    pupil.midGrade = Val(txtMidterm.Text)
    pupil.finGrade = Val(txtFinal.Text)
    section.Add pupil
    'Clear Text Boxes
    txtName.Text = ""
    txtSSN.Text = ""
    txtMidterm.Text = ""
    txtFinal.Text = ""
    picGrades.Print "Student added."
  End Sub

  Private Sub cmdCalculate_Click()
    Dim i As Integer, grade As String
    picGrades.Cls
    For i = 1 To section.Count
      picGrades.Print section.Item(i).Name; _
                    Tab(28); section.Item(i).SocSecNum; _
                    Tab(48); section.Item(i).CalcSemGrade
    Next i
  End Sub

  Private Sub cmdQuit_Click()
    End
  End Sub

  Private Sub Form_Load()
    'Initially, regular student should be selected
    optReg = True
  End Sub
```

[Run, type in data for Al Adams, press the Add Student button, repeat the process for Brittany Brown and Carol Cole, press the Calculate Grades button, and then enter data for Daniel Doyle.]

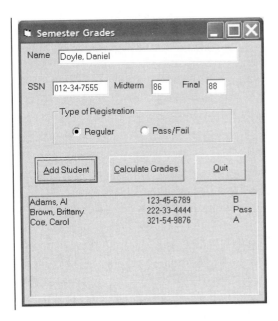

Keys

The items in a collection are automatically paired with the numbers from 1 on. Visual Basic provides an alternative device for accessing a specific item. At the time an item is added to a collection, we can associate a key for the item via a statement of the form

```
collectionName.Add objectName, keyString
```

After that, the object can be referred to as *collectionName.Item(keyString)*. A property of the object can be accessed with

```
collectionName.Item(keyString).property
```

For instance, consider the situation of Example 1. If we are using social security number as a key, and the object *pupil* contains the data for Brittany Brown, then the statement

```
section.Add pupil, "222-33-4444"
```

would assign the string "222-33-4444" as a key for her data. Then her name property can be accessed with

```
section.Item("222-33-4444").Name
```

EXAMPLE 2 The following program extends Example 1 so that the grade for an individual student can be displayed by giving a social security number. There are no changes in the two classes. In the Sub cmdAdd_Click procedure of the form code, line

```
section.Add pupil
```

is changed to

```
section.Add pupil, txtSSN.Text
```

An additional command button (cmdDisplay) with the caption "Display Single Grade" is placed on the form and the following event procedure for this button is added.

```
Private Sub cmdDisplay_Click()
  Dim ssn As String
  ssn = InputBox("Enter the student's social security number.")
  picGrades.Cls
  picGrades.Print section.Item(ssn).Name; _
                  Tab(28); section.Item(ssn).SocSecNum; _
                  Tab(48); section.Item(ssn).CalcSemGrade
End Sub
```

When this command button is pressed, the input box in Figure 13.1 appears. To obtain the output in Figure 13.2, run the program, enter the same data as in the execution of Example 1, press the "Display Single Grade" button, type 222-33-4444 into the input box, and press Enter.

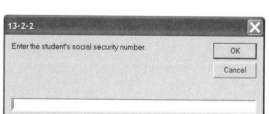

Figure 13.1 Input box

Figure 13.2 Output of program

Events

In the previous section we drew a parallel between objects and controls and showed how to define properties and methods for classes. In addition to the two predefined events for classes, Initialize and Terminate, other events can be defined by the programmer to communicate changes of properties, errors, and the progress of lengthy operations. Such events are called **user-defined events**. The statement for triggering an event is located in the class module and the event is dealt with in the form code. Suppose that the event is named User-DefinedEvent and has the arguments $arg1$, $arg2$, and so on. In the class module, the statement

```
Public Event UserDefinedEvent(arg1, arg2, ...)
```

should be placed in the (Declarations) section of (General), and the statement

```
RaiseEvent UserDefinedEvent(arg1, arg2, ...)
```

should be placed at the locations in the class module code at which the event should be triggered. In the form code, an instance of the class, call it *object1*, must be declared with a statement of the type

```
Dim WithEvents object1 As ClassName
```

in order to be able to respond to the event. That is, the keyword WithEvents must be inserted into the object variable declaration statement. (**Note:** You cannot use the New keyword along with the WithEvents keyword.) The header of an event procedure for *object1* will be

```
Private Sub object1_UserDefinedEvent(par1, par2, ...)
```

EXAMPLE 3 Consider the circle class defined in Example 3 of Section 13.1. Add a user-defined event that is triggered whenever the center of a circle changes. The event should have parameters to pass the center and radius of the circle. The form code should use the event to determine if part (or all) of the drawn circle will fall outside the form. If so, the event procedure should display the message "Circle Off Screen" in a label and cause all future circles to be drawn in red.

SOLUTION Let's call the event PositionChanged.

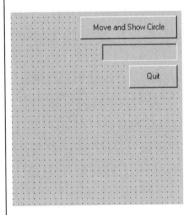

Control	Property	Setting
frmCircles	BorderStyle	0-None
cmdMove	Caption	Move and Show Circle
lblCaution	BorderStyle	1-Fixed Single
	Caption	(blank)
cmdQuit	Caption	Quit

```
'Class module for CCircle
Private m_x As Integer  'Dist from center of circle to left side of form
Private m_y As Integer  'Distance from center of circle to top of form
Private m_r As Integer  'Radius of circle
Public Event PositionChanged(x As Integer, y as Integer, r As Integer)
'Event is triggered by a change in the center of the circle

Private Sub Class_Initialize()
  'Set the initial center of the circle to the upper
  'left corner of the form, and set its radius to 500.
  m_x = 0
  m_y = 0
  m_r = 500
End Sub
```

```
Public Property Get Xcoord() As Integer
  Xcoord = m_x
End Property

Public Property Let Xcoord(ByVal vNewValue As Integer)
  m_x = vNewValue
End Property

Public Property Get Ycoord() As Integer
  Ycoord = m_y
End Property

Public Property Let Ycoord(ByVal vNewValue As Integer)
  m_y = vNewValue
End Property

Public Sub Show()
  'Display the circle.
  'See discussion of Circle method in Section 10.4.
  frmCircles.Circle (m_x, m_y), m_r
End Sub

Public Sub Move(Dist)
  'Move the center of the circle Dist twips to the right
  'and Dist twips down.
  m_x = m_x + Dist
  m_y = m_y + Dist
  RaiseEvent PositionChanged(m_x, m_y, m_r)
  Call Show
End Sub

'Form code
Dim WithEvents round As CCircle

Private Sub Form_Load()
  Set round = New CCircle
End Sub

Private Sub cmdMove_Click()
  round.Move(500)
End Sub

Private Sub round_PositionChanged(x As Integer, y As Integer, _
                                  r As Integer)
  'This event is triggered when the center of the circle changes.
  'The code determines if part of the circle is off the screen.
  If (x + r > frmCircles.Width) Or (y + r > frmCircles.Height) Then
      lblCaution.Caption = "Circle Off Screen"
      frmCircles.ForeColor = vbRed 'Make future circles red
  End If
End Sub

Private Sub cmdQuit_Click()
  End
End Sub
```

[Run and press the "Move and Show Circle" button seven times. **Note:** The last circle will be colored red.]

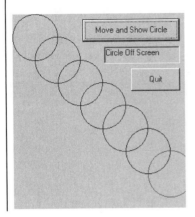

Comments

1. Perhaps a better name for "user-defined events" would be "programmer-defined events."

2. A statement of the form

```
collectionName.Add objectName, keyString
```

can also be written as

```
collectionName.Add Item:=objectName, Key:=keyString
```

3. The WithEvents keyword cannot be inserted into a declaration statement of the form

```
Dim objectName As Object
```

It can only be used when a specific class follows the word "As."

4. Collections require more memory than arrays and slow down execution time. If either a collection or an array would suffice, choose an array. This will often be the case when the number of items is fixed. For instance, a deck of cards should be represented as an array of card objects rather than a collection of card objects.

 PRACTICE PROBLEMS 13.2

Consider the program in Example 1, but assume that there are no Pass/Fail students. Therefore, in the form code, the statement Dim pupil As Object should be replaced by Dim pupil As CStudent and the cmdAdd method should be altered accordingly.

1. Alter the Property Let SocSecNum procedure to raise the event ImproperSSN when the social security number does not have 11 characters. The event should pass the length of the social security number and the student's name to the form code.

2. What statement must be placed in the general declarations section of the class module?

3. Write an event procedure for the event ImproperSocSecNum.

4. What statement in the form code must be altered?

EXERCISES 13.2

1. In Example 1, modify the event procedure cmdCalculate_Click() so that only the students who received a grade of A or Pass are displayed.

The CD accompanying this textbook contains the file STATES.TXT which provides data on the 50 states. (This file is used in Exercises 2 through 6.) Each record contains five pieces of information about a single state: name, abbreviation, date it entered the union, area (in square miles), and population in the year 2000. The records are ordered by the date of entry into the union. The first three records are

"Delaware", "DE", "Dec. 7, 1787", 2489, 783600
"Pennsylvania", "PA", "Dec. 12, 1787", 46058, 12281054
"New Jersey", "NJ", "Dec. 18, 1787", 8722, 8414350

2. Create a class CState with five properties to hold the information about a single state, and a method that calculates the density (people per square mile) of the state.

3. Write a program that requests a state's abbreviation in a message box and displays the name of the state and the date the state entered the union. The program should use a collection of CState objects.

4. Write a program that requests a state's name in a message box and displays the state's abbreviation, density, and date of entrance into the union.

5. Write a program that displays the names of the states and their densities in a list box ordered by density. The program should use a collection of CState objects.

6. Write a program that reads the data from the file into a collection of CState objects and raises an event whenever the population of a state exceeds ten million. States with a large population should have their names and populations displayed in a picture box by the corresponding event procedure.

7. Consider the program described in the opening paragraph of the Practice Problems. Add an event that is raised when the grade entered for a student is negative or greater than 100. Show all changes that must be made, and write an event procedure for the event.

8. Consider the class CPairOfDice discussed in Exercise 20 of Section 13.1. Add the event SnakeEyes that is raised whenever two ones appear during a roll of the dice. Write a program that uses the event.

9. Consider the class CStopWatch discussed in Exercise 21 of Section 13.1. Add the event MidnightPassed which is triggered if midnight occurs between the invocations of the Start and Stop methods. Write a program that uses the event.

10. Consider the CFraction class in Exercise 26 of Section 13.1. Add the event ZeroDenominator, which is triggered whenever a denominator is set to 0. Write a program that uses the event.

✔✔ **Solutions to Practice Problems 13.2**

1.
```
Property Let SocSecNum(ByVal vNum As String)
    If Len(vNum) = 11 Then
        m_ssn = vNum
    Else
        RaiseEvent ImproperSSN(Len(vNum),m_name)
    End If
End Property
```

2. `Public Event ImproperSSN(length As Integer, studentName As String)`

3.
```
Private Sub pupil_ImproperSSN(length As Integer, studentName As string)
    MsgBox "The social security number entered for " & _
        studentName & " consisted of" & Str(length) & _
        " characters. Reenter the data for " & studentName & "."
End Sub
```

4. The statement

`Dim pupil As CStudent`

must be changed to

`Dim WithEvents pupil As CStudent`

and moved to the general declarations section.

13.3 CLASS RELATIONSHIPS

The three relationships between classes are "use," "containment," and "inheritance." One class **uses** another class if it manipulates objects of that class. We say that class A **contains** class B when a member variable of class A is an object of type class B. **Inheritance** is a process by which one class (the child class), inherits the properties, methods, and events of another class (the parent class). Visual Basic does not support the strict academic definition of inheritance. In this section, we present programs that illustrate "use" (Example 1) and "containment" (Example 2).

In this section we will be setting variables to existing objects. In that case, the proper statement is

`Set objVar = existingObject`

EXAMPLE 1 Write a program to create and control two airplane objects (referred to as a *bomber* and a *plane*) and a bomb object. The airplane object should keep track of its location (that is, the number of twips from the left side and the top side of the form), be capable of moving in a direction (Forward, Up, or Down) specified by the user from a combo box, and be able to drop a bomb when so commanded.

The last task will be carried out by the bomb object. In the event that a bomb dropped from the bomber hits the plane, the plane should disappear. The airplanes and the bomb will have physical representations as pictures inside image controls. By their locations we mean the upper-left corners of their respective image controls. The picture files AIRPLANE.BMP and BOMB.BMP can be found in the Pictures directory of the CD accompanying this textbook.

SOLUTION

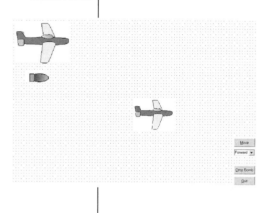

Object	Property	Setting
frmPlanes	BackColor	(white)
	BorderStyle	0-None
	WindowState	2-Maximized
imgBomberPic	Picture	AIRPLANE.BMP
	Stretch	True
imgPlanePic	Picture	AIRPLANE.BMP
	Stretch	True
imgBombPic	Picture	BOMB.BMP
	Stretch	True
	Visible	False
cboDirection	List	Forward
		Up
		Down
	Text	Forward
cmdMove	Caption	Move Bomber
cmdDropBomb	Caption	Drop Bomb
cmdQuit	Caption	Quit

```
'Class module for CPlane
Private m_imgPlane As Image 'image control associated with plane

Property Let imagePlane(newPlane As Image)
  Set m_imgPlane = newPlane
End Property

Public Function Present() As Boolean
  'Determine if the plane is visible
  'Will be needed by the bomb object.
  If m_imgPlane.Visible Then
      Present = True
    Else
      Present = False
  End If
End Function

Public Function X() As Integer
  X = m_imgPlane.Left
End Function

Public Function Y() As Integer
  Y = m_imgPlane.Top
End Function
```

```
Public Function W() As Integer
 W = m_imgPlane.Width
End Function

Public Function H() As Integer
  H = m_imgPlane.Height
End Function

Public Sub Fly(ByVal dir As String, ByVal Height As Integer, ByVal Width As Integer)
  m_imgPlane.Visible = True
  'Meanings of variables
  'dir     Direction of airplane (Forward, Up, or Down)
  'Height  Height of form
  'Width   Width of form
  If dir = "Up" Then
      'Prevent airplane from rising off the screen.
      If (m_imgPlane.Top - 500) >= 0 Then
        m_imgPlane.Top = m_imgPlane.Top - 500
      End If
    ElseIf dir = "Down" Then
      'Prevent airplane from falling off the screen.
      If (m_imgPlane.Top + m_imgPlane.Height + 500) <= Height Then
          m_imgPlane.Top = m_imgPlane.Top + 500
      End If
    ElseIf dir = "Forward" Then
      'Prevent airplane from moving off the screen.
      If (m_imgPlane.Left + m_imgPlane.Width + 500) <= Width Then
          m_imgPlane.Left = m_imgPlane.Left + 500
      End If
  End If
End Sub

Public Sub Destroy()
  m_imgPlane.Visible = False
End Sub

Private Sub Class_Terminate()
  Set m_imgPlane = Nothing
End Sub

'Class module for CBomb
Private imgBomb As Image
Public Event BombPositionChanged(X As Integer, Y As Integer, _
                                 W As Integer, H As Integer)
Property Let imageBomb(bomb As Image)
  Set imgBomb = bomb
End Property

Public Sub GoDown(plane As CPlane, ByVal FormHeight As Integer)
  Dim j As Integer
  imgBomb.Left = plane.X + 0.5 * plane.W
  imgBomb.Top = plane.Y + plane.H
  imgBomb.Visible = True
```

```
   Do While imgBomb.Top < FormHeight
     imgBomb.Top = imgBomb.Top + 5
     RaiseEvent BombPositionChanged(imgBomb.Left, imgBomb.Top, _
                                    imgBomb.Width, imgBomb.Height)

     'Pause
     For j = 1 To 2000
     Next j
   Loop
End Sub

Public Sub Destroy()
  imgBomb.Visible = False
End Sub

Private Sub Class_Terminate()
  Set imgBomb = Nothing
End Sub

'Form code
Dim bomber As CPlane
Dim plane As CPlane
Dim WithEvents bomb As CBomb

Private Sub Form_Load()
  Set bomber = New CPlane
  Set plane = New CPlane
  Set bomb = New CBomb
  bomber.imagePlane = imgBomberPic
  plane.imagePlane = imgPlanePic
  bomb.imageBomb = imgBombPic
End Sub

Private Sub cmdMove_Click()
  bomber.Fly cboDirection.Text, frmPlanes.Height, frmPlanes.Width
End Sub

Private Sub cmdDropBomb_Click()
  bomb.GoDown bomber, frmPlanes.Height
End Sub

Private Sub cmdQuit_Click()
  End
End Sub

Private Sub bomb_BombPositionChanged(X As Integer, Y As Integer, H As Integer, W As Integer)
  'Check to see if Plane is hit, i.e. the bomb is inside plane or vice versa.
  If plane.Present() Then
      If (plane.X <= X) And (plane.X + plane.W >= X) And _
         (plane.Y <= Y) And (plane.Y + plane.H >= Y) Or _
         (X <= plane.X) And (X + W >= plane.X) And _
         (Y <= plane.Y) And (Y + H >= plane.Y) Then
```

```
            plane.Destroy
            bomb.Destroy
          End If
      End If
  End If
End Sub
```

[Run, press the Move button twice, and then press the Drop Bomb button.]

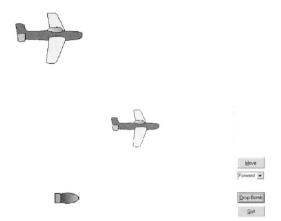

EXAMPLE 2 Write a program to deal a five-card poker hand. The program should have a deck-of-cards object containing an array of 52 card objects.

SOLUTION Our card object will have two properties, Denomination and Suit, and one method, IdentifyCard. The IdentifyCard method returns a string such as "Ace of Spades."

In the DeckOfCards object, the Initialize event procedure assigns denominations and suits to the 52 cards. The method ReadCard(n) returns the string identifying the nth card of the deck. The method ShuffleDeck uses Rnd to mix-up the cards while making 200 passes through the deck. The event Shuffling(n As Integer, nMax As Integer) is triggered during each shuffling pass through the deck and its parameters communicate the number of the pass and the total number of passes, so that the program that uses it can keep track of the progress.

Object	Property	Setting
frmPokerHand	Caption	Poker Hand
picHand		
cmdShuffle	Caption	&Shuffle
cmdDeal	Caption	&Deal
cmdQuit	Caption	&Quit

```
'Class module for CCard
Private m_Denomination As String
Private m_Suit As String

Public Property Let Denomination(ByVal vDenom As String)
  m_Denomination = vDenom
End Property
```

```
Public Property Let Suit(ByVal vSuit As String)
  m_Suit = vSuit
End Property

Public Property Get Denomination() As String
  Denomination = m_Denomination
End Property

Public Property Get Suit() As String
  Suit = m_Suit
End Property

Public Function IdentifyCard() As String
  Dim Denom As String
  Select Case Val(m_Denomination)
    Case 1
      Denom = "Ace"
    Case Is <= 10
      Denom = m_Denomination
    Case 11
      Denom = "Jack"
    Case 12
      Denom = "Queen"
    Case 13
      Denom = "King"
  End Select
  IdentifyCard = Denom & " of " & m_Suit
End Function

'Class module for CDeckOfCards
Dim m_deck(1 To 52) As CCard    'Class CDeckOfCards contains class CCard
Public Event Shuffling(n As Integer, nMax As Integer)

Private Sub Class_Initialize()
  Dim i As Integer
  For i = 1 To 52
    Set m_deck(i) = New CCard
    'Make the first thirteen cards hearts, the
    'next thirteen cards diamonds, and so on.
    Select Case i
      Case Is <= 13
        m_deck(i).Suit = "Hearts"
      Case Is <= 26
        m_deck(i).Suit = "Diamonds"
      Case Is <= 39
        m_deck(i).Suit = "Clubs"
      Case Else
        m_deck(i).Suit = "Spades"
    End Select
    'Assign numbers from 1 through 13 to the
    'cards of each suit.
    If (i Mod 13 = 0) Then
        m_deck(i).Denomination = Str(13)
```

```vb
      Else
         m_deck(i).Denomination = Str(i Mod 13)
      End If
   Next i
End Sub

Public Function ReadCard(cardNum As Integer) As String
   ReadCard = m_deck(cardNum).IdentifyCard
End Function

Private Sub Swap(ByVal i As Integer, ByVal j As Integer)
   'Swap the ith and jth card in the deck
   Dim tempCard As CCard
   Set tempCard = m_deck(i)
   Set m_deck(i) = m_deck(j)
   Set m_deck(j) = tempCard
End Sub

Public Sub ShuffleDeck()
   'Do 200 passes through the deck. On each pass
   'swap each card with a randomly selected card.
   Dim index As Integer, i As Integer, k As Integer
   Randomize   'Initialize random number generator
   For i = 1 To 200
     For k = 1 To 52
       index = Int((52 * Rnd) + 1)
       Call Swap(k, index)
     Next k
     RaiseEvent Shuffling(i, 200)
   Next i
End Sub

'Form Code
Dim WithEvents cards As CDeckOfCards

Private Sub Form_Load()
   Set cards = New CDeckOfCards
End Sub

Private Sub cmdShuffle_Click()
   cards.ShuffleDeck
End Sub

Private Sub cmdDeal_Click()
Dim str As String
Dim i As Integer
   picHand.Cls
   For i = 1 To 5
     str = cards.ReadCard(i)
     picHand.Print str
   Next i
End Sub
```

```
Private Sub cards_Shuffling(n As Integer, nMax As Integer)
  'n is the number of the specific pass through the deck (1, 2, 3..)
  'nMax is the total number of passes when the deck is shuffled
  picHand.Cls
  picHand.Print "Shuffling Pass:"; n; "out of"; nMax
End Sub

Private Sub cmdQuit_Click()
  End
End Sub
```

[Run, click on the Shuffle button, and click on the Deal button after the shuffling is complete.]

Comment

1. Example 1 illustrates "use" since the GoDown object of the bomb object receives a plane object. In general, class A uses Class B if an object of class B is sent a message by a property or method of class A, or a method or property of class A returns, receives, or creates objects of class B.

➤ EXERCISES 13.3

1. Write a program for the fraction calculator shown in Figure 13.3. After the numerators and denominators of the two fractions to the left of the equals sign are placed in the four text boxes, one of four operation buttons should be pressed. The result appears to the right of the equals sign. The program should use a Calculator class, which contains three members of the type CFraction discussed in Exercise 26 of Section 13.1.

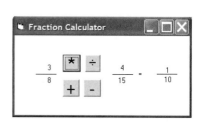

Figure 13.3 Sample output for Exercise 1.

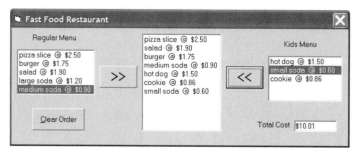

Figure 13.4 Sample output for Exercise 2.

2. Write a program that takes orders at a fast food restaurant. See Figure 13.4. The restaurant has two menus, a regular menu and a kids menu. An item is ordered by highlighting it in one of the list boxes and then pushing the >> or << button to place it in the order list box in the center of the form. As each item is ordered, a running total is displayed in the label at the lower right part of the form. The program should use a Menu class, which contains a Food class. (The contents of each of the three list boxes should be treated as Menu objects.) A Food object should hold the name and price of a single food item. A Menu object should have a MenuChanged event that can be used by the form code to update the cost of the order.

3. Write a program for a simple game in which each of two players rolls a pair of dice. The person with the highest tally wins. See Figure 13.5. The program should use a Game class (CHighRoller) having two member variables of the type CPairOfDice discussed in Exercise 19 of Section 13.1.

Figure 13.5 Sample output for Exercise 3.

4. Write a program to produce an employee's weekly paycheck receipt. The receipt should contain the employee's name, amount earned for the week, total amount earned for the year, FICA tax deduction, withholding tax deduction, and take-home amount. The program should use an Employee class (CEmployee) and a Tax class (CTax). The Tax class must have properties for the amount earned for the week, the prior total amount earned for the year, the number of withholding exemptions, and marital status. It should have methods for computing FICA and withholding taxes. The Employee class should store the employee's name, number of withholding allowances, marital status, hours worked this week, hourly salary, and previous amount earned for the year. The Employee class should use the Tax class to calculate the taxes to be deducted. The formula for calculating the FICA tax is given in Exercise 25 of Section 13.1. To compute the withholding amount, multiply the number of withholding allowances by $58.65, subtract the product from the amount earned, and use Table 13.1 or Table 13.2.

Adjusted Weekly Income	Income Tax Withheld
$0 to $51	$0
Over $51 to $164	10% of amount over $51
Over $164 to $579	$11.30 + 15% of excess over $164
Over $579 to $1,268	$73.55 + 27% of amount over $579
Over $1,268 to $2,792	$259.58 + 30% of amount over $1,268
Over $2,792 to $6,032	$716.78 + 35% of amount over $2,792
Over $6,032	$1,850.78 + 38.6% of amount over $6,032

Table 13.1 2003 Federal income tax withheld for a single person paid weekly.

Adjusted Weekly Income	Income Tax Withheld
$0 to $124	$0
Over $124 to $355	10% of amount over $124
Over $355 to $1,007	$23.10 + 15% of excess over $355
Over $1,007 to $2,150	$120.90 + 27% of amount over $1,007
Over $2,150 to $3,454	$429.51 + 30% of amount over $2,150
Over $3,454 to $6,093	$820.71 + 35% of amount over $3,454
Over $6,093	$1,744.36 + 38.6% of amount over $6,093

Table 13.2 2003 Federal income tax withheld for a married person paid weekly.

CHAPTER 13   SUMMARY

1. An *object* is an entity that stores data, has methods that manipulate the data, and can trigger events. A *class* is a template from which objects are created. A *method* specifies the way in which an object's data are manipulated. An *event* is a message sent by an object to signal the occurrence of an action.

2. Classes are defined in a separate module called a *class module*. Data are stored in member variables and accessed by procedures called *properties*.

3. Property Let and Property Get procedures are used to set and retrieve values of member variables. These procedures can also be used to enforce constraints and carry out validation.

4. The Initialize and Terminate event procedures are automatically invoked when an object is created and falls out of scope, respectively.

5. An object variable is declared in a program with a statement of the form `Dim objectName As className` and created with a statement of the form `Set objectName = New className`.

6. A *collection* is a convenient device for grouping together diverse objects. Objects are added to collections with the Add method and removed with the Remove method. The number of objects in a collection is determined with the Count property and an object is returned by the Item method using either an index number or a key.

7. Events are declared in the general declarations section of a class module with a statement of the form `Public Event UserDefinedEvent(arg1, arg2, ...)` and triggered with a RaiseEvent statement. In the form code, the declaration statement for an object must include the keyword WithEvents in order for the events coming from the object to be processed.

8. Objects interact through *use* and *containment*.

CHAPTER 13 PROGRAMMING PROJECTS

1. *Son of Deep Blue.* Write a program that plays a game of tic-tac-toe in which a person competes with the computer. The game should be played in a control array of nine labels. See Figure 13.6. After the user moves by placing an X in a label, the program should determine the location for the O. The program should use a tic-tac-toe object that raises events when a player moves and when the game is over. The outcome of the game should be announced in a message box.

Figure 13.6 Tic-Tac-Toe.

2. *Bank Account.* Write a program to maintain a person's Savings and Checking accounts. The program should keep track of and display the balances in both accounts, and maintain a list of transactions (deposits, withdrawals, fund transfers, and check clearings) separately for each account. The two lists of transactions should be stored in sequential files so that they will persist between program sessions.

Consider the form in Figure 13.7. The two dropdown combo boxes should each contain the items Checking and Savings. Each of the four frames corresponds to a type of transaction. (When Savings is selected in the Account combo box, the Check frame should disappear.) The user makes a transaction by typing data into the text boxes of a frame and pressing the command button. The items appearing in the transactions list box should correspond to the type of account that has been selected. The caption of the second label in the Transfer frame should toggle between "to Checking" and "to Savings" depending on the item selected in the "Transfer from" combo box. If a transaction cannot be carried out, a message (such as "Insufficient funds") should be displayed.

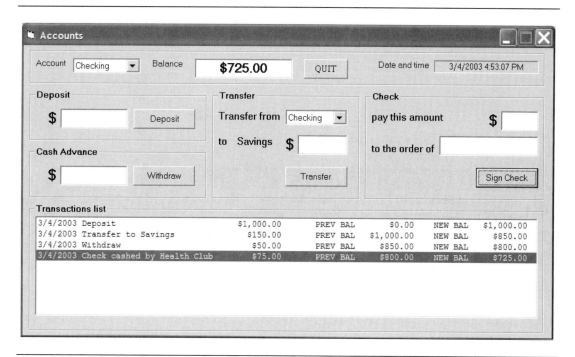

Figure 13.7 Bank accounts.

The program should use two classes, CTransaction and CAccount. The class CTransaction should have properties for transaction type, amount, paid to, previous balance, new balance, and transaction date. It should have a method that puts the data into a string that can be added to the Transaction list box, and methods that place data into and retrieve data from a sequential file.

The class CAccount, which will have both a checking account and a savings account as instances, should contain a collection of CTransaction objects. In addition, it should have properties for account type (Checking or Savings) and balance. It should have methods to carry out a transaction (if possible), to display the list of transactions, and to load and retrieve the set of transactions into or from a sequential file. The events InsufficientFunds and TransactionCommitted should be triggered at appropriate times. [**Hint:** In order to make CAccount object to display a list of transactions, a list box should be passed to a method as an argument. The method might begin with `Public Sub EnumerateTransactions(LB As ListBox).`]

3. Write a program that records the weekly payroll of a department that hires both salaried and hourly employees. The program should accept user input and display the number of employees, the number of salaried employees, the total payroll, and the average number of hours worked. The classes CSalariedEmployee and CHourlyEmployee both should contain Name, Rate, and HoursWorked properties. (The Rate text box should be filled in with the weekly salary for salaried workers and the hourly wage for hourly workers.) Each class should have a CalcGrossPay function that returns the appropriate weekly pay. A sample output is shown in Figure 13.8.

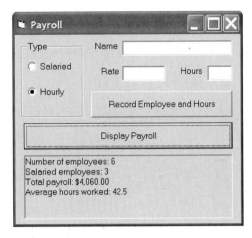

Figure 13.8 Payroll.

4. Write a program for the game BlackJack. See Figure 13.9. The program should use a BlackJack class (CBlackJack) that contains a member variable of the type CDeckOfCards presented in Example 2 of Section 13.3.

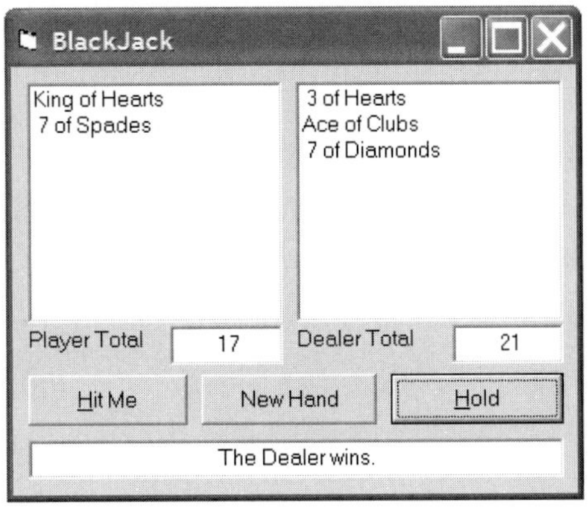

Figure 13.9 BlackJack.

14 Communicating with Other Applications

14.1 OLE

OLE, which stands for Object Linking and Embedding, is a technology that allows programmers to use Visual Basic to interact with applications such as spreadsheets and word processors. The three types of OLE are known as automation, linking, and embedding. With automation, you control an application from outside. With linking and embedding, you bring an application into your program. In this section, OLE is illustrated with Microsoft Excel and Word. However, the programs and walkthroughs can be modified for other spreadsheet and word processing software packages.

OLE Automation

The objects in the Visual Basic Toolbox have both properties and methods, and Visual Basic programs control them by manipulating their properties and methods. In general, anything that can be controlled in this way is called an **object**. In particular, an Excel spreadsheet or a Word document can be specified as an **OLE Automation object**.

We have worked extensively with the data types String, Integer, and Single. There are eight other data types, including one called **Object**. A variable that has been declared as an Object variable can be assigned to refer to an OLE Automation object. The CreateObject function is used to create an OLE Automation object and the Set statement is used to assign the object to an object variable. For instance, the pair of statements

```
Dim objExcel As Object
Set objExcel = CreateObject("Excel.sheet")
```

creates an Excel spreadsheet object and assigns it to the Object variable objExcel. The pair of statements

```
Dim objWord As Object
Set objWord = CreateObject("Word.Basic")
```

creates a Word document object and assigns it to the Object variable objWord. After the object is no longer needed, a statement of the form

```
Set objVar = Nothing
```

should be executed to discontinue association of objVar with the specific object and release all the resources associated with the previously referenced object.

An object is controlled by manipulating its properties and methods. For instance, the statement

```
objExcel.Application.Cells(4, 3).Value = "49"
```

places the number 49 into the cell in the fourth row and third column (that is, C4) of the spreadsheet. Some other Excel statements are

```
objExcel.Application.Visible = True              'Display spreadsheet
objExcel.Application.Cells(4, 3).Font.Bold = True    'Make cell bold
objExcel.Application.Cells(7, 3).Formula = "=SUM(C1:C5)"   'Specify that
                'cell C7 hold the sum of the numbers in cells C1 through C5
objExcel.Application.Quit                         'Exit Excel
```

With the Word object, the statement

```
objWord.Insert = "We'll always have Paris."
```

inserts the sentence into the document at the current insertion point. Some other Word statements are

```
objWord.FileNewDefault       'Create a new document based on
                             'the Normal template
objWord.WordLeft             'Move the insertion point left one word
                             '(Counts period as a word.)
objWord.Bold                 'Change font to bold
objWord.FileSaveAs filespec  'Save document with specified name
objWord.FilePrint            'Print the current document
objWord.FileClose            'Close the current document
```

OLE Automation involves the following four steps:

1. Declare an Object variable with a Dim statement.

2. Create an OLE Automation object with a CreateObject function and assign it to the variable with a Set statement.

3. Transfer commands and/or data to the OLE Automation object to carry out the desired task.

4. Close the object and assign the value Nothing to the Object variable.

EXAMPLE 1   The following program, which requires that Microsoft Excel be present in your computer, creates a spreadsheet for college expenses and uses the spreadsheet to add up the values for the different categories. The user should place numbers into the text boxes and then press the first command button to tabulate total college expenses. This process can be repeated as many times as desired.

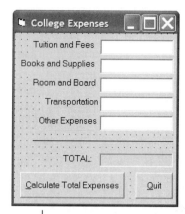

Object	Property	Setting
frm14_1_1	Caption	College Expenses
lblTuitNFees	Caption	Tuition and Fees
txtTuitNFees	Text	(blank)
lblBooksNSuppl	Caption	Books and Supplies
txtBooksNSuppl	Text	(blank)
lblBoard	Caption	Room and Board
txtBoard	Text	(blank)
lblTransportation	Caption	Transportation
txtTransportation	Text	(blank)
lblOther	Caption	Other Expenses
txtOther	Text	(blank)
Line1		
lblTotal	Caption	TOTAL:
lblHoldTotal	Caption	(blank)
cmdCalculate	Caption	&Calculate Total Expenses
cmdQuit	Caption	&Quit

```
Dim objExcel As Object        'In (Declarations) section of (General)

Private Sub cmdCalculate_Click()
  Set objExcel = CreateObject("Excel.Sheet")
  'Make Excel visible
  objExcel.Application.Visible = True
  'Fill in Rows Values
  objExcel.Application.Cells(1, 3).Value = txtTuitNFees.Text
  objExcel.Application.Cells(2, 3).Value = txtBooksNSuppl.Text
  objExcel.Application.Cells(3, 3).Value = txtBoard.Text
  objExcel.Application.Cells(4, 3).Value = txtTransportation.Text
  objExcel.Application.Cells(5, 3).Value = txtOther.Text
  'Set up a cell to total the expenses
  objExcel.Application.Cells(6, 3).Formula = "=SUM(C1:C5)"
  objExcel.Application.Cells(6, 3).Font.Bold = True
  'Set total as the contents of this cell
  lblHoldTotal = objExcel.Application.Cells(6, 3).Value
  'Make Excel invisible
  objExcel.Application.Visible = False
End Sub

Private Sub cmdQuit_Click()
  'Close Excel
  objExcel.Application.Quit
  'Release the object variable
  Set objExcel = Nothing
  End
End Sub
```

[Run, place numbers into the text boxes, and click on the Calculate Total Expenses button. **Note:** If the form is not visible, click on the College icon in the Window's task bar at the bottom of the screen.]

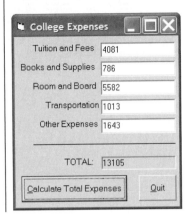

EXAMPLE 2

The following program creates a Word document, prints the contents of the document, and saves the document to a file.

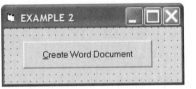

Object	Property	Setting
frm14_1_2	Caption	EXAMPLE 2
cmdCreate	Caption	&Create Word Document

```
Private Sub cmdCreate_Click()
  Dim objWord As Object
  Set objWord = CreateObject("Word.Basic")
  objWord.FileNewDefault
  objWord.Insert "I can resist everything."
  objWord.Wordleft
  objWord.Bold
  objWord.Insert " except temptation"
  objWord.FilePrint      'Make sure your printer is on
  objWord.FileSaveAs "QUOTE.DOC"
  objWord.FileClose
  Set objWord = Nothing
End Sub
```

[Run, and click the command button. The file QUOTE.DOC will be created and the printer will produce the following output.]

```
I can resist everything except temptation.
```

The OLE Container Control

An OLE Container control provides a bridge to Windows applications, such as spreadsheets and word processors. For instance, it can hold an Excel spreadsheet or a Word document. The application can be either linked or embedded through the OLE Container control. With **linking**, a link is established to the data associated with the application and only a snapshot of the data is displayed. Other applications can access the object's data and modify them. For example, if you link a text file to a Visual Basic application, the text file can be modified by any application linked to it. The modified version appears in all documents linked to this text. With **embedding**, all the application's data are actually contained in the OLE Container control and no other application has access to the data.

When you place an OLE Container control on a form, the dialog box in Figure 14.1 appears. You can select an application from the list and then press the OK button (or double-click on the application) to insert it into the control. Alternately, you can click on the "Create from File" option button to produce the dialog box in Figure 14.2. From this second dialog box, you specify a file (such as a Word .DOC file or an Excel .XLS file) by typing it into the text box or clicking the Browse command button and selecting it from a standard file selection dialog box. After the file has been selected, you have the option of checking the Link check box before clicking on the OK button to insert the contents of the file into the OLE Container control.

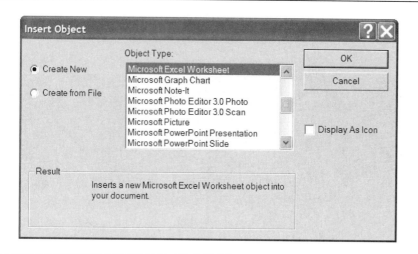

Figure 14.1 An Insert Object dialog box.

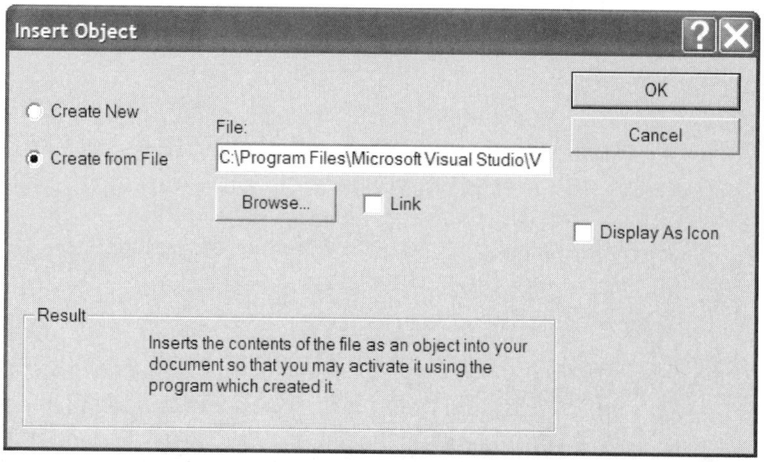

Figure 14.2 Dialog box for inserting contents of a file into an OLE Container control.

An Embedding Walkthrough Using Excel

1. Press Alt/**F**ile/**N**ew Project and click on OK.

2. Click the OLE icon in the Toolbox and use the single-click-draw technique to create a very large rectangle on the form.

3. The Insert Object dialog box appears. Double-click on "Microsoft Excel Worksheet" in the Object Type list.

Excel will be invoked and you will be able to create a spreadsheet. (Most likely, the Excel menu bar will replace the Visual Basic menu bar. In some cases, the Excel menu bar will appear on the form just below the title bar.)

4. Enter data into cells as shown in the first three rows of the spreadsheet in Figure 14.3.

5. Drag to select cells A1 through F3.

6. If you are using Excel 97 or a later version, click Insert, click Chart, and then proceed to Step 8. If you are using Excel 95, click Insert, then Chart, and then On This Sheet.

7. (A new mouse pointer consisting of a thin plus sign and a small bar chart appears.) Move the mouse pointer to cell A5, drag to the bottom-right corner of the OLE Container control, and then release the left mouse button.

A Chart Wizard dialog box appears.

8. Click on the Finish button.

Your spreadsheet should be similar to the one in Figure 14.3.

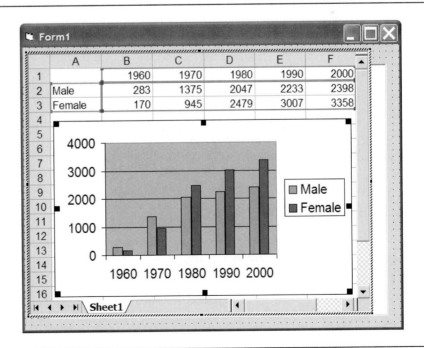

Figure 14.3 An Excel spreadsheet.

9. Click on the form to exit Excel.

   The values you created in Excel are now displayed in the OLE rectangle without any Excel embellishments. If necessary, you can resize the OLE rectangle to show any hidden material.

10. Run the program.

11. Double-click on the OLE rectangle to reinvoke Excel.

12. Change the value in one of the cells and then click on any other cell.

    Notice that the change is reflected in the bar chart.

13. Click the End icon to end the program.

    Notice that the changes to the data and graph have been lost. They are permanently gone.

14. Add a command button to the form and caption it Save Sheet.

15. Double-click on the command button to open the Command1_Click event procedure code window.

16. With Excel 97 or a later version, enter the following program lines into this code window. (With Excel 95, delete `worksheets("sheet1")`.)

    ```
    OLE1.Object.worksheets("sheet1").SaveAs "C:\MySheet.xls"
    ```

17. Run the program, double-click on the OLE rectangle to invoke Excel, change the contents of one of the cells, and click on another cell.

18. Click twice on the Save Sheet command button.

19. Click the End icon to end the program.

    Again the changes to the data and graph have been lost. However, the saved file now can be used to recover the changes if you so desire. To do so, go to the SourceDoc property of OLE1, click on the ellipsis, type C:\ MYSHEET.XLS into the text box, click on the OK button, and click on Yes in the "Delete Current Embedded Object?" message box.

A Linking Walkthrough Using Word

1. Before starting Visual Basic, invoke Word, type in a few sentences, and save the document. In this walkthrough we assume that the document you have created now resides on drive A and is named MYWORK.DOC.

2. Invoke Visual Basic.

3. Click the OLE icon in the Toolbox and use the single-click-draw technique to create a large rectangle on the form.

4. Click on the "Create from File" option button, type A:\MYWORK.DOC into the text box, click the Link check box, and click on the OK button.

   The document saved in MYWORK. DOC is displayed in the OLE rectangle.

5. Run the program and double-click the OLE rectangle. The complete Word program is invoked and the document in MYWORK.DOC is displayed.

6. Make some changes to the document, and then press Alt/File/Save and Alt/File/Exit to save your changes and exit Word. The modified document is displayed in the OLE rectangle on the Visual Basic form.

7. End the program and display the form if it is hidden.

   Notice that the document in the OLE rectangle is the original document, not the modified version. Visual Basic maintains an image of this original document in the program to display at run time if it is unable to display the latest version of the data (document).

8. Run the program.

   The document is still the original version.

9. Double-click on the OLE rectangle to invoke Word.

   Notice that the document displayed is the modified version.

10. Exit back to Visual Basic and then end the Visual Basic program.

11. Double-click on the form and add the code

    ```
    OLE1.Action = 6  'Update OLE image
    ```

    to the Form_Load event procedure.

12. Run the program.

    Notice that Visual Basic has updated the document to the last version saved while in Word even though you have not yet accessed Word by double-clicking.

Comments

1. The proper Automation statements can depend on the version of Office installed and on the configuration of the computer. We successfully tested the statements given in this section with several versions and configurations. However, there is a chance that some of the statements will not work on your computer.

2. An embedded application in the container OLE1 can be made into an OLE Automation object by a pair of statements of the form

   ```
   Dim objVar As Object
   Set objVar = OLE1.Object
   ```

3. After an Excel spreadsheet has been opened as an object, data can be assigned to and read from a single cell with statements such as

   ```
   objExcel.Application.Cells(4, 2).Value = "49"
   num = objExcel.Application.Cells(1, 3).Value
   ```

   These statements can be replaced by the following statements that use the standard spreadsheet notation for cells.

   ```
   objExcel.Application.Range("B4").Value = "49"
   num = objExcel.Application.Range("C1").Value
   ```

4. A linked or embedded application can be activated by double-clicking on the OLE container. It can also be activated with the code

```
OLE1.Action = 7
```

and deactivated with the code

```
OLE1.Action = 9
```

5. The OLE Automation function GetObject, which is similar to CreateObject, can be used to access existing Excel spreadsheets. For instance, if a worksheet resides in the root directory on a diskette in drive A and has the name EXPENSES.XLS, then the spreadsheet can be accessed with the pair of statements

```
Dim objExcel As Object
Set objExcel = GetObject("A:\EXPENSES.XLS")
```

6. Some other Word statements for use in OLE Automation are

```
objWord.FileOpen filespec      'Open the specified document
objWord.FontSize n             'Assign the value n to the font size
objWord.StartOfLine            'Move the insertion point to the
                               'beginning of the current line
objWord.EndOfLine              'Move the insertion point to the
                               'end of the current line
objWord.StartOfDocument        'Move the insertion point to the
                               'beginning of the document
objWord.EndOfDocument          'Move the insertion point to the
                               'end of the document
objWord.FileSave               'Save the current document
```

7. The following key combinations can be used to carry out tasks with an embedded Excel application:

Ctrl+;	Insert the date in the current cell
Alt+=	Sum continuous column of numbers containing the current cell
Ctrl+Z	Undo the last operation
Shift+F3	Invoke the Function Wizard
F7	Check spelling

8. The standard prefix for the name of an OLE container control is *ole*.

✔ **PRACTICE PROBLEM 14.1**

1. Redo the "Linking Walkthrough Using Word", but do not click the Link check box in Step 4. What differences do you notice as you continue the walkthrough?

➤ **EXERCISES 14.1**

Exercises 1 through 3 apply to a form containing a command button, a text box, and an OLE container (oleExcel) with an embedded Excel 97 (or later version) worksheet. Run the program, double-click oleExcel, enter numbers into some of the cells, click on the text box to move the focus away from the spreadsheet, and then click on cmdDisplay. What will appear in txtOutput? (**Note:** The first two lines of each event procedure make the contents of objExcel into an OLE Automation object.) If you are using Excel 95, delete "**worksheets("Sheet1")**".

1.
```
Private Sub cmdDisplay_Click()
    Dim objExcel As Object
    Set objExcel = oleExcel.Object
    Dim n As Integer
    Dim sumVar As Integer
    sumVar = 0
    For n = 1 To 3
      sumVar = sumVar + objExcel.worksheets("sheet1").Cells(n, 1).Value
    Next n
    txtOutput.Text = sumVar
    Set objExcel = Nothing
End Sub
```

2.
```
Private Sub cmdDisplay_Click()
    Dim objExcel As Object
    Set objExcel = oleExcel.Object
    Dim strVar As String
    If objExcel.worksheets("sheet1").Cells(1, 1) > _
              objExcel.worksheets("sheet1").Cells(2, 1) Then
        strVar = "A1 is greater than A2."
      Else
        strVar = "A2 is less than or equal to A1."
    End If
    txtOutput.Text = strVar
    Set objExcel = Nothing
End Sub
```

3.
```
Private Sub cmdDisplay_Click()
    Dim objExcel As Object
    Set objExcel = oleExcel.Object
    objExcel.worksheets("sheet1").Cells(25, 25).Formula = "=MAX(A1:A3)"
    txtOutput.Text = objExcel.worksheets("sheet1").Cells(25, 25).Value
    Set objExcel = Nothing
End Sub
```

4. Suppose the sequential file NUMBERS.TXT contains a sequence of numbers. Write an OLE Automation program that reads the numbers from the file and uses a spreadsheet to calculate their average. (**Note:** A function such as AVERAGE(C1:C3) averages the numbers in the specified block of cells.)

5. Write a program similar to Example 1 that allows you to input grades for three exams and then uses a spreadsheet to determine the average grade. (**Note:** A function such as AVERAGE(C1:C3) averages the numbers in the specified block of cells.)

6. Write an OLE Automation program to open the document created in Example 2 and insert "A Quotation by Oscar Wilde." at the beginning of the document. (**Note:** The statement objWord.Insert Chr(13) inserts a carriage return and line feed.)

7. Write an OLE Automation program to open the document created in Example 2, and add another paragraph to the end of the document. One possibility is "I always pass on good advice. It is the only thing to do with it. It is never of any use to oneself."

8. Write a program with a text box, two command buttons, and a word processor embedded in an OLE Container control. The program should use the word processor to correct the spelling of a sentence typed into the text box. When the first command button is clicked, the contents of the text box should be placed into the clipboard and the word processor activated. The user can place the sentence into the document with Ctrl+V, press F7 to invoke the spell checker, select the corrected sentence as a block, and press Ctrl+C to put the corrected sentence into the clipboard. When the second command button is pressed, the word processor should be deactivated and the contents of the clipboard should replace the contents of the text box.

9. Write a program with a form containing a command button, a text box, and an OLE container (oleExcel) with an embedded spreadsheet as in Figure 14.3. After you run the program, double-click oleExcel, enter the three grades, and then click on cmdDisplay, the semester grade should be displayed in the text box. The semester grade is obtained by throwing out the lowest grade and averaging the other two grades.

✔✔ **Solution to Practice Problem 14.1**

1. In Step 5, when the OLE rectangle is double-clicked, the complete version of Word is not invoked. Instead, the standard Toolbar is overlaid in the middle of the screen. In Step 6, the document cannot be saved because the menu bar is not present, and neither clicking on the Save icon nor pressing Ctrl+S works.

14.2 ACCESSING THE INTERNET WITH VISUAL BASIC

What Is the Internet?

The Internet began in the late 1960s as a project funded by the Defense Department's Advanced Research Projects Agency (ARPA) and initially was known as ARPANET. Over time, many research institutions and universities connected to this network. Eventually, the National Science Foundation took over ARPANET and ultimately it became what we now know as the Internet. Recent years have seen an amazing amount of growth in this global network.

The Internet often is confused with one of its most popular components, the **World Wide Web** (WWW) or "the Web." The Internet is much more than the Web. It also consists of electronic mail (e-mail), file transfer (FTP), newsgroups, and remote login capabilities. E-mail allows people to send messages to one another over the Internet. FTP allows people to transfer files from one machine to another. This is often the preferred method of retrieving shareware or freeware programs over the Internet. Usenet is a large collection of electronic discussion groups called newsgroups. There are newsgroups dedicated to every topic imaginable. People can post messages that all members of the group can read and answer.

The World Wide Web is made up of documents called pages, which contain pictures and text. The pages are accessed through programs called **Web browsers,** of which the best known are Netscape, Safari, and Internet Explorer. Web pages usually include links to other pages. These links are often set apart from the regular text by using boldface, underlining, or color. When you click on a link, you call up the page referred to by that link. These links used for connecting documents are called **hyperlinks.**

To access an initial Web page, you must specify an address called a Uniform Resource Locator (**URL**). You can do this by typing in a URL (or Locator) text box found toward the top of your browser, or typing in the dialog box that appears when selecting the Open command from the File menu, or clicking the Open button in the Toolbar.

A Web Browser Walkthrough

1. Connect to the Internet either through your commercial service provider or by using your school's network computers.

2. Start up a Web browser such as Netscape or Internet Explorer.

3. In the Location or URL text box toward the top of the browser, type the URL http://www.whitehouse.gov

4. Press Enter.

   After a little wait, you will see the White House Web page loaded into your browser.

5. Click on one of the highlighted or underlined phrases (links) in the document.

   The page associated with this link will load. For instance, if you click on "The President" you will see a page with information about the President.

6. Click on some other links to see what pages are brought up.

7. When you are through exploring the White House page, try other URL addresses such as:

Microsoft's Visual Basic Page	http://msdn.microsoft.com/vbasic
Google Search Engine	http://www.google.com
Prentice-Hall's Home Page	http://www.prenhall.com

The remainder of this section is devoted to using Visual Basic to integrate the Microsoft Internet Explorer Web browser into our programs. The requirements for this task are as follows:

1. A modem, or a direct Internet connection.

2. Microsoft Internet Explorer 4.0 (or higher) must be installed.

To Add the Web Browser Control to Your Visual Basic Toolbox

1. Invoke Visual Basic.

2. Press Ctrl+T to invoke the Components dialog box.

3. Click the check box next to Microsoft Internet Controls.

4. Click the OK button.

The Web browser icon should now appear in your Toolbox.

EXAMPLE I The following program creates a simplified Web browser. (Before running the program, be sure you are connected to the Internet as discussed above.) The primary task of the program, accessing the Web, is accomplished with the single statement

```
WebBrowser1.Navigate(txtURL.Text)
```

The On Error Resume Next statement specifies that when a run-time error occurs, control goes to the statement immediately following the statement where the error occurred, where execution continues. This statement is needed because the LocationURL of the Web browser control can easily return an error and crash the program. (For instance, this would happen if the intended Web site was down.)

After you run the program as specified in what follows, click on one of the links. **Note:** The home page of Internet Explorer will also be the home page of the Web browser control.

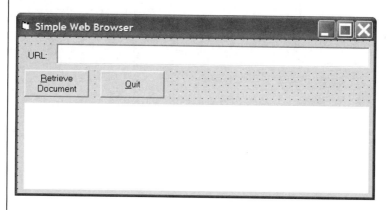

Object	Property	Setting
frm14_2_1	Caption	Simple Web Browser
lblURL	Caption	URL:
txtURL	Text	(blank)
cmdRetrieve	Caption	&Retrieve Document
	Default	True
cmdQuit	Caption	&Quit
WebBrowser1		

```
Private Sub Form_Load()
  WebBrowser1.GoHome              'Calls up Internet Explorer's home page
End Sub
```

```
Private Sub cmdRetrieve_Click()
  'Calls up the URL typed in the text box
  WebBrowser1.Navigate(txtURL.Text)
End Sub

Private Sub Form_Resize()
  'Resizes the WebBrowser control with the Form,
  'as long as the form is not minimized.
  'occurs when the Form is first displayed
  If frm14_2_1.WindowState <> 1 Then
      WebBrowser1.Width = frm14_2_1.ScaleWidth - (2 * WebBrowser.Left)
      WebBrowser1.Height = frm14_2_1.ScaleHeight - WebBrowser.Top - _
                           WebBrowser.Left
  End If
End Sub

Private Sub WebBrowser1_NavigateComplete2 (ByVal pDisp As Object, _
                                           URL As Variant)
  'Is activated when the HTML control finishes retrieving the
  'requested Web page.
  'Updates the text box to display the URL of the current page.
  On Error Resume Next   'Eliminates error messages
  txtURL.Text = WebBrowser1.LocationURL
End Sub

Private Sub cmdQuit_Click()
  End
End Sub
```

[Run. The Internet Explorer's home page will be displayed. Type http://www.whitehouse.gov/ into the text box, and click on the "Retrieve Document" command button.]

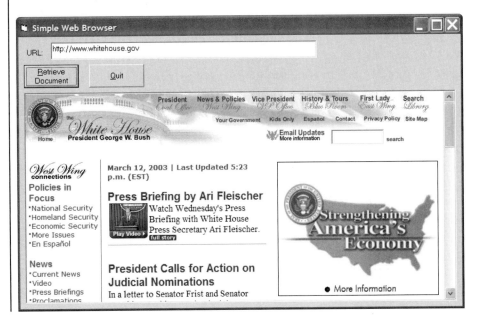

EXAMPLE 2

The following enhancement of Example 1 adds a label that shows the status of the Web browser control, a command button that returns you back to the most recently accessed page, and a command button that displays the Prentice-Hall web site. (The picture of the Prentice-Hall trademark is contained in the Pictures directory of the accompanying CD.)

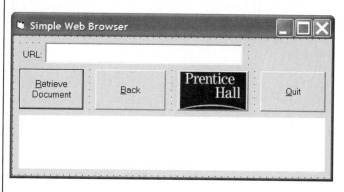

Object	Property	Setting
frm14_2_2	Caption	Simple Web Browser
lblURL	Caption	URL:
txtURL	Text	(blank)
lblStatus	Caption	(blank)
cmdRetrieve	Caption	&Retrieve Document
	Default	True
cmdBack	Caption	&Back
cmdPH	Caption	(none)
	Style	Graphical
	Picture	PHICON.BMP
cmdQuit	Caption	&Quit
WebBrowser1		

Add the following code to the program in Example 1.

```
Private Sub WebBrowser1_StatusTextChange(ByVal Text As String)
  'Event is called whenever the address of the page being
  'displayed changes. The address is assigned to the string Text.
  lblStatus.Caption = Text
End Sub

Private Sub cmdBack_Click()
  WebBrowser1.GoBack     'Return to the previous Web site or page
End Sub

Private Sub cmdPH_Click()
  WebBrowser1.Navigate ("http://www.prenhall.com")
End Sub
```

[Run. After the Internet Explorer home page appears, click on the command button with the picture of the Prentice-Hall trademark.]

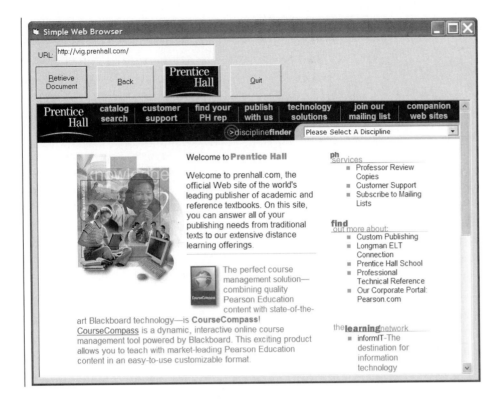

Comments

1. The abbreviation HTTP stands for HyperText Transfer Protocol.

2. Some additional properties of the Web browser control are

LocationURL	Gives the URL of the current page.
LocationName	Gives the title of the current page.
Busy	Has the value True if the control is downloading a file or navigating to a new location.

3. Some additional methods of the Web browser control are

GoForward	Undoes the most recent GoBack method.
GoSearch	Goes to the user's Web searching page.
Stop	Cancels the current operation of the control.

4. Some additional events of the Web browser control are

BeforeNavigate	Triggered right before the control moves to a new location.
ProgressChange	Triggered periodically as the downloading continues.
DownloadComplete	Triggered when the download is complete, halted, or failed.

5. If a file on your disk is an HTML document, you can view it as a Web page with the statement `WebBrowser1.Navigate "filespec"`.

6. A good book about the Internet is

K. Hafner and M. Lyon, *Where Wizards Stay Up Late: The Origins of the Internet*, Simon & Schuster, 1996.

PRACTICE PROBLEM 14.2

1. Can a Web browser really be written with just one line of code?

EXERCISES 14.2

1. What is the difference between the Internet and the World Wide Web?

2. Suppose the sequential file CENSORED.TXT contains a list of URLs that you do not want accessed. Modify Example 1 so that the user will not be able to visit these Web pages.

3. Modify the program in Example 2 to contain a Forward button.

4. Modify the program in Example 2 to inform the user when the downloading of the requested Web page is complete.

5. Implement a history list for the Web browser of Example 2. This list should be displayed in a list box and should contain the URL addresses of the last ten Web addresses visited. The user should be able to revisit one of these 10 sites by double-clicking on the appropriate address.

6. Add a What's Cool list of interesting URL addresses to the Web browser from Example 2. One such list is stored in the file COOL.TXT on the CD accompanying this book. When the program is loaded, the contents of the file should be placed into a list box. The user should be able to visit one of the interesting sites by double-clicking on its address in the list box.

7. Add a BookMarks feature to the Web browser in Example 2. Bookmarks are listed addresses that you frequently use. Create a sequential file called BOOKMARKS.TXT containing a few addresses. When you load the program, the contents of BOOKMARKS.TXT should be displayed in a list box. The user should be able to visit one of these sites by double-clicking on its address in the list box. Also, the user should be able to create a new bookmark by adding the address in the text box to both the list box and the sequential file.

8. Enhance the program in Exercise 7 to allow the user to delete a bookmark.

9. Type the following text into Windows Notepad and save it with the name WELCOME.HTM. Then write a program to view this file as a Web page.

```
<BODY>
<I> Welcome </I> to <B>Visual Basic 6.0 </B>
</BODY>
```

10. Experiment with the program in Exercise 9 to determine the values of the LocationURL and LocationName properties of the Web Browser control when the control is looking at an HTML file on a disk.

Solution to Practice Problem 14.2

1. Yes. If the program in Example 1 is simplified to consist solely of the procedure cmdRetrieve_Click(), it will still browse the Web.

14.3   WEB PAGE PROGRAMMING WITH VBSCRIPT

Note: This section requires that the Internet Explorer Web browser be installed on your computer.

Web browsers display Web pages created as text files, called HTML[1] documents. The text files can be written with Notepad or any other word processor. VBScript is a subset of the Visual Basic programming language that is used to make Web pages interactive. (You can use any VBScript code in VB itself.) In this section, we learn how to create Web pages with HTML, add controls to Web pages, and write VBScript code that manipulates these controls.

HTML

Here is a typical line in an HTML document.

<B>This sentence will be printed in bold.</B>

The items <B> and </B> are called **tags**. Here the letter B stands for Bold and the pair of tags tells the browser to display everything between them in boldface. The first tag is called the **begin tag** and the second the **end tag**. Most tags come in pairs in which the second tag differs from the first only in the addition of a slash (/). The combination of a pair of tags and the data characters enclosed by them is called an **element**. In general, a tag defines a format to apply or an action to take. A pair of tags tells the browser what to do with the text between the tags. Some pairs of tags and their effect on the text between them are as follows.

<I>, </I>	Display the text in italics
<U>, </U>	Display the text underlined.
<Hn>, </Hn>	Display the text in a size n header ($1 \leq n \leq 6$)
<BIG>, </BIG>	Display the text one font size larger.
<SMALL>, </SMALL>	Display the text one font size smaller.
<CENTER>, </CENTER>	Center the text.
<TITLE>, </TITLE>	Place the text in the Web page title bar.

An example of a tag that does not come in pairs is <P>, which tells the browser to start a new paragraph and insert a blank line. A similar tag is <BR>, which inserts a carriage return and a line feed to start a new line. The lines

```
Line One
Line Two
```

in an HTML document will be displayed as

```
Line One Line Two
```

in the Web page, since browsers combine all the white space (including spaces, tabs, and line breaks) into a single space. On the other hand,

```
Line One <BR> Line Two
```

---

1. HTML stands for HyperText Markup Language

will be displayed as

```
Line One
Line Two
```

and

```
Line One <P> Line Two
```

will be displayed as

```
Line One
```

```
Line Two
```

Sometimes the begin tag of a pair contains additional information needed to carry out a task. The pair of tags <A HREF=*address*> and </A> create a hyperlink to the Web page with the specified address and the text between the tags underlined. For instance, the element

<A HREF="http://www.prenhall.com/"> This is a link to Prentice-Hall.</A>

in an HTML document will be displayed by the browser as

This is a link to Prentice-Hall.

When you click anywhere on this link, the browser will move to the Prentice-Hall Web site.

HTML documents consist of two parts, the head and the body, delineated by the pairs of tags <HEAD>, </HEAD> and <BODY>, </BODY>. In addition, the entire HTML document is usually enclosed in the pair of tags <HTML>, </HTML>. The HTML document in Figure 14.4 produces the Web page shown in Figure 14.5.

```
NEWVB.HTM - Notepad
File  Edit  Format  View  Help
<HTML>
  <HEAD>
    <TITLE>Features in Visual Basic 6.0</TITLE>
  </HEAD>
  <BODY>
    <CENTER>
      <H1>What's New in Language Features</H1>
    </CENTER>
    <H4>Resizable Arrays Can Be Assigned</H4>
    <I>Variable-sized arrays</I> can now appear on the left side of an
assignment. Fixed-sized arrays cannot appear on the left side of an
assignment, although they can appear on the right.
    <H4>Functions Can Return Arrays</H4>
    Functions and properties procedures <B>will</B> be able to return arrays.
  </BODY>
</HTML>
```

Figure 14.4 HTML document.

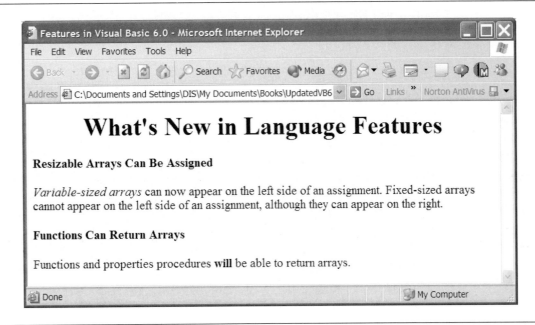

Figure 14.5 Web page.

Displaying a Web Page for an HTML Document

Suppose you have created the HTML document of Figure 14.4 in Notepad. The following walkthrough shows how to go back and forth between the HTML document and its associated Web page.

1. Save the Notepad document in a file with the extension .*HTM.* (**Note:** As a precaution against accidentally saving the file with the extension .*TXT,* set the "Save as type:" combo box to "All Files.") Do not exit Notepad.

2. Locate the file with Windows Explorer.

3. Double-click on the file. (Internet Explorer will be invoked and will display the Web page shown in Figure 14.5.)

4. Switch to the HTML document in Notepad. (One way to do this is to press Alt +Tab one or more times and then release the Alt key when the rectangle surrounds the Notepad icon.)

5. Make a change in the document. (For instance, change "What's" to "What is".)

6. Save the Notepad document.

7. Switch to Internet Explorer.

8. Press the Refresh button on the Toolbar. The Web page will now appear with "What's" changed to "What is".

Placing HTML Controls on a Form

Controls similar to some of the Visual Basic controls can be placed on a Web page using HTML. We will refer to these as **HTML controls**. HTML controls usually have different control and property names than their Visual Basic counterparts. Table 14.1 shows some Visual Basic controls that have comparable HTML controls, and Table 14.2 shows some property name changes.

Visual Basic Control	Equivalent HTML Control
CommandButton	button
TextBox	text
CheckBox	checkbox

Table 14.1 Comparable controls.

Visual Basic Property	Equivalent HTML Property
Text	VALUE
Caption	VALUE
Width	SIZE
Value	CHECKED

Table 14.2 Comparable properties.

An HTML control is placed on a Web page with an element of the form

```
<INPUT TYPE=controlType NAME=controlName ... otherSettings>
```

For instance, the element

```
<INPUT TYPE=text NAME="txtBox" VALUE="" SIZE=20>
```

places a text control with the name *txtBox* on a Web page. The control is initially empty and is capable of holding about 20 characters. The element

```
<INPUT TYPE=button NAME="cmdShow" VALUE="Show Greeting">
```

places a command button named *cmdShow* with caption "Show Greeting" on a Web page. The element

```
<INPUT TYPE=checkbox NAME="chkBox" VALUE=True>
```

places a checked check box named *chkBox* on a Web page. (The caption for the check box is typed in following the element.)

EXAMPLE I

The following HTML document produces the Web page shown in Figure 14.6.

```
<HTML>
  <HEAD>
    <TITLE>My First Web Page</TITLE>
  </HEAD>

  <BODY>
    <H1>Hello</H1>
    Type your name into the text box.
    <INPUT TYPE=text NAME="txtBox" VALUE="" SIZE=20>
    <BR><BR>
    <INPUT TYPE=checkbox NAME="chkBox" CHECKED=True>
    Display name in uppercase.
    <BR><BR>
    <INPUT TYPE=button NAME="cmdShow" VALUE="Show Greeting">
  </BODY>
</HTML>
```

Figure 14.6 Web page produced by Example 1.

Using VBScript with HTML Forms

The VBScript programming language is a variant of Visual Basic. It has most of the familiar features, such as If blocks, Do loops, Select Case blocks, procedures, and arrays. However, VBScript has some differences from Visual Basic. Certain events and methods have different names in the two languages. Table 14.3 shows a few of these differences. In VBScript, all variables are of type Variant and are declared with a statement of the form Dim *variableName*. Some additional differences between Visual Basic and VBScript are listed in Comments 5 and 6.

Visual Basic	Equivalent in HTML
Click event	onClick
DblClick event	onDblClick
GotFocus event	onFocus
LostFocus event	onBlur
SetFocus method	focus

Table 14.3 Comparable events and methods.

Code is written into a SCRIPT element with begin tag

```
<SCRIPT LANGUAGE="VBSCRIPT">
```

and end tag </SCRIPT>. The element can be placed in either the head or body section of the HTML document. Usually it is placed in the head section, as in Example 2.

EXAMPLE 2

The following enhancement of Example 1 uses VBScript to add functionality to the text and button controls. Figure 14.7 shows the output produced after the user types his name into the text control and clicks on the button control.

```
<HTML>
  <HEAD>
    <TITLE>My First Web Page</TITLE>
    <SCRIPT LANGUAGE="VBSCRIPT">
      Sub cmdShow_onClick()
        Dim msg
        msg = txtBox.Value
        If chkBox.Checked = True Then
           MsgBox "Greetings " & UCase(msg)
         Else
           MsgBox "Greetings " & msg
        End If
      End Sub
    </SCRIPT>
  </HEAD>

  <BODY>
    <H1>Hello</H1>
    Type your name into the text box.
    <INPUT TYPE=text NAME="txtBox" VALUE="" SIZE=20>
    <BR><BR>
    <INPUT TYPE=checkbox NAME="chkBox" CHECKED=True>
     Display name in uppercase.
    <BR><BR>
    <INPUT TYPE=button NAME="cmdShow" VALUE="Show Greeting">
  </BODY>
</HTML>
```

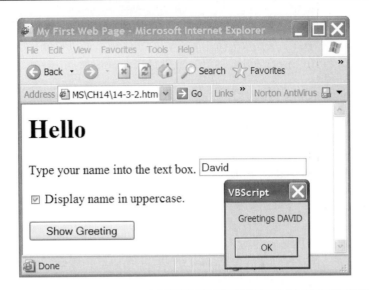

Figure 14.7 A possible outcome produced by Example 2.

Comments

1. HTML tags are not case sensitive. For instance, <b> has the same effect as <B>.

2. If you use a TITLE element, it must be placed inside the HEAD portion of an HTML document.

3. VBScript programs can contain code that is not in any procedure. If so, this code is executed by Internet Explorer as soon as the Web page is displayed. It is analogous to Visual Basic code found in the Form_Load event procedure.

4. Some features of Visual Basic that are not available in VBScript are ranges of values and the Is keyword in Case clauses, Str and Val functions, the Open statement, the On Error GoTo statement, arrays declared with lower bound ≤ 0, line labels, collections, and picture box controls.

5. If i is the index of a For...Next loop, in Visual Basic the final statement should be Next i. In VBScript, the i must be dropped from the final statement.

✔ PRACTICE PROBLEMS 14.3

What is the effect of each of the following portions of an HTML document?

1. <I>The <B>future</B> isn't what it used to be.</I>

2.
```
<SCRIPT LANGUAGE="VBSCRIPT">
  Dim word
  word = "untie!"
  Call Connect(word)
  Sub Connect(word)
    MsgBox "Bad spellers of the world, " & word
  End Sub
</SCRIPT>
```

➤ **EXERCISES 14.3**

In Exercises 1 through 4, determine what will be displayed on the Web page by the portion of the HTML document shown.

1. `<I>Keep cool,</I> <B>but don't freeze.</B><BR>Found on a jar of mayonnaise.`

2. `So little time<P>and so little to do.`

3. `Would you like to visit the <A HREF="http://www.prenhall.com">Prentice-Hall</A> Web site?`

4. `Talk is cheap because <BIG>supply</BIG> exceeds demand.`

In Exercises 5 through 8, find the errors.

5.
```
<SCRIPT LANGUAGE="VBSCRIPT">
  Sub cmdShow_Click()
    Dim nom
    nom = <B>txtFirstName.text</B>
    MsgBox "Greetings " & nom
  End Sub
</SCRIPT>
```

6.
```
<SCRIPT LANGUAGE="VBSCRIPT">
  Sub txtBox_onFocus()
    Dim num As Integer
    num = InputBox("Enter a whole number:")
    txtBox.Value = num
  End Sub
</SCRIPT>
```

7.
```
<SCRIPT>
  Sub cmdShow_onClick()
    MsgBox "Keep cool"
  End Sub
</SCRIPT>
```

8. Start slow <i> and taper off.<i>

In Exercises 9 through 14, conjecture on the effect of the line of code. Then test your guess in a Web page.

9. `document.Title = "My Second Web Page"`

10. `MsgBox(document.LastModified)`

11. `txtBox.Style.Color = "Red"`

12. `document.bgColor = "Blue"`

13. `txtBox.Style.FontWeight = "Bold"`

14. `cmdShow.Style.FontStyle = "Italic"`

15. Create a Web page with a text box, a command button, and two check boxes. The check boxes should have captions "Red" and "Bold". When the command button is clicked, the word "VBScript" should be displayed in the text box in the color and style determined by the status of the check boxes. (**Note:** The statement `txtBox.Style.FontWeight = "Normal"` resets the font to its default state.)

16. Rework Example 6 of Section 3.4 as a Web page.

17. Create a Web page that displays the date and time in a text box as soon as the Web page appears. Use the functions Date and Time.

18. Create a Web page that displays the message "Welcome to my Web page." as soon as the Web page appears.

19. Create a Web page containing a text box and a command button. Instruct the user to enter a word into the text box and push the command button to see the word written backwards.

20. Table 14.4 gives the number of colleges in each of the New England states. Create a Web page with a text box and a command button. The user should be instructed to type the name of one of the New England states into the text box and then press the command button. When the command button is pressed, the number of colleges in the state should be displayed in a message dialog box.

State	Colleges	State	Colleges
Connecticut	42	New Hampshire	30
Maine	31	Rhode Island	14
Massachusetts	117	Vermont	22

Table 14.4 Colleges in New England.

✔✔ **Solutions to Practice Problems 14.3**

1. *The **future** isn't what it used to be.*

2. As soon as the Web page appears, a message box containing the statement "Bad spellers of the world, untie!" will appear.

CHAPTER 14 **SUMMARY**

1. OLE, a technology developed by Microsoft, gives Visual Basic access to other applications.

2. OLE Automation allows you to control other applications with Visual Basic code. The other application is declared as an object with the Set statement and CreateObject function.

3. Other applications can be embedded in or linked to a form with the OLE Container control.

4. The WebBrowser control can be used to create a browser for the World Wide Web.

5. The document-formatting language used by Web browsers is called *HTML*. *Tags* are used to mark up text with display instructions. The combination of a pair of tags and the text enclosed is called an *element*.

6. *VBScript* is a variant of Visual Basic that is used to make Web pages interactive.

15 Visual Basic .NET

15.1 FUNDAMENTALS OF VISUAL BASIC .NET

In the year 2002, Microsoft released Visual Basic .NET (abbreviated VB.NET), a major revision of Visual Basic. Programs written in VB.NET are executed by a program called the .NET runtime (also known as the Common Language Runtime, or CLR). By targeting the .NET runtime as opposed to the Windows operating system, programs written in VB.NET can be executed on other operating systems and devices that have the .NET runtime installed, such as cell phones and handheld computers. Furthermore, VB.NET programs can interact with programs written in other languages that target the .NET runtime (such as C#.NET and C++.NET). The collection of .NET programming languages are packaged together with the .NET runtime as Visual Studio .NET.

VB.NET is a totally object-oriented language that requires a Windows NT, Windows 2000, Windows XP, or later operating system. VB.NET is not backward compatible with VB 6.0. However, most of the topics covered in this book carry over to VB.NET with slight changes. This chapter explains the new features in VB.NET and show how to make the transition from programming in VB 6.0 to programming in VB.NET. After reading this chapter, you will be able to convert most of the VB 6.0 programs in this book into VB.NET code. (**Note:** The CD accompanying this book does not contain VB.NET.)

Invoking VB.NET: To invoke VB.NET, click the Start button, point to Programs, point to Microsoft Visual Studio.NET, and click on Microsoft Visual Studio.NET in the final list. The screen that appears is similar to the one in Figure 15.1. The top part consists of menu names and icons for tools. The remainder of the screen consists primarily of four rectangular windows. The large rectangular window containing the word "Start" is known as the **Start Window** or the **Visual Studio Home Page**.

VB.NET programs are also known as **applications**, **solutions**, or **projects**, and each is saved (as several files and subfolders) in its own folder. Before starting a new program, you should use Window's Explorer to create a folder to hold the folders for the programs. For instance, you might create a subfolder of My Documents named "VB.NET Programs."

One way to begin the creation of a new program is to click on File in the menu bar at the top of the screen, hover the cursor over New, and then click on Project to produce a "New Project" dialog box similar to the one in Figure 15.2. Alternately, you can click on the button captioned "New Project" in the Start Window. (The number of icons appearing in the Templates window depends on the version of VB.NET that has been installed.)

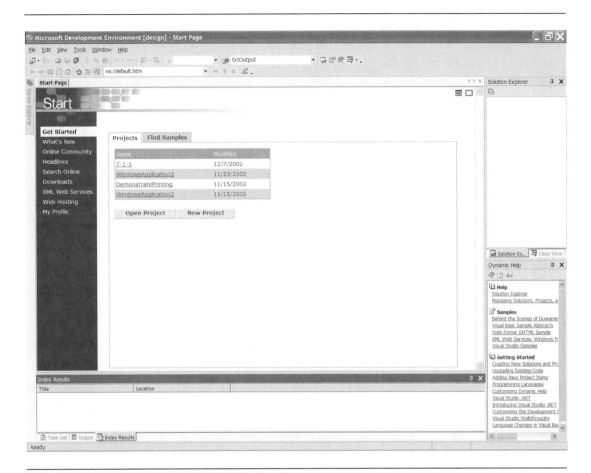

Figure 15.1 The Visual Studio Start screen.

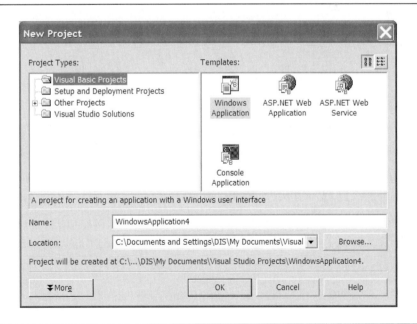

Figure 15.2 A New Project dialog box (using the Standard edition of VB.NET).

The top part of the New Project box contains a list of Project Types on the left and a collection of icons on the right. In this book, we will always select Visual Basic Projects as the project type and will always choose the Windows Application icon. Most likely these two selections will already be highlighted. If not, click on Visual Basic Projects and Windows Application.

We must now give a name to the program and decide where to store it. (This differs from VB 6.0, where we don't name a program until it is saved.) If we do not choose a name, the program will receive a default name of "Windows-Application" followed by a number. We must also specify a location—that is, a folder to contain the program when it is saved. (You can click on the Browse button and search for the folder to hold the programs. Some of the program files will be saved in subfolders of that folder.) After the name and location are specified, click on the OK button to bring up the initial VB.NET screen. See Figure 15.3.

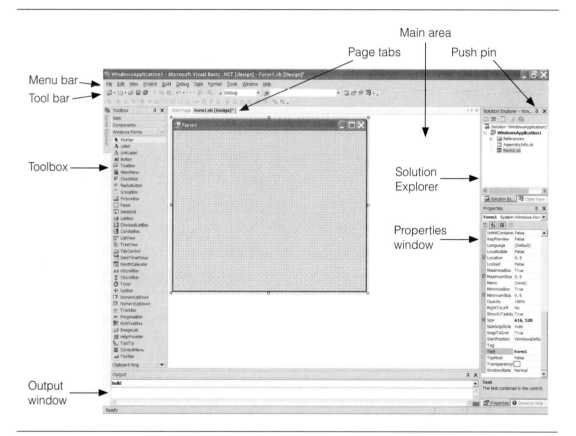

Figure 15.3 The initial VB.NET screen.

Note: When opening or closing your programs, use *Open Solution* and *Close Solution* from the File menu, not *Open* and *Close*.

The **Solution Explorer window** plays a role similar to that of the Project Explorer window in VB 6.0. There is no Form Layout window; however, the location of the form during run time can be specified by the form's StartPosition and Location properties.

New Feature: Auto Hide

Auto Hide allows you to enlarge your code window by having certain windows disappear behind a tab while not in use. Notice that the Toolbox, Properties, and Solution Explorer windows each have a push pin icon in their title bar. When Auto Hide is enabled on one of these windows, the window is hidden and the name and icon of a window are visible on a tab at the edge of the screen. When you move the cursor over the tab, the window slides back into view and is ready for use. When the window loses focus, it automatically slides back to its tab on the edge of the screen. To toggle the Auto Hide feature of a window between enabled and disabled, click on the push pin. The push pin will be vertical when Auto Hide is disabled and horizontal when it is enabled.

The Code Window

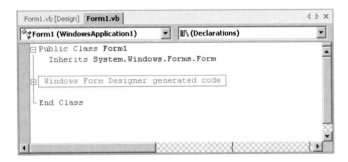

Figure 15.4 Code window for a new program.

Figure 15.4 shows a typical VB.NET Code window for a new program. The tab in the title bar, labeled Form1.vb, corresponds to the Code window. You press the other tab, labeled Form1.vb [Design], when you want to return to the Form Design window. Just below the title bar are two dropdown list boxes. The left box is called the Class Name Box, and the right box the Method Name box. (When you hover the mouse pointer over one of these list boxes, its type appears in the tooltip.) The rectangle

> Windows Form Designer generated code

corresponds to a collapsed block of code, which holds information about the form and the controls placed on the form. We need not be concerned with this hidden code. However, if you would like to see it, click on the plus sign in the little square to the left of the rectangle. (To collapse the code back into the rectangle, click on the minus sign in the little square to the left of #Region.) We place our program code between the rectangle and the words "End Class."

The Declaration Statement of an Event Procedure

With VB.NET, the first line of an event procedure, called the declaration statement, normally has the form

```
Private Sub objectName_event(ByVal sender As System.Object,
               ByVal e As System.EventArgs) Handles objectName.event
```

Since we do not need to use the parameters inside the parentheses for the events considered in this book, for the sake of readability we substitute ellipses. However, the parameters will automatically appear in all the programs. (Essentially, the word "sender" carries a reference to the object that triggered the event, and the letter "e" carries some additional information related to the corresponding event.) The structure of an event procedure is

```
Private Sub objectName_event(...) Handles objectName.event
   statements
End Sub
```

where the three dots (that is, the ellipses) represent

```
ByVal sender As System.Object, ByVal e As System.EventArgs
```

The event that triggers the procedure is actually identified by the term *objectName.event*. Actually, several events can trigger the same event procedure. If so, they would each appear, separated by commas, after the word "Handles." The term *objectName_event* is the name of the procedure and can be changed to whatever you like.

Changes in Fundamental Controls

In Chapters 3 through 11, all of the programs relied on forms, labels, text boxes, command buttons, and picture boxes. Six minor changes to these objects are as follows.

1. Command buttons are called buttons, and the prefix for naming them is *btn*. Their default name has changed from Command1 to Button1.

2. The default name for a text box has been changed from VB 6.0's Text1 to TextBox1.

3. The Caption property of forms, labels, and buttons in VB 6.0, is called the Text property in VB.NET.

4. The Alignment property for a label or text box in VB 6.0 is called the TextAlign property in VB.NET.

5. The SetFocus method is called the Focus method in VB.NET. The LostFocus and GotFocus events are replaced by the Leave and Enter events in VB.NET.

6. The default name of the form is Form1. However, the name of the form never appears in code. The keyword Me is used instead to refer to the form. (For instance, the statement Me.Text = "SALES DATA" places the words

SALES DATA in the form's title bar.) Also, changing the name of the form requires several steps. Therefore, we tend to not change the name and just leave it as Form1.

There is a major change with regard to the picture box control. Our favorite method of displaying output is not available in VB.NET. The Print method cannot be used to display text in a picture box. Of course, lost along with the Print method is the ability to create print zones with commas. However, there is an alternative that not only makes text easier to display, but also provides greater flexibility with print zones. The solution is to write text to a list box and use the String.Format function to format the lines of text into zones.

String.Format Function

With the String.Format function, not only can we specify the size of each zone in a line of text, but can also specify whether the text will be left- or right-justified within each zone and can format it as currency, percentages, and various numeric formats. Figure 15.5 shows a table in a list box that was formatted with the String.Format function and had its font name set to Courier New. (**Note:** Endowment is in billions and the final column tells what fraction of the student body attended public secondary schools.)

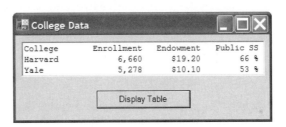

Figure 15.5 Formatting specified by a String.Format function.

If *item* is a number or string, then the statement

```
lstBox.Items.Add(item)
```

displays the value of *item* in the list box. The output shown in the list box for Figure 15.5 was obtained with the following code.

```
fmtStr = "{0,-10}{1,14:N0}{2,12:C}{3,12:P0}"
lstBox.Items.Clear
lstBox.Items.Add(String.Format(fmtStr, "College", "Endowment", _
                               "Enrollment", "Public SS"))
lstBox.Items.Add(String.Format(fmtStr, "Harvard", 6660, 19.2, 0.659))
lstBox.Items.Add(String.Format(fmtStr, "Yale", 5278, 10.1, 0.532))
```

The format string *fmtStr* specifies four zones. Let's call them zone0, zone1, zone2, and zone3. The four zones have widths 10, 14, 12, and 12. The text displayed in a zone is right-justified unless the number for the zone width is preceded with a minus sign. Therefore, zone0 is left-justified and the other three zones are right-justified. In addition, the characters following the colons specify special numeric formatting. (String data are not affected.) The characters N0, C, and P0 produce the same formatting as FormatNumber(arg, 0), FormatCurrency(arg, 2), and FormatPercent(arg, 0), respectively. Consider the last line in the code above. It uses *fmtStr* to place Yale left-justified into zone0, 5278 right-justified as a whole number into zone 1, 10.1 right-justified in currency format into zone2, and .532 right-justified as a whole number percent into zone 3.

There is no restriction on the number and widths of the zones. The width, w, and formatting of the nth zone, where $n = 0, 1, 2, \ldots$, is specified in a format string by a pair of braces of the form {n, w:*formatting symbols*}. If w is preceded by a minus sign, the text appearing in the zone will be left-justified; otherwise it will be right-justified. The most used formatting symbols consist of a letter (N for number, C for currency, or P for percent) followed by an optional digit specifying the number of decimal places to be displayed. If there is no digit after the letter, two decimal places are displayed. Table 15.1 contains some examples of such formatting.

Zone format term	Number to be formatted	Number displayed
{0,12:N3}	1234.5679	1,234.568
{0,12:N0}	34.6	35
{0,12:C1}	1234.567	$1,234.6
{0,12:P}	0.569	56.90 %

Table 15.1 Formatting a zone.

The format strings considered so far consist of a sequence of pairs of curly brackets. We also can insert spaces between successive pairs of brackets. If so, the corresponding zones in the output will be separated by those spaces. The instance, the lines of code

```
Dim fmtStr As String = "{0, 5}  {1, -5}"
'Line above has two spaces after the first right curly bracket
lstOutput.Items.Add("12345678901234567890")
lstOutput.Items.Add(String.Format(fmtStr, 1, 2))
```

produce the output

```
12345678901234567890
    1  2
```

New Feature: ReadOnly Property of Text boxes

The default value of the ReadOnly property of a text box is False. When the property is set to True, the program can display output in the text box, but the user cannot edit the contents of the text box. Therefore, the combination of list boxes and read-only text boxes provide a good alternative to picture boxes and labels for displaying output.

Specifying Colors

The background and foreground colors of an object can be specified with statements of the form

```
object.BackColor = Color.hue
object.ForeColor = Color.hue
```

where *hue* can be any one of 141 colors ranging (in alphabetical order) from AliceBlue to YellowGreen. After you type the word Color followed by a period, the colors appear in a dropdown list box from which you can select your choice. All the standard colors, such as Red, Blue, Green, and Yellow, are in the list.

Left, Right, and Mid Functions

The Mid function works the same in VB.NET as in VB 6.0. However, the functions Left and Right must be replaced by Microsoft.VisualBasic.Left and Microsoft.VisualBasic.Right. These functions are intended for backward compatibility. Another alternative is to replace Left(*str*, n) with Mid(*str*, 1, n), and to replace Right(*str*, n) with Mid(*str*, Len(*str*) − n + 1) .

New Feature: Initializing Variables During Declaration

In VB.NET, the default value of a numeric variable is 0 and the default of a string variable is the keyword Nothing. The default value is also known as the initial value. The initial value can be set to a value other than zero or Nothing. To specify a different initial value, follow the declaration statement with an equal sign followed by the initial value. The statement

```
Dim interestRate As Single = 5.25
```

declares *interestRate* to be a variable of type Single and gives it the initial value 5.25. The statement

```
Dim film As String = "Chicago"
```

declares *film* to be a variable of type String and gives it the initial value "Chicago".

An error occurs whenever an attempt is made to perform a string operation on Nothing or to display it in a text box or list box. Therefore, unless a string variable is guaranteed to be assigned a value before being used, you should initialize it—even if you just assign the empty string to it.

New Feature: Random Object

Random numbers are easy to generate in VB.NET due to the **Random object.** A **random number generator** is declared in VB.NET with a statement of the form

```
Dim randomNum As New Random()
```

If *m* and *n* are whole numbers, with *m* < *n*, then the value of

```
randomNum.Next(m, n)
```

is a randomly selected whole number from *m* through *n*, including *m* but excluding *n*. The following VB.NET event procedure simulates the rolling of a pair of dice.

```
Private Sub btnRollDice_Click(...) Handles btnRollDice.Click
  Dim randomNum As New Random()
  Dim num1 As Integer, num2 As Integer
  'Display the outcome of rolling a pair of dice
  num1 = randomNum.Next(1, 7)
  num2 = randomNum.Next(1, 7)
  txtNumbers.Text = num1 & "   " & num2
End Sub
```

Passing by Value and by Reference

In VB 6.0, the use of ByRef and ByVal in the declaration line of a general procedure is optional. If neither of these keywords is used, then ByRef is implied. In VB.NET, either ByRef or ByVal *must* precede every parameter. If neither of the keywords is typed in preceding one of the parameters, the editor will automatically insert ByVal before the parameter. Therefore, by default, variables are passed by value.

Some Font Properties are Read-Only

The font properties that specify the name and style of the font are usually specified at design time. The settings of these properties can be displayed in code with statements such as

```
txtBox.Text = txtBox.Font.Name
txtBox.Text = txtBox.Font.Size
```

However, they cannot be altered in code with statements of the form

```
txtBox.Font.Name = "Courier New"
txtBox.Font.Bold = True
txtBox.Font.Size = 16
```

The properties of the font are therefore said to be read-only. To change the font for a control, a new font must be assigned using the following syntax:

```
txtBox.Font = New Font("fontname", fontsize, FontStyle.style)
```

For example, to set the font to Courier New, 16 point, Bold, as above:

```
txtBox.Font = New Font("Courier New", 16, FontStyle.Bold)
```

Changes in Controls and Objects Discussed in Chapter 11

VB.NET does not have a line, shape, or image control. As alternatives, VB. NET's label control can be used to draw lines and rectangular shapes, and VB.NET's picture box control has most of the capabilities of VB 6.0's image control. The picture box control's Image property specifies the picture to be displayed, and the SizeMode property has the same capabilities as the image control's stretch property. In code, a picture is placed into a picture box with a statement of the form `picBox.Image = Image.FromFile (filespec)`.

The VB 6.0 frame control has been replaced by VB.NET's group box control, and VB 6.0's option button control has been renamed radio button in VB.NET.

The drive, directory, and file list box controls are not available in VB.NET. However, their functionality can be achieved with VB.NET's OpenFileDialog and SaveFileDialog controls. The common dialog control from VB 6.0, which was an amalgam of five controls, has been replaced in VB.NET by five individual controls.

For the check box and radio button controls, the Value property of VB 6.0 has been replaced in VB.NET with the Checked property (whose value is either True or False). In VB.NET, menus are created with the MainMenu control found in the Toolbox instead of VB 6.0's Menu Editor, which was invoked from the Tools menu.

With VB.NET, a timer control is turned off with `Timer1.Enabled = False` instead of with `Timer1.Interval = 0`. The Timer event of VB 6.0 has been replaced with the Tick event in VB.NET. In VB.NET, the Timer control is visible not on the form in the Form designer but in a separate pane at the bottom part of the Form designer.

The Max and Min properties for scroll bars of VB 6.0 have been changed to Maximum and Minimum. The default value for Maximum is 100. (The Max property had a default value of 32,767.) In VB 6.0 Min could be set to a value greater than Max; in VB.NET this is not allowed.

In VB.NET, a primary form (usually called Form1) is displayed when the program is executed. Secondary forms may be defined and displayed using the form's ShowDialog method.

The two most important controls from Chapter 11 are the list box and combo box controls. Their default event procedure (that is, the event procedure generated automatically in the Code window when you double-click on a list box or combo box in the Form designer) has changed from Click in VB 6.0 to SelectedIndexChanged in VB.NET. Also, in VB.NET, list boxes no longer have an ItemData property. Table 15.2 shows some name changes for their methods and properties.

VB 6.0	VB.NET
AddItem method	Items.Add
RemoveItem method	Items.RemoveAt
Clear method	Items.Clear
Style property	DropDownStyle
ListIndex property	SelectedIndex
Text property	SelectedItem

Table 15.2 List box and combo box name changes.

Object-Oriented Programming

In VB.NET, classes are written in the Form's Code window using Class blocks. VB 6.0 has separate Property Let and Property Get procedures. VB.NET has a Property block that contains Set and Get procedures. VB 6.0's Initialize event is called New in VB.NET and takes optional parameters. VB.NET's classes have full object-oriented capability, including inheritance, polymorphism, and abstraction.

Miscellaneous Changes in VB.NET

1. In VB.NET Option Explicit is the default setting and therefore will be in effect unless the line Option Explicit Off is inserted at the top of the Code window.

2. The DblClick event procedure of VB 6.0 is called DoubleClick in VB.NET.

3. The built-in functions Sqr and Round from VB 6.0 are replaced in VB.NET by the functions Math.Sqrt and Math.Round.

4. VB 6.0's Printer object is not available in VB.NET. The printing capabilities in VB.NET are much more flexible and powerful. However, they are also significantly more complex.

5. The VB 6.0 statement

   ```
   MsgBox prompt, , title
   ```

   is written in VB.NET as

   ```
   MsgBox(prompt, , title)
   ```

   In general, all procedure and function calls in VB.NET have parentheses, even if no parameters are being passed.

6. In VB.NET, the declaration line for the Form_Load event procedure is

   ```
   Private Sub Form1_Load(...) Handles MyBase.Load
   ```

7. For the picture box control, the Picture property of VB 6.0 has been replaced in VB.NET by the Image property. In VB.NET, the picture box control has a StretchImage property that is analogous to the Stretch property for the image control in VB 6.0.

8. Graphics is much more complex in VB.NET than in VB 6.0. For instance, VB.NET does not have a Scale method.

9. The SelText property of a text box in VB 6.0 is called SelectedText in VB.NET.

10. In the record type of VB 6.0 discussed in Chapter 9, the word Type is replaced by the word Structure in VB.NET. Also, each field must be specified with a Dim statement.

11. VB.NET does not support fixed-length strings.

12. Although VB.NET allows you to declare an array of controls, they are not as easy to program as the control arrays of VB 6.0. The ease of handling event procedures is lost.

1. How would the following VB 6.0 statement be written in VB.NET?

```
Text1.BackColor = vbRed
```

2. What is the effect of the following lines of code?

```
Dim randomNum As New Random()
Label2.Text = Chr(randomNum.Next(65, 91))
```

EXERCISES 15.1

In Exercises 1 through 8, determine the output displayed by the lines of code.

1.
```
lblGreeting.TextAlign = HorizontalAlignment.Center
lblGreeting.ForeColor = Color.Red
lblGreeting.Text = "Hello"
```

2.
```
btnPushMe.Text = "Push Me"
Me.Text = "Caption property changed to Text property"
```

3.
```
Me.Text = "Who are you?"
Button1.Text = "I'm a Button."
```

4.
```
TextBox1.TextAlign = HorizontalAlignment.Right
TextBox1.BackColor = Color.Blue
TextBox1.Text = "Blue"
```

5.
```
Dim sales As Single = 123.67
lstBox.Items.Add(sales)
```

6.
```
Dim state As String = "Maryland"
lstBox.Items.Add("U of " & Microsoft.VisualBasic.Left(state, 1))
```

7.
```
Dim state As String = "MARYLAND"
txtBox.Text = Mid(state, 1, 1) & Mid(state, Len(state))
```

8.
```
Dim num As Integer = 50
MsgBox(Str(num), , "Number of States")
```

In Exercises 9 through 18, determine the output produced by the lines of code. Assume that Courier New is the font for the list box.

9.
```
Dim fmtStr As String = "{0,-5}{1,5}"
lstOutput.Items.Add("12345678901234567890")
lstOutput.Items.Add(String.Format(fmtStr, 1, 2))
```

10.
```
Dim fmtStr As String = "{0,5}{1,5}"
lstOutput.Items.Add("12345678901234567890")
lstOutput.Items.Add(String.Format(fmtStr, 1, 2))
```

11.
```
Dim fmtStr As String = "{0,5}{1,-5}"
lstOutput.Items.Add("12345678901234567890")
lstOutput.Items.Add(String.Format(fmtStr, 1, 2))
```

12.
```
Dim fmtStr As String = "{0,-5}{1,-5}"
lstOutput.Items.Add("12345678901234567890")
lstOutput.Items.Add(String.Format(fmtStr, 1, 2))
```

13.
```
Dim fmtStr As String = "{0,3}{1,10}"
lstOutput.Items.Add("12345678901234567890")
lstOutput.Items.Add(String.Format(fmtStr, "A", "Alice"))
```

14.
```
Dim fmtStr As String = "{0,-13}{1,-10}{2,-17:N0}"
lstOutput.Items.Add("1234567890123456789012345678901")
lstOutput.Items.Add(String.Format(fmtStr, "Mountain", "Place", "Ht (ft)"))
lstOutput.Items.Add(String.Format(fmtStr, "K2", "Kashmir", 28250))
```

15.
```
Dim fmtStr As String = "{0,11}   {1,-11}"   'Three spaces
lstOutput.Items.Add("12345678901234567890")
lstOutput.Items.Add(String.Format(fmtStr, "College", "Mascot"))
lstOutput.Items.Add(String.Format(fmtStr, "Univ. of MD", "Terrapins"))
lstOutput.Items.Add(String.Format(fmtStr, "Duke", "Blue Devils"))
```

16.
```
'Toss coin twice
Dim fmtStr As String = "{0,8}  {1,-7}"   'Two spaces
lstOutput.Items.Add("12345678901234567890")
lstOutput.Items.Add(String.Format(fmtStr, "Number", "Percent"))
lstOutput.Items.Add(String.Format(fmtStr, "of Heads", "of time"))
fmtStr = "{0,8}  {1,-7:P0}"
lstOutput.Items.Add(String.Format(fmtStr, 0, 1 / 4))
lstOutput.Items.Add(String.Format(fmtStr, 1, 1 / 2))
lstOutput.Items.Add(String.Format(fmtStr, 2, 1 / 4))
```

17.
```
'Elements in a 150 Pound Person
Dim fmtStr As String = "{0,-7}  {1,-7}  {2,-7}"   'Two spaces
lstOutput.Items.Add("12345678901234567890")
lstOutput.Items.Add(String.Format(fmtStr, "Element", "Weight", "Percent"))
fmtStr = "{0,-7}  {1,-7:N1}  {2,-7:P1}"
lstOutput.Items.Add(String.Format(fmtStr, "Oxygen", 97.5, 97.5 / 150))
lstOutput.Items.Add(String.Format(fmtStr, "Carbon", 27, 27 / 150))
```

18.
```
Dim fmtStr As String = "{0,10}   {1,-10}"   'Three spaces
lstOutput.Items.Add("12345678901234567890")
lstOutput.Items.Add(String.Format(fmtStr, "", "Tuition"))
lstOutput.Items.Add(String.Format(fmtStr, "College", "& Fees"))
fmtStr = "{0,10}   {1,-10:C0}"
lstOutput.Items.Add(String.Format(fmtStr, "Stanford", 25917))
lstOutput.Items.Add(String.Format(fmtStr, "Harvard", 24441))
```

In Exercises 19 through 22, describe the effect of executing the statement(s).

19.
```
Dim randomNum As New Random()
txtBox.Text = CStr(randomNum.Next(1, 10))
```

20.
```
Dim randomNum As New Random()
Dim number As Integer
'Assume the array Pres() contains the names of the U.S. Presidents
'with subscripts ranging from 1 through 43
number = randomNum.Next(1, 44)
txtBox.Text = Pres(number)
```

21.
```
Dim randomNum As New Random()
'95 characters can be produced by the computer keyboard
MsgBox(Chr(randomNum.Next(32, 127), , "Keyboard"))
```

22.
```
Dim randomNum As New Random()
Dim number As Integer, temp As String
'Suppose the array states() contains the names of the 50
'states with subscripts ranging from 1 through 50
number = randomNum.Next(1, 51)
lstBox.Items.Add(states(number))
temp = states(number)
states(number) = states(50)
states(50) = temp
lstBox.Items.Add(states(randomNum.Next(1, 50)))
```

In Exercises 23 through 36, write a single line of code to carry out the task.

23. Display the string "Visual Basic .NET" in the title bar of the form.

24. Declare the variable *bird* to be of type String and assign it the value "oriole".

25. Declare the variable *trombones* to be of type Integer and assign it the value 76.

26. Use a function to display the first five letters of the string "United States" in TextBox1.

27. Add the string "Sequoia" to the list box lstTrees.

28. Add the number 7 to the combo box cboLucky.

29. Change the foreground color of Button1 to green.

30. Display "Delaware" in a message dialog box with the words "First State" in its title bar.

31. Place a check mark in the small square of CheckBox1.

32. Turn on RadioButton1.

33. Use a function to display the last five letters of "Visual Basic" in TextBox1.

34. Turn off Timer1.

35. Move the scroll box of HScrollBar2 to its rightmost position.

36. Display the square root of 2 in lstBox.

In Exercises 37 and 38, write some lines of code to carry out the task.

37. Select the answer to a multiple-choice question at random and display it in a message dialog box. Assume the possible choices are A, B, C, D, and E.

38. Select an even number from 2 through 100 at random and display it in a label.

In Exercises 39 through 50 convert the VB 6.0 program to a VB.NET program.

39. Section 3.3, Example 1   **40.** Section 3.5, Example 5

41. Section 3.6, Example 1   **42.** Section 3.6, Example 6

43. Section 3.6, Example 8   **44.** Section 4.1, Example 5

45. Section 4.2, Example 7   **46.** Section 4.3, Example 2

47. Section 11.1, Example 1   **48.** Section 11.1, Example 3

49. Section 11.2, Example 1   **50.** Section 11.2, Example 3

51. In 2002, worldwide PC shipments totaled more than 132 million units. Table 15.3 shows the number of units (in thousands) shipped by leading companies. Write a program to produce the table shown in Figure 15.6.

Company	Shipments (thousands of units)
Hewlett-Packard	21,478
Dell	20,112
IBM	7,928
NEC	4,550
Toshiba	4,237
Others	74,046
Total	132,351

Table 15.3 Worldwide PC shipments in 2002.

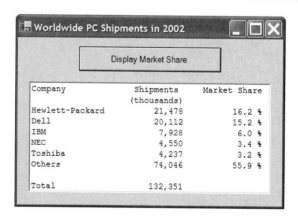

Figure 15.6 Output of Exercise 51.

52. Write a VB.NET program to create the digital clock described in Exercise 44 of Section 11.2.

✔✔ **Solutions to Practice Problems 15.1**

1. `TextBox1.BackColor = Color.Red`

2. The lines of code select a letter at random from the alphabet and display it in a label.

15.2 ARRAYS, SEQUENTIAL FILES, AND DATABASES

Arrays, sequential files, and databases are all constructs for holding and processing many pieces of data. There are some major differences in the way they are handled in VB 6.0 and in VB.NET.

Arrays

In VB.NET arrays, indices must have 0 as lower bound and must be declared with a Dim statement of the form

```
Dim arrayName() As VarType
```

and have the range given later, or with

```
Dim arrayName(n) As VarType
```

Whereas in VB 6.0 the upper bound n can only be a constant, in VB.NET it also can be a variable or expression. Although ReDim cannot be used to declare an array, it can be used to resize *any* array. The form of the ReDim statement is

```
ReDim arrayName(m)
```

which loses the current contents of the array, or with

```
ReDim Preserve arrayName(m)
```

which keeps the current values of the array. **Note:** Since the type cannot be changed, the "As *DataType*" clause cannot appear at the end of a ReDim statement.

When an array is passed to a procedure in VB.NET, the argument in the Call statement consists of the name of the array, written *without* a trailing empty set of parentheses. The corresponding parameter in the declaration statement for the procedure must consist of an array name *with* a trailing empty set of parentheses. Like all other parameters, the array parameter must be preceded with ByVal or ByRef and followed with an "As VarType" clause. The method GetUpperBound simplifies working with arrays that have been passed to a procedure. The value of *arrayName*.GetUpperBound(0) is the upper bound of the array.

Like ordinary variables, array variables can be declared and assigned initial values at the same time. A statement of the form

```
Dim arrayName() As VarType = {value0, value1, value2,... valueN}
```

declares an array having upper bound N and assigns *value0* to *arrayName*(0), *value1* to *arrayName*(1), *value2* to *arrayName*(2), ..., and *valueN* to *arrayName*(N). For instance, in Example 2 of Section 7.1, the Dim statement and Form1_Load event procedure can be replaced by the single line

```
Dim teamName() As String = _
            {"", "Red Sox", "Giants", "White Sox", "Cubs", "Cubs"}
```

Sequential Files

In Section 1.2 we used Notepad to create the sequential file (containing names, hourly wages, and hours worked) shown in Figure 15.7. Each record appears on a single line and the fields are separated by commas. This design is known as **CSV format**. (**Note:** CSV is an abbreviation for *Comma Separated Values*.).

"Mike Jones", 7.35, 35
"John Smith", 6.75, 33

Figure 15.7 A sequential file in CSV format.

Figure 15.8 shows the same data with the fields appearing on separate lines. This design is known as **LSV format**, where LSV stands for *Line Separated Values*.

Mike Jones
7.35
35
John Smith
6.75
33

Figure 15.8 A sequential file in LSV format.

In VB.NET, sequential files are easiest to read if they are in LSV format. In this section we learn how to manage such files in VB.NET and how to convert a file in CSV format to one in LSV format. In VB.NET, data is read from a sequential file with an object called a **StreamReader** and is written to or appended to a sequential file with an object called a **StreamWriter**.

A StreamReader as an object that can read a stream of characters coming from a disk or coming over the Internet. A statement of the form

```
Dim sr As IO.StreamReader
```

declares the variable *sr* to be of type StreamReader. Then a statement of the form

```
sr = IO.File.OpenText(filespec)
```

opens the specified file for input. The declaration and assignment statements above can be combined into the single statement

```
Dim sr As IO.StreamReader = IO.File.OpenText(filespec)
```

Lines of data can be read in order, one at a time, from the file with the ReadLine method. Each piece of data is retrieved as a string. A statement of the form

```
strVar = sr.ReadLine
```

causes the program to look in the file for the next unread line of data and assign it to the variable *strVar*. The data can be assigned to a numeric variable if it is first converted to a numeric type with a statement such as

```
numVar = Val(sr.ReadLine)
```

The **Peek method** can be used to determine when the end of a text file has been reached. At any time, the value of

```
sr.Peek
```

is the ANSI value of the first character of the line about to be read with Read-Line. If the end of the file has been reached, the value of sr.Peek is –1.

After the desired items have been read from the file, the communications link can be terminated with the statement

```
sr.Close()
```

An attempt to open a nonexistent file for input terminates the program with the error message beginning "An unhandled exception of type 'System.IO. FileNotFound' exception occurred." There is a method that tells us whether a certain file has already been created. If the value of

```
IO.File.Exists(filespec)
```

is True, then the specified file exists. Therefore, prudence dictates that files be opened for input with code such as

```
Dim sr As IO.StreamReader
If IO.File.Exists(filespec) Then
  sr = IO.File.OpenText(filespec)
Else
  message = "Either no file has yet been created or the file named " & _
            filespec & " is not where expected."
  MsgBox(message, , "File Not Found")
End If
```

Note: Each VB.NET program is contained in a folder with the name you specified in the New Project window. This folder holds the files for the program and contains two subfolders named *bin* and *obj*. If no path is specified for a file, VB.NET will look for the file in the *bin* subfolder for the program. For the programs given in this book, we will assume that all files accessed are contained in the *bin* folder for the program.

EXAMPLE 1 The following program uses the file STAFF.TXT shown in Figure 15.8 to display the weekly earnings of each employee.

```
Private Sub btnShowEarnings_Click(...) Handles btnShowEarnings.Click
  Dim nom As String, hourlyWage As Single, hoursWorked as Single
  Dim sr As IO.StreamReader = IO.File.OpenText("STAFF.TXT")
```

```
  Do Until sr.Peek = -1
    nom = sr.ReadLine
    hourlyWage = Val(sr.ReadLine)
    hoursWorked = Val(sr.ReadLine)
    lstOutput.Items.Add(nom & "  " & FormatCurrency(hourlyWage * hoursWorked))
  Loop
End Sub
```

[Run, and then click on the button. The following output is displayed in the list box.]

```
Mike Jones  $257.35
John Smith  $222.75
```

A sequential file is opened for output with a pair of statements of the form

```
Dim sw As IO.StreamWriter
sw = IO.File.CreateText(filespec)
```

or the single statement

```
Dim sw As IO.StreamWriter = IO.File.CreateText(filespec)
```

where *sw* is a variable name. A sequential file is opened for append with a pair of statements of the form

```
Dim sw As IO.StreamWriter
sw = IO.File.AppendText(filespec)
```

or the single statement

```
Dim sw As IO.StreamWriter = IO.File.AppendText(filespec)
```

Then lines of data are placed into the file with the WriteLine statement. If *datum* is either a piece of string or numeric data, then the statement

```
sw.WriteLine(datum)
```

writes the information into a new line of the file. After all data has been written to the file, it can be closed with the statement

```
sw.Close()
```

The Name and Kill statements of VB 6.0 are replaced in VB.NET by IO.File.Move and IO.File.Delete. For instance,

```
Name oldfilespec As newfilespec
```

becomes

```
IO.File.Move(oldfilespec, newfilespec).
```

Changing the Format of a Sequential File

We can write simple programs to convert text files from CSV format to LSV format, and vice versa. However, we will have to make a few assumptions and discuss some new functions.

Both VB 6.0 and VB.NET have the two functions Replace and Split that facilitate working with CSV formatted files. If *strng* is a string, possibly containing quotation marks, then the value of

```
Replace(strng, Chr(34), "")
```

is the value of *strng* with all quotation marks removed. Split can convert a string containing commas into a String array where the zeroth element contains the text preceding the first comma, the first element contains the text between the first and second commas, . . . , and the last element contains the text following the last comma. For instance, suppose the String array *employees*() has been declared without an upper bound, and the string variable *strVar* has the value "Bob, 23.50, 45". Then the statement

```
employees = Split(strVar, ",")
```

sets the upper bound of *employees*() to 2 and sets *employees*(0) = "Bob", *employees*(1) = "23.50", *employees*(2) = "45". In the line of code above, the character comma is called the **delimiter**[1] for the Split function.

EXAMPLE 2   The following program illustrates the use of the Split function.

```
Private Sub btnRead_Click(...) Handles btnRead.Click
  Dim stateData() As String, line As String, i As Integer
  Dim sr As IO.StreamReader = IO.File.OpenText("STATES.TXT")
  'Suppose the first line of STATES.TXT is
  ' "California", 1850, "Sacramento", "Eureka"
  line = sr.ReadLine
  line = Replace(line, Chr(34), "")    'Strip out all quotation marks
  stateData = Split(line, ",")
  For i = 0 To stateData.GetUpperBound(0)
    stateData(i) = Trim(stateData(i))    'Get rid of extraneous spaces
    lstOutput.Items.Add(stateData(i))
  Next i
End Sub
```

[Run, and then click the button. The following is displayed in the list box.]

```
California
1850
Sacramento
Eureka
```

---

1. In the general form of the Split function, any character can be used as the delimiter.

EXAMPLE 3

The following program converts any CSV file to an LSV file and then displays the contents of the new file. We will assume that the file to be converted is located in the *bin* folder for the program.

```
Private Sub btnConvert_Click(...) Handles btnConvert.Click
  Dim line As String, fields() As String
  Dim fromFile As String, toFile As String
  Dim i As Integer
  Dim sr As IO.StreamReader
  Dim sw As IO.StreamWriter
  fromFile = InputBox("Name of original file:", "Convert from CSV to LSV")
  toFile = InputBox("Name of converted file:", "Convert from CSV to LSV")
  sr = IO.File.OpenText(fromFile)
  sw = IO.File.CreateText(toFile)
  Do While (sr.Peek() <> -1)
    line = sr.ReadLine()
    line = Replace(line, Chr(34), "")    'Strip out all quotation marks
    fields = Split(line, ",")
    For i = 0 To fields.GetUpperBound(0)
      sw.WriteLine(Trim(fields(i)))
    Next i
  Loop
  sr.Close()
  sw.Close()
  sr = IO.File.OpenText(toFile)
  Do While (sr.Peek() <> -1)
    lstFile.Items.Add(sr.ReadLine)
  Loop
  sr.Close()
End Sub
```

[Run, press the button, and respond to the two requests with csvSTATES.TXT and STATES.TXT. Assume that the file csvSTATES.TXT contains the two lines "California", 1850, "Sacramento", "Eureka" and "New York", 1788, "Albany", "Excelsior". The following will be displayed in the list box.]

California
1850
Sacramento
Eureka
New York
1788
Albany
Excelsior

The reverse of the Split function is the Join function, which concatenates the elements of a string array into a string containing the elements separated by a specified delimiter. For instance, the code

```
Dim greatLakes() As String ={"Huron","Ontario","Michigan","Erie","Superior"}
Dim lakes As String
lakes = Join(greatLakes, ",")
txtOutput.Text = lakes
```

produces the output

```
Huron,Ontario,Michigan,Erie,Superior
```

Note: Whenever we created sequential files with Notepad, we always put quotation marks around the strings. However, the quotation marks were not necessary. The Input # statement retrieves data from the file properly whether or not the strings are surrounded by quotation marks. Therefore, the Join statement can be used to convert LSV files to CSV files.

Databases in VB.NET

In Chapter 12, we accessed data from databases using the ADO data control. VB.NET uses a newer technology called ADO.NET that allows programs to access data seamlessly from a variety of data sources. We will show how to access a database directly through code (without using a control) by using a DataTable object.

A DataTable object holds the contents of a table as a rectangular array. (A data table is similar to a two-dimensional array; it has rows and columns.) The following six lines of code create a DataTable variable named *dt* and fill it with the contents of the Cities table from the database MEGACITIES2.MDB:

```
Dim dt As New DataTable()
Dim connStr As String = "Provider=Microsoft.Jet.OLEDB.4.0;" & _
                        "Data Source = MEGACITIES2.MDB"
Dim sqlStr As String = "SELECT * FROM Cities"
Dim dataAdapter As New OleDb.OleDbDataAdapter(sqlStr, connStr)
dataAdapter.Fill(dt)
dataAdapter.Dispose()
```

For the time being, treat the six lines of code as boilerplate to be inserted into a program. The first statement, which declares *dt* to be a variable of type DataTable, is often placed in the Declarations section of the Code window. The next two statements have the following general form:

```
Dim connStr As String = "Provider=Microsoft.Jet.OLEDB.4.0;" & _
                        "Data Source = DataBaseName"
Dim sqlStr As String = "SELECT * FROM TableName"
```

where the database is assumed to be in the *bin* subfolder of the program folder. After the six lines of code are executed, the value of

```
dt.Rows.Count
```

is the number of records in the table, and the value of

```
dt.Columns.Count
```

is the number of columns in the table. The records are numbered 0 through dt.Rows.Count - 1, and the fields are numbered 0 through dt.Columns.Count - 1. The value of

```
dt.Columns(j)
```

is the name of the *j*th field. The value of

```
dt.Rows(i)(j)
```

is the entry in the *j*th field of the *i*th record. The value of

```
dt.Rows(i)(fieldName)
```

is the entry in the specified field of the *i*th record. In Table 15.4, *dt* holds the Cities table of MEGACITIES2.MDB.

Expression	Value
dt.Rows.Count	10
dt.Columns.Count	4
dt.Rows(3)(1)	USA
dt.Rows(2)("city")	Calcutta

Table 15.4 Some values from Cities table of MEGACITIES2.MDB.

EXAMPLE 4 The following program displays one record at a time from the Cities table of the MEGACITIES2.MDB database. The user can move forward or backward through the records, or specify the city to be displayed.

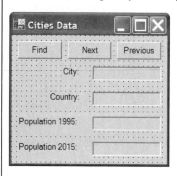

Object	Property	Setting
Form1	Text	Cities Data
btnFind	Text	Find
btnNext	Text	Next
btnPrevious	Text	Previous
lblCity	Text	City:
txtCity	ReadOnly	True
	Text	(blank)
lblCountry	Text	Country:
txtCountry	ReadOnly	True
	Text	(blank)
lblPop1995	Text	Population 1995:
txtPop1995	ReadOnly	True
	Text	(blank)
lblPop2015	Text	Population 2015:
txtPop2015	ReadOnly	True
	Text	(blank)

```
Dim dt As New DataTable()
Dim rowIndex As Integer

Private Sub Form1_Load(...) Handles MyBase.Load
  'Get data from the database, put it into the DataTable object dt,
  'and display the initial record's data in text boxes
  Dim connStr As String = "Provider = Microsoft.Jet.OLEDB.4.0;" & _
                    "Data Source = MEGACITIES2.MDB"
```

```
    Dim sqlStr As String = "SELECT * FROM Cities"
    Dim dataAdapter As New OleDb.OleDbDataAdapter(sqlStr, connStr)
    dataAdapter.Fill(dt)
    dataAdapter.Dispose()
    rowIndex = 0
    Call UpdateTextBoxes()
  End Sub

  Private Sub btnFind_Click(...) Handles btnFind.Click
    'Search through each row looking for the requested city.
    'Update the fields if that city is found.
    'Otherwise, display a message box.
    Dim cityName As String
    Dim i As Integer
    Dim cityFound As Boolean = False
    cityName = InputBox("Enter the name of the city to search for.")
    For i = 0 To (dt.Rows.Count - 1)
      If dt.Rows(i)("city") = cityName Then
        cityFound = True
        rowIndex = i
        Call UpdateTextBoxes()
      End If
    Next i
    If (Not cityFound) Then
      MsgBox("Cannot find the requested city")
    End If
  End Sub

  Private Sub btnNext_Click(...) Handles btnNext.Click
    'Show the next record if the current one is not the last
    If (rowIndex < dt.Rows.Count - 1) Then
      rowIndex = rowIndex + 1
      Call UpdateTextBoxes()
    End If
  End Sub

  Private Sub btnPrevious_Click(...) Handles btnPrevious.Click
    'Show the previous record if the current one is not the first
    If (rowIndex > 0) Then
      rowIndex = rowIndex - 1
      Call UpdateTextBoxes()
    End If
  End Sub

  Private Sub UpdateTextBoxes()
    'Display the contents of the row specified by the variable rowIndex
    txtCity.Text = dt.Rows(rowIndex)("city")
    txtCountry.Text = dt.Rows(rowIndex)("country")
    txtPop1995.Text = dt.Rows(rowIndex)("pop1995")
    txtPop2015.Text = dt.Rows(rowIndex)("pop2015")
  End Sub
```

[Run, and then click the Next button three times.]

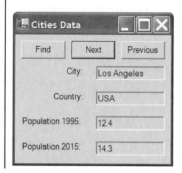

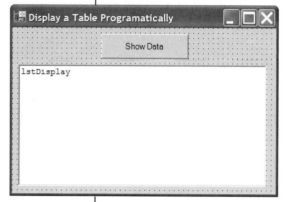

EXAMPLE 5 The following program displays the contents of the Cities table of MEGA-CITIES2.MDB in a list box, along with the percentage increases for the populations.

Object	Property	Setting
Form1	Text	Display a Table Programatically
btnShow	Text	Show Data
lstDisplay		

```
Private Sub btnShow_Click(...) Handles btnShow.Click
  Dim fmtStr As String = "{0,-15}{1,-10}{2,7:N1}{3,7:N1}{4,7:P0}"
  Dim percentIncrease As Single
  Dim i As Integer
  'Place contents of Cities table into a DataTable
  Dim dt As New DataTable()
  Dim connStr As String = "Provider=Microsoft.Jet.OLEDB.4.0;" & _
                          "Data Source = MEGACITIES2.MDB"
  Dim sqlStr As String = "SELECT * FROM Cities"
  Dim dataAdapter As New OleDb.OleDbDataAdapter(sqlStr, connStr)
  dataAdapter.Fill(dt)
  dataAdapter.Dispose()
  'Fill the list box
  lstDisplay.Items.Add(String.Format(fmtStr, "CITY", "COUNTRY", _
    "1995", "2015", "INCR."))
  For i = 0 To dt.Rows.Count - 1
    percentIncrease = (Val(dt.Rows(i)("pop2015")) - _
        Val(dt.Rows(i)("pop1995"))) / Val(dt.Rows(i)("pop1995"))
    lstDisplay.Items.Add(String.Format(fmtStr, dt.Rows(i)(0), _
        dt.Rows(i)(1), dt.Rows(i)(2), dt.Rows(i)(3), percentIncrease))
  Next i
End Sub
```

[Run, and click the button.]

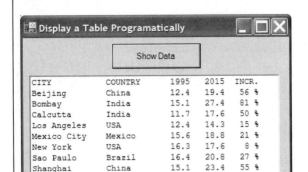

In Example 2, we placed information from a data table into a list box one line at a time. However, a data table can be bound to a list box and have information transferred automatically into the list box. The statement

```
lstBox.DataSource = dt
```

binds the list box to the data table, and the statement

```
lstBox.DisplayMember = fieldName
```

displays the contents of the specified field in the list box.

EXAMPLE 6 The following program uses a list box to display a column of data from a data table. When a particular country is selected, the event procedure retrieves the country's currency from the corresponding record and displays it in a text box.

Object	Property	Setting
Form1	Text	Currency
lstCountries		
lblCurrency	Text	Currency:
txtCurrency	ReadOnly	True
	Text	(blank)

```
Dim dt As New DataTable()

Private Sub Form1_Load(...) Handles MyBase.Load
    Dim connStr As String = "Provider = Microsoft.Jet.OLEDB.4.0;" & _
                    "Data Source = MEGACITIES2.MDB"
    Dim sqlStr As String = "SELECT * FROM Countries"
    Dim dataAdapter As New OleDb.OleDbDataAdapter(sqlStr, connStr)
    dataAdapter.Fill(dt)
    dataAdapter.Dispose()
```

```
        lstCountries.DataSource = dt   'Bind the list box to the data table
        lstCountries.DisplayMember = "country"  'Display the country field
    End Sub

    Private Sub lstCountries_SelectedIndexChanged(...) _
                            Handles lstCountries.SelectedIndexChanged
        txtCurrency.Text = dt.Rows(lstCountries.SelectedIndex)("currency")
    End Sub
```

[Run, and click on one of the countries.]

In the above example, a data table was bound to a ListBox control that displayed an entire column. The entire table can be displayed by binding the data table to a DataGrid with a statement such as

```
DataGrid1.DataSource = dt
```

Note: In VB.NET the DataGrid control is in the Toolbox.

The programs presented above all contained a statement of the form

```
Dim sqlStr As String = "SELECT * FROM tableName"
```

that created an entire existing table as a view. Replacing this string with a different SQL string will result in a different "virtual" table for the data table when it is filled by the data adapter.

 PRACTICE PROBLEMS 15.2

1. How many elements are there in an array having upper bound 100?

2. What is the error in the following VB.NET statement?

```
ReDim scores(5) As Integer
```

3. Give a situation in which it is necessary to use the pair of statements

```
Dim sr As IO.StreamReader
sr = IO.File.OpenText(filespec)
```

rather than the single statement

```
Dim sr As IO.StreamReader = IO.File.OpenText(filespec)
```

➤ **EXERCISES 15.2**

In Exercises 1 through 12, determine the output displayed by the lines of code.

1. ```
Dim twinCities() As String = {"", "Minneapolis", "St. Paul"}
txtBox.Text = twinCities(1)
```

2. ```
Dim riceKrispies() As String = {"Snap", "Krackle", "Pop"}
txtBox.Text = riceKrispies(1)
```

3. ```
Dim ships(1) As String
ships(0) = "Nina"
ships(1) = "Pinta"
ReDim ships(2)
ships(2) = "Santa Maria"
txtBox.Text = ships(1)
```

4. ```
Dim fabFour() As String = {"", "John", "Paul", "Ringo"}
Dim i As Integer
ReDim Preserve fabFour(4)
fabFour(4) = "George"
For i = 1 To 4
  lstOutput.Items.Add(fabFour(i))
Next i
```

5. ```
Dim liberalArts() As String = {"grammar", "logic", "rhetoric", _
                     "arithmetic", "music", "geometry", "astronomy"}
txtBox.Text = Str(liberalArts.GetUpperBound(0))
```

6. ```
Dim num As Integer = 5
Dim scores(num) As Integer, i As Integer
For i = 0 To num
  scores(i) = i + 10
Next i
lstOutput.Items.Add(scores(num))
txtBox.Text = Str(scores.GetUpperBound(0))
```

7. ```
Dim allVowelWords() As String, line As String
line = "abstemious,dialogue,facetious,sequoia,education"
allVowelWords = Split(line, ",")
txtOutput.Text = allVowelWords(2)
```

8. ```
Dim orderWords() As String   'Letters in alphabetical order
Dim line As String = "bijoux, biopsy, almost"
orderWords = Split(line, ",")
txtOutput.Text = Trim(orderWords(orderWords.GetUpperBound(0)))
```

9. ```
Dim notes() As String = {"A","B","C","D","E","F","G"}
txtOutput.Text = Join(notes, ",")
```

10. ```
Dim line As String = "I came, I saw, I conquered."
Dim temp() As String
temp = Split(line, ",")
txtOutput.Text = Join(temp, ",")
```

11.
```
Dim sr As IO.StreamReader = IO.File.OpenText("DATA.TXT")
Dim nom As String
nom = sr.ReadLine
lstBox.Items.Add(nom)
nom = Replace(nom, Chr(34), "")
lstBox.Items.Add(nom)
```

(Assume that the first line of the file DATA.TXT is "Maryland", "MD", 12407.)

12.
```
Dim sr As IO.StreamWriter = IO.File.CreateText("DATA.TXT")
txtBox.Text = IO.File.Exists("DATA.TXT")
```

In Exercises 13 through 18, assume that the file DATA.TXT (shown to the right of the code) has been accessed with the statement `Dim sr As IO.Stream-Reader = IO.File.OpenText("DATA.TXT")`. Determine the output displayed by the lines of code.

13.
```
Dim num As Single
num = Val(sr.ReadLine)
txtOutput.Text = Str(num * num)
```
DATA.TXT
4

14.
```
Dim word As String
word = sr.ReadLine
txtOutput.Text = "un" & word
```
DATA.TXT
speakable

15.
```
Dim str1 As String, str2 As String
str1 = sr.ReadLine
str2 = sr.ReadLine
txtOutput.Text = str1 & str2
```
DATA.TXT
base
ball

16.
```
Dim yrOfBirth As Single, curYr As Single
yrOfBirth = Val(sr.ReadLine)
curYr = Val(sr.ReadLine) 'Current year
txtOutput.Text = "Age: " & curYr - yrOfBirth
```
DATA.TXT
1983
2003

17.
```
Dim building As String
Dim numRooms As Single
building = sr.ReadLine
numRooms = Val(sr.ReadLine)
txtOutput.Text = "The " & building " has" & Str(numRooms) & " rooms."
```
DATA.TXT
White House
132

18.
```
Dim major As String
Dim percent As Single
major = sr.ReadLine
percent = Val(sr.ReadLine)
txtOutput.Text = "In 2002, " & Str(percent) & _
            "% of entering college freshmen majored in " & major & "."
```
DATA.TXT
Computer Science
2.2

In Exercises 19 through 22, determine the output displayed in the text box when the button is clicked.

19.
```
Private Sub btnDisplay_Click(...) Handles btnDisplay.Click
    Dim salutation As String
    Dim sw As IO.StreamWriter = IO.File.CreateText("GREETINGS.TXT")
```

```
      sw.WriteLine("Hello")
      sw.WriteLine("Aloha")
      sw.Close()
      Dim sr As IO.StreamReader = IO.File.OpenText("GREETINGS.TXT")
      salutation = sr.ReadLine
      txtOutput.Text = salutation
      sr.Close()
    End Sub
```

20.
```
    Private Sub btnDisplay_Click(...) Handles btnDisplay.Click
      Dim salutation As String, welcome As String
      Dim sw As IO.StreamWriter = IO.File.CreateText("GREETINGS.TXT")
      sw.WriteLine("Hello")
      sw.WriteLine("Aloha")
      sw.Close()
      Dim sr As StreamReader = IO.File.OpenText("GREETINGS.TXT")
      salutation = sr.ReadLine
      welcome = sr.ReadLine
      txtOutput.Text = welcome
      sr.Close()
    End Sub
```

21.
```
    Private Sub btnDisplay_Click(...) Handles btnDisplay.Click
      Dim salutation As String
      Dim sw As IO.StreamWriter = IO.File.CreateText("GREETINGS.TXT")
      sw.WriteLine("Hello")
      sw.WriteLine("Aloha")
      sw.WriteLine("Bon Jour")
      sw.Close()
      Dim sr As IO.StreamReader = IO.File.OpenText("GREETINGS.TXT")
      Do While (sr.Peek <> -1)
        salutation = sr.ReadLine
        txtOutput.Text = salutation
      Loop
      sr.Close()
    End Sub
```

22. Assume the contents of the file GREETING.TXT are as shown in Figure 15.9.

```
    Private Sub btnDisplay_Click(...) Handles btnDisplay.Click
      Dim file As String, welcome As String
      Dim salutation As Integer
      file = "GREETING.TXT"
      Dim sw As IO.StreamWriter = IO.File.AppendText(file)
      sw.WriteLine("Buenos Dias")
      sw.Close()
      Dim sr As IO.StreamReader = IO.File.OpenText(file)
      For salutation = 1 To 4
        welcome= sr.ReadLine
        txtOutput.Text = welcome
      Next salutation
      sr.Close()
    End Sub
```

```
Hello
Aloha
Bon Jour
```

Figure 15.9 Contents of the file GREETING.TXT.

Exercises 23 through 29 refer to the database MEGACITIES2.MDB presented in Chapter 12. In these exercises, describe the output displayed when the button is clicked.

23.
```
Private Sub btnDisplay_Click(...) Handles btnDisplay.Click
    Dim i As Integer, sum As Single
    Dim dt As New DataTable()
    Dim connStr As String = "Provider=Microsoft.Jet.OLEDB.4.0;" & _
                        "Data Source = MEGACITIES2.MDB"
    Dim sqlStr As String = "SELECT * FROM Cities"
    Dim dataAdapter As New OleDb.OleDbDataAdapter(sqlStr, connStr)
    dataAdapter.Fill(dt)
    dataAdapter.Dispose()
    sum = 0
    For i = 0 To dt.Rows.Count - 1
      sum = sum + Val(dt.Rows(i)("pop2015"))
    Next i
    txtOutput.Text = Str(sum) & " million"
End Sub
```

24.
```
Private Sub btnDisplay_Click(...) Handles btnDisplay.Click
    Dim i As Integer
    Dim dt As New DataTable()
    Dim connStr As String = "Provider=Microsoft.Jet.OLEDB.4.0;" & _
                        "Data Source = MEGACITIES2.MDB"
    Dim sqlStr As String = "SELECT * FROM Cities"
    Dim dataAdapter As New OleDb.OleDbDataAdapter(sqlStr, connStr)
    dataAdapter.Fill(dt)
    dataAdapter.Dispose()
    For i = 0 To dt.Rows.Count - 1
      If Val(dt.Rows(i)("pop2015")) > 25 Then
        lstOutput.Items.Add(dt.Rows(i)(0))
      End If
    Next i
End Sub
```

25.
```
Private Sub btnDisplay_Click(...) Handles btnDisplay.Click
    Dim i As Integer
    Dim dt As New DataTable()
    Dim connStr As String = "Provider=Microsoft.Jet.OLEDB.4.0;" & _
                        "Data Source = MEGACITIES2.MDB"
    Dim sqlStr As String = "SELECT * FROM Countries"
    Dim dataAdapter As New OleDb.OleDbDataAdapter(sqlStr, connStr)
    dataAdapter.Fill(dt)
    dataAdapter.Dispose()
```

```
      For i = 0 To dt.Rows.Count - 1
        If Len(dt.Rows(i)("country")) = 5 Then
            lstOutput.Items.Add(dt.Rows(i)(0))
        End If
      Next i
    End Sub
```

26.
```
Private Sub btnDisplay_Click(...) Handles btnDisplay.Click
    Dim i As Integer
    Dim dt As New DataTable()
    Dim connStr As String = "Provider=Microsoft.Jet.OLEDB.4.0;" & _
                            "Data Source = MEGACITIES2.MDB"
    Dim sqlStr As String = "SELECT * FROM Countries"
    Dim dataAdapter As New OleDb.OleDbDataAdapter(sqlStr, connStr)
    dataAdapter.Fill(dt)
    dataAdapter.Dispose()
    For i = 0 To dt.Columns.Count - 1
      lstOutput.Items.Add(dt.Columns(i))
    Next i
End Sub
```

27.
```
Private Sub btnDisplay_Click(...) Handles btnDisplay.Click
    Dim dt As New DataTable()
    Dim connStr As String = "Provider = Microsoft.Jet.OLEDB.4.0;" & _
                            "Data Source = MEGACITIES.MDB"
    Dim sqlStr As String = "SELECT * FROM Countries"
    Dim dataAdapter As New OleDb.OleDbDataAdapter(sqlStr, connStr)
    dataAdapter.Fill(dt)
    dataAdapter.Dispose()
    lstCountries.DataSource = dt
    lstCountries.DisplayMember = "currency"
End Sub
```

28.
```
Private Sub btnDisplay_Click(...) Handles btnDisplay.Click
    Dim dt As New DataTable()
    Dim connStr As String = "Provider = Microsoft.Jet.OLEDB.4.0;" & _
                            "Data Source = MEGACITIES.MDB"
    Dim sqlStr As String = "SELECT * FROM Cities"
    Dim dataAdapter As New OleDb.OleDbDataAdapter(sqlStr, connStr)
    dataAdapter.Fill(dt)
    dataAdapter.Dispose()
    txtCurrency.Text = dt.Rows(1)("country")
End Sub
```

29.
```
Private Sub btnDisplay_Click(...) Handles btnDisplay.Click
    Dim dt As New DataTable()
    Dim sqlStr As String = "SELECT city FROM Cities WHERE " & _
                           "country = 'China' ORDER BY city ASC"
    Dim connStr As String = "Provider = Microsoft.Jet.OLEDB.4.0;" & _
                            "Data Source = MEGACITIES2.MDB"
    Dim dataAdapter As New OleDb.OleDbDataAdapter(sqlStr, connStr)
    dataAdapter.Fill(dt)
    dataAdapter.Dispose()
    DataGrid1.DataSource = dt
End Sub
```

In Exercises 30 through 32, identify the errors.

30. `Dim scores(5 To 10) As Integer`

31. `Dim primaryColors(3) As String = {"", "red", "blue", "yellow"}`

32. `Dim sw As StreamWriter = File.AppendText("YOB.TXT")`

In Exercises 33 and 34, identify any errors. Assume that the contents of the file GREETING.TXT are as shown in Figure 15.9.

33.
```
Private Sub btnDisplay_Click(...) Handles btnDisplay.Click
   Dim sw As IO.StreamWriter = IO.File.CreateText("GREETINGS.TXT")
   Dim word As String
   word = sw.ReadLine
   txtOutput.Text = word
   sw.Close()
End Sub
```

34.
```
Private Sub btnDisplay_Click(...) Handles btnDisplay.Click
   Dim sr As IO.StreamReader = IO.File.OpenText("GREETING.TXT")
   "GREETING.TXT".Close
End Sub
```

In Exercises 35 through 38, describe the effect of executing the statement(s).

35.
```
For i = 0 To mountains.GetUpperBound(0)
   lstBox.Items.Add(mountains(i))
Next i
```

36. `txtBox.Text = rivers.GetUpperBound(0)`

37.
```
Dim sr As IO.StreamReader   'In declarations section

Private Sub btnAccess_Click(...) Handles btnAccess.Click
   sr = IO.File.OpenText("GREETINGS.TXT")
End Sub
```

38. `txtBox.Text = Chr(sr.Peek)`

In Exercises 39 through 44, write a single line of code to carry out the task.

39. Declare the array *oceans*() to have upper bound 5 and contain the values Atlantic, Pacific, Indian, Arctic, and Antarctic in the elements with subscripts 1 through 5.

40. Declare the array *bigThree*() to have upper bound 2 and contain the values Ford, Chrysler, General Motors.

41. Change the upper bound of the array *towns*() to 100

42. Display the upper bound of the array *colors*() in a message dialog box.

43. Open the file PLACES.TXT for append.

44. Read the next character from the file identified by *sr* and display the character in a text box.

In Exercises 45 through 54, use the database MEGACITIES2.MDB.

45. Write a program to place in a list box the names of the countries in the Countries table in the order they appear in the table.

46. Write a program to place in a list box the names of the countries in the Countries table in the reverse order that they appear in the table.

47. Write a program to place in a list box the names of the cities in the Cities table whose populations are projected to exceed 20 million in the year 2015.

48. Write a program to place in a list box the names of the cities in the Cities table whose 1995 populations are between 12 and 16 million.

49. Write a program to place in a list box the names of the countries in the Countries table, where each name is followed by a hyphen and the name of its currency.

50. Write a program to find and display the city in the Cities table that will experience the greatest percentage growth from 1995 to 2015.[**Note:** The percentage growth is $100 * (pop2015 - pop1995) / pop1995$.]

51. Write a program to place the countries from the Countries table in a list box in descending order of their 1995 populations.

52. Write a program to place the cities from the Cities table in a list box in descending order of their percentage population growth from 1995 to 2015.

53. Write a program to display in a data grid the *name* and *currency* of each city from the table Cities in a data grid.

54. Write a program to display in a data grid the names and 1995 populations of the countries in the table Country. The countries should be displayed in descending order of their populations.

In Exercises 55 through 70 convert the VB 6.0 program to a VB.NET program.

55. Section 7.1, Example 1   **56.** Section 7.1, Example 3

57. Section 7.1, Example 4   **58.** Section 7.1, Example 5

59. Section 7.1, Example 7   **60.** Section 7.2, Example 4

61. Section 7.4, Example 2   **62.** Section 7.5, Example 1

63. Section 3.5, Example 2   **64.** Section 8.1, Example 2

65. Section 12.1, Example 1   **66.** Section 12.3, Example 1

67. Section 12.2, Example 2

68. Redo Exercise 51 of Section 15.1. However, assume that the file PCS.TXT contains the information in Table 15.3 in LSV format. That is, the first two lines contain the entries Hewlett-Packard and 21478.

69. The file MEMBERS.TXT contains the names of the 100 members of a club. Randomly select people to serve as President, Treasurer, and Secretary. **Note:** A person cannot hold more than one office.

70. Redo Exercise 51 of Section 15.1 by using a pair of parallel arrays to hold the company names and amounts of shipments. The data should be entered into the arrays when they are declared.

71. Write a program to convert any LSV file to a CSV file and then display the contents of the new file. Assume that the file to be converted is located in the *bin* folder for the program. **Note:** In addition to supplying the filenames, the user also must provide the number of fields in each record of the LSV file.

✔✔ **Solutions to Practice Problems 15.2**

1. The array would have 101 elements, since in VB.NET the first subscript is 0. In many situations, we prefer to begin with the element having subscript 1 when assigning values and therefore give the values "" or 0 to the element with subscript 0.

2. Since ReDim cannot be used to declare a variable in VB.NET, the statement must be intended to change the size of an already declared array. Since the array variable would have been given a data type when it was declared, there is no need for the clause "As Integer." Actually, VB.NET does not allow any "As *DataType*" clause to appear in a ReDim statement. Therefore, the proper statement is

```
ReDim scores(5)
```

3. When the StreamReader variable *sr* is a form-level variable. The first statement should be placed in the Declaration section of the Code window and the second statement in a procedure. Also, when the value of the variable *filespec* is determined at run time.

CHAPTER 15   SUMMARY

Most of the programming constructs (such as procedure, decision structures, loops, arrays) taught in the VB 6.0 part of this book carry over to VB.NET with only minor changes. The names of some controls, properties, methods, and events have changed. The main new concepts of concern to us are the use of format strings to display output in a list box, the use of StreamReader and StreamWriter objects to read and write sequential files, and the use of the data table object to manipulate database information.

CHAPTER 15   PROGRAMMING PROJECTS

1. Work Programming Project 9 in Chapter 6 (chain-link sentence) as a VB.NET program. Use the functions Replace and Split.

2. Work Programming Project 8 of Chapter 11 (*The Underdog and the World Series*) as a VB.NET program.

3. Convert the Recording Checks and Deposits case study from Chapter 8 to a VB.NET program. Instead of printing a report, display the report (properly formatted) in a list box.

ANSI Value	Character	ANSI Value	Character	ANSI Value	Character
000	(null)	040	(	080	P
001	□	041	)	081	Q
002	□	042	*	082	R
003	□	043	+	083	S
004	□	044	,	084	T
005	□	045	-	085	U
006	□	046	.	086	V
007	□	047	/	087	W
008	□	048	0	088	X
009	(tab)	049	1	089	Y
010	(line feed)	050	2	090	Z
011	□	051	3	091	[
012	□	052	4	092	\
013	(carriage return)	053	5	093	]
014	□	054	6	094	^
015	□	055	7	095	_
016	□	056	8	096	`
017	□	057	9	097	a
018	□	058	:	098	b
019	□	059	;	099	c
020	□	060	<	100	d
021	□	061	=	101	e
022	□	062	>	102	f
023	□	063	?	103	g
024	□	064	@	104	h
025	□	065	A	105	i
026	□	066	B	106	j
027	□	067	C	107	k
028	□	068	D	108	l
029	□	069	E	109	m
030	□	070	F	110	n
031	□	071	G	111	o
032	(space)	072	H	112	p
033	!	073	I	113	q
034	"	074	J	114	r
035	#	075	K	115	s
036	$	076	L	116	t
037	%	077	M	117	u
038	&	078	N	118	v
039	'	079	O	119	w

ANSI Value	Character	ANSI Value	Character	ANSI Value	Character
120	x	166	¦	212	Ô
121	y	167	§	213	Õ
122	z	168	¨	214	Ö
123	{	169	©	215	×
124	|	170	ª	216	Ø
125	}	171	«	217	Ù
126	~	172	¬	218	Ú
127	□	173	–	219	Û
128	□	174	®	220	Ü
129	□	175	‾	221	Ý
130	‚	176	°	222	Þ
131	ƒ	177	±	223	ß
132	„	178	²	224	à
133	…	179	³	225	á
134	†	180	´	226	â
135	‡	181	µ	227	ã
136	^	182	¶	228	ä
137	‰	183	·	229	å
138	Š	184	‚	230	æ
139	‹	185	¹	231	ç
140	Œ	186	º	232	è
141	□	187	»	233	é
142	□	188	¼	234	ê
143	□	189	½	235	ë
144	□	190	¾	236	ì
145	'	191	¿	237	í
146	'	192	À	238	î
147	"	193	Á	239	ï
148	"	194	Â	240	õ
149	•	195	Ã	241	ñ
150	–	196	Ä	242	ò
151	—	197	Å	243	ó
152	~	198	Æ	244	ô
153	™	199	Ç	245	õ
154	š	200	È	246	ö
155	›	201	É	247	÷
156	œ	202	Ê	248	ø
157	□	203	Ë	249	ù
158	□	204	Ì	250	ú
159	Ÿ	205	Í	251	û
160	□	206	Î	252	ü
161	¡	207	Ï	253	ý
162	¢	208	Ð	254	þ
163	£	209	Ñ	255	
164	¤	210	Ò		
165	¥	211	Ó		

How To

HOW TO: Install, Invoke, and Exit Visual Basic

A. Install the Working Model Edition of Visual Basic

1. Place the CD accompanying this book into your CD drive. In about five seconds you will most likely hear a whirring sound from the CD drive.
2. Double-click on My Computer in the Windows Desktop. A window showing the different disk drives will appear.
3. Double-click on the icon containing a picture of a CD (along with a drive) and having "Schneider_Update" and the drive letter below the icon. A list of folders and files will appear. (**Note:** With Windows XP, click on the Start button, and then click on the My Computer icon in the upper-right section of the start menu.)
4. Double-click on the icon labeled "Setup.exe". (The icon is a colorful sideways 8.) A large window with the words "Visual Basic 6.0 Working Model" will appear.
5. The title bar of the large window says "Installation Wizard for Visual Basic 6.0 Working Model." The installation wizard will guide you through the installation process. Click on Next to continue.
6. An End User License Agreement will appear. After reading the agreement, click on the the circle to the left of the sentence "I accept the agreement." and then click on Next.
7. The next window to appear has spaces for an ID number, your name, and your company's name. Ignore the ID number. Just type in your name and, optionally, a company name, and then click Next.

If you are using Windows XP, skip steps 8 and 9.

8. Visual Basic 6.0 requires that you have Internet Explorer 4.0 or later version on your computer. If a recent version is not present, the Installation Wizard will install it for you. If so, successive windows will guide you through the installation. At some point you will be required to restart your computer. We recommend doing the standard installation and using the recommended destination folder.
9. You might next be guided through the installation of DCOM98, which is also needed by Visual Basic 6.0. After installing DCOM98, the installation wizard will automatically restart your computer and then continue with the installation of VB 6.0. **Note:** If another window is covering the Installation Wizard window, then click on the Installation Wizard window. If you can't find the Installation Wizard window, repeat Steps 1–5.

You will now be guided through the installation of the Working Model Edition VB 6.0. At the end of the installation, Visual Basic will be invoked.

10. The next window requests the name of the Common Install Folder. We recommend that you simply click on Next, which will accept the default folder and copy some files into it.
11. The next window to appear is the Visual Basic 6.0 Working Model Setup. Click on Continue.
12. The next screen shows your Product ID number and possibly requests your name. Enter your name if requested and then click on OK.
13. The next window asks you to choose between Typical and Custom installations. We recommend that you click on the Typical icon.
14. About one minute is required for the VB 6.0 Working Model to be installed. If the next screen to appear gives you the opportunity to restart Windows, click on Restart Windows. Otherwise, click on the OK button.
15. The next window to appear gives you the opportunity to register your copy of VB 6.0 over the Web. Uncheck the Register Now box and click on Finish.

B. Invoke Visual Basic after installation.

1. Click the Start button.
2. Point to Programs. (**Note:** With Windows XP, point to All Programs.)
3. Point to Microsoft Visual Basic 6.0. (A new panel will open on the right.)
4. In the new panel, click on Microsoft Visual Basic 6.0.

C. Exit Visual Basic.

1. Press the Esc key.
2. Press Alt/F/X.
3. If an unsaved program is present, Visual Basic will prompt you about saving it.

Note: In many situations, Step 1 is not needed.

HOW TO: Manage Programs

A. Run a program from Visual Basic.

1. Click on the Start icon (right arrowhead) in the Toolbar.

or

1. Press F5.

or

1. Press Alt/R and make a selection from the Run menu.

B. Save the current program on a disk.

1. Press Alt/F/V [or click the Save Project icon (shows a diskette) on the Toolbar].
2. Fill in the requested information. Do not give an extension as part of the project name or the file name. Two files will be created—one with

extension .VBP and the other with extension .FRM. The .VBP file holds a list of files related to the project. The .FRM file actually holds the program.

Note: After a program has been saved once, updated versions can be saved with the same filenames by pressing Alt/F/V. Alt/F/E and Alt/F/A are used to save the program with new file names.

C. Begin a new program.

1. Press Alt/F/N.
2. If an unsaved program is present, Visual Basic will prompt you about saving it.

D. Open a program stored on a disk.

1. Press Alt/F/O [or click the Open Project icon (shows an open folder) on the Toolbar].
2. Click on one of the two tabs, Existing or Recent.
3. If you selected Existing, choose a folder for the "Look in:" box, type a filename into the "File name:" box, and press the Enter key. Alternatively, double-click on one of the filenames displayed in the large box in the middle of the dialog box.
4. If you selected Recent, double-click on one of the files in the list.

Note 1: In Steps 3 and 4, if an unsaved program is present, Visual Basic will prompt you about saving it.

Note 2: The form or code for the program may not appear, but they can be accessed through the Project Explorer window by opening the Forms folder, clicking on the name of the form, and then clicking on either the View object or the View Code button.

E. Use the Project Explorer.

Note: Just below the Project Explorer title bar are three icons (View Code, View Object, and Toggle Folders), and below them is the List window. At any time, one item in the List window [such as a form (contained in the Forms folder) or a module] can be selected.

1. Click on View Code to see the code associated with the selected item.
2. Click on View Object to see the Object (usually the form) associated with the selected item.

F. Display the form associated with a program.

1. Press Alt/V/B. (If the selection Object is grayed, first run and then terminate the program.)

   or

1. Press Shift+F7.

   or

1. Press Alt/V/P to activate the Project Explorer window.
2. Select the name of the form.
3. Click on the View Object button.

HOW TO: Use the Editor

A. Select (or highlight) text.

    1. Move the cursor to the beginning or end of the text.
    2. Hold down a Shift key and use the direction keys to highlight a block of text.
    3. Release the Shift key.

    or

    1. Move the mouse to the beginning or end of the text.
    2. Hold down the left mouse button and move the mouse to the other end of the text.
    3. Release the left mouse button.

Note 1: To deselect text, press a direction key or click outside the text.

Note 2: To select a word, double-click on it. To select a line, move the mouse pointer just far enough into the left margin so that the pointer changes to an arrow, and then single-click there.

B. Cut a line of a program.

    1. Move the cursor to the line.
    2. Press Ctrl+Y.

    or

    1. Mark the line as a block. (See item A of this section.)
    2. Press Alt/E/T or press Ctrl+X.

Note: In the preceding maneuvers, the line is placed in the clipboard and can be retrieved by pressing Ctrl+V. To delete the line without placing it in the clipboard, mark it as a block and press Del.

C. Move a line within the Code window.

    1. Move the cursor to the line and press Ctrl+Y.
    2. Move the cursor to the target location.
    3. Press Ctrl+V.

D. Use the clipboard to move or duplicate statements.

    1. Mark the statements as a block.
    2. Press Ctrl+X to delete the block and place it into the clipboard, or press Ctrl+C to place a copy of the block into the clipboard.
    3. Move the cursor to the location where you desire to place the block.
    4. Press Ctrl+V to place a copy of the text from the clipboard at the cursor position.

E. Search for specific text in the program.

    1. Press Alt/E/F or Ctrl+F.
    2. Type sought-after text into the rectangle.
    3. Select desired options if different from the defaults.
    4. Press the Enter key.
    5. To repeat the search, press Find Next or press Cancel and then F3.

F. Find and Replace.

1. Press Alt/E/E or Ctrl+H.
2. Type sought-after text into first rectangle.
3. Press Tab.
4. Type replacement text into second rectangle.
5. Select desired options if different from the defaults.
6. Press the Enter key.
7. Press Replace to make the change, or press Replace All to make all such changes.

G. Undo a change to the code.

1. Press Alt/E/U or Ctrl+Z to undo the last change made to a line.

HOW TO: Get Help

(Available only with Learning, Professional, and Enterprise Editions.)

A. Obtain information about a Visual Basic topic.

1. Press Alt/H/M.
2. Click on the Index tab and follow the instructions.
3. To display a topic, double-click on it.
4. If a second list pops up, double-click on an item from it.

B. View the syntax and purpose of a Visual Basic keyword.

1. Type the word into a Code window.
2. Place the cursor on, or just following, the keyword.
3. Press F1.

C. Display an ANSI table.

1. Press Alt/H/M and click on the Index tab.
2. Type ANSI and press the Enter key.
3. To move between the displays for ANSI characters 0-127 and 128-255, click on "See Also," and then click on the Display button.

D. Obtain a list of Visual Basic's reserved words.

1. Press Alt/H/M.
2. Type "keywords", press the down-arrow key, and double-click on a category of keywords from the list below the blue bar.

E. Obtain a list of shortcut keys.

1. Press Alt/H/M and click on the Contents tab.
2. Double-click on the Additional Information book.
3. Double-click on the Keyboard Guide book.
4. Double-click on one of the collections of shortcut keys.

F. Obtain information about a control.

1. Click on the control at design time.
2. Press F1.

G. Exit Help.

1. Press Esc.

HOW TO: Manipulate a Dialog Box

A. Use a dialog box.

A dialog box contains three types of items: rectangles (text or list boxes), option lists, and command buttons. An option list is a sequence of option buttons or check boxes of the form ○ *option* or ☐ *option*.

1. Move from item to item with the Tab key. (The movement is from left to right and top to bottom. Use Shift+Tab to reverse the direction.)
2. Inside a rectangle, either type in the requested information, or use the direction keys to make a selection.
3. In an option list, an option button of the form ○ *option* can be selected with the direction keys. A dot inside the circle indicates that the option has been selected.
4. In an option list, a check box of the form ☐ *option* can be checked or unchecked by pressing the spacebar. An **X** or ✓ inside the square indicates that the option has been checked.
5. A highlighted command button is invoked by pressing the Enter key.

B. Cancel a dialog box

1. Press the Esc key.

or

1. Press the Tab key until the command button captioned "Cancel" is highlighted and then press the Enter key.

HOW TO: Use Menus

A. Open a dropdown menu.

1. Click on the menu name.

or

1. Press Alt.
2. Press the underlined letter in the name of the menu. Alternatively, use the Right Arrow key to move the highlighted cursor bar to the menu name, and then press the Down Arrow key.

B. Make a selection from a dropdown menu.

1. Open the dropdown menu.
2. Click on the desired item.

or

1. Open the dropdown menu. One letter in each item that is eligible to be used will be underlined.
2. Press the underlined letter. Alternatively, use the Down Arrow key to move the cursor bar to the desired item and then press the Enter key.

C. Obtain information about the selections in a dropdown menu.

1. Press Alt/H/M and click on the Contents tab.
2. Double-click on the Interface Reference book
3. Double-click on the Menu book

4. Double-click on the name of the menu of interest.
5. Double-click on the selection of interest.

D. Look at all the menus in the menu bar.

1. Press Alt/F.
2. Press the Right Arrow key to cycle through available menus.

E. Close a dropdown menu.

1. Press the Esc key or click anywhere outside the menu.

HOW TO: Utilize the Windows Environment

A. Place text in the Windows clipboard.

1. Mark the text as a block as described in the How to Use the Editor section.
2. Press Ctrl+C.

B. Access Windows Notepad.

1. Click the Start button.
2. Point to Programs.
3. Point to Accessories.
4. Click Notepad.

C. Display all characters in a font.

1. Click the Start button.
2. Point to Programs.
3. Point to Accessories.
4. Click Character Map.
5. Click on the underlined down arrow at the right end of the Font box.
6. Highlight the desired font, and press the Enter key, or click on the desired font.

D. Display an ANSI or ASCII code for a character with a code above 128.

1. Proceed as described in item C above to display the font containing the character of interest.
2. Click on the character of interest. Displayed at the right end of the bottom line of the font table is Alt+0xxx, where xxx is the code for the character.

HOW TO: Design a Form

A. Display the Toolbox.

1. Press Alt/V/X.

B. Place a new control on the form.

Option I: (new control with default size and position)

1. Double-click on the control's icon in the Toolbox. The new control appears at the center of the form.
2. Size and position the control as described in items G and H, which follow.

Option II: (a single new control sized and positioned as it is created)

1. Click on the control's icon in the Toolbox.
2. Move the mouse to the approximate position on the form desired for the upper-left corner of the control.
3. Press and hold the left mouse button.
4. Move the mouse to the position on the form desired for the lower-right corner of the control. A dashed box will indicate the overall shape of the new control.
5. Release the left mouse button.
6. The control can be resized and repositioned as described in items G and H.

Option III: (multiple instances of the same control)

1. Click on the control's icon in the Toolbox, while holding down the Ctrl key.
2. Repeatedly use Steps 2 to 5 of Option II to create instances of the control.
3. When finished creating instances of this control, click on the arrow icon in the Toolbox.

C. Create a related group of controls.

1. Place a picture box or frame control on the form to hold the related group of controls.
2. Use Option II or III in item B of this section to place controls in the picture box or frame.

D. Select a particular control.

1. Click on the control.

or

1. Press the Tab key until the control is selected.

E. Delete a control.

1. Select the control to be deleted.
2. Press the Del key.

F. Delete a related group of controls.

1. Select the picture box or frame holding the related group of controls.
2. Press the Del key.

G. Move a control, related group of controls, or form to a new location.

1. Move the mouse onto the control, the picture box or frame containing the related group of controls, or the title bar of the form.
2. Drag the object to the new location.

H. Change the size of a control.

1. Select the desired control.
2. Move the mouse to one of the eight sizing handles located around the edge of the control. The mouse pointer will change to a double-arrow, which points in the direction that resizing can occur.
3. Drag to the desired size.

I. Change the size of a Project Container window.

> 1. Move the mouse to the edge or corner of the window that is to be stretched or shrunk. The mouse pointer will change to a double-arrow, which points in the direction that resizing can occur.
> 2. Drag to the desired size.

J. Use the Color palette to set foreground and background colors.

> 1. Select the desired control or the form.
> 2. Press Alt/V/L to activate the Color palette.
> 3. If the Color palette obscures the object you are working with, you may wish to use the mouse to grab the Color palette by its title bar and move it so that at least some of the object shows.
> 4. To set the foreground color, click on the square within a square at the far left in the Color palette and click on the desired color from the palette.
> 5. To set the background color, click on the region within the outer square but outside the inner square and click on the desired color from the palette.
>
> or
>
> 1. Select the desired control or the form.
> 2. Press Alt/V/W or F4 to activate the Properties window.
> 3. To set the foreground color, click on the down-arrow to the right of the ForeColor settings box, click on the Palette tab, and click on the desired color.
> 4. To set the background color, click on the down-arrow to the right of the BackColor settings box, click on the Palette tab, and click on the desired color.

HOW TO: Work with the Properties of an Object

A. Activate the Properties window.

> 1. Press Alt/V/W.
>
> or
>
> 1. Press F4.
>
> or
>
> 1. Click on an object on the form with the right mouse button.
> 2. In the shortcut menu, click on Properties.

B. Highlight a property in the Properties window.

> 1. Activate the Properties window, and press the Enter key.
> 2. Use the Up or Down Arrow keys to move the highlight bar to the desired property.
>
> or
>
> 1. Activate the Properties window.
> 2. Click on the up or down arrow located at the ends of the vertical scroll bar at the right side of the Properties window until the desired property is visible.
> 3. Click on the desired property.

C. Select or specify a setting for a property.

1. Highlight the property whose setting is to be changed.
2. Click on the settings box or press Tab to place the cursor in the settings box.
   a. If a black down-arrow appears at the right end of the settings box, click on the down-arrow to display a list of all allowed settings, and then click on the desired setting.
   b. If an ellipsis (three periods: . . .) appears at the right end of the settings box, press F4 or click on the ellipsis to display a dialog box. Answer the questions in the dialog box, and click on OK or Open, as appropriate.
   c. If the cursor moves to the settings box, type in the new setting for the property.

D. Change a property setting of an object.

1. Select the desired object.
2. Activate the Properties window.
3. Highlight the property whose setting is to be changed.
4. Select or specify the new setting for the property.

E. Let a label change size to accommodate its caption.

1. Set the label's AutoSize property to True. (The label will shrink to the smallest size needed to hold the current caption. If the caption is changed, the label will automatically grow or shrink horizontally to accommodate the new caption. If the WordWrap property is set to True as well, the label will grow and shrink vertically, keeping the same width.)

F. Let a label caption use more than one line.

1. Set the label's WordWrap property to True. [If the label is not wide enough to accommodate the entire caption on one line, part of the caption will wrap to additional lines. If the label height is too small, then part or all of these wrapped lines will not be visible (unless the AutoSize property is set to True).]

G. Let a text box display more than one line.

1. Set the text box's MultiLine property to True. (If the text box is not wide enough to accommodate the text entered by the user, the text will scroll down to new lines. If the text box is not tall enough, lines will scroll up out of view, but can be redisplayed by moving the cursor up.)

H. Assign an access key to a label or command button.

1. When assigning a value to the Caption property, precede the desired access-key character with an ampersand (&).

I. Allow a particular command button to be activated by a press of the Enter key.

1. Set the command button's Default property to True.

Note: Setting the Default property True for one command button automatically sets the property to False for all the other command buttons on the form.

J. Adjust the order in which the Tab key moves the focus.

1. Select the first control in the tabbing sequence.
2. Change the setting of the TabIndex property for this control to 0.
3. Select the next control in the tabbing sequence.
4. Change the setting of the TabIndex property for this control to 1.
5. Repeat Steps 3 and 4 (adding 1 to the Tab Index property) until all controls on the form have been assigned a new TabIndex setting.

Note: In Steps 2 and 4, if an object is moved to another position in the sequence, then the TabIndex property for the other objects will be renumbered accordingly.

K. Allow the pressing of Esc to activate a particular command button.

1. Set the command button's Cancel property to True. (Setting the Cancel property to True for one command button automatically sets it to False for all other command buttons.)

L. Keep the contents of a picture box from being erased accidentally.

1. Set the picture box's AutoRedraw property to True. (The default is False. Unless the property is set to True, the contents will be erased when the picture box is obscured by another window.)

HOW TO: Manage Procedures

A. Access the Code window.

1. Press Alt/V/C or F7. (If the Code window does not appear, run and then terminate the program.)

   or

1. Press Alt/V/P to activate the Project Explorer window.
2. Select the name of the form.
3. Click on the "View Code" button.

B. Look at an existing procedure.

1. Access the Code window.
2. Press Ctrl+Down Arrow or Ctrl+Up Arrow to see all the procedures.

   or

1. Access the Code window.
2. Click on the down arrow at the right of the Object box and then select an object. [For general procedures select (General) as the Object.]
3. Click on the down arrow at the right of the Procedure box and then select a procedure.

C. Create a general procedure.

1. Access the Code window.
2. Move to a blank line that is not inside a procedure.
3. Type Private Sub (for a Sub procedure) or Private Function (for a Function procedure) followed by the name of the procedure and any parameters.

4. Press the Enter key. (The Code window will now display the new procedure heading and an End Sub or End Function statement.)

5. Type the procedure into the Code Window.

or

1. Access the Code window.

2. Press Alt/T/P. (A dialog box will appear.)

3. Type the name of the procedure into the Name rectangle.

4. Select the type of procedure.

5. Select the Scope by clicking on Public or Private. (In this book, we always use Private.)

6. Press the Enter key. (The Code window will now display the new procedure heading and an End Sub or End Function statement.)

7. Type the procedure into the Code Window.

D. Alter a procedure.

1. View the procedure in the Code Window as described in item B of this section.

2. Make changes as needed.

E. Remove a procedure.

1. Bring the procedure into the Code Window as described in item B of this section.

2. Mark the entire procedure as a block. That is,
   a. Press Ctrl+PgUp to move the cursor to the beginning of the procedure.
   b. Hold down the Shift key and press Ctrl+PgDn to move the cursor to the start of the next procedure.

3. Press the Del key.

F. Insert an existing procedure into a program.

1. Open the program containing the procedure.

2. View the procedure in the Code Window as described in item B of this section.

3. Mark the entire procedure as a block, as described in step 2 of item E of this section.

4. Press Ctrl+C to place the procedure into the clipboard.

5. Open the program in which the procedure is to be inserted and access the Code Window.

6. Move the cursor to a blank line.

7. Press Ctrl+V to place the contents of the clipboard into the program.

HOW TO: Manage Windows

A. Enlarge the active window to fill the entire screen.

1. Click on the Maximize button (page icon; second icon from the right) on the title bar of the window.

2. To return the window to its original size, click on the Restore (double-page) button that has replaced the Maximize button.

B. Move a window.

    1. Move the mouse to the title bar of the window.
    2. Drag the window to the desired location.

C. Change the size of a window.

    1. Move the mouse to the edge of the window that is to be adjusted or to the corner joining the two edges to be adjusted.
    2. When the mouse becomes a double arrow, drag the edge or corner until the window has the desired size.

D. Close a window.

    1. Click on the X button on the far right corner of the title bar.

HOW TO: Use the Printer

A. Obtain a printout of a program.

    1. Press Alt/F/P.
    2. Press the Enter key.

Note: To print just the text selected as a block or the active (current) window, use the direction keys to select the desired option.

B. Obtain a printout of the form during run time.

    1. Place the statement PrintForm in the Form_Click( ) or other appropriate procedure of the program which will be executed at the point when the desired output will be on the form.

HOW TO: Use the Debugger

A. Stop a program at a specified line.

    1. Place the cursor on the desired line.
    2. Press F9 or Alt/D/T to highlight the line in red. (This highlighted line is called a *breakpoint*. When the program is run, it will stop at the breakpoint before executing the statement.)

Note: To remove this breakpoint, repeat Steps 1 and 2.

B. Remove all breakpoints.

    1. Press Alt/D/C or Ctrl+Shift+F9.

C. Run a program one statement at a time.

    1. Press F8. The first executable statement will be highlighted. (An event must first occur for which an event procedure has been written.)
    2. Press F8 each time you want to execute the currently highlighted statement.

Note: You will probably need to press Alt+Tab to switch back and forth between the form and the VB environment. Also, to guarantee that output is retained while stepping through the program, the AutoRedraw property of the form and any picture boxes may need to be set to True.

D. Run the program one statement at a time, but execute each general procedure call without stepping through the statements in the procedure one at a time.

1. Press Shift+F8. The first executable statement will be highlighted.
2. Press Shift+F8 each time you want to execute the currently highlighted statement.

E. Continue execution of a program that has been suspended.

1. Press F5.

Note: Each time an attempt is made to change a suspended program in a way that would prevent the program from continuing, Visual Basic displays a dialog box warning that the program will have to be restarted from the beginning and gives the option to cancel the attempted change.

F. Have further stepping begin at the line containing the cursor (no variables are cleared).

1. Press Alt/D/R or Ctrl+F8.

G. Set the next statement to be run in the current procedure.

1. Place the cursor anywhere in the desired statement.
2. Press Alt/D/N or Ctrl+F9.

H. Determine the value of an expression during run time.

1. Press Alt/D/A (Add Watch)
2. Type the expression into the Expression text box, adjust other entries in the dialog box (if necessary), and click on OK.

Note: The value of the expression will appear in the Watch window during break mode.

or

1. In Break mode, hover the cursor over the variable to have its value displayed.

Visual Basic Statements, Functions, Methods, Properties, Events, Data Types, and Operators

This appendix applies to the following objects: form, printer, text box, command button, label, and picture box. The last four are also called *controls*. Terms in brackets follow some of the discussions. These terms refer to supporting topics presented at the end of this appendix.

Abs The function Abs strips the minus signs from negative numbers while leaving other numbers unchanged. If x is any number, then the value of Abs(x) is the absolute value of x.

Action The type of a common dialog box can be determined by the setting of the Action property (1-Open, 2-Save As, 3-Color, 4-Font, 5-Print). This use is obsolete. Instead, use the methods ShowOpen, ShowSave, ShowColor, ShowFont, and ShowPrinter. For an OLE control, the setting of the Action property during run time determines the action to take.

Add A statement of the form *collectionName*.Add *objectName* adds the named object to a collection. A statement of the form *collectionName*.Add *objectName keyString* adds the named object to a collection with the key keyString.

AddItem The AddItem method adds an additional item to a list box or combo box and adds an additional row to a grid. A statement of the form List1.AddItem *str* inserts the string either at the end of the list (if Sorted = False) or in its proper alphabetical position (if Sorted = True). The statement List1.AddItem *str, n* inserts the item at the position with index *n*. The use of an index is not recommended when Sorted = True. The statement MSFlexGrid1.AddItem "", *n* inserts a new row into the grid at position *n*.

AddNew The AddNew method is used with a data control to set the stage for the addition of a new record to the end of a file. It clears any controls bound to the data control. The actual addition takes place after Value and Update statements are executed.

Alignment The Alignment property of a text box or label affects how the text assigned to the Text property is displayed. If the Alignment property is set to 0 (the default), text is displayed left-justified; if set to 1, text is right-justified; and if set to 2, text is centered.

And (Logical Operator) The logical expression *condition1* And *condition2* is true only if both *condition1* and *condition2* are true. For example, (3<7) And ("abc">"a") is true because 3<7 is true as is "abc">"a". Also, ("apple">"ape") And ("earth">"moon") is false because "earth">"moon" is false.

And (Bitwise Operator) The expression *byte1* And *byte2* is evaluated by expressing each byte as an 8-tuple binary number and then Anding together corresponding digits, where 1 And 1 equals 1, 1 And 0, 0 And 1, and 0 And 0 all equal 0. For example, the expression 37 And 157 translated to binary 8-tuples becomes 00100101 And 10011101. Anding together corresponding digits gives the binary 8-tuple 00000101 or decimal 5. Thus, 37 And 157 is 5.

Array If *arglist* is a comma-delimited list of values, then the value of the function Array(*arglist*) is a variant containing an array of these values. See Dim for discussion of arrays.

Asc Characters are stored as numbers from 0 to 255. If *str* is a string of characters, then Asc(*str*) is the number corresponding to the first character of *str*. For any n from 0 to 255, Asc(Chr(n)) is n.

Atn The trigonometric function Atn, or *arctangent*, is the inverse of the tangent function. For any number x, Atn(x) is an angle in radians between $-pi/2$ and $pi/2$ whose tangent is x. [radians]

AutoRedraw The AutoRedraw property determines what happens to graphics and Printed material on a form or picture box after another object (for example, another picture box) or program temporarily obscures part of the form or picture box. If AutoRedraw is True, then Visual Basic will restore the graphics and Printed material from a copy that it has saved in memory. If AutoRedraw is False, then Visual Basic does not keep track of graphics and Printed material that have been obscured, but it does invoke the Paint event of the form or picture box when the obstruction is removed. Thus, only graphics and Printed material generated by the Paint event will be restored when AutoRedraw is False.

AutoSize If the AutoSize property of a label or picture box is True, Visual Basic automatically sets the width and height of the label so that the entire caption can be accommodated. If the AutoSize property is False, the size of the label is not adjusted by Visual Basic, and captions are clipped if they do not fit.

BackColor The BackColor property determines the background color of an object. For a command button, the background color is valid only when the style property is set to "1-Graphical." (Such a command button can display a picture.) If the BackColor of a form or picture box is changed while a program is running, all graphics and Printed text directly on the form or picture box are erased. [color]

BackStyle The BackStyle property of a label or shape is opaque (1) by default. The rectangular, square, circular, or oval region associated with the control is filled with the control's background color and possibly caption. If the BackStyle is set to transparent (0), whatever is behind the control remains visible; the background color of the control essentially becomes "see through."

Beep The statement Beep produces a sound of frequency 800 Hz that lasts a fraction of a second.

BOF When the BOF property of a data control is True, the current record position in the file is before the first record.

Boolean A variable of type Boolean requires 2 bytes of memory and holds either the value True or False. If boolVar is a Boolean variable, then the statement Print boolVar displays True when the value is True and displays False when the value is False.

BorderColor The BorderColor property determines the color of a line or shape control. [color]

BorderStyle The BorderStyle property determines the border style for a form [0-none, 1-fixed single, 2-sizeable (default), 3-fixed double, 4-Fixed ToolWindow, 5-Sizable ToolWindow], line or shape [0-transparent, 1-solid, 2-dash, 3-dot, 4-dash-dot, 5-dash-dot-dot, 6-inside solid], grid image, label, picture box, and text box [0-none, 1-fixed single (default)]. You cannot change the borders of forms and text boxes during run time.

BorderWidth The BorderWidth property (with settings from 1 through 8192) determines the thickness of a line or shape control.

Byte A variable of type Byte uses a single byte of memory and holds a value from 0 to 255.

Call A statement of the form Call *ProcedureName*(*argList*) is used to execute the named Sub procedure, passing to it the variables and values in the list of arguments. Arrays appearing in the list of arguments should be specified by the array name followed by empty parentheses. The value of a variable argument may be altered by the Sub procedure unless the variable is surrounded by parentheses. After the statements in the Sub procedure have been executed, program execution continues with the statement following Call. **Note:** The keyword Call may be omitted. In this case, the parentheses are omitted and the statement is written *ProcedureName argList*.

Cancel The Cancel property provides a means of responding when the user presses the Esc key. At most one command button on a form may have its Cancel property set to True. If the Esc key is pressed while the program is running, Visual Basic will execute the click event procedure of the command button whose Cancel property is True.

Caption The Caption property holds the text that is to appear as the caption for a form, command button, data control, or label. If an ampersand (&) is placed in the caption of a command button or label, the ampersand will not be displayed, but the character following the ampersand will become an underlined access key. Access keys provide a quick way to access a command button or the control (usually a text box) following (in tab index order) a label. Access keys are activated by holding down the Alt key and pressing the access key character.

CBool The function CBool converts byte, currency, double-integer, integer, long integer, and single-precision numbers to the Boolean values True or False. Nonzero values are converted to True and zero is converted to False. If x is any number, then the value of CBool(x) is the Boolean value determined by x.

CByte The function CByte converts integer, long integer, single-precision, double-precision, and currency numbers to byte numbers. If x is any number, then the value of CByte(x) is the byte number determined by x.

CCur The function CCur converts byte integer, long integer, single-precision, and double-precision numbers to currency numbers. If x is any number, then the value of CCur(x) is the currency number determined by x.

CDate The function CDate converts byte, currency, double-integer, integer, long integer, and single-precision numbers to dates. If x is any number, then the value of CDate(x) is the date determined by x.

CDbl The function CDbl converts byte, integer, long integer, single-precision, and currency numbers to double-precision numbers. If x is any number, then the value of CDbl(x) is the double-precision number determined by x.

Change The Change event occurs when the contents of a combo box, folder list box, drive list box, label, picture box, scroll bar, or text box are altered in a specific way. The alterations are: (a) change of text (combo box or text box), (b) user selects a new directory or drive (directory and drive list boxes), (c) scroll box moves, (d) change of Caption property (label), and (e) change of Picture property (picture box).

ChDir The statement ChDir *path* changes the current folder on the specified disk drive to the subfolder specified by *path*. For example, ChDir "C:\" specifies the root folder of the C drive as the current folder. Omitting a drive letter in *path* causes the default drive to be used.

ChDrive The statement ChDrive *drive* changes the default drive to the drive specified by *drive*. For example, ChDrive "A" specifies the A drive as the new default drive.

Chr If n is a number from 0 to 255, then a statement of the form *objectName*.Print Chr(n) displays the nth character of the current font.

CInt The function CInt converts byte, long integer, single-precision, double-precision, and currency numbers to integer numbers. If x is any number from -32768 to 32767, the value of CInt(x) is the (possibly rounded) integer constant that x determines.

Circle The graphics method *objectName*.Circle (x, y), r, c, $r1$, $r2$, a draws on *objectName* a portion, or all, of an ellipse. The center of the ellipse is the point (x, y) and the longer radius is r. The color of the ellipse is determined by c. If $r1$ and $r2$ are present, then the computer draws only the portion of the ellipse that extends from the radius line at an angle of Abs($r1$) radians with the horizontal radius line to the radius line at an angle of Abs($r2$) radians with the horizontal radius line in a counterclockwise direction. If either $r1$ or $r2$ is negative, the computer also draws its radius line. The ratio of the length of the vertical diameter to the length of the horizontal diameter will be a. After the Circle method is executed, the value of *objectName*.CurrentX becomes x and the value of *objectName*.CurrentY becomes y. [color] [coordinate systems] [radians]

Clear The method ClipBoard.Clear clears the clipboard, setting its contents to the null string. The statements List1.Clear and Combo1.Clear remove all items from the control's list.

Click The Click event applies to check boxes, combo boxes, command buttons, directory list boxes, file list boxes, forms, frames, grids, images, labels, list boxes, menu items, OLE controls, option buttons, picture boxes, and text boxes. A Click event occurs whenever the left mouse button is pressed and released while the mouse cursor is over the control or over a blank area on the form. In the case of a command button, the Click event is also called if the spacebar or Enter key is pressed while the command button has the focus, or if the button's access key is used.

CLng The function CLng converts byte, integer, single-precision, double-precision, and currency numbers to long integer numbers. If x is any number from

–2,147,483,648 to 2,147,483,647, the value of CLng(*x*) is the (possibly rounded) long integer constant that *x* determines.

Close The statement Close #*n* closes the file that has been opened with reference number *n*. By itself, Close closes all open files. The Close method for a data control closes the database.

Cls The method *formName*.Cls clears the form *formName* of all text and graphics that have been placed directly on the form with methods like *formName*.Print, *formName*.Circle, and so on. The method *pictureBox*.Cls clears the named picture box. The Cls method resets the CurrentX and CurrentY properties of the cleared object to the coordinates of the upper-left corner [usually (0, 0)].

Col and **Row** The Col and Row properties specify the current cell of a grid. The statements MSFlexGrid1.Col = *m* and MSFlexGrid1.Row = *n* specify the cell in column *m* and row *n* to be the current cell. The statement MSFlexGrid1.Text = *str* places the string into the current cell. When the user clicks on a nonfixed cell, its column number is assigned to the Col property and its row number is assigned to the Row property.

ColAlignment The statement MSFlexGrid1.ColAlignment(*m*) = *n*, aligns the text in column *m* both vertically and horizontally according to the following table.

n	Horizontally	Vertically
0	Left	Top
1	Left	Centered
2	Left	Bottom
3	Centered	Top
4	Centered	Centered
5	Centered	Bottom
6	Right	Top
7	Right	Centered
8	Right	Bottom
9	Strings left-justified, Numbers right-justified	

Color The value of the Color property of a Color common dialog box identifies the selected color.

Cols and **Rows** The Cols and Rows properties of a grid specify the numbers of rows and columns.

ColWidth The statement MSFlexGrid1.Colwidth(*m*) = *n* specifies that column *m* of the grid be *n* twips wide. (There are about 1440 twips in an inch.)

Const The statement Const *constantName* As *DataType* = *expression* causes Visual Basic to treat every occurrence of *constantName* as the value of the expression. This replacement takes place before any lines of the program are executed. A *constantName* may appear in only one Const statement and may not appear on the left side of an assignment statement. We call *constantName* a "symbolic constant" or "named constant."

Control The Control data type may be used in the parameter lists of Sub and Function definitions to allow the passing of control names to the procedure.

ControlBox The ControlBox property determines whether or not a form has a Control-menu button displayed in the upper left corner. If the ControlBox property is set to True (the default), the Control-menu button is displayed. Among the operations available from the Control-menu button is the ability to close the form and thereby end the program. If the ControlBox property of a form is set to False, the Control-menu button is not displayed. Because, in this case, the user cannot end the program by using the Control-menu button or by pressing Alt+F4, it is important to provide a command button for this purpose.

Connect The Connect property of a data control identifies the format (such as Access, FoxPro, Dbase) of the database determined by the DatabaseName property.

Cos The value of the trigonometric function $\text{Cos}(x)$ is the cosine of an angle of x radians. [radians]

Count The value of *collectionName*.Count is the number of objects in the collection.

CreateObject If *appName* is the name of an application and *objectType* is the type or class of the object to create, then the value of the function CreateObject(*appName. objectType*) is an OLE Automation object. For instance, CreateObject("Excel.sheet") creates an Excel worksheet and CreateObject("Word. Basic") creates a Word document.

CSng The function CSng converts byte, integer, long integer, and double-precision numbers to single-precision numbers. If x is any number, the value of $\text{CSng}(x)$ is the single-precision number that x determines.

CStr The function CStr converts byte, integer, long integer, single-precision, double-precision, currency, and variant numbers to strings. If x is any number, the value of $\text{CStr}(x)$ is the string determined by x. Unlike the Str function, CStr does not place a space in front of positive numbers. [variant]

CurDir The value of the function CurDir(*drive*) is a string specifying the current folder on the drive specified by *drive*. The value of CurDir("") or CurDir is a string specifying the current folder on the default drive.

Currency The currency data type is extremely useful for calculations involving money. A variable of type Currency requires 8 bytes of memory and can hold any number from –922,337,203,685,477.5808 to 922,337,203,685,477.5807 with at most four decimal places. Currency values and variables may be indicated by the type tag @: 21436587.01@, Balance@.

CurrentX, CurrentY The properties CurrentX and CurrentY give the horizontal and vertical coordinates of the point on a form, picture box, or the printer at which the next Print or graphics method will begin. Initially, CurrentX and CurrentY are the coordinates of the upper-left corner of the object. [coordinate systems]

CVar The function CVar converts strings and byte, integer, long integer, single-precision, double-precision, and currency numbers to variants. If x is any string or number, the value of $\text{CVar}(x)$ is the variant determined by x. [variant]

CVDate The function CVDate converts a numeric or string expression to an equivalent serial date. If x is any expression representing a valid date, the value of $\text{CVDate}(x)$ is the serial date determined by x. Valid numeric values are –

657434 (January 1, 100 AD.) to 2958465 (December 31, 9999). Valid string expressions either look like one of these valid numeric values (for example, "19497" corresponding to May 18, 1953) or look like a date (for example, "10 Feb 1955", "August 13, 1958", etc.) [date]

DatabaseName The value of the DatabaseName property of a data control is the filespec of the file containing the database.

DataField After the DataSource property of a data-aware control has been set to bind the control to a data control, the DataField property is set to a field of the table accessed by the data control.

DataSource To bind a data-aware control to a data control at design time, set the value of the DataSource property of the data-aware control to the name of the data control.

Date (Function) The value of the function Date is the current date. If *dateStr* is a string representing a date, the statement Date = *dateStr* changes the date as specified by *dateStr*.

Date (Data Type) A variable of type Date uses 8 bytes of memory and holds numbers representing dates from Jan. 1, 100 to Dec. 31, 9999. Literal date values can be assigned to date variables with statements such as *dateVar* = #5/12/1999#, *dateVar* = #5 Jan, 1997#, and *dateVar* = #February 10, 2004#. However, values of *dateVar* are displayed in the form month/day/year (for example, 5/12/99).

DateSerial The value of the function DateSerial(*year*, *month*, *day*) is the serial date corresponding to the given year, month, and day. Values from 0 to 9999 are acceptable for *year*, with 0 to 99 interpreted as 1900 to 1999. Values of 1 to 12 for *month*, and 1 to 31 for *day* are normal, but any integer value is acceptable. Often, numeric expressions are used for *month* or *day* that evaluate to numbers outside these ranges. For example, DateSerial(2003, 2, 10 + 90) is the date 90 days after Feb. 10, 2003. [date]

DateValue The value of the function DateValue(*str*) is the serial date corresponding to the date given in *str*. DateValue recognizes the following date formats: "2-10-1955", "2/10/1955", "February 10, 1955", "Feb 10, 1955", "10-Feb-1955", and "10 February 1955". For the years 1900 through 1999, the initial "19" is optional. [date]

Day The function Day extracts the day of the month from a serial date. If *d* is any valid serial date, the value of Day(*d*) is an integer from 1 to 31 giving the day of the month recorded as part of the date and time stored in *d*. [date]

DblClick The DblClick event applies to combo boxes, file list boxes, forms, frames, grids, images, labels, list boxes, OLE controls, option buttons, picture boxes, and text boxes. A DblClick event occurs whenever the left mouse button is pressed and released twice, in quick succession, while the mouse cursor is over the control or over a blank area on the form. Double-clicking on an object will first cause that object's Click event to occur, followed by its DblClick event. *Note:* When you double-click on an item in a drive list box, the item is automatically assigned to the Path property. When you double-click on an item in a file list box, the item is automatically assigned to the FileName property.

Default When the Default property of a command button is set to True and the focus is on an object that is not another command button, pressing the enter key has the same effect as clicking on the button. At most, one command button on a form can have True as the value of its Default property.

DefInt, DefLng, DefSng, DefDbl, DefStr, DefCur, DefVar, DefByte, DefBool, DefDate, DefObj   A variable can be assigned a type by either a type-declaration tag or an As clause. A statement of the form DefInt *letter* specifies that any "untyped" variable whose name begins with the specified letter will have integer type. A statement of the form DefInt *letter1*-*letter2* specifies that all "untyped" variables whose names begin with a letter in the range *letter1* through *letter2* will have integer type. The statements DefLng, DefSng, DefDbl, DefStr, DefCur, DefVar, DefByte, DefBool, DefDate, and DefObj specify the corresponding types for long integer, single-precision, double-precision, string, currency, variant, byte, boolean, date, and object variables, respectively. Def*Type* statements are placed in the (Declarations) section of (General). [variant]

Delete   The Delete method for a data control deletes the current record.

Dim   The statement Dim *arrayName*(*m* To *n*) As *variableType* declares an array with subscripts ranging from *m* to *n*, inclusive, where *m* and *n* are in the normal integer range of –32768 to 32767. The *variableType* must be Integer, Long, Single, Double, Currency, String, String*n*, Variant, Boolean, Byte, Date, or a user-defined type. A statement of the form Dim *arrayName*(*m* To *n*, *p* To *q*) As *variableType* declares a doubly subscripted, or two-dimensional, array. Three- and higher-dimensional arrays are declared similarly. If *m* and *p* are zero, the preceding Dim statements may be changed to Dim *arrayName*(*n*) As *variableType* and Dim *arrayName*(*n*, *q*) As *variableType*. The statement Dim *arrayName*( ) As *variableType* defines an array whose size is initially unknown but must be established by a ReDim statement before the array can be accessed. The statement Dim *variableName* As *variableType* specifies the type of data that will be stored in *variableName*. Variables and arrays Dimmed in the (Declarations) section of (General) are available to all procedures. In procedures, Dim is used to declare variables, but ReDim is often used to dimension arrays. [dynamic vs. static] [variant]

Dir   If *fileTemplate* specifies a file (or a collection of files by including ? or *), then the value of the function Dir(*fileTemplate*) is the filename of the first file matching the pattern specified by *fileTemplate*. If this value is not the null string, the value of the function Dir is the name of the next file that matches the previously specified pattern. For example, the value of Dir("*.VBP") will be the name of the first file in the current folder of the default drive whose name has the .VBP extension. [filespec]

Do/Loop   A statement of the form Do, Do While *cond*, or Do Until *cond* is used to mark the beginning of a block of statements that will be repeated. A statement of the form Loop, Loop While *cond*, or Loop Until *cond* is used to mark the end of the block. Each time a statement containing While or Until followed by a condition is encountered, the truth value of the condition determines whether the block should be repeated or whether the program should jump to the statement immediately following the block. A Do loop may also be exited at any point with an Exit Do statement.

DoEvents   Executing the statement DoEvents permits Visual Basic to act on any events may have occurred while the current event procedure has been executing.

Double   A variable of type Double requires 8 bytes of memory and can hold 0, the numbers from 4.94065×10^{-324} to $1.797693134862316 \times 10^{308}$ with at most 17 significant digits, and the negatives of these numbers. Double values and variables may be indicated by the type tag #: 2.718281828459045#, Pi#.

DrawMode   The property DrawMode determines whether graphics are drawn in black, white, foreground color, or some interaction of these colors with the current contents of the form or picture box. The following table lists the allowed values for the DrawMode property and the rules for what RGB color number will be assigned at a given point when the RGB color number for the color currently displayed at that point is *display* and the RGB color number for the draw color is *draw*. [color]

DrawMode	Color Produced	
1	&H00000000& (Black)	
2	Not draw And Not display	(inverse of #15)
3	display And Not draw	(inverse of #14)
4	Not draw	(inverse of #13)
5	draw And Not display	(inverse of #12)
6	Not display	(inverse of #11)
7	draw Xor display	
8	Not draw Or Not display	(inverse of #9)
9	draw And display	
10	Not (draw Xor display)	(inverse of #7)
11	display	(transparent)
12	display Or Not draw	
13	draw (draw color)	
14	draw Or Not display	
15	draw Or display	
16	&H00FFFFFF& (White)	

DrawStyle   When DrawWidth is 1 for a form or picture box (the default), the property DrawStyle determines whether graphics are drawn using a solid line or some combinations of dots and dashes. Use a DrawStyle of 0 (the default) for solid lines, 1 for dashed lines, 2 for dotted lines, 3 for dash-dot lines, or 4 for dash-dot-dot lines. A DrawStyle of 5 produces "invisible" graphics.

When thick lines are drawn as a result of setting DrawWidth to values greater than 1, graphics are always drawn using solid lines. In this case, DrawStyle can be used either to center the thick line over where a line with a DrawWidth of 1 would be drawn or, when drawing closed figures like ellipses and rectangles, to place the thick line just inside where the line with a DrawWidth of 1 would be drawn. To draw thick graphics inside the normal closed figure, use a DrawStyle of 6. DrawStyles 1 through 4 will center thick graphics over the normal location.

DrawWidth   The property DrawWidth determines the width in pixels of the lines that are drawn by graphics methods. The default is 1 pixel. Values from 1 to 32,767 are permitted.

Drive   The Drive property of a drive list box gives the contents of the currently selected item.

Enabled   The property Enabled determines whether or not a form or control responds to events. If the Enabled property of a form or control is set to True (the default), and if an event occurs for which an event procedure has been written, the event procedure will be executed. When the Enabled property of a form or control is set to False, all events relating to that control are ignored; no event procedures are executed.

End The statement End terminates the execution of the program and closes all files. Also, the statements End Def, End Function, End If, End Select, End Sub, and End Type are used to denote the conclusion of multiline function definitions, function blocks, If blocks, Select Case blocks, Sub procedures, and user-defined, record-type declarations.

EndDoc The method Printer.EndDoc is used to indicate that the document currently being printed is complete and should be released to the printer.

Environ Visual Basic has an environment table consisting of equations of the form "*name=value*" that is inherited from DOS when Windows is invoked. If *name* is the left side of an equation in Visual Basic's environment table, then the value of the function Environ("*name*") will be the string consisting of the right side of the equation. The value of Environ(*n*) is the *n*th equation in Visual Basic's environment table.

EOF Suppose a file has been opened for sequential input with reference number *n*. The value of the function EOF(*n*) will be True (–1) if the end of the file has been reached and False (0) otherwise. [**Note:** The logical condition Not EOF(*n*) is true until the end of the file is reached.] When used with a communications file, EOF(*n*) will be true if the communications buffer is empty and false if the buffer contains data.

Err After an error occurs during the execution of a program, the value of Err.Number will be a number identifying the type of error. Err.Number is used in conjunction with the On Error statement. If *n* is a whole number from 0 to 32,767, then the statement Err.Raise *n* generates the run-time error associated with the number *n*.

Eqv The logical expression *condition1* Eqv *condition2* is true if *condition1* and *condition2* are both true or both false. For example, (1>2) Eqv ("xyz"<"a") is true because both 1>2 and "xyz"<"a" are false, whereas ("apple">"ape") Eqv ("earth"> "moon") is false because "apple">"ape" is true but "earth">"moon" is false.

Erase For static arrays, the statement Erase *arrayName* resets each array element to its default value. For dynamic arrays, the statement Erase *arrayName* deletes the array from memory. **Note:** After a dynamic array has been Erased, it may be ReDimensioned. However, the number of dimensions must be the same as before. [dynamic vs. static]

Error (Statement) The statement Error *n* simulates the occurrence of the run-time error identified by the number *n*, where *n* may range from 1 to 32,767. It is a useful debugging tool.

Error (Function) The value of the function Error is the error message corresponding to the run-time error that has most recently occurred. The value of the function Error(*errNum*) is the error message corresponding to the run-time error designated by *errNum*.

Event A statement of the form Public Event *UserDefinedEvent*(arg1, arg2, . . .), appearing in the general declarations section of a class module, declares a user-defined event and passes the arguments to the event procedure. After this declaration is made, the RaiseEvent statement can be used to fire the event.

Exit The Exit statement may be used in any of five forms: Exit For, Exit Sub, Exit Function, Exit Property, Exit Def, and Exit Do. The Exit statement causes program execution to jump out of the specified structure prematurely: Exit For jumps out of a For/Next loop to the statement following Next, Exit Sub jumps out of a Sub procedure to the statement following the Call statement, and so on.

Exp The value of the function Exp(x) is e^x, where e (about 2.71828) is the base of the natural logarithm function.

False A keyword of Boolean type. False is used when setting the value of properties that are either True or False. For example, Picture1.Font.Italic = False.

Fields The Fields property of a recordset is used to read or set the Value property of the Recordset. For instance, a statement of the form Print Data1.RecordSet.Fields(*fieldName*).Value displays the value in the specified field of the current record of the database table associated with the data control. The preceding Print statement can be abbreviated to Print Data1.RecordSet(*fieldName*).

FileAttr After a file has been opened with reference number n, the value of the function FileAttr (n, 1) is 1, 2, 4, 8, or 32 depending on whether the file was opened for Input, Output, Append, Random, or Binary, respectively. The value of the function FileAttr (n, 2) is the file's DOS file handle, a number that uniquely identifies the file and is used in assembly language programming.

FileCopy The statement FileCopy *source*, *destination* creates the file specified by *destination* by making a copy of the file specified by *source*. Both *source* and *destination* may specify drive and path information. If the file specified by *destination* already exists, it will be overwritten without a warning being issued.

FileDateTime The value of the function FileDateTime(*filename*) is a string giving the date and time that the file specified by the *filename* was created or last modified.

FileLen The value of the function FileLen(*filename*) is the length in characters (bytes) of the file specified by *filename*.

FileName The FileName property of a file list box is the contents of the currently selected item.

FillColor When the FillStyle property of a form or picture box is set to a value other than the default of 1, the property FillColor determines what color is used to paint the interior of ellipses and rectangles drawn with the Circle and Line graphics methods. The FillColor property may be assigned any valid RGB color number. The default value for FillColor is black (0). [color]

FillStyle The property FillStyle determines what pattern is used to paint the interior of ellipses and rectangles drawn on forms or picture boxes with the Circle and Line methods. The default value for FillStyle is transparent (1), which means that interiors are not painted. Other values available for FillStyle are solid (0), horizontal lines (2), vertical lines (3), diagonals running upward to the right (4), diagonals running downward to the right (5), vertical and horizontal lines [crosshatched] (6), and diagonal crosshatched (7). **Note:** Using BF in a Line method has the same effect as setting the FillStyle to 0 and the FillColor to the color of the bordering line.

FindFirst, FindLast, FindNext, FindPrevious A statement of the form Data1.RecordSet.Find*What criteria* selects a new current record in the table of the database associated with the data control in the expected way, based on the specifications of the string *criteria*.

Fix The value of the function Fix(*x*) is the whole number obtained by discarding the decimal part of the number *x*.

FixedAlignment The statement MSFlexGrid1.FixedAlignment(*m*) = *n*, where *n* = 0 (left-align (default)), 1 (right-align), or 2 (centered), aligns the text in the fixed cells of the *m*th column of the grid.

FixedCols and **FixedRows** The FixedCols and FixedRows properties of a grid specify the number of fixed rows and fixed columns of a grid. Fixed rows and columns are used for headings and never disappear due to scrolling.

Flags The Flags property of a common dialog box sets a variety of options.

Font.Bold or **FontBold** These properties determine whether the characters Printed on a form, picture box, or printer, or assigned to a text box, command button, or label appear in bold or normal type. If the property is set to True (the default), then for a form, picture box, or printer, subsequent Printed characters appear bold. For a text box, command button, or label, the text or caption is immediately changed to bold. If the property is set to False, subsequent characters are Printed in normal type and characters assigned to the text or caption property change immediately to normal type.

FontCount The value of the property Screen.FontCount is the number of fonts available for use on the screen. Similarly, the value of the property Printer. FontCount is the number of fonts available on the printer. The FontCount property is set according to your Windows environment and is generally used to determine the limit on the index for the Fonts property.

Font.Italic or **FontItalic** These properties determine whether or not the characters Printed on a form, picture box, or printer, or assigned to a text box, command button, or label appear in italic or upright type. If the property is set to True, then for a form, picture box, or printer, subsequent characters appear in italic. For a text box, command button, or label, the text or caption is immediately changed to italic. If the property is set to False (the default), subsequent characters are Printed in upright type and characters assigned to the text or caption property change immediately to upright type.

Font.Name or **FontName** These properties determine what type face is used when characters are Printed on a form, picture box, or printer, or assigned to a text box, command button, or label. If the property of a form, picture box, or printer is set to a font obtained from the Fonts property, all subsequently Printed characters will appear in the new type face. When the property of a text box, command button, or label is set to a new font, characters assigned to the text or caption property change immediately to the new type face.

Fonts The value of the property Screen.Fonts(*fontNum*) is the name of a screen font available in the current Windows environment. The index *fontNum* can range from 0 to Screen.FontCount–1. Similarly, the value of the property Printer.Fonts(*fontNum*) is the name of an available printer font. The values in the Fonts property are set by your Windows environment and are generally used to determine which fonts are available for setting the FontName property.

Font.Size or **FontSize** These properties determine the size, in points, of characters Printed on forms, picture boxes, and the printer or displayed in text boxes and on command buttons and labels. Available font sizes depend on your Windows environment, but will always be between 1 and 2048. Default font sizes are usually between 8 and 12 point. *Note:* One point equals 1/72nd of an inch.

Font.StrikeThrough or **FontStrikeThru** These properties determine whether or not the characters Printed on a form, picture box, or printer, or assigned to a text box, command button, or label appear in a strikethru or standard font. If the property is set to True, then for a form, picture box, or printer, subsequent Printed characters appear with a horizontal line through the middle of each character. For a text box, command button, or label, the text or caption is immediately changed so that a horizontal line goes through the middle of each character. If the property is set to False (the default), subsequent characters are Printed in standard type, and characters assigned to text or caption property change immediately to standard type.

FontTransparent The property FontTransparent determines the degree to which characters Printed to forms and picture boxes obscure existing text and graphics. If the FontTransparent property is set to True (the default), the existing text and graphics are obscured only by the dots (pixels) needed to actually form the new character. If the FontTransparent property is set to False, then all text and graphics are obscured within the character box (small rectangle surrounding a character) associated with the new character. Those dots (pixels) not needed to form the character are changed to the background color.

Font.Underline or **FontUnderline** These properties determine whether or not the characters printed on a form, picture box, or printer, or assigned to a text box, command button, or label appear with an underline. If the property is set to True, then for a form, picture box, or printer, subsequent characters Printed appear underlined. For a text box, command button, or label, the text or caption is immediately changed to underlined. If the property is set to False (the default), subsequent characters are Printed without underlines, and characters assigned to the text or caption property change immediately to nonunderlined.

For Each/Next A multistatement block beginning with For Each *var* In *arrayName* and ending with Next *var*, where *arrayName* is an array of type variant and *var* is a variant variable, executes the statements inside the block for each element of the array.

For/Next The statement For *index* = *a* To *b* Step *s* sets the value of the variable *index* to *a* and repeatedly executes the statements between itself and the statement Next *index*. Each time the Next statement is reached, *s* is added to the value of *index*. This process continues until the value of *index* passes *b*. Although the numbers *a*, *b*, and *s* may have any numeric type, the lower the precision of the type, the faster the loop executes. The statement For *index* = *a* To *b* is equivalent to the statement For *index* = *a* To *b* Step 1. The index following the word Next is optional.

ForeColor The property ForeColor determines the color used to display text, captions, graphics, and Printed characters. If the ForeColor property of a form or picture box is changed, subsequent characters will appear in the new color. For a text box, command button, or label, text or caption is immediately changed to the new color. [color]

Format The value of the function Format(*expression*, *str*) is a string representing *expression* (a number, date, time, or string) formatted according to the rules given by *str*. Format is useful when assigning values to the Text property and when Printing to a form, picture box, or the printer.

Numeric output can be formatted with commas, leading and trailing zeros, preceding or trailing signs (+ or –), and exponential notation. This is accomplished either by using for *str* the name of one of several predefined numeric formats or by combining in *str* one or more of the following special numeric formatting characters: #, 0, decimal point (period), comma, %, E–, and E+. The expression to be formatted can evaluate to one of the numeric types or a string representing a number.

Predefined numeric formats include "General Number," which displays a number as is; "Currency," which displays a number with a leading dollar sign and with commas every three digits to the left of the decimal, displays two decimal places, and encloses negative numbers in parentheses; "Fixed," which displays two digits to the right and at least one digit to the left of the decimal point; "Standard," which displays a number with commas and two decimal places but does not use parentheses for negative numbers; "Percent," which multiplies the value by 100 and displays a percent sign after two decimal places; and "Scientific," which displays numbers in standard scientific notation. For example, Format(–5432.352, "Currency") gives the string "($5,432.35)".

The symbol # designates a place for a digit. If the number being formatted does not need all the places provided by the #'s given in *str*, the extra #'s are ignored. The symbol 0, like #, designates a place for a digit. However, if the number being formatted does not need all the places provided by the 0's given in *str*, the character 0 is displayed in the extra places. If the number being converted has more whole-part digits than there is space reserved by #'s and 0's, additional space is used as if the format string had more #'s at its beginning. For example, Format(56, "####") yields "56", Format(56, "#") yields "56", Format(0, "#") yields "", Format(56, "0000") yields "0056", Format(56, "0") yields "56", and Format(0, "0") yields "0".

The decimal point symbol (.) marks the location of the decimal place. It separates the format rules into two sections, one applying to the whole part of the number and the other to the decimal part. When included in the format string, a decimal point will always appear in the resulting string. For example, Format(56.246, "#.##") yields "56.25", Format(.246, "#.##") yields ".25", Format(.246, "0.##") yields "0.25", and Format(56.2, "0.00") yields "52.20".

The comma symbol (,) placed to the left of the decimal point between #'s and/or 0's causes commas to be displayed to the left of every third digit to the left of the decimal point, as appropriate. If commas are placed to the immediate left of the decimal point (or to the right of all #'s and 0's when the decimal-point symbol is not used), then before the number is formatted, it is divided by 1000 for each comma, but commas will not appear in the result. In order to divide by 1000's and display commas in the result, use format strings like "#,#,.00", which displays the number with commas in units of thousands, and "#,#,,.00", which displays the number with commas in units of millions. For example, Format(1234000, "#,#") yields "1,234,000", Format(1234000, "#,") yields "1234", Format(1234000, "#,.") yields "1234.", Format(1234000, "#,,.0") yields "1.2", and Format(1234000, "#,0,.0") yields "1,234.0".

The percent symbol (%) placed to the right of all #'s, 0's, and any decimal point causes the number to be converted to a percentage (multiplied by 100) before formatting and the symbol % to be displayed. For example, Format(.05624, "#.##%") yields "5.62%", and Format(1.23, "#%") yields "123%".

The symbols E+ and E− placed to the right of all #'s, 0's, and any decimal point cause the number to be displayed in scientific notation. Places for the digits in the exponent must be reserved to the right of E+ or E− with #'s or 0's. When E+ is used and the exponent is positive, a plus sign appears in front of the exponent in the result. When E− is used and the exponent is positive, no sign or space precedes the exponent. When scientific notation is used, each position reserved by #'s to the left of the decimal point is used whenever possible. For example, Format(1234.56, "#.##E+##") yields "1.23E+3", Format(1234.56, "##.##E−##") yields "12.34E2", Format(1234, "###.00E+##") yields "123.40E+1", and Format(123, "###E+00") yields "123E+00".

Date and time output can be formatted using numbers or names for months, putting the day, month, and year in any order desired, using 12-hour or 24-hour notation, and so on. This is accomplished either by letting *str* be the name of one of several predefined date/time formats or by combining in *str* one or more special date/time formatting characters. The expression to be formatted can evaluate to a number that falls within the range of valid serial dates or to a string representing a date/time.

Predefined date/time formats include "General Date," which displays a date in mm/dd/yyyy format and, if appropriate, a time in hh:mm:ss PM format; "Long Date," which displays the day of week, the full name of month, the day, and a four-digit year; "Medium Date," which displays the day, abbreviated month name, and two-digit year; "Short Date," which displays "mm/dd/yy"; "Long Time," which displays the time in hh:mm:ss PM format; "Medium Time," which displays time in hh:mm PM format; and "Short Time," which display time in 24-hour format as hh:mm. For example, let dt = DateSerial(55,2,10) + TimeSerial(21,45,30). Then Format(dt, "General Date") yields "2/10/55 9:45:30 PM", Format(dt, "Medium Date") yields "10-Feb-55", and Format(dt, "Short Time") yields "21:45".

Format symbols for the day, month, and year include d (day as number but no leading zero), dd (day as number with leading zero), ddd (day as three-letter name), dddd (day as full name), m (month as number but no leading zero), mm (month as number with leading zero), mmm (month as three-letter name), mmmm (month as full name), yy (year as two-digit number), and yyyy (year as four-digit number). Separators such as slash, dash, and period may be used as desired to connect day, month, and year symbols into a final format. For example, Format("August 13, 1958", "dddd, d.mmm.yy") yields "Wednesday, 13.Aug.58" and Format("July 4, 1776", "ddd: mmmm dd, yyyy") yields "Thu: July 04, 1776". Additional format symbols for dates include w (day-of-week as number 1–7), ww (week-of-year as number 1–53), q (quarter-of-year as number 1–4), y (day-of-year as number 1–366), ddddd (same as short date), and dddddd (same as long date).

Format symbols for the second, minute, and hour include s (seconds with no leading zero), ss (seconds as two-digit number), n (minutes with no leading zero), nn (minutes as two-digit number), h (hours with no leading zero), hh (hours as two-digit number), AM/PM (use 12-hour clock and uppercase), am/pm (use 12-hour clock and lowercase), A/P (use 12-hour clock and single uppercase letter), a/p (use 12-hour clock and single lowercase letter), and ttttt (same as general date). Separators such as colons and periods may be used as desired to connect hour, minute, and second symbols into a final format. For example, Format("14:04:01", "h:nn AM/PM") yields "2:04 PM", Format("14:04:01", "h.n.s") yields "14.4.1", and Format(0.75, "h:nna/p") yields "6:00p".

String output can be formatted as all uppercase, all lowercase, left-justified or right-justified. Symbols used to format strings are @ (define a field for at least as many characters as there are @ symbols; if fewer characters than @ symbols, fill remainder of field with spaces; if more characters than @ symbols, display the extra characters—don't clip), & (reserve space for entire output string), < (convert all characters to lowercase before displaying), > (convert all characters to uppercase before displaying), ! (left justify within field defined by @ symbols; default is to right justify). For example, Format("Red", "@") yields "Red", Format("Red", "@@@@@@") yields "   Red" (3 leading spaces), Format("Red", "!>@@@@@@") yields "RED   " (3 trailing spaces), and Format("Red", "<&") yields "red".

FormatCurrency The value of the function FormatCurrency(*exp*) is the string representation of the expression as dollars and cents. Fractional values are preceded by a leading zero, and negative values are surrounded by parentheses instead of beginning with a minus sign. FormatCurrency(*exp*, *r*) displays a value rounded to *r* decimal places. The function has additional optional parameters. FormatCurrency(*exp*, , vbFalse) suppresses leading zeros for fractional values. FormatCurrency(*exp*, , , vbFalse) uses minus signs for negative numbers.

FormatNumber The value of the function FormatNumber(*exp*, *r*) is the string representation of the expression as a number with *r* decimal places. Fractional values are preceded by a leading zero. FormatNumber(*exp*) displays a value rounded to 2 decimal places. The function has additional optional parameters. FormatNumber(*exp*, , vbFalse) suppresses leading zeros for fractional values. FormatNumber(*exp*, , , vbTrue) surrounds a negative value with parentheses instead of a leading minus sign. FormatNumber(exp, , , , vbFalse) suppresses commas.

FormatPercent The value of the function FormatPercent(*exp*, *r*) is the string representation of the expression as a percentage (multiplied by 100) with *r* decimal places. Fractional values are preceded by a leading zero. FormatPercent(*exp*) displays the percentage rounded to 2 decimal places. The function has additional optional parameters. FormatPercent(*exp*, , vbFalse) suppresses leading zeros for fractional values. FormatPercent(*exp*, , , vbTrue) surrounds a negative value with parentheses instead of a leading minus sign.

FreeFile When files are opened, they are assigned a reference number from 1 to 255. At any time, the value of the function FreeFile is the next available reference number.

FromPage and **ToPage** The FromPage and ToPage properties of a Print common dialog box identify the values selected for the From and To text boxes.

Function A function is a multistatement block usually beginning with a statement such as Private Function *FunctionName*(*parList*) As *returnType*, followed on subsequent lines by one or more statements for carrying out the task of the function, and ending with the statement End Function. The parameter list, *parList*, is a list of variables through which values will be passed to the function when the function is called. Parameter types may be numeric, (variable-length) string, variant, object, user-defined record type, or array. The types of the parameters may be specified with type-declaration tags, Def*Type* statements, or As clauses. Array names appearing in the parameter list should be followed by an empty pair of parentheses. Functions are named with the same conventions as variables. The value of a variable argument used in calling a function may be altered by the function unless the variable is surrounded by parentheses. The value returned can be of any type (declared in *returnType*). Variables appearing in a function are local to the function unless they have been declared in the (Declarations) section of (General) and are not redeclared in Dim or Static statements within the function. A statement of the form Function *Function-Name(parList)* Static specifies that all variables local to the function be treated as static by default; that is, they are invisible outside of the function but retain their values between function calls. Functions may invoke themselves (called *recursion*) or other procedures. However, no procedure may be defined inside a function.

Get User-defined record types provide an efficient means of working with random-access files. After a user-defined record type is defined and a variable of that type, call it *recVar*, is declared, the file is opened with a length equal to Len (*recVar*). The *r*th record of the random-access file is retrieved and assigned to *recVar* with the statement Get #*n*, *r*, *recVar*.

The Get statement is also used to retrieve data from a binary file and assign it to any type of variable. Suppose *var* is a variable that holds a value consisting of *b* bytes. (For instance, if *var* is an integer variable, then *b* is 2. If *var* is an ordinary string variable, then *b* will equal the length of the string currently assigned to it.) The statement Get #*n*, *p*, *var* assigns to the variable *var*, the *b* consecutive bytes beginning with the byte in position *p* of the binary file having reference number *n*. (**Note:** The positions are numbered 1, 2, 3, ...) If *p* is omitted, then the current file position is used as the beginning position. [binary file]

GetAttr The value of the function GetAttr(*filename*) is a number indicating the file attributes associated with the file specified by *filename*. Let *attrib* be a variable holding the value returned by GetAttr. Then the file specified by *filename* is a read-only file if *attrib* And 1 = 1, is a hidden file if *attrib* And 2 = 2, is a system file if *attrib* And 4 = 4, is a volume label if *attrib* And 8 = 8, is a folder name if *attrib* And 16 = 16, or has been modified since the last backup if *attrib* And 32 = 32. See SetAttr.

GetObject If *filespec* specifies a file for an application that supports OLE Automation, then the value of the function GetObject(*filespec*) is an OLE Automation object.

GetText The value of the method ClipBoard.GetText is a string containing a copy of the data currently stored in the clipboard.

Global The Global statement is used to create variables, including arrays, that are available to all procedures in all forms and BAS modules associated with a project. The Global statement must be placed in the (Declarations) section of a BAS module and has the same structure as a Dim statement. For example, the statement `Global classList(1 to 30) As String, numStudents As Integer` creates an array and a variable for use in all procedures of the project.

GoSub A statement of the form GoSub *lineLabel* causes a jump to the first statement following the specified line label. When the statement Return is reached, the program jumps back to the statement following the GoSub statement. The GoSub statement and its target must be in the same procedure. [line label] [subroutine]

GotFocus A GotFocus event occurs when an object receives the focus, either through a user action or through code, via the SetFocus method.

GoTo The statement GoTo *lineLabel* causes an unconditional jump to the first statement after the specified line label. The GoTo statement and its target must be in the same procedure. [line label]

GridLines Grid lines are the light gray lines in a grid that separate columns and rows. The GridLines property determines whether the grid lines are visible (GridLines = True) or not (GridLines = False.)

Height The property Height determines the vertical size of an object. Height is measured in units of twips. For the Printer object, Height may be read (ph = Printer.Height is OK) but not assigned (Printer.Height = 100 causes an error).

Hex If *n* is a whole number from 0 to 2,147,483,647, then the value of the function Hex(*n*) is the string consisting of the hexadecimal representation of *n*.

Hide The Hide method removes a form from the screen.

Hour The function Hour extracts the hours from a serial date. If *d* is any valid serial date, then the value of Hour(*d*) is a whole number from 0 to 23 indicating the hours recorded as part of the date and time store in *d*. [date]

If (Block) A block of statements beginning with a statement of the form If *condition* Then and ending with the statement End If indicates that the group of statements between If and End If are to be executed only when *condition* is true. If the group of statements is separated into two parts by an Else statement, then the first part will be executed when *condition* is true and the second part when *condition* is false. Statements of the form ElseIf *condition* may also appear and define groups of statements to be executed when alternate conditions are true.

If (Single Line) A statement of the form If *condition* Then *action* causes the program to take the specified action if *condition* is true. Otherwise, execution continues at the next line. A statement of the form If *condition* Then *action1* Else *action2* causes the program to take *action1* if *condition* is true and *action2* if *condition* is false.

If TypeOf To test for the type of a control when the control name is passed to a procedure, use If TypeOf *controlName* Is *controlType* Then *action1* Else *action2* in either the single line or block form of the If statement. ElseIf TypeOf is also permitted. For *controlType*, use one of the control names that appear in the Form Design ToolBox (CommandButton, Label, TextBox, etc.)—for example, If TypeOf objectPassed Is Label Then. . . .

Imp The logical expression *condition1* Imp *condition2* is true except when *condition1* is true and *condition2* is false. For example, (3<7) Imp ("abc">"a") is true because both 3<7 and "abc">"a" are true, and ("apple">"ape") Imp ("earth"> "moon") is false because "apple">"ape" is true but "earth">"moon" is false. Imp is an abbreviation for "logically implies."

Index When a control is part of a Control array, it is identified by the number specified by its Index property.

Input The statement *strVar* = Input(*n*, *m*) assigns the next *n* characters from the file with reference number *m* (opened in Input or Binary mode) to *strVar*.

Input # The statement Input #*n*, *var* reads the next item of data from a sequential file that has been opened for Input with reference number *n* and assigns the item to the variable *var*. The statement Input #*n*, *var1*, *var2*, . . . reads a sequence of values and assigns them to the variables.

InputBox The value of the function InputBox(*prompt*) is the string entered by the user in response to the prompt given by *prompt*. The InputBox function automatically displays the prompt, a text box for user input, an OK button, and a Cancel button in a dialog box in the center of the screen. If the user selects Cancel, the value of the function is the null string (""). For greater control, use the function InputBox(*prompt, title, defaultStr, xpos, ypos*), which places the caption *title* in the title bar of the dialog box, displays *defaultStr* as the default value in the text box, and positions the upper-left corner of the dialog box at coordinates (*xpos, ypos*) on the screen. [coordinate systems]

InStr The value of the function InStr(*str1, str2*) is the position of the string *str2* in the string *str1*. The value of InStr(*n, str1, str2*) is the first position at or after the *n*th character of *str1* that the string *str2* occurs. If *str2* does not appear as a substring of *str1*, the value is 0.

Int The value of the function Int(*x*) is the greatest whole number that is less than or equal to *x*.

Integer A variable of type Integer requires 2 bytes of memory and can hold the whole numbers from –32,768 to 32,767. Integer values and variables may be indicated by the type tag %: 345%, Count%.

Interval The Interval property of a Timer control is set to the number of milliseconds (1 to 65535) required to trigger a Timer event.

IsDate The value of the function IsDate(*str*) is True if the string *str* represents a date between January 1, 100 and December 31, 9999. Otherwise, the value is False. [date]

IsEmpty The value of the function IsEmpty(*v*) is True if *v* is a variable of unspecified type (that is, is a variant) that has not yet been assigned a value. In all other cases the value of IsEmpty is False. [variant]

IsNull The value of the function IsNull(*v*) is True if *v* is a variant variable that has been assigned the special value Null. In all other cases the value of IsNull is False. [variant]

IsNumeric The value of the function IsNumeric(*v*) is True if *v* is a number, numeric variable, or a variant variable that has been assigned a number or a string that could be obtained by Formatting a number. In all other cases the value of IsNumeric is False. [variant]

Item The value of *collectionName*.Item(*n*) is the *n*th object in the named collection. The value of *collectionName*.Item(*keyString*) is the *n*th object in the named collection, where *keyString* is the key given to the object when it was added to the collection. If the value of *n* or *keyString* doesn't match an existing object of the collection, an error occurs.

ItemData When you create a list or combo box, Visual Basic automatically creates a long integer array referred to as ItemData. The statement List1. ItemData(*m*) = *n* assigns the value *n* to the *m*th subscripted variable of the array. It is commonly used with the NewIndex property to associate a number with each item in a list, and thereby create a minidatabase. The ItemData property is especially useful for lists in which Sorted = True.

KeyPress The KeyPress event applies to command buttons, text boxes, and picture boxes. A KeyPress event occurs whenever the user presses a key while one of the preceding controls has the focus. A code identifying which key was pressed will be passed to the event procedure in the KeyAscii parameter. This information can then be used to determine what action should be taken when a given key is pressed.

Kill The statement Kill "*filespec*" deletes the specified disk file. [filespec]

LargeChange When a scroll bar is clicked between the scroll box and one of the arrow buttons, the Value property of the scroll bar changes by the value of the LargeChange property and the scroll box moves accordingly.

LBound For a one-dimensional array *arrayName*, the value of the function LBound(*arrayName*) is the smallest subscript value that may be used. For any array *arrayName*, the value of the function LBound(*arrayName*, n) is the smallest subscript value that may be used for the nth subscript of the array. For example, after the statement Dim example(1 To 31, 1 To 12, 1990 To 1999) is executed, the value of LBound(example, 3) is the smallest value allowed for the third subscript of example( ), which is 1990.

LCase The value of the string function LCase(*str*) is a string identical to *str* except that all uppercase letters are changed to lowercase.

Left (Property) The property Left determines the position of the left edge of a form or control. The units of measure are twips for forms. The units of measure for a control are determined by the ScaleMode property of the container (form, picture box, etc.) upon which the control has been placed, with the position of the control measured from the edge of its container using the coordinate system established by the various Scale. . . properties for the container. By default, the unit of measure for a container is twips, with a value of 0 for the Left property placing the control against the left edge of the container.

Left (Function) The value of the function Left(*str*, n) is the string consisting of the leftmost n characters of *str*. If n is greater than the number of characters in *str*, the value of the function is *str*.

Len The value of Len(*str*) is the number of characters in the string *str*. If *var* is not a variable-length string variable, the value of Len(*var*) is the number of bytes needed to hold the value of the variable in memory. That is, Len(*var*) is 1, 2, 2, 4, 4, 8, or 8 for byte, Boolean, integer, long integer, single-precision, double-precision, and currency variables. Len(*var*), when *var* is a variable with a user-defined record type, is the number of bytes of memory needed to store the value of the variable. If *var* is a variant variable, Len(*var*) is the number of bytes needed to store var as a string. [variant]

Let The statement Let *var* = *expr* assigns the value of the expression to the variable. If *var* is a fixed-length string variable with length n and Len(*expr*) is greater than n, then just the first n characters of *expr* are assigned to *var*. If Len(*expr*) < n, then *expr* is padded on the right with spaces and assigned to *var*. If *var* has a user-defined type, then *expr* must be of the same type. The statement *var* = *expr* is equivalent to Let *var* = *expr*.

Line The graphics method *objectName*.Line ($x1$, $y1$)–($x2$, $y2$) draws a line connecting the two points. The graphics method *objectName*.Line –($x2$, $y2$) draws a line from the point (*objectName*.CurrentX, *objectName*.CurrentY) to the specified point. The object *objectName* can be a form, picture box, or the Printer. The line is in color c if *objectName*.Line (*x1*, *y1*)–(*x2*, *y2*), c is executed. The statement *objectName*.Line (*x1*, *y1*)–(*x2*, *y2*), ,B draws a rectangle with the two points as opposite vertices. (If B is replaced by BF, a solid rectangle is drawn.) After a Line method is executed, the value of *objectName*.CurrentX becomes *x2* and the value of *objectName*.CurrentY becomes *y2*. [color] [coordinate systems]

Line Input # After a file has been opened as a sequential file for Input with reference number n, the statement Line Input #n, *str* assigns to the string variable *str* the string of characters from the current location in the file up to the next pair of carriage return/line feed characters.

List The List property of a combo box, directory list box, drive list box, file list box, or list box is used to access items in the list. When one of these controls is created, Visual Basic automatically creates the string array List to hold the list of items stored in the control. The value of List1.List(n) is the item of List1 having index n. The value of List1.List (List1.ListIndex) is the item (string) currently highlighted in list box List1.

ListCount For a list or combo box, the value of List1.ListCount or Combo1. ListCount is the number of items currently in the list. For a directory list box, drive list box, or file list box, the value of *control*.ListCount is the number of subfolders in the current folder, the number of drives on the computer, or the number of files in the current directory that match the Pattern property, respectively.

ListIndex The ListIndex property gives the index of the currently selected item is a combo box, directory list box, drive list box, file list box, or list box.

Load (Event) The Load event applies only to forms and usually occurs only once, immediately when a program starts. This is the appropriate place to put code that should be executed every time a program is run, regardless of the user's actions.

Load (Statement) If *controlName* is the name of a control in a control array whose Index property was assigned a value during form design and *num* is a whole number that has not yet been used as an index for the *controlName*() array, then the statement Load *controlName*(*num*) copies properties of *controlName*(0) and creates the element *controlName*(*num*) of the *controlName*() array.

LoadPicture The statement *objectName*.Picture = LoadPicture(*pictureFile*), where *objectName* is a form or picture box, places the picture defined in the file specified by *pictureFile* on *objectName*.

Loc This function gives the current location in a sequential, random-access, or binary file. For a sequential file with reference number n, Loc(n) is the number of blocks of 128 characters read from or written to the file since it was opened. For a random-access file, Loc(n) is the current record (either the last record read or written, or the record identified in a Seek statement). For a binary file, Loc(n) is the number of bytes from the beginning of the file to the last byte read or written. For communications, the value of Loc(n) is the number of bytes waiting in the communications buffer with reference number n. [binary file]

Lock The Lock command is intended for use in programs that operate on a network. After a file has been opened with reference number n, the statement Lock #n denies access to the file by any other process. For a random-access file, the statement Lock #n, *r1* To *r2* denies access to records *r1* through *r2* by any other process. For a binary file, this statement denies access to bytes *r1* through *r2*. The statement Lock #*n*, *r1* locks only record (or byte) *r1*. For a sequential file, all forms of the Lock statement have the same effect as Lock #*n*. The Unlock statement is used to remove locks from files. All locks should be removed before a file is closed or the program is terminated. [binary file]

LOF After a file has been opened with reference number *n*, the number of characters in the file (that is, the length of the file) is given by LOF(*n*). For communications, the value of LOF(*n*) equals the number of bytes waiting in the communications buffer with reference number *n*.

Log If *x* is a positive number, the value of Log(*x*) is the natural logarithm (base e) of *x*.

Long A variable of type Long requires 4 bytes of memory and can hold the whole numbers from –2,147,483,648 to 2,147,483,647. Long values and variables may be indicated by the type tag &: 12345678&, Population&.

LostFocus A LostFocus event occurs when an object loses the focus, either through a user action or through code, via the SetFocus method.

LSet If *strVar* is a string variable, then the statement LSet *strVar* = *str* replaces the value of *strVar* with a string of the same length consisting of *str* truncated or padded on the right with spaces. LSet also can be used to assign a record of one user-defined type to a record of a different user-defined type.

LTrim The value of the function LTrim(*str*) is the string obtained by removing all the spaces from the beginning of the string *str*. The string *str* may be of either fixed or variable length.

Max and **Min** The Max and Min properties of scroll bars give the values of horizontal (vertical) scroll bars when the scroll box is at the right (bottom) and left (top) arrows, respectively.

MaxButton The MaxButton property determines whether or not a form has a Maximize button in the upper-right corner. If the value of the MaxButton property is set to True (the default), a Maximize button is displayed when the program is run. The user then has the option to click on the Maximize button to cause the form to enlarge and fill the entire screen. If the value of the MaxButton property is set to False, the maximize button is not displayed when the program is run, and the user is thus unable to "maximize" the form.

MaxLength The property MaxLength determines the maximum number of characters that a text box will accept. If the MaxLength property for a text box is set to 0 (the default), an unlimited number of characters may be entered in the text box.

Mid The value of the function Mid(*str*, *m*, *n*) is the substring of *str* beginning with the *m*th character of *str* and containing up to *n* characters. If the parameter *n* is omitted, Mid(*str*, *m*) is all the characters of *str* from the *m*th character on. The statement Mid(*str*, *m*, *n*) = *str2* replaces the characters of *str*, beginning with the *m*th character, by the first *n* characters of the string *str2*.

MinButton The MinButton property determines whether or not a form has a Minimize button in the upper-right corner. If the value of the MinButton property is set to True (the default), a Minimize button is displayed when the program is run. The user then has the option to click on the Minimize button to cause the form to be replaced by a small icon in the Taskbar at the bottom of the screen. If the value of the MinButton property is set to False, the Minimize button is not displayed when the program is run, and the user is thus unable to "minimize" the form.

Minute The function Minute extracts the minutes from a serial date. If *d* is any valid serial date, the value of Minute(*d*) is a whole number from 0 to 59 giving the minutes recorded as part of the date and time stored in *d*. [date]

MkDir The statement MkDir *path\dirName* creates a subfolder named *dirName* in the folder specified by *path*.

Mod The value of the expression *num1* Mod *num2* is the whole-number remainder when *num1* is divided by *num2*. If either *num1* or *num2* is not a whole number, it is rounded to a whole number before the Mod operation is performed. If one or both of *num1* and *num2* are negative, the result of the Mod operation will have the same sign as *num1*. For example, 25 Mod 7 is 4, 18.7 Mod 3.2 is 1, –35 Mod –4 is –3, and 27 Mod –6 is 3.

Month The function Month extracts the month from a serial date. If *d* is any valid serial date, the value of Month(*d*) is a whole number from 1 to 12 giving the month recorded as part of the date and time stored in *d*. [date]

MousePointer The property MousePointer determines what shape the mouse pointer takes when the mouse is over a particular form or control. Valid values for the MousePointer property are whole numbers from 0 to 12. A value of 0 (the default) indicates that the mouse pointer should take on the normal shape for the control it is over. (The normal shape over text boxes is an I-beam, and for a form, picture box, label, or command button it is an arrow.) Use a MousePointer value of 1 for an arrow, 2 for crosshairs, 3 for an I-beam, 4 for a small square within a square, 5 for a four-pointed arrow, 6 for a double arrow pointing up to the right and down to the left, 7 for a double arrow pointing up and down, 8 for a double arrow pointing up to the left and down to the right, 9 for a double arrow pointing left and right, 10 for an up arrow, 11 for an hourglass, and 12 for a "do not" symbol (circle with diagonal line).

Move The method *objectName*.Move *xpos, ypos* moves the named form or control so that its upper left corner has coordinates (*xpos, ypos*). For forms, positioning is relative to the upper left corner of the screen. For controls, positioning is relative to the upper left corner of the form, frame, or picture box to which the control is attached. The method *objectName*.Move *xpos, ypos, width, height* also resizes the named form or control to be *width* units wide and *height* units high. The Move method may be used whether or not a form or control is visible. If you wish to specify just a new width for an object, you CANNOT use *objectName*.Move , , *width*. Instead, use *objectName*.Move *objectName*.Left, *objectName*.Top, *width*. Similar considerations apply for changing just *ypos*, *height*, *width* and *height*, and so on.

MoveFirst, MoveLast, MoveNext, MovePrevious The data control methods MoveNext, MovePrevious, MoveLast, and MoveFirst select new current records in the expected way.

MsgBox (Statement and Function) The statement MsgBox *prompt* displays *prompt* in a dialog box with an OK button. The more general statement MsgBox *prompt, buttons, title* displays *prompt* in a dialog box with *title* in the Title bar and containing from one to three buttons as determined by the value of *buttons*. The value of *buttons* also determines which button is the default (has the focus) and which, if any, of four icons is displayed. The value to use for *buttons* can be computed as follows:

$$buttons = set\ number + default\ number + icon\ number$$

where set number, default number, and icon number are determined from the following tables:

Buttons Set	Set Number
OK	0
OK, Cancel	1
Abort, Retry, Ignore	2
Yes, No, Cancel	3
Yes, No	4
Retry, Cancel	5

Focus Default	Default Number
First Button	0
Second Button	256
Third Button	512

Icon	Icon Number
Stop sign	16
Question mark	32
Exclamation mark	48
Information	64

The value of the function MsgBox(*prompt, buttons, title*) indicates which of the displayed buttons the user pushed; in all other aspects the MsgBox statement and function act in the same manner. The values returned for each of the possible buttons pressed are 1 for OK, 2 for Cancel (or Esc), 3 for Abort, 4 for Retry, 5 for Ignore, 6 for Yes, and 7 for No.

MultiLine The property MultiLine determines whether or not a text box can accept and display multiple lines. If the MultiLine property of a text box is set to True, then text entered in the text box will wrap to a new line when the right side of the text box is reached. Pressing the Enter key will also start a new line. If the MultiLine property of a text box is set to False (the default), input is restricted to a single line that scrolls if more input is entered than can be displayed within the width of the text box.

Name (Property) The property Name is used at design time to give a meaningful name to a form or control. This new name will then be used by Visual Basic in naming all event procedures for the form or control.

Name (Statement) The statement Name "*filespec1*" As "*filespec2*" is used to change the name and/or the folder of *filespec1* to the name and/or folder specified by *filespec2*. The two filespecs must refer to the same drive. [filespec]

New The keyword New is used with Set, to create an instance of a class. A typical statement is Set *objectVariable* As New *className*.

NewIndex The NewIndex property of a combo box or list box gives the index number of the item most recently added to the list.

NewPage The method Printer.NewPage indicates that the current page of output is complete and should be sent to the printer.

Not (Bitwise Operator) The expression Not *byte1* is evaluated by expressing the byte as an 8-tuple binary number and then Notting each individual digit, where Not 1 is equal to 0, while Not 0 is equal to 1. For example, the expression Not 37 translated to binary 8-tuples becomes Not 00100101. Notting each digit gives the binary 8-tuple 11011010 or decimal 218; thus Not 37 is 218.

Not (Logical Operator) The logical expression Not *condition1* is true if *condition1* is false and false if *condition1* is true. For example, Not (3<7) is false because 3<7 is true, and Not ("earth">"moon") is true because "earth">"moon" is false.

Nothing The keyword Nothing is used with Set to discontinue the association of an object variable with a specific object. A typical statement is Set *objectVariable* = Nothing. Assigning Nothing to an object variable releases all the system and memory resources associated with the previously referenced object when no other variable refers to it.

Now The value of the function Now( ) is the serial date for the current date and time as recorded on the computer's internal clock. [date]

Oct If *n* is a whole number between 0 and 2,147,483,647, Oct(*n*) is the octal (that is, base 8) representation of *n*.

On Error The statement On Error GoTo *lineLabel* sets up error-trapping. An error then causes a jump to the error-handling routine beginning with the first statement following the specified line label. The On Error statement and its target must be in the same procedure. [line label]

On...GoSub and **On...GoTo** The statement On *expression* GoSub *lineLabel1*, *lineLabel2*, . . . causes a GoSub to *lineLabel1*, *lineLabel2*, . . . depending on whether the value of the expression is 1, 2, ... Similarly, the GoTo variation causes an unconditional jump to the appropriate line label. The GoSub or GoTo statement and its target must be in the same procedure. [line label]

Open The statement Open "*filespec*" For *mode* As #*n* allows access to the file *filespec* in one of the following modes: Input (information can be read sequentially from the file), Output (a new file is created and information can be written sequentially to it), Append (information can be added sequentially to the end of a file), or Binary (information can be read or written in an arbitrary fashion). The statement Open "*filespec*" For Random As #*n* Len = *g* allows random access to the file *filespec* in which each record has length *g*. Throughout the program, the file is referred to by the reference number *n* (from 1 through 255). Another variation of the Open statement is Open "LPT1" For Output As #*n*, which allows access to the printer as if it were a sequential file.

In a network environment, two enhancements to the Open statement are available. Visual Basic accesses data files in two ways: it reads from them or writes to them. When several processes may utilize a file at the same time, accurate file handling requires that certain types of access be denied to anyone but the person who has opened the file. The statement Open "*filespec*" For *mode* Lock Read As #*n* or Open "*filespec*" For Random Lock Read As #*n* Len = *g* opens the specified file and forbids any other process from reading the file as long as the file is open. Lock Write forbids any other process from writing to the file as long as the file is open. Lock Read Write forbids any other process from reading or writing to the file as long as the file is open. Lock Shared grants full access to any other process, except when a file is currently opened and locked by a process for a certain access mode, then another process attempting to open the file for the same mode will receive the message "Permission denied" and be denied access. [filespec] [binary file]

Option Base After the statement Option Base m is executed, where m is 0 or 1, a statement of the form Dim *arrayName*(n) defines an array with subscripts ranging from m to n. Visual Basic's extended Dim statement, which permits both lower and upper subscript bounds to be specified for each array, achieves a wider range of results, making its use preferable to Option Base.

Option Compare The statement Option Compare Text, placed in the (Declarations) section of (General), causes string comparisons to be case-insensitive. Thus, if Option Compare Text is in effect, the comparison "make" = "MaKe" will be true. The statement Option Compare Binary placed in the (Declarations) section produces the default comparison rules, which are case-sensitive and use the character order given in the ANSI/ASCII character tables.

Option Explicit If the statement Option Explicit appears in the (Declarations) section of (General), each variable must be declared before it is used. A variable is declared by appearing in a Const, Dim, Global, ReDim, or Static statement, or by appearing as a parameter in a Sub or Function definition.

Or (Bitwise Operator) The expression *byte1* Or *byte2* is evaluated by expressing each byte as an 8-tuple binary number and then Oring together corresponding digits, where 1 Or 1, 1 Or 0, and 0 Or 1 are all equal to 1, while 0 And 0 is equal to 0. For example, the expression 37 Or 157 translated to binary 8-tuples becomes 00100101 Or 10011101. Oring together corresponding digits gives the binary 8-tuple 10111101 or decimal 189. Thus, 37 Or 157 is 189.

Or (Logical Operator) The logical expression *condition1* Or *condition2* is true except when both *condition1* and *condition2* are false. For example, ("apple">"ape") Or ("earth">"moon") is true because "apple">"ape" is true, and (1>2) Or ("moon"< "earth") is false because both (1>2) and ("moon"<"earth") are false.

Path The Path property for a directory list box is the contents of the currently selected item, and for a files list box is the path identifying the folder whose files are displayed.

PathChange For a files list box, the PathChange event is triggered by a change in the value of the Path property.

Pattern The Pattern property of a files list box uses wildcard characters to determine which file names are displayed. A typical statement is File1.Pattern = "*.TXT."

PatternChange For a files list box, the PatternChange event is triggered by a change in the value of the Pattern property.

Picture The property Picture allows a form, command button, option button, check box, or picture box to be assigned a picture or icon for display. If *iconOrPicture* is a file defining an icon or bitmapped picture, then *objectName*.Picture = LoadPicture(*iconOrPicture*) places the icon or picture on the object identified by *objectName*.

Point The value of the method *objectName*.Point(x, y) is the RGB number of the color of the point with coordinates (x, y) on the form or picture box identified by *objectName*. Thus, if the point with coordinates (x, y) has been painted using color RGB(r, g, b), then the value of Point(x, y) will be $r+256*g+65536*b$. If the coordinates (x, y) identify a point that is not on *objectName*, the value of Point(x, y) will be –1. [color] [coordinate systems]

Print   The print method is used to display data on the screen or printer. The statement *objectName*.Print *expression* displays the value of the expression at the current position of the cursor in the named object (form, picture box, or Printer) and moves the cursor to the beginning of the next line. (Numbers are displayed with a trailing space and positive numbers with a leading space.) If the statement is followed by a semicolon or comma, the cursor will not move to the next line after the display, but will move to the next position or print zone, respectively. Several expressions may be placed in the same Print method if separated by semicolons (to display them adjacent to one another) or by commas (to display them in successive zones).

Print #   After a file has been opened as a sequential file for output or append with reference number n, the statement Print #n, *expression* places the value of the expression into the file in the same way the Print method displays it in a picture box.

Printer   The Printer object provides access to the printer. Methods available are Print to send text to the printer, NewPage to execute a form feed to begin a new page, EndDoc to complete the printing process, and the graphics methods. Many properties available for forms and picture boxes, such as fonts and scaling, are also available for the printer.

PrintForm   The method *formName*.PrintForm prints on the printer an image of the named form and all its contents.

Property Get/End Property   A Property Get procedure is a multistatement block in a class module beginning with a statement of the form Public Property Get *name(parList)*, followed on subsequent lines by one or more statements for carrying out the task of the procedure, and ending with the statement End Property. The parameter list *parList* is a list of variables through which values will be passed to the procedure when the property value of an associated object is retrieved. The name and data type of each parameter in a Property Get procedure must be the same as the corresponding parameter in a Property Let procedure (if one exists).

Property Let/End Property   A Property Let procedure is a multistatement block in a class module beginning with a statement of the form Public Property Let *name(parList)*, followed on subsequent lines by one or more statements for carrying out the task of the procedure, and ending with the statement End Property. The parameter list *parList* is a list of variables through which values will be passed to the procedure when an assignment is made to the property of an associated object. The name and data type of each parameter in a Property Let procedure must be the same as the corresponding parameter in a Property Get procedure (if one exists).

PSet   The graphics method *objectName*.PSet(x, y) displays the point with coordinates (x, y) in the foreground color. The method *objectName*.PSet(x, y), c causes the point (x, y) to be displayed in the RGB color specified by c. The size of the point is determined by the value of the DrawWidth property. The actual color(s) displayed depend on the values of the DrawMode and DrawStyle properties. After a PSet method is executed, the value of *objectName*.CurrentX becomes *x* and the value of *objectName*.CurrentY becomes *y*. [color] [coordinate systems]

Put   The Put statement is used to place data into a random-access file. Suppose *recVar* is a variable of a user-defined record type and that a file has been opened with a statement of the form Open *fileName* For Random As #*n* Len = Len(*recVar*). The statement Put #*n*, *r*, *recVar* places the value of *recVar* in the *r*th record of the file.

   The Put statement is also used to place data into a file opened as a binary file. Suppose *var* is a variable that holds a value consisting of *b* bytes. (For instance, if *var* is an integer variable, then *b* is 2. If *var* is an ordinary string variable, then *b* will equal the length of the string currently assigned to it.) The statement Put #*n*, *p*, *var* writes the successive bytes of *var* into the *b* consecutive locations beginning with position *p* in the binary file with reference number *n*. (**Note:** The positions are numbered 1, 2, 3, ...) If *p* is omitted, the current file position is used as the beginning position. [binary file]

QBColor   The function QBColor provides easy access to 16 standard colors. If *colorAttrib* is a whole number from 0 to 15, the value of the functions QBColor(*colorAttrib*) is the RGB color number associated with *colorAttrib*. The following table names the colors produced by each of the possible values of *colorAttrib*.

0 Black	4 Red	8 Gray	12 Light Red
1 Blue	5 Magenta	9 Light Blue	13 Light Magenta
2 Green	6 Brown	10 Light Green	14 Yellow
3 Cyan	7 White	11 Light Cyan	15 Intense White

RaiseEvent   After an event has been declared in the general declarations section of a class module, the statement RaiseEvent *EventName(arg1, arg2, . . .)* generates the event.

Randomize   The statement Randomize automatically uses the computer's clock to seed the random-number generator. If a program includes a Randomize statement in the Form_Load event procedure, the list of numbers generated by Rnd will vary each time the program is executed. Randomize *n* seeds the generator with a number determined by *n*. If a program does not seed the random-number generator or seeds it with a set number, the list of numbers generated by Rnd will be the same each time the program is executed.

RecordCount   The value of Data1.Recordset.RecordCount is the number of records in the database table associated with the data control.

RecordSource   The value of the RecordSource property of a data control is the table of the database determined by the DatabaseName property. The value can also be an SQL statement used to specify a virtual table.

ReDim   The statement ReDim *arrayName*(...) erases the array from memory and recreates it. The information inside the parentheses has the same form and produces the same results as that in a Dim statement. After the ReDimensioning, all elements have their default values. Although the ranges of the subscripts may be changed, the number of dimensions must be the same as in the original Dimensioning of the array. ReDim may be used only within procedures; it may not be used in the (Declarations) section of (General). To establish an array that is available to all procedures and also can be resized, Dim it with empty parentheses in the (Declarations) section of (General) and then ReDim it as needed within appropriate procedures.

Refresh The method *objectName*.Refresh causes the named form or control to be refreshed, that is, redrawn reflecting any changes made to its properties. Generally, refreshing occurs automatically, but if not, it may be forced with the Refresh method.

Rem The statement Rem allows documentation to be placed in a program. A line of the form Rem *comment* is ignored during execution. The Rem statement may be abbreviated as an apostrophe.

Remove A statement of the form *collectionName*.Remove *n* deletes the *n*th object from the collection and automatically reduces the object numbers from *n* on by 1 so that there is no gap in the numbers. A statement of the form *collectionName*.Remove *keyString* deletes the object identified by the key *keyString*. If the value of *n* or *keyString* doesn't match an existing object of the collection, an error occurs.

RemoveItem The RemoveItem method deletes items from list and combo boxes and deletes rows from grids. The statement List1.RemoveItem *n* (where *n* is 0, 1, . . .) deletes the item with index *n*. For instance, List1.RemoveItem 0 deletes the top item and List1.RemoveItem ListCount − 1 deletes the bottom item in the list. The statement MSFlexGrid1.RemoveItem *n* deletes row *n* from the grid.

Reset The statement Reset closes all open files. Using Reset is equivalent to using Close with no file reference numbers.

Resume When the statement Resume is encountered at the end of an error-handling routine, the program branches back to the statement in which the error was encountered. The variations Resume *lineLabel* and Resume Next cause the program to branch to the first statement following the indicated line label or to the statement following the statement in which the error occurred, respectively. (The combination of On Error and Resume Next is similar to the combination GoSub and Return.) [line label]

Return When the statement Return is encountered at the end of a subroutine, the program branches back to the statement following the one containing the most recently executed GoSub. The variation Return *lineLabel* causes the program to branch back to the first statement following the indicated line label. [line label] [subroutine]

RGB The value of the function RGB(*red, green, blue*) is the color number corresponding to a mixture of *red* red, *green* green, and *blue* blue. This color number is assigned to color properties or used in graphics methods to produce text or graphics in a particular color. Each of the three color components may have a value from 0 to 255. The color produced using RGB(0, 0, 0) is black, RGB(255, 255, 255) is white, RGB(255, 0, 0) is bright red, RGB(10, 0, 0) is a dark red, and so on. (The value of the function RGB(*r, g, b*) is the long integer $r + 256*g + 65536*b$.) [color]

Right The value of the function Right(*str, n*) is the string consisting of the rightmost *n* characters of *str*. If *n* is greater than the number of characters of *str*, then the value of the function is *str*.

RmDir If *path* specifies a folder containing no files or subfolder, then the statement RmDir *path* removes the folder.

Rnd The value of the function Rnd is a randomly selected number from 0 to 1, not including 1. The value of Int($n*$Rnd)+1 is a random whole number from 1 to n.

Round The value of the function Round(n, r) is the number n rounded to r decimal places. If r is omitted, n is rounded to a whole number.

RowHeight The statement MSFlexGrid1.RowHeight(m) = n specifies that row m of the grid be n twips high. (There are about 1440 twips in an inch.)

RSet If *str1* is a string variable, the statement RSet *str1* = *str2* replaces the value of *str1* with a string of the same length consisting of *str2* truncated or padded on the left with spaces.

RTrim The value of the function RTrim(*str*) is the string obtained by removing all the spaces from the end of the string *str*. The string *str* may be either fixed-length or variable-length.

Scale The method *objectName*.Scale (*x1, y1*)–(*x2, y2*) defines a coordinate system for the form, picture box, or printer identified by *objectName*. This coordinate system has horizontal values ranging from *x1* at the left edge of *objectName* to *x2* at the right edge and vertical values ranging from *y1* at the top edge of *objectName* to *y2* at the bottom edge. Subsequent graphics methods and control positioning place figures and controls in accordance with this new coordinate system. As a result of using the Scale method, the ScaleMode property of *objectName* is set to 0, the ScaleLeft property to *x1*, the ScaleTop property to *y1*, the ScaleHeight property to *y2–y1*, and the ScaleWidth property to *x2–x1*. The method *objectName*.Scale without arguments resets the coordinate system of *objectName* to the default coordinate system where the unit of measure is twips and the upper-left corner of *objectName* has coordinates (0, 0).

ScaleHeight The property ScaleHeight determines the vertical scale on a form or picture box. After the statement *objectName*.ScaleHeight = *hght* is executed, the vertical coordinates range from *objectName*.ScaleTop at the top edge of *objectName* to *objectName*.ScaleTop + *hght* at the bottom edge. The default value of the ScaleHeight property is the height of *objectName* when measured in the units specified by *objectName's* ScaleMode property.

ScaleLeft The property ScaleLeft determines the horizontal coordinate of the left edge of a form or picture box. After the statement *objectName*.ScaleLeft = *left* is executed, the horizontal coordinates will range from *left* at the left edge of *objectName* to *left* + *objectName*.ScaleWidth at the right edge. The default value of the ScaleLeft property is 0.

ScaleMode The property ScaleMode determines the horizontal and vertical unit of measure for the coordinate system on a form or picture box. If the ScaleMode property of a form or picture box is set to 1 (the default), the unit of measure becomes twips. Other possible values for ScaleMode are 2 for points (72 points = 1 inch), 3 for pixels, 4 for characters (1 horizontal unit = 120 twips; 1 vertical unit = 240 twips), 5 for inches, 6 for millimeters, and 7 for centimeters. A value of 0 for the ScaleMode property indicates that units of measure are to be determined from the current settings of the ScaleHeight and ScaleWidth properties. Visual Basic automatically sets the ScaleMode property of an object to 0 when any of the object's Scale... properties are assigned values.

ScaleTop The property ScaleTop determines the vertical coordinate of the top edge of a form or picture box. After the statement *objectName*.ScaleTop = *top* is executed, the vertical coordinates range from *top* at the top edge of *objectName* to *top* + *objectName*.ScaleHeight at the bottom edge. The default value for the ScaleTop property is 0.

ScaleWidth The property ScaleWidth determines the horizontal scale on a form or picture box. After the statement *objectName*.ScaleWidth = *wdth* is executed, the horizontal coordinates range from *objectName*.ScaleLeft at the left edge of *objectName* to *objectName*.ScaleLeft + *wdth* at the right edge. The default value of the ScaleWidth property is the width of *objectName* when measured in the units specified by *objectName*'s ScaleMode property.

ScrollBars The ScrollBars property of a grid or text box specifies whether the control has horizontal (setting = 1), vertical (setting = 2), both (setting = 3), or no (setting = 0) scroll bars. In order for a text box to have scroll bars, the MultiLine property must be set to True.

Second The function Second extracts the seconds from a serial date. If *d* is any valid serial date, the value of Second(*d*) is a whole number from 0 to 59 giving the seconds recorded as part of the date and time stored in *d*. [date]

Seek The statement Seek #*n*, *p* sets the current file position in the binary or random-access file referenced by *n* to the *p*th byte or record of the file, respectively. After the statement is executed, the next Get or Put statement will read or write bytes, respectively, beginning with the *p*th byte or record. The value of the function Seek(*n*) is the current file position either in bytes or by record number. After a Put or Get statement is executed, the value of Seek(*n*) is the number of the next byte or record. [binary file]

Select Case The Select Case statement provides a compact method of selecting for execution one of several blocks of statements based on the value of an expression. The Select Case block begins with a line of the form Select Case *expression* and ends with the statement End Select. In between are clauses of the form Case *valueList* and perhaps the clause Case Else. The items in the *valueList* may be individual values or ranges of values such as "*a* To *b*" or "Is < *a*". Each of these Case statements is followed by a block of zero or more statements. The block of statements following the first Case *valueList* statement for which *valueList* includes the value of *expression* is the only block of statements executed. If none of the value lists includes the value of expression and a Case Else statement is present, then the block of statements following the Case Else statement is executed.

SendKeys The statement SendKeys *str* places in the keyboard buffer the characters and keystrokes specified by *str*. The effect is exactly the same as if the user had typed the series of characters/keystrokes at the keyboard. The statement SendKeys *str*, True places keystrokes in the keyboard buffer and waits until these keystrokes are processed (used) before allowing program execution to continue with the next statement in the procedure containing the SendKeys statement. Keystrokes can be specified that do not have a displayable character or that result from using the Shift, Ctrl, or Alt keys.

Set Essentially, Set is "Let for objects." Whereas the Let statement is used to assign ordinary values to variables or properties, the Set statement is used to assign objects to variables or properties.

The statement Set *controlVar* = *objectExpression* associates the name *controlVar* with the object identified by *objectExpression*. For example, if the statements Dim Scenery As PictureBox and Set Scenery = Picture1 are executed, then Scenery becomes another name for Picture1, and references like Scenery.Print *message* are equivalent to Picture1.Print *message*. Also, the Set statement assigns an object to an object variable. When you want to release the memory used for the object, execute Set *objVar* = Nothing.

SetAttr The statement SetAttr *fileName, attribute* sets the file attribute of the file specified by *fileName*. A file's attribute can be 0 for "Normal" or a combination of 1, 2, or 4 for "Read-only", "Hidden", and "System." In addition, a file can be marked as "changed since last backup" by adding 32 to its attribute. Thus, for example, if a file's attribute is set to 35 (1 + 2 + 32), the file is classified as a Read-only Hidden file that has been changed since the last backup.

SetFocus The method *objectName*.SetFocus moves the focus to the named form or control. Only the object with the focus can receive user input from the keyboard or the mouse. If *objectName* is a form, the form's default control, if any, receives the focus. Disabled and invisible objects cannot receive the focus. If an attempt is made to set focus to a control that cannot receive the focus, the next control in tab order receives the focus.

SetText The method ClipBoard.SetText *info* replaces the contents of the clipboard with the string *info*.

Sgn The value of the function $Sgn(x)$ is 1, 0, or –1, depending on whether x is positive, zero, or negative, respectively.

Shell If *command* is a DOS command, the function Shell(*command*) causes *command* to be executed. If the DOS command requires user input, execution of the Visual Basic program will be suspended until the user input is supplied. Using the function Shell with no arguments suspends program execution and invokes a copy of DOS. Entering the command Exit resumes execution of the Visual Basic program. The value returned by the Shell function is a number used by Windows to identify the new task being performed.

Show The Show method makes an invisible form visible. The statement Form1.Show 1 also makes a form modal. No user input to any other form will be accepted until the modal form is hidden.

Sin For any number x, the value of the trigonometric function $Sin(x)$ is the sine of the angle of x radians. [radians]

Single A variable of type Single requires 4 bytes of memory and can hold 0, the numbers from 1.40129×10^{-45} to 3.40283×10^{38} with at most seven significant digits, and the negatives of these numbers. Single values and variables may be indicated by the type tag !: 32.156!, Meters!.

SmallChange When a scroll bar arrow button is clicked, the Value property of the scroll bar changes by the value of the SmallChange property and the scroll box moves accordingly.

Sorted When the Sorted property of a list or combo box is set to True, the items are automatically presented in alphabetical order.

Space If n is an integer from 0 to 32767, the value of the function Space(n) is the string consisting of n spaces.

Spc The function Spc is used in Print and Print# statements to generate spaces. For instance, the statement Print *str1*; Spc(*n*); *str2* skips *n* spaces between the displays of the two strings.

Sqr For any nonnegative number *x*, the value of the square root function Sqr(*x*) is the non-negative number whose square is *x*.

Static A statement of the form Static *var1*, *var2*, . . . can be used at the beginning of the definition of a procedure to specify that the variables *var1*, *var2*, . . . are static local variables in the procedure. Memory for static variables is permanently set aside by Visual Basic, allowing static variables to retain their values between successive calls of the procedure. The type of each variable is either determined by a Def*Type* statement, a type-declaration tag, or an As clause. Static variables have no connection to variables of the same name outside the procedure, and so may be named without regard to "outside" variables. Arrays created in a procedure by Dim or ReDim are lost when the procedure is exited. Arrays that are local to a procedure yet retained from one invocation of the procedure to the next can be created by dimensioning the array in the procedure with a Static statement rather than a Dim or ReDim statement. Dimensions for static arrays must be numeric constants. A local static array whose size is to be determined at run time is declared by listing its name followed by empty parentheses in a Static statement, and then dimensioning the array in a subsequent ReDim statement.

Stop The statement Stop suspends the execution of a program. Execution can be resumed beginning with the first statement after the Stop statement by pressing F5.

Str The Str function converts numbers to strings. The value of the function Str(*n*) is the string consisting of the number *n* in the form normally displayed by a print statement.

StrComp The value of the function StrComp(*str1*, *str2*, *compMode*) is −1, 0, 1, or Null, depending on whether *str1* < *str2*, *str1* = *str2*, *str1* > *str2*, or either of *str1* and *str2* is Null. The comparison will be case-sensitive if *compMode* is 0 and case-insensitive if *compMode* is 1.

StrConv The value of StrConv(*str*, 3) is the value of *str* with the first letter of every word converted to uppercase. The value of StrConv(*str*, 1) is the same as UCase(*str*) and the value of StrConv(*str*, 2) is the same as LCase(*str*).

Stretch When the Stretch property of an image control is set to False (the default value), the image control will hold the picture at its normal size. If the Stretch property is set to True, the picture will be resized to fit the image control

String (Data Type) A variable of type String can hold a string of up to 32,767 characters. String values are enclosed in quotes. String variables can be indicated by the type tag $: FirstName$. A variable of type String*n holds a string of *n* characters, where *n* is a whole number from 1 to 32,767. Variables of this type have no type tag and must be declared in a Dim, Global, or Static statement. Until assigned a value, these variables contain a string of *n* Chr(0)'s.

String (Function) If *n* is a whole number from 0 to 32767, the value of String(*n*, *str*) is the string consisting of the first character of *str* repeated *n* times. If *m* is a whole number from 0 to 255, the value of the function String(*n*, *m*) is the string consisting of the character with ANSI value *m* repeated *n* times.

Style The Style property of a combo box determines whether the list is always visible (Style = 1) or whether the list drops down when the user clicks on the arrow and then disappears after a selection is made (Style = 0).

Sub/End Sub A Sub procedure is a multistatement block beginning with a statement of the form Sub *ProcedureName(parList)*, followed on subsequent lines by one or more statements for carrying out the task of the Sub procedure, and ending with the statement End Sub. The parameter list *parList* is a list of variables through which values will be passed to the Sub procedure whenever the function is called. (See the discussion of Call.) Parameters may be numeric or (variable-length) string variables as well as arrays.

Tab The function Tab(*n*) is used in Print and Print# statements to move the cursor to position *n* and place spaces in all skipped-over positions. If *n* is less than the cursor position, the cursor is moved to the *n*th position of the next line.

TabIndex The property TabIndex determines the order in which the tab key moves the focus about the objects on a form. Visual Basic automatically assigns successive tab indexes as new controls are created at design time. Visual Basic also automatically prevents two controls on the same form from having the same tab index by renumbering controls with higher tab indexes when the designer or program directly assigns a new tab index to a control.

Tan For any number x (except for $x = \pi/2, -\pi/2, 3 * \pi/2, -3 * \pi/2$, and so on), the value of the trigonometric function Tan(x) is the tangent of the angle of x radians. [radians]

Text For a text box, the Text property holds the information assigned to a text box. A statement of the form *textBoxName*.Text = *str* changes the contents of *textBoxName* to the string specified by *str*. A statement of the form *str* = *textBoxName*.Text assigns the contents of *textBoxName* to *str*. For a list or combo box, *control*.Text is the contents of the currently highlighted item or the item in the text box, respectively. For a grid, MSFlexGrid1.Text is the contents of the active cell.

TextHeight This method applies to forms, picture boxes, and printer objects. The value of the method *objectName*.TextHeight(*str*) is the amount of vertical space required to display the contents of *str* using the font currently assigned for *objectName*. These contents may include multiple lines of text resulting from the use of carriage-return/line-feed pairs (Chr(13) + Chr(10)) in *str*. The units of height are those specified by the ScaleMode and ScaleHeight properties of *objectName*. (The default is twips.)

TextWidth This method applies to forms, picture boxes, and printer objects. The value of the method *objectName*.TextWidth(*strVar*) is the amount of horizontal space required to display the contents of *strVar* using the font currently assigned for *objectName*. When carriage return/line feed pairs (Chr(13) + Chr(10)) create multiple lines in *strVar*, this will be the space required for the longest line.

Time The value of the function Time is the current time expressed as a string of the form hh:mm:ss. (The hours range from 0 to 23, as in military time.) If *timeStr* is such a string, the statement Time = *timeStr* sets the computer's internal clock to the corresponding time.

Timer (Function) The value of the function Timer is the number of seconds from midnight to the time currently stored in the computer's internal clock.

Timer (Event) The Timer event is triggered by the passage of the amount of time specified by the Interval property of a timer control whose Enabled property is set to True.

TimeSerial The value of the function TimeSerial(*hour, minute, second*) is the serial date corresponding to the given hour, minute, and second. Values from 0 (midnight) to 23 (11 p.m.) for *hour*, and 0 to 59 for both *minute* and *second* are normal, but any Integer value may be used. Often, numeric expressions are used for *hour*, *minute*, or *second* that evaluate to numbers outside these ranges. For example, TimeSerial(15–5, 20–30, 0) is the serial time 5 hours and 30 minutes before 3:20 p.m.

TimeValue The value of the function TimeValue(*str*) is the serial date corresponding to the time given in *str*. TimeValue recognizes both the 24-hour and 12-hour time formats: "13:45:24" or "1:45:24PM".

Top The property Top determines the position of the top edge of a form or control. The units of measure are twips for forms. The units of measure for a control are determined by the ScaleMode property of the container (form, picture box, etc.) on which the control has been placed, with the position of the control measure from the edge of its container using the coordinate system established by the various Scale... properties for the container. By default, the unit of measure for a container is twips, with a value of 0 for the Top property placing the control against the top edge of the container.

Trim The value of the function Trim(*str*) is the string obtained by removing all the spaces from the beginning and end of the string *str*. The string *str* may be either fixed-length or variable-length.

True A keyword of the Boolean type, True is used when setting the value of properties that are either True or False. For example, Picture1.Font.Italic = True.

Type/End Type A multistatement block beginning the Type *typeName* and ending with End Type creates a user-defined record type. Each statement inside the block has the form *elt* As *type*, where *elt* is a variable and *type* is either Integer, Boolean, Byte, Date, Long, Single, Double, Currency, Variant, String*n (that is, fixed-length string), or another user-defined record type. After a statement of the form Dim *var* As *typeName* appears, the element corresponding to the statement *elt* As *type* is referred to as *var.elt*. Type declaration blocks must be placed in the (Declarations) section of a BAS module. [variant]

TypeName If var is variable, then the value of the function TypeName(var) is a string identifying the type of the variable. The possible values of the function are Byte, Integer, Long, Single, Double, Currency, Date, String, Boolean, Error, Empty (uninitialized), Null (no valid data), Object (an object that supports OLE Automation), Unknown (an OLE Automation object whose type is unknown), and Nothing (an object variable that doesn't refer to an object).

UBound For a one-dimensional array *arrayName*, the value of the function UBound(*arrayName*) is the largest subscript value that may be used. For any array *arrayName*, the value of the function UBound(*arrayName*, n) is the largest subscript value that may be used for the *n*th subscript of the array. For example, after the statement Dim example(1 To 31, 1 To 12, 1990 To 1999) is executed, the value of UBound(example, 3) is the largest value allowed for the third subscript of example( ), which is 1999.

UCase The value of the string function UCase(*str*) is a string identical to *str* except that all lowercase letters are changed to uppercase.

Unlock The Unlock command is intended for use in programs that operate on a network. After a Lock statement has been used to deny access to all or part of a file (see the discussion of Lock for details), a corresponding Unlock statement can be used to restore access. Suppose a data file has been opened as reference number *n*. The locks established by the statements Lock #n; Lock #n, *r1*; and Lock #n, *r1* To *r2* are undone by the statements Unlock #n; Unlock #n, *r1*; and Unlock #n, *r1* To *r2*, respectively. There must be an exact correspondence between the locking and the unlocking statements used in a program; that is, each set of paired statements must refer to the same range of record numbers or bytes.

Update The Update method of a data control is used to save changes made to the database.

Val The Val function is used to convert strings to numbers. If the leading characters of the string *str* correspond to a number, then Val(*str*) will be the number represented by these characters. For any number *n*, Val(Str(*n*)) is *n*.

Validate The Validate event procedure is activated whenever the current record of a database table is about to be changed. The heading of the procedure has the form Private Sub Data1_Validate(Action As Integer, Save As Integer), where the value of Action identifies the specific operation that triggered the event and the value of Save specifies whether data bound to the control has changed. You can change the value of the Action argument to convert one operation into another.

Value The Value property of a scroll bar is a number between the values of the Min and Max properties of the scroll bar that is related to the position of the scroll box. The Value property of an option button is True when the button is on and False when the button is off. The Value property of a check box is 0 (unchecked), 1 (checked), or 2 (grayed). The Value property of Fields("*fieldName*") reads the contents of a field of the current record.

Variant A variable of type variant can be assigned numbers, strings, and several other types of data. Variant variables are written without type-declaration tags. [variant]

VarType The value of the function VarType(*var*) is a number indicating the type of value stored in *var*. This function is primarily used to check the type of data stored in a variant variable. Some values returned by VarType are 0 for "Empty," 1 for "Null," 2 for Integer, 3 for Long Integer, 4 for Single Precision, 5 for Double Precision, 6 for Currency, 7 for Date, 8 for String, 9 for OLE Automation object, 10 for Error, 11 for Boolean, 13 for Non-OLE Automation object, and 17 for Byte. For nonvariant arrays, the number assigned is 8192 plus the number assigned to the type of the array. [variant]

Visible The property Visible determines whether or not a form or control is displayed. If the Visible property of an object is True, the object will be displayed (if not covered by other objects) and respond to events if its Enabled property is

True. If the Visible property of an object is set to False, the object will not be displayed and cannot respond to events.

WeekDay The value of the function WeekDay(d) is a number giving the day of the week for the date stored in d. These values will range from 1 for Sunday to 7 for Saturday.

While/Wend A While ... Wend loop is a sequence of statements beginning with a statement of the form While *condition* and ending with the statement Wend. After the While statement is executed, the computer repeatedly executes the entire sequence of statements inside the loop as long as the condition is true.

Width (Property) The property Width determines the horizontal size of an object. Width is measured in units of twips. For the Printer object, Width may be read (pw = Printer.Width is OK) but not assigned (Printer.Width = 100 causes an error).

Width (Statement) If s is an integer less than 255 and n is the reference number of a file opened in sequential mode, the statement Width #n, s causes Visual Basic to permit at most s characters to be printed on a single line in the file. Visual Basic will send a carriage-return/line-feed pair to the file after s characters have been printed on a line, even if the Print # or Write # statement would not otherwise start a new line at that point. The statement Width #n, 0 specifies infinite width; that is, a carriage-return/line-feed pair will be sent to the printer only when requested by Print # or Write #.

With/End With A multistatement block begun by With *recName* or With *objName* and ended by End With is used to assign values to the fields of the named record variable or to properties of the named object. The statements inside the block have the form .*fieldName* = *fieldValue* or .*propertyName* = *propertyValue*. When you use this block, you only have to refer to the record variable or object once instead of referring to it with each assignment.

WithEvents If a class has events attached to it, and form code intends to make use of these events, then the keyword WithEvents should be inserted into the statement declaring an instance of the class. A typical declaration statement is Private WithEvents *objectVariable* As *className*.

WordWrap The WordWrap property of a label with AutoSize property set to True determines whether or not long captions will wrap. (When a label's AutoSize property is False, word wrap always occurs, but the additional lines will not be visible if the label is not tall enough.) Assume a label's AutoSize property is True. If its WordWrap property is set to True, long captions will wrap to multiple lines; if its WordWrap property is False (the default), the caption will always occupy a single line. If a label has its WordWrap and AutoSize properties set to True, the label's horizontal length is determined by the length of its longest word, with long captions being accommodated by having the label expand vertically so that word wrap can spread the caption over several lines. If a label's WordWrap property is set to False while its AutoSize property is True, the label will be one line high and will expand or shrink horizontally to exactly accommodate its caption.

Write # After a sequential file is opened for output or append with reference number n, the statement Write #n, *exp1*, *exp2*, . . . records the values of the expressions one after the other into the file. Strings appear surrounded by quotation marks, numbers do not have leading or trailing spaces, all commas in the expressions are recorded, and the characters for carriage return and line feed are placed following the data.

Xor (Logical Operator) The logical expression *condition1* Xor *condition2* is true if *condition1* is true or *condition2* is true, but not if both are true. For example, (3<7) Xor ("abc">"a") is false because both 3<7 and "abc">"a" are true, and ("apple">"ape") Xor ("earth">"moon") is true because "apple">"ape" is true and "earth">"moon" is false.

Xor (Bitwise Operator) The expression *byte1* Xor *byte2* is evaluated by expressing each byte as an 8-tuple binary number and then Xoring together corresponding digits, where 1 Xor 0 and 0 Xor 1 both equal 1, while 1 Xor 1 and 0 Xor 0 both equal 0. For example, the expression 37 Xor 157 translated to binary 8-tuples becomes 00100101 Xor 10011101. Xoring together corresponding digits gives the binary 8-tuple 10111000 or decimal 184. Thus, 37 Xor 157 is 184.

Year The function Year extracts the year from a serial date. If *d* is any valid serial date, then the value of Year(*d*) is a whole number from 100 to 9999 giving the year recorded as part of the date and time stored in *d*. [date]

Supporting Topics

[binary file]: A file that has been opened with a statement of the form Open "*filespec*" For Binary As #*n* is regarded simply as a sequence of characters occupying positions 1, 2, 3, ... At any time, a specific location in the file is designated as the "current position." The Seek statement can be used to set the current position. Collections of consecutive characters are written to and read from the file beginning at the current position with Put and Get statements, respectively. After a Put or Get statement is executed, the position following the last position accessed becomes the new current position.

[color]: Numbers written in base 16 are referred to as hexadecimal numbers. They are written with the digits 0, 1, 2, 3, 4, 5, 6, 7, 8, 9, A (=10), B (=11), C (=12), D (=13), E (=14), and F (=15). A hexadecimal number such as *rst* corresponds to the decimal integer $t + 16 * s + 16^2 * r$. Each color in Visual Basic is identified by a long integer (usually expressed as a hexadecimal number of the form &H...&) and referred to as an RGB color number. This number specifies the amounts of red, green, and blue combined to produce the color. The amount of any color is a relative quantity, with 0 representing none of the color and 255 representing the maximum available. Thus, black corresponds to 0 units each of red, green, and blue, and white corresponds to 255 units each of red, green, and blue. The RGB color number corresponding to *r* units of red, *g* units of green, and *b* units of blue is $r + 256 * g + 65536 * b$, which is the value returned by the function RGB(r, g, b). Hexadecimal notation provides a fairly easy means of specifying RGB color numbers. If the amount of red desired is expressed as a two-digit hexadecimal number, *rr*, the amount of green in hexadecimal as *gg*, and the amount of blue in hexadecimal as *bb*, then the RGB color number for this color is &H00*bbggrr*&. For example, the RGB color number for a bright green would come from 255 (FF in hexadecimal) units of green, so the RGB color number in hexadecimal is &H0000FF00&.

[coordinate systems]: The default coordinate system for a form, picture box, or the printer defines the upper-left corner as the point (0, 0). In this coordinate system, the point (x, y) lies x units to the right of and y units below the upper-left corner. The unit of measure in the default coordinate system is a twip. A twip is defined as 1/1440 of an inch (though varying screen sizes may result in 1440 twips not appearing as exactly an inch on the screen). Custom coordinate systems can be created using the Scale method and ScaleMode property.

[date]: Functions dealing with dates and times use the type 7 variant data type. Dates and times are stored as serial dates, double-precision numbers, with the whole part recording the date and the decimal part recording the time. Valid whole parts range from −657434 to 2958465, which correspond to all days from January 1, 100 to December, 31, 9999. A whole part of 0 corresponds to December 30, 1899. All decimal parts are valid, with .0 corresponding to midnight, .25 corresponding to 6 a.m., .5 corresponding to noon, and so on. In general, the decimal equivalent of $sec/86400$ corresponds to sec seconds past midnight. If a given date corresponds to a negative whole part, then times on that day are obtained by adding a negative decimal part to the negative whole part. For example, October, 24, 1898, corresponds to a whole part of −432. A time of 6 p.m. corresponds to .75, so a time of 6 p.m. on 10/24/1898 corresponds to −432 +−.75 = −432.75.

[dynamic vs. static arrays]: Visual Basic uses two methods of storing arrays: dynamic and static. The memory locations for a static array are set aside the instant the program is executed, and this portion of memory may not be freed for any other purpose. The memory locations for a dynamic array are assigned when a particular procedure requests that an array be created (a Dim or ReDim statement is encountered) and *can* be freed for other purposes. Although dynamic arrays are more flexible, static arrays can be accessed faster. Arrays Dimensioned in the (Declarations) section of (General) use static allocation, except for arrays declared using empty parentheses. Arrays created in procedures use dynamic allocation.

[filespec]: The filespec of a file on disk is a string consisting of the letter of the drive, a colon, and the name of the file. If folders are being used, the file name is preceded by the identifying path.

[line label]: Program lines that are the destinations of statements such as GoTo and GoSub are identified by placing a line label at the beginning of the program line or alone on the line proceeding the program line. Line labels may be placed only at the beginning of a line, are named using the same rules as variables, and are followed by a colon. Line numbers may be used in place of line labels, but program readability is greatly improved by using descriptive line labels.

[radians]: The radian system of measurement measures angles in terms of a distance around the circumference of the circle of radius 1. If the vertex of an angle between 0 and 360 degrees is placed at the center of the circle, the length of the arc of the circle contained between the two sides of the angle is the radian measure of the angle. An angle of d degrees has a radian measure of (pi/180) $* d$ radians.

[subroutine]: A subroutine is a sequence of statements beginning with a line label and ending with a Return statement. A subroutine is meant to be branched to by a GoSub statement and is usually placed after an Exit Sub or Exit Function statement at the bottom of a procedure so that it cannot be entered inadvertently.

[variant]: Variant is a generic variable type. Any variable that is used without a type declaration tag ($, %, &, !, #, @) or without being declared as a specific type using an As clause or a Def*Type* statement is treated as a variant variable. A variable of type Variant can hold any type of data. When values are assigned to a variant variable, Visual Basic keeps track of the "type" of data that has been stored. Visual Basic recognizes many types of data: type 0 for "Empty" (nothing yet has been stored in the variable; the default), type 1 for "Null" (the special value Null has been assigned to the variable), type 2 for Integer, type 3 for Long integer, type 4 for Single precision, type 5 for Double precision, type 6 for Currency, type 7 for Date/time, type 8 for String, type 10 for Error, type 11 for Boolean, and type 17 for Byte. A single variant variable may be assigned different data types at different points in a program, although this is usually not a good programming technique. The data assigned to a variant array need not all be of the same type. As a result, a variant array can be used in much the same way as a user-defined type to store related data.

Visual Basic Debugging Tools

Errors in programs are called *bugs* and the process of finding and correcting them is called *debugging*. Since Visual Basic does not discover errors due to faulty logic, they present the most difficulties in debugging. One method of discovering a logical error is by **desk-checking**, that is, tracing the values of variables on paper by writing down their expected value after "mentally executing" each line in the program. Desk checking is rudimentary and highly impractical except for small programs.

Another method of debugging involves placing Print methods at strategic points in the program and displaying the values of selected variables or expressions until the error is detected. After correcting the error, the Print methods are removed. For many programming environments, desk checking and Print methods are the only debugging methods available to the programmer.

The Visual Basic debugger offers an alternative to desk checking and Print methods. It allows you to pause during the execution of your program in order to view and alter values of variables. These values can be accessed through the Immediate, Watch, and Locals windows, known collectively as the three Debug windows.

The Three Program Modes

At any time, a program is in one of three modes—design mode, run mode, or break mode. The current mode is displayed in the Visual Basic title bar.

Title bar during design mode.

Title bar during run mode.

Title bar during break mode.

With the program in design mode, you place controls on a form, set their initial properties, and write code. Run mode is initiated by pressing F5 or the Start button. Break mode is invoked automatically when a run-time error occurs. While a program is running, you can manually invoke Break mode by pressing Ctrl+Break, clicking on Break in the Run menu, or clicking on the Break icon ▌▌ (located between the Start and Stop icons). While the program is in break mode, you can use the Immediate window to examine and change values of variables and object settings. When you enter Break mode, the Start button on the Toolbar changes to a Continue button. You can click on it to proceed with the execution of the program.

The Immediate Window

You can set the focus to the Immediate window by clicking on it (if visible), by pressing Ctrl+G, or by choosing "Immediate Window" from the View menu. Although the Immediate window can be used during design time, it is primarily used in Break mode. When you type a statement into the Immediate window and press the Enter key, the statement is executed at once. A statement of the form

```
Print expression
```

displays the value of the expression on the next line of the Immediate window. In Figure D.1, three statements have been executed. (When the program was interrupted, the variable *numVar* had the value 10.) In addition to displaying values of expressions, the Immediate window also is commonly used to change the value of a variable with an assignment statement before continuing to run the program. **Note 1:** Any statement in the Immediate window can be executed again by placing the cursor anywhere on the statement and pressing the Enter key. **Note 2:** In earlier versions of Visual Basic the Immediate window was called the Debug window.

Figure D.1 Three Print statements executed in the Immediate window.

The Watch Window

You can designate an expression as a watch expression or a break expression. Break expressions are of two varieties: those that cause a break when they become true and those that cause a break when they change value. At any time, the Watch window shows the current values of all watch and break expressions. In the Watch window of Figure D.2, the type of each expression is specified by an icon as shown in Table D.1.

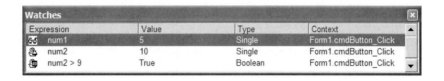

Watches			
Expression	Value	Type	Context
num1	5	Single	Form1.cmdButton_Click
num2	10	Single	Form1.cmdButton_Click
num2 > 9	True	Boolean	Form1.cmdButton_Click

Figure D.2 The Watch window.

Icon	Type of expression
	Watch expression
	Break when expression is true
	Break when expression has changed

Table D.1 Watch type icons.

The easiest way to add an expression to the Watch window is to right-click on a variable in the code window and then click on "Add Watch" to call up an Add Watch dialog box. You can then alter the expression in the Expression text box and select one of the three Watch types. To delete an expression from the Watch window, right-click on the expression and then click on "Delete Watch." To alter an expression in the Watch window, right-click on the expression and click on "Edit Watch."

The Locals Window

The Locals window, invoked by clicking on "Locals Window" in the View menu, is a feature that was new to Visual Basic in version 5.0. This window automatically displays the names, values, and types of all variables in the current procedure. See Figure D.3. You can alter the values of variables at any time. In addition, you can examine and change properties of controls through the Locals window.

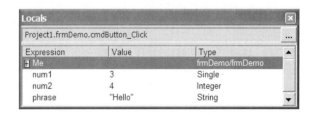

Figure D.3 The Locals window.

Stepping Through a Program

The program can be executed one statement at a time, with each press of an appropriate function key executing a statement. This process is called **stepping** (or **stepping into**). After each step, values of variables, expressions, and conditions can be displayed in the debugging windows, and the values of variables can be changed.

When a procedure is called, the lines of the procedure can be executed one at a time, referred to as **stepping into** the procedure, or the entire procedure can be executed at once, referred to as **stepping over** a procedure. A step over a procedure is called a **procedure step**. In addition, you can execute the remainder of the current procedure at once, referred to as **stepping out** of the procedure.

Stepping begins with the first line of the first event procedure invoked by the user. Program execution normally proceeds in order through the statements in the event procedure. However, at any time the programmer can specify the next statement to be executed.

As another debugging tool, Visual Basic allows the programmer to specify certain lines as **breakpoints**. Then, when the program is run, execution will stop at the first breakpoint reached. The programmer can then either step through the program or continue execution to the next breakpoint.

The tasks discussed previously are summarized below, along with a means to carry out each task. The tasks invoked with function keys can also be produced from the menu bar.

Step Into:	Press F8
Step Over:	Press Shift+F8
Step Out:	Press Ctrl+Shift+F8
Set a breakpoint:	Move cursor to line, press F9
Remove a breakpoint:	Move cursor to line containing breakpoint, press F9
Clear all breakpoints:	Press Ctrl+Shift+F9
Set next statement:	Press Ctrl+F9
Continue execution to next breakpoint or the end of the program:	Press F5
Run to cursor:	Press Ctrl+F8

Six Walkthroughs

The following walkthroughs use the debugging tools with the programming structures covered in Chapters 3, 4, 5, and 6.

Stepping Through an Elementary Program: Chapter 3

The following walkthrough demonstrates several capabilities of the debugger.

1. Create a form with a command button (cmdButton) and a picture box (picBox). Set the AutoRedraw property of the picture box to True. (During the debugging process, the entire form will be covered. The True setting for AutoRedraw prevents the contents of the picture box from being erased.)

2. Double-click on the command button and enter the following event procedure:

```
Private Sub cmdButton_Click()
  Dim num As Single
  picBox.Cls
  num = Val(InputBox("Enter a number:"))
  num = num + 1
  num = num + 2
  picBox.Print num
End Sub
```

3. Press F8, click the command button, and press F8 again. A yellow arrow points to the picBox.Cls statement, and the statement is highlighted in yellow. This indicates that the picBox.Cls statement is the next statement to be executed. (Pressing F8 is referred to as stepping. You can also step to the next statement of a program with the Step Into option from the Debug menu.)

4. Press F8. The picBox.Cls statement is executed and the statement involving InputBox is designated as the next statement to be executed.

5. Press F8 to execute the statement containing InputBox. Respond to the request by typing 5 and clicking the OK button.

6. Press F8 again to execute the statement num = num + 1.

7. Let the mouse hover over any occurrence of the variable *num* for a second or so. The current value of the variable will be displayed in a small box. See Figure D.4.

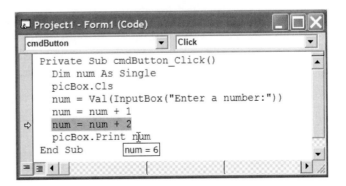

Figure D.4 Obtaining the value of a variable.

8. Click on the End icon to end the program.

9. Move the cursor to the line

```
num = num + 2
```

and then press F9. A red dot appears to the left of the line and the line is displayed in white text on a red background. This indicates that the line is a breakpoint. (Pressing F9 is referred to as toggling a breakpoint. You also can toggle a breakpoint with the Toggle Breakpoint option from the Debug menu.)

10. Press F5 and click on the command button. Respond to the request by entering 5. The program executes the first three lines and stops at the breakpoint. The breakpoint line is not executed.

11. Open the Immediate window by pressing Ctrl+G. If necessary, clear the contents of the window. Type the statement

```
Print "num ="; num
```

into the Immediate window, and then press Enter to execute the statement. The appearance of "num = 6" on the next line of the Immediate window confirms that the breakpoint line was not executed.

12. Press F7 to return to the Code window.

13. Move the cursor to the line num = num + 1 and then press Ctrl+F9 to specify that line as the next line to be executed. (You can also use the Set Next Statement option from the Debug menu.)

14. Press F8 to execute the selected line.

15. Press Ctrl+G to return to the Immediate window. Move the cursor to the line containing the Print method and press Enter to confirm that the value of *num* is now 7, and then return to the Code window.

16. Move the cursor to the breakpoint line and press F9 to deselect the line as a breakpoint.

17. Press F5 to execute the remaining lines of the program. Observe that the value displayed in the picture box is 9.

General Comment: As you step through a program, the form will become hidden from view. However, the form will be represented by a button on the Windows taskbar at the bottom of the screen. The button will contain the name of the form. You can see the form at any time by clicking on its button.

Stepping Through a Program Containing a General Procedure: Chapter 4

The following walkthrough uses the single-stepping feature of the debugger to trace the flow through procedures.

1. Create a form with a command button (cmdButton) and a picture box (picBox). Set the AutoRedraw property of the picture box to True. Then enter the following two procedures:

```
Private Sub cmdButton_Click()
  Dim p As Single, b As Single
  picBox.Cls
  p = 1000     'Principal
  Call GetBalance(p, b)
  picBox.Print "The balance is"; b
End Sub

Private Sub GetBalance(prin As Single, bal As Single)
  'Calculate the balance at 5% interest rate
  Dim interest As Single
  interest = .05 * prin
  bal = prin + interest
End Sub
```

2. Press F8, click the command button, and press F8 again. The picBox.Cls statement is highlighted to indicate that it is the next statement to be executed.

3. Press F8 two more times. The Call statement is highlighted.

4. Press F8 once and observe that the heading of the Sub procedure GetBalance is now highlighted in yellow.

5. Press F8 three times to execute the assignment statements and to highlight the End Sub statement. (Notice that the Dim and Rem statements were skipped.)

6. Press F8 and notice that the yellow highlight has moved back to the cmdButton_Click event procedure and is on the statement immediately following the Call statement.

7. Click on the End icon to end the program.

8. Repeat Steps 2 and 3, and then press Shift+F8 to step over the procedure GetBalance. The procedure has been executed in its entirety.

9. Click on the End icon to end the program.

Communication Between Arguments and Parameters

The following walkthrough uses the Locals window to monitor the values of arguments and parameters during the execution of a program.

1. If you have not already done so, type the preceding program into the Code window.

2. Press F8 and click on the command button.

3. Select "Locals Window" from the View window. Notice that the variables from the cmdButton_Click event procedure appear in the Locals window.

4. Press F8 three more times to highlight the Call statement. Notice that the value of the variable *p* has changed.

5. Press F8 to call the Sub procedure. Notice that the variables displayed in the Locals window are now those of the procedure GetBalance.

6. Press F8 three times to execute the procedure.

7. Press F8 to return to cmdButton_Click event procedure. Notice that the value of the variable *b* has inherited the value of the variable *bal*.

8. Click on the End icon to end the program.

Stepping Through Programs Containing Selection Structures: Chapter 5

If Blocks

The following walkthrough demonstrates how an If statement evaluates a condition to determine whether to take an action.

1. Create a form with a command button (cmdButton) and a picture box (picBox). Set the AutoRedraw property of the picture box to True. Then open the Code window and enter the following procedure:

```
Private Sub cmdButton_Click()
   Dim wage As Single
   picBox.Cls
   wage = Val(InputBox("wage:"))
   If wage < 5.15 Then
       picBox.Print "Below minimum wage."
     Else
       picBox.Print "Wage Ok."
   End If
End Sub
```

2. Press F8, click the command button, and press F8 twice. The picBox.Cls statement will be highlighted and executed, and then the statement containing InputBox will be highlighted.

3. Press F8 once to execute the statement containing InputBox. Type a wage of 3.25, and press the Enter key. The If statement is highlighted, but has not been executed.

4. Press F8 once, and notice that the highlight for the current statement has jumped to the statement `picBox.Print "Below minimum wage."` Because the condition "wage < 5.15" is true, the action associated with Then was selected.

5. Press F8 to execute the picBox.Print statement. Notice that Else is skipped and End If is highlighted.

6. Press F8 again. We are through with the If block, and the statement following the If block, End Sub, is highlighted.

7. Click on the End icon to end the program.

8. If desired, try stepping through the program again with 5.75 entered as the wage. Since the condition "wage < 5.15" will be false, the Else action will be executed instead of the Then action.

Select Case Blocks

The following walkthrough illustrates how a Select Case block uses the selector to choose from among several actions.

1. Create a form with a command button (cmdButton) and a picture box (picBox). Set the AutoRedraw property of the picture box to True. Then open the Code window and enter the following procedure:

```
Private Sub cmdButton_Click()
  Dim age As Single, price As Single
  picBox.Cls
  age = Val(InputBox("age:"))
  Select Case age
    Case Is < 12
      price = 0
    Case Is < 18
      price = 3.5
    Case Is> >= 65
      price = 4
    Case Else
      price = 5.5
  End Select
  picBox.Print "Your ticket price is ";FormatCurrency(price)
End Sub
```

2. Press F8, click on the command button, and press F8 twice. The picBox.Cls statement will be highlighted and executed, and then the statement containing InputBox will be highlighted.

3. Press F8 once to execute the statement containing InputBox. Type an age of 8 and press the Enter key. The Select Case statement is highlighted, but has not been executed.

4. Press F8 twice, and observe that the action associated with "Case Is < 12" is highlighted.

5. Press F8 once to execute the assignment statement. Notice that End Select is highlighted. This demonstrates that when more than one Case clause is true, only the first is acted upon.

6. Click on the End icon to end the program.

7. If desired, step through the program again, entering a different age and predicting which Case clause will be acted upon. (Some possible ages to try are 12, 14, 18, 33, and 67.)

Stepping Through a Program Containing a Do Loop: Chapter 6

Do Loops

The following walkthrough demonstrates use of the Immediate window to monitor the value of a condition in a Do loop that searches for a name.

1. Access Windows Notepad, enter the following line of data, and save the file on the A drive with the name DATA.TXT

```
Bert, Ernie, Grover, Oscar
```

2. Return to Visual Basic. Create a form with a command button (cmdButton) and a picture box (picBox). Set the AutoRedraw property of the picture box to True. Then double-click on the command button and enter the following procedure:

```
Private Sub cmdButton_Click()
  'Look for a specific name
  Dim searchName As String, nom As String
  picBox.Cls
  searchName = InputBox("Name:")  'Name to search for in list
  Open "A:DATA.TXT" For Input As #1
  nom = ""
  Do While (nom <> searchName) And Not EOF(1)
    Input #1, nom
  Loop
  Close #1
  If nom = searchName Then
      picBox.Print nom
    Else
      picBox.Print "Name not found"
  End If
End Sub
```

3. Press F8 and click on the command button. The heading of the event procedure is highlighted in yellow.

4. Double-click on the variable *searchName*, click the right mouse button, click on "Add Watch," and click on OK. The variable *searchName* has been added to the Watch window.

5. Repeat Step 4 for the variable *nom*.

6. Drag the mouse across the words

```
(nom <> searchName) And Not EOF(1)
```

to highlight them. Then click the right mouse button, click on "Add Watch," and click on OK. Widen the Watch window as much as possible in order to see the entire expression.

7. Press F8 three more times to execute the picBox.Cls statement and the statement containing InputBox. Enter the name "Ernie" at the prompt.

8. Press F8 repeatedly until the entire event procedure has been executed. Pause after each keypress and notice how the values of the expressions in the Watch window change.

9. Click on the End icon to end the program.

To Selected Odd-Numbered Exercises

CHAPTER 1

Exercises 1.2

1. The program is busy carrying out a task; please wait.

3. Double-clicking means clicking the left mouse button twice in quick succession.

5. Cursor

7. Starting with an uppercase W, Windows refers to Microsoft's Windows program. Starting with a lowercase w, windows refers to the rectangular regions of the screen in which different programs are displayed.

9. Double-click on the Notepad icon.

11. A toggle is a key like the Ins, NumLock, and CapsLock keys that changes keyboard operations back and forth between two different typing modes.

13. PgDn

15. Backspace

17. NumLock

19. CapsLock

21. End

23. Shift

25. Alt/F/P

27. Ctrl+Home

29. Alt

31. Alt

33. Alt/F/A

35. End/Enter

Exercises 1.3

1. A file name cannot contain a question mark.

3. Forward slashes (/) are not allowed in filespecs. Use a backslash (\) to separate folders in a filespec.

5. 4

7. 4 (Answers may vary)

9. Files are sorted by size.

11. Files are sorted by the date they were last modified.

13. Create a new directory called TEMP on your hard drive and then copy the file from the first diskette to TEMP. Place the second diskette in the diskette drive and then copy the file from TEMP to the second diskette. Delete the file and TEMP from the hard drive.

CHAPTER 3

Exercises 3.1

1. Command buttons appear to be pushed down and then let up when they are clicked.

3. After a command button is clicked, its border becomes boldfaced, and a rectangle of small dots is visible inside the border.

(In Exercises 7 through 27, begin by pressing Alt/F/N to create a new form.)

7. Click on the Properties window or Press F4 to activate the Properties window.
Click on the Caption property.
Type in "CHECKING ACCOUNT".

9. Double-click the text box icon in the Toolbox.
Activate the Properties window and highlight the BackColor property.

Click on the down-arrow to the right of the Settings box.
Click on the Palette tab.
Click on the desired yellow in the palette.
Click on the Text property.
Click on the Settings box and delete "Text1".
Click on the form to see the empty, yellow text box.

11. Double-click on the text box icon in the Toolbox.

    Activate the Properties window and highlight the Text property.

    Type the requested sentence.

    Highlight the MultiLine property.

    Double-click on the highlighted MultiLine property to change its value to True.

    Highlight the Alignment property.

    Double-click twice on the highlighted Alignment property to change its value to 2-Center.

    Click on the form.

    Use the mouse to resize the text box so that the sentence occupies three lines.

13. Double-click on the text box icon in the Toolbox.

    Activate the Properties window and highlight the Text property.

    Type "VISUAL BASIC".

    Highlight the Font property.

    Click on the ellipsis to the right of the Settings box.

    Click on "Courier" in the Font box and click OK.

    Resize the text box to accommodate its text.

    Click on the form to see the resulting text box.

15. Double-click on the command button icon in the Toolbox.

    Activate the Properties window and highlight the Caption property.

    Type "PUSH".

    Highlight the Font property and click on the ellipsis.

    Click on Italic in the Font Style box.

    Click on 24 in the Size box.

    Click OK.

    Click on the form to see the resulting command button.

    Resize the command button to accommodate its caption.

17. Double-click on the command button icon in the Toolbox.

    Activate the Properties window and highlight the Caption property.

    Type "PUS&H".

    Click on the form to see the resulting command button.

19. Double-click on the label icon in the Toolbox.

    Activate the Properties window and highlight the Caption property.

    Type "ALIAS".

    Click on the form to see the resulting label.

21. Double-click on the label icon in the Toolbox.

    Activate the Properties window and highlight the Alignment property.

    Double-click twice on the highlighted Alignment property to change its value to "2-Center".

    Highlight the Caption property.

    Type "ALIAS".

    Double-click on the BorderStyle property to change its value to "1–Fixed Single".

    Highlight the Font property and click on the ellipsis.

    Click on Italic in the Font Style box and click OK.

    Click on the form to see the resulting label.

23. Double-click on the label icon in the Toolbox.

    Activate the Properties window and highlight the Font property.

    Click on the ellipsis to the right of the Settings box.

    Click on Wingdings in the Font box.

    Click on the largest size available (72) in the Size list box.

    Click OK.

    Highlight the Caption property.

    Change the caption setting to a less than sign by pressing <.

    Click on the label and enlarge it.

    (If you didn't know that the less than symbol corresponded to a diskette in the Wingdings font, you could double-click on the diskette character in the Character Map, click the Copy button, highlight the Caption property of the label, and press Ctrl+V. The less than character would appear in the Caption settings box.)

25. Double-click on the picture box icon in the Toolbox.

    Activate the Properties window and highlight the BackColor property.

    Click on the down-arrow to the right of the Settings box.

    Click on the Palette tab.

    Click on the desired yellow in the palette.

    Click on the form to see the yellow picture box.

27. Double-click on the picture box icon in the Toolbox.

    Increase the size of the picture box so that it can easily hold two standard size command buttons.

    Click (do NOT double-click) on the command button icon in the Toolbox.

    Move the mouse to the desired location in the picture box where you want the upper-left corner of the first command button to be.

    Press and hold the left mouse button and drag the mouse down and to the right until the rectangle attains the size desired for the first command button

    Release the left mouse button.

    Repeat the preceding four steps (starting with clicking on the command button icon in the Toolbox) to place the second command button on the picture box.

29. Create a new project. Change the form's caption to "Dynamic Duo". Place two command buttons on the form. Enter as the caption of the first "&Batman" and of the second "&Robin". Increase the font size for both command buttons to 14.

31. Create a new project. Change the form's caption to "Fill in the Blank". Place a label, a text box, and another label on the form at appropriate locations. Change the caption of the first label to "Toto, I don't think we're in" and of the second label to "A Quote from the Wizard of Oz". Delete "Text1" from the Text property of the text box. Resize and position the labels as needed.

33. Create a new project. Change the form's caption to "An Uncle's Advice". Place a picture box on the form and increase its size to provide plenty of space. Place on the picture box five labels and three command buttons. Change the captions of each label to the appropriate text. Change the BorderStyle property of the last label to "1–Fixed Single". Change the captions of the command buttons to "1", "2", and "3". Resize and position the labels and command buttons as is appropriate. Finally, the size of the picture box and form can be adjusted down as appropriate.

35. Create a new project. Change the form's caption to "Picture Box." Place a picture box and a label on the form. Change the label's Caption property to the sentence shown. Change the label's BackColor property to white, and its Font Size property to 14. Access the picture box's Picture property and select the picture file PICBOX.BMP from the Pictures folder on the CD accompanying this textbook.

Exercises 3.2

1. The word Hello.

3. The word Hello in italic letters.

5. The text box vanishes; nothing is visible.

7. The word Hello in green letters.

9. The word Hello in big, fixed-width letters.

11. The name of the control has been given but not the property being assigned. frmHi ="Hello" needs to be changed to frmHi.Caption = "Hello".

13. Text boxes do not have a Caption property. Information to be displayed in a text box must be assigned to the Text property.

15. Only 0 and 1 are valid values for the BorderStyle property of a label.

17. `lblTwo.Caption = "E.T. phone home."`

19. `txtBox.ForeColor = vbRed`
`txtBox.Text = "The stuff that dreams are made of."`

21. `txtBox.Text = ""`

23. `lblTwo.Visible = False`

25. `picBox.BackColor = vbBlue`

27. `txtBox.Font.Bold = True`
`txtBox.Font.Italic = True`
`txtBox.Text = "Hello"`

29. `cmdButton.SetFocus`

31. `lblTwo.BorderStyle = 1`
`lblTwo.Alignment = 2`

37.
```
Private Sub cmdLeft_Click()
   lblShow.Alignment = 0
   lblShow.Caption = "Left Justify"
End Sub

Private Sub cmdCenter_Click()
   lblShow.Alignment = 2
   lblShow.Caption = "Center"
End Sub

Private Sub cmdRight_Click()
   lblShow.Alignment = 1
   lblShow.Caption = "Right Justify"
End Sub
```

41. The size of the text box is changed. When the left- or right-arrow keys are pressed, the right side of the text box moves to the left or right accordingly. When the up- or down-arrow keys are pressed, the bottom side of the text box moves up or down accordingly.

43. The button is centered vertically on the form.

45. (a) All three text boxes move to the left in unison.
   (b) All three text boxes become narrower by the same amount.
   (c) The text on all three text boxes changes to Blue.

39.
```
Private Sub cmdRed_Click()
   txtShow.BackColor = vbRed
End Sub

Private Sub cmdBlue_Click()
   txtShow.BackColor = vbBlue
End Sub

Private Sub cmdWhite_Click()
   txtShow.ForeColor = vbWhite
End Sub

Private Sub cmdYellow_Click()
   txtShow.ForeColor = vbYellow
End Sub
```

41.
```
Private Sub txtLife_GotFocus()
   txtQuote.Text = "I like life, it's something to do."
End Sub

Private Sub txtFuture_GotFocus()
   txtQuote.Text = "The future isn't what it used to be."
End Sub

Private Sub txtTruth_GotFocus()
   txtQuote.Text = "Tell the truth and run."
End Sub
```

43.

Object	Property	Setting
cmdLarge	Caption	Large
cmdSmall	Caption	Small
cmdBold	Caption	Bold
cmdItalics	Caption	Italic
txtShow	Text	Hello World.

```
Private Sub cmdLarge_Click()
   txtShow.Font.Size = 18
End Sub

Private Sub cmdSmall_Click()
   txtShow.Font.Size = 8
End Sub

Private Sub cmdBold_Click()
   txtShow.Font.Bold = True
   txtShow.Font.Italic = False
End Sub

Private Sub cmdItalics_Click()
   txtShow.Font.Italic = True
   txtShow.Font.Bold = False
End Sub
```

45.

Object	Property	Setting
frmEx45	Caption	Face
lblFace	Font.Name	Wingdings
	Caption	K
	Font.Size	24
cmdVanish	Caption	Vanish
cmdReappear	Caption	Reappear

```
Private Sub cmdVanish_Click()
  lblFace.Visible = False
End Sub


Private Sub cmdReappear_Click()
  lblFace.Visible = True
End Sub
```

47.

Object	Property	Setting
cmdPush1	Caption	Push Me
cmdPush2	Caption	Push Me
cmdPush3	Caption	Push Me
cmdPush4	Caption	Push Me

```
Private Sub cmdPush1_Click()
  cmdPush1.Visible = False
  cmdPush2.Visible = True
  cmdPush3.Visible = True
  cmdPush4.Visible = True
End Sub

Private Sub cmdPush2_Click()
  cmdPush1.Visible = True
  cmdPush2.Visible = False
  cmdPush3.Visible = True
  cmdPush4.Visible = True
End Sub

Private Sub cmdPush3_Click()
  cmdPush1.Visible = True
  cmdPush2.Visible = True
  cmdPush3.Visible = False
  cmdPush4.Visible = True
End Sub

Private Sub cmdPush4_Click()
  cmdPush1.Visible = True
  cmdPush2.Visible = True
  cmdPush3.Visible = True
  cmdPush4.Visible = False
End Sub
```

Exercises 3.3

1. 12

3. .03125

5. 8

7. 3E+15

9. 4E–20

11. Not Valid

13. Valid

15. Not valid

17. 10

19. 16

21. 9

23.
```
Private Sub cmdCompute_Click()
  picOutput.Cls
  picOutput.Print 7 * 8 + 5
End Sub
```

25.
```
Private Sub cmdCompute_Click()
  picOutput.Cls
  picOutput.Print .055 * 20
End Sub
```

27.
```
Private Sub cmdCompute_Click()
  picOutput.Cls
  picOutput.Print 17 * (3 + 162)
End Sub
```

29.

x	y
–	–
2	–
2	6
11	6
11	6
11	6
11	7
–	–

31. 6

33. 1 2 3 4
11

35. 1
64

37. 27 12

39. The third line should read c = a + b

41. The first line should not contain a comma. The second line should not contain a dollar sign.

43. picOutput.Print 1; 2; 1 + 2

45.
```
Private Sub cmdCompute_Click()
  picOutput.Cls
  revenue = 98456
  costs = 45000
  profit = revenue - costs
  picOutput.Print profit
End Sub
```

47.
```
Private Sub cmdCompute_Click()
    picOutput.Cls
    price = 19.95
    discountPercent = 30
    markDown = (discountPercent / 100) * price
    price = price - markDown
    picOutput.Print price
End Sub
```

49.
```
Private Sub cmdCompute_Click()
    picOutput.Cls
    balance = 100
    balance = balance + balance * .05
    balance = balance + balance * .05
    balance = balance + balance * .05
    picOutput.Print balance
End Sub
```

51.
```
Private Sub cmdCompute_Click()
    picOutput.Cls
    balance = 100
    balance = balance * (1.05 ^ 10)
    picOutput.Print balance
End Sub
```

53.
```
Private Sub cmdCompute_Click()
    picOutput.Cls
    acres = 30
    yieldPerAcre = 18
    corn = yieldPerAcre * acres
    picOutput.Print corn
End Sub
```

55.
```
Private Sub cmdCompute_Click()
    picOutput.Cls
    distance = 233
    elapsedTime = 7 - 2
    averageSpeed = distance / elapsedTime
    picOutput.Print averageSpeed
End Sub
```

57.
```
Private Sub cmdCompute_Click()
    picOutput.Cls
    waterPerPersonPerDay = 1600
    people = 300000000
    days = 365
    waterUsed = waterPerPersonPerDay * people * days
    picOutput.Print waterUsed
End Sub
```

Exercises 3.4

1.
```
Hello
1234
```

3. `12 12 TWELVE`

5. `A ROSE IS A ROSE IS A ROSE`

7. `  1234 Main Street`

9. `"We're all in this alone."  Lily Tomlin`

11.
```
 17 2
-20 16
```

13. `The number of digits in 3567 is 4`

15. The variable phone should be declared as type String, not Single.

17. The sentence in the second line should be enclosed by quotation marks.

19. End is a keyword and cannot be used as a variable name.

21.
```
Private Sub txtBox_KeyPress(KeyAscii As Integer)
    KeyAscii = Asc("*")
End Sub
```

23.
```
Private Sub cmdDisplay_Click()
    picOutput.Cls
    Dim firstName As String, middleName As String
    Dim lastName As String, yearOfBirth As Integer
    firstName = "Thomas"
    middleName = "Alva"
    lastName = "Edison"
    yearOfBirth = 1847
    picOutput.Print firstName; " "; middleName; " ";
    picOutput.Print lastName; ","; yearOfBirth
End Sub
```

25.
```
Private Sub cmdDisplay_Click()
    picOutput.Cls
    Dim publisher As String
    publisher = "Prentice Hall, Inc."
    picOutput.Print Chr(169); " "; publisher
End Sub
```

27.
```
Private Sub cmdClearX_Click()
    txtNum1.Text = ""
End Sub

Private Sub cmdClearY_Click()
    txtNum2.Text = ""
End Sub

Private Sub cmdCompute_Click()
    picSum.Print Val(txtNum1.Text) + Val(txtNum2.Text)
End Sub

Private Sub cmdClearSum_Click()
    picSum.Cls
End Sub
```

29.
```
Private Sub cmdCompute_Click()
    lblNumMiles.Caption = Str(Val(txtNumSec.Text) / 5)
End Sub
```

31.
```
Private Sub cmdCompute_Click()
    Dim cycling As Single, running As Single
    Dim swimming As Single, pounds As Single
    picWtLoss.Cls
    cycling = Val(txtCycle.Text)
    running = Val(txtRun.Text)
    swimming = Val(txtSwim.Text)
    pounds = (200*cycling + 475*running + 275*swimming) / 3500
    picWtLoss.Print pounds; "pounds were lost."
End Sub
```

33.

Object	Property	Setting
frmEx33	Caption	Net Income
lblRevenue	Caption	Revenue
txtRevenue	Text	(blank)
lblExpenses	Caption	Expenses
txtExpenses	Text	(blank)
cmdCompute	Caption	Display Net Income
picOutput		

```
Private Sub cmdCompute_Click()
  Dim income As Single
  picOutput.Cls
  income = Val(txtRevenue.Text) - Val(txtExpenses.Text)
  picOutput.Print "The company's net income is"; income
End Sub
```

35.

Object	Property	Setting
frmEx35	Caption	Price-to-Earnings Ratio
lblPrice	Caption	Price
txtPrice	Text	(blank)
lblEarnings	Caption	Earnings
txtEarnings	Text	(blank)
cmdCompute	Caption	Compute PER
picOutput		

```
Private Sub cmdCompute_Click()
  Dim per As Single
  picOutput.Cls
  per = Val(txtPrice.Text) / Val(txtEarnings.Text)
  picOutput.Print "The price-to-earnings ratio is"; per
End Sub
```

37.

Object	Property	Setting
frmEx37	Caption	Grass Seed
lblOunces	Caption	Ounces of seed recommended for 2000 square feet of lawn
txtOunces	Text	(blank)
lblLawnWidth	Caption	Width of lawn in feet
txtLawnWidth	Text	(blank)
lblLawnLength	Caption	Length of lawn in feet
txtLawnLength	Text	(blank)
cmdCompute	Caption	&Display Seed Needed
picOutput		

```
Private Sub cmdCompute_Click()
  Dim lbSeedPerFt As Single, area As Single, grassSeed As Single
  picOutput.Cls
  lbSeedPerFt = (Val(txtOunces.Text) / 16) / 2000
  area = Val(txtLawnWidth.Text) * Val(txtLawnLength.Text)
  grassSeed = lbSeedPerFt * area
  picOutput.Print grassSeed; "pounds of grass seed are needed."
End Sub
```

39.

Object	Property	Setting
cmdIncrement	Caption	Increment
lblCounter	Caption	0

```
Private Sub cmdIncrement_Click()
  lblCounter.Caption = Str(Val(lblCounter.Caption) + 1)
End Sub
```

41.

Object	Property	Setting
frmEx41	Caption	Tipping
lblAmount	Caption	Amount of bill:
txtAmount	Text	(blank)
lblPercentTip	Caption	Percentage Tip:
txtPercentTip	Text	(blank)
cmdComputeTip	Caption	&Compute Tip
picOutput		

```
Private Sub cmdComputeTip_Click()
  picOutput.Cls
  picOutput.Print "The tip is"; Val(txtAmount.Text) * Val(txtPercentTip.Text) / 100; "dollars."
End Sub
```

Exercises 3.5

1. 16

3. baseball

5. Age: 20

7. setup

9. The White House has 132 rooms.

11. 1 OneTwo 2
  2
  1

13. Harvard Universty is 367 years old.

15. You might win 180 dollars.

17. Hello John Jones

19. 1 one   won

21. one   two

23. 1234567890
        5

25. 1234567890
    one two

27. 12345678901234
    one

              two

29. The Input #1 statement will assign "John Smith" to str1, leaving nothing left to assign to str2. An "Input past end of file" error will occur.

31. Each line in the file consists of three items, but the Input #1 statements are reading just two. As a result, the second Input#1 statement will assign the numeric data 102 to the string variable *building* and 0 to *ht*. This is not what was intended.

33. The response is to be used as a number, so the input from the user should not contain commas. With the given user response, the value in the variable statePop will be 8.

35. It should be "Printer.Font.Name". Also, the name of the font to the right of the equal sign must be surrounded by quotes.

37. Commas cannot be used to format the caption of a label. Also, the value of the caption must be surrounded by quotation marks. The programmer might have intended

```
lblTwo.Caption = " 1          2"
```

39. When assigning properties of the form, the correct object name is Form1 (or whatever the form is named), not Form. Also, Tab(5) and semicolons can only be used with a Print method.

41.

category	amount	total
(undefined)	(undefined)	(undefined)
""	(undefined)	(undefined)
""	0	(undefined)
""	0	0
""	0	0
"phone"	35.25	0
"phone"	35.25	35.25
"postage"	14.75	35.25
"postage"	14.75	50
"postage"	14.75	50
"postage	14.75	50
(undefined)	(undefined)	(undefined)

43.
```
Private Sub cmdDisplay_Click()
    picOutput.Cls
    Dim major As String, percent01 As Single, percent02 As Single
    Open "MAJORS.TXT" For Input As #1
    Input #1, major, percent01, percent02
    picOutput.Print "The change in the percentage of college freshmen who ";
    picOutput.Print "intended to major in "; major; " was "; _
                    percent02 - percent01
    Input #1, major, percent01, percent02
    picOutput.Print "The change in the percentage of college freshmen who ";
    picOutput.Print "intended to major in "; major; " was "; _
                    percent02 - percent01
    Close #1
End Sub
```

45.
```
Private Sub cmdDisplay_Click()
    picOutput.Cls
    Dim begOfYearPrice As Single, endOfYearPrice As Single, percentIncrease As Single
    begOfYearPrice = 200
    endOfYearPrice = Val(InputBox("Enter price at the end of the year:"))
    percentIncrease = 100 * (endOfYearPrice - begOfYearPrice) / begOfYearPrice
    picOutput.Print "The percent increase for the year is"; percentIncrease
End Sub
```

47. `MsgBox "The future isn't what it used to be."`

49.
```
Private Sub cmdSummarize_Click()
    Dim account As String, beginningBalance As Single
    Dim deposits As Single, withdrawals As Single
    Dim endOfMonth As Single, total As Single
    'Report checking account activity
    picReport.Cls
    Open "3-5-E49.TXT" For Input As #1
    '1st account
    Input #1, account, beginningBalance, deposits, withdrawals
    endOfMonth = beginningBalance + deposits - withdrawals
    total = endOfMonth
    picReport.Print "Monthly balance for account "; account; " is $"; endOfMonth
    '2nd account
    Input #1, account, beginningBalance, deposits, withdrawals
    endOfMonth = beginningBalance + deposits - withdrawals
    total = total + endOfMonth
    picReport.Print "Monthly balance for account "; account; " is $"; endOfMonth
```

```
        '3rd account
        Input #1, account, beginningBalance, deposits, withdrawals
        endOfMonth = beginningBalance + deposits - withdrawals
        total = total + endOfMonth
        picReport.Print "Monthly balance for account "; account; " is $"; endOfMonth
        picReport.Print "Total for all accounts is $"; total
        Close #1
    End Sub
51. Private Sub cmdComputeAvg_Click()
        Dim socNmb As String, exam1 As Single, exam2 As Single, exam3 As Single
        Dim final As Single, average As Single, total As Single
        'Compute semester averages
        picOutput.Cls
        Open "3-5-E51.TXT" For Input As #1
        '1st student
        Input #1, socNmb, exam1, exam2, exam3, final
        average = (exam1 + exam2 + exam3 + final * 2) / 5
        total = average
        picOutput.Print "Semester average for "; socNmb; " is"; average
        '2nd student
        Input #1, socNmb, exam1, exam2, exam3, final
        average = (exam1 + exam2 + exam3 + final * 2) / 5
        total = total + average
        picOutput.Print "Semester average for "; socNmb; " is"; average
        '3rd student
        Input #1, socNmb, exam1, exam2, exam3, final
        average = (exam1 + exam2 + exam3 + final * 2) / 5
        total = total + average
        picOutput.Print "Semester average for "; socNmb; " is"; average
        picOutput.Print "Class average is"; total / 3
        Close #1
    End Sub
53. Private Sub cmdCompute_Click()
        Dim athlete As String, sport As String
        Dim winnings As Single, endorsements As Single
        'Display a table of sports salaries
        picOutput.Cls
        picOutput.Print , , " Salary or"
        picOutput.Print "Athlete", "Sport", " Winnings", " Endorsements", " Total"
        Open "3-5-E53.TXT" For Input As #1
        Input #1, athlete, sport, winnings, endorsements
        picOutput.Print athlete, sport, winnings, endorsements, winnings + endorsements
        Input #1, athlete, sport, winnings, endorsements
        picOutput.Print athlete, sport, winnings, endorsements, winnings + endorsements
        Input #1, athlete, sport, winnings, endorsements
        picOutput.Print athlete, sport, winnings, endorsements, winnings + endorsements
        Input #1, athlete, sport, winnings, endorsements
        picOutput.Print athlete, sport, winnings, endorsements, winnings + endorsements
        Close #1
    End Sub
55. Private Sub txtPhoneNum_GotFocus()
        MsgBox "Be sure to include the area code!", , ""
    End Sub
57. Private Sub cmdCompute_Click()
        Dim price As Single, quantity As Single, revenue As Single
        picOutput.Cls
        Open "3-5-E57.TXT" For Input As #1
        Input #1, price
        Input #1, quantity
        revenue = price * quantity
        picOutput.Print "The revenue is"; revenue
        Close #1
    End Sub
```

Exercises 3.6

1. MCD'S
3. 10
5. 6
7. 3.128
9. AB
11. e
13. 4
15. 0
17. now
19. 2
21. 3
23. -3
25. 1.67
27. 0
29. Lul
31. ullaby
33. LULLABY
35. 0
37. by
39. 8lab
41. Today is Thu
43. o
45. I guess your answer is yes
47. 1937 YANKEES
49. -12.346

51. 12,345.00
53. 0.1
55. 12345
57. 1.20
59. 12
61. $1,234.50
63. ($1,234,567.00)
65. -$1,234.00
67. $3,200.00
69. 4%
71. -5.000%
73. 10,000.00%
75. 75.0%
77. tomorrow's date
79. Friday, December 31, 1999
81. the current year
83. Manhattan $24.00
85. Name   Salary
    Bill $123,000.00
87. 1234567890
             abcd
89. 1234567890
          1234.559
91. 1234567890
              $25.00

93. The two arguments of Left should be interchanged.

95. Cannot take the square root of a negative number.

97. The second argument of Format must be a string; @@@@@@@ should be "@@@@@@@".

99. The function name Format is missing in front of the parenthesis.

101. Yes

103. No

105. No, the second will have a leading space.

107. Integers from 10 through 19

109. Integers from 1 through 52

111. The 26 lowercase letters a through z

113. 2 * Rnd + 2

115. Int(2 * Rnd)

117. Chr(Int(7 * Rnd) + 65)

119. `'Display an area code from a phone number entered in the form xxx-xxx-xxxx`
```
picOutput.Print Left(txtPhone.Text, 3)
```

121.
```
Private Sub cmdDisplay_Click()
    Dim grad As Integer
    'Display number of graduation tickets
    picOutput.Cls
    grad = Val(InputBox("Enter number of graduates:"))
    picOutput.Print Int(2000 / grad); "tickets will be distributed to each student"
End Sub
```

123.
```
Private Sub cmdDisplay_Click()
    Dim q As Single, h As Single, c As Single
    'Compute optimal inventory size
    q = Val(InputBox("Enter quantity:"))
    h = Val(InputBox("Enter ordering cost:"))
    c = Val(InputBox("Enter storage cost:"))
    picOutput.Print "The optimum inventory size is"; Sqr(2 * q * h / c)
End Sub
```

125.

Object	Property	Setting
frmDOB	Caption	Day of Birth
lblDOB	Caption	Date of Birth (mm-dd-yyyy)
txtDOB	Text	(blank)
cmdDay	Caption	Determine Day of Birth
picOutput		

```
Private Sub cmdDay_Click()
    Dim when As String, comma As Integer
    'Determine day of the week person was born
    when = FormatDateTime(txtDOB.Text, vbLongDate)
    comma = InStr(when, ",")
    picOutput.Print "You were born on a "; Left(when, comma - 1); "."
End Sub
```

127.
```
Private Sub cmdComputeChange_Click()
    Dim cents As Integer, quarters As Integer
    'Quarters in change
    cents = Val(InputBox("Number of cents (between 1 and 99):"))
    quarters = Int(cents / 25)
    picResult.Cls
    picResult.Print "The change will contain"; quarters; "quarters."
End Sub
```

129.

Object	Property	Setting
frmBaseball	Caption	Baseball
lblAtBats	Caption	Times at bat
txtAtBats	Text	(blank)
lblHits	Caption	Hits
txtHits	Text	(blank)
cmdCalculate	Caption	Calculate Batting Average
picAverage		

```
Private Sub cmdCalculate_Click()
    Dim ave As String
    ave = FormatNumber(txtHits / txtAtBats, 3, vbFalse)
    picAverage.Print "Batting average: "; ave
End Sub
```

131.
```
Private Sub cmdFindDigits_Click()
    Dim num As String, ptPos As Integer
    'Determine number of digits before and after the decimal point
    num = InputBox("Enter a number containing a decimal point:")
    ptPos = InStr(num, ".")
    picOutput.Cls
    picOutput.Print "There are"; ptPos - 1; "digits before the decimal point"
    picOutput.Print "and"; Len(num) - ptPos; "digits after the decimal point."
End Sub
```

133.

Object	Property	Setting
frmCompoundInterest	Caption	Compound Interest
lblPrincipal	Caption	Principal
txtPrincipal	Text	(blank)
lblInterestRate	Caption	Interest Rate
txtInterestRate	Text	(blank)
cmdCompute	Caption	Compute Balance
lblBalance	Caption	Balance after 10 years
lblOutput	Caption	(blank)

```
Private Sub cmdCompute_Click()
    Dim principal As Single, intRate As Single, balance As Single
    'Show growth of money in a savings account
    principal = Val(txtPrincipal.Text)
    txtPrincipal.Text = FormatCurrency(principal)
    intRate = Val(txtInterestRate.Text)
    txtInterestRate.Text = FormatPercent(intRate)
    balance = principal * (1 + intRate) ^ 10
    lblOutput.Caption = FormatCurrency(balance)
End Sub
```

```
      Private Sub txtPrincipal_GotFocus()
        txtPrincipal.Text = ""
      End Sub

      Private Sub txtInterestRate_GotFocus()
        txtInterestRate.Text = ""
      End Sub
135.  Private Sub cmdPrintStateData_Click()
        Dim state As String, capital As String
        Dim population As Single, area As Single
        Dim nicePop As String, niceArea As String, niceDens As String
        'State data
        Open "STATES.TXT" For Input As #1
        Printer.Font.Name = "Courier New"
        Printer.Font.Bold = True
        Printer.Print "State"; Tab(12); "Capital"; Tab(24); "Population";
        Printer.Print Tab(38); "Area"; Tab(48); "Density"
        Printer.Font.Bold = False
        'Process first state
        Input #1, state, capital, population, area
        nicePop = FormatNumber(population, 0)
        niceArea = FormatNumber(area, 0)
        niceDens = FormatNumber(population / area)
        Printer.Print state; Tab(12); capital; Tab(24); Format(nicePop, "@@@@@@@@@@");
        Printer.Print Tab(38); Format(niceArea, "@@@@@@"); Tab(48); Format(niceDens, "@@@@@@")
        'Process second state
        Input #1, state, capital, population, area
        nicePop = FormatNumber(population, 0)
        niceArea = FormatNumber(area, 0)
        niceDens = FormatNumber(population / area)
        Printer.Print state; Tab(12); capital; Tab(24); Format(nicePop, "@@@@@@@@@@");
        Printer.Print Tab(38); Format(niceArea, "@@@@@@"); Tab(48); Format(niceDens, "@@@@@@")
        'Process third state
        Input #1, state, capital, population, area
        nicePop = FormatNumber(population, 0)
        niceArea = FormatNumber(area, 0)
        niceDens = FormatNumber(population / area)
        Printer.Print state; Tab(12); capital; Tab(24); Format(nicePop, "@@@@@@@@@@");
        Printer.Print Tab(38); Format(niceArea, "@@@@@@"); Tab(48); Format(niceDens, "@@@@@@")
        Close #1
        Printer.EndDoc
      End Sub
137.  Private Sub cmdPrintRndDate_Click()
        Dim m As Integer, y As Integer
        'Select a random month and year during the 1990s
        Randomize
        m = Int(12 * Rnd) + 1
        y = Int(10 * Rnd) + 1990
        picOutput.Cls
        picOutput.Print m; "/"; y
      End Sub
139.  Private Sub txtNyahNyah_KeyPress(KeyAscii As Integer)
        'Replace the user's keystroke with a random uppercase letter from A to Z
        Randomize
        KeyAscii = Int(26 * Rnd) + 65
      End Sub
```

CHAPTER 4

Exercises 4.1

1. It isn't easy being green.
          Kermit the frog

3. Why do clocks run clockwise?
Because they were invented in the northern
hemisphere, where sundials move clockwise.

5. Divorced, beheaded, died,
Divorced, beheaded, survived.

7. Keep cool, but don't freeze.
Source: A jar of mayonnaise.

9. 88 keys on a piano

11. It was the best of times.
It was the worst of times.

13. Your name has 7 letters.
The first letter is G

15. abcde

17. 144 items in a gross

19. 30% of M&M's Plain Chocolate Candies are brown.

21. 1440 minutes in a day

23. t is the 6 th letter of the word.

25. The May 2001 salary survey of readers of the Visual
Basic Programmers Journal gave average salaries of
database developers according to the database used.

Sybase SQL Server programmers earned $75,633.
Oracle programmers earned $73,607.
Microsoft SQL Server programmers earned $68,295.

27. President Clinton is a graduate of Georgetown University
President Bush is a graduate of Yale University

29. The first 6 letters are Visual

31. The negative of worldly is unworldly

33. 24 blackbirds baked in a pie.

35. There is a parameter in the Sub procedure, but no argument
in
the statement calling the Sub procedure.

37. Since *Print* is a keyword, it cannot be used as the name of a

Sub procedure.

39.
```
Private Sub cmdDisplay_Click()
    Dim num As Integer
    'Display a lucky number
    picOutput.Cls
    num = 7
    Call Lucky(num)
End Sub

Private Sub Lucky(num As Integer)
    'Display message
    picOutput.Print num; "is a lucky number."
End Sub
```

41.
```
Private Sub cmdDisplay_Click()
    Dim tree As String, ht As Single
    'Information about trees
    picOutput.Cls
    Open "TREES.TXT" For Input As #1
    Input #1, tree, ht
    Call Tallest(tree, ht)
    Input #1, tree, ht
    Call Tallest(tree, ht)
    Close #1
End Sub

Private Sub Tallest(tree As String, ht As Single)
    'Display information about tree
    picOutput.Print "The tallest "; tree; " in the U.S. is"; ht; "feet."
End Sub
```

43.
```
Private Sub cmdCompute_Click()
    Dim num As Single
    'Given a number, display its triple
    picResult.Cls
    num = Val(InputBox("Enter a number:"))
    Call Triple(num)
End Sub

Private Sub Triple(num As Single)
    'Multiply the value of the number by 3
    picResult.Print "The number's triple is"; 3 * num
End Sub
```

45.
```
Private Sub cmdDisplay_Click()
    Dim word As String, col As Integer
    'Enter a word and column number to display
    picOutput.Cls
    word = InputBox("Enter a word:")
    col = Val(InputBox("Enter a column number between 1 and 10:"))
    Call PlaceNShow(word, col)
End Sub

Private Sub PlaceNShow(word As String, col As Integer)
    'Display the word at the given column number
    picOutput.Print Tab(col); word
End Sub
```

47.
```
Private Sub cmdDisplay_Click()
  'Intended college majors
  picOutput.Cls
  Call DisplaySource
  Call Majors(16.2, "business")
  Call Majors(2.2, "computer science")
End Sub

Private Sub DisplaySource()
  'Display the source of the information
  picOutput.Print "According to a 2002 survey of college freshmen"
  picOutput.Print "taken by the Higher Educational Research Institute:"
  picOutput.Print
End Sub

Private Sub Majors(students As Single, field As String)
  'Display the information about major
  picOutput.Print students; "percent said they intend to major in "; field
End Sub
```

49.
```
Private Sub cmdDisplay_Click()
  Dim num As Single
  'Favorite number
  picOutput.Cls
  num = Val(txtBox.Text)
  Call Sum (num)
  Call Product(num)
End Sub

Private Sub Sum(num As Single)
  picOutput.Print "The sum of your favorite number with itself is"; num + num
End Sub

Private Sub Product(num As Single)
  picOutput.Print "The product of your favorite number with itself is"; num * num
End Sub
```

51.
```
Private Sub cmdDisplay_Click()
  Dim animal As String, sound As String
  'Old McDonald Had a Farm
  picOldMcDonald.Cls
  Open "FARM.TXT" For Input As #1
  Input #1, animal, sound
  Call ShowVerse(animal, sound)
  picOldMcDonald.Print
  Input #1, animal, sound
  Call ShowVerse(animal, sound)
  picOldMcDonald.Print
  Input #1, animal, sound
  Call ShowVerse(animal, sound)
  picOldMcDonald.Print
  Input #1, animal, sound
  Call ShowVerse(animal, sound)
  Close #1
End Sub

Private Sub ShowVerse(animal As String, sound As String)
  'Display a verse from Old McDonald Had a Farm
  picOldMcDonald.Print "Old McDonald had a farm. Eyi eyi oh."
  picOldMcDonald.Print "And on his farm he had a "; animal; ".  Eyi eyi oh."
  picOldMcDonald.Print "With a "; sound; " "; sound; " here, ";
  picOldMcDonald.Print "and a "; sound; " "; sound; " there."
  picOldMcDonald.Print "Here a "; sound; ", there a "; sound;
  picOldMcDonald.Print ", everywhere a "; sound; " "; sound; "."
  picOldMcDonald.Print "Old McDonald had a farm. Eyi eyi oh."
End Sub
```

53.
```
Private Sub cmdDisplay_Click()
    'Display a table for occupation growth
    picOutput.Cls
    Open "GROWTH.TXT" For Input As #1
    picOutput.Print "Occupation"; Tab(40); 1998; Tab(48); 2008; Tab(56); "Increase"
    picOutput.Print
    Call ComputeIncrease
    Call ComputeIncrease
    Call ComputeIncrease
    Call ComputeIncrease
    Close #1
End Sub

Private Sub ComputeIncrease()
    Dim occupation As String, num98 As Single, num08 As Single, perIncrease As Single
    'Read data and compute percent increase, display all data
    Input #1, occupation, num98, num08
    perIncrease = (num08 - num98) / num98
    picOutput.Print occupation; Tab(40); num98; Tab(48); num08; Tab(58); FormatPercent(perIncrease, 0)
End Sub
```

Exercises 4.2

1. 9

3. Can Can

5. 25

7. Less is more

9. Gabriel was born in the year 1980

11. Buckeyes

13. 0

15. 1 1

17.
```
4 overwhelming
8 whelming
4 whelming
4 ming
4 whelming
```

19. The variable *c* should be a parameter in the Sub procedure. That is, the Sub statement should be `Private Sub Sum (x As Single, y As Single, c As Single)`. Also, the Dim statement in the Sub procedure should be deleted.

21.
```
Private Sub cmdCompute_Click()
    Dim price As Single, tax As Single, cost As Single
    'Calculate sales tax
    picOutput.Cls
    Call InputPrice(price)
    Call Compute(price, tax, cost)
    Call ShowData(price, tax, cost)
End Sub

Private Sub InputPrice(price As Single)
    'Get the price of the item
    price = Val(InputBox("Enter the price of the item:"))
End Sub

Private Sub Compute(price As Single, tax As Single, _
        cost As Single)
    'Calculate the cost
    tax = .05 * price
    cost = price + tax
End Sub

Private Sub ShowData(price As Single, tax As Single, _
        cost As Single)
    'Display bill
    picOutput.Print "Price: "; price
    picOutput.Print "Tax: "; tax
    picOutput.Print "--------------"
    picOutput.Print "Cost: "; cost
End Sub
```

23.
```
Private Sub cmdDisplay_Click()
    Dim length As Single, width As Single, area As Single
    'Compute area of rectangle
    picOutput.Cls
    Call InputSize(length, width)
    Call ComputeArea(length, width, area)
    Call ShowArea(area)
End Sub

Private Sub InputSize(length As Single, width As Single)
    'Get the dimensions of the rectangle
    length = Val(txtLength.Text)
    width = Val(txtWidth.Text)
End Sub
```

```
        Private Sub ComputeArea(length As Single, width As Single, area As Single)
          'Calculate the area
          area = length * width
        End Sub

        Private Sub ShowArea(area As Single)
          'Display the area of the rectangle
          picOutput.Print "The area of the rectangle is"; area
        End Sub
```

25. `Dim nom As String   'place in the (Declarations) section of (General)`

27.
```
    Private Sub cmdDisplay_Click()
        Dim first As String, last As String, fInit As String, lInit As String
        'Display initials
        picOutput.Cls
        Call InputNames(first, last)
        Call ExtractInitials(first, last, fInit, lInit)
        Call DisplayInitials(fInit, lInit)
    End Sub

    Private Sub InputNames(first As String, last As String)
      'Get the person's first and last name
      first = InputBox("Enter your first name:")
      last = InputBox("Enter your last name:")
    End Sub

    Private Sub ExtractInitials(first As String, last As String, fInit As String, lInit As String)
      'Determine the initials of the first and last names
      fInit = Left(first,1)
      lInit = Left(last,1)
    End Sub

    Private Sub DisplayInitials(fInit As String, lInit As String)
      'Display the initials
      picOutput.Print "The initials are "; fInit; "."; lInit; "."
    End Sub
```

29.
```
    Private Sub cmdCompute_Click()
        Dim cost As Single, price As Single, markup As Single
        'Calculate percentage markup
        picMarkup.Cls
        Call InputAmounts(cost, price)
        Call ComputeMarkup(cost, price, markup)
        Call DisplayMarkup(markup)
    End Sub

    Private Sub InputAmounts(cost As Single, price As Single)
      cost = Val(InputBox("Enter the cost:"))
      price = Val(InputBox("Enter the selling price:"))
    End Sub

    Private Sub ComputeMarkup(cost As Single, price As Single, markup As Single)
      markup = (price - cost) / cost
    End Sub

    Private Sub DisplayMarkup(markup As Single)
      picMarkup.Print "The markup is "; FormatPercent(markup)
    End Sub
```

31.
```
    Private Sub cmdCompute_Click()
        Dim nom As String, atBats As Integer, hits As Integer, ave As Single
        'Calculate batting average
        picAverage.Cls
        Open "4-2-E31.TXT" For Input As #1
        Call ReadStats(nom, atBats, hits)
        Call ComputeAverage(atBats, hits, ave)
        Call DisplayInfo(nom, ave)
        Close #1
    End Sub
```

```
    Private Sub ReadStats(nom As String, atBats As Integer, hits As Integer)
      Input #1, nom, atBats, hits
    End Sub


    Private Sub ComputeAverage(atBats As Integer, hits As Integer, ave As Single)
      ave = hits / atBats
    End Sub


    Private Sub DisplayInfo(nom As String, ave As Single)
      picAverage.Print "Name", "Batting Average"
      picAverage.Print nom, FormatNumber(ave, 3, vbFalse)
    End Sub
```

33.
```
    Private Sub cmdDisplay_Click()
      'Display Hat Rack mall comparison table
      picTable.Cls
      picTable.Print Tab(15); "Rent per"
      picTable.Print Tab(15); "Square"; Tab(25); "Total"; Tab(35); "Monthly"
      picTable.Print "Mall Name"; Tab(15); "Foot"; Tab(25); "Feet"; Tab(35); "Rent"
      picTable.Print
      Open "MALLS.TXT" For Input As #1
      Call DisplayInfo
      Call DisplayInfo
      Call DisplayInfo
      Close #1
    End Sub


    Private Sub ComputeRent(rentPerSqFoot As Single, feet As Single, total As Single)
      'Compute monthly rent given rent/foot and number of feet
      total = rentPerSqFoot * feet
    End Sub


    Private Sub DisplayInfo()
      Dim mall As String, rentPerSqrFoot As Single, squareFeet As Single, rent As Single
      'Display the information for a single mall
      Input #1, mall, rentPerSqFoot, squareFeet
      Call ComputeRent(rentPerSqFoot, squareFeet, rent)
      picTable.Print mall; Tab(15); FormatCurrency(rentPerSqFoot); Tab(25); squareFeet; Tab(35); FormatCurrency(rent)
    End Sub
```

35.
```
    Dim total As Single  'In (Declarations) section of (General)


    Private Sub cmdProcessItem_Click()
      Dim item As String, price As Single
      'Process item; display part of sales receipt
      Call InputData(item, price)
      total = total + price
      Call ShowData(item, price)
      txtItem.Text = ""
      txtPrice.Text = ""
      txtItem.SetFocus
    End Sub


    Private Sub cmdDisplay_Click()
      Dim tax As Single
      'Display sum, tax, and total
      tax = total * .05
      tax = Round(tax, 2)
      picReceipt.Print Tab(15); "-------"
      Call ShowData("Sum", total)
      Call ShowData("Tax", tax)
      Call ShowData("Total", total + tax)
    End Sub
```

```
Private Sub InputData(item As String, price As Single)
  'Input item name and price
  item = txtItem.Text
  price = Val(txtPrice.Text)
End Sub
```

```
Private Sub ShowData(strItem As String, numItem As Single)
  'Display data on specified line
  picReceipt.Print strItem; Tab(15); FormatNumber(numItem)
End Sub
```

Exercises 4.3

1. 203

3. The population will double in 24 years.

5. Volume of cylinder having base area 3.14159
and height 2 is 6.28318
Volume of cylinder having base area 28.27431
and height 4 is 113.0972

7. train

9. moral has the negative amoral
political has the negative apolitical

11. The first line of the function definition should end with
As String not *As Single*.

13.
```
Private Sub cmdCompute_Click()
    Dim radius As Single, height As Single
    'Tin Needed for a Tin Can
    picOutput.Cls
    Call InputDims(radius, height)
    Call ShowAmount(radius, height)
End Sub
```

```
Private Sub InputDims(radius As Single, height As Single)
  radius = Val(InputBox("Enter radius of can:"))
  height = Val(InputBox("Enter height of can:"))
End Sub
```

```
Private Sub ShowAmount(radius As Single, height As Single)
  picOutput.Print "A can of radius"; radius; "and height"; height
  picOutput.Print "requires"; CanArea(radius, height); "square centimeters to make."
End Sub
```

```
Private Function CanArea(radius As Single, height As Single) As Single
  'Calculate surface area of a cylindrical can
  CanArea = 6.28 * (radius * radius + radius * height)
End Function
```

15.
```
Private Sub cmdCalculate_Click()
    picResult.Cls
    picResult.Print "Your BMI is": BMI(Val(txtWeight), Val(txtHeight))
End Sub
```

```
Private Function BMI(w As Single, h As Single) As Single
  'Calculate body mass index
  BMI = Round(703 * w / h ^ 2)
End Function
```

17.
```
Private Sub cmdCompute_Click()
    Dim popcorn As Single, butter As Single, bucket As Single, price As Single
    'Popcorn Profits
    picProfit.Cls
    Call InputAmounts(popcorn, butter, bucket, price)
    Call ShowProfit(popcorn, butter, bucket, price)
End Sub
```

```
Private Sub InputAmounts(popcorn As Single, butter As Single, bucket As Single, price As Single)
  popcorn = Val(InputBox("What is the cost (in dollars) of the popcorn kernels?"))
  butter = Val(InputBox("What is the cost (in dollars) of the butter?"))
  bucket = Val(InputBox("What is the cost(in dollars) of the bucket?"))
  price = Val(InputBox("What is the sale price?"))
End Sub
```

```
    Private Function Profit(popcorn As Single, butter As Single, bucket As Single, price As Single) As Single
      'Calculate the profit on a bucket of popcorn
      Profit = price - (popcorn + butter + bucket)
    End Function


    Private Sub ShowProfit(popcorn As Single, butter As Single, bucket As Single, price As Single)
      picProfit.Print "The profit is ";
      picProfit.Print FormatCurrency(Profit(popcorn, butter, bucket, price))
    End Sub
```

19.
```
    Private Sub cmdCompute_Click()
      Dim weight As Single
      'Original Cost of Airmail
      picCost.Cls
      Call InputWeight(weight)
      Call ShowCost(weight)
    End Sub


    Private Function Ceil(x As Single) As Single
      Ceil = -Int(-x)
    End Function


    Private Function Cost(weight As Single) As Single
      'Calculate the cost of an airmail letter
      Cost = .05 + .1 * Ceil(weight - 1)
    End Function


    Private Sub InputWeight(weight As Single)
      weight = Val(txtOunces.Text)
    End Sub


    Private Sub ShowCost(weight As Single)
      picCost.Print "The cost of mailing the letter is "; FormatCurrency(Cost(weight))
    End Sub
```

21.
```
    Private Sub cmdGreetSenator_Click()
      Dim nom As String
      'Display a greeting for a senator
      picGreeting.Cls
      nom = InputBox("Enter the senator's name:")
      picGreeting.Print
      picGreeting.Print "The Honorable "; nom
      picGreeting.Print "United States Senate"
      picGreeting.Print "Washington, DC 20001"
      picGreeting.Print
      picGreeting.Print "Dear Senator "; LastName(nom); ","
    End Sub


    Private Function LastName(nom As String) As String
      Dim spaceNmb As Integer
      'Determine the last name of a two-part name
      spaceNmb = InStr(nom, " ")
      LastName = Mid(nom, spaceNmb + 1, Len(nom) - spaceNmb)
    End Function
```

CHAPTER 5

Exercises 5.1

1. True		13. True	
3. True		15. True	
5. True		17. False	
7. True		19. False	
9. False		21. False	
11. False		23. True	

25. Equivalent

27. Not Equivalent

29. Equivalent

31. Not Equivalent

33. Equivalent

35. a <= b

37. (a >= b) Or (c = d)

39. (a = "") Or (a >= b) Or (Len(a) >= 5)

Exercises 5.2

1. Less than ten

3. tomorrow is another day.

5. 10

7. Cost of call: $11.26

9. The number of vowels is 2

11. positive

13. Incorrect conditional. Should be If (1 < num) And (num < 3) Then

15. no Then

17. Comparing numeric and string data

19. Incorrect condition. Should be If (j = 4) Or (k = 4) Then

21. a = 5

23.
```
If j = 7 Then
    b = 1
  Else
    b = 2
End If
```

25.
```
message = "Is Alaska bigger than Texas and California combined?"
answer = InputBox(message)
If UCase(Left(answer, 1)) = "Y" Then
    picOutput.Print "Correct"
  Else
    picOutput.Print "Wrong"
End If
```

27.
```
Private Sub cmdComputeTip_Click()
    Dim cost As Single, tip As Single
    'Give server a tip
    picTip.Cls
    cost = Val(InputBox("Enter cost of meal:"))
    tip = cost * .15
    If tip < 1 Then
        tip = 1
    End If
    picTip.Print "Leave "; FormatCurrency(tip); " for the tip."
End Sub
```

29.
```
Private Sub cmdOrderDisks_Click()
    Dim num As Single, cost As Single
    'Order diskettes
    picCost.Cls
    num = Val(InputBox("Number of diskettes:"))
    If num < 100 Then
        cost = .25 * num    '25 cents each
      Else
        cost = .2 * num     '20 cents each
    End If
    picCost.Print "The cost is "; FormatCurrency(cost)
End Sub
```

31.
```
Private Sub txtNum_KeyPress(KeyAscii As Integer)
    If (KeyAscii < Asc("0")) Or (KeyAscii > Asc("9")) Then
        'Ignore all keystrokes except the digits 0 through 9
        KeyAscii = 0
    End If
End Sub
```

33.
```
Private Sub cmdProcessWithdrawal_Click()
    Dim balance As Single, amount As Single
    'Savings account withdrawal
    picBalance.Cls
    balance = Val(InputBox("Current balance:"))
    amount = Val(InputBox("Amount of withdrawal:"))
    If (balance >= amount) Then
        balance = balance - amount
        picBalance.Print "New balance is "; FormatCurrency(balance)
        If balance < 150 Then
            picBalance.Print "Balance below $150"
        End If
      Else
        picBalance.Print "Withdrawal denied."
    End If
End Sub
```

35.
```
Private Sub cmdRunLottery_Click()
    Dim d1 As Integer, d2 As Integer, d3 As Integer, lucky As String
    'Select three digits at random
    picLuckySeven.Cls
    Randomize
    d1 = Int(10 * Rnd)
    d2 = Int(10 * Rnd)
    d3 = Int(10 * Rnd)
    lucky = "Lucky seven"
    picLuckySeven.Print d1; d2; d3
    If d1 = 7 Then
        If (d2 = 7) Or (d3 = 7) Then
            picLuckySeven.Print lucky
        End If
      Else
        If (d2 = 7) And (d3 = 7) Then
            picLuckySeven.Print lucky
        End If
    End If
End Sub
```

37.
```
Private Sub cmdConvert_Click()
    Dim word As String, first As String
    'Convert to Pig Latin
    picPigLatin.Cls
    word = InputBox("Enter a word (use all lowercase):")
    first = Left(word, 1)
    If InStr("aeiou", first) <> 0 Then
        word = word & "way"
      Else
        word = Mid(word, 2, Len(word) - 1) & first & "ay"
    End If
    picPigLatin.Print "The word in pig latin is "; word
End Sub
```

39.
```
Dim status As Integer  'In (Declarations) section of (General)

Private Sub cmdBogart_Click()
  If status = 0 Then
      picCasablanca.Print "I came to Casablanca for the waters."
      status = 1
    ElseIf status = 1 Then
      picCasablanca.Print "I was misinformed."
      status = 0
  End If
End Sub

Sub cmdRaines_Click ()
  picCasablanca.Print "But we're in the middle of the desert."
End Sub
```

41.

Object	Property	Setting
frmPresident Quiz	Caption	Yankee Doodle President
lblQuestion	Caption	Which U.S. President was born on July 4?
txtAnswer	Text	(blank)
cmdCheckAnswer	Caption	Check Answer
lblCount	Caption	0
lblGuesses	Caption	guesses so far.

```
Private Sub cmdCheckAnswer_Click()
  Dim msg As String
  'lblCount keeps track of the number of guesses; increase number of guesses by 1
  lblCount.Caption = FormatNumber(Val(lblCount.Caption) + 1, 0)
  If InStr(UCase(txtAnswer.Text), "COOLIDGE") > 0 Then
      MsgBox "Calvin Coolidge was born on July 4, 1872.", , "Correct"
      End
    ElseIf Val(lblCount.Caption) = 3 Then
      msg = "He once said, 'If you don't say anything,"
      msg = msg & " you won't be called upon to repeat it.'"
      MsgBox msg, , "Hint"
    ElseIf Val(lblCount.Caption) = 7 Then
      MsgBox "His nickname was 'Silent Cal.'", , "Hint"
    ElseIf Val(lblCount.Caption) = 10 Then
      MsgBox "Calvin Coolidge was born on July 4, 1872.", , "You've run out of guesses"
      End
    End If
End Sub
```

43.
```
Private Sub cmdCalcNJTax_Click()
  Dim income As Single, tax As Single
  'Calculate New Jersey state income tax
  picNJTax.Cls
  income = Val(InputBox("Taxable income:"))
  If income <= 20000 Then
      tax = .02 * income
    Else
      If income <= 50000 Then
          tax = 400 + .025 * (income - 20000)
        Else
          tax = 1150 + .035 * (income - 50000)
      End If
  End If
  picNJTax.Print "Tax is "; FormatCurrency(tax)
End Sub
```

Exercises 5.3

1. The price is $3.75
The price is $3.75

3. Mesozoic Era
Paleozoic Era
?

5. Nope.
He worked with the developer, von Neumann, on the ENIAC.
Correct.

7. The less things change, the more they remain the same.
Less is more.
Time keeps everything from happening at once.

9. Should have a Case clause.

11. Case a = "Bob" should be Case "Bob"

13. Error in second Case.

15. Logical error: >= "Peach" should be >= "PEACH"
Syntax error: "ORANGE TO PEACH" should be "ORANGE" To "PEACH"

17. Valid

19. Invalid

21. Valid

23.
```
Select Case a
  Case 1
    picOutput.Print "one"
  Case Is > 5
    picOutput.Print "two"
End Select
```

25.
```
Select Case a
  Case 2
    picOutput.Print "yes"
  Case Is < 5
    picOutput.Print "no"
End Select
```

27.
```
Private Sub cmdDescribe_Click()
    Dim percent As Single
    'Determine degree of cloudiness
    picCloudCover.Cls
    percent = Val(InputBox("Percentage of cloud cover:"))
    Select Case percent
      Case 0 To 30
        picCloudCover.Print "Clear"
      Case 31 To 70
        picCloudCover.Print "Partly cloudy"
      Case 71 To 99
        picCloudCover.Print "Cloudy"
      Case 100
        picCloudCover.Print "Overcast"
      Case Else
        picCloudCover.Print "Percentage must be between 0 And 100."
    End Select
End Sub
```

29.
```
Private Sub cmdFindNumDays_Click()
    Dim monthName As String, days As Integer
    'Give number of days in month
    picNumDays.Cls
    Call InputMonth(monthName)
    Call GetDays(monthName, days)
    Call ShowDays(days, monthName)
End Sub

Private Sub InputMonth(monthName As String)
    'Input a month of the year
    monthName = InputBox("Enter a month (do not abbreviate):")
End Sub

Private Sub GetDays(monthName As String, days As Integer)
    Dim answer As String
    'Compute number of days in the month
    Select Case UCase(monthName)
      Case "FEBRUARY"
        answer = InputBox("Is it a leap year?")
        If UCase(Left(answer, 1)) = "Y" Then
            days = 29
          Else
            days = 28
        End If
      Case "APRIL", "JUNE", "SEPTEMBER", "NOVEMBER"
        days = 30
      Case "JANUARY","MARCH","MAY","JULY","AUGUST","OCTOBER","DECEMBER"
        days = 31
    End Select
End Sub

Private Sub ShowDays(days As Integer, monthName As String)
    'Report number of days in month
    picNumDays.Print monthName; " has"; days; "days."
End Sub
```

31.
```
Private Sub cmdAssign_Click()
    Dim score As Integer
    'Give letter grade for number score
    picLetterGrade.Cls
    Call InputScore(score)
    Call ShowGrade(score)
End Sub

Private Function Grade(score As Integer) As String
    'Return letter grade for score
    Select Case score
        Case 90 To 100
            Grade = "A"
        Case 80 To 89
            Grade = "B"
        Case 70 To 79
            Grade = "C"
        Case 60 To 69
            Grade = "D"
        Case 0 To 59
            Grade = "F"
        Case Else
            Grade = "Invalid"
    End Select
End Function

Private Sub InputScore(score As Integer)
    'Input a number score
    score = Val(InputBox("What is the score?"))
End Sub

Private Sub ShowGrade(score As Integer)
    'Show letter grade for score
    picLetterGrade.Print "The letter grade is "; Grade(score)
End Sub
```

33.
```
Private Sub cmdCompute_Click()
    Dim amount As Single, reward As Single
    'Determine cash award
    picReward.Cls
    amount = Val(InputBox("How much was recovered?"))
    Select Case amount
        Case Is <= 75000
            reward = .1 * amount
        Case Is <= 100000
            reward = 7500 + .05 * (amount - 75000)
        Case Is > 100000
            reward = 8750 + .01 * (amount - 100000)
            If reward > 50000 Then
                reward = 50000
            End If
    End Select
    picReward.Print "The amount given as reward is "; _
                    FormatCurrency(reward)
End Sub
```

35.

Object	Property	Setting
frmEx5_3_35	Caption	Presidential Trivia
lblQuestion	Caption	Last name of one of the five most recent Presidents
txtName	Text	(blank)
cmdGetFacts	Caption	Get Facts
picTrivia		

```
Private Sub cmdGetFacts_Click()
    Dim pres As String, state As String, trivia As String, midInit As String
    pres = txtName.Text
    Select Case UCase(pres)
        Case "CARTER"
            state = "Georgia"
            trivia = "The only soft drink served in the Carter "
            trivia = trivia & "White House was Coca-Cola."
        Case "REAGAN"
            state = "California"
            trivia = "His secret service code name was Rawhide."
        Case "BUSH"
            state = "Texas"
            midInit = InputBox("What is his middle initial, P (father) or W (son):?", _
                               "WHICH ONE?")
            If UCase(midInit) = "P" Then
                trivia = "He was the third left-handed president."
            Else
                trivia = "He once owned the Texas Rangers baseball team."
            End If
        Case "CLINTON"
            state = "Arkansas"
            trivia = "In college he did a good imitation of Elvis Presley."
        Case Else
            state = ""
            trivia = ""
    End Select
```

```
    If state <> "" Then
        picTrivia.Cls
        picTrivia.Print "President "; pres; "'s ";
        picTrivia.Print "home state was "; state; "."
        picTrivia.Print trivia
    End If
    txtName.Text = ""
    txtName.SetFocus
End Sub
```

37.
```
Private Sub cmdHumor_Click()
    lblSentence.Caption = HumorMsg(Val(txtNumber.Text))
End Sub


Private Sub cmdInsult_Click()
    lblSentence.Caption = InsultMsg(Val(txtNumber.Text))
End Sub


Private Function HumorMsg(num As Integer) As String
  Dim temp As String
  Select Case num
    Case 1
      HumorMsg = "I can resist everything except temptation"
    Case 2
      HumorMsg = "I just heard from Bill Bailey. He's not coming home."
    Case 3
      temp = "I have enough money to last the rest of my life,"
      HumorMsg = temp & " unless I buy something."
    Case Else
      HumorMsg = ""
      txtNumber.Text = ""
  End Select
End Function


Private Function InsultMsg(num As Integer) As String
  Select Case num
    Case 1
      InsultMsg = "How much would you charge to haunt a house?"
    Case 2
      InsultMsg = "I bet you have no more friends than an alarm clock."
    Case 3
      InsultMsg = "When your IQ rises to 30, sell."
    Case Else
      InsultMsg = ""
      txtNumber.Text = ""
  End Select
End Function
```

CHAPTER 6

Exercises 6.1

1. 17

3. You are a super programmer!

5. 2

7. The value of q keeps growing until the program crashes when the value exceeds the upper limit for a variable of type Single.

9. Do and Loop interchanged.

11. `While num >= 7`

13. `Until response <> "Y"`

15. `Until nom = ""`

17. `Until (a <= 1) Or (a >= 3)`

19. `While n = 0`

21.
```
Private Sub cmdDisplay_Click()
    Dim nom As String, num As Integer
    'Request and display three names
    picOutput.Cls
    num = 0
    Do While num < 3
      nom = InputBox("Enter a name:")
      picOutput.Print nom
      num = num + 1
    Loop
End Sub
```

23.
```
Private Sub cmdDisplayConvTable_Click()
    Dim celsius As Single
    'Convert Celsius to Fahrenheit
    picTempTable.Cls
    picTempTable.Print "Celsius"; Tab(10); "Fahrenheit"
    celsius = -40
    Do While celsius <= 40
      Call ShowFahrenheit(celsius)
      celsius = celsius + 5
    Loop
End Sub

Private Function Fahrenheit(celsius As Single) As Single
    'Convert Celsius to Fahrenheit
    Fahrenheit = (9 / 5) * celsius + 32
End Function

Private Sub ShowFahrenheit(celsius As Single)
    'Give Fahrenheit equivalent
    picTempTable.Print celsius; Tab(10); Fahrenheit(celsius)
End Sub
```

25.
```
Private Sub cmdComputeOdds_Click()
    Dim counter As Integer, sevens As Integer, dieOne As Integer, dieTwo As Integer
    Randomize
    counter = 0
    sevens = 0
    Do While sevens < 10
      dieOne = Int(6 * Rnd) + 1
      dieTwo = Int(6 * Rnd) + 1
      counter = counter + 1
      If dieOne + dieTwo = 7 Then
          sevens = sevens + 1
      End If
    Loop
    picOdds.Cls
    picOdds.Print "The approximate odds of two die totaling seven is 1 in ";
    picOdds.Print FormatNumber(counter / sevens)
End Sub
```

27.
```
Private Sub cmdDisplay_Click()
    Dim x As Integer, y As Integer, z As Integer
    'First terms in the Fibonacci sequence
    x = 1
    y = 1
    z = x + y
    picFibonacci.Cls
    picFibonacci.Print "Terms in the Fibonacci sequence between 1 and 100 are:"
    picFibonacci.Print x; y;
    Do While z <= 100
        picFibonacci.Print z;
        x = y
        y = z
        z = x + y
    Loop
End Sub
```

29.
```
Private Sub cmdDisplay_Click()
    Dim minuteHandPos As Single, hourHandPos As Single, difference As Single
    'When after 6:30 do clock hands exactly overlap?
    minuteHandPos = 0
    hourHandPos = 30
    Do While hourHandPos - minuteHandPos >= .0001
      difference = hourHandPos - minuteHandPos
      minuteHandPos = minuteHandPos + difference
      hourHandPos = hourHandPos + difference / 12
    Loop
    picOutput.Print "The hands overlap at"; minuteHandPos; "minutes after six."
End Sub
```

31.
```
Private Sub cmdBounceBall_Click()
    Dim height As Single, bounceFactor As Single, bounces As Integer, distance As Single
    'Bounce a ball and find total distance traveled
    picTotalDistance.Cls
    Call InputData(height, bounceFactor)
    Call BounceBall(height, bounceFactor, bounces, distance)
    Call ShowData(bounces, distance)
End Sub

Private Sub InputData(height As Single, bounceFactor As Single)
    Dim prompt As String
    'Input height and coefficient of restitution
    prompt = "What is the coefficient of restitution of the ball (0 to 1)? " _
            & "Examples are .7 for a tennis ball, .75 for a basketball, " _
            & ".9 for a super ball, and .3 for a softball."
    bounceFactor = Val(InputBox(prompt))
    height = Val(InputBox("From how many meters will the ball be dropped?"))
    height = height * 100        ' convert to centimeters
End Sub

Private Sub BounceBall(hght As Single, bFactor As Single, bounces As Integer, dist As Single)
    bounces = 1            ' first bounce
    dist = hght
    Do While hght * bFactor >= 10
        bounces = bounces + 1
        hght = hght * bFactor
        dist = dist + 2 * hght        ' up then down again
    Loop
End Sub

Private Sub ShowData(bounces As Integer, distance As Single)
    picTotalDistance.Print "The ball bounced"; bounces; "times and traveled about ";
    picTotalDistance.Print FormatNumber(distance / 100); " meters."
End Sub
```

33.
```
Private Sub cmdEstimate_Click()
    Dim amt As Single, yrs As Integer
    'Years to deplete savings account
    picResult.Cls
    amt = Val(InputBox("Enter initial amount in account:"))
    yrs = 0
    If amt * 1.05 - 1000 >= amt Then
        picResult.Print "Account will never be depleted."
      Else
        Do
          amt = amt * 1.05 - 1000
          yrs = yrs + 1
        Loop Until amt <= 0
        picResult.Print "It takes"; yrs; "years to deplete the account."
    End If
End Sub
```

35.
```
Private Sub cmdDetermineAge_Click()
    Dim age As Integer
    'Solution to age problem
    picResult.Cls
    age = 1
    Do While (1980 + age) <> (age * age)
        age = age + 1
    Loop
    picResult.Print "The solution is"; age; "years old."
End Sub
```

37.
```
Private Sub cmdCapSentence_Click()
    'Capitalize entire sentence
    picOutput.Cls
    picOutput.Print UCase(txtSentence.Text)
End Sub
```

```
Private Sub cmdCapInitial_Click()
  Dim info As String, word As String
  'Capitalize first letter of each word
  picOutput.Cls
  info = LTrim(txtSentence.Text) 'discard any leading spaces
  Do While info <> ""
    word = NextWord(info)
    picOutput.Print UCase(Left(word, 1)); Mid(word, 2); " ";
  Loop
End Sub

Private Function NextWord(info As String) As String
  Dim spacePos As Integer
  'Take word from beginning of info; space assumed to be the word separator
  spacePos = InStr(info, " ")
  If spacePos = 0 Then
      NextWord = info
      info = ""
    Else
      NextWord = Left(info, spacePos - 1)
      info = LTrim(Mid(info, spacePos))
  End If
End Function
```

39.
```
Private Sub cmdFindGCD_Click()
  Dim m As Single, n As Single, t As Single, q As Single
  'Greatest common divisor
  picGCD.Cls
  Call InputIntegers(m, n)
  Do While n <> 0
    t = n
    n = m Mod n
    m = t
  Loop
  picGCD.Print "The greatest common divisor is"; m
End Sub

Private Sub InputIntegers(m As Single, n As Single)
  'Input two integers
  m = Val(InputBox("Enter first integer:", "GCD"))
  n = Val(InputBox("Enter second integer:", "GCD"))
End Sub
```

Exercises 6.2

1. 13

3. pie
   cake
   melon

5.
```
   A
Apple
Apricot
Avocado

   B
Banana
Blueberry

   G
Grape

   L
Lemon
Lime
```

7. A group of ducks is called a brace

9. counters

11. Loop statement missing. Also, loop cannot be entered because the value of num is 0.

13. Last president in file will not be printed.

15.
```
Private Sub cmdDisplay_Click()
    Dim largest As Single, num as Single
    'Find largest of a collection of numbers
    picOutput.Cls
    largest = 0
    Open "6-2-E15.TXT" For Input As #1
    Do While Not EOF(1)
      Input #1, num
      If num > largest Then
          largest = num
      End If
    Loop
    picOutput.Print "The largest number is"; largest
End Sub
```

17.
```
Private Sub cmdDisplay_Click()
    Dim total As Single, numGrades As Integer, grade As Single
    Dim average As Single, aaCount As Integer
    'Display percentage of grades that are above average
    picOutput.Cls
    Open "FINAL.TXT" For Input As #1
    total = 0
    numGrades = 0
    Do While Not EOF(1)
      Input #1, grade
      total = total + grade
      numGrades = numGrades + 1
    Loop
    Close #1
    If numGrades > 0 Then
        average = total / numGrades
        aaCount = 0
        Open "FINAL.TXT" For Input As #1
        Do While Not EOF(1)
          Input #1, grade
          If grade > average Then
              aaCount = aaCount + 1
          End If
        Loop
        Close #1
        picOutput.Print FormatPercent(aaCount / numGrades); " of grades are above the average of ";
        picOutput.Print FormatNumber(average)
    End If
End Sub
```

19.
```
Private Sub cmdShowPresident_Click()
    Dim n As Integer, num As Integer, nom As String
    'Display the name of the nth president
    n = Val(txtPresNum.Text)
    If (1 <= n) And (n <= 43) Then
        picPresident.Cls
        Open "USPRES.TXT" For Input As #1
        num = 0
        Do
          Input #1, nom
          num = num + 1
        Loop Until num = n
        picPresident.Print nom; " was President number"; n
        Close #1
    End If
End Sub
```

21.
```
Private Sub cmdTestAlgorithm_Click()
    Dim n As Single, numSteps As Single
    'Generate sequence with algorithm
    picResult.Cls
    n = Val(txtInitialNum.Text)
    numSteps = 0
    Do While n <> 1
      numSteps = numSteps + 1
      If (n / 2) = Int(n / 2) Then
          n = n / 2
          picResult.Print n;
        Else
          n = (3 * n) + 1
          picResult.Print n;
      End If
      'Move to next line after each ten numbers are displayed
      If numSteps Mod 10 = 0 Then
        picResult.Print
      End If
    Loop
    picResult.Print
    picResult.Print "It took"; numSteps; "steps to reach 1."
End Sub
```

23.
```
Private Sub cmdProcessSonnet_Click()
    Dim totalWords As Integer, lineCount As Integer, sonnetLine As String
    Dim wordCount As Integer, word As String
    'Analyze a Shakespeare sonnet
    picAnalysis.Cls
    totalWords = 0
    lineCount = 0
    Open "SONNET.TXT" For Input As #1
    Do While Not EOF(1)
      Input #1, sonnetLine
      lineCount = lineCount + 1
      wordCount = 0
      Do While sonnetLine <> ""
        word = nextWord(sonnetLine)
        wordCount = wordCount + 1
      Loop
      totalWords = totalWords + wordCount
    Loop
    Close #1
    picAnalysis.Print "The sonnet contains an average of"; totalWords / lineCount
    picAnalysis.Print "words per line and a total of "; totalWords; "words."
End Sub

Private Function NextWord(info As String) As String
    Dim spacePos As Integer
    'Take word from beginning of info; space assumed to be the word separator
    'This function modifies the parameter
    spacePos = InStr(info, " ")
    If spacePos = 0 Then
        NextWord = info
        info = ""
      Else
        NextWord = Left(info, spacePos - 1)
        info = LTrim(Mid(info, spacePos))
    End If
End Function
```

25.
```
Private Sub cmdRemoveParens_Click()
    Dim sentence As String, parensFlag As Boolean, position As Integer, letter As String
    'Remove parentheses and their contents from a sentence
    picOutput.Cls
    sentence = txtSentence.Text
    parensFlag = False
    position = 1
    Do Until position > Len(sentence)
      letter = Mid(sentence, position, 1)
      Select Case letter
        Case "("
          parensFlag = True
        Case ")"
          parensFlag = False
          position = position + 1
        Case Else
          If Not parensFlag Then
              picOutput.Print letter;
          End If
      End Select
      position = position + 1
    Loop
End Sub
```

27.
```
Private Sub cmdDisplay_Click()
    Dim money As Single, liquid As String, price As Single
    'Display liquids available given an amount of money
    picOutput.Cls
    money = Val(txtAmount.Text)
    picOutput.Print "You can purchase one gallon of any of the following liquids."
    Open "LIQUIDS.TXT" For Input As #1
    Do While Not EOF(1)
      Input #1, liquid, price
      If price <= money Then
          picOutput.Print liquid
      End If
    Loop
    Close #1
End Sub
```

Exercises 6.3

1. Pass # 1
Pass # 2
Pass # 3
Pass # 4

3.   2   4   6   8 Who do we appreciate?

5.   5   6   7   8   9   10   11   12   13

7. Steve Cram   3:46.31
Steve Scott   3:51.6
Mary Slaney   4:20.5

9. 1   4   7   10
2   5   8   11
3   6   9   12

11. *******Hooray*******

13. Loop is never executed because 1 is less than 25.5 and the step is negative.

15. A For statement can only have one Next statement.

17.
```
Private Sub cmdDisplay_Click()
    Dim num As Integer
    For num = 1 To 10 Step 2
      picOutput.Print num
    Next num
End Sub
```

19.
```
Private Sub cmdDisplay_Click()
    Dim i As Integer
    'Display a row of 10 stars
    picOutput.Cls
    For i = 1 To 10
      picOutput.Print "*";
    Next i
End Sub
```

21.
```
Private Sub cmdDisplay_Click()
    Dim i As Integer, j As Integer
    'Display 10 x 10 array of stars
    picOutput.Cls
    For i = 1 To 10
      For j = 1 To 10
        picOutput.Print "*";
      Next j
      picOutput.Print
    Next i
End Sub
```

23.
```
Private Sub cmdComputeSum_Click()
    Dim sum As Single, denominator As Integer
    'Compute the sum 1 + 1/2 + 1/3 + 1/4 + ... + 1/100
    picOutput.Cls
    sum = 0
    For denominator = 1 To 100
      sum = sum + (1 / denominator)
    Next denominator
    picOutput.Print "The sum is"; sum
End Sub
```

25.
```
Private Sub cmdAnalyzeOptions_Click()
    Dim result1 As Single, result2 As Single
    'Compare salaries
    picResults.Cls
    result1 = Option1
    result2 = Option2
    picResults.Print "Option 1 = "; FormatCurrency(result1)
    picResults.Print "Option 2 = "; FormatCurrency(result2)
    If result1 > result2 Then
        picResults.Print "Option 1";
      Else
        picResults.Print "Option 2";
    End If
    picResults.Print " pays better"
End Sub

Private Function Option1() As Single
  Dim i As Integer, sum As Single
  'Compute total salary for 10 days,
  'with a flat salary of $100/day
  sum = 0
  For i = 1 To 10
    sum = sum + 100
  Next i
  Option1 = sum
End Function

Private Function Option2() As Single
  Dim i As Integer, daySalary As Single, sum As Single
  'Compute the total salary for 10 days,
  'starting at $1 and doubling each day
  sum = 0
  daySalary = 1
  For i = 1 To 10
    sum = sum + daySalary
    daySalary = daySalary * 2
  Next i
  Option2 = sum
End Function
```

27.
```
Private Sub cmdCompIdealWeights_Click()
    Dim lower As Integer, upper As Integer
    'Ideal weights for men and women
    picWeightTable.Cls
    Call InputBounds(lower, upper)
    Call ShowWeights(lower, upper)
End Sub

Private Function IdealMan(height As Integer) As Single
    'Compute the ideal weight of a man given the height
    IdealMan = 4 * height - 128
End Function

Private Function IdealWoman(height As Integer) As Single
    'Compute the ideal weight of a woman given the height
    IdealWoman = 3.5 * height - 108
End Function

Private Sub InputBounds(lower As Integer, upper As Integer)
    'Input the lower and upper bounds on height
    lower = Val(InputBox("Enter lower bound on height in inches:"))
    upper = Val(InputBox("Enter upper bound on height in inches:"))
End Sub

Private Sub ShowWeights(lower As Integer, upper As Integer)
    Dim height As Integer
    'Display table of weights
    picWeightTable.Print
    picWeightTable.Print "Height", "Wt - Women", "Wt - Men"
    picWeightTable.Print
    For height = lower To upper
        picWeightTable.Print height, IdealWoman(height), IdealMan(height)
    Next height
End Sub
```

29.
```
Private Sub cmdCountSibilants_Click()
    'Number of sibilants in sentence
    picResults.Cls
    picResults.Print "There are"; Sibilants(txtSentence.Text); "sibilants."
End Sub

Private Function Sibilants(sentence As String) As Integer
    Dim numSibs As Integer, i As Integer, letter As String
    'Count number of sibilants
    numSibs = 0
    For i = 1 To Len(sentence)
        letter = UCase(Mid(sentence, i, 1))
        If (letter = "S") Or (letter = "Z") Then
            numSibs = numSibs + 1
        End If
    Next i
    Sibilants = numSibs
End Function
```

31.
```
Private Sub cmdCalcBalance_Click()
    Dim amt As Single, yearNum As Integer
    'Calculate balance after 10 years.
    picBalance.Cls
    amt = 800
    For yearNum = 1 To 10
        amt = amt * 1.04 + 100
    Next yearNum
    picBalance.Print "The final amount is "; FormatCurrency(amt)
End Sub
```

33.
```
Private Sub cmdDecay_Click()
    Dim grams As Single, yearNum As Integer
    'Radioactive decay
    picOutput.Cls
    grams = 10
    For yearNum = 1 To 5
      grams = .88 * grams
    Next yearNum
    picOutput.Print "Of 10 grams of cobalt 60,"
    picOutput.Print FormatNumber(grams); " grams remain after 5 years."
End Sub
```

35.
```
Private Sub cmdDraw_Click()
    Dim stars As Integer, i As Integer
    'Draw a hollow box
    picOutput.Cls
    picOutput.Font.Name = "Courier New"
    stars = Val(Inputbox("Number of stars?"))
    Call DrawSide(stars)
    For i = 1 To stars - 2
      Call DrawRow(stars)
    Next i
    Call DrawSide(stars)
End Sub

Private Sub DrawSide(stars As Integer)
  Dim i As Integer
  'Draw a solid side of stars
  For i = 1 To stars
    picOutput.Print "*";
  Next i
  picOutput.Print
End Sub

Private Sub DrawRow(stars As Integer)
  Dim i As Integer
  'Draw a row (put spaces between the two stars)
  picOutput.Print "*";
  For i = 1 To stars - 2
    picOutput.Print " ";
  Next i
  picOutput.Print "*"
End Sub
```

37.
```
Private Sub cmdDisplay_Click()
    Dim m As Integer, n As Integer, row As Integer, col As Integer
    'Create a multiplication table
    picTable.Cls
    picTable.Font.Name = "Courier New"
    m = Val(InputBox("Enter number of rows:"))
    n = Val(InputBox("Enter number of columns:"))
    For row = 1 To m
      For col = 1 To n
        picTable.Print Format(row * col, "@@@@@@");
      Next col
      picTable.Print
    Next row
End Sub
```

39.
```
Private Sub cmdCompute_Click()
    Dim testValue As Single, amount As Single, i As Integer
    'Gambling casino problem
    picLoser.Cls
    testValue = 4
    Do
      testValue = testValue + 1    'Start test with $5
      amount = testValue
      For i = 1 To 3        'One iteration for each casino
        amount = amount - 1      'Entrance fee
        amount = amount / 2      'Funds lost
        amount = amount - 1      'Exit fee
      Next i
    Loop Until amount = 0
    picLoser.Print "Starting amount = "; FormatCurrency(testValue)
End Sub
```

41.
```
Private Sub cmdSelectWord_Click()
    Dim which As Integer, i As Integer, word As String
    'Select random word from file of 20 words
    Randomize
    picOutput.Cls
    which = Int(20 * Rnd) + 1
    Open "6-3-E41.TXT" For Input As #1
    For i = 1 To which
      Input #1, word
    Next i
    picOutput.Print "The selected word is "; word; "."
    Close #1
End Sub
```

43.
```
Private Sub cmdPickWinner_Click()
    Dim entries As Integer, nom As String
    Dim which As Integer, i As Integer, word As String
    'Select random name from file with unknown number of names
    Randomize
    picWinner.Cls
    entries = 0
    Open "6-3-E43.TXT" For Input As #1
    Do While Not EOF(1)
      Input #1, nom
      entries = entries + 1
    Loop
    Close #1
    which = Int(entries * Rnd) + 1
    Open "6-3-E43.TXT" For Input As #1
    For i = 1 To which
      Input #1, nom
    Next i
    picWinner.Print "The winner is "; nom
    Close #1
End Sub
```

CHAPTER 7

Exercises 7.1

1. 3 7 0

3. Stuhldreher
Crowley

5. 6 2 9 11 3 4

7. The Dim statement in the (Declarations) section of (General) dimensions companies() with subscripts from 1 to 100 and makes companies available to all procedures. Therefore, the ReDim statement in the Form_Load event procedure produces the error message "Array already dimensioned." First line should be Dim companies() As String

9. Array subscript out of range (when k > 4).

11. Improper syntax in first Dim statement.

13.

river(1)	river(2)	river(3)	river(4)	river(5)
Thames	Ohio	Amazon	Volga	Nile

river(1)	river(2)	river(3)	river(4)	river(5)
Ohio	Amazon	Volga	Nile	Thames

15. (a) 2
(b) 7
(c) 10
(d) 9

17. Replace lines 18 through 24 with

```
'Display all names and difference from average
picTopStudents.Cls
For student = 1 To 8
  picTopStudents.Print nom(student), score(student) -
average
Next student
```

19. `Dim bestPicture(1993 To 2003) As String`

21.
```
Dim marx(1 To 4) As String 'In (Declarations) section
                                'of (General)
Private Sub Form_Load()
  marx(1) = "Chico"
  marx(2) = "Harpo"
  marx(3) = "Groucho"
  marx(4) = "Zeppo"
End Sub
```

23.
```
Dim i As Integer
'Store in b() the reverse of the values in a()
For i = 1 To 4
  b(i) = a(5 - i)
Next i
```

25.
```
Dim i As Integer, k As Integer
'Display the elements of the array a()
For i = 1 To 26 Step 5
  For k = 0 To 4
    picArray.Print Tab(10 * k + 1); a(i + k);
  Next k
  picArray.Print
Next i
```

27.
```
Dim i As Integer, differFlag As Boolean
'Compare arrays a() and b() for same values
differFlag = False
For i = 1 To 10
  If a(i) <> b(i) Then
      differFlag = True
  End If
Next i
If differFlag Then
    picOutput.Print "The arrays are not identical."
  Else
    picOutput.Print "The arrays have identical values."
End If
```

29.
```
Dim i As Integer
'Curve grades by adding 7
For i = 1 To 12
  grades(i) = grades(i) + 7
Next i
```

31.
```
Private Sub cmdDisplay_Click()
    Dim range As Integer, dataElement As Integer, score As Integer, interval As Integer
    'Create and display the frequency of scores
    Dim frequency(1 To 5) As Integer
    'Set array elements to 0
    For range = 1 To 5
      frequency(range) = 0
    Next range
    'Read scores, count scores in each of five intervals
    Open "7-1-E31.TXT" For Input As #1
    For dataElement = 1 To 30
      Input #1, score
      range = Int(score / 10) + 1    'Number in the range of 1-5
      frequency(range) = frequency(range) + 1
    Next dataElement
    Close #1
    'Display frequency in each interval
    picTable.Cls
    picTable.Print "Interval"; Tab(12); "Frequency"
    picTable.Print
    For interval = 1 To 5
      picTable.Print 10 * (interval - 1); "to"; 10 * interval - 1;
      picTable.Print Tab(14); frequency(interval)
    Next interval
End Sub
```

33.
```
Private Sub cmdDisplay_Click()
    Dim i As Integer, total As Single
    Dim nom(1 To 10) As String, stores(1 To 10) As Single
    'Display names, percentage of total stores for top ten pizza chains
    'Read from text file and record names and number of stores
    'Compute total stores
    Open "7-1-E33.TXT" For Input As #1
    total = 0                     'Total stores
    For i = 1 To 10
      Input #1, nom(i), stores(i)
      total = total + stores(i)
    Next i
    Close #1
    'Display names and percentage of total stores
    picOutput.Cls
    picOutput.Print "Name"; Tab(30); "Percentage of stores"
    For i = 1 To 10
      picOutput.Print nom(i); Tab(30); FormatPercent(stores(i) / total)
    Next i
End Sub
```

35.
```
Dim monthNames(1 To 12) As Single   'In (Declarations) section of (General)

Private Sub Form_Load()
  monthNames(1) = "January"
  monthNames(2) = "February"
  monthNames(3) = "March"
  monthNames(4) = "April"
  monthNames(5) = "May"
  monthNames(6) = "June"
  monthNames(7) = "July"
  monthNames(8) = "August"
  monthNames(9) = "September"
  monthNames(10) = "October"
  monthNames(11) = "November"
  monthNames(12) = "December"
End Sub

Private Sub cmdDisplay_Click()
  Dim monthNum As Integer
  'Display month name
  picOutput.Cls
  monthNum = Val(InputBox("Enter month number:"))
  If (monthNum > 0) And (monthNum < 13) Then
      picOutput.Print "Month name is "; monthNames(monthNum)
    Else
      MsgBox ("Number must be between 1 and 12.", , "Error"
  End If
End Sub
```

37.
```
Dim color() As String     'Holds the colors, initial upper bound 50
Dim counter As Integer    'The number of colors stored

Private Sub Form_Load()
  Dim ub As Integer   'Upper bound of array
  'Load the colors from the file into the array
  ReDim color(1 To 50)
  counter = 0
  'Loop over all lines of the file
  ub = 50
  Open "COLORS.TXT" For Input As #1
  Do While Not EOF(1)
    'If out of room then increase the size of the array
    If counter >= ub Then
        ReDim Preserve color(1 To ub + 10)
        ub = ub + 10
    End If
    counter = counter + 1
    Input #1, color(counter)
  Loop
  Close #1
End Sub

Private Sub cmdDisplay_Click()
  Dim i As Integer
  Dim letter As String
  'Display all colors that begin with a letter
  letter = UCase(txtLetter)
  picColors.Cls
  For i = 1 To counter
    'If letter matches first letter in color, display it
    If Left(color(i), 1) = letter Then
        picColors.Print color(i)
    End If
  Next i
End Sub
```

39.
```
Private Sub cmdDisplay_Click()
    Dim i As Integer, roll As Integer
    Dim results(1 To 6) As Integer
    'Report results of 1000 rolls of a die
    Randomize
    picOutput.Cls
    For i = 1 To 1000
      roll = Int(6 * Rnd) + 1
►     results(roll) = results(roll) + 1
    Next i
    For i = 1 to 6
       picOutput.Print i; "came up"; results(i); "times."
    Next i
End Sub
```

Exercises 7.2

1. No.

3. Michigan

5. less than
greater than
equals
less than

7. The total rainfall for the first quarter is 10

9. You can't display an entire array with one statement.
Change picOutput.Print city to picOutput.Print city (1).

11. *n* is incremented by 1 even if the user enters 0 to stop and
see the product. Move the incrementing inside the If
block just before the statement num(n) = number.

13.
```
Private Sub CopyArray(a() As Integer, b() As Integer)
    Dim i As Integer
    'Place a's values in b
    For i = 1 to UBound(a)
      b(i) = a(i)
    Next i
End Sub
```

15.
```
Private Sub Ascending()
    Dim orderFlag As Boolean, i As Integer
    'Determine if array is ascending
    orderFlag = True
    i = 1
    Do While (i < UBound(scores)) And (orderFlag)
      If scores(i) > scores(i + 1) Then
         orderFlag = False
      End If
      i = i + 1
    Loop
    If orderFlag Then
       picOutput.Print "Array is ascending."
     Else
       picOutput.Print "Array is not ascending."
    End If
End Sub
```

17.
```
Private Sub WhatOrder()
  Dim ascendFlag As Boolean, descendFlag As Boolean, i As Integer
  'Determine if order is ascending, descending, both, or neither
  ascendFlag = True
  descendFlag = True
  For i = 1 To UBound(scores) - 1
    If scores(i) > scores(i + 1) Then
        ascendFlag = False
      ElseIf scores(i) < scores(i + 1) Then
        descendFlag = False
    End If
  Next i
  If ascendFlag And descendFlag Then
      picOutput.Print "Array is both ascending and descending"
    ElseIf (Not ascendFlag) And (Not descendFlag) Then
      picOutput.Print "Array is neither ascending nor descending."
    ElseIf ascendFlag Then
      picOutput.Print "Array is ascending."
    Else
      picOutput.Print "Array is descending."
  End If
End Sub
```

19.
```
Private Sub MergeOrderedWithDups()
  Dim indexA As Integer, indexB As Integer, indexC As Integer
  Dim doneA As Boolean, doneB As Boolean
  'Merge ascending arrays, with duplications
  ReDim c(1 To 40) As Single
  indexA = 1
  indexB = 1
  doneA = False
  doneB = False
  For indexC = 1 To 40
    If ((a(indexA) <= b(indexB)) And Not doneA) Or doneB Then
        c(indexC) = a(indexA)
        If indexA < 20 Then
            indexA = indexA + 1
          Else
            doneA = True
        End If
      Else
        c(indexC) = b(indexB)
        If indexB < 20 Then
            indexB = indexB + 1
          Else
            doneB = True
        End If
    End If
  Next indexC
End Sub
```

21.
```
Dim state(1 To 50) As String    'In (Declarations) section of (General)
Dim numStates As Integer
'Maintain a list of states

Private Sub cmdInsState_Click()
  Dim nom As String, i As Integer, j As Integer
  'Enter a new state in the correct position
  If numStates = UBound(state) Then
      MsgBox "Fifty states have already been entered.", , ""
    Else
      nom = txtState.Text
      state(numStates + 1) = nom
      i = 1
      'Find the place to insert the state
      Do While state(i) < nom
        i = i + 1
      Loop
```

```
            If (nom = state(i)) And (i <= numStates) Then
                MsgBox "State is already in the list."
              Else   'Shift elements up by 1, insert state
                For j = numStates To i Step -1
                    state(j + 1) = state(j)
                Next j
                state(i) = nom
                numStates = numStates + 1
            End If
        End If
        txtState = ""
        txtState.SetFocus
    End Sub

    Private Sub cmdDelState_Click()
        Dim nom As String, i As Integer, k As Integer
        'Delete a state from the list
        nom = txtState.Text
        i = 1
        Do While (i < numStates) And (nom > state(i))
            i = i + 1
        Loop
        If (numStates = 0) Or (nom <> state(i)) Then
            MsgBox "State is not in the list"
          Else   ' Shift rest of array down by 1
            numStates = numStates - 1
            For k = i To numStates
                state(k) = state(k + 1)
            Next k
        End If
        txtState = ""
        txtState.SetFocus
    End Sub

    Private Sub cmdDisplay_Click()
        Dim i As Integer
        'Display the states in the list
        picStates.Cls
        For i = 1 To numStates
            picStates.Print state(i)
        Next i
        txtState.SetFocus
    End Sub

    Private Sub cmdQuit_Click()
        End
    End Sub
```

23.
```
    Dim grades(1 To 100) As Integer   'In (Declarations) section of (General)
    Dim numScores As Integer
    'Report the number of students scoring above the class average

    Private Sub cmdRecordScore_Click()
        If numScores = 100 Then
            MsgBox "100 scores have been entered. Cannot process more data.", , "Array Full"
          Else
            numScores = numScores + 1
            grades(numScores) = Val(txtScore.Text)
        End If
        txtScore.Text = ""
        txtScore.SetFocus
    End Sub

    Private Sub cmdCalcAverage_Click()
        Dim average As Single, aboveAverage As Integer
        picOutput.Cls
        average = Avg(grades(), numScores)
        aboveAverage = AboveAvg(grades(), numScores, average)
        picOutput.Print aboveAverage; "students scored above the average of"; average
    End Sub
```

```
Private Function Avg(scores() As Integer, num As Integer) As Single
  'Compute the average
  Dim sum As Integer, i As Integer
  sum = 0
  For i = 1 To num
    sum = sum + scores(i)
  Next i
  If num <> 0 Then
      Avg = sum / num
    Else
      Avg = 0
  End If
End Function


Private Function AboveAvg(scores() As Integer, num As Integer, classAvg As Single) As Integer
  Dim i As Integer, tot As Integer
  'Count number of scores above average
  For i = 1 To num
    If scores(i) > classAvg Then
        tot = tot + 1
    End If
  Next i
  AboveAvg = tot
End Function
```

25.
```
Private Sub cmdSelectPeople_Click()
  'Choose 40 people from a text file containing 100 names
  Dim person(1 To 100) As Integer
  Call ClearArray(person())
  Call SelectPeople(person())
  Call ShowPeople(person())
End Sub

Private Sub ClearArray(person() As Integer)
  Dim i As Integer
  'Clear all array elements (no one selected yet)
  For i = 1 To 100
    person(i) = 0
  Next i
End Sub

Private Sub SelectPeople(person() As Integer)
  Dim i As Integer, num As Integer
  'Select 40 people (person i selected when person(i) = 1)
  Randomize
  For i = 1 To 40
    Do
      num = Int(Rnd * 100) + 1
    Loop Until person(num) = 0
    person(num) = 1
  Next i
End Sub

Private Sub ShowPeople(person() As Integer)
  Dim i As Integer, nom As String
  'Display selected people
  picOutput.Cls
  Open "7-2-E25.TXT" For Input As #1
  For i = 1 To 100
    Input #1, nom
    If person(i) = 1 Then
        picOutput.Print nom
    End If
  Next i
  Close #1
End Sub
```

Exercises 7.3

5. The width of the text box is cut in half.

7. The text box will move left or right so that the upper-left corner of the text box is of equal distance from the top and the left edge of the form.

9. The text box will extend all the way across the form. If the left edge of the text box is not at the left edge of the form, then part of the text box will extend beyond the right edge of the form but will not be visible.

15.
```
Private Sub cmdButton_Click(Index As Integer)
  Dim othrIdx As Integer
  othrIdx = (Index + 1) Mod 2
  cmdButton(Index).Left = cmdButton(othrIdx).Left + cmdButton(othrIdx).Width + 100
End Sub
```

17.
```
Private Sub cmdButton_Click(Index As Integer)
  cmdButton(Index).Width = 2 * cmdButton(Index).Width
End Sub
```

19.
```
Load txtBox(1)
txtBox(1).Top = txtBox(0).Top + txtBox(0).Height + 100
txtBox(1).Visible = True
```

21. The first line of the event procedure should not have (1) in it, but instead should have (Index As Integer) after Click.

23. The index of the For loop should start at 1, not 0, or If i > 0 Then . . . End If should be put around the Load statement and the statement that sets the Top property. With a value of zero for *i*, an attempt will be made to load lblID(0), which has already been created at design time, and to set the Top property of lblID(0) based on the Top and Height properties of lblID(–1), which cannot be done.

11.
```
Private Sub cmdButton_Click(Index As Integer)
  cmdButton(Index).Visible = False
End Sub
```

13.
```
Private Sub cmdButton_Click(Index As Integer)
  Dim otherIndex As Integer
  otherIndex = (Index + 1) Mod 2
  cmdButton(Index).Font.Italic = True
  cmdButton(otherIndex).Font.Italic = False
End Sub
```

25. Home expenses for winter were $4,271.66

27. Summer bills exceeded winter by $67.09

29. The form displays a vertical column of four text boxes, separated from each other by one-half the height of a text box and labeled on the left with "Row #". The column is headed by "Col 1".

31. The form displays a horizontal row of four touching text boxes labeled above by "Col #". The row is labeled on the left by "Row 1".

33.
```
Private Sub txtWinter_LostFocus(Index As Integer)
  'recompute totals
  Call Retotal
End Sub

Private Sub txtSpring_LostFocus(Index As Integer)
  'recompute totals
  Call Retotal
End Sub

Private Sub txtSummer_LostFocus(Index As Integer)
  'recompute totals
  Call Retotal
End Sub

Private Sub txtFall_LostFocus(Index As Integer)
  'recompute totals
  Call Retotal
End Sub

Private Sub Retotal()
  Dim total(1 To 4) As Single
  Dim i As Integer, cTotal As Single
  'recompute totals
  For i = 1 To 4
    total(1) = total(1) + Val(txtWinter(i).Text)
    total(2) = total(2) + Val(txtSpring(i).Text)
    total(3) = total(3) + Val(txtSummer(i).Text)
    total(4) = total(4) + Val(txtFall(i).Text)
  Next i
  For i = 1 to 4
    lblQuarterTot(i).Caption = Str(total(i))
  Next i
```

```
    For i = 1 to 4
      cTotal = 0
      cTotal = Val(txtWinter(i).Text) + Val(txtSpring(i).Text)
      cTotal = cTotal + Val(txtSummer(i).Text) + Val(txtFall(i).Text)
      lblCategTot(i).Caption = Str(cTotal)
    Next i
  End Sub
```

35.
```
  Private Sub picTrafficLight_LostFocus(Index As Integer)
      picTrafficLight(Index).BackColor = vbWhite
  End Sub

  Private Sub picTrafficLight_GotFocus(Index As Integer)
    Select Case Index
      Case 0
        picTrafficLight(0).BackColor = vbYellow
      Case 1
        picTrafficLight(1).BackColor = vbRed
      Case 2
        picTrafficLight(2).BackColor = vbGreen
    End Select
  End Sub
```

37.
```
  Dim correctNum As Single   'In (Declarations) section of (General)

  Private Sub Form_Load()
    Open "7-3-E37.TXT" For Input As #1
    Call GetQuestion
  End Sub

  Private Sub GetQuestion()
    Dim i As Integer, info As String
    For i = 0 to 4
      Input #1, info          'obtain question and 4 possible answers
      lblSentence(i).Caption = info
    Next i
    Input #1, correctNum     'number of the correct answer
  End Sub

  Private Sub cmdAnswer_Click(Index As Integer)
    If Index = correctNum Then
        Call CorrectAnswer
    Else
        Call IncorrectAnswer
    End If
  End Sub

  Private Sub CorrectAnswer()
    Dim response As String
    If Not EOF(1) Then
        Call GetQuestion
    Else
      MsgBox "There are no more questions.", , ""
      Close #1
      End
    End If
  End Sub

  Private Sub IncorrectAnswer()            Private Sub cmdQuit_Click()
    MsgBox "Incorrect, Try Again", , ""      Close #1
  End Sub                                     End
                                           End Sub
```

Exercises 7.4

1. 200 100

3. 11 7 Numbers interchanged.

5. Items not properly swapped.

7. Sequential

9. 4 swaps

11. $(n-1) + (n-2) + \ldots + 1$ or $n(n-1)/2$

13. 4 swaps

15. 8 comparisons

17. Go through the list once and count the number of times that each of the four integers occurs. Then list the determined number of 1's, followed by the determined number of 2's, etc.

19. 16; 8 1/2; 5

21.
```
Private Sub TripleSwap(x As Single, y As Single, z As
Single)
  Dim temp As Single
  'Interchange the values of x, y, and z
  temp = x
  x = y
  y = z
  z = temp
End Sub
```

23.
```
Private Sub cmdDisplay_Click()
  'Display major events and crowd estimates in alphabetical order
  Dim majorEvent(1 To 9) As String, crowd(1 To 9) As Integer
  Call ReadData(majorEvent(), crowd())
  Call SortData(majorEvent(), crowd())
  Call ShowData(majorEvent(), crowd())
End Sub

Private Sub ReadData(majorEvent() As String, crowd() As Integer)
  Dim i As Integer
  'Read major event names, crowd estimates
  Open "7-4-E23.TXT" For Input As #1
  For i = 1 To UBound(majorEvent)
    Input #1, majorEvent(i), crowd(i)
  Next i
  Close #1
End Sub

Private Sub SortData(majorEvent() As String, crowd() As Integer)
  Dim elements As Integer, gap As Integer, doneFlag As Boolean, index As Integer
  Dim strTemp As String, numTemp As Integer
  'Shell sort data by majorEvent names
  elements = UBound(majorEvent)
  gap = Int(elements / 2)
  doneFlag = False
  Do While gap >= 1
    Do
      doneFlag = True
      For index = 1 To elements - gap
        If majorEvent(index) > majorEvent(index + gap) Then
            'swap majorEvents
            strTemp = majorEvent(index)
            majorEvent(index) = majorEvent(index + gap)
            majorEvent(index + gap) = strTemp
            'swap crowd
            numTemp = crowd(index)
            crowd(index) = crowd(index + gap)
            crowd(index + gap) = numTemp
            doneFlag = False
        End If
      Next index
    Loop Until doneFlag
    gap = Int(gap / 2)
  Loop
End Sub

Private Sub ShowData(majorEvent() As String, crowd() As Integer)
  Dim i As Integer, temp As String
  'Display major event names and crowd estimates
  picEvents.Cls
  picEvents.Print "Event"; Tab(40); "Crowd Estimate (in thousands)"
  picEvents.Print
  For i = 1 To UBound(majorEvent)
    temp = FormatNumber(crowd(i), 0)
    picEvents.Print majorEvent(i); Tab(46); Format(temp,"@@@@@")
  Next i
End Sub
```

25.
```
Private Sub cmdDisplay_Click()
  Dim wordList(1 To 11) As String
  'Input list of words, insert additional word, display entire list
  picWords.Cls
  Call InputWords(wordList())
  Call InsertWord(wordList())
  Call ShowWords(wordList())
End Sub

Private Sub InputWords(wordList() As String)
  Dim i As Integer
  'Input first 10 words
  picWords.Print "Input ten words in alphabetical order."
  For i = 1 To 10
    wordList(i) = InputBox("Enter word number " & Str(i) & ":")
  Next i
End Sub

Private Sub InsertWord(wordList() As String)
  Dim word As String, i As Integer, k As Integer
  'Insert eleventh word in alphabetical order.
  'Put it at end to start with.
  picWords.Print
  word = InputBox("Word to add:", "")
  wordList(11) = word
  i = 1
  Do While word > wordList(i)     'Terminate when a word greater than the new word
    i = i + 1                     'is found or when the new word is reached (i = 11)
  Loop
  'New word belongs in slot i; move elements i through 10 up one slot
  'If it belongs in last place (i = 11), this loop will be skipped
  For k = 10 To i Step -1
    wordList(k + 1) = wordList(k)
  Next k
  wordList(i) = word
End Sub

Private Sub ShowWords(wordList() As String)
  Dim i As Integer
  'Show list of eleven words
  picWords.Cls
  For i = 1 To 11
    picWords.Print wordList(i); " "
  Next i
End Sub
```

27.
```
Private Sub cmdDisplay_Click()
  Dim nums(1 To 2000) As Integer
  Dim dist(0 To 63) As Integer
  'Tabulate frequencies in an array of 2000 numbers
  Call FillArray(nums())
  Call GetOccurrences(nums(), dist())
  Call ShowDistribution(dist())
End Sub

Private Sub FillArray(nums() As Integer)
  Dim i As Integer
  'Generate numbers from 0 to 63 and place in array
  nums(1) = 5
  For i = 2 To 2000
    nums(i) = (9 * nums(i - 1) + 7) Mod 64
  Next i
End Sub

Private Sub GetOccurrences(nums() As Integer, dist() As Integer)
  Dim i As Integer
  'Record occurrences for each number
  For i = 1 To 2000
    dist(nums(i)) = dist(nums(i)) + 1
  Next i
End Sub
```

```
    Private Sub ShowDistribution(dist() As Integer)
      Dim colWid As Integer, col As Integer, colNum As Integer, i As Integer
      'Display distribution array
      picDistribution.Cls
      colWid = 12                      'Width allotted for a column
      For colNum = 0 To 3              'Display headings at top of four column
        col = colWid * colNum + 1
        picDistribution.Print Tab(col); " # Occur";
      Next colNum
      picDistribution.Print
      For i = 1 To 63                  'Display numbers & count of occurrences
        colNum = (i - 1) Mod 4
        col = colWid * colNum + 1
        picDistribution.Print Tab(col); i; Tab(col + 4); dist(i);
        If col = 3 Then
            picDistribution.Print
        End If
      Next i
    End Sub
```

29.
```
    Dim codes() As String   'In (Declarations) section of (General)

    Private Sub Form_Load()
      Dim i As Integer
      ReDim codes(Asc("A") To Asc("Z")) As String
      Open "7-4-E29.TXT" For Input As #1
      For i = Asc("A") To Asc("Z")
        Input #1, codes(i)
      Next i
      Close #1
    End Sub


    Private Sub cmdConvertToMorse_Click()
      Dim word As String
      'Encode word in Morse Code
      word = UCase(txtWord.Text)
      Call ShowCode(word)
    End Sub


    Private Sub ShowCode(word As String)
      Dim index As Integer, letter As String
      'Show code for each index in word
      picMorse.Cls
      For index = 1 To Len(word)
        letter = Mid(word, index, 1)
        picMorse.Print codes(Asc(letter)), letter
      Next index
    End Sub
```

31.
```
    Private Sub cmdCalcAvg_Click()
      Dim nom As String
      Dim score(1 To 7) As Integer
      'Compute average of five highest test scores out of seven
      Call InputData(nom, score())
      Call SortData(score())
      Call ShowData(nom, score())
    End Sub


    Private Sub InputData(nom As String, score() As Integer)
      Dim i As Integer
      'Input student's name and seven test scores
      nom = InputBox("Student's name:")
      For i = 1 To 7
        score(i) = Val(InputBox("Test score " & Str(i) & ":"))
      Next i
    End Sub
```

```
Private Sub SortData(score() As Integer)
  Dim passNum As Integer, index As Integer, temp As Integer
  'Bubble sort scores in descending order
  For passNum = 1 To 6
    For index = 1 To 7 - passNum
      If score(index) < score(index + 1) Then
          temp = score(index)
          score(index) = score(index + 1)
          score(index + 1) = temp
      End If
    Next index
  Next passNum
End Sub


Private Sub ShowData(nom As String, score() As Integer)
  Dim sum As Integer, passNum As Integer
  picAvg.Cls
  sum = 0
  For passNum = 1 To 5
    sum = sum + score(passNum)
  Next passNum
  picAvg.Print nom, sum / 5
End Sub
```

33.
```
Private Sub cmdCalcMedian_Click()
    Dim n As Integer
    'Input array of measurements and determine their median
    Call InputNumberOfMeasurements(n)
    ReDim nums(1 To n) As Single
    Call InputNums(nums())
    Call DisplayMedian(nums())
End Sub

Private Sub InputNumberOfMeasurements(n As Integer)
    'Input number of measurements
    n = Val(InputBox("Number of measurements:"))
End Sub

Private Sub InputNums(nums() As Single)
  Dim i As Integer
  'Input list of measurements
  For i = 1 To UBound(nums)
    nums(i) = Val(InputBox("Enter measurement #" & Str(i) & ":"))
  Next i
End Sub

Private Sub DisplayMedian(nums() As Single)
  'Display the median of the n measurements
  picMedian.Cls
  picMedian.Print "The median is"; Median(nums())
End Sub

Private Function Median(nums() As Single) As Single
  Dim n As Integer, m As Integer
  Call SortNums(nums())
  n = UBound(nums)
  If Int(n / 2) = n / 2 Then               'n is even
      m = n / 2
      Median = (nums(m) + nums(m + 1)) / 2 'Median is average of two middle measurements
    Else                                   'n is odd
      Median = nums((n + 1) / 2)           'Median is the middle measurement
  End If
End Function


Private Sub SortNums(nums() As Single)
  Dim n As Integer, i As Integer, j As Integer, temp As Single
  'Bubble sort list of numbers
  n = UBound(nums)
```

```
      For i = 1 To n - 1
        For j = 1 To n - i
          If nums(j) > nums(j + 1) Then
              temp = nums(j)
              nums(j) = nums(j + 1)
              nums(j + 1) = temp
          End If
        Next j
      Next i
    End Sub
```

Exercises 7.5

1. 12

3. Dorothy

5. 4 1 6
    5 8 2

7. 1 3 5

9. The dimension statement should read Dim a(1 To 4, 1 To 3) As Integer (currently, the error is Subscript Out of Range.)

11.
```
Private Sub FillArray(a() As Single)
  Dim row As Integer, col As Integer
  'Fill an array
  For row = 1 To 10
    For col = 1 To 10
      a(row, col) = col
    Next col
  Next row
End Sub
```

13.
```
Private Sub Exchange(a() As Single)
  Dim col As Integer, temp As Single
  'Interchange values of 2nd and 3rd row
  For col = 1 To 10
    temp = a(2, col)
    a(2, col) - a(3, col)
    a(3, col) = temp
  Next col
End Sub
```

15.
```
Private Sub cmdDisplay_Click()
  Dim inv(1 To 2, 1 To 3) As Single, sales(1 To 2, 1 To 3) As Single
  'Program to calculate inventory
  Call ReadArrays(inv(), sales())
  Call ShowInventory(inv(), sales())
End Sub

Private Sub ReadArrays(inv() As Single, sales() As Single)
  Dim store As Integer, item As Integer
  'Read beginning inventory and sales for day
  'Beginning inventory is assumed to reside in BEGINV.TXT
  'Sales for day is assumed to reside in SALES.TXT
  Open "BEGINV.TXT" For Input As #1
  Open "SALES.TXT" For Input As #2
  For store = 1 To 2
    For item = 1 To 3
      Input #1, inv(store, item)
      Input #2, sales(store, item)
    Next item
  Next store
  Close #1
  Close #2
End Sub

Private Sub ShowInventory(inv() As Single, sales() As Single)
  Dim total As Single, store As Integer, item As Integer
  'Calculate and show inventory at end of the day
  picInventory.Cls
  total = 0
  For store = 1 To 2
    For item = 1 To 3
      inv(store, item) = inv(store, item) - sales(store, item)
      picInventory.Print inv(store, item),
      total = total + inv(store, item)
    Next item
    picInventory.Print
  Next store
  picInventory.Print "Total inventory is now"; total
End Sub
```

```
17. Private Sub cmdCompute_Click()
      'Compute course enrollments by campus, no. of students by course
      picEnroll.Cls
      Dim enrollment(1 To 3, 1 To 10) As Single
      Call ReadData(enrollment())
      Call ShowCampusTotals(enrollment())
      Call ShowCourseTotals(enrollment())
    End Sub

    Private Sub ReadData(enrollment() As Single)
      Dim campus As Integer, course As Integer
      'Read enrollment data
      'Course enrollment data are assumed to reside in ENROLL.TXT
      Open "ENROLL.TXT" For Input As #1
      For campus = 1 To 3
        For course = 1 To 10
          Input #1, enrollment(campus, course)
        Next course
      Next campus
      Close #1
    End Sub

    Private Sub ShowCampusTotals(enrollment() As Single)
      Dim campus As Integer, total As Single, course As Integer
      'Compute and show total enrollments for each campus
      For campus = 1 To 3
        total = 0
        For course = 1 To 10
          total = total + enrollment(campus, course)
        Next course
        picEnroll.Print "The total course enrollments on campus"; campus; "is"; total
      Next campus
    End Sub

    Private Sub ShowCourseTotals(enrollment() As Single)
      Dim course As Integer, total As Single, campus As Integer
      'Compute total enrollment for each course
      For course = 1 To 10
        total = 0
        For campus = 1 To 3
          total = total + enrollment(campus, course)
        Next campus
        picEnroll.Print "The total enrollment in course"; course; "is"; total
      Next course
    End Sub

19. Private Sub cmdCalcGolfStats_Click()
      Dim nom(1 To 3) As String, score(1 To 3, 1 To 4) As Integer
      'Compute golf statistics
      picStats.Cls
      Call ReadData(nom(), score())
      Call ComputeTotalScore(nom(), score())
      Call ComputeAveScore(nom(), score())
    End Sub

    Private Sub ReadData(nom() As String, score() As Integer)
      Dim player As Integer, round As Integer
      'Results of 2003 Buick Invitational assumed to reside in GOLF.TXT
      'Read names and scores
      Open "GOLF.TXT" For Input As #1
      For player = 1 To 3
        Input #1, nom(player)
        For round = 1 To 4
          Input #1, score(player, round)
        Next round
      Next player
      Close #1
    End Sub
```

```
   Private Sub ComputeTotalScore(nom() As String, score() As Integer)
     Dim player As Integer, total As Integer, round As Integer
     'Compute total score for each player
     For player = 1 To 3
       total = 0
       For round = 1 To 4
         total = total + score(player, round)
       Next round
       picStats.Print "The total score for "; nom(player); " was"; total
     Next player
     picStats.Print
   End Sub


   Private Sub ComputeAveScore(nom() As String, score() As Integer)
     Dim round As Integer, total As Integer, player As Integer
     'Compute average score for each round
     For round = 1 To 4
       total = 0
       For player = 1 To 3
         total = total + score(player, round)
       Next player
       picStats.Print "The average for round"; round; "was"; FormatNumber(total / 3)
     Next round
   End Sub
```

21.
```
    'In the (Declarations) section of (General)
    Dim prog(1 To 3) As String, univ(1 To 3, 1 To 5) As String


    Private Sub cmdDisplayRankings_Click()
      Dim university As String
      'Access information from University Rankings Table
      university = Trim(txtUnivName.Text)
      Call ShowRankings(university)
    End Sub


    Private Sub Form_Load()
      Dim dept As Integer, ranking As Integer
      'Read university rankings in three departments
      Open "RANKINGS.TXT" For Input As #1
      'The first line of the file is "Business", "U of PA", "U of IN", "U of MI", "UC Berkeley", "U of VA"
      For dept = 1 To 3
        Input #1, prog(dept)
        For ranking = 1 To 5
          Input #1, univ(dept, ranking)
        Next ranking
      Next dept
      Close #1
    End Sub


    Private Sub ShowRankings(university As String)
      Dim foundFlag As Boolean, dept As Integer, ranking As Integer
      'Show rankings of university
      picRankings.Cls
      picRankings.Print university; " departments ranked in the top 5:"
      foundFlag = False
      For dept = 1 To 3
        For ranking = 1 To 5
          If univ(dept, ranking) = university Then
              picRankings.Print prog(dept), ranking
              foundFlag = True
          End If
        Next ranking
      Next dept
      If Not foundFlag Then
          picRankings.Print "Sorry! No information listed."
      End If
      txtUnivName.Text = ""
      txtUnivName.SetFocus
    End Sub
```

23.

Object	Property	Setting
lblStudent	Caption	Name of Student #1:
txtStudent	Text	(blank)
lblExam()	Index	1 to 5
	Caption	Exam # Grade
txtExam()	Index	1 to 5
	Text	(blank)
cmdRecordData	Caption	Record Student Data
picGrades		

```
'In (Declarations) section of (General)
Dim nom(1 To 15) As String, score(1 To 15, 1 To 5) As Integer
Dim student As Integer

Private Sub cmdRecordData_Click()
  Dim exam As Integer
  'Record name and five exam scores for another student
  'Exam scores are entered in a control array of five text boxes
  'When last student is entered, process data and prevent further data entry
  student = student + 1
  nom(student) = txtStudent.Text
  For exam = 1 To 5
    score(student, exam) = Val(txtExam(exam).Text)
  Next exam
  If student = UBound(nom) Then
      Call ProcessData
      cmdRecordData.Visible = False
    Else
      txtStudent.Text = ""
      For exam = 1 To 5
        txtExam(exam).Text = ""
      Next exam
      lblStudent.Caption = "Name of student #" & FormatNumber(student + 1, 0) & ":"
      txtStudent.SetFocus
  End If
End Sub

Private Sub ProcessData()
  'Analyze exam scores
  picGrades.Cls
  Call ShowAverages(nom(), score())
  Call SortScores(score())
  Call ShowMedians(score())
End Sub

Private Sub ShowAverages(nom() As String, score() As Integer)
  Dim index As Integer, sum As Integer, exam As Integer
  'Compute and show semester score averages
  picGrades.Print "Name"; Tab(15); "Semester average"
  For index = 1 To UBound(nom)
    sum = 0
    For exam = 1 To 5
      sum = sum + score(index, exam)
    Next exam
    picGrades.Print nom(index); Tab(20); FormatNumber(sum / 5, 0)
  Next index
End Sub

Private Sub SortScores(score() As Integer)
  Dim entries As Integer, exam As Integer, passNum As Integer
  Dim index As Integer, temp As Integer
  'Bubble sort scores
  entries = UBound(nom)
```

```
    For exam = 1 To 5
      For passNum = 1 To entries - 1
        For index = 1 To entries - passNum
          If score(index, exam) > score(index + 1, exam) Then
              temp = score(index, exam)
              score(index, exam) = score(index + 1, exam)
              score(index + 1, exam) = temp
          End If
        Next index
      Next passNum
    Next exam
  End Sub

  Private Sub ShowMedians(score() As Integer)
    Dim entries As Integer, exam As Integer, middle As Integer
    'Show medians for each exam
    entries = UBound(nom)
    For exam = 1 To 5
      picGrades.Print "The median on exam"; exam; "was";
      If Int(entries / 2) = entries / 2 Then    'If even number of entries
          middle = entries / 2          'First index of the two "middle" entries
          picGrades.Print (score(middle, exam) + score(middle + 1, exam)) / 2
      Else
          middle = (entries + 1) / 2
          picGrades.Print score(middle, exam)
      End If
    Next exam
  End Sub
```

25.
```
  Private Sub cmdCalcTotSales_Click()
    'Compute total sales for each store and for entire company
    Dim sales(1 To 3, 1 To 5) As Integer, cost(1 To 5) As Single
    Call ReadData(sales(), cost())
    Call ShowRevenues(sales(), cost())
  End Sub

  Private Sub ReadData(sales() As Integer, cost() As Single)
    Dim store As Integer, item As Integer
    'Read sales and cost
    Open "7-5-E25B.TXT" For Input As #1
    For store = 1 To 3
      For item = 1 To 5
        Input #1, sales(store, item)
      Next item
    Next store
    Close #1
    Open "7-5-E25A.TXT" For Input As #1
    For item = 1 To 5
      Input #1, cost(item)
    Next item
    Close #1
  End Sub

  Private Sub ShowRevenues(sales() As Integer, cost() As Single)
    Dim totalRevenue As Single, store As Integer, storeRevenue As Single
    Dim item As Integer, totalStr As String
    'Compute and show revenues
    picTotalSales.Font.Name = "Courier New"
    picTotalSales.Cls
    picTotalSales.Print "Store"; Tab(12); "Total"
    totalRevenue = 0
```

```
    For store = 1 To 3
      storeRevenue = 0
      For item = 1 To 5
        storeRevenue = storeRevenue + sales(store, item) * cost(item)
      Next item
      totalRevenue = totalRevenue + storeRevenue
      totalStr = FormatCurrency(storeRevenue)
      picTotalSales.Print " "; store; Tab(7); Format(totalStr, "@@@@@@@@@")
    Next store
    picTotalSales.Print "Total revenue for the company was "; FormatCurrency(totalRevenue)
End Sub
```

CHAPTER 8

Exercises 8.1

1. `Hello`

3. `Hello`
`Aloha`
`Bon Jour`

5. Copies Hello and Bon Jour into the file
"WELCOME.TXT".

7. No quotes surrounding file name.

9. Using EOF(1) as the terminating value in a For loop.

11. In the Open statement, remove the quotation marks
surrounding nom. Otherwise, the new file will have the
name NOM instead of the intended name
NEWGREET.TXT

13.
```
Private Sub cmdCreateFile_Click()
    'Create file of names and prices of items bought by cowboys
    Open "COWBOY.TXT" For Output As #1
    Write #1, "Colt Peacemaker", 12.2
    Write #1, "Holster", 2
    Write #1, "Levi Strauss Jeans", 1.35
    Write #1, "Saddle", 40
    Write #1, "Stetson", 10
    Close #1
    MsgBox "File has been created."
End Sub
```

15.
```
Private Sub cmdAddItem_Click()
    'Add Winchester rifle to end of file COWBOY.TXT
    Open "COWBOY.TXT" For Append As #1
    Write #1, "Winchester rifle", 20.5
    Close #1
    MsgBox "Item added to file."
End Sub
```

17.
```
Private Sub cmdAddItem_Click()
    Dim newItem As String, newPrice As Single
    'Insert an item into COWBOY.TXT file in proper sequence
    Call InputItemData(newItem, newPrice)
    Call AddItemData(newItem, newPrice)
End Sub

Private Sub AddItemData(newItem As String, newPrice As Single)
Dim insertedFlag As Boolean, item As String, price As Single
    'Create second COWBOY file with new inserted item
    Open "COWBOY.TXT" For Input As #1
    Open "COWBOY2.TXT" For Output As #2
    insertedFlag = False        'Tells if item has been inserted
    Do While Not EOF(1)
      Input #1, item, price
      If (Not insertedFlag) And (item >= newItem) Then
          Write #2, newItem, newPrice
          insertedFlag = True
      End If
      Write #2, item, price
    Loop
    Close #1
    If Not insertedFlag Then
        Write #2, newItem, newPrice
    End If
    Close #2
End Sub

Private Sub InputItemData(newItem As String, newPrice As
Single)
    'Input new item name and price
    newItem = InputBox("New item to be inserted:")
    newPrice = Val(InputBox("Price of the new item:"))
End Sub
```

19.
```
Private Sub cmdRemoveItem_Click()
    Dim item As String, price As Single
    'Produce COWBOY4.TXT with Holster removed
    Open "COWBOY.TXT" For Input As #1
    Open "COWBOY4.TXT" For Output As #2
    Do While Not EOF(1)
      Input #1, item, price
      If item <> "Holster" Then
          Write #2, item, price
      End If
    Loop
    Close #2
    Close #1
End Sub
```

23.
```
Private Sub cmdProcess_Click()
    Dim searchTitle As String, filename As String
    Dim title As String, copies As Integer
    'Access publisher's inventory files
    picInventory.Cls
    Call InputData(searchTitle, filename)
    Open filename For Input As #1
    title = ""
    Do While (title <> searchTitle) And (Not EOF(1))
      Input #1, title, copies
      title = UCase(title)
    Loop
    If (title = searchTitle) And (searchTitle <> "") Then
        picInventory.Print "No. of copies in inventory:"; copies
      Else
        picInventory.Print "Book is not listed."
    End If
    Close #1
End Sub
```

```
Private Sub InputData(searchTitle As String, filename _
  As String)
  Dim bookType As String
  'Input book name and determine file name
  searchTitle = UCase(txtTitle.Text)
  bookType = txtType.Text
  If UCase(bookType) = "H" Then
      filename = "HARDBACK.INV"
    Else
      filename = "PAPERBCK.INV"
  End If
End Sub
```

21.
```
Private Sub cmdFind_Click()
    Dim search As String, nom As String, yob As Integer
    'Search for a name in YOB.TXT
    picOutput.Cls
    search = txtName.Text
    Open "YOB.TXT" For Input As #1
    nom = ""
    Do While (search > nom) And (Not EOF(1))
      Input #1, nom, yob
    Loop
    Close #1
    If (nom = search) And (search <> "") Then
        picOutput.Print nom; "'s age is"; 2003 - yob
      Else
        picOutput.Print search; " is not in YOB.TXT"
    End If
End Sub
```

25.
```
Private Sub cmdDelOpenFile_Click()
    On Error GoTo ErrorHandler
    Dim item As String, price As Single
    picOutput.Cls
    Open "COWBOY.TXT" For Input As #1
    Input #1, item, price
    picOutput.Print item, price
    Kill "COWBOY.TXT"
    Input #1, item, price
    picOutput.Print item, price
    Close #1
    Exit Sub
ErrorHandler:
    '55 = file already open
    If Err.Number = 55 Then
      picOutput.Print "ERROR"; Err.Number; ":Can't kill file"
    End If
    'Skip line that tries to kill the open file
    Resume Next
End Sub
```

Exercises 8.2

1.
```
Private Sub cmdCreateFile_Click()
    'Add initial batting average record to AVERAGE.TXT
    Write #1, txtPlayer.Text, 0, 0     'Initialize counters
    txtPlayer.Text = ""
    txtPlayer.SetFocus
End Sub
```

```
Private Sub cmdQuit_Click()
  Close #1
  End
End Sub
```

```
Private Sub Form_Load()
  Open "AVERAGE.TXT" For Output As #1
End Sub
```

3.
```
Private Sub cmdAddPlayer_Click()
    'Add a player to the end of the file AVERAGE.TXT
    Write #1, txtPlayer.Text, 0, 0
    txtPlayer.Text = ""
    txtPlayer.SetFocus
End Sub
```

```
Private Sub cmdQuit_Click()
  Close #1
  End
End Sub
```

```
Private Sub Form_Load()
  Open "AVERAGE.TXT" For Append As #1
End Sub
```

5.
```
Private Sub cmdProcess_Click()
    Dim nom As String, subscriber As String
    'NY Times subscribers on your block
    Open "BLOCK.TXT" For Input As #1
    Open "TIMES.TXT" For Input As #2
    Open "NAMES.TXT" For Output As #3
    subscriber = ""
    Do While Not EOF(1)
      Input #1, nom
      Do While (subscriber < nom) And (Not EOF(2))
        Input #2, subscriber
      Loop
      If subscriber = nom Then
          Write #3, subscriber
      End If
    Loop
    Close #1
    Close #2
    Close #3
End Sub
```

7.
```
Private Sub cmdCountRepeats_Click()
    Dim max As Single, lastNum As Single, numRepeats As Single, number As Single
    'Count maximum number of repeated integers
    picOutput.Cls
    Open "NUMBERS.TXT" For Input As #1
    max = 0
    lastNum = 0
    numRepeats = 0
    Do While Not EOF(1)
      Input #1, number
      If number <> lastNum Then
          If numRepeats > max Then
              max = numRepeats
          End If
          lastNum = number
          numRepeats = 1
        Else
          numRepeats = numRepeats + 1
      End If
    Loop
    picOutput.Print "The maximum number of repeats is"; max
    Close #1
End Sub
```

9.
```
Private Sub cmdProcessTicketSales_Click()
    Dim cntrlVar As Integer, gradeTotal As Integer, total As Integer
    Dim grade As Integer, nom As String, nmbTix As Integer
    'Display student raffle ticket totals
    picOutput.Cls
    Open "RAFFLE.TXT" For Input As #1
    cntrlVar = 0
    gradeTotal = 0
    total = 0
    Do While Not EOF(1)
      Input #1, grade, nom, nmbTix
      If cntrlVar = 0 Then        'Reset cntrlVar after first grade is read
          cntrlVar = grade
      End If
      If (grade <> cntrlVar) Then    'Display gradeTotal if new grade found
          picOutput.Print "Grade"; cntrlVar; "sold"; gradeTotal; "tickets"
          total = total + gradeTotal
          gradeTotal = 0
          cntrlVar = grade
      End If
      gradeTotal = gradeTotal + nmbTix
```

```
      If EOF(1) Then              'At end-of-file, print last grade's total
          picOutput.Print "Grade"; cntrlVar; "sold"; gradeTotal; "tickets"
          total = total + gradeTotal
      End If
    Loop
    picOutput.Print
    picOutput.Print "Total = "; total
    Close #1
  End Sub
```

11.
```
    Private Sub cmdUpdate_Click()
      Dim mstName As String, mstNmb As String, nom As String, newNmb As String
      'Update phone number master file
      Open "MASTER.TXT" For Input As #1
      Open "MOVED.TXT" For Input As #2
      Open "TEMP.TXT" For Output As #3
      Do While Not EOF(2)
        Input #2, nom, newNmb
        Do
          Input #1, mstName, mstNmb
          If mstName = nom Then
              Write #3, mstName, newNmb
            Else
              Write #3, mstName, mstNmb
          End If
        Loop Until mstName = nom
      Loop
      Do While Not EOF(1)
        Input #1, mstName, mstNmb
        Write #3, mstName, mstNmb
      Loop
      Close #1
      Close #2
      Close #3
      Open "MASTER.TXT" For Output As #1
      Open "TEMP.TXT" For Input As #2
      Do While Not EOF(2)
        Input #2, mstName, mstNmb
        Write #1, mstName, mstNmb
      Loop
      Close #1
      Close #2
      Kill "TEMP.TXT"
    End Sub
```

CHAPTER 9

Exercises 9.1

1.
```
    Pacific   Mississipp
```

3.
```
    heights are same
     170
    eye colors are same
```

5. The variables used in the assignment statements are invalid. They should be astrology.nom and astrology.sign.

7. `employee.name = "Bob"` is invalid and there is no End Type statement.

9. Number is an invalid data type.

11.
```
    Public Type planet
      planetName As String * 20
      distanceFromSun As Single
    End Type
```

13.
```
    Public Type car
      make As String * 20
      model As String * 20
      yr As Integer
      mileage As Single
    End Type
```

15.
```
    Private Sub cmdDisplay_Click ()
      Dim word1 As String * 14
      Dim word2 As String * 14
      Dim word3 As String * 14
      'Input three words and display them in first three zones
      picOutput.Cls
      picOutput.Font.Name = "Courier New"
      word1 = txtWord1.Text
      word2 = txtWord2.Text
      word3 = txtWord3.Text
      picOutput.Print word1; word2; word3
    End Sub
```

Exercises 9.2

1. VA

3. TX
   WI
   VA
   3

5. Virginia Tech   VA   1872
   Harvard   MA   1636

7. Milwaukee Area Tech. Col.   WI   1912

9. Cannot take length of a variable type. Should be Len(actor).

11. Cannot print record variable.

13.
```
Public Type typeNums
   num1 As Single
   num2 As Single
   num3 As Single
End Type

Dim numbers As typeNums
Open "NUMBERS.DAT" For Random As #1 Len = Len(numbers)
```

15.
```
'In BAS module
Public Type typePerson
   nom As String * 15
   yob As Integer
End Type

'in Form Module
Private Sub cmdConvertFile_Click()
   Dim recNum As Single, nom As String, yob As Integer
   'Make random file YOB.DAT from sequential file YOB.TXT
   Dim person As typePerson
   Open "YOB.TXT" For Input As #1
   Open "YOB.DAT" For Random As #2 Len = Len(person)
   recNum = 1
   Do While Not EOF(1)
      Input #1, nom, yob
      person.nom = nom
      person.yob = yob
      Put #2, recNum, person
      recNum = recNum + 1
   Loop
   Close #1
   Close #2
End Sub
```

CHAPTER 10

Exercises 10.1

1. `picBox.Scale (-1, 30)-(7, -5)`

3.
```
picBox.Line (-1, 0)-(4, 0)      'x-axis
picBox.Line (0, -8)-(0, 40)     'y-axis
```

5.
```
Private Sub cmdDraw_Click()
   'Draw axes and line
   picOutput.Scale (-2, 240)-(12, -40)
   picOutput.Line (-2, 0)-(12, 0)       'Draw x-axis
   picOutput.Line (0, -40)-(0, 240)     'Draw y-axis
   picOutput.Line (3, 200)-(10, 150)    'Draw line
   picOutput.Circle (3, 200), .05
   picOutput.Circle (10, 150), .05
End Sub
```

7.
```
Private Sub cmdDraw_Click()
   'Draw axes and line
   picOutput.Scale (-.2 * 4, 1.2 * .5)-(1.2 * 4, -.2 * .5)
   picOutput.Line (-.2 * 4, 0)-(1.2 * 4, 0)    'Draw x-axis
   picOutput.Line (0, -.2 * .5)-(0, 1.2 * .5)  'Draw y-axis
   picOutput.Line (2, .5)-(4, .3)              'Draw line
   picOutput.Circle (2, .5), .03
   picOutput.Circle (4, .3), .03
End Sub
```

9.
```
Private Sub cmdDraw_Click()
   'Draw a circle in the center of the picture box
   picOutput.Scale (-10, 10)-(10, -10)
   picOutput.Circle (0, 0), 4
End Sub
```

11.
```
Private Sub cmdDraw_Click()
   'Draw a tick mark at 70 on the y-axis
   picOutput.Scale (-10, 100)-(100, -10)
   picOutput.Line (-10, 0)-(100, 0)     'x-axis
   picOutput.Line (0, -10)-(0, 100)     'y-axis
   picOutput.Line (-1, 70)-(1, 70)
End Sub
```

13.
```
Private Sub cmdDraw_Click()
   'Draw points in the 4 corners of the picture box
   picOutput.Scale (0, 10)-(10, 0)
   picOutput.Circle (0, 0), 1
   picOutput.Circle (0, 10), 1
   picOutput.Circle (10, 0), 1
   picOutput.Circle (10, 10), 1
End Sub
```

15.
```
Private Sub cmdDraw_Click()
   'Draw a rectangle
   picOutput.Scale (0, 10)-(10, 0)
   picOutput.Line (1, 1)-(1, 6)
   picOutput.Line (1, 6)-(6, 6)
   picOutput.Line (6, 6)-(6, 1)
   picOutput.Line (6, 1)-(1, 1)
End Sub
```

17.
```
Private Sub cmdDraw_Click()
   Dim r As Single
   'Draw five concentric circles
   picOutput.Scale (0, 10)-(10, 0)
   For r = .5 To 2.5 Step .5
      picOutput.Circle (5, 5), r
   Next r
End Sub
```

19.
```
Private Sub cmdDraw_Click()
   'Draw a circle and tangent line
   picOutput.Scale (0, 10)-(10, 0)
   picOutput.Circle (5, 5), 1
   picOutput.Line (6, 0)-(6, 10)
End Sub
```

21. The circle will be smaller.

23. The circle will be the same size as in Exercise 21.

25.
```
Private Sub cmdDraw_Click()
    Dim maxX As Single, maxY As Single, x As Single
    'Graph the Square Function
    maxX = 10
    maxY = maxX * maxX
    picOutput.Cls
    picOutput.Scale (-.2 * maxX, 1.2 * maxY)-(1.2 * maxX, -.2 * maxY)
    picOutput.Line (-.2 * maxX, 0)-(1.2 * maxX, 0)   'Draw x-axis
    picOutput.Line (0, -.2 * maxY)-(0, 1.2 * maxY)   'Draw y-axis
    For x = 0 To maxX Step .01
        picOutput.PSet (x, x * x)
    Next x
End Sub
```

27.
```
Private Sub cmdDraw_Click()
    Dim maxNum As Integer, interval As Single
    Dim i As Integer, xPos As Single, ticLabel As String
    'Draw a number line
    maxNum = Val(InputBox("Enter maximum number to be displayed:"))
    picOutput.Cls
    picOutput.Scale (-10, 10)-(110, -10)
    picOutput.Line (0, 0)-(100, 0)          'Draw x-axis
    interval = 100 / (maxNum + 1)
    For i = 1 To maxNum
        xPos = interval * i
        picOutput.Line (xPos, -.5)-(xPos, .5)
        ticLabel = FormatNumber(i, 0)
        picOutput.CurrentX = interval * i - picOutput.TextWidth(ticLabel) / 2
        picOutput.CurrentY = -1
        picOutput.Print ticLabel;
    Next i
End Sub
```

29.
```
Private Sub cmdDraw_Click()
    Dim x As Integer, y As Integer
    'Draw a sheet of graph paper
    picOutput.Scale (0, 50)-(100, 0)
    For x = 0 To 100 Step 5
        picOutput.Line (x, 0)-(x, 50)
    Next x
    For y = 0 To 50 Step 5
        picOutput.Line (0, y)-(100, y)
    Next y
End Sub
```

Exercises 10.2

1. `picOutput.Scale (-1, 3120)-(6, -520)`

Exercises 10.3

1. The variable numYears will have to be increased and the new data added to the text file.

11. `picOutput.Scale (-7.5, 5)-(2.5, -5)`

13. Only procedure DrawData needs to be changed
```
Private Sub DrawData(male() As Single, female() As Single, numYears As Integer)
    Dim i As Integer
    'Draw rectangles
    For i = 1 To numYears
        picEnroll.Line (i - .4, male(i))-(i, 0), , BF
        picEnroll.Line (i - .2, female(i))-(i + .2, 0), , B
    Next i
End Sub
```

Exercises 10.4

1. Counterclockwise the numbers are 0, .15, .45, .70, and .90.

3. Assume that the data .15, .30, .25, .20, and .10 have been placed in the file 10-4-E3.TXT.

```
Private Sub cmdDraw_Click()
  Dim circumf As Single, i As Integer, startAngle As Single, stopAngle As Single, radius As Single
  Dim percent(1 To 5) As Single, cumPercent(0 To 5) As Single
  'Draw circle and radius lines and fill one sector
  picOutput.Scale (-10, 10)-(10, -10)
  radius = 5
  circumf = 2 * 3.14159
  cumPercent(0) = .0000001 'a "zero" that can be made negative
  Open "10-4-E3.TXT" For Input As #1
  For i = 1 To 5
    Input #1, percent(i)
    cumPercent(i) = cumPercent(i - 1) + percent(i)
    startAngle = cumPercent(i - 1) * circumf
    stopAngle = cumPercent(i) * circumf
    If percent(i) = .1 Then
        picOutput.FillStyle = 0 'solid fill
      Else
        picOutput.FillStyle = 1 'transparent fill
    End If
    picOutput.Circle (0, 0), radius, , -startAngle, -stopAngle
  Next i
  Close #1
End Sub
```

9.
```
Private Sub cmdDraw_Click()
  Dim circumf As Single
  'Draw Pacman
  picOutput.Scale (-4, 4)-(4, -4)
  circumf = 2 * 3.14159
  picOutput.Circle (0, 0), 2, , -(1 / 8) * circumf, -(7 / 8) * circumf
End Sub
```

CHAPTER 11

Exercises 11.1

1. The currently selected item in lstBox, Mozart, is displayed in picOutput.

3. The last item in lstBox, Tchaikovsky, is displayed in picOutput.

5. Brahms is added to the list (after Beethoven) and is displayed in picOutput.

7. The currently selected item in lstBox, Mozart, is deleted.

9. All items are removed from lstBox.

11. Chopin is removed from the list. (Mozart is not removed because the deletion of Chopin changes the index of Mozart from 3 to 2 while the value of *n* in the next pass through the For...Next loop is 3.)

13. `picOutput.Print cboBox.List(0)`

15. `picOutput.Print cboBox.List(0)`

25.
```
Private Sub cmdDisplay_Click()
  Dim i As Integer, total As Single
  total = 0
  For i = 0 to lstNumbers.ListCount - 1
    total = total + Val(lstNumbers.List(i))
  Next i
  picOutput.Print "The average of the numbers is"; total / lstNumbers.ListCount
End Sub
```

17. `cboBox.RemoveItem 1`

19. `cboBox.AddItem "Cervantes"    'Will appear first in the list`

21.
```
Private Sub DeleteMs()
  Dim i As Integer
  'Delete all items beginning with M
  i = 0
  Do While i <= cboBox.ListCount - 1
    If Left(cboBox.List(i), 1) = "M" Then
        cboBox.RemoveItem i
      Else
        i = i + 1
    End If
  Loop
End Sub
```

23. `picOutput.Print cboBox.List(cboBox.NewIndex)`

27.
```
Private Sub cmdDisplay_Click()
   Dim i As Integer
   For i = 0 to lstNumbers.ListCount - 1 Step 2
     picOutput.Print lstNumbers.List(i)
   Next i
End Sub
```

29.
```
Private Sub cmdDisplay_Click()
   Dim i As Integer, largest As Single, smallest As Single
   largest = Val(lstNumbers.List(0))
   smallest = largest
   For i = 1 to lstNumbers.ListCount - 1
     If Val(lstNumbers.List(i)) < smallest Then
         smallest = Val(lstNumbers.List(i))
       ElseIf Val(lstNumbers.List(i)) > largest Then
         largest = Val(lstNumbers.List(i))
     End If
   Next i
   picOutput.Print "The spread of the numbers is"; largest - smallest
End Sub
```

31.

Object	Property	Setting
frmStates	Caption	State Facts
lstStates	Sorted	True
picStates		

```
Dim nickName(1 To 4) As String, motto(1 To 4) As String    'In (Declarations) section of (General)


Private Sub Form_Load()
  Dim i As Integer, state As String
  Open "STATEINF.TXT" For Input As #1
  For i = 1 To 4
    Input #1, state, nickName(i), motto(i)
    lstStates.AddItem state
    lstStates.ItemData(lstStates.NewIndex) = i
  Next i
  Close #1
End Sub


Private Sub lstStates_DblClick()
  picStates.Cls
  picStates.Print "Nickname: "; nickName(lstStates.ItemData(lstStates.ListIndex))
  picStates.Print "Motto: "; motto(lstStates.ItemData(lstStates.ListIndex))
End Sub
```

35.

Object	Property	Setting
frmLengths	Caption	Length Converter
lblFrom	Caption	From
lblTo	Caption	To
lstFrom		
lstTo		
lblLength	Caption	Length to be converted
txtLength	Text	(blank)
cmdConvert	Caption	Convert
lblConverted	Caption	Converted Length
lblNewLen	Caption	(blank)

```
Private Sub Form_Load()
  lstFrom.AddItem "inch"
  lstFrom.AddItem "feet"
  lstFrom.AddItem "yard"
  lstFrom.AddItem "meter"
  lstFrom.AddItem "mile"
  lstTo.AddItem "inch"
  lstTo.AddItem "feet"
  lstTo.AddItem "yard"
  lstTo.AddItem "meter"
  lstTo.AddItem "mile"
End Sub
```

```
Private Sub cmdConvert_Click()
  Dim fromFactor As Single, toFactor As Single, newDist As Single
  'fromFactor is # of inches in "from" unit
  Select Case lstFrom.ListIndex
    Case 0
      fromFactor = 1
    Case 1
      fromFactor = 12
    Case 2
      fromFactor = 36
    Case 3
      fromFactor = 100 / 2.54 '100 centimeters / 2.54 cm per inch
    Case 4
      fromFactor = 63360      '5280 feet per mile * 12 inches per foot
  End Select
  'toFactor is # of inches in "to" units
  Select Case lstTo.ListIndex
    Case 0
      toFactor = 1
    Case 1
      toFactor = 12
    Case 2
      toFactor = 36
    Case 3
      toFactor = 100 / 2.54 '100 centimeters / 2.54 cm per inch
    Case 4
      toFactor = 63360       '5280 feet per mile * 12 inches per foot
  End Select
  newDist = Val(txtLength.Text) * fromFactor / toFactor
  If newDist >= 1 Then
      lblNewLen.Caption = FormatNumber(newDist)
    Else
      lblNewLen.Caption = FormatNumber(newDist, 6)
  End If
End Sub
```

Exercises 11.2

1. The word "Income" becomes the caption embedded in the top of Frame1.

3. The Check1 check box becomes unchecked.

5. The Option1 option button becomes unselected.

7. The scroll box will move to its rightmost position.

9. Clicking on the arrow on either end of the scroll bar will move the scroll box the same ("large") distance as clicking on the bar between the scroll box and an arrow.

11. The Timer1 control is disabled (that is, stopped).

13. The Shape1 control becomes an oval.

15. The Shape1 control becomes filled with a crosshatch pattern.

17. The thickness of the Line1 control doubles.

19. `Frame1.Left = Frame1.Left + 100`

21. `Option2.Value = False`

23. `HScroll2.Value = HScroll2.Min + (HScroll2.Max - HScroll2.Min) / 3`

25.
```
Dim flag As Boolean 'In (Declarations) section of (General)
Private Sub Form_Load()
  flag = False
  Timer1.Interval = 65000   'One minute and five seconds
  Timer1.Enabled = True
End Sub

Private Sub Timer1_Timer()
  If Not flag Then
      flag = True
    Else
      flag = False
      Call TheEvent  'The procedure is invoked every 2 minutes and 10 seconds.
  End If
End Sub
```

27. `Shape1.FillStyle = 3`

29. Option2 is selected (True) and Option1 is unselected (False).

31. Check boxes, Combo list boxes, Horizontal scroll bars, List boxes, Option buttons, and Vertical scroll bars can receive the focus.

33. Yes, the option buttons attached to a frame will become invisible if the frame is made invisible.

35.
```
Private Sub cmdDisplay_Click()
    Dim numChecked As Integer
    numChecked = 0
    If Check1.Value = 1 Then
        numChecked = numChecked + 1
    End If
    If Check2.Value = 1 Then
        numChecked = numChecked + 1
    End If
    If Check3.Value = 1 Then
        numChecked = numChecked + 1
    End If
    picOutput.Cls
    picOutput.Print "You have checked"; numChecked; "check
box";
    If numChecked <> 1 Then
        picOutput.Print "es."
    Else
        picOutput.Print "."
    End If
End Sub
```

39.

Object	Property	Setting
frmStyle	Caption	Font Style
fraSize	Caption	Size
fraEffect	Caption	Special Effects
opt8pt	Caption	8.25
opt12pt	Caption	12
opt18pt	Caption	18
chkBold	Caption	&Bold
chkItalic	Caption	&Italic
chkUnderline	Caption	&Underline
txtInfo	Text	Visual Basic

```
Private Sub Form_Load()
   'Make sure effects reflect initial check box settings
   txtInfo.Font.Bold = False
   txtInfo.Font.Italic = False
   txtInfo.Font.Underline = False
End Sub

Private Sub chkBold_Click()
  If chkBold.Value = 1 Then
      txtInfo.Font.Bold = True
    Else
      txtInfo.Font.Bold = False
  End If
End Sub

Private Sub chkItalic_Click()
  If chkItalic.Value = 1 Then
      txtInfo.Font.Italic = True
    Else
      txtInfo.Font.Italic = False
  End If
End Sub

Private Sub chkUnderline_Click()
  If chkUnderline.Value = 1 Then
      txtInfo.Font.Underline = True
    Else
      txtInfo.Font.Underline = False
  End If
End Sub

Private Sub opt8pt_Click()
  txtInfo.Font.Size = 8.25
End Sub

Private Sub opt12pt_Click()
  txtInfo.Font.Size = 12
End Sub

Private Sub opt18pt_Click()
  txtInfo.Font.Size = 18
End Sub
```

43.

Object	Property	Setting
frmTemp	Caption	Temperatures
vsbFahren	Max	32
	Min	212
	LargeChange	5
vsbCelsius	Max	0
	Min	100
	LargeChange	5
lblFVal	Caption	32
lblFHigh	Caption	212
lblFLow	Caption	32
lblFahren	Caption	Fahrenheit
lblCVal	Caption	0
lblCHigh	Caption	100
lblCLow	Caption	0
lblCelsius	Caption	Celsius

```
Private Sub vsbFahren_Change()
  Dim c As Integer
    lblFVal.Caption = Str(vsbFahren.Value)
    c = (5 / 9) * (vsbFahren.Value - 32)
    vsbCelsius.Value = c
    lblCVal.Caption = Str(vsbCelsius.Value)
End Sub

Private Sub vsbCelsius_Change()
  Dim f As Integer
    lblCVal.Caption = Str(vsbCelsius.Value)
    f = (9 / 5) * vsbCelsius.Value + 32
    vsbFahren.Value = f
    lblFVal.Caption = Str(vsbFahren.Value)
End Sub
```

Exercises 11.3

1. The number of columns in msgFlex will change to 5.

3. The height of row number 3 (the 4th row) in msgFlex will be set to 400 twips.

5. The first two columns of msgFlex will become fixed (will not scroll) and cannot receive the focus.

7. The current cell becomes a cell in row number 3 (the 4th row) of msgFlex.

9. The string "Income" will be displayed in the current cell of msgFlex.

11. Information in each cell in column number 3 (the 4th column) of msgFlex will be centered.

13. The grid lines will disappear from the nonfixed rows and columns of msgFlex.

15. Any scroll bars displayed on msgFlex will disappear.

17. The menu item mnuCut is ungrayed and, if selected, will generate a click event.

19. The menu item mnuSave appears without a check mark to its left.

21. The contents of the Clipboard are deleted.

23. The text currently selected in txtBox, if any, is copied into the Clipboard.

25. frmTwo is made visible (but not modal).

27. frmOne becomes hidden.

29. A Color common dialog box is opened.

31. If an Open common dialog box is displayed after this statement is executed, the "Files of type" dropdown combo box will give the user the choice of displaying all files or just files with the extension .TXT.

33. `msgFlex.Rows = 7`

35. `msgFlex.ColWidth(0) = 3000`

37. `msgFlex.FixedRows = 2`

39. `msgFlex.Col = 2`

41. `picBox.Print msgFlex.Text`

43. `msgFlex.ColAlignment(1) = 7`

45. `msgFlex.GridLines = 1    'flexGridFlat`

47. `mnuExit.Enabled = 0`

49. `mnuNormal.Checked = True`

51. `street = Clipboard.GetText()`

53. `Clipboard.SetText "Happy"`

55. `txtBox.SelText = Clipboard.GetText()`

57. `txtBox.SelText = ""`

59. `frmTwo.Show 1`

61. `frmTwo.Hide`

63. `dlgOpen.ShowOpen`

65. The string " 32" is displayed in the cell in 5th row and 6th column of msgFlex.

69.

Object	Property	Setting
frmOrder	Caption	Order Form
msgOrder	Cols	3
	Rows	4
	FixedCols	0
cmdTotal	Caption	Compute Total
picTotal		

```
Private Sub Form_Load()
  'Set column widths and overall grid size
  msgOrder.ColWidth(0) = 2000
  msgOrder.ColWidth(2) = 1000
  msgOrder.Width = 3000 + msgOrder.ColWidth(1) + 75
  msgOrder.Height = 4 * msgOrder.RowHeight(0) + 100
  'Assign column headings
  msgOrder.Col = 0
  msgOrder.Row = 0
  msgOrder.Text = "Description"
  msgOrder.Col = 1
  msgOrder.Text = "Qty."
```

```
    msgOrder.Col = 2
    msgOrder.Text = "Price Each"
    'Make first description field the active cell
    msgOrder.Row = 1
    msgOrder.Col = 0
  End Sub

  Private Sub cmdTotal_Click()
    Dim total As Single, i As Integer
    Dim qty As Integer, price As Single
    total = 0
    For i = 1 To 3
      msgOrder.Row = i
      msgOrder.Col = 1
      qty = Val(msgOrder.Text)
      msgOrder.Col = 2
      price = Val(msgOrder.Text)
      total = total + qty * price
    Next i
    picTotal.Cls
    picTotal.Print FormatNumber(total)
  End Sub

  Private Sub msgOrder_Click()
    Dim info As String
    If msgOrder.Row > 0 Then
        If msgOrder.Col = 0 Then
            msgOrder.Text = InputBox("Enter description:")
          ElseIf msgOrder.Col = 1 Then
            msgOrder.Text = InputBox("Enter quantity:")
          ElseIf msgOrder.Col = 2 Then
            info = InputBox("Enter price each:")
            msgOrder.Text = FormatNumber(Val(info))
        End If
    End If
  End Sub
```

73. The following changes are required to the solution given in Example 2:

Revise the procedure ShowTotals as shown in what follows.
Add the procedure TotalCol as shown in what follows.
In the procedure msgSprdSht_Click, change the Dim statement to

```
Dim temp As String, message As String, adjCol As Integer
```

and replace the statement

```
Call ShowTotals
```

with the statements

```
adjCol = msgSprdSht.Col
Call TotalCol(msgSprdSht.Col)
```

```
Private Sub ShowTotals()
  Dim colNum As Integer
  'Compute and display total of each numeric column
  msgSprdSht.Row = numRows - 1
  msgSprdSht.Col = 0
  msgSprdSht.Text = "Total"
  For colNum = 1 To numCols - 1
    Call TotalCol(colNum)
  Next colNum
End Sub

Private Sub TotalCol(colNum As Integer)
  Dim total As Single, rowNum As Integer
  total = 0
  For rowNum = 1 To numRows - 3
    msgSprdSht.Row = rowNum
    msgSprdSht.Col = colNum
    total = total + Val(msgSprdSht.Text)
  Next rowNum
```

```
      msgSprdSht.Row = numRows - 2
      msgSprdSht.Text = "----------------"
      msgSprdSht.Row = numRows - 1
      msgSprdSht.Text = FormatCurrency(total)
   End Sub
```

75.

Object	Property	Setting
frmMain	Caption	Number to Dial
cmdShow	Caption	Show Push Buttons
lblNumber	Caption	(blank)

```
   Private Sub cmdShow_Click()
     frmDialPad.Show 1
   End Sub
```

Object	Property	Setting
frmDialPad	Caption	Push Buttons
msgDialPad	Cols	3
	FixedCols	0
	FixedRows	0
	Rows	4
	ScrollBars	0 – none
lblPhone	Caption	(blank)
cmdClear	Caption	Clear
cmdEnter	Caption	Enter

```
   Dim charList As String  'In (Declarations) section of (General) in frmDialPad

   Private Sub cmdClear_Click()
     lblPhone.Caption = ""
   End Sub

   Private Sub cmdEnter_Click()
     frmMain.lblNumber.Caption = lblPhone.Caption
     frmDialPad.Hide
   End Sub

   Private Sub Form_Load()
     Dim i As Integer, j As Integer, place As Integer
     msgDialPad.Font.Size = 18
     charList = "123456789*0#"
     For i = 0 To 3
       msgDialPad.RowHeight(i) = 400
     Next i
     For j = 0 To 2
       msgDialPad.ColWidth(j) = 400
     Next j
     For i = 0 To 3
       For j = 0 To 2
         msgDialPad.Row = i
         msgDialPad.Col = j
         place = 3 * i + j + 1
         msgDialPad.Text = Mid(charList, place, 1)
       Next j
     Next i
     msgDialPad.Width = 3 * msgDialPad.ColWidth(0) + 88
     msgDialPad.Height = 4 * msgDialPad.RowHeight(0) + 108
   End Sub

   Private Sub msgDialPad_Click()
     Dim place As Integer
     If Len(lblPhone.Caption) = 3 Then
         lblPhone.Caption = lblPhone.Caption & "-"
     End If
     place = 3 * msgDialPad.Row + msgDialPad.Col + 1
     lblPhone.Caption = lblPhone.Caption & Mid(charList, place, 1)
   End Sub
```

CHAPTER 12

Exercises 12.1

1.
Object	Property	Setting
adoCountries	ConnectionString	MEGACITIES1.MDB
	RecordSource	Countries
lstCountries	DataSource	adoCountries
cmdList	Caption	List Countries

```
Private Sub cmdList_Click()
  adoCountries.Recordset.MoveFirst
  Do While Not adoCountries.Recordset.EOF
    lstCountry.AddItem adoCountries.Recordset.Fields("country").Value
    adoCountries.Recordset.MoveNext
  Loop
End Sub
```

3.
Object	Property	Setting
adoCities	ConnectionString	MEGACITIES1.MDB
	RecordSource	Cities
	Caption	Cities
lstCities	DataSource	adoCities
cmdDisplay	Caption	Display Populous Cities

```
Private Sub cmdDisplay_Click()
  adoCities.Recordset.MoveFirst
  Do While Not adoCities.Recordset.EOF
    If adoCities.Recordset.Fields("pop2015").Value > 20 Then
        lstCities.AddItem adoCities.Recordset.Fields("city").Value
    End If
    adoCities.Recordset.MoveNext
  Loop
End Sub
```

15. PubID, Name, Company Name, Address, City, State, Zip, Telephone, Fax, Comments

19. field

21. The current record is advanced to the next record in the table, but recycles back to the first record in the table when the end of the table is reached.

25.
Object	Property	Setting
adoRates	ConnectionString	EXCHANGERATES.MDB
	RecordSource	Rates
	Caption	Rates
dlCurrencies	RowSource	adoRate
	ListField	Name
lblRate	Caption	Rate per US Dollar
txtRate	Text	(blank)

```
Private Sub dlCurrencies_Click()
  adoRates.Recordset.MoveFirst
  Do While adoRates.Recordset.Fields("name") <> dlCurrencies.Text
    adoRates.Recordset.MoveNext
  Loop
  txtRate.Text = adoRates.Recordset.Fields("DollarRate").Value
End Sub
```

31.
Object	Property	Setting
adoPlayers	ConnectionString	BASEBALL.MDB
	RecordSource	Players
	Caption	Baseball
picDisplay	DataSource	adoPlayers
cmdShow	Caption	Show Top Player

```
Private Sub cmdShow_Click()
  Dim batAvg As Single   'Batting average for current record
  Dim maxAvg As Single   'Highest batting average found
  'Reminder: Don't forget that at least one control must be
```

```
'bound to the ADO data control for the data control to be
'used. Therefore, we set the picDisplay DataSource to adoPlayers.
'Make one pass to find the highest batting average,
'then a second pass to find all players with that average.
maxAvg = 0
picDisplay.Cls
adoPlayers.Recordset.MoveFirst
Do While (adoPlayers.Recordset.EOF <> True)
  batAvg = adoPlayers.Recordset.Fields("hits") / _
         adoPlayers.Recordset.Fields("atBats")
  If batAvg > maxAvg Then
     maxAvg = batAvg
  End If
  adoPlayers.Recordset.MoveNext
Loop
adoPlayers.Recordset.MoveFirst
Do While (adoPlayers.Recordset.EOF <> True)
  batAvg = adoPlayers.Recordset.Fields("hits") / _
         adoPlayers.Recordset.Fields("atBats")
  If (batAvg = maxAvg) Then
     picDisplay.Print adoPlayers.Recordset.Fields("name")
  End If
  adoPlayers.Recordset.MoveNext
Loop
End Sub
```

Exercises 12.2

1. Could cause a problem if the country was not one of the countries in the Countries table.

3. No problem.

5. Au_ID

7. ISBN

9. None

11. B

13. A

15. D

17. C

19. Beijing

21. Los Angeles

23.
```
adoCities.RecordSource = "SELECT * FROM Cities ORDER BY pop2015 ASC"
adoCities.Refresh
adoCities.Recordset.MoveFirst
adoCities.Recordset.Find "country = 'China'"
```

25.

Object	Property	Setting
frmDBMan	Caption	Database Management
cmdAlphabetical	Caption	&Alphabetical Order
cmd1995Pop	Caption	Order by &1995 Population
cmd2015Pop	Caption	Order by &2015 Population
cmdAlphCoCity	Caption	Alphabetical Order by Country and City
dlCities	ListField	city
	RowSource	adoCities
adoCities	Caption	Large World Cities
	ConnectionString	MEGACITIES2.MDB
	RecordSource	Cities
cmdQuit	Caption	Exit

```
Private Sub cmd1995Pop_Click()
  Dim strSQL As String
  strSQL = "SELECT * FROM Cities ORDER BY pop1995 ASC"
  adoCities.RecordSource = strSQL
  adoCities.Refresh
End Sub

Private Sub cmd2015Pop_Click()
  Dim strSQL As String
  strSQL = "SELECT * FROM Cities ORDER BY pop2015 ASC"
  adoCities.RecordSource = strSQL
  adoCities.Refresh
End Sub
```

```
Private Sub cmdAlphabetical_Click()
  Dim strSQL As String
  strSQL = "SELECT * FROM Cities ORDER BY City ASC"
  adoCities.RecordSource = strSQL
  adoCities.Refresh
End Sub

Private Sub cmdAlphCoCity_Click()
  Dim strSQL As String
  'Order alphabetically by country and city
  strSQL = "SELECT * FROM Cities ORDER BY country, city ASC"
  adoCities.RecordSource = strSQL
  adoCities.Refresh
End Sub

Private Sub cmdQuit_Click()
  End
End Sub
```

Exercises 12.3

1. `SELECT * FROM Countries WHERE country Like 'I*' ORDER BY pop1995 ASC`

3. `SELECT country, currency FROM Countries WHERE pop1995>100 AND pop1995<200 ORDER BY pop1995 ASC`

5. `SELECT * FROM Cities WHERE country='China' ORDER BY pop2015 DESC`

7. `SELECT * FROM Cities WHERE pop1995>15 AND pop1995<16 ORDER BY pop1995 ASC, pop2015 ASC`

9. `SELECT city,Cities.pop2015,currency FROM Cities INNER JOIN Countries ON Countries.country=Cities.country WHERE Countries.country='India' ORDER BY pop2015 DESC`

15. Suppose the two tables are named Lines and Actors.

Object	Property	Setting
frmFilms	Caption	Famous Movie Lines
adoLines	Caption	Famous Lines
	ConnectionString	LINES.MDB
	RecordSource	SELECT famousLine, maleLead FROM Lines INNER JOIN Actors ON Lines.film=Actors.film
adoFilms	DataSource	adoLines

17. OLYMPICSNEW.MDB is an empty database created in Visual Data Manager with the same structure as OLYMPICS.MDB, except for the year field which is now of type Integer.

Object	Property	Setting
frmOlympics	Caption	Summer Olympics
adoNew	Caption	New database
	ConnectionString	OLYMPICSNEW.MDB
	RecordSource	Summer
cmdCopy	Caption	&Copy and Update the Database
cmdExit	Caption	Done
	Enabled	False
adoOld	Caption	Old database
	ConnectionString	OLYMPICS.MDB
	RecordSource	Summer
dgOld	DataSource	adoOld
dgNew	DataSource	adoNew

```
Private Sub cmdCopy_Click()
  Dim yrStr As String   ' gets the 2-character year from old DB
  Dim yrInt As Integer  ' holds the integer year for new DB
  Dim century As Integer
  Dim site As String, mostMedals As String
```

```
'Modify old Olympics database, with 2 chars for year, and copy into new DB with year stored as integer
'Get first record; should be 1896 Olympics
adoOld.Recordset.MoveFirst
Call GetOldData(yrStr, site, mostMedals)
yrInt = Val(yrStr) + 1800
Call PutNewData(yrInt, site, mostMedals)
adoOld.Recordset.MoveNext
'Read old database, fill new database
century = 1900
Do While Not datOld.Recordset.EOF
  Call GetOldData(yrStr, site, mostMedals)
  yrInt = Val(yrStr) + century
  Call PutNewData(yrInt, site, mostMedals)
  adoOld.Recordset.MoveNext
Loop
'Insert 1996 and 2000 Summer Olympics
Call PutNewData(1996, "Atlanta", "USA")
Call PutNewData(2000, "Sydney", "USA")
cmdExit.Enabled = True
cmdCopy.Enabled = False
adoNew.Refresh
End Sub

Private Sub GetOldData(yr As String, site As String, mostMedals As String)
  'Get data from current record of old database
  yr = adoOld.Recordset.Fields("year").Value
  site = adoOld.Recordset.Fields("site").Value
  mostMedals = adoOld.Recordset.Fields("mostMedals").Value
End Sub

Private Sub PutNewData(yr As Integer, site As String, mostMedals As String)
  'Add record at end of new database
  adoNew.Recordset.AddNew
  adoNew.Recordset.Fields("year").Value = yr
  adoNew.Recordset.Fields("site").Value = site
  adoNew.Recordset.Fields("mostMedals").Value = mostMedals
  adoNew.Recordset.Update
End Sub

Private Sub cmdExit_Click()
  End
End Sub
```

CHAPTER 13

Exercises 13.1

1. Any negative grade will be recorded as 0 and any grade greater than 100 will be recorded as 100.

3. `Property Get midGrade() As Single`
   `  midGrade = m_midterm`
   `End Property`

5. The object variable *scholar* was not set to refer to an object of type CStudent before being used. Either the top line should be changed to `Dim scholar As New CStudent` or the line `Set Scholar = New CStudent` should be added at the beginning of the procedure.

7. The variable *m_Name*, which is a Private member variable of the class CStudent, was assigned a value from outside the CStudent class code.

9. The method CalcSemGrade returns a value, but cannot set a value.

11. The member variable *m_ssn* will have the value "999-99-9999" whenever an instance of the class is created.

13. None.

15. Add the following lines to the Form_Load event procedure, and change 500 to −500 in the cmdMove_Click event procedure.

    `round.Xcoord = frmCircles.Width`
    `round.Ycoord = frmCircles.Height`

17.
```
'Class module for CSquare
Private m_length As Single
Private m_perimeter As Single
Private m_area As Single

Public Property Get Length() As Single
  Length = m_length
End Property

Public Property Let Length(ByVal vSide As Single)
  m_length = vSide
  m_perimeter = 4 * vSide
  m_area = vSide * vSide
End Property

Public Property Get Perimeter() As Single
  Perimeter = m_perimeter
End Property

Public Property Let Perimeter(ByVal vAround As Single)
  m_perimeter = vAround
  m_length = vAround / 4
  m_area = m_length * m_length
End Property

Public Property Get Area() As Single
  Area = m_area
End Property

Public Property Let Area(ByVal vRegion As Single)
  m_area = vRegion
  m_length = Sqr(vRegion)
  m_perimeter = 4 * m_length
End Property
```

Exercises 13.2

1.
```
Private Sub cmdCalculate_Click()
  Dim i As Integer, grade As String
  picGrades.Cls
  For i = 1 To section.Count
    If (section.Item(I).CalcSemGrade = "A") Or (section.Item(I).CalcSemGrade = "Pass") Then
      picGrades.Print section.Item(i).Name; Tab(28); section.Item(i).SocSecNum(); _
                  Tab(48); section.Item(i).CalcSemGrade
    End If
  Next i
End Sub
```

3.
```
'State Class (CState)
Private m_name As String
Private m_abbrev As String
Private m_enterDate As String
Private m_pop2000 As Single
Private m_area As Single

Property Let StateName(ByVal vNom As String)
  m_name = vNom
End Property

Property Get StateName() As String
  StateName = m_name
End Property

Property Let Abbrv(ByVal vNom As String)
  m_abbrev = vNom
End Property
```

```
Property Get Abbrv() As String
  Abbrv = m_abbrev
End Property

Property Let EnterUnion(ByVal vWhen As String)
  m_enterDate = vWhen
End Property

Property Get EnterUnion() As String
  EnterUnion = m_enterDate
End Property

Property Let StatePop(ByVal vPopulation As Single)
  m_pop2000 = vPopulation
End Property

Property Get StatePop() As Single
  StatePop = m_pop2000
End Property

Property Let LandArea(ByVal vArea As Single)
  m_area = vArea
End Property

Property Get LandArea() As Single
  LandArea = m_area
End Property

Public Function Density() As Single
  Density = m_pop2000 / m_area
End Function

'Form code
Dim USstates As New Collection

Private Sub cmdAbbrev_Click()
  st = InputBox("Enter an abbreviation")
  txtState.Text = USstates.Item(st).StateName & _
                "    " & USstates.Item(st).EnterUnion
End Sub

Private Sub Form_Load()
  Dim state As CState
  Dim sname As String, dat As String
  Dim abbrev As String
  Dim pop As Long, area As Single, i As Integer
  'Read in the state date and put
  'it into the collection
  Open "STATES.TXT" For Input As #1
  For i = 1 To 50
    Set state = New CState
    Input #1, sname, abbrev, dat, area, pop
    state.StateName = sname
    state.Abbrv = abbrev
    state.EnterUnion = dat
    state.LandArea = area
    state.StatePop = pop
    USstates.Add state, abbrev
    Set state = Nothing
  Next i
  Close #1
End Sub
```

Exercises 13.3

1.
```
'Fraction Class (CFraction)
Private m_numerator As Integer
Private m_denominator As Integer

Property Let Num(ByVal vNum As Integer)
  m_numerator = vNum
End Property'

Property Get Num() As Integer
  Num = m_numerator
End Property

Property Let Den(ByVal vDen As Integer)
  m_denominator = vDen
End Property

Property Get Den() As Integer
  Den = m_denominator
End Property

Public Sub Reduce()
  Dim T As Integer, N As Integer
  Dim M As Integer, done As Boolean
  Dim GCD As Integer
  N = m_numerator
  M = m_denominator
  done = False
  Do While (Not done)
    If (N <> 0) Then
        T = N
        N = M Mod N
        M = T
      Else
        GCD = M
        done = True
    End If
  Loop
  m_numerator = m_numerator / GCD
  m_denominator = m_denominator / GCD
End Sub

'Calculator Class (CCalculator)
Private m_frac1 As CFraction
Private m_frac2 As CFraction
Private m_result As CFraction

Property Let Frac1(ByVal vFrac As CFraction)
  Set m_frac1 = vFrac
End Property

Property Let Frac2(ByVal vFrac As CFraction)
  Set m_frac2 = vFrac
End Property

Property Get result() As CFraction
  Set result = m_result
End Property

Public Function Add() As CFraction
  'Add the two fractions
  Set m_result = New CFraction
  m_frac1.Reduce
  m_frac2.Reduce
  m_result.Den = m_frac1.Den * m_frac2.Den
  m_result.Num = m_frac1.Num * m_frac2.Den + _
             m_frac2.Num _ * m_frac1.Den
  m_result.Reduce
  Set Add = m_result
End Function
```

```
Public Function Subtract() As CFraction
  'Subtract the two fractions
  Set m_result = New CFraction
  m_frac1.Reduce
  m_frac2.Reduce
  m_result.Den = m_frac1.Den * m_frac2.Den
  m_result.Num = m_frac1.Num * m_frac2.Den - m_frac2.Num *
m_frac1.Den
  m_result.Reduce
  Set Subtract = m_result
End Function

Public Function Multiply() As CFraction
  'Multiply the two fractions
  Set m_result = New CFraction
  m_frac1.Reduce
  m_frac2.Reduce
  m_result.Num = m_frac1.Num * m_frac2.Num
  m_result.Den = m_frac1.Den * m_frac2.Den
  m_result.Reduce
  Set Multiply = m_result
End Function

Public Function Divide() As CFraction
  'Divide the two fractions
  Set m_result = New CFraction
  m_frac1.Reduce
  m_frac2.Reduce
  m_result.Num = m_frac1.Num * m_frac2.Den
  m_result.Den = m_frac1.Den * m_frac2.Num
  m_result.Reduce
  Set Divide = m_result
End Function

'Form code
Dim Calc As New CCalculator

Private Sub Init()
  Dim Fraction1 As New CFraction, Fraction2 As New CFraction
  Fraction1.Num = Val(txtNum1.Text)
  Fraction1.Den = Val(txtDen1.Text)
  Fraction2.Num = Val(txtNum2.Text)
  Fraction2.Den = Val(txtDen2.Text)
  Calc.Frac1 = Fraction1
  Calc.Frac2 = Fraction2
End Sub

Private Sub DisplayResult(result As CFraction)
  'Display the result
  lblResNum.Caption = Str(result.Num)
  lblResDen.Caption = Str(result.Den)
End Sub

Private Sub cmdAdd_Click()
  Call Init
  Call DisplayResult(Calc.Add)
End Sub

Private Sub cmdSubtract_Click()
  Call Init
  Call DisplayResult(Calc.Subtract)
End Sub

Private Sub cmdMultiply_Click()
  Call Init
  Call DisplayResult(Calc.Multiply)
End Sub

Private Sub cmdDivide_Click()
  Call Init
  Call DisplayResult(Calc.Divide)
End Sub
```

CHAPTER 14

Exercises 14.1

1. The sum of the first three cells in the first column of the spreadsheet.

3. The largest of the first three numbers in the first column of the spreadsheet.

Exercises 14.2

1. The World Wide Web is just one component of the Internet.

Exercises 14.3

1. *Keep cool,* **but don't freeze.**
Found on a jar of mayonnaise.

3. Would you like to visit the <u>Prentice-Hall</u> Web site?

5. HTML formatting tags cannot be used inside a VBScript program.

7. The scripting language is not identified in the begin tag.

15.
```
<HTML>
  <HEAD>
    <TITLE>Exercise 14-3-E15</TITLE>
    <SCRIPT LANGUAGE="VBSCRIPT">
      Sub cmdShowText_onClick
        If (chkRed.Checked = True) Then
            txtBox.Style.Color="Red"
         Else
            txtBox.Style.Color="Black"
        End If
        If (chkBold.Checked = True) Then
            txtBox.Style.FontWeight="Bold"
         Else
            txtBox.Style.FontWeight="Normal"
        End If
        txtBox.Value="VBScript"
      End Sub
    </SCRIPT>
  </HEAD>

  <BODY>
    <INPUT TYPE="CheckBox" NAME="chkRed" CHECKED="False"> Red<BR>
    <INPUT TYPE="CheckBox" NAME="chkBold" CHECKED="False"> Bold<BR>
    <INPUT TYPE="Text" NAME="txtBox" SIZE="10">
    <INPUT TYPE="Button" NAME="cmdShowText" VALUE="Show Text">
  </BODY>
</HTML>
```

9. The caption in the title bar will be changed to "My Second Web Page."

11. The foreground color of the text in txtBox will be changed to red.

13. The text inside txtBox will displayed as bold.

CHAPTER 15

Exercises 15.1

1. The word Hello in red letters centered in the label.

3. The sentence "Who are you?" appears in the form's title bar, and the phrase "I'm a Button" appears as the caption of the button.

5. The number 123.67 is added to the list box.

7. The abbreviation MD appears in the text box.

9.
```
12345678901234567890
  1        2
```

11.
```
12345678901234567890
  12
```

13.
```
12345678901234567890
   A      Alice
```

15.
```
12345678901234567890
     College    Mascot
  Univ. of MD   Terrapins
       Duke     Blue Devils
```

17.
```
12345678901234567890
Element  Weight  Percent
Oxygen   97.5    65.0
Carbon   27.0    18.0 %
```

19. Display a randomly chosen number from 1 through 9.

21. Display a randomly chosen character from the computer's keyboard.

23. `Me.Text = "Visual Basic .NET"`

25. `Dim trombones As Integer = 76`

27. `lstTrees.Items.Add("Sequoia")`

29. `Button1.ForeColor = Color.Green`

31. `CheckBox1.Checked = True`

33. `TextBox1.Text = Mid("Visual Basic", Len("Visual Basic") − 4, 5)`

35. `HScrollBar2.Value = HScrollBar2.Maximum`

37.
```
Dim randomNum As New Random()
MsgBox(Chr(randomNum.Next(65, 70)))
```

41.
```
Private Sub btnEvaluate_Click(...) Handles btnEvaluate.Click
  Dim n As Single, root As Single
  n = 6.76
  root = Math.Sqrt(n)
  lstResults.Items.Clear()
  lstResults.Items.Add(root)
  lstResults.Items.Add(Int(n))
  lstResults.Items.Add(Math.Round(n, 1))
End Sub
```

43.
```
Private Sub btnSelect_Click(...) Handles btnSelect.Click
  'Display the winning lottery numbers
  Dim randomNum As New Random()
  Dim num1 As Integer, num2 As Integer, num3 As Integer
  num1 = randomNum.Next(0, 10)
  num2 = randomNum.Next(0, 10)
  num3 = randomNum.Next(0, 10)
  txtNumbers.Text = num1 & "   " & num2 & "   " & num3
End Sub
```

47.
```
Private Sub lstOxys_SelectedIndexChanged(...) Handles _
          lstOxys.SelectedIndexChanged
  txtSelected.Text = "The selected item is " & _
                  lstOxys.SelectedItems(lstOxys.SelectedIndex)
End Sub

Private Sub btnAdd_Click(...) Handles btnAdd.Click
  Dim item As String
  item = InputBox("Item to Add:")
  lstOxys.Items.Add(item)
End Sub

Private Sub lstOxys_DoubleClick(...) Handles lstOxys.DoubleClick
  lstOxys.Items.RemoveAt(lstOxys.SelectedIndex)
  txtSelected.Text = ""
End Sub
```

49.
```
Private Sub Tally(...) Handles chkDrugs.Click, _
              chkDental.Click, chkVision.Click, chkMedical.Click
  Dim sum As Single = 0
  If chkDrugs.Checked Then
    sum = sum + 12.51
  End If
  If chkDental.Checked Then
    sum = sum + 9.68
  End If
  If chkVision.Checked Then
    sum = sum + 1.5
  End If
  If chkMedical.Checked Then
    sum = sum + 25.25
  End If
  txtTotal.Text = FormatCurrency(sum)
End Sub
```

51.
```
Private Sub btnDisplay_Click(...) Handles btnDisplay.Click
  Dim fmtStr As String = "{0, -15}    {1,12:N0}    {2, 12:P1}"
  Dim total As Single = 132351
  lstOutput.Items.Add(String.Format(fmtStr, "Company", _
                            "Shipments ", "Market Share"))
  lstOutput.Items.Add(String.Format(fmtStr, "", "(thousands)", ""))
  lstOutput.Items.Add(String.Format(fmtStr, "Hewlett-Packard", _
                            21478, 21478 / total))
  lstOutput.Items.Add(String.Format(fmtStr, "Dell", 20112, 20112 / total))
  lstOutput.Items.Add(String.Format(fmtStr, "IBM", 7928, 7928 / total))
  lstOutput.Items.Add(String.Format(fmtStr, "NEC", 4550, 4550 / total))
  lstOutput.Items.Add(String.Format(fmtStr, "Toshiba", 4237, 4237 / total))
  lstOutput.Items.Add(String.Format(fmtStr, "Others", 74046, 74046 / total))
  lstOutput.Items.Add("")
  lstOutput.Items.Add(String.Format(fmtStr, "Total", total, ""))
End Sub
```

Exercises 15.2

1. `Minneapolis`

3. `""`

5. `6`

7. `facetious`

9. `ABCDEFG`

11. `"Maryland", "MD", 12407`
    `Maryland, MD, 12407`

13. `16`

15. `baseball`

17. `The White House has 132 rooms.`

19. `Hello`

21. `Bon Jour`

23. The sum of the 2015 populations of the ten cities.

25. The countries whose names are five letters long.

27. The list box will display the currency of countries in the Countries table.

29. The names of the cities in China.

31. primaryColors(3) should be replaced with primaryColors()

33. A StreamWriter cannot be used to read from a file.

35. Display all the elements of the array.

37. Open the file GREETINGS.TXT for output.

39. ```
Dim ocean() As String = {"", "Atlantic", "Pacific", _
                         "Indian", "Arctic", "Antarctic"}
```

41. `ReDim towns(100) or ReDim Preserve towns(100)`

43. `Dim sw As IO.StreamWriter = IO.File.AppendText("PLACES.TXT")`

45. ```
Private Sub btnDisplay_Click(...) Handles btnDisplay.Click
    Dim i As Integer
    Dim dt As New DataTable()
    Dim connStr As String = "Provider=Microsoft.Jet.OLEDB.4.0;" & _
                        "Data Source = MEGACITIES2.MDB "
    Dim sqlStr As String = "SELECT * FROM Countries"
    Dim dataAdapter As New OleDb.OleDbDataAdapter(sqlStr, connStr)
    dataAdapter.Fill(dt)
    dataAdapter.Dispose()
    For i = 0 To dt.Rows.Count - 1
      lstCountries.Items.Add(dt.Rows(i)("country"))
    Next i
End Sub
```

51. ```
Private Sub btnDisplay_Click(...) Handles btnDisplay.Click
    Dim i As Integer
    Dim dt As New DataTable()
    Dim connStr As String = "Provider=Microsoft.Jet.OLEDB.4.0;" & _
                        "Data Source = MEGACITIES2.MDB "
    Dim sqlStr As String = "SELECT * FROM Countries ORDER BY pop1995 DESC"
    Dim dataAdapter As New OleDb.OleDbDataAdapter(sqlStr, connStr)
    dataAdapter.Fill(dt)
    dataAdapter.Dispose()
    lstCountries.DataSource = dt
    lstCountries.DisplayMember = "country"
End Sub
```

53. ```
Private Sub btnDisplay_Click(...) Handles btnDisplay.Click
    Dim i As Integer
    Dim dt As New DataTable()
    Dim connStr As String = "Provider=Microsoft.Jet.OLEDB.4.0;" & _
                        "Data Source = MEGACITIES2.MDB "
    Dim sqlStr As String = "SELECT city, currency FROM Cities " & _
            "INNER JOIN Countries ON Cities.country=Countries.country"
    Dim dataAdapter As New OleDb.OleDbDataAdapter(sqlStr, connStr)
    dataAdapter.Fill(dt)
    dataAdapter.Dispose()
    DataGrid1.DataSource = dt
End Sub
```

55.
```
Private Sub btnWhoWon_Click(...) Handles btnWhoWon.Click
    Dim teamName(5) As String
    Dim n As Integer
    'Place World Series Winners into the array
    teamName(1) = "Red Sox"
    teamName(2) = "Giants"
    teamName(3) = "White Sox"
    teamName(4) = "Cubs"
    teamName(5) = "Cubs"
    'Access array
    n = Val(txtNumber.Text)
    txtWinner.Text = "The " & teamName(n) & " won World Series number " & n
End Sub
```

63.
```
Private Sub btnCompute_Click(...) Handles btnCompute.Click
    Dim sr As IO.StreamReader = IO.File.OpenText("STAFF.TXT")
    Dim name As String
    Dim hourlyWage As Single, hoursWorked As Single, salary As Single
    'The text file is placed in the bin subfolder of the folder 3-5-3
    name = sr.ReadLine
    hourlyWage = Val(sr.ReadLine)
    hoursWorked = Val(sr.ReadLine)
    salary = hourlyWage * hoursWorked
    lstPayroll.Items.Add(name & "    " & FormatCurrency(salary))
    name = sr.ReadLine
    hourlyWage = Val(sr.ReadLine)
    hoursWorked = Val(sr.ReadLine)
    sr.Close()
    salary = hourlyWage * hoursWorked
    lstPayroll.Items.Add(name & "    " & FormatCurrency(salary))
End Sub
```

65.
```
Dim dt As New DataTable()

Private Sub Form1_Load(...) Handles MyBase.Load
    Dim connStr As String = "Provider = Microsoft.Jet.OLEDB.4.0;" & _
                            "Data Source = MEGACITIES2.MDB"
    Dim sqlStr As String = "SELECT * FROM Countries"
    Dim dataAdapter As New OleDb.OleDbDataAdapter(sqlStr, connStr)
    dataAdapter.Fill(dt)
    dataAdapter.Dispose()
    lstCountries.DataSource = dt  'Bind the list box to the data table
    lstCountries.DisplayMember = "country"  'Display the specified field
End Sub

Private Sub lstCountries_SelectedIndexChanged(...) Handles _
                                    lstCountries.SelectedIndexChanged
    txtCurrency.Text = dt.Rows(lstCountries.SelectedIndex)("currency")
End Sub
```

67.
```
Private Sub btnFindCities_Click(...) Handles btnFindCities.Click
    UpdateListBox("SELECT city FROM Cities WHERE country = '" & _
                  txtCountry.Text & "' ORDER BY city ASC")
End Sub

Sub UpdateListBox(ByVal sqlStr As String)
    'Declare and populate the data table
    Dim dt As New DataTable()
    Dim connStr As String = "Provider = Microsoft.Jet.OLEDB.4.0;" & _
                            "Data Source = MEGACITIES2.MDB"
    Dim dataAdapter As New OleDb.OleDbDataAdapter(sqlStr, connStr)
    dataAdapter.Fill(dt)
    dataAdapter.Dispose()
    'Display the names of the cities in the specified country
    If dt.Rows.Count = 0 Then
        MsgBox("No cities from that country in the database")
    Else
        lstDisplay.DataSource = dt
        lstDisplay.DisplayMember = "city"
    End If
End Sub
```

INDEX

ACCOMPANYING CD

The CD in this book contains the files needed to install the Working Model Edition of Visual Basic 6.0. To install the software, follow the steps in the first part of Appendix B.

In addition, the CD contains all the programs from the examples and case studies of this textbook, all of the TXT files and databases needed for the exercises, and several BMP (picture) files. The programs (and TXT files) are contained in the folder PRO-GRAMS, in subfolders called CH03, CH04, CH05, and so on. The picture files are contained in the folder PICTURES. We recommend that you copy the entire contents of the folder PROGRAMS onto your hard drive or a diskette.

Every folder and file on the CD has its Read-only attribute turned on. Unless their Read-only attributes are turned off, text files and program files cannot be altered, database files cannot be read by Visual Basic, and VB.NET programs will not run. Follow these steps to turn off the Read-only attributes of folders and files located on a hard drive or diskette:

1. Locate the folder or file with Windows Explorer or My Computer.

2. Right-click on the folder or file, and click on Properties in the dropdown list.

3. In the Attributes section of the Properties window, delete the check mark from the Read-only box, and click on OK.

4. If a Confirm Attribute Changes window appears, select "Apply changes to this folder, subfolders and files", and click on OK.

Note: The above steps can be applied to a selected collection of folders and files. This is especially useful with Windows 95 and Windows 98 which do not support step 4.

Each VB 6.0 program has a name of the form *chapter-section-number*.VBP. For instance, the program in Chapter 3, Section 2, Example 4 has the name 3-2-4.VBP. Many of the programs make use of TXT files that are also in the subfolder. When one of these programs accesses a text file, the filespec for the text file is preceded with App.Path. This tells Visual Basic to look for the program in the folder from which the program has been opened.

END-USER LICENSE AGREEMENT FOR MICROSOFT SOFTWARE

IMPORTANT—READ CAREFULLY: This Microsoft End-User License Agreement ("EULA") is a legal agreement between you (either an individual or a single entity) and Microsoft Corporation for the Microsoft software product identified above, which includes computer software and may include associated media, printed materials, and "online" or electronic documentation ("SOFTWARE PRODUCT"). The SOFTWARE PRODUCT also includes any updates and supplements to the original SOFTWARE PRODUCT provided to you by Microsoft. Any software provided along with the SOFTWARE PRODUCT that is associated with a separate end-user license agreement is licensed to you under the terms of that license agreement. By installing, copying, downloading, accessing or otherwise using the SOFTWARE PRODUCT, you agree to be bound by the terms of this EULA. If you do not agree to the terms of this EULA, do not install , copy , or otherwise use the SOFTWARE PRODUCT.

Software PRODUCT LICENSE

The SOFTWARE PRODUCT is protected by copyright laws and international copyright treaties, as well as other intellectual property laws and treaties. The SOFTWARE PRODUCT is licensed, not sold.

1. **GRANT OF LICENSE.** This EULA grants you the following rights:

1.1 **License Grant.** You may install and use one copy of the SOFTWARE PRODUCT on a single computer. You may also store or install a copy of the SOFTWARE PRODUCT on a storage device, such as a network server, used only to install or run the SOFTWARE PRODUCT over an internal network; however, you must acquire and dedicate a license for each separate computer on or from which the SOFTWARE PRODUCT is installed, used, accessed, displayed or run.

1.2 **Academic Use.** You must be a "Qualified Educational User" to use the SOFTWARE PRODUCT in the manner described in this section. To determine whether you are a Qualified Educational User, please contact the Microsoft Sales Information Center/One Microsoft Way/Redmond, WA 98052-6399 or the Microsoft subsidiary serving your country. If you are a Qualified Educational User, you may either:

(i) exercise the rights granted in Section 1.1, OR

(ii) if you intend to use the SOFTWARE PRODUCT solely for instructional purposes in connection with a class or other educational program, this EULA grants you the following alternative license models:

(A) Per Computer Model. For every valid license you have acquired for the SOFTWARE PRODUCT, you may install a single copy of the SOFTWARE PRODUCT on a single computer for access and use by an unlimited number of student end users at your educational institution, provided that all such end users comply with all other terms of this EULA, OR

(B) Per License Model. If you have multiple licenses for the SOFTWARE PRODUCT, then at any time you may have as many copies of the SOFTWARE PRODUCT in use as you have licenses, provided that such use is limited to student or faculty end users at your educational institution and provided that all such end users comply with all other terms of this EULA. For purposes of this subsection, the SOFTWARE PRODUCT is "in use" on a computer when it is loaded into the temporary memory (i.e., RAM) or installed into the permanent memory (e.g., hard disk, CD ROM, or other storage device) of that computer, except that a copy installed on a network server for the sole purpose of distribution to other computers is not "in use". If the anticipated number of users of the SOFTWARE PRODUCT will exceed the number of applicable licenses, then you must have a reasonable mechanism or process in place to ensure that the number of persons using the SOFTWARE PRODUCT concurrently does not exceed the number of licenses.

2. DESCRIPTION OF OTHER RIGHTS AND LIMITATIONS.

- **Limitations on Reverse Engineering, Decompilation, and Disassembly.** You may not reverse engineer, decompile, or disassemble the SOFTWARE PRODUCT, except and only to the extent that such activity is expressly permitted by applicable law notwithstanding this limitation.

- **Separation of Components.** The SOFTWARE PRODUCT is licensed as a single product. Its component parts may not be separated for use on more than one computer.

- **Rental.** You may not rent, lease or lend the SOFTWARE PRODUCT.

- **Trademarks.** This EULA does not grant you any rights in connection with any trademarks or service marks of Mirosoft

- **Software Transfer.** The initial user of the SOFTWARE PRODUCT may make a one-time permanent transfer of this EULA and SOFTWARE PRODUCT only directly to an end user. This transfer must include all of the SOFTWARE PRODUCT (including all component parts, the media and printed materials, any upgrades, this EULA, and, if applicable, the Certificate of Authenticity). Such transfer may not be by way of consignment or any other indirect transfer. The transferee of such one-time transfer must agree to comply with the terms of this EULA, including the obligation not to further transfer this EULA and SOFTWARE PRODUCT.

- **Termination.** Without prejudice to any other rights, Microsoft may terminate this EULA if you fail to comply with the terms and conditions of this EULA. In such event, you must destroy all copies of the SOFTWARE PRODUCT and all of its component parts.

4. **COPYRIGHT.** All title and intellectual property rights in and to the SOFTWARE PRODUCT (including but not limited to any images, photographs, animations, video, audio, music, text, and "applets" incorporated into the SOFTWARE PRODUCT), the accompanying printed materials, and any copies of the SOFTWARE PRODUCT are owned by Microsoft or its suppliers. All title and intellectual property rights in and to the content which may be accessed through use of the SOFTWARE PRODUCT is the property of the respective content owner and may be protected by applicable copyright or other intellectual property laws and treaties. This EULA grants you no rights to use such content. All rights not expressly granted are reserved by Microsoft.

5. **BACKUP COPY.** After installation of one copy of the SOFTWARE PRODUCT pursuant to this EULA, you may keep the original media on which the SOFTWARE PRODUCT was provided by Microsoft solely for backup or archival purposes. If the original media is required to use the SOFTWARE PRODUCT on the COMPUTER, you may make one copy of the SOFTWARE PRODUCT solely for backup or archival purposes. Except as expressly provided in this EULA, you may not otherwise make copies of the SOFTWARE PRODUCT or the printed materials accompanying the SOFTWARE PRODUCT.

6. **U.S. GOVERNMENT RESTRICTED RIGHTS.** The SOFTWARE PRODUCT and documentation are provided with RESTRICTED RIGHTS. Use, duplication, or disclosure by the Government is subject to restrictions as set forth in subparagraph (c)(1)(ii) of the Rights in Technical Data and Computer Software clause at DFARS 252.227-7013 or subparagraphs (c)(1) and (2) of the Commercial Computer Software—Restricted Rights at 48 CFR 52.227-19, as applicable. Manufacturer is Microsoft Corporation/One Microsoft Way/Redmond, WA 98052-6399.

7. **EXPORT RESTRICTIONS.** You agree that you will not export or re-export the SOFTWARE PRODUCT, any part thereof, or any process or service that is the direct product of the SOFTWARE PRODUCT (the foregoing collectively referred to as the "Restricted Components"), to any country, person, entity or end user subject to U.S. export restrictions. You specifically agree not to export or re-export any of the Restricted Components (i) to any country to which the U.S. has embargoed or restricted the export of goods or services, which currently include, but are not necessarily limited to Cuba, Iran, Iraq, Libya, North Korea, Sudan and Syria, or to any national of any such country, wherever located, who intends to transmit or transport the Restricted Components back to such country; (ii) to any end-user who you know or have reason to know will utilize the Restricted Components in the design, development or production of nuclear, chemical or biological weapons; or (iii) to any end-user who has been prohibited from participating in U.S. export transactions by any federal agency of the U.S. government. You warrant and represent that neither the BXA nor any other U.S. federal agency has suspended, revoked, or denied your export privileges.

8. **NOTE ON JAVA SUPPORT.** THE SOFTWARE PRODUCT MAY CONTAIN SUPPORT FOR PROGRAMS WRITTEN IN JAVA. JAVA TECHNOLOGY IS NOT FAULT TOLERANT AND IS NOT DESIGNED, MANUFACTURED, OR INTENDED FOR USE OR RESALE AS ON-LINE CONTROL EQUIPMENT IN HAZARDOUS ENVIRONMENTS REQUIRING FAIL-SAFE PERFORMANCE, SUCH AS IN THE OPERATION OF NUCLEAR FACILITIES, AIRCRAFT NAVIGATION OR COMMUNICATION SYSTEMS, AIR TRAFFIC CONTROL, DIRECT LIFE SUPPORT MACHINES, OR WEAPONS SYSTEMS, IN WHICH THE FAILURE OF JAVA TECHNOLOGY COULD LEAD DIRECTLY TO DEATH, PERSONAL INJURY, OR SEVERE PHYSICAL OR ENVIRONMENTAL DAMAGE.

MISCELLANEOUS

If you acquired this product in the United States, this EULA is governed by the laws of the State of Washington.

If you acquired this product in Canada, this EULA is governed by the laws of the Province of Ontario, Canada. Each of the parties hereto irrevocably attorns to the jurisdiction of the courts of the Province of Ontario and further agrees to commence any litigation which may arise hereunder in the courts located in the Judicial District of York, Province of Ontario.

If this product was acquired outside the United States, then local law may apply.

Should you have any questions concerning this EULA, or if you desire to contact Microsoft for any reason, please contact Microsoft, or write: Microsoft Sales Information Center/One Microsoft Way/ Redmond, WA 98052-6399.

LIMITED WARRANTY

LIMITED WARRANTY. Microsoft warrants that (a) the SOFTWARE PRODUCT will perform substantially in accordance with the accompanying written materials for a period of ninety (90) days from the date of receipt, and (b) any Support Services provided by Microsoft shall be substantially as described in applicable written materials provided to you by Microsoft, and Microsoft support engineers will make commercially reasonable efforts to solve any problem. To the extent allowed by applicable law, implied warranties on the SOFTWARE PRODUCT, if any, are limited to ninety (90) days. Some states/jurisdictions do not allow limitations on duration of an implied warranty, so the above limitation may not apply to you.

CUSTOMER REMEDIES. Microsoft's and its suppliers' entire liability and your exclusive remedy shall be, at Microsoft's option, either (a) return of the price paid, if any, or (b) repair or replacement of the SOFTWARE PRODUCT that does not meet Microsoft's Limited Warranty and that is returned to Microsoft with a copy of your receipt. This Limited Warranty is void if failure of the SOFTWARE PRODUCT has resulted from accident, abuse, or misapplication. Any replacement SOFTWARE PRODUCT will be warranted for the remainder of the original warranty period or thirty (30) days, whichever is longer. Outside the United States, neither these remedies nor any product support services offered by Microsoft are available without proof of purchase from an authorized international source.

NO OTHER WARRANTIES. **To the maximum extent permitted by applicable law, Microsoft and its suppliers disclaim all other warranties and conditions, either express or implied, including, but not limited to, implied warranties OR CONDITIONS of merchantability, fitness for a particular purpose, title and non-infringement, with regard to the SOFTWARE PRODUCT, and the provision of or failure to provide Support Services. This limited warranty gives you specific legal rights. You may have others, which vary from state/jurisdiction to state/jurisdiction.**

LIMITATION OF LIABILITY. **TO THE MAXIMUM EXTENT PERMITTED BY APPLICABLE LAW, IN NO EVENT SHALL MICROSOFT OR ITS SUPPLIERS BE LIABLE FOR ANY SPECIAL, INCIDENTAL, INDIRECT, OR CONSEQUENTIAL DAMAGES WHATSOEVER (INCLUDING, WITHOUT LIMITATION, DAMAGES FOR LOSS OF BUSINESS PROFITS, BUSINESS INTERRUPTION, LOSS OF BUSINESS INFORMATION, OR ANY OTHER PECUNIARY LOSS) ARISING OUT OF THE USE OF OR INABILITY TO USE THE SOFTWARE PRODUCT OR THE FAILURE TO PROVIDE SUPPORT SERVICES, EVEN IF MICROSOFT HAS BEEN ADVISED OF THE POSSIBILITY OF SUCH DAMAGES. IN ANY CASE, MICROSOFT'S ENTIRE LIABILITY UNDER ANY PROVISION OF THIS EULA SHALL BE LIMITED TO THE GREATER OF THE AMOUNT ACTUALLY PAID BY YOU FOR THE SOFTWARE PRODUCT OR U.S.$5.00; PROVIDED, HOWEVER, IF YOU HAVE ENTERED INTO A MICROSOFT SUPPORT SERVICES AGREEMENT, MICROSOFT'S ENTIRE LIABILITY REGARDING SUPPORT SERVICES SHALL BE GOVERNED BY THE TERMS OF THAT AGREEMENT. BECAUSE SOME STATES/JURISDICTIONS DO NOT ALLOW THE EXCLUSION OR LIMITATION OF LIABILITY, THE ABOVE LIMITATION MAY NOT APPLY TO YOU.**